FIVE HUNDRED YEARS

EXPLORING AMERICAN TRADITIONS

THIRD EDITION

Scott E. Casper   **Richard O. Davies**

Pearson
Custom
Publishing

PEARSON CUSTOM PUBLISHING
75 Arlington Street, Suite 300, Boston, MA 02116
A Pearson Education Company

Copyright Acknowledgments

Contents

Introduction

Five hundred years! It seems an absolute folly to try to compress the major ideas and themes that constitute "American traditions" into just a few hundred pages. Perhaps it is useful to begin by dissecting the phrase "American traditions" itself. At least since the writer Hector St. John Crevecoeur asked "What then is this American, this new man?" in the late 1700s, people have debated what exactly it means to be "American." For instance, does living in the United States of America make one an American? Unlike any other nation in the world, the United States has prided itself upon its ability to accept individuals representing many diverse cultures and races. But what happens to those diverse individuals; when do they become Americans? Some have argued that America is a melting pot, in which individuals are assimilated—their ethnic and cultural particulars melted out or melted together, resulting in a composite "American-ness." Others respond that the United States is a multicultural society of distinct and, to some extent, unassimilated peoples and cultures—and that this very multiplicity is what makes "American-ness." Is American-ness a product of being in this place, or of believing in some shared set of values or ideals? And if the latter, what are we to make of the times when America has fallen far short of its promise of providing all with full access to the so-called American Dream?

The concept of "traditions" is no less complex. When does an idea become a "tradition"? And what happens to an idea in the process of becoming a tradition? In the readings that follow, you will be able to trace connections: ideas that have recurred throughout American history, similar questions that elicit new answers in new circumstances. But like different interpretations of a piece of music, these themes sound different in different voices. Traditions do not travel through time unaltered—or, if they do, they often begin to seem stale, unapplicable to new situations. Rather, traditions, once established, provide sources for others to draw on for their own aims. The Declaration of Independence, written in 1776, becomes the model for a feminist declaration of women's rights in 1848. That declaration, in turn, remains an inspiration for a women's-rights movement that achieves the right to vote seventy-two years later. And two generations after that, in the 1960s, a new women's movement emerges, asserting women's desire to participate fully in the worlds of work and politics. Is this a "tradition"? Only in hindsight. After all, the men who drafted and issued the Declaration of Independence—before the United States had actually even won independence from Great Britain—neither imagined nor desired that their vision of political equality would include women. And the authors of the 1848 Seneca Falls Declaration were ridiculed by most Americans. And after winning the right to vote in 1920, the women's movement collapsed. Nonetheless, common themes run through all these events, however different the voices, interpretations, and contexts.

Perhaps, like the "melting pot vs. multicultural society" issue, the true "American traditions" are a series of recurring questions, rather than any single set of answers. What is the meaning of the "American Dream"? What is the proper balance between individual liberties and rights and the good of a larger community? What kinds of political and economic systems are most suited to American ideals? And how and why have answers to these questions differed or remained constant? As you read the selections in this volume, consider both content and context: what the authors said, how they expressed their ideas, why they expressed them the way they did. This will enable you to draw connections and to consider individual works in relation to the cultural, political, and social surroundings in which they were originally written.

The texts in this book are all original sources, written over the last five hundred years to describe, comment on, or influence life and events in America. We have attempted to select works that provide a broad, though by no means comprehensive, exposure to ideas and questions that have helped create the foundations of American politics, society, and culture. This collection provides you with the opportunity to sample for yourself many of the important ideas that have contributed to erecting the structure of contemporary American civilization. It also provides you with a complex variety of voices—some famous, some not.

Finally, it provides you with a wide range of genres and forms: selections from political pamphlets, novels, paintings, sports reporting, poetry, photographs, children's literature, maps, speeches, and more.

Many people have contributed to the creation of this book, from conceiving its framework to suggesting selections for inclusion. We are grateful to all of them: Kathy Boardman, Michael Branch, Linda Curcio, Dennis Dworkin, Jerome Edwards, David Fenimore, Cheryll Glotfelty, Jen Huntley-Smith, Greg Jones, Leah Magennis, John Marini, Gaye McCollum, Thomas Nickles, Eric Porter, Elizabeth Raymond, Catherine Ramirez, Bernard Schopen, and John Yarnevich. We greatly appreciate the encouragement and support of Phillip Boardman, who has been this book's most consistent champion from the outset. We would also like to thank our students, whose responses to the earlier editions of the book have helped us as we shaped this edition.

American traditions are extraordinarily rich and diverse. In exploring some of the voices and works that have helped to shape them, we can learn much about ourselves and the fabric of our own lives.

Scott E. Casper
Richard O. Davies
University of Nevada, Reno

1. Early Encounters

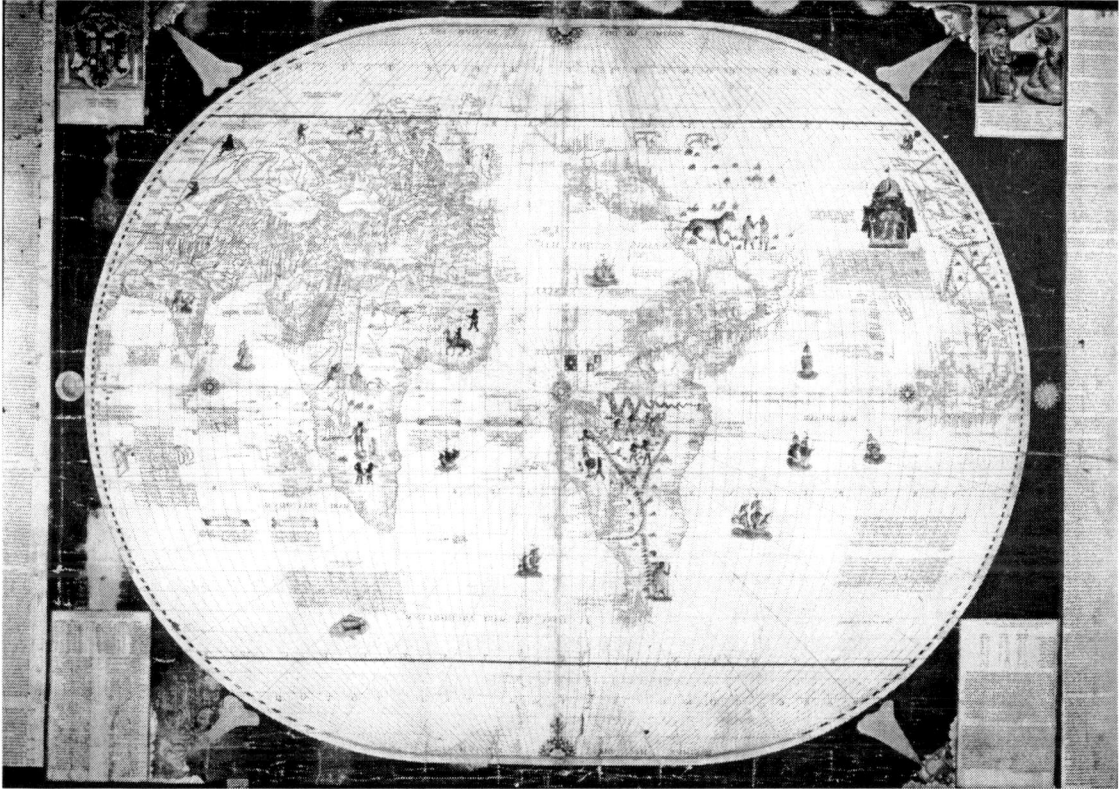

Oval World Map, 1544 by Sebastian Cabot. Biblotheque Nationale de France.

Maps seem like objective, visual representations of physical space. But look closer, and they capture ideas, experiences, and world view as well as places. The simplest road map today probably identifies sites that somebody considers meaningful: schools, parks, churches, government buildings. It marks human interaction with the landscape. It distinguishes one-lane roads from interstate highways, and it marks the boundaries between cities or states, or between land and water. In contrast, the Abstract Expressionist painting on the front cover of this book, Jasper Johns's 1961 *Map*, offers a commentary on the familiar United States map, and on the whole process of mapmaking. The boundaries between states are blurred. So are the boundaries between the United States and the Canadian provinces and Mexican states. Even the oceans aren't entirely blue. Four centuries earlier, Europeans of various nations—Portugal, Spain, France, England—were seeking to "discover" and possess places and peoples across the oceans. Making maps became a way of marking territory, like Columbus planting the Spanish flag on the shores of San Salvador. Sebastian Cabot's 1544 *Oval World Map* revealed a European view of the "New World." Who or what populates the Americas, Africa, Asia? What features of the landscape find their way into the map? And how does Cabot represent the Europeans themselves? All of these questions help us enter the colonizers' mental maps as well as their physical ones.

1

Chronology

1441:	African slaves first brought to Portugal
1492:	Christopher Columbus first arrives in the Caribbean
1514:	Bartholome de las Casas begins preaching against the conquest
1515:	Hernan Cortes lands in Mexico
1534:	Frenchman Jacques Cartier first explores the St. Lawrence River
1550:	Tobacco introduced to Europe
1584–1587:	Walter Raleigh's colony on Roanoke Island
1607:	English found Jamestown (Virginia)
1608:	French found Quebec
1609:	Spanish found Santa Fe (now New Mexico)
1619:	First Africans brought to Virginia
1620:	Pilgrim emigration to Plymouth
1622:	Indian uprising in Virginia
1625:	Jesuit missionaries arrive in New France
1629:	Puritans begin settlement of Massachusetts Bay
1662:	Virginia law makes slavery hereditary

Introduction

For nearly two centuries, Americans have read in their schoolbooks that "Christopher Columbus discovered America." This compact sentence, however, contains at least two problems. The name "America" would have been alien to Columbus (1451–1506), who traveled in search of the East Indies and landed on what would later be called the North American continent quite by accident. Europeans named this continent America later, after a merchant from Florence named Amerigo Vespucci who traveled with a Portuguese expedition and wrote accounts of his experiences. The other problem lies in the concept of discovery. From a European perspective, Columbus "discovered" America. But from the perspective of the millions of people already living in the Americas in 1492, Columbus hardly ranked as a discoverer. Perhaps another definition of "discover"—a common definition several hundred years ago—fits better. To discover, for most seventeenth- and eighteenth-century English speakers, meant to *uncover*: to reveal something that already existed. To Europeans, this was precisely Columbus's achievement.

In the last twenty years, the European uncovering of the "New World" has become the subject of great controversy. Once celebrated without question, the explorations of the fifteenth and sixteenth centuries now possess other meanings as well. What was for Europeans a discovery was for the native inhabitants of the Americas largely a disaster. Unbeknownst to European explorers and their crews, they brought with them diseases to which they, but not the peoples of the New World, had developed immunity. As a result, millions of native Americans died of illnesses like smallpox within a few generations of contact with Europeans. Other exchanges were not as destructive. Culinary transmissions (Europeans introduced native Americans to sugar; native Americans introduced Europeans to corn, tomatoes, and peppers) transformed agriculture and diet on both sides of the Atlantic, and the introduction of the horse in America profoundly altered many native societies. Because "discovery" is a loaded term—it takes the point of view of the discoverer, and it suggests an altogether positive process—historians and other scholars have come to use terms like "encounter" to describe what happened in America between 1492 and the 1600s. Such terms consider the meeting of cultures from both sides, how each looked at itself and the other. They also allow us to avoid reducing history to a simplistic story of "good guys" (either heroic discoverers *or* noble, victimized Indians) and "bad guys." Both European societies and native American societies housed immense creativity and violence, complex social structures and often-brutal social customs. To suggest otherwise—to make these encounters into tales of heroes, villains, and victims, or into struggles between the "civilized" and the "savage"—is to ignore the complexity of cultures and the people who created and inhabited them.

This complexity is clear from the readings that follow. European methods of colonizing the New World were by no means monolithic; different nations adopted diverse colonial practices. The Spanish policy emphasized extracting resources, using Indians and later enslaved Africans as laborers, but not establishing large new societies of Spanish migrants in America. England, by contrast, "transplanted" its society into the New World, founding colonies of English inhabitants along the east coast of what is now the United States. (The word plantation, usually reserved now to describe large Southern slaveholding farms, came from "transplantation," which the English used to describe all their colonies in America.) The English settlers, while they learned agricultural methods from the eastern Indian tribes, also attempted to distance their societies from native ones. French settlement occurred primarily in the interior of the continent, in Canada and around the Great Lakes; French fur traders and trappers created extensive trading relationships with native inhabitants, living among them and sometimes intermarrying. European travelers and colonizers often wrote about the land, people, and cultures they encountered in America. Some drew pictures of what they saw in the New World—such as Thomas Harriot's engraving of an Algonquian Indian village called Secota (located in modern-day Virginia) that appears in this chapter. When engravings like this one were published in England, writers often accompanied them with descriptions (such as John White's description of Secota). Travelers' accounts often reveal much about the Europeans' own perspectives: witness the early description of relations between the English and Native Americans by the English scientist Harriot (1560–1621). Even maps, such as the "Oval World Map" made in 1544 by Italian explorer Sebastian Cabot (1476?–1557), contain elements that reveal Europeans' view of the lands they had "discovered."

The first permanent English settlement in America, at Jamestown, Virginia, nearly perished in its first year. The London Company, chartered in 1606 by King James I, received exclusive rights to colonize the southern part of English North America, and sent 144 men on its initial expedition. The 104 who survived the trip called their new colony Jamestown, but they chose a poor site to settle. Jamestown rested on swampy ground, a prime location for malaria (a disease to which Europeans possessed no immunity) but not for agriculture. Within a year only 38 of the original colonists survived. The company sent new men (the first women and children came in 1609), including Captain John Smith (1580–1631)—who took over the colony and quickly established order. Thanks to Smith's efforts, Jamestown survived its first years. It became prosperous several years later when colonists realized the potential of tobacco on the Virginia soil. The resulting need for additional laborers led to two solutions, the importation of English indentured servants (who would work for a specified period and then receive their freedom and land) and the importation of African slaves. Slavery initially resembled indentured servitude: many of the early slaves received their freedom after a period of work. By the end of the century, slavery had become harsher and more permanent, and the condition of slavery was passed from mothers to their children. The early Virginians' relationships with their Indian neighbors were often troubled and sometimes worse: Smith raided Indian villages for food, his successors led attacks on Indian towns, and in 1622 an Indian attack left 347 colonists dead. Smith's 1608 description of the Indians and the speech by their leader Powhatan (1550?–1618) to Smith the following year offer a glimpse of this encounter.

French colonization produced its own relationships between colonizers and native peoples, which were often less strife-ridden than the English experiences. Because French explorers, traders, and missionaries lived in closer contact with Native Americans than did most English settlers, they observed the cultures of the Great Lakes tribes in detail, as the missionary Paul LeJeune's account indicates. By the same token, the Indians in these regions (including the Micmacs) had similarly complex views of these European newcomers. By the late 1600s France and England would become embroiled in a century-long global conflict for international supremacy. In America, that conflict would involve Native Americans as well as European colonists. In the imperial wars of the 1700s—particularly the French and Indian War of 1754–1763—both France and England forged alliances with Indian tribes. When England prevailed in 1763, the French lost their North American possessions, including Canada. With the French went their system of Native American relations. The system that emerged in its place, beginning before the American Revolution, sprang from English colonists' desire to inhabit ever more of the North American continent in the name of cultivation and "civilization."

CHRISTOPHER COLUMBUS

Letter to the Sovereigns on His First Voyage (1493)

Sir, forasmuch as I know that you will take pleasure in the great triumph with which Our Lord has crowned my voyage, I write this to you, from which you will learn how, in twenty days I reached the Indies with the fleet which the most illustrious King and Queen, our lords, gave to me. And there I found very many islands filled with people without number, and of them all have I taken possession for Their Highnesses, by proclamation and with the royal standard displayed, and nobody objected. To the first island which I found I gave the name *Sant Salvador*, in recognition of His Heavenly Majesty, who marvelously hath given all this; the Indians call it *Guanahani*. To the second I gave the name *Isla de Santa María de Concepción*; to the third, *Ferrandina*; to the fourth, *La Isla Bella*; to the fifth, *La Isla Juana*; and so to each one I gave a new name.

When I reached Juana, I followed its coast to the westward, and I found it to be so long that I thought it must be the mainland, the province of Catayo. And since I found neither towns nor cities along the coast, but only small villages, with the people of which I could not have speech because they all fled forthwith, I went forward on the same course, thinking that I should not fail to find great cities and towns. And, at the end of many leagues, seeing that there was no change and that the coast was bearing me northwards, which was contrary to my desire since winter was already beginning and I proposed to go thence to the south, and as moreover the wind was favorable, I determined not to wait for a change of weather and backtracked to a certain harbor already noted, and thence I sent two men upcountry to learn if there were a king or great cities. They traveled for three days and found an infinite number of small villages and people without number, but nothing of importance; hence they returned.

I understood sufficiently from other Indians, whom I had already taken, that continually this land was an island, and so I followed its coast eastward 107 leagues up to where it ended. And from that cape I saw toward the east another island, distant 18 leagues from the former, to which I at once gave the name *La Spañola*. And I went there and followed its northern part, as I had in the case of Juana, to the eastward for 178 great leagues in a straight line. As Juana, so all the others are very fertile to an excessive degree, and this one especially. In it there are many harbors on the sea coast, beyond comparison with others which I know in Christendom, and numerous rivers, good and large, which is marvelous. Its lands are lofty and in it there are many sierras and very high mountains, to which the island *Centrefrei* is not comparable. All are most beautiful, of a thousand shapes, and all accessible, and filled with trees of a thousand kinds and tall, and they seem to touch the sky; and I am told that they never lose their foliage, which I can believe, for I saw them as green and beautiful as they are in Spain in May, and some of them were flowering, some with fruit, and some in another condition, according to their quality. And there were singing the nightingale and other little birds of a thousand kinds in the month of November, there where I went. There are palm trees of six or eight kinds, which are a wonder to behold because of their beautiful variety, and so are the other trees and fruits and plants; therein are marvelous pine groves, and extensive meadow country; and there is honey, and there are many kinds of birds and a great variety of fruits. Upcountry there are many mines of metals, and the population is innumerable. *La Spañola* is marvelous, the sierras and the mountains and the plains and the meadows and the lands are so beautiful and rich for planting and sowing, and for livestock of every sort, and for building towns and villages. The harbors of the sea here are such as you could not believe it without seeing them; and so the rivers, many and great, and good streams, the most of which bear gold. And the trees and fruits and plants have great differences from those of La Juana; in this [island] there are many spices and great mines of gold and of other metals.

The people of this island and of all the other islands which I have found and seen, or have not seen, all go naked, men and women, as their mothers bore them, except that some women cover one place only with the leaf of a plant or with a net of cotton which they make for that purpose. They have no iron or steel or weapons, nor are they capable of using them, although they are well-built people of handsome stature, because they are wondrous timid. They have no other arms than arms of canes, [cut] when they are in seed time, to the ends of which they fix a sharp little stick; and they dare not make use of these, for oftentimes it has happened that I have sent ashore two or three men to some town to have speech, and people without number have come out to them, and as soon as they saw them coming, they fled; even a father would not stay for his son; and this not because wrong has been done to anyone; on the contrary, at every point where I have been and have been able to have speech, I have given them of all that I had, such as cloth and many other things, without receiving anything for it; but they are like that, timid beyond cure. It is true that after they have been reassured and have lost this fear, they are so artless and so free with all they possess, that no one would believe it without having seen it. Of anything they have, if you ask them for it, they never say no; rather they invite the person to share it, and show as much love as if they were giving their hearts; and whether the thing be of value or of small price, at once they are content with whatever little thing of whatever kind may be given to them. I forbade that they should be given things so worthless as pieces of broken crockery and broken glass, and lace points, although when they were able to get them, they thought they had the best jewel in the world; thus it was learned that a sailor for a lace point received gold to the weight of two and a half *castellanos,* and others much more for other things which were worth much less; yea, for new *blancas,* for them they would give all that they had, although it might be two or three castellanos' weight of gold or an ar- roba or two of spun cotton; they even took pieces of the broken hoops of the wine casks and, like animals, gave what they had, so that it seemed to me to be wrong and I forbade it, and I gave them a thousand good, pleasing things which I had brought, in order that they might be fond of us, and furthermore might become Christians and be inclined to the love and service of Their Highnesses and of the whole Castilian nation, and try to help us and to give us of the things which they have in abundance and which are necessary to us. And they know neither sect nor idolatry, with the excep- tion that all believe that the source of all power and goodness is in the sky, and they believe very firmly that I, with these ships and people, came from the sky, and in this belief they everywhere re- ceived me, after they had overcome their fear. And this does not result from their being ignorant (for they are of a very keen intelligence and men who navigate all those seas, so that it is wondrous the good account they give of everything), but because they have never seen people clothed or ships like ours.

And as soon as I arrived in the Indies, in the first island which I found, I took by force some of them in order that they might learn [Castilian] and give me information of what they had in those parts; it so worked out that they soon understood us, and we them, either by speech or signs, and they have been very serviceable. I still have them with me, and they are still of the opinion that I come from the sky, in spite of all the intercourse which they have had with me, and they were the first to announce this wherever I went, and the others went running from house to house and to the neighboring towns with loud cries of, "Come! Come! See the people from the sky!" They all came, men and women alike, as soon as they had confidence in us, so that not one, big or little, remained behind, and all brought something to eat and drink, which they gave with marvelous love. In all the islands they have very many *canoas* like rowing *fustes,* some bigger and some smaller, and some are bigger than a *fusta* of eighteen benches. They are not so beamy, because they are made of a single log, but a *fusta* could not keep up with them by rowing, since they make incredible speed, and in these they navigate all those islands, which are innumerable, and carry their merchandise. Some of these canoes I have seen with 70 and 80 men on board, each with his oar.

In all these islands, I saw no great diversity in the appearance of the people or in their manners and language, but they all understand one another, which is a very singular thing, on account of which I hope that Their Highnesses will determine upon their conversion to our holy faith, towards which they are much inclined.

I have already said how I went 107 leagues in a straight line from west to east along the coast of the island Juana, and as a result of that voyage I can say that this island is larger than England and Scotland together; for, beyond these 107 leagues, there remain to the westward two provinces where I have not been, one of which they call Avan, and there the people are born with tails. Those provinces cannot have a length of less than 50 or 60 leagues, as I could understand from those Indians whom I retain and who know all the islands. The other, *Española,* in circuit is greater than all Spain, from *Colonya* by the coast to *Fuenterauia* in Vizcaya, since I went along one side 188 great leagues in a straight line from west to east. It is a desirable land and, once seen, is never to be relinquished; and in it, although of all I have taken possession for their Highnesses and all are more richly supplied than I know or could tell, I hold them all for their Highnesses, which they may dispose of as absolutely as of the realms of Castile. In this *Española,* in the most convenient place and in the best district for the gold mines and for all trade both with this continent and with that over there belong to the Grand Khan, where there will be great trade and profit, I have taken possession of a large town to which I gave the name *La Villa de Nauidad,* and in it I have built a fort and defenses, which already, at this moment, will be all complete, and I have left in it enough people for such a purpose, with arms and artillery and provisions for more than a year, and a fusta, and a master of the sea in all [maritime] arts to build others; and great friendship with the king of that land, to such an extent that he took pride in calling me and treating me as brother; and even if he were to change his mind and offer insult to these people, neither he nor his people know the use of arms and they go naked, as I have already said, and are the most timid people in the world, so that merely the people whom I have left there could destroy all that land; and the island is without danger for their persons, if they know how to behave themselves.

In all these islands, it appears, all the men are content with one woman, but to their *Maioral,* or king, they give up to twenty. It appears to me that the women work more than the men. I have been unable to learn whether they hold private property, but it appeared true to me that all took a share in anything that one had, especially in victuals.

In these islands I have so far found no human monstrosities, as many expected, on the contrary, among all these people good looks are esteemed; nor are they Negroes, as in Guinea, but with flowing hair, and they are not born where there is excessive force in the solar rays; it is true that the sun there has great strength, although it is distant from the Equator 26 degrees. In these islands, where there are high mountains, the cold this winter was severe, but they endure it through habit and with the help of food which they eat with many and excessively hot spices. Thus I have neither found monsters nor had report of any, except in an island which is the second at the entrance to the Indies, which is inhabited by a people who are regarded in all the islands as very ferocious and who eat human flesh; they have many canoes with which they range all the islands of India and pillage and take as much as they can; they are no more malformed than the others, except that they have the custom of wearing their hair long like women, and they use bows and arrows of the same stems of cane with a little piece of wood at the tip for want of iron, which they have not. They are ferocious toward these other people, who are exceedingly great cowards, but I make no more account of them than of the rest. These are those who have intercourse with the women of *Matremomio,* which is the first island met on the way from Spain to the Indies, in which there is not one man. These women use no feminine exercises, but bows and arrows of cane, like the abovesaid; and they arm and cover themselves with plates of copper, of which they have plenty. In another island which they assure me is larger than *Española,* the people have no hair. In this there is countless gold, and from it and from the other islands I bring with me *Indios* as evidence.

In conclusion, to speak only of that which has been accomplished on this voyage, which was so hasty, Their Highnesses can see that I shall give them as much gold as they want if Their Highnesses will render me a little help; besides spice and cotton, as much as Their Highnesses shall command; and gum mastic, as much as they shall order shipped, and which, up to now, has been found only in Greece, in the island of Chios, and the Seignory sell it for what it pleases; and aloe wood, as much as they shall order shipped, and slaves, as many as they shall order, who will be idolaters. And I believe that I have found rhubarb and cinnamon, and I shall find a thousand other things of value, which the people whom I have left there will have discovered, for I tarried nowhere, provided the wind allowed me to sail, except in the town of Navidad, where I stayed [to have it] secured and well seated. And the truth is I should have done much more if the vessels had served me as the occasion required.

This is enough. And the Eternal God, Our Lord, Who gives to all those who walk in His way victory over things which appear impossible; and this was notably one. For, although men have talked or have written of these lands, all was conjecture, without getting a look at it, but amounted only to this; that those who heard for the most part listened and judged it more a fable than that there was anything in it, however, small.

So, since our Redeemer has given this triumph to our most illustrious King and Queen, and to their renowned realms, in so great a matter, for this all Christendom ought to feel joyful and make great celebrations and give solemn thanks to the Holy Trinity with many solemn prayers for the great exaltation which it will have, in the turning of so many peoples to our holy faith, and afterwards for material benefits, since not only Spain but all Christians will hence have refreshment and profit. This is exactly what has been done, though in brief.

Done on board the caravel off the Canary Islands, on the fifteenth of February, year 1493.

At your service.

The Admiral

Thomas Harriot

from A Briefe and True Report of the
New Found Land of Virginia (1590)

Of the Nature and Manners of the People

It resteth I speak a word or two of the natural inhabitants, their natures and manners, . . . as that you may know, how that they in respect of troubling our inhabiting and planting, are not to be feared, but that they shall have cause both to fear and love us, that shall inhabit with them.

They are a people clothed with loose mantles made of Deer skins, & aprons of the same round about their middles; all else naked; of such a difference of statures only as we in England, having no edge tools or weapons of iron or steel to offend us withal, neither know they how to make any: those weapons that they have, are only bows made of Witch hazel, & arrows of reeds, flat edged truncheons also of wood about a yard long, neither have they anything to defend themselves but targets made of barks, and some armours made of sticks wickered together with thread. . . .

Their manner of wars amongst themselves is either by sudden surprising one another most commonly about the dawning of the day, or moonlight, or else by ambushes, or some subtle devices. Set battles are very rare, except it fall out where there are many trees, where either part may have some hope of defence, after the delivery of every arrow, in leaping behind some or other.

If there fall out any wars between us & them, what their fight is likely to be, we having advantages against them so many manner of ways, as by our discipline, our strange weapons and devices else, especially by ordinance great and small, it may be easily imagined; by the experience we have had in some places, the turning up of their heels against us in running away was their best defence. In respect of us they are a people poor, and for want of skill and judgment in the knowledge and use of our things, do esteem our trifles before things of greater value: Notwithstanding in their proper manner considering the want of such means as we have, they seem very ingenious; For although they have no such tools, nor any such crafts, sciences and arts as we; yet in those things they do, they show excellence of wit. And by how much they upon due consideration shall find our manner of knowledges and crafts to exceed theirs in perfection, and speed for doing or execution, by so much the more is it probable that they should desire our friendships & love, and have the greater respect for pleasing and obeying us. Whereby may be hoped if means of good government be used, that they may in short time be brought to civility and the embracing of true religion.

Some religion they have already, which although it be far from the truth, yet being as it is, there is hope it may be the easier and sooner reformed.

They believe that there are many Gods which they call *Montóac,* but of different sorts and degrees; one only chief and great God, which hath been from all eternity. Who as they affirm when he purposed to make the world, made first other gods of a principal order to be as means and instruments to be used in the creation and government to follow; and after the Sun, Moon, and Stars as petty gods, and the instruments of the other order more principal. First they say were made waters, out of which by the gods was made all diversity of creatures that are visible or invisible.

For mankind they say a woman was made first, which by the working of one of the gods, conceived and brought forth children: And in such sort they say they had their beginning. But how many years or ages have passed since, they say they can make no relation, having no letters nor other such means as we to keep records of the particularities of times past, but only tradition from father to son. . . .

They believe also the immortality of the soul, that after this life as soon as the soul is departed from the body, according to the works it hath done, it is either carried to heaven the habitacle of gods, there to enjoy perpetual bliss and happiness, or else to a great pit or hole, which they think to be in the furthest parts of their part of the world toward the sunset, there to burn continually: the place they call *Popogusso.* . . .

Most things they saw with us, as Mathematical instruments, sea compasses, the virtue of the lodestone in drawing iron, a perspective glass whereby was showed many strange sights, burning glasses, wildfire works, guns, books, writing and reading, spring clocks that seem to go of themselves, and many other things that we had, were so strange unto them, and so far exceeded their capacities to comprehend the reason and means how they should be made and done, that they thought they were rather the works of gods than of men, or at the leastwise they had been given and taught us of the gods. Which made many of them to have such opinion of us, as that if they knew not the truth of god and religion already, it was rather to be had from us, whom God so specially loved than from a people that were so simple, as they found themselves to be in comparison of us. Whereupon greater credit was given unto that we spoke of concerning such matters.

Many times and in every town where I came, according as I was able, I made declaration of the contents of the Bible; that therein was set forth the true and only GOD, and his mighty works, that therein was contained the true doctrine of salvation through Christ, with many particularities of Miracles and chief points of religion, as I was able then to utter, and thought fit for the time. And although I told them the book materially & of itself was not of any such virtue, as I thought they did conceive, but only the doctrine therein contained; yet would many be glad to touch it, to embrace it, to kiss it, to hold it to their breasts and heads, and stroke over all their body with it; to show their hungry desire of that knowledge which was spoken of.

The *Wiroans* with whom we dwelt called *Wingina,* and many of his people would be glad many times to be with us at our prayers, and many times call upon us both in his own town, as also in others whither he sometimes accompanied us, to pray and sing Psalms; hoping thereby to be partaker of the same effects which we by that means also expected.

Twice this *Wiroans* was so grievously sick that he was like to die, and as he lay languishing, doubting of any help by his own priests, and thinking he was in such danger for offending us and thereby our god, sent for some of us to pray and be a means to our God that it would please him either that he might live, or after death dwell with him in bliss, so likewise were the requests of many others in the like case.

On a time also when their corn began to wither by reason of a drought which happened extraordinarily, fearing that it had come to pass by reason that in something they had displeased us, many would come to us & desire us to pray to our God of England, that he would preserve their corn, promising that when it was ripe we also should be partakers of the fruit.

There could at no time happen any strange sickness, losses, hurts, or any other cross unto them, but that they would impute to us the cause or means thereof for offending or not pleasing us.

One other rare and strange accident, leaving others, will I mention before I end, which moved the whole country that either knew or heard of us, to have us in wonderful admiration.

There was no town where we had any subtle device practiced against us, we leaving it unpunished or not revenged (because we sought by all means possible to win them by gentleness) but that within a few days after our departure from every such town, the people began to die very fast, and many in short space; in some towns about twenty, in some forty, in some sixty, & in one six score, which in truth was very many in respect of their numbers. This happened in no place that we could learn but where we had been where they used some practice against us, and after such time; The disease also was so strange, that they neither knew what it was, nor how to cure it; the like by report of the oldest men in the country never happened before, time out of mind. A thing specially observed by us, as also by the natural inhabitants themselves.

Insomuch that when some of the inhabitants which were our friends & especially the *Wiroans Wingina* had observed such effects in four or five towns to follow their wicked practices, they were persuaded that it was the work of our God through our means, and that we by him might kill and slay whom we would without weapons and not come near them.

And thereupon when it had happened that they had understanding that any of their enemies had abused us in our journeys, hearing that we had wrought no revenge with our weapons, & fearing upon some cause the matter should so rest: did come and entreat us that we would be a means to our God that they as others that had dealt ill with us might in like sort die; alleging how much it would be for our credit and profit as also theirs; and hoping furthermore that we would do so much at their requests in respect of the friendship we profess them.

Whose entreaties although we showed that they were ungodly, affirming that our God would not subject himself to any such prayers and requests of men: that indeed all things have been and were to be done according to his good pleasure as he had ordained: and that we to show ourselves his true servants ought rather to make petition for the contrary, that they with them might live together with us, be made partakers of his truth & serve him in righteousness; but notwithstanding in such sort, that we refer that as all other things, to be done according to his divine will & pleasure, and as by his wisdom he had ordained to be best.

Yet because the effect fell out so suddenly and shortly after according to their desires, they thought nevertheless it came to pass by our means, and that we in using such speeches unto them did but dissemble the matter, and therefore came unto us to give us thanks in their manner that although we satisfied them not in promise, yet in deeds and effect we had fulfilled their desires.

This marvelous accident in all the country wrought so strange opinions of us, that some people could not tell whether to think us gods or men, and the rather because that all the space of their sickness, there was no man of ours known to die, or that was especially sick: they noted also that we had no women among us, neither that we did care for any of theirs.

Some therefore were of opinion that we were not born of women, and therefore not mortal, but that we were men of an old generation many years past then risen again to immortality. . . .

The Towne of Secota

Their townes that are not inclosed with poles aire commonlye fayrer. Then suche as are inclosed, as appereth in this figure which livelye expresseth the towne of Secotam. For the howses are Scattered heer and ther, and they have gardein expressed by the letter E. wherin groweth Tobacco which the inhabitants call Uppowoc. They have also groaves wherin thei take deer, and fields wherin they sowe their corne. In their corne fields they builde as yt weare a scaffolde wher on they sett a cottage like to a rownde chaire, signiffied by F. wherin they place one to watche for there are suche nomber of fowles, and beasts, that unless they keepe the better watche, they would soone devoure all their corne. For which cause the watcheman maketh continual cryes and noyse. They sowe their corne with a certaine distance noted by H. other wise one stalke would choke the growthe of another and the corne would not come unto his rypeurs[1] G. For the leaves therof are large, like unto the leaves of great reedes. They have also a severall broade plotte C. whear they meete with their neighbours, to celebrate their cheefe solemne feastes . . . and a place D. whear after they have ended their feaste they make merrie togither. Over against this place they have a rownd plott B. wher they assemble themselves to make their solemne prayers. Not far from which place ther is a lardge buildinge A. wherin are the tombes of their kings and princes . . . likewise they have garden notted bey the letter I. wherin they use to sowe pompions.[2] Also a place marked with K. wherin the make a fyre att their solemne feasts, and hard without the towne a river L. from whence they fetche their water. This people therfore voyde of all covetousnes lyve cherfullye and att their harts ease. Butt they solemnise their feasts in the nigt, and therefore they keepe verye great fyres to avoyde darkenes, ant to testifie their Joye.

[1]Ripeness.
[2]Pumpkins.

JOHN SMITH

on The Chesapeake Indians (1608)

The land is not populous, for the men be fewe; their far greater number is of women and children. Within 60 miles of *James* Towne there are about some 5000 people, but of able men fit for their warres scarse 1500. To nourish so many together they have yet no means, because they make so small a benefit of their land, be it never so fertill.

6 or 700 have been the most [that] hath seen together, when they gathered themselves to have surprised *Captaine Smyth at Pamaunke,* having but 15 to withstand the worst of their furie. As small as the proportion of ground that hath yet beene discoverd, is in comparison of that yet unknowne. The people differ very much in stature, especially in language, as before is expressed.

Since being very great as the *Sesquesahamocks,* others very little as the *Wighcocomocoes:* but generally tall and straight, of a comely proportion, and of a colour browne, when they are of any age, but they are borne white. Their haire is generally black; but few have any beards. The men weare halfe their heads shaven, the other halfe long. For Barbers they use their women, who with 2 shels will grate away the haire, of any fashion they please. The women are cut in many fashions agreeable to their yeares, but ever some part remaineth long.

They are very strong, of an able body and full of agilitie, able to endure to lie in the woods under a tree by the fire, in the worst of winter, or in the weedes and grasse, in *Ambuscado* in the Sommer.

They are inconstant in everie thing, but what feare constraineth them to keepe. Craftie, timerous, quicke of apprehension and very ingenuous. Some are of disposition fearful, some bold, most cautelous, all *Savage.* Generally covetous of copper, beads, and such like trash. They are soone moved to anger, and so malitious, that they seldome forget an injury: they seldome steale one from another, least their conjurors should reveale it, and so they be pursued and punished. That they are thus feared is certaine, but that any can reveale their offences by conjuration I am doubtful. Their women are carefull not to bee suspected of dishonesty without the leave of their husbands.

Each household knoweth their owne lands and gardens, and most live of their owne labours.

For their apparell, they are some time covered with the skinnes of wilde beasts, which in winter are dressed with the haire, but in sommer without. The better sort use large mantels of deare skins not much differing in fashion from the Irish mantels. Some imbrodered with white beads, some with copper, other painted after their manner. But the common sort have scarce to cover their nakednesse but with grasse, the leaves of trees, or such like. We have seen some use mantels made of Turkey feathers, so prettily wrought and woven with threeds that nothing could bee discerned but the feathers, that was exceeding warme and very handsome. But the women are alwaies covered about their midles with a skin and very shamefast to be seene bare.

They adorne themselves most with copper beads and paintings. Their women some have their legs, hands, breasts and face cunningly imbrodered with diverse workes, as beasts, serpentes, artificially wrought into their flesh with blacke spots. In each eare commonly they have 3 great holes, whereat they hange chaines, bracelets, or copper. Some of their men weare in those holes, a small greene and yellow coloured snake, neare halfe a yard in length, which crawling and lapping her selfe about his necke often times familiarly would kiss his lips. Others wear a dead Rat tied by the tail. Some on their heads weare the wing of a bird or some large feather, with a Rattell. Those Rattels are somewhat like the chape of a Rapier but lesse, which they take from the taile of a snake. Many have the whole skinne of a hawke or some strange fowle, stuffed with the wings abroad. Others a broad peece of copper, and some the hand of their enemy dryed. Their heads and shoulders are painted red with the roote *Pocone* braied to powder mixed with oyle; this they hold in somer to preserve them from the heate, and in winter from the cold. Many other formes of paintings they use, but he is the most gallant that is the most monstrous to behould.

Their buildings and habitations are for the most part by the rivers or not farre distant from some fresh spring. Their houses are built like our Arbors of small young springs bowed and tyed, and so close covered with mats or the barkes of trees very handsomely, that notwithstanding either winde raine or weather, they are as warme as stooves, but very smoaky, yet at the toppe of the house there is a hole made for the smoake to goe into right over the fire.

Against the fire they lie on little hurdles of Reedes covered with a mat, borne from the ground a foote and more by a hurdle of wood. On these round about the house, they lie heads and points one by thother against the fire: some covered with mats, some with skins, and some starke naked lie on the ground, from 6 to 20 in a house.

Their houses are in the midst of their fields or gardens; which are smal plots of ground, some 20, some 40, some 100, some 200, some more, some lesse. Some times from 2 to 100 of these houses [are] togither, or but a little separated by groves of trees. Neare their habitations is little small wood, or old trees on the ground, by reason of their burning of them for fire. So that a man may gallop a horse amongst these woods any waie, but where the creekes or Rivers shall hinder.

Men women and children have their severall names according to the severall humor of their Parents. Their women (they say) are easilie delivered of childe, yet doe they love children verie dearly. To make them hardy, in the coldest mornings they wash them in the rivers, and by painting and ointments so tanne their skins, that after year or two, no weather will hurt them.

The men bestowe their times in fishing, hunting, wars, and such manlike exercises, scorning to be seene in any woman like exercise, which is the cause that the women be verie painefull and the men often idle. The women and children do the rest of the worke. They make mats, baskets, pots, morters, pound their corne, make their bread, prepare their victuals, plant their corne, gather their corne, beare all kind of burdens, and such like. . . .

POWHATAN

Speech to Captain John Smith (1609)

Captaine Smith, you may understand that I having seene the death of all my people thrice, and not any one living of these three generations but my selfe; I know the difference of Peace and Warre better than any in my Country. But now I am old and ere long must die, my brethren, namely Opitchapam, Opechancanough, and Kekataugh my two sisters, and their two daughters, are distinctly each others successors. I wish their experience no lesse then mine, and your love to them no lesse then mine to you. But this bruit from Nandsamund, that you are come to destroy my Country, so much affrighteth all my people as they dare not visit you. What will it availe you to take that by force you may quickly have by love, or to destroy them that provide you food. What can you get by warre, when we can hide our provisions and fly to the woods? whereby you must famish by wronging us your friends. And why are you thus jealous of our loves seeing us unarmed, and both doe, and are willing still to feede you, with that you cannot get but by our labours? Thinke you I am so simple, not to know it is better to eate good meate, lye well, and sleepe quietly with my women and children, laugh and be merry with you, have copper, hatchets, or what I want being your friend: then be forced to flie from all, to lie cold in the woods, feede upon Acornes, rootes, and such trash, and be so hunted by you, that I can neither rest, eate, nor sleepe; but my tyred men must watch, and if a twig but breake, every one cryeth there commeth Captaine Smith: then must I fly I know not whether: and thus with miserable feare, end my miserable life, leaving my pleasures to such youths as you, which through your rash unadvisednesse may quickly as miserably end, for want of that, you never know where to finde. Let this therefore assure you of our loves, and every yeare our friendly trade shall furnish you with Corne; and now also, if you would come in friendly manner to see us, and not thus with your guns and swords as to invade your foes.

Paul Le Jeune

on Montagnais Indian Cosmology (1634)

I have already reported that the Savages believe that a certain one named Atachocam had created the world, and that one named Messou had restored it. I have questioned upon this subject the famous Sorcerer and the old man with whom I passed the Winter; they answered that they did not know who was the first Author of the world,—that it was perhaps Atahocham, but that was not certain; that they only spoke of Atahocam as one speaks of a thing so far distant that nothing sure can be known about it; . . .

As to the Messou, they hold that he restored the world, which was destroyed in the flood; whence it appears that they have some tradition of that great universal deluge which happened in the time of Noah. . . .

They also say that all animals, of every species, have an elder brother, who is, as it were, the source and origin of all individuals, and this elder brother is wonderfully great and powerful. . . . Now these elders of all the animals are the juniors of the Messou. Behold him well related, this worthy restorer of the Universe, he is elder brother to all beasts. If any one, when asleep, sees the elder or progenitor of some animals, he will have a fortunate chase; if he sees the elder of the Beavers, he will take Beavers; if he sees the elder of the Elks, he will take Elks, possessing the juniors through the favor of their senior whom he has seen in the dream. . . .

Their Religion, or rather their superstition, consists besides in praying; but O, my God, what prayers they make! In the morning, when the little children come out from their Cabins, they shout, *Cacouakhi, Pakhais Amiscouakhi, Pakhais Mousouakhi, Pakhais,* "Come Porcupines; come, Beavers; come, Elk;" and this is all of their prayers.

When the Savages sneeze, and sometimes even at other times, during the Winter, they cry out in a loud voice, *Etouctaian miraouinam an Mirouscamikhi,* "I shall be very glad to see the Spring."

At other times, I have heard them pray for the Spring, or for deliverance from evils and other similar things; and they express all these things in the form of desires, crying out as loudly as they can, "I would be very glad if this day would continue, if the wind would change," etc. I could not say to whom these wishes are addressed, for they themselves do not know, at least those whom I have asked have not been able to enlighten me. . . .

These are some of their superstitions. How much dust there is in their eyes, and how much trouble there will be to remove it that they may see the beautiful light of truth! I believe, nevertheless, that any one who knew their language perfectly, in order to give them good reasons promptly, would soon make them laugh at their own stupidity; for sometimes I have made them ashamed and confused, although I speak almost entirely by my hands, I mean by signs. . . .

In order to have some conception of the beauty of this edifice, its construction must be described. I shall speak from knowledge, for I have often helped to build it. Now, when we arrived at the place where we were to camp, the women, armed with axes, went here and there in the great forests, cutting the framework of the hostelry where we were to lodge; meantime the men, having drawn the plan thereof, cleared away the snow with their snowshoes, or with shovels which they make and carry expressly for this purpose. Imagine now a great ring or square in the snow, two, three or four feet deep, according to the weather or the place where they encamp. This depth of snow makes a white wall for us, which surrounds us on all sides, except the end where it is broken through to form the door. The framework having been brought, which consists of twenty or thirty poles, more or less, according to the size of the cabin, it is planted, not upon the ground but upon the snow; then they throw upon these poles, which converge a little at the top, two or three rolls of bark sewed together, beginning at the bottom, and behold, the house is made. The ground inside, as well as the wall of snow which extends all around the cabin, is covered with little branches of fir; and, as a finishing touch, a wretched skin is fastened to two poles to serve as a door, the doorposts being the snow itself. . . .

You cannot stand upright in this house, as much on account of its low roof as the suffocating smoke; and consequently you must always lie down, or sit flat upon the ground, the usual posture of the Savages. When you go out, the cold, the snow, and the danger of getting lost in these great woods drive you in again more quickly than the wind, and keep you a prisoner in a dungeon which has neither lock nor key.

This prison, in addition to the uncomfortable position that one must occupy upon a bed of earth, has four other great discomforts,—cold, heat, smoke, and dogs. As to the cold, you have the snow at your head with only a pine branch between, often nothing but your hat, and the winds are free to enter in a thousand places. . . . When I lay down at night I could study through this opening both the Stars and the Moon as easily as if I had been in the open fields.

Nevertheless, the cold did not annoy me as much as the heat from the fire. A little place like their cabins is easily heated by a good fire, which sometimes roasted and broiled me on all sides, for the cabin was so narrow that I could not protect myself against the heat. You cannot move to right or left, for the Savages, your neighbors, are at your elbows; you cannot withdraw to the rear, for you encounter the wall of snow, or the bark of the cabin which shuts you in. I did not know what position to take. Had I stretched myself out, the place was so narrow that my legs would have been halfway in the fire; to roll myself up in a ball, and crouch down in their way, was a position I could not retain as long as they could; my clothes were all scorched and burned. You will ask me perhaps if the snow at our backs did not melt under so much heat. I answer, "no;" that if sometimes the heat softened it in the least, the cold immediately turned it into ice. I will say, however, that both the cold and the heat are endurable, and that some remedy may be found for these two evils.

But, as to the smoke, I confess to you that it is martyrdom. It almost killed me, and made me weep continually, although I had neither grief nor sadness in my heart. It sometimes grounded all of us who were in the cabin; that is, it caused us to place our mouths against the earth in order to breathe. For, although the Savages were accustomed to this torment, yet occasionally it became so dense that they, as well as I, were compelled to prostrate themselves, and as it were to eat the earth, so as not to drink the smoke. I have sometimes remained several hours in this position, especially during the most severe cold and when it snowed; for it was then the smoke assailed us with the greatest fury, seizing us by the throat, nose, and eyes. . . .

As to the dogs, which I have mentioned as one of the discomforts of the Savages' houses, I do not know that I ought to blame them, for they have sometimes rendered me good service. . . . These poor beasts, not being able to live outdoors, came and lay down sometimes upon my shoulders, sometimes upon my feet, and as I only had one blanket to serve both as covering and mattress, I was not sorry for this protection, willingly restoring to them a part of the heat which I drew from them. It is true that, as they were large and numerous, they occasionally crowded and annoyed me so much, that in giving me a little heat they robbed me of my sleep, so that I very often drove them away. . . .

CHRESTIEN LECLERQ

A Micmac Indian Response to the French

(c. 1677)

I am greatly astonished that the French have so little cleverness, as they seem to exhibit in the matter of which thou hast just told me on their behalf, in the effort to persuade us to convert our poles, our barks, and our wigwams into those houses of stone and of wood which are tall and lofty, according to their account, as these trees. Very well! But why now, . . . do men of five to six feet in height need houses which are sixty to eighty? For, in fact, as thou knowest very well thyself, Patriarch—do we not find in our own all the conveniences and the advantages that you have with yours, such as reposing, drinking, sleeping, eating, and amusing ourselves with our friends when we wish? This is not all, . . . my brother, hast thou as much ingenuity and cleverness as the Indians, who carry their houses and their wigwams with them so that they may lodge wheresoever they please, independently of any seignior whatsoever? Thou art not as bold nor as stout as we, because when thou goest on a voyage thou canst not carry upon thy shoulders thy buildings and thy edifices. Therefore it is necessary that thou preparest as many lodgings as thou makest changes of residence, or else thou lodgest in a hired house which does not belong to thee. As for us, we find ourselves secure from all these inconveniences, and we can always say, more truly than thou, that we are at home everywhere, because we set up our wigwams with ease wheresoever we go, and without asking permission of anybody. Thou reproachest us, very inappropriately, that our country is a little hell in contrast with France, which thou comparest to a terrestrial paradise, inasmuch as it yields thee, so thou sayest, every kind of provision in abundance. Thou sayest of us also that we are the most miserable and most unhappy of all men, living without religion, without manners, without honour, without social order, and, in a word, without any rules, like the beasts in our woods and our forests, lacking bread, wine, and a thousand other comforts which thou hast in superfluity in Europe. Well, my brother, if thou dost not yet know the real feelings which our Indians have towards thy country and towards all thy nation, it is proper that I inform thee at once. I beg thee now to believe that, all miserable as we seem in thine eyes, we consider ourselves nevertheless much happier than thou in this, that we are very content with the little that we have; and believe also once for all, I pray, that thou deceivest thyself greatly if thou thinkest to persuade us that thy country is better than ours. For if France, as thou sayest, is a little terrestrial paradise, art thou sensible to leave it? And why abandon wives, children, relatives, and friends? Why risk thy life and thy property every year, and why venture thyself with such risk, in any season whatsoever, to the storms and tempests of the sea in order to come to a strange and barbarous country which thou considerest the poorest and least fortunate of the world? Besides, since we are wholly convinced of the contrary, we scarcely take the trouble to go to France, because we fear, with good reason, lest we find little satisfaction there, seeing, in our own experience, that those who are natives thereof leave it every year in order to enrich themselves on our shores. We believe, further, that you are also incomparably poorer than we, and that you are only simple journeymen, valets, servants, and slaves, all masters and grand captains though you may appear, seeing that you glory in our old rags and in our miserable suits of beaver which can no longer be of use to us, and that you find among us, in the fishery for cod which you make in these parts, the wherewithal to comfort your misery and the poverty which oppresses you. As to us, we find all our riches and all our conveniences among ourselves, without trouble and without exposing our lives to the dangers in which you find yourselves constantly through your long voyages. And, whilst feeling compassion for you in the sweetness of our repose, we wonder at the anxieties and cares which you give yourselves night and day in order to load your ship. We see also that all your people live, as a rule, only upon cod which you catch among us. It is everlastingly nothing but cod—cod in the morning, cod at midday, cod at evening, and always cod, until things come to such a pass that if you wish some good morsels, it is at our expense; and you are obliged to have recourse to the Indians, whom you despise so much, and to beg them to go a-hunting that you may be regaled. Now tell me this one little thing, if thou hast any sense: Which of these two is the wisest and happiest—he who labours without ceasing and only obtains, and that with great trouble, enough to live on, or he who rests in comfort and finds all that he needs in the pleasure of hunting and fishing? It is true, . . . that we have not always had the use of bread and of wine which your France produces; but, in fact, before the arrival of the French in these parts, did not the Gaspesians live much longer than now? And if we have not any longer among us any of those old men of a hundred and thirty to forty years, it is only because we are gradually adopting your manner of living, for experience is making it very plain that those of us live longest who, despising your bread, your wine, and your brandy, are content with the custom of our ancestors and of all the Gaspesian nation. Learn now, my brother, once for all, because I must open to thee my heart: there is no Indian who does not consider himself infinitely more happy and more powerful than the French.

2. Puritanism in History and Literature

A		In *Adam's* Fall We Sinned all.	N		*Nightengales* fing In Time of Spring.
B		Thy Life to Mend This *Book* Attend.	O		The *Royal Oak* it was the Tree That fav'd His Royal Majeftie.
C		The *Cat* doth play And after flay.	P		*Peter* denies His Lord and cries
D		A *Dog* will bite A Thief at night.	Q		Queen *Efther* comes in Royal State To Save the JEWS from difmal Fate
E		An *Eagle's* flight Is out of fight.	R		*Rachel* doth mourn For her fifft born.
F		The Idle *Fool* Is whipt at School.	S		*Samuel* anoints Whom God appoints.
G		As runs the *Glafs* Mans life doth pafs.	T		*Time* cuts down all Both great and fmall.
H		My *Book* and *Heart* Shall never part.	U		*Uriah's* beauteous Wif Made David feek his Life.
J		*Job* feels the Rod Yet bleffes GOD.	W		*Whales* in the Sea God's Voice obey.
K		Our *KING* the good No man of blood.	X		*Xerxes* the great did die, And fo muft you & I.
L		The *Lion* bold The *Lamb* doth hold.	Y		*Youth* forward flips Death foonest nips.
M		The *Moon* gives light In time of night.	Z		*Zacheus* he Did climb the Tree His Lord to fee.

The New England Primer, 1727.

Like maps, textbooks—including the one you're reading now—are created for specific reasons and particular audiences. Benjamin Harris, a Massachusetts printer, first published *The New England Primer* in 1683. In this little book for little children, the ABCs became an alphabet of Puritan beliefs, from original sin ("In Adam's Fall/We Sinned all.") to the importance of individual literacy ("My Book and Heart/Shall never part."). The first printer in British North America had set up shop in Cambridge in 1639. In 1647 Massachusetts Bay Colony had required that towns with fifty or more families support a public school, and that towns of a hundred families support a grammar school that included Latin. The message of literacy was nothing new. But by 1683, more non-Puritans were migrating to New England, descendants of the original settlers were "falling away" from their parents' and grandparents' faith, and secular books shared bookstore space with religious ones. *The New England Primer*, then, may have aimed to do more than just reinforce a people's existing faith. At the same time, it offered potential profit to its publisher: for centuries, textbooks have been the bedrock of publishers' success. English law prohibited colonial printers from publishing English Bibles; most literary works wouldn't sell enough copies to recoup a small printer's expenses. So little books like almanacs, sermons, and schoolbooks became the colonial printer's staples. Reprinted and revised, *The New England Primer* kept selling for over a hundred years.

Chronology

1629:   Puritans begin settlement of Massachusetts Bay

1636:   Harvard College founded

1637:   Pequot War in New England

1639:   First printing press established in Massachusetts

1644:   Dissenter Roger Williams receives charter to found Rhode Island

1647:   Massachusetts law establishing first public schools in British America

1664:   New York founded when English take New Netherland

1675:   King Philip's War

1681:   Pennsylvania founded by Quaker William Penn

1683:   *New-England Primer* first published

1692:   Witchcraft trials in Salem, Massachusetts

Introduction

When we use the word "puritan" today, images of repression are usually not far behind. "Puritans" are people with stern moral codes, which they seek to impose on others: they are hostile to social pleasures—their own and those of others. This definition of "puritan" has colored the way we think about the seventeenth-century Puritans, the English religious dissenters who settled in the place they called "New England" in the 1630s. But where did our definition come from? Does it represent the Puritans as they were—or as they wished to present themselves? Or was it an image created later, by writers like Nathaniel Hawthorne, whose 1850 novel *The Scarlet Letter* portrayed the Puritans as morally rigid and hypocritical?

To understand the Puritans in their own terms, we must consider their status in England in the early 1600s. England was officially a Protestant nation, whose national religion was the Church of England (or Anglican Church). But it had become Protestant for political rather than religious reasons: in 1529 King Henry VIII had broken with the Catholic Church and established the Church of England when the Pope refused to grant him a divorce. By the end of the 1500s, some Anglicans came to believe that the Church of England was little more than Catholicism with the English monarch instead of the Pope at its head: its rituals and beliefs seemed little different from those of Roman Catholicism. These Anglicans sought to "purify" their church: to simplify rituals, reduce the power of bishops (whom the monarch appointed), and reform the clergy to emphasize theological learning. These "Puritans" did not seek to leave the Anglican Church, unlike the "Separatists"—including the Pilgrims who came to Plymouth Rock in 1620—who wanted to establish their own congregations. Rather, they hoped to reform it. The Puritans were unlike the Pilgrims in other ways as well. The Pilgrims who came to Plymouth had first emigrated from England to Holland, where they were excluded from mercantile guilds and found their children adopting Dutch ways and intermarrying with the Dutch. For them, America was a refuge, a place to separate from both persecution and cultural and religious dilution. For the Puritans who came a decade later, coming to America was part of a larger mission: not just escaping religious and economic persecution, but establishing a society that would be a model for the one they had left.

John Winthrop (1588–1649), the leader of the Puritan emigrants to America in 1630, expressed many of the Puritans' ideas and aspirations in his sermon "A Model of Christian Charity," which he delivered aboard the ship *Arbella* carrying his community across the Atlantic. Drawn from Calvinist theology, the concept of predestination implied that God had a relationship with each individual and had predetermined who would be saved and who would be damned. In Puritan theology, individuals could do nothing about their predestination: God's grace alone, not good deeds, determined their fates. However, one's behavior in life was a sign of whether one would be saved: in other words, piety and industriousness in this world could indicate salvation in the next—even if it could do nothing to guarantee salvation. Beyond individual predestination, Winthrop indicated a vision for the Puritan community as a whole. It was to be a "city on a hill" for others (both the native peoples in America and Anglicans at home in Old England) to emulate. Puritans argued that they had an "errand into the wilderness," a covenant with God to establish a new society, to bring order out of the seeming chaos of the new world. And this covenant was communal: God had made it not with particular individuals, but with the community as a whole. The community

23

was at the heart of Puritan religion *and* everyday life. When first established, a New England Puritan town might measure two hundred square miles, but its residents settled within a very small radius of each other. Rather than move to the outskirts of town to settle farms remote from their fellow Puritans, they made their homes near the center of town, which contained their church (which was often also their meeting hall) and cemetery. Town governance also reflected the communitarian model: conducted in town meetings, it depended on the idea that the inhabitants shared a common purpose.

In addition to Winthrop's sermon, which reminded Puritans of what they were about to create, the page from the *New England Primer*, one of the colony's earliest schoolbooks, offers a glimpse into how Puritan values were passed to children. Anne Bradstreet (1612–1672), one of the Puritans aboard the *Arbella* in 1630, became the first important poet in British North America. Her father was the second governor of the Massachusetts colony (after Winthrop), and in 1647 her brother-in-law took copies of her early poems back to England, where they were published unbeknownst to her. The first of her poems here, "The Prologue," was the introduction in that volume. The second, written later about the burning of her house, reflects one of the stark realities of life on the frontier (where she lived with her husband and children). Together the poems suggest her sense of herself as a woman poet in Puritan society.

On and beyond the borders of Puritan settlement, of course, lived Native Americans: Narragansetts, Wampanoags, Pequots, and others. The early Puritan settlers established friendly relations with these native inhabitants, who taught the newcomers critical agricultural methods and entered into trade with the English colonists. Some Puritans, like the minister John Eliot (1604–1690), sought to convert Indians to Christianity. Eliot, the "Indian Apostle," wrote a series of "dialogues" to assist Indians he had trained to become Christian missionaries among their own people. In the dialogue here, the Christianized Indian Piumbukhou tries to teach his unconverted relatives about the Bible. By the 1660s, however, conversion efforts were giving way to tensions as the English colonists continued to press into Indian territory. As early as 1637, the Pequot tribe had been nearly destroyed in a war with settlers in the Connecticut River Valley. In 1675 a deadlier conflict, known as King Philip's War (after the English name for the Wampanoag leader), broke out between several tribes and the colonists of Massachusetts Bay, Plymouth, and Connecticut. Over a thousand colonists died in the early years of the conflict, but eventually the white settlers prevailed, crushing the tribes, killing or capturing between three and five thousand Indians and enslaving another thousand, and killing their leaders. (In the map of New England—originally published in England in 1675—that appears at the end of this chapter, we can see contemporary evidence of this warfare.)

Even before the start of King Philip's War, numerous leaders of Puritan New England had begun to lament a social problem they called "declension." The colonists seemed to be falling away from the faith and communitarian spirit of the original settlers. Ministers preached sermons on the subject; the Indian attack that started King Philip's War seemed to be God's punishment for the colonists' breach of their covenant. Soon after the war erupted, the Massachusetts General Court (the colonial legislature) passed a law to restore the colony's moral order—and thus renew its favor in God's eyes. Declension, however, was difficult to reverse by legislation. In part, fears of declension were built into the image of the "city on a hill": even in the optimism of 1630, John Winthrop had warned the first settlers what would happen if they broke their divine covenant. What Puritan ministers observed with horror in the 1670s did have some basis in reality. By the 1670s, the children and grandchildren of the first settlers no longer remained united by the fear of monarchial persecution that had knit their parents together. Moreover, as a second and third generation arose—and the population of New England towns multiplied—colonists moved outward from town centers to the land on the periphery, and regional disagreements emerged within the towns. Perhaps most important, by the late seventeenth century non-Puritan immigrants from England were coming to New England in growing numbers: when Puritan leaders decried declension, they may well have been looking at a society in which many inhabitants had never been Puritan at all.

It is important to remember that the Puritans of New England made up just one part of the British colonies in seventeenth-century North America. When we think of the foundations of American society, however, we often tend to think of the Puritans—even though they were dominant in only a few colonies and even though their period of real political and social control was relatively short. Our perception stems in part from the Puritans' assiduous record-keeping: highly literate (unlike many of the early Virginia colonists), they left numerous volumes of public documents, diaries, and letters. And perhaps the Puritans make more attractive ancestors because they possessed a social ideal, a belief in the "city on a hill" that would be used by American leaders for the next 350 years. (The early Virginians, by contrast, came to the New World almost exclusively for material gain.) But making the Puritans into the precursors of American democracy—or, conversely, the precursors of American hypocrisy and repression—fails to understand them in their own terms. Perhaps, instead, the Puritans' place as American founders lies in introducing questions that have persisted ever since, about the basis for community, the community's relationship to those inside and outside it, and the implications of a sense of mission.

JOHN WINTHROP

from A Model of Christian Charity (1630)

God Almighty in His most holy and wise providence hath so disposed of the condition of mankind as in all times some must be rich, some poor, some high and eminent in power and dignity, others mean and in subjection.

THE REASON HEREOF:

First, to hold conformity with the rest of His works, being delighted to show forth the glory of His wisdom in the variety and difference of the creatures and the glory of His power, in ordering all these differences for the preservation and good of the whole, and the glory of His greatness; that as it is the glory of princes to have many officers, so this great King will have many stewards, counting Himself more honored in dispensing His gifts to man by man, than if He did it by His own immediate hand.

Secondly, that He might have the more occasion to manifest the work of His Spirit: first, upon the wicked in moderating and restraining them, so that the rich and mighty should not eat up the poor, nor the poor and despised rise up against their superiors and shake off their yoke; secondly, in the regenerate, in exercising His graces in them: as in the great ones, their love, mercy, gentleness, temperance, etc.; in the poor and inferior sort, their faith, patience, obedience, etc.

Thirdly, that every man might have need of other [men], and from hence they might be all knit more nearly together in the bond of brotherly affection. From hence it appears plainly that no man is made more honorable than another or more wealthy, etc., out of any particular and singular respect to himself but for the glory of his creator and the common good of the creature, man. Therefore God still reserves the property of these gifts to Himself, as [in] Ezekial 16:17; He there calls wealth His gold and His silver, etc. [In] Proverbs 3:9 He claims their service as His due, "Honor the Lord with thy riches," etc. All men being thus (by divine providence) ranked into two sorts, rich and poor, under the first are comprehended all such as are able to live comfortably by their own means duly improved; and all others are poor, according to the former distribution. There are two rules whereby we are to walk, one towards another: justice and mercy. These are always distinguished in their act and in their object, yet may they both concur in the same subject in each respect: as sometimes there may be an occasion of showing mercy to a rich man in some sudden danger of distress, and also doing of mere justice to a poor man in regard of some particular contract. There is likewise a double law by which we are regulated in our conversation, one towards another, in both the former respects, the law of nature and the law of grace, or the moral law or the law of the Gospel, to omit the rule of justice as not properly belonging to this purpose, otherwise than it may fall into consideration in some particular cases. By the first of these laws, man, as he was enabled so withal, [is] commanded to love his neighbor as himself; upon this ground stand all the precepts of the moral law, which concerns our dealings with men. To apply this to the works of mercy, this law requires two things: first, that every man afford his help to another in every want or distress; secondly, that he perform this out of the same affection which makes him careful of his own good according to that of our savior, Matthew 7:12: "Whatsoever ye would that men should do to you." This was practiced by Abraham and Lot in entertaining the angels and the old man of Gibea.

The law of grace or the Gospel hath some difference from the former, as in these respects: first, the law of nature was given to man in the estate of innocency, this [law] of the Gospel [was given to man] in the estate of regeneracy. Secondly, the former propounds one man to another as the same flesh and image of God, this as a brother in Christ also, and in the communion of the same spirit, and so teacheth us to put a difference between Christians and others. Do good to all, especially to "the household of faith." Upon this ground the Israelites were to put a difference between the brethren of such as were strangers though not of the Canaanites. Thirdly, the law of nature could give no rules for dealing with enemies, for all are to be considered as friends in the estate of innocency; but the Gospel commands love to an enemy. Proof: "If thine enemy hunger, feed him;" "love your enemies, do good to them that hate you," Matthew 5:44.

This law of the Gospel propounds likewise a difference of seasons and occasions. There is a time when a Christian must sell all and give to the poor as they did in the apostles' times. There is a time also when a Christian (though they give not all yet) must give beyond their ability, as they of Macedonia, II Corinthians 8, 9. Likewise, community of perils calls for extraordinary liberality and so doth community in some special service for the church. Lastly, when there is no other means whereby our Christian brother may be relieved in this distress, we must help him beyond our ability, rather than tempt God in putting Him upon help by miraculous or extraordinary means.

It rests now to make some application of this discourse by the present design which gave the occasion of writing it. Herein are four things to be propounded: first, the persons; secondly, the work, thirdly, the end; fourthly, the means.

1. For the persons, we are a company professing ourselves fellow members of Christ, in which respect only, though we were absent from each other many miles, and had our employments as far distant, yet we ought to account ourselves knit together by this bond of love, and live in the exercise of it, if we would have comfort of our being in Christ. This was notorious in the practice of the Christians in former times, as is testified of the Waldenses from the mouth of one of the adversaries, Aeneas Sylvius: *Mutuo solent amare penè antequam norint*—they used to love any of their own religion even before they were acquainted with them.

2. For the work we have in hand, it is by mutual consent, through a special overruling providence and a more than an ordinary approbation of the churches of Christ, to seek out a place of cohabitation and consortship under a due form of government both civil and ecclesiastical. In such cases as this, the care of the public must oversway all private respects by which not only conscience but mere civil policy doth bind us; for it is a true rule that particular estates cannot subsist in the ruin of the public.

3. The end is to improve our lives to do more service to the Lord, the comfort and increase of the body of Christ whereof we are members, [so] that ourselves and posterity may be the better preserved from the common corruptions of this evil world, to serve the Lord and work out our salvation under the power and purity of His holy ordinances.

4. For the means whereby this must be effected, they are twofold: a conformity with the work and the end we aim at; these we see are extraordinary, therefore we must not content ourselves with usual ordinary means. Whatsoever we did or ought to have done when we lived in England, the same must we do, and more also where we go. That which the most in their churches maintain as a truth in profession only, we must bring into familiar and constant practice: as in this duty of love we must love brotherly without dissimulation; we must "love one another with a pure heart fervently;" we must "bear one another's burdens;" we must not look only on our own things but

also on the things of our brethren. Neither must we think that the Lord will bear with such failings at our hands as He doth from those among whom we have lived.

Thus stands the cause between God and us: we are entered into covenant with Him for this work; we have taken out a commission; the Lord hath given us leave to draw our own articles. We have professed to enterprise these actions upon these and these ends; we have hereupon besought Him of favor and blessing. Now if the Lord shall please to hear us and bring us in peace to the place we desire, then hath He ratified this covenant and sealed our commission, [and He] will expect a strict performance of the articles contained in it. But if we shall neglect the observation of these articles which are the ends we have propounded and, dissembling with our God, shall fall to embrace this present world and prosecute our carnal intentions, seeking great things for ourselves and our posterity, the Lord will surely break out in wrath against us, be revenged of such a perjured people, and make us know the price of the breach of such a covenant.

Now the only way to avoid this shipwreck and to provide for our posterity is to follow the counsel of Micah: to do justly, to love mercy, to walk humbly with our God. For this end, we must be knit together in this work as one man. We must entertain each other in brotherly affection; we must be willing to abridge ourselves of our superfluities, for the supply of others' necessities; we must uphold a familiar commerce together in all meekness, gentleness, patience and liberality. We must delight in each other, make others' conditions our own, rejoice together, mourn together, labor and suffer together, always having before our eyes our commission and community in the work, our community as members of the same body. So shall we "keep the unity of the spirit in the bond of peace," the Lord will be our God and delight to dwell among us, as His own people, and [He] will command a blessing upon us in all our ways, so that we shall see much more of His wisdom, power, goodness, and truth than formerly we have been acquainted with. We shall find that the God of Israel is among us, when ten of us shall be able to resist a thousand of our enemies, when He shall make us a praise and glory [so] that men shall say of succeeding plantations, "The Lord make it like that of New England," for we must consider that we shall be as a city upon a hill, the eyes of all people are upon us. So that if we shall deal falsely with our God in this work we have undertaken, and so cause Him to withdraw His present help from us, we shall be made a story and a by-word through the world; we shall open the mouths of enemies to speak evil of the ways of God and all professors for God's sake; we shall shame the faces of many of God's worthy servants and cause their prayers to be turned into curses upon us, till we be consumed out of the good land whither we are going. And to shut up this discourse with that exhortation of Moses, that faithful servant of the Lord, in his last farewell to Israel, Deuteronomy 30: Beloved, there is now set before us "life and good, death and evil," in that we are commanded this day to love the Lord our God and to love one another, to walk in His ways and to keep His commandments, and His ordinance, and His laws, and the articles of our covenant with Him [so] that we may live and be multiplied and [so] that the Lord our God may bless us in the land whither we go to possess it. But if our hearts shall turn away so that we will not obey, but shall be seduced and worship other gods, our pleasures and profits, and serve them, it is propounded unto us this day, we shall surely perish out of the good land whither we pass over this vast sea to possess it.

> Therefore, let us choose life,
> that we, and our seed,
> may live; by obeying His
> voice and cleaving to Him,
> for He is our life and
> our prosperity.

ANNE BRADSTREET
"The Prologue" (1650)

1

To sing of wars, of captains, and of kings,
Of cities founded, commonwealths begun,
For my mean pen are too superior things:
Or how they all, or each their dates have run
Let poets and historians set these forth,
My obscure lines shall not so dim their worth.

2

But when my wond'ring eyes and envious heart
Great Bartas' sugared lines do but read o'er,
Fool I do grudge the Muses did not part
'Twixt him and me that overfluent store:
A Bartas can do what a Bartas will
But simple I, according to my skill.

3

From schoolboy's tongue no rhet'ric we expect,
Nor yet a sweet consort from broken strings,
Nor perfect beauty where's a main defect:
My foolish, broken, blemished Muse so sings,
And this to mend, alas, no art is able,
'Cause nature made it so irreparable.

4

Nor can I, like that fluent sweet tongued Greek,
Who lisped at first, in future times speak plain.
By art he gladly found what he did seek,
A full requital of his striving pain.
Art can do much, but this maxim's most sure:
A weak or wounded brain admits no cure.

5

I am obnoxious to each carping tongue
Who says my hand a needle better fits,
A poet's pen all scorn I should thus wrong,

For such despite they cast on female wits:
If what I do prove well, it won't advance,
They'll say it's stol'n, or else it was by chance.

6

But sure the antique Greeks were far more mild,
Else of our sex, why feigned they those nine
And poesy made Calliope's own child;
So 'mongst the rest they placed the arts divine:
But this weak knot they will full soon untie,
The Greeks did nought, but play the fools and lie.

7

Let Greeks be Greeks, and women what they are,
Men have precedency and still excel,
It is but vain unjustly to wage war;
Men can do best, and women know it well.
Preeminence in all and each is yours;
Yet grant some small acknowledgement of ours.

8

And oh ye high flown quills that soar the skies,
And ever with your prey still catch your praise,
If e'er you deign these lowly lines your eyes,
Give thyme or parsley wreath, I ask no bays;
This mean and unrefined ore of mine
Will make your glist'ring gold but more to shine.

Anne Bradstreet
"Upon the Burning of Our House, July 10th, 1666" (1666)

In silent night when rest I took
For sorrow near I did not look
I wakened was with thund'ring noise
And piteous shrieks of dreadful voice.
That fearful sound of "Fire!" and "Fire!"
Let no man know is my desire.

I, starting up, the light did spy,
And to my God my heart did cry
To strengthen me in my distress
And not to leave me succorless.
Then, coming out, beheld a space
The flame consume my dwelling place.

And when I could no longer look,
I blest His name that gave and took,
That laid my goods now in the dust.
Yea, so it was, and so 'twas just.
It was His own, it was not mine,
Far be it that I should repine;

He might of all justly bereft
But yet sufficient for us left.
When by the ruins oft I past
My sorrowing eyes aside did cast,
And here and there the places spy
Where oft I sat and long did lie:

Here stood that trunk, and there that chest,
There lay that store I counted best.
My pleasant things in ashes lie,
And them behold no more shall I.
Under thy roof no guest shall sit,
Nor at thy table eat a bit.

No pleasant tale shall e'er be told,
Nor things recounted done of old.
No candle e'er shall shine in thee,
Nor bridegroom's voice e'er heard shall be.
In silence ever shall thou lie
Adieu, Adieu, all's vanity.

Then straight I 'gin my heart to chide,
And did thy wealth on earth abide?
Didst fix thy hope on mold'ring dust?
The arm of flesh didst make thy trust?
Raise up thy thoughts above the sky
That dunghill mists away may fly.

Thou hast an house on high erect,
Framed by that mighty Architect,
With glory richly furnished,
Stands permanent though this be fled.
It's purchased and paid for too
By Him who hath enough to do.

A price so vast as is unknown
Yet by His gift is made thine own;
There's wealth enough, I need no more,
Farewell, my pelf, farewell my store.
The world no longer let me love,
My hope and treasure lies above.

John Eliot

A Dialogue Between Piumbukhou and His Unconverted Relatives

(c. 1671)

KINSMAN: I had rather that my actions of love should testify how welcome you are, and how glad I am of this your kind visitation, than that I should say it in a multitude of words. But in one word, you are very welcome into my heart, and I account it among the best of the joys of this day, that I see your face, and enjoy your company in my habitation.

KINSWOMAN: It is an addition to the joys of this day, to see the face of my loving kinsman. And I wish you had come a little earlier, that you might have taken part with us in the joys of this day, wherein we have had all the delights that could be desired, in our merry meeting, and dancing.

And I pray cousin, how doth your wife, my loving kinswoman, is she yet living? And is she not yet weary of your new way of praying to God? And what pleasure have you in those ways?

PIUMBUKHOU: My wife doth remember her love to you. She is in good health of body, and her soul is in a good condition. She is entered into the light of the knowledge of God, and of Christ. She is entered into the narrow way of heavenly joys, and she doth greatly desire that you would turn from these ways of darkness in which you so much delight, and come taste and see how good the Lord is.

And whereas you wish I had come sooner, to have shared with you in your delights of this day. Alas, they are no delights, but griefs to me, to see that you do still delight in them. I am like a man that have tasted of sweet wine and honey, which have so altered the taste of my mouth, that I abhor to taste of your sinful and foolish pleasures, as the mouth doth abhor to taste the most filthy and stinking dung, the most sour grapes, or most bitter gall. Our joys in the knowledge of God, and of Jesus Christ, which we are taught in the Book of God, and feel in our heart, is sweeter to our soul, than honey is unto the mouth and taste.

KINSWOMAN: We have all the delights that the flesh and blood of man can devise and delight in and we taste and feel the delights of them, and would you make us believe that you have found out new joys and delights, in comparison of which all our delights do stink like dung? Would you make us believe that we have neither eyes to see, nor ears to hear, nor mouth to taste? Ha, ha, he! I appeal to the sense and sight and feeling of the company present, whether this be so.

ALL: You say very true. Ha, ha, he!

PIUMBUKHOU: Hearken to me, my friends, and see if I do not give a clear answer unto this seeming difficulty. Your dogs take as much delight in these meetings, and the same kinds of delight as you do. They delight in each others company. They provoke each other to lust, and enjoy the pleasures of lust as you do. They eat and play and sleep as you do. What joys have you more than dogs have to delight the body of flesh and blood?

But all mankind have an higher and better part than the body. We have a soul, and that soul shall never die. Our soul is to converse with God, and to converse in such things as do concern God, and heaven, and an eternal estate, either in happiness with God, if we walk with him and serve him in this life, or in misery and torment with the Devil, if we serve him in this life. The service of God doth consist in virtue, and wisdom, and delights of the soul, which will reach to heaven, and abide forever.

But the service of the Devil is in committing sins of the flesh, which defile both body and soul, and reach to hell, and will turn all to fire and flame to torment your souls and bodies in all eternity.

Now consider, all your pleasures and delights are such as defile you with sin, and will turn to flame, to burn and torment you. They provoke God to wrath, who hath created the prison of hell to torment you, and the more you have took pleasure in sin, the greater are your offences against God, and the greater shall be your torments.

But we that pray to God repent of our old sins, and by faith in Christ we seek for, and find a pardon for what is past, and grace and strength to reform for time to come. So that our joys are soul joys in godliness, and virtue, and hope of glory in another world when we die.

Your joys are bodily, fleshly, such as dogs have, and will all turn to flames in hell to torment you.

KINSMAN: If these things be so, we had need to cease laughing, and fall to weeping, and see if we can draw water from our mournful eyes to quench these tormenting flames. My heart trembles to hear these things. I never heard so much before, nor have I any thing to say to the contrary, but that these things may be so. But how shall I know that you say true? Our forefathers were (many of them) wise men, and we have wise men now living. They all delight in these our delights. They have taught us nothing about our soul, and God, and heaven, and hell, and joy and torment in the life to come. Are you wiser than our fathers? May not we rather think that *English* men have invented these stories to amaze us and fear us out of our old customs, and bring us to stand in awe of them, that they might wipe us of our lands, and drive us into corners, to seek new ways of living, and new places too? And be beholding to them for that which is our own, and was ours, before we knew them.

ALL: You say right.

PIUMBUKHOU: The Book of God is no invention of Englishmen. It is the holy law of God himself, which was given unto man by God, before Englishmen had any knowledge of God, and all the knowledge which they have, they have it out of the Book of God. And this book is given to us as well as to them, and it is as free for us to search the scriptures as for them. So that we have our instruction from a higher hand, than the hand of man. It is the great Lord

God of heaven and earth, who teacheth us these great things of which we speak. Yet this is also true, that we have great cause to be thankful to the English, and to thank God for them. For they had a good country of their own, but by ships sailing into these parts of the world, they heard of us, and of our country, and of our nakedness, ignorance of God, and wild condition. God put it into their hearts to desire to come hither, and teach us the good knowledge of God; and their King gave them leave so to do, and in our country to have their liberty to serve God according to the word of God. And being come hither, we gave them leave freely to live among us. They have purchased of us a great part of those lands which they possess. They love us, they do us right, and no wrong willingly. If any do us wrong, it is without the consent of their rulers, and upon our complaints our wrongs are righted. They are (many of them, especially the ruling part) good men, and desire to do us good. God put it into the heart of one of their ministers (as you all know) to teach us the knowledge of God, by the word of God, and hath translated the holy Book of God into our language, so that we can perfectly know the mind and counsel of God. And out of this book have I learned all that I say unto you, and therefore you need no more doubt of the truth of it, then you have cause to doubt that the heaven is over our head, the sun shineth, the earth is under our feet, we walk and live upon it, and breathe in the air. For as we see with our eyes these things to be so, so we read with our own eyes these things which I speak of, to be written in God's own book, and we feel the truth thereof in our own hearts.

KINSWOMAN: Cousin, you have wearied your legs this day with a long journey to come and visit us, and you weary your tongue with long discourses. I am willing to comfort and refresh you with a short supper.

ALL: Ha, ha, he. Though short, if sweet that has good favor to a man that is weary. Ha, ha, he.

KINSWOMAN: You make long and learned discourses to us which we do not well understand. I think our best answer is to stop your mouth, and fill your belly with a good supper, and when your belly is full you will be content to take rest yourself, and give us leave to be at rest from these gastering and heart-trembling discourses. We are well as we are, and desire not to be troubled with these new wise sayings.

THE MASSACHUSETTS GENERAL COURT
Provoking Evils (1675)

Whereas the most wise & holy God, for several years past, hath not only warned us by his word, but chastized us with his rods, inflicting upon us many general (though lesser) judgments, but we have neither heard the word nor rod as wee ought, so as to be effectually humbled for our sins to repent of them, reform, and amend our ways; hence it is the righteous God hath heightened our calamity, and given commission to the barbarous heathen to rise up against us, and to become a smart rod and severe scourge to us, in burning & depopulating several hopeful plantations, murdering many of our people of all sorts, and seeming as it were to cast us off, and putting us to shame, and not going forth with our armies, hereby speaking aloud to us to search and try our ways, and turn again unto the Lord our God, from whom wee have departed with a great backsliding.

1. The Court, apprehending there is too great a neglect of discipline in the churches, and especially respecting those that are their children, through the non acknowledgment of them according to the order of the gospel; in watching over them, as well as chattechising of them, inquiring into their spiritual estates, that, being brought to take hold of the covenant, they may acknowledge & be acknowledged according to their relations to God & to his church, and their obligations to be the Lords, and to approve themselves so to be by a suitable profession & conversation; and do therefore solemnly recommend it unto the respective elders and brethren of the several churches throughout this jurisdiction to take effectual course for reformation herein.

2. Whereas there is manifest pride openly appearing amongst us in that long hair, like women's hair, is worn by some men, either their own or others hair made into perewiggs, and by some women wearing borders of hair, and their cutting, curling, & immodest laying out their hair, which practice doth prevail & increase, especially amongst the younger sort,—

This Court doth declare against this ill custom as offensive to them, and divers sober Christians amongst us, and therefore doe hereby exhort and advise all persons to use moderation in this respect; and further, doe empower all grand juries to present to the County Court such persons, whither male or female, whom they shall judge to exceed in the premises; and the County Courts are hereby authorized to proceed against such delinquents either by admonition, fine, or correction, according to their good discretion.

3. Notwithstanding the wholesome laws already made by this Court for restraining excess in apparel, yet through corruption in many, and neglect of due execution of those laws, the evil of pride in apparel, both for costliness in the poorer sort, & vain, new, strange fashions, both in poor & rich, with naked breasts and arms, or, as it were, pinioned with the addition of superstitious ribbons both on hair & apparel; for redress whereof, it is ordered by this Court, that the County Courts, from time to time, doe give strict charge to present all such persons as they shall judge to exceed in that kind, and if the grand jury shall neglect their duty herein, the County Court shall impose a fine upon them at their discretion.

And it is further ordered, that the County Court, single magistrate, Commissioners Court in Boston, have hereby power to summon all such persons so offending before them, and for the first offense to admonish them, and for each offense of that kind afterwards to impose a fine of ten shillings upon them, or, if unable to pay, to inflict such punishment as shall be by them thought most suitable to the nature of the offense; and the same judges above named are hereby empowered to judge of and execute the laws already extant against such excess.

Whereas it may be found amongst us, that men's thresholds are set up by Gods thresholds, and mans posts besides Gods posts, especially in the open meetings of Quakers, whose damnable heresies, abominable idolatries, are hereby promoted, embraced, and practiced, to the scandal of religion, hazard of souls, and provocation of divine jealousy against this people, for prevention & reformation whereof, it is ordered by this Court and the authority thereof, that every person found at a Quakers meeting shall be apprehended, ex officio, by the constable, and by warrant from a magistrate or commissioner shall be committed to the house of correction, and there to have the discipline of the house applied to them, and to be kept to work, with bread & water, for three days, and then released, or else shall pay five pounds in money as a fine to the county for such offense; and all constables neglecting their duty in not faithfully executing this order shall incur the penalty of four pounds, upon conviction, one third whereof to the informer.

And touching the law of importation of Quakers, that it may be more strictly executed, and none transgressing to escape punishment,—

It is hereby ordered, that the penalty to that law averred be in no case abated to less than twenty pounds.

4. Whereas there is so much profanes amongst us in persons turning their backs upon the public worship before it be finished and the blessing pronounced,—

It is ordered by this Court, that the officers of the churches, or select-men, shall take care to prevent such disorders, by appointing persons to shut the meeting house doors, or any other meet way to attain the end.

5. Whereas there is much disorder & rudeness in youth in many congregations in time of the worship of God, whereby sin & profaneness is greatly increased, for reformation whereof,—

It is ordered by this Court, that the select men doe appoint such place or places in the meeting house for children or youth to sit in where they may be most together and in public view, and that the officers of the churches, or select-men, doe appoint some grave & sober person or persons to take a particular care of and inspection over them, who are hereby required to present a list of the names of such, who, by their own observance or the information of others, shall be found delinquent, to the next magistrate or Court, who are empowered for the first offense to admonish them, for the second offense to impose a fine of five shillings on their parents or governors, or order the children to be whipped, and if incorrigible, to be whipped with ten stripes, or sent to the house of correction for three days.

6. Whereas the name of God is prophaned by common swearing and cursing in ordinary communication, which is a sin that grows amongst us, and many hear such oaths and curses, and conceals the same from authority, for reformation whereof, it is ordered by this Court, that the laws already in force against this sin be vigorously prosecuted; and, as addition thereunto, it is further ordered, that all such persons who shall at any time hear profane oaths and curses spoken by any person or persons, and shall neglect to disclose the same to some magistrate, commissioner, or constable, such persons shall incur the same penalty provided in that law against swearers.

7. Whereas the shameful and scandalous sin of excessive drinking, tipling, & company keeping in taverns, &c, ordinaries, grows upon us, for reformation whereof,—

It is commended to the care of the respective County Courts not to license any more public houses then are absolutely necessary in any town, and to take care that none be licensed but persons of approved sobriety and fidelity to law and good order; and that licensed houses be regulated in their improvement for the refreshing & entertainment of travelers & strangers only, and all town dwellers are hereby strictly enjoined & required to forbear spending their time or estates in such common houses of entertainment, to drink & tiple, upon penalty of five shillings for every offense, or, if poor, to be whipped, at the discretion of the judge, not exceeding five stripes; and every ordinary keeper, permitting persons to transgress as above said, shall incur the penalty of five shillings for each offense in that kind; and any magistrate, commissioner, or selectmen are empowered & required vigorously to putt the abovesaid law in execution.

And, further, it is ordered, that all private, unlicensed houses of entertainment be diligently searched out, and the penalty of this law strictly imposed; and that all such houses may be the better discovered, the select-men of every town shall choose some sober and discrete persons, to be authorized from the County Court, each of whom shall take the charge of ten or twelve families of his neighborhood, and shall diligently inspect them, and present the names of such persons so transgressing to the magistrate, commissioners, or selectmen of the town, who shall return the same to be proceeded with by the next County Court as the law directs; and the persons so chosen and authorized, and attending their duty faithfully therein, shall have one third of the fines allowed them; but, if neglect of their duty, and shall be so judged by authority, they shall incur the same penalty provided against unlicensed houses.

8. Whereas there is a woeful breach of the fifth commandment to be found amongst us, in contempt of authority, civil, ecclesiastical, and domestical, this Court doth declare, that sin is highly provoking to the Lord, against which he hath borne severe testimony in his word, especially in that remarkable judgments upon Chorah and his company, and therefore doe strictly require & command all persons under this government to reform so great an evil, least God from heaven punish offenders herein by some remarkable judgments. And it is further ordered, that all County Courts, magistrates, commissioners, selectmen, and grand jurors, according to their several capacities, doe take strict care that the laws already made & provided in this case be duly executed, and particularly that evil of inferiors absenting themselves out of the families whereunto they belong in the night, and meeting with corrupt company without leave, and against the mind & to the great grief of their superiors, which evil practice is of a very perilous nature, and the root of much disorder.

It is therefore ordered by this Court, that whatever inferior shall be legally convicted of such an evil practice, such persons shall be punished with admonition for the first offense, with fine not exceeding ten shillings, or whipping not exceeding five stripes, for all offenses of like nature afterwards.

9. Whereas the sin of idleness (which is a sin of Sodom) doth greatly increase, notwithstanding the wholesome laws in force against the same, as an addition to that law,—

This Court doth order, that the constable, with such other person or persons whom the selectmen shall appoint, shall inspect particular families, and present a list of the names of all idle persons to the selectmen, who are hereby strictly required to proceed with them as already the law directs, and in case of obstinacy, by charging the constable with them, who shall convey them to some magistrate, by him to be committed to the house of correction.

10. Whereas there is oppression in the midst of us, not only by such shopkeepers and merchants who set excessive prizes on their goods, also by mechanics but *also by mechanics* and day laborers, who are daily guilty of that evil, for redress whereof, & as an addition to the law, title Oppression, it is ordered by this Court, that any person that judgeth himself oppressed by shopkeepers or merchants in setting excessive prizes on their goods, have hereby liberty to make their complaint to the grand jurors, or otherwise by petition to the County Court immediately, who shall send to the person accused, and if the Court, upon examination, judge the person complaining in-

jured, they shall cause the offendor to return double the overplus, or more then the equal price, to the injured person, and also impose a fine on the offenders at the discretion of the Court; and if any person judge himself oppressed by mechanics or day laborers, they may make complaint thereof to the selectmen of the town, who if upon the examination doe find such complaint just, having respect to the quality of the pay, and the length or shortness of the day labor, they shall cause the offender to make double restitution to the party injured, and pay a fine of double the value exceeding the due price.

11. Whereas there is a loose & sinful custom of going or riding from town to town, and that oft times men & women together, upon pretense of going to lecture, but it appears to be merely to drink & revel in ordinaries & taverns, which is in itself scandalous and it is to be feared a notable means to debauch our youth and hazard the chastity of such as are drawn forth thereunto, for prevention whereof,—

It is ordered by this Court, that all single persons who, merely for their pleasure, take such journeys, & frequent such ordinaries, shall be reputed and accounted riotous & unsober persons, and of ill behavior, and shall be liable to be summoned to appear before any County Court, magistrate, or commissioner, & being thereof convicted, shall give bond & sufficient sureties for the good behavior in twenty pounds, and upon refusal so to doe, shall be committed to prison for ten days, or pay a fine of forty shillings for each offense. . . .

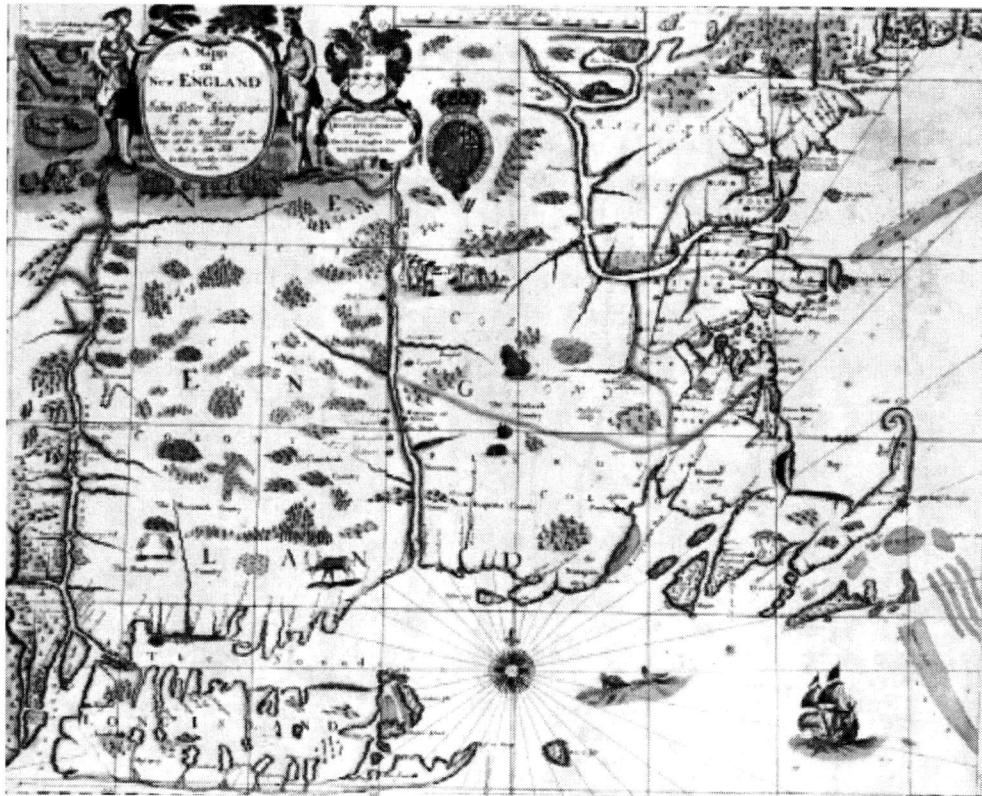

Map of New England, 1675. Courtesy of Map Collection, Yale University Library.

3. Intellectual and Political Revolutions, 1760–1820

The Washington Family, 1798 by Edward Savage. Courtesy of Winterthur Museum.

What's in a family picture? If the family was George Washington's, the meaning might be national as well as personal. In the 1790s, Edward Savage painted likenesses of George and Martha Washington and Martha's two grandchildren, whom George and Martha were raising. By 1796 he completed a family portrait, a huge painting now at the National Gallery of Art in Washington, D.C. Two years later he finished an engraving, which he offered for sale. *The Washington Family,* like Noah Webster's 1783 *American Spelling Book,* helped define America. Here the different segments of society–men and women, black and white–exist in harmonious hierarchy, the white men inhabiting one side and their dependents the other. George Washington is now the Father of His Country, not a young, revolutionary general. He still wears his uniform and spurs, but has removed his hat and joined the family circle. Young George Washington Parke Custis rests one hand on a globe, long a symbol of world power in portraits of European monarchs. Martha Washington and Eleanor Custis gaze at George, whose own eyes seem to focus on something beyond the picture itself–a man with a view toward something loftier. On the table, a map of the new national capital at Washington might remind viewers that George Washington had planned the city himself, or that America had a seat of national power (even if most Americans had little to do with the national government). In the background, a sweeping vista suggests the nation's boundless future. And everyone knows his or her place; nobody is trying to foment a second American Revolution.

Chronology

1740s: Religious Great Awakening begins in the Northeast

1753:   French start building forts from Lake Erie to the Ohio

1754–1763:   French and Indian War (Seven Years' War in Europe, 1756–1763)

1763:   Treaty of Paris ends Seven Years' War

1763:   Proclamation Line bars colonial settlement west of the Appalachians

1764:   Sugar Act

1765:   Stamp Act

1770:   Boston Massacre

1775:   War breaks out at Lexington and Concord

1776:   Thomas Paine's *Common Sense* (January)

Declaration of Independence (July)

1777:   Slavery abolished in Vermont

1783:   Treaty of Paris ends American Revolution

Noah Webster's *American Spelling Book*

1786:   Shays' Rebellion, Massachusetts

1787:   United States Constitution drafted

1787–1788:   Ratification debates

1789:   George Washington elected first President

1793:   Cotton gin invented

Introduction

When the thirteen British colonies in North America declared independence from Great Britain and renamed themselves the "United States of America" on July 4, 1776, it was by no means certain that their independence would last. War had already been raging for over fourteen months, and on that very day 32,000 British troops sailed into New York harbor. Within months, British armies controlled New York City and maintained substantial military advantages over the colonists—many of whom had little desire to break with their "mother country." When the last battles ended in 1781, the military phase of the "American Revolution" was over. But how revolutionary was this "revolution"? It eliminated the authority of the English king and parliament over the North American colonies (now states), but how did it change the lives or social structures of the people in those states?

Much had changed in the colonies between King Philip's War in the 1670s and the outbreak of revolution a century later. The population of the mainland colonies had grown phenomenally, from just over 75,000 inhabitants (not counting Native Americans) in 1660 to over 1.6 million a century later—a twenty-one-fold increase. Even more dramatic was the increase in the colonial black population: in 1660, three thousand blacks lived in the mainland colonies, about four percent of the total population. By 1760, blacks—most of them enslaved—numbered 326,000, more than twenty percent of the colonial population. In a century, slavery had become a primary labor system in Virginia, Maryland, and the Carolinas, and an important social and economic institution as well in New York, New Jersey, and Delaware.

In the mid-1600s, the English colonies in North America had been outposts of Great Britain. Clustered mainly along the Atlantic coastline, the colonists lived on the periphery—the outer edge—of the British empire. London was the commercial and cultural center of the empire. By 1750, colonial cities like Philadelphia, New York, and Boston were developing their own peripheries, regions to the west that depended on them for finished goods, newspapers, and commercial centers. The colonies remained overwhelmingly agricultural: more than 95% of colonists lived in rural areas, and most of those earned their livelihood as farmers. At the same time, colonial America was becoming increasingly complex economically, with rising artisan trades and mercantile sectors in the major cities. Ironically, as the colonies expanded they came to look *more*, not less, like English society. Like England, they developed stratifications of wealth, ranging from extremely rich merchants and professional men at the top to landless workers and unemployed paupers at the bottom, particularly in the cities. The merchants and professionals sought to become as "English" as possible, adopting the fashions and consumer styles of the English gentry. Many of the leaders of the American Revolution—George Washington, Thomas Jefferson, John Hancock—came from this colonial elite.

Within this colonial elite, too, the ideas of the European Enlightenment took the firmest root in America. The Enlightenment might be described as a massive intellectual movement, even a revolution, of the late-seventeenth and eighteenth centuries. The philosopher John Locke was among the most widely read Enlightenment figures: in his *Essay on Human Understanding*, Locke argued that God had not predetermined the human mind, that it was instead a *tabula rasa*, a blank slate. What God had furnished, according to Locke, was reason and the ability to acquire knowledge. Therefore, human beings possessed the power to improve their world by using their reason. Science, too, was central to Enlightenment thought: it could provide the methods to investigate and understand the world. The language of reason, science, and "natural laws"—fixed principles of the universe that humans could learn through investigation—became a staple of Enlightenment writings, on both sides of the Atlantic.

The colonial leaders of the revolt against England thus were perhaps the most "English" of the colonists: schooled in European ideas, dressed in the clothing of the English gentry, many of them living in homes modeled from English architectural styles. Why, then, would they have led a revolt against the very nation they sought to emulate culturally? In part, their revolt represented the assertiveness of an elite that had begun to recognize the boundaries of its authority. No matter how powerful within the colonies, their governance was always subject to the laws of King and Parliament—a legislature in which they could not sit and were not represented. In part, it stemmed from another set of ideas they had imbibed from English political theory: the concept that power and liberty were always and inherently in conflict, an idea especially persuasive to those who felt their liberty threatened. For example, from the standpoint of Parliament, its tax on colonial sugar imports (1764) served to pay for British administration of the colonies after the French and Indian War, in which England had nearly bankrupted itself defending the colonies against the French. From the standpoint of some colonists, the tax encroached upon their liberties. Over the next ten years, a cycle developed in which more and more colonists perceived British governmental actions as a conspiracy against colonial liberty. Even when hostilities broke out in April 1775 at Lexington and Concord, though, a majority of colonists may still have favored reconciling with their "mother country."

Thomas Paine's pamphlet *Common Sense,* published in January 1776, helped to sway public opinion toward complete American independence. Paine (1737–1809), who had moved from London to Philadelphia just two years earlier, employed a variety of rhetorical strategies to make his argument; within weeks thousands of copies of the pamphlet had been printed. Over 120,000 copies rolled from printing presses across the colonies by May 1776, making *Common Sense* the biggest publishing sensation in American history to that point. Even before Paine's best-selling pamphlet, artists and engravers had been producing pictures to fuel colonial resistance. *The Bloody Massacre perpetrated in King Street,* engraved by the Boston silversmith Paul Revere (1735–1818) shortly after the "Boston Massacre" of 1770, portrayed British soldiers in ways designed to stir colonial anger: the "redcoats" were an organized army, firing on command at colonists. (Never mind that the colonists may well have provoked the attack; the historical record is far from clear.) Amos Doolittle, another Massachusetts patriot, engraved the first visual illustrations of the opening battles: his *The Battle of Lexington* appeared in December 1775, just eight months after the battle. It, too, depicted events from a distinctly colonial vantage point.

On May 10, 1776, the Continental Congress (an extralegal body containing representatives of the thirteen colonies) called on the colonies to form their own governments—an act tantamount to declaring colonial independence. After Virginia's Richard Henry Lee introduced a resolution for independence on June 7, Congress appointed a five-man committee to draft a declaration. Thomas Jefferson (1743–1826) drafted the document, which explained in universal language the large reasons for independence, then detailed the particular grievances. Jefferson's early version of the Declaration of Independence and the final version are printed here. Soon after Jefferson's Declaration became public, twenty-three-year-old Lemuel Haynes (1753–1833)—a Massachusetts soldier in the American army, and the son of a black father and a white mother who had been raised as an indentured servant in the home of a farmer and minister—drew on Jefferson's words and ideas to make a further plea, for the end of slavery. Haynes's work, which was never published until 1983, suggests the limits of the American "revolution."

After the war ended, new questions arose. For instance, how was the new nation to be governed? The colonial experience led many (including Jefferson) to argue for strictly limited government, centered in the states and towns. Jefferson envisioned an agrarian republic, made up of educated, primarily self-governing farmers, whose self-sufficiency would make them the best citizens because they depended on no other for their livelihood. As society became more urban and moved toward manufacturing, Jefferson argued, it became more corrupt: citizens became less truly independent, and thus less able to place the common good above the interests of those who paid them. Other leaders of the Revolution, however, took a different view. During the war, the Continental Congress had encountered numerous difficulties raising an army and the money to pay for troops and supplies. Individual state governments had often resisted or ignored Congress, and under the Articles of Confederation (the agreement between the thirteen states) Congress had little power to enforce its requests. Men like Alexander Hamilton (1757–1804), who had seen the problems of such a system, favored a stronger central government. Events after the war reinforced their views. Social unrest in the 1780s—including Shays's Rebellion, in which mobs of farmers in western Massachusetts protested debt enforcement by shutting down courthouses—persuaded others of a need for central authority. The Shays "Rebels," who called themselves "Regulators," argued that they were simply pursuing the vision of the American Revolution, protesting a corrupt state government. When that government sent troops to crush the rebellion, it indicated its view of where revolution stopped.

Buoyed by the increasing number of state leaders who favored stronger national government, twelve states (all but Rhode Island) sent delegates to Philadelphia in the summer of 1787 to revise the Articles of Confederation. The delegates, who came to be known as the Constitutional Convention, went further: they scrapped the Articles and wrote an entirely new Constitution, creating a far more powerful national government divided into three branches (executive, legislative, and judicial). Their work aroused fierce controversy when they revealed it in late September; indeed, several major states seemed likely to reject this new Constitution, including New York. To generate support for ratification, Hamilton, James Madison (1751–1836), and John Jay wrote a series of essays for New York newspapers. These essays, published under the pseudonym of "Publius," titled *The Federalist Papers,* and reprinted in other states, made the case for adopting the Constitution. Numerous opponents—labeled Antifederalists—also took to the press. The Constitution won ratification, but not easily: in Virginia, the ratification convention approved it by an 89–79 vote; in New York, the margin was 30 to 27.

Creating a national constitution meant that the United States would have the skeleton of a political structure; it did not, however, mean that citizens of this new nation would necessarily think of themselves as "Americans." Artists like Benjamin Turner produced assertive engravings like *America Guided by Wisdom*—combining American symbols with classical Greek ones to suggest the new nation's place in the world's progress—but what did "American" mean? Numerous cultural entrepreneurs emerged to promote a national identity, none more enthusiastically than Noah Webster (1758–1843). A Connecticut schoolteacher, Webster argued in the 1780s that a new nation needed its own language, complete with spellings defined by American usage, not aristocratic British custom. Escaping English cultural dominance was not Webster's sole aim: he also sought to create cultural unity in a new nation that stretched from Maine to Georgia and as far west as Kentucky. To do so, he wrote spelling books, grammar books, and readers for America's youth. Not surprisingly, Webster became an ardent Federalist, for his dream of cultural union meshed well with Hamilton and Madison's objective of a strong national government. Webster's 1790 essay on American education, printed here, gives a glimpse of his vision for the new nation. It also indicates his idea about how the different sexes should be educated, an issue addressed by Judith Sargent

Murray (1751–1820) in the same year. Murray, like Lemuel Haynes and the Shays rebels, questioned the extent of the American "revolution."

Race remained the new nation's greatest dilemma, and nobody exemplified that dilemma better than Thomas Jefferson. As a Virginia planter, Jefferson owned slaves. He probably had a long-term sexual relationship with one of those slaves, Sally Hemings, though the nature of that relationship can never be fully known. As a revolutionary, Jefferson envisioned the end of slavery itself and wrote some of the most eloquent words against human bondage. He supported various proposals for emancipating slaves in his native Virginia–usually proposals for gradual emancipation, connected to schemes for African colonization of freed American slaves. As an Enlightenment scientist, Jefferson believed in the study of racial characteristics: what made black people different from white people? Did difference lie largely, or entirely, in the fact that black people had been enslaved? All of these questions emerged in Jefferson's *Notes on the State of Virginia,* a book he wrote in the early 1780s. A French diplomat in America sent a questionnaire about America to members of the Continental Congress; the questions found their way to Jefferson, whose answers about Virginia (ranging from statistics about land and climate to descriptions of customs) gave the fullest picture of any American state in this era. In the chapter on "Laws," excerpted here, Jefferson described recent proposals to change Virginia's legal code—and offered a lengthy, complex commentary on African Americans' abilities and potential. Six years after *Notes on the State of Virginia* was published (1785), Benjamin Banneker (1731–1806), an African-American mathematician, astronomer, and almanac maker, wrote to Jefferson—who was now the nation's first Secretary of State. Banneker challenged Jefferson to extend equality to all men regardless of race, offering his own almanac as testimony to the scientific achievement that people of African descent could accomplish. Days later, Jefferson replied. Their letters reveal yet again Jefferson's—and America's—complex and conflicted beliefs about race.

Perhaps, too, these complexities indicated the extent to which this was indeed a revolutionary age. The intellectual revolution of the Enlightenment and the political revolution of 1776 had led to new questions, far beyond those imagined possible by many of the men who had declared independence from the British king.

THOMAS PAINE

from Common Sense (1776)

Introduction

Perhaps the sentiments contained in the following pages, are not yet sufficiently fashionable to procure them general favour; a long habit of not thinking a thing *wrong*, gives it a superficial appearance of being *right*, and raises at first a formidable outcry in defence of custom. But the tumult soon subsides. Time makes more converts than reason. . . .

The cause of America is in a great measure the cause of all mankind. Many circumstances hath, and will arise, which are not local, but universal, and through which the principles of all Lovers of Mankind are affected, and in the Event of which, their Affections are interested. The laying a Country desolate with Fire and Sword, declaring War against the natural rights of all Mankind, and extirpating the Defenders thereof from the Face of the Earth, is the concern of every Man to whom Nature hath given the Power of feeling. . . .

Thoughts on the Present State of American Affairs

In the following pages I offer nothing more than simple facts, plain arguments, and common sense; and have no other preliminaries to settle with the reader, than that he will divest himself of prejudice and prepossession, and suffer his reason and his feelings to determine for themselves; that he will put *on*, or rather that he will not put *off*, the true character of a man, and generously enlarge his views beyond the present day.

Volumes have been written on the subject of the struggle between England and America. Men of all ranks have embarked in the controversy, from different motives, and with various designs; but all have been ineffectual, and the period of debate is closed. Arms, as the last resource, decide the contest; the appeal was the choice of the king, and the continent hath accepted the challenge. . . .

The sun never shined on a cause of greater worth. 'Tis not the affair of a city, a country, a province, or a kingdom, but of a continent—of at least one eighth part of the habitable globe. 'Tis not the concern of a day, a year, or an age; posterity are virtually involved in the contest, and will be more or less affected, even to the end of time, by the proceedings now. Now is the seed time of continental union, faith and honour. The least fracture now will be like a name engraved with the point of a pin on the tender rind of a young oak; the wound will enlarge with the tree, and posterity read it in full grown characters. . . .

I have heard it asserted by some, that as America hath flourished under her former connection with Great Britain, that the same connection is necessary towards her future happiness, and will always have the same effect. Nothing can be more fallacious than this kind of argument. We may as well assert, that because a child has thrived upon milk, that it is never to have meat; or that the first twenty years of our lives is to become a precedent for the next twenty. But even this is admitting more than is true, for I answer roundly, that America would have flourished as much, and probably much more, had no European power had any thing to do with her. The commerce by which she hath enriched herself are the necessaries of life, and will always have a market while eating is the custom of Europe.

But she has protected us, say some. That she hath engrossed us is true, and defended the continent at our expense as well as her own is admitted, and she would have defended Turkey from the same motive, viz. the sake of trade and dominion.

Alas, we have been long led away by ancient prejudices, and made large sacrifices to superstition. We have boasted the protection of Great Britain, without considering, that her motive was *interest* not *attachment*; that she did not protect us from *our enemies* on *our account*, but from *her enemies* on *her own account*, from those who had no quarrel with us on any *other account*, and who will always be our enemies on the *same account*. Let Britain wave her pretensions to the continent, or the continent throw off the dependence, and we should be at peace with France and Spain were they at war with Britain. The miseries of Hanover last war ought to warn us against connections.

It hath lately been asserted in parliament, that the colonies have no relation to each other but through the parent country, *i.e.* that Pennsylvania and the Jerseys, and so on for the rest, are sister colonies by the way of England; this is certainly a very round-about way of proving relationship, but it is the nearest and only true way of proving enemyship, if I may so call it. France and Spain never were, nor perhaps ever will be our enemies as *Americans,* but as our being the *subjects of Great Britain.*

But Britain is the parent country, say some. Then the more shame upon her conduct. Even brutes do not devour their young, nor savages make war upon their families; wherefore the assertion, if true, turns to her reproach; but it happens not to be true, or only partly so, and the phrase *parent* or *mother country* hath been Jesuitically adopted by the — and his parasites, with a low papistical design of gaining an unfair bias on the credulous weakness of our minds. Europe, and not England, is the parent country of America. This new world hath been the asylum for the persecuted lovers of civil and religious liberty from *every part* of Europe. Hither have they fled, not from the tender embraces of the mother, but from the cruelty of the monster; and it is so far true of England, that the same tyranny which drove the first emigrants from home, pursues their descendants still.

In this extensive quarter of the globe, we forget the narrow limits of three hundred and sixty miles (the extent of England) and carry our friendship on a larger scale; we claim brotherhood with every European Christian, and triumph in the generosity of the sentiment.

It is pleasant to observe by what regular gradations we surmount the force of local prejudice, as we enlarge our acquaintance with the world. A man born in any town in England divided into parishes, will naturally associate most with his fellow parishioners (because their interests in many cases will be common) and distinguish him by the name of *neighbour;* if he meet him but a few miles from home, he drops the narrow idea of a street, and salutes him by the name of *townsman;* if he travels out of the county, and meet him in any other, he forgets the minor divisions of street and town, and calls him *countryman, i.e. countyman;* but if in their foreign excursions they should associate in France or any other part of *Europe,* their local remembrance would be enlarged into that of *Englishmen.* And by a just parity of reasoning, all Europeans meeting in America, or any other quarter of the globe, are *countrymen;* for England, Holland, Germany, or Sweden, when compared with the whole, stand in the same places on the larger scale, which the divisions of street, town, and county do on the smaller ones; distinctions too limited for continental minds. Not one third of the inhabitants, even of this province, are of English descent. Wherefore I reprobate the phrase of parent or mother country applied to England only, as being false, selfish, narrow and ungenerous.

But admitting that we were all of English descent, what does it amount to? Nothing. Britain, being now an open enemy, extinguishes every other name and title: And to say that reconciliation is our duty, is truly farcical. The first king of England, of the present line (William the Conqueror) was a Frenchman, and half the peers of England are descendants from the same country; wherefore by the same method of reasoning, England ought to be governed by France. . . .

I challenge the warmest advocate for reconciliation, to shew, a single advantage that this continent can reap, by being connected with Great Britain. I repeat the challenge, not a single advantage is derived. Our corn will fetch its price in any market in Europe, and our imported goods must be paid for buy them where we will.

But the injuries and disadvantages we sustain by that connection, are without number; and our duty to mankind at large, as well as to ourselves, instruct us to renounce the alliance: Because, any submission to, or dependence on Great Britain, tends directly to involve this continent in European wars and quarrels; and sets us at variance with nations, who would otherwise seek our friendship, and against whom, we have neither anger nor complaint. As Europe is our market for trade, we ought to form no partial connection with any part of it. It is the true interest of America to steer clear of European contentions, which she never can do, while by her dependence on Britain, she is made the make-weight in the scale of British politics.

Europe is too thickly planted with kingdoms to be long at peace, and whenever a war breaks out between England and any foreign power, the trade of America goes to ruin, *because of her connection with Britain.* . . . Every thing that is right or natural pleads for separation. The blood of the slain, the weeping voice of nature cries, 'TIS TIME TO PART. Even the distance at which the Almighty hath placed England and America, is a strong and natural proof, that the authority of the one, over the other, was never the design of Heaven. The time likewise at which the continent was discovered, adds weight to the argument, and the manner in which it was peopled encreases the force of it. The reformation was preceded by the discovery of America, as if the Almighty graciously meant to open a sanctuary to the persecuted in future years, when home should afford neither friendship nor safety.

The authority of Great Britain over this continent, is a form of government, which sooner or later must have an end: And a serious mind can draw no true pleasure by looking forward, under the painful and positive conviction, that what he calls 'the present constitution' is merely temporary. . . .

It is the good fortune of many to live distant from the scene of sorrow; the evil is not sufficiently brought to *their* doors to make *them* feel the precariousness with which all American property is possessed. But let our imaginations transport us for a few moments to Boston, that seat of wretchedness will teach us wisdom, and instruct us for ever to renounce a power in whom we can have no trust. The inhabitants of that unfortunate city, who but a few months ago were in ease and affluence, have now no other alternative than to stay and starve, or turn out to beg. Endangered by the fire of their friends if they continue within the city, and plundered by the soldiery if they leave it. In their present condition they are prisoners without the hope of redemption, and in a general attack for their relief, they would be exposed to the fury of both armies.

Men of passive tempers look somewhat lightly over the offences of Britain, and, still hoping for the best, are apt to call out, *'Come we shall be friends again for all this.'* But examine the passions and feelings of mankind. Bring the doctrine of reconciliation to the touchstone of nature, and then tell me, whether you can hereafter love, honour, and faithfully serve the power that hath carried fire and sword into your land? If you cannot do all these, then are you only deceiving yourselves, and by your delay bringing ruin upon posterity. Your future connection with Britain, whom you can neither love nor honour, will be forced and unnatural, and being formed only on the plan of present convenience, will in a little time fall into a relapse more wretched than the first. But if you say, you can still pass the violations over, then I ask, Hath your house been burnt? Hath your property been destroyed before your face? Are your wife and children destitute of a bed to lie on, or bread to live on? Have you lost a parent or a child by their hands, and yourself the ruined and wretched survivor? If you have not, then are you not a judge of those who have. But if you have, and can still shake hands with the murderers, then are you unworthy the name of husband, father, friend, or lover, and whatever may be your rank or title in life, you have the heart of a coward, and the spirit of a sycophant. . . .

It is repugnant to reason, to the universal order of things, to all examples from the former ages, to suppose, that this continent can longer remain subject to any external power. The most sanguine in Britain does not think so. The utmost stretch of human wisdom cannot, at this time compass a plan short of separation, which can promise the continent even a year's security. Reconciliation is and was a falacious dream. Nature hath deserted the connection, and Art cannot supply her place. For, as Milton wisely expressed, 'Never can true reconcilement grow where wounds of deadly hate have pierced so deep.' . . .

Small islands not capable of protecting themselves, are the proper objects for kingdoms to take under their care; but there is something very absurd, in supposing a continent to be perpetually governed by an island. In no instance hath nature made the satellite larger than its primary planet, and as England and America, with respect to each other, reverses the common order of nature, it is evident they belong to different systems: England to Europe, America to itself. . . .

If there is any true cause of fear respecting independence, it is because no plan is yet laid down. Men do not see their way out—Wherefore, as an opening into that business, I offer the following hints; at the same time modestly affirming, that I have no other opinion of them myself, than that they may be the means of giving rise to something better. Could the straggling thoughts of individuals be collected, they would frequently form materials for wise and able men to improve to useful matter.

LET the assemblies be annual, with a President only. The representation more equal. Their business wholly domestic, and subject to the authority of a Continental Congress.

Let each colony be divided into six, eight, or ten, convenient districts, each district to send a proper number of delegates to Congress, so that each colony send at least thirty. The whole number in Congress will be at least 390. Each Congress to sit and to choose a president by the following method. When the delegates are met, let a colony be taken from the whole thirteen colonies by lot, after which let the whole Congress choose (by ballot) a president from out of the delegates of that province. In the next Congress, let a colony be taken by lot from twelve only, omitting that colony from which the president was taken in the former Congress, and so proceeding on till the whole thirteen shall have had their proper rotation. And in order that nothing may pass into a law but what is satisfactorily just, not less than three fifths of the Congress to be called a majority.—He that will promote discord, under a government so equally formed as this, would join Lucifer in his revolt.

But as there is a peculiar delicacy, from whom, or in what manner, this business must first arise, and as it seems most agreeable and consistent, that it should come from some intermediate body between the governed and the governors, that is between the Congress and the people, let a CONTINENTAL CONFERENCE be held, in the following manner, and for the following purpose.

A committee of twenty-six members of Congress, viz. two for each colony. Two members for each house of assembly, or Provincial convention; and five representatives of the people at large, to be chosen in the capital city or town of each province, for, and in behalf of the whole province, by as many qualified voters as shall think proper to attend from all parts of the province for that purpose; or, if more convenient, the representatives may be chosen in two or three of the most populous parts thereof. In this conference, thus assembled, will be united, the two grand principles of business, *knowledge* and *power*. The members of Congress, Assemblies, or Conventions, by having had experience in national concerns, will be able and useful counsellors, and the whole, being empowered by the people will have a truly legal authority.

The conferring members being met, let their business be to frame a CONTINENTAL CHARTER, or Charter of the United Colonies; (answering to what is called the Magna Charta of England) fixing the number and manner of choosing members of Congress, members of Assembly, with their date of sitting, and drawing the line of business and jurisdiction between them: (Always remembering, that our strength is continental, not provincial:) Securing freedom and property to all men, and above all things the free exercise of religion, according to the dictates of conscience; with such other matter as is necessary for a charter to contain. Immediately after which, the said conference

The Bloody Massacre perpetrated in King Street on March 5, 1770 by Paul Revere. Copyright © 2000 by Museum of Fine Arts, Boston. All rights reserved. Courtesy of Museum of Fine Arts, Boston.

to dissolve, and the bodies which shall be chosen conformable to the said charter, to be the legislators and governors of this continent and for the time being: Whose peace and happiness, may God preserve, Amen.

Should any body of men be hereafter delegated for this or some similar purpose, I offer them the following extracts from that wise observer on governments *Dragonetti.* 'The science', says he, 'of the politician consists in fixing the true point of happiness and freedom. Those men would deserve the gratitude of ages, who should discover a mode of government that contained the greatest sum of individual happiness, with the least national expense.'—*Dragonetti on Virtue and Rewards.*

But where says some is the King of America? I'll tell you Friend, he reigns above, and doth not make havoc of mankind like the Royal — of Britain. Yet that we may not appear to be defective even in earthly honours, let a day be solemnly set apart for proclaiming the charter; let it be brought forth placed on the divine law, the word of God; let a crown be placed thereon, by which the world may

know, that so far as we approve of monarchy, that in America THE LAW IS KING. For as in absolute governments the King is law, so in free countries the law *ought* to be King; and there ought to be no other. But lest any ill use should afterwards arise, let the crown at the conclusion of the ceremony be demolished, and scattered among the people whose right it is. . . .

Ye that tell us of harmony and reconciliation, can ye restore to us the time that is past? Can ye give to prostitution its former innocence? Neither can ye reconcile Britain and America. The last cord now is broken, the people of England are presenting addresses against us. There are injuries which nature cannot forgive; she would cease to be nature if she did. As well can the lover forgive the ravisher of his mistress, as the continent forgive the murders of Britain. The Almighty hath implanted in us these unextinguishable feelings for good and wise purposes. They are the guardians of his image in our hearts. They distinguish us from the herd of common animals. The social compact would dis-

solve, and justice be extirpated from the earth, or have only a casual existence were we callous to the touches of affection. The robber and the murderer, would often escape unpunished, did not the injuries which our tempers sustain, provoke us into justice.

O ye that love mankind! Ye that dare oppose, not only the tyranny, but the tyrant, stand forth! Every spot of the old world is over-run with oppression. Freedom hath been hunted round the globe. Asia, and Africa, have long expelled her.—Europe regards her like a stranger, and England hath given her warning to depart. O! receive the fugitive, and prepare in time an asylum for mankind.

The Battle of Lexington, April 19, 1775 by Amos Dolittle. Courtesy of Chicago Historical Society.

Thomas Jefferson

Declaration of Independence, original and final drafts (1776)

[note: The text is taken from Jefferson's *Autobiography.* The form of the Declaration as reported is printed in roman type, the parts stricken by Congress are bracketed in italics, while the parts substituted are in small capitals. Eds.]

[July 4, 1776]

When, in the course of human events, it becomes necessary for one people to dissolve the political bands which have connected them with another, and to assume among the powers of the earth the separate and equal station to which the laws of nature and of nature's God entitle them, a decent respect to the opinions of mankind requires that they should declare the causes which impel them to the separation.

We hold these truths to be self evident: that all men are created equal; that they are endowed by their Creator with CERTAIN [*inherent and*] inalienable rights; that among these are life, liberty, and the pursuit of happiness; that to secure these rights, governments are instituted among men, deriving their just powers from the consent of the governed; that whenever any form of government becomes destructive of these ends, it is the right of the people to alter or to abolish it, and to institute new government, laying its foundation on such principles, and organizing its powers in such form, as to them shall seem most likely to effect their safety and happiness. Prudence, indeed, will dictate that governments long established should not be changed for light and transient causes; and accordingly all experience hath shown that mankind are more disposed to suffer while evils are sufferable, than to right themselves by abolishing the forms to which they are accustomed. But when a long train of abuses and usurpations, [*begun at a distinguished period and*] pursuing invariably the same object, evinces a design to reduce them under absolute despotism, it is their right, it is their duty to throw off such government, and to provide new guards for their future security. Such has been the patient sufferance of these colonies; and such is now the necessity which constrains them to ALTER [*expunge*] their former systems of government. The history of the present king of Great Britain is a history of REPEATED [*unremitting*] injuries and usurpations, ALL HAVING [*among which appears no solitary fact to contradict the uniform tenor of the rest, but all have*] in direct object the establishment of an absolute tyranny over these states. To prove this, let facts be submitted to a candid world [*for the truth of which we pledge a faith yet unsullied by falsehood*].

He has refused his assent to laws the most wholesome and necessary for the public good.

He has forbidden his governors to pass laws of immediate and pressing importance, unless suspended in their operation till his assent should be obtained; and, when so suspended, he has utterly neglected to attend to them.

He has refused to pass other laws for the accommodation of large districts of people, unless those people would relinquish the right of representation in the legislature, a right inestimable to them, and formidable to tyrants only.

He has called together legislative bodies at places unusual, uncomfortable, and distant from the depository of their public records, for the sole purpose of fatiguing them into compliance with his measures.

He has dissolved representative houses repeatedly [*and continually*] for opposing with manly firmness his invasions on the rights of the people.

He has refused for a long time after which dissolutions to cause others to be elected, whereby the legislative powers, incapable of annihilation, have returned to the people at large for their exercise, the state remaining, in the meantime, exposed to all the dangers of invasion from without and convulsions within.

He has endeavored to prevent the population of these states; for that purpose obstructing the laws for naturalization of foreigners, refusing to pass others to encourage their migrations hither, and raising the conditions of new appropriations of lands.

He has OBSTRUCTED [*suffered*] the administration of justice BY [*totally to cease in some of these states*] refusing his assent to laws for establishing judiciary powers.

He has made [*our*] judges dependent on his will alone for the tenure of their offices, and the amount and payment of their salaries.

He has erected a multitude of new offices, [*by a self-assumed power*] and sent hither swarms of new officers to harass our people and eat out their substance.

He has kept among us in times of peace standing armies [*and ships of war*] without the consent of our legislatures.

He has affected to render the military independent of, and superior to, the civil power.

He has combined with others to subject us to a jurisdiction foreign to our constitutions and unacknowledged by our laws, giving his assent to their acts of pretended legislation for quartering large bodies of armed troops among us; for protecting them by a mock trial from punishment for any murders which they should commit on the inhabitants of these states; for cutting off our trade with all parts of the world; for imposing taxes on us without our consent; for depriving us IN MANY CASES of the benefits of trial by jury; for transporting us beyond seas to be tried for pretended offences; for abolishing the free system of English laws in a neighboring province, establishing therein an arbitrary government, and enlarging its boundaries, so as to render it at once an example and fit instrument for introducing the same absolute rule into these COLONIES [*states*]; for taking away our charters, abolishing our most valuable laws, and altering fundamentally the forms of our governments; for suspending our own legislatures, and declaring themselves invested with power to legislate for us in all cases whatsoever.

He has abdicated government here BY DECLARING US OUT OF HIS PROTECTION, AND WAGING WAR AGAINST US [*withdrawing his governors, and declaring us out of his allegiance and protection*].

He has plundered our seas, ravaged our coasts, burnt our towns, and destroyed the lives of our people.

He is at this time transporting large armies of foreign mercenaries to complete the works of death, desolation and tyranny already begun with circumstances of cruelty and perfidy SCARCELY PARALLELED IN THE MOST BARBAROUS AGES, AND TOTALLY unworthy the head of a civilized nation.

He has constrained our fellow citizens taken captive on the high seas, to bear arms against their country, to become the executioners of their friends and brethren, or to fall themselves by their hands.

He has EXCITED DOMESTIC INSURRECTION AMONG US, AND HAS endeavored to bring on the inhabitants of our frontiers, the merciless Indian savages, whose known rule of warfare is an undistinguished destruction of all ages, sexes and conditions [*of existence*].

[*He has incited treasonable insurrections of our fellow citizens, with the allurements of forfeiture and confiscation of our property.*

He has waged cruel war against human nature itself, violating its most sacred rights of life and liberty in the persons of a distant people who never offended him, captivating and carrying them into slavery in another hemisphere, or to incur miserable death in their transportation hither. This piratical warfare, the opprobrium of INFIDEL powers, is the warfare of the CHRISTIAN king of Great Britain. Determined to keep open a market where MEN should be bought and sold, he has prostituted his negative for suppressing every legislative attempt to prohibit or to restrain this execrable commerce. And that this assemblage of horrors might want no fact of distinguished die, he is now exciting those very people to rise in arms among us, and to purchase that liberty of which he has deprived them, by murdering the people on whom he also obtruded them: thus paying off former crimes committed against the LIBERTIES of one people, with crimes which he urges them to commit against the LIVES of another.]

In every stage of these oppressions we have petitioned for redress in the most humble terms: our repeated petitions have been answered only by repeated injuries.

A prince whose character is thus marked by every act which may define a tyrant is unfit to be the ruler of a FREE people [*who mean to be free. Future ages will scarcely believe that the hardiness of one man adventured, within the short compass of twelve years only, to lay a foundation so broad and so undisguised for tyranny over a people fostered and fixed in principles of freedom.*]

Nor have we been wanting in attentions to our British brethren. We have warned them from time to time of attempts by their legislature to extend AN UNWARRANTABLE [*a*] jurisdiction over US [*these our states*]. We have reminded them of the circumstances of our emigration and settlement here, [*no one of which could warrant so strange a pretension: that these were effected at the expense of our own blood and treasure, unassisted by the wealth or the strength of Great Britain: that in constituting indeed our several forms of government, we had adopted one common king, thereby laying a foundation for perpetual league and amity with them: but that submission to their parliament was no part of our constitution, nor ever in idea, if history may be credited: and,*] we HAVE appealed to their native justice and magnanimity AND WE HAVE CONJURED THEM BY [*as well as to*] the ties of our common kindred to disavow these usurpations which WOULD INEVITABLY [*were likely to*] interrupt our connection and correspondence. They too have been deaf to the voice of justice and of consanguinity. WE MUST THEREFORE [*and when occasions have been given them, by the regular course of their laws, of removing from their councils the disturbers of our harmony, they have, by their free election, re-established them in power. At this very time too, they are permitting their chief magistrate to send over not only soldiers of our common blood, but Scotch and foreign mercenaries to invade and destroy us. These facts have given the last stab to agonizing affection, and manly spirit bids us to renounce forever these unfeeling brethren. We must endeavor to forget our former love for them, and hold them as we hold the rest of mankind, enemies in war, in peace friends. We might have a free and a great people together; but a communication of grandeur and of freedom, it seems, is below their dignity. Be it so, since they will have it. The road to happiness and to glory is open to us, too. We will tread it apart from them, and*] acquiesce in the necessity which denounces our [*eternal*] separation AND HOLD THEM AS WE HOLD THE REST OF MANKIND, ENEMIES IN WAR, IN PEACE FRIENDS!

We, therefore, the representatives of the United States of America in General Congress assembled, appealing to the supreme judge of the world for the rectitude of our intentions, do in the name, and by the authority of the good people of these COLONIES, SOLEMNLY PUBLISH AND DECLARE, THAT THESE UNITED COLONIES ARE, AND OF RIGHT OUGHT TO BE FREE AND INDEPENDENT STATES; THAT THEY ARE ABSOLVED FROM ALL ALLEGIANCE TO THE BRITISH CROWN, AND THAT ALL POLITICAL CONNECTION BETWEEN THEM AND THE STATE OF GREAT BRITAIN IS, AND OUGHT TO BE, TOTALLY DISSOLVED; [*states reject and renounce all allegiance and subjection to the kings of Great Britain and all others who may hereafter claim by, through or under them; we utterly dissolve all political connection which may heretofore have subsisted between us and the people or parliament of Great Britain: and finally we do assert and declare these colonies to be free and independent states,*] and that as free and independent states, they have full power to levy war, conclude peace, contract alliances, establish commerce, and to do all other acts and things which independent states may of right do.

And for the support of this declaration, with a firm reliance on the protection of divine providence, we mutually pledge to each other our lives, our fortunes, and our sacred honor.

Lemuel Haynes

from Liberty Further Extended (1776)

[Note: spelling and punctuation have been modernized from original manuscript.]

> We hold these truths to be self-Evident, that all men are created Equal, that they are Endowed By their Creator with certain unalienable rights, that among these are Life, Liberty, and the pursuit of happiness.
>
> —Congress.

. . . Liberty, and freedom, is an innate principle, which is unmovably placed in the human species; and to see a man aspire after it, is not enigmatical, seeing he acts no ways incompatibly with his own nature; consequently, he that would infringe upon a man's liberty may reasonably expect to meet with opposition, seeing the defendant cannot comply to nonresistance, unless he counteracts the very laws of nature.

Liberty is a jewel which was handed down to man from the cabinet of heaven, and is coeval with his existence. And as it proceed from the Supreme Legislature of the universe, so it is he which has a sole right to take away; therefore, he that would take away a man's liberty assumes a prerogative that belongs to another, and acts out of his own domain.

One man may boast a superiority above another in point of natural privilege; yet if he can produce no convincive arguments in vindication of this pre-eminence his hypothesis is to be suspected. To affirm, that an Englishman has a right to his liberty, is a truth which has been so clearly evinced, especially of late, that to spend time illustrating this, would be but superfluous tautology. But I query, whether liberty is so contracted a principle as to be confined to any nation under heaven; nay, I think it not hyperbolical to affirm, that even an African, has equally as good a right to his liberty in common with Englishmen.

I know that those that are concerned in the slave-trade, do pretend to bring arguments in vindication of their practice; yet if we give them a candid examination, we shall find them (even those of the most cogent kind) to be essentially deficient. We live in a day wherein *liberty and freedom* is the subject of many millions' concern; and the important struggle hath already caused great effusion of blood; men seem to manifest the most sanguine resolution not to let their natural rights go without their lives go with them; a resolution, one would think every one that has the least love to his country, or future posterity, would fully confide in; yet while we are so zealous to maintain, and foster our own invaded rights, it cannot be thought impertinent for us candidly to reflect on our own conduct, and I doubt not but that we shall find subsisting in the midst of us, that may with propriety be styled [called] oppression, nay, much greater oppression, than that which Englishmen seem so much to spurn at. I mean an oppression which they, themselves, impose upon others.

It is not my business to enquire into every particular practice, that is practiced in this land, that may come under this odious character; but, what I have in view, is to humbly offer some free thoughts, on the practice of *slave-keeping*. Oppression is not spoken of, nor ranked in the sacred oracles, among the least of those sins, that are the procuring cause of those signal judgments, which God is pleased to bring upon the children of men. Therefore let us attend. I mean to write with freedom, yet with the greatest submission.

And the main proposition, which I intend for some brief illustration, is this: namely, that an *African*, or, in other terms, *that a Negro may justly challenge, and has an undeniable right to his liberty: Consequently, the practice of slave-keeping, which so much abounds in this land, is illicit.*

Every privilege that mankind enjoy have their origin from God; and whatever acts are passed in any earthly court, which are derogatory to those edicts that are passed in the Court of Heaven, the act is *void*. If I have a particular privilege granted to me by God, . . . then he that would infringe upon my benefit, assumes an unreasonable and tyrannic power.

It hath pleased God to *make of one blood all nations of men, for to dwell upon the face of the Earth.* Acts 17, 26. And as all are of one species, so there are the same laws, and aspiring principles placed in all nations; and the effect that these laws will produce, are similar to each other. Consequently we may suppose that what is precious to one man, is precious to another, and what is irksome, or intolerable to one man, is so to another, considered in a law of nature. Therefore we may reasonably conclude, that liberty is equally as precious to a *black man*, as it is to a *white one*, and bondage equally as intolerable to the one as it is to the other: seeing it effects the laws of nature equally as much in the one as does in the other. But, as I observed before, those privileges that are granted to us by the divine being, no one has the least right to take them from us without our consent; and there is not the least precept, or practice, in the Sacred Scriptures, that constitutes a black man a slave, any more than a white one.

Shall a man's color be the decisive criterion whereby to judge of his natural right? Or because a man is not of the same color with his neighbor, shall he be deprived of those things that distinguisheth him from the beasts of the field?

I would ask, whence is it that an Englishman is so far distinguished from an African in point of natural privilege? Did he receive it in his original constitution? or by some subsequent grant? Or does he boast of some higher descent that gives him this preeminence? For my part I can find no such revelation. It is a lamentable consequence of the fall, that mankind have an insatiable thirst after superiority one over another. So that however common or prevalent the practice may be, it does not amount, even to a circumstance, that the practice is warrantable.

God has been pleased to distinguish some men from others, as to natural abilities, but not as to natural *right*, as they came out of his hands.

But sometimes men by their flagitious practice forfeit their liberty into the hands of men, by becoming unfit for society; but have the *Africans* ever as a nation forfeited their liberty in this manner? Whatever individuals have done, yet, I believe, no such challenge can be made upon them, as a body. As there should be some rule whereby to govern the conduct of men, so it is the duty and interest of a community, to form a system of *law*, that is calculated to promote the commercial interest of each other, and so long as it produces so blessed an effect, it should be maintained. But when, instead of contributing to the well being of the community, it proves baneful to its subjects over whom it extends, then it is high time to call it in question. Should any ask, where shall we find any system of law whereby to regulate our moral conduct? I think there is none so explicit and indefinite, as that which was given by the blessed savior of the world. *As you would that men should do unto you, do you even so to them.* One would think, that the mention of the precept, would strike conviction to the heart of these slavetraders, unless an avaricious disposition governs the laws of humanity.

If we strictly adhere to the rule, we shall not impose anything upon others, but what we should be willing should be imposed upon us were we in their condition. . . .

O! what an immense deal of African blood hath been shed by the inhuman cruelty of Englishmen! that reside in a Christian land! Both at home, and in their own country? they being the fomenters of those wars, that is absolutely necessary, in order to carry on this cursed trade; and in their emigration into these colonies? and by their merciless masters, in some parts at least? O ye that have made yourselves drunk with human blood! although you may go with impunity here in this life, yet God will hear the cries of that innocent blood, which cries from the sea, and from the ground against you, like the blood of Abel, more pealful than thunder, *vengeance! vengeance!* What will you do in that day when God shall make inquisition for blood? he will make you drink the vials of his indignation which like a potable stream shall be poured out without the least mixture of mercy. Believe it, Sirs, there shall not a drop of blood, which you have spilt unjustly, be lost in forgetfulness. But it shall bleed afresh, and testify against you, in the day when God shall deal with sinners. . . .

Can you wash your hands, and say, I am clean from this sin? Perhaps you will dare to say it before men, but dare you say it before the tremendous tribunal of that God before whom we must all, in a few precarious moments, appear? Then whatever fair glosses we may have put upon our conduct, that God whose eyes pervade the utmost extent of human thought, and surveys with one intuitive view, the affairs of men; he will examine into the matter himself, and will set every thing upon its own basis; and impartiality shall be seen flourishing throughout that solemn assembly. Alas! shall men hazard their precious souls for a little of the transitory things of time. *O Sirs!* Let that pity and compassion which is peculiar to mankind, especially to English-men, no longer lie dormant in your breast; let it run free through disinterested benevolence, then how would these iron yokes spontaneously fall from the galled necks of the oppressed! And that disparity, in point of natural privilege which is the bane of society, would be case upon the utmost coasts of oblivion. . . . Therefore is it not high time to undo these heavy burdens, and let the oppressed go free? And while you manifest such a noble and magnanimous spirit, to maintain inviolably your own natural rights, and militate so much against despotism, as it hath respect unto yourselves, you do not assume the same usurpations, and are no less tyrannic. Pray let there be a congruity amidst your conduct, lest you fall amongst that class the inspired penman speaks of, *Romans* 2.21 and on: *Thou therefore which teacheth another, teachest thou not thy Self? thou that preachest a man should not steal, dost thou steal? thou that sayest, a man should not commit adultery, dost thou commit adultery? thou that abhorreth idols, dost thou commit sacrilege? thou that makest thy boast of the law, though breaking the law dishonorest thou God?* While you thus sway your tyrant scepter over others, you have nothing to expect but to share in the bitter pill. 'Twas an excellent note that I lately read in a modern piece, and it was this. "O when shall America be consistently engaged in the cause of liberty!" If you have any love to yourselves, or any love to this land, if you have any love to your fellow-men, break these intolerable yokes, and let their names be remembered no more, lest they be retorted on your own necks, and you sink under them, for God will not hold you guiltless.

HECTOR ST. JOHN DE CREVECOEUR

"What Is an American?"
from *Letters from an American Farmer* (1782)

I wish I could be acquainted with the feelings and thoughts which must agitate the heart and present themselves to the mind of an enlightened Englishman, when he first lands on this continent. He must greatly rejoice that he lived at a time to see this fair country discovered and settled; he must necessarily feel a share of national pride, when he views the chain of settlements which embellishes these extended shores. When he says to himself, this is the work of my countrymen, who, when convulsed by factions, afflicted by a variety of miseries and wants, restless and impatient, took refuge here. They brought along with them their national genius, to which they principally owe what liberty they enjoy, and what substance they possess. Here he sees the industry of his native country displayed in a new manner, and traces in their works the embryos of all the arts, sciences, and ingenuity which flourish in Europe. Here he beholds fair cities, substantial villages, extensive fields, an immense country filled with decent houses, good roads, orchards, meadows, and bridges, where an hundred years ago all was wild, woody, and uncultivated! What a train of pleasing ideas this fair spectacle must suggest; it is a prospect which must inspire a good citizen with the most heartfelt pleasure. The difficulty consists in the manner of viewing so extensive a scene. He is arrived on a new continent; a modern society offers itself to his contemplation, different from what he had hitherto seen. It is not composed, as in Europe, of great lords who possess everything, and of a herd of people who have nothing. Here are no aristocratical families, no courts, no kings, no bishops, no ecclesiastical dominion, no invisible power giving to a few a very visible one; no great manufacturers employing thousands, no great refinements of luxury. The rich and the poor are not so far removed from each other as they are in Europe. Some few towns excepted, we are all tillers of the earth, from Nova Scotia to West Florida. We are a people of cultivators, scattered over an immense territory, communicating with each other by means of good roads and navigable rivers, united by the silken bands of mild government, all respecting the laws, without dreading their power, because they are equitable. We are all animated with the spirit of an industry which is unfettered and unrestrained, because each person works for himself. . . . We have no princes, for whom we toil, starve, and bleed: we are the most perfect society now existing in the world. Here man is free as he ought to be; nor is this pleasing equality so transitory as many others are. Many ages will not see the shores of our great lakes replenished with inland nations, nor the unknown bounds of North America entirely peopled. Who can tell how far it extends? Who can tell the millions of men whom it will feed and contain? for no European foot has as yet travelled half the extent of this mighty continent!

The next wish of this traveller will be to know whence came all these people? they are a mixture of English, Scotch, Irish, French, Dutch, Germans, and Swedes. From this promiscuous breed, that race now called Americans have arisen. The eastern provinces must indeed be excepted, as being the unmixed descendants of Englishmen. . . .

In this great American asylum, the poor of Europe have by some means met together, and in consequence of various causes; to what purpose should they ask one another what countrymen they are? Alas, two thirds of them had no country. Can a wretch who wanders about, who works and starves, whose life is a continual scene of sore affliction or pinching penury; can that man call England or any other kingdom his country? A country that had no bread for him, whose fields procured him no harvest, who met with nothing but the frowns of the rich, the severity of the laws, with jails and punishments; who owned not a single foot of the extensive surface of this planet? No! urged by a variety of motives, here they came. Every thing has tended to regenerate them; new laws, a new mode of living, a new social system; here they are become men: in Europe they were as so many useless plants, wanting vegetative mould, and refreshing showers; they withered, and were mowed down by want, hunger, and war; but now by the power of transplantation, like all other plants they have taken root and flourished! Formerly they were not numbered in any civil lists of their country, except in those of the poor; here they rank as citizens. By what invisible power has this surprising metamorphosis been performed? By that of the laws and that of their industry. . . .

What attachment can a poor European emigrant have for a country where he had nothing? The knowledge of the language, the love of a few kindred as poor as himself, were the only cords that tied him: his country is now that which gives him land, bread, protection, and consequence. What then is the American, this new man? He is either an European, or the descendant of an European, hence that strange mixture of blood, which you will find in no other country. I could point out to you a family whose grandfather was an Englishman, whose wife was Dutch, whose son married a French woman, and whose present four sons have now four wives of different nations. *He is* an American, who, leaving behind him all his ancient prejudices and manners, receives new ones from the new mode of life he has embraced, the new government he obeys, and the new rank he holds. He becomes an American by being received in the broad lap of our great *Alma Mater*. Here individuals of all nations are melted into a new race of men, whose labours and posterity will one day cause great changes in the world. Americans are the western pilgrims, who are carrying along with them that great mass of arts, sciences, vigour, and industry which began long since in the east; they will finish the great circle. The Americans were once scattered all over Europe; here they are incorporated into one of the finest systems of population which has ever appeared, and which will hereafter become distinct by the power of the different climates they inhabit. The American ought therefore to love this country much better than that wherein either he or his forefathers were born. Here the rewards of his industry follow with equal steps the progress of his labour; his labour is founded on the basis of nature, *self-interest*; can it want a stronger allurement? Wives and children, who before in vain demanded of him a morsel of bread, now, fat and frolicsome, gladly help their father to clear those fields whence exuberant crops are to arise to feed and to clothe them all; without any part being claimed, either by a despotic prince, a rich abbot, or a mighty lord. Here religion demands but little of him; a small voluntary salary to the minister, and gratitude to God; can he refuse these? The American is a new man, who acts upon new principles; he must therefore entertain new ideas, and form new opinions. From involuntary idleness, servile dependence, penury, and useless labour, he has passed to toils of a very different nature, rewarded by ample subsistence.—This is an American.

British America is divided into many provinces, forming a large association, scattered along a coast 1500 miles extent and about 200 wide. This society I would fain examine, at least such as it appears in the middle provinces; if it does not afford that variety of tinges and gradations which may be observed in Europe, we have colours peculiar to ourselves. For instance, it is natural to conceive that those who live near the sea, must be very different from those who live in the woods; the intermediate space will afford a separate and distinct class.

Men are like plants; the goodness and flavour of the fruit proceeds from the peculiar soil and exposition in which they grow. We are nothing but what we derive from the air we breathe, the climate we inhabit, the government we obey, the system of religion we profess, and the nature of our employment. . . .

Those who live near the sea, feed more on fish than on flesh, and often encounter that boisterous element. This renders them more bold and enterprising; this leads them to neglect the confined occupations of the land. They see and converse with a variety of people, their intercourse with mankind becomes extensive. The sea inspires them with a love of traffic, a desire of transporting produce from one place to another; and leads them to a variety of resources which supply the place of labour. Those who inhabit the middle settlements, by far the most numerous, must be very different; the simple cultivation of the earth purifies them, but the indulgences of the government, the soft remonstrances of religion, the rank of independent freeholders, must necessarily inspire them with sentiments, very little known in Europe among people of the same class. What do I say? Europe has no such class of men; the early knowledge they acquire, the early bargains they make, give them a great degree of sagacity. As freemen they will be litigious; pride and obstinacy are often the cause of law suits; the nature of our laws and governments may be another. As citizens it is easy to imagine, that they will carefully read the newspapers, enter into every political disquisition, freely blame or censure governors and others. As farmers they will be careful and anxious to get as much as they can, because what they get is their own. As northern men they will love the cheerful cup. As Christians, religion curbs them not in their opinions; the general indulgence leaves every one to think for themselves in spiritual matters; the laws inspect our actions, our thoughts are left to God. Industry, good living, selfishness, litigiousness, country politics, the pride of freemen, religious indifference, are their characteristics. If you recede still farther from the sea, you will come into more modern settlements; they exhibit the same strong lineaments, in a ruder appearance. Religion seems to have still less influence, and their manners are less improved.

Now we arrive near the great woods, near the last inhabited districts; there men seem to be placed still farther beyond the reach of government, which in some measure leaves them to themselves. How can it pervade every corner; as they were driven there by misfortunes, necessity of beginnings, desire of acquiring large tracts of land, idleness, frequent want of economy, ancient debts; the reunion of such people does not afford a very pleasing spectacle. When discord, want of unity and friendship; when either drunkenness or idleness prevail in such remote districts; contention, inactivity, and wretchedness must ensue. There are not the same remedies to these evils as in a long established community. The few magistrates they have, are in general little better than the rest; they are often in a perfect state of war; that of man against man, sometimes decided by blows, sometimes by means of the law; that of man against every wild inhabitant of these venerable woods, of which they are come to dispossess them. There men appear to be no better than carnivorous animals of a superior rank, living on the flesh of wild animals when they can catch them, and when they are not able, they subsist on grain. He who would wish to see America in its proper light, and have a true idea of its feeble beginnings and barbarous rudiments, must visit our extended line of frontiers where the last settlers dwell, and where he may see the first labours of settlement, the mode of clearing the earth, in all their different appearances; where men are wholly left dependent on their native tempers, and on the spur of uncertain industry, which often fails when not sanctified by the efficacy of a few moral rules. There, remote from the power of example and check of shame, many families exhibit the most hideous parts of our society. They are a kind of forlorn hope, preceding by ten or twelve years the most respectable army of veterans which come after them. In that space, prosperity will polish some, vice and the law will drive off the rest, who

uniting again with others like themselves will recede still farther; making room for more industrious people, who will finish their improvements, convert the loghouse into a convenient habitation,
and rejoicing that the first heavy labours are finished, will change in a few years that hitherto barbarous country into a fine fertile, well regulated district. Such is our progress, such is the march of
the Europeans toward the interior parts of this continent. . . .

Exclusive of those general characteristics, each province has its own, founded on the government, climate, mode of husbandry, customs, and peculiarity of circumstances. Europeans submit in-
sensibly to these great powers, and become, in the course of a few generations, not only Americans
in general, but either Pennsylvanians, Virginians, or provincials under some other name. Whoever
traverses the continent must easily observe those strong differences, which will grow more evident
in time. The inhabitants of Canada, Massachusetts, the middle provinces, the southern ones will be
as different as their climates; their only points of unity will be those of religion and language. . . .

But to return to our back settlers. I must tell you, that there is something in the proximity of
the woods, which is very singular. It is with men as it is with the plants and animals that grow and
live in the forests; they are entirely different from those that live in the plains. . . . By living in or
near the woods, their actions are regulated by the wildness of the neighbourhood. The deer often
come to eat their grain, the wolves to destroy their sheep, the bears to kill their hogs, the foxes to
catch their poultry. This surrounding hostility immediately puts the gun into their hands; they
watch these animals, they kill some; and thus by defending their property, they soon become professed hunters: this is the progress; once hunters, farewell to the plough. The chase renders them
ferocious, gloomy, and unsociable; a hunter wants no neighbour, he rather hates them, because he
dreads the competition. In a little time their success in the woods makes them neglect their tillage.
They trust to the natural fecundity of the earth, and therefore do little; carelessness in fencing often
exposes what little they sow to destruction; they are not at home to watch; in order therefore to
make up the deficiency, they go oftener to the woods. That new mode of life brings along with it a
new set of manners, which I cannot easily describe. These new manners being grafted on the old
stock, produce a strange sort of lawless profligacy, the impressions of which are indelible. The
manners of the Indian natives are respectable, compared with this European medley. Their wives
and children live in sloth and inactivity; and having no proper pursuits, you may judge what education the latter receive. Their tender minds have nothing else to contemplate but the example of
their parents; like them they grow up a mongrel breed, half civilised, half savage, except nature
stamps on them some constitutional propensities. . . . To all these reasons you must add, their
lonely situation, and you cannot imagine what an effect on manners the great distances they live
from each other has! Consider one of the last settlements in its first view: of what is it composed?
Europeans who have not that sufficient share of knowledge they ought to have, in order to prosper; people who have suddenly passed from oppression, dread of government, and fear of laws,
into the unlimited freedom of the woods. This sudden change must have a very great effect on
most men, and on that class particularly. Eating of wild meat, whatever you may think, tends to
alter their temper: though all the proof I can adduce, is, that I have seen it: and having no place of
worship to resort to, what little society this might afford is denied them. The Sunday meetings, exclusive of religious benefits, were the only social bonds that might have inspired them with some
degree of emulation in neatness. Is it then surprising to see men thus situated, immersed in great
and heavy labours, degenerate a little? It is rather a wonder the effect is not more diffusive. . . .
Thus our bad people are those who are half cultivators and half hunters; and the worst of them are
those who have degenerated altogether into the hunting state. As old ploughmen and new men of
the woods, as Europeans and new made Indians, they contract the vices of both; they adopt the
moroseness and ferocity of a native, without his mildness, or even his industry at home. . . . Hunting is but a licentious idle life, and if it does not always pervert good dispositions; yet, when it is

united with bad luck, it leads to want: want stimulates that propensity to rapacity and injustice, too natural to needy men, which is the fatal gradation. After this explanation of the effects which follow by living in the woods, shall we yet vainly flatter ourselves with the hope of converting the Indians? We should rather begin with converting our back-settlers; and now if I dare mention the name of religion, its sweet accents would be lost in the immensity of these woods. Men thus placed are not fit either to receive or remember its mild instructions; they want temples and ministers, but as soon as men cease to remain at home, and begin to lead an erratic life, let them be either tawny or white, they cease to be its disciples.

Thus have I faintly and imperfectly endeavoured to trace our society from the sea to our woods! yet you must not imagine that every person who moves back, acts upon the same principles, or falls into the same degeneracy. Many families carry with them all their decency of conduct, purity of morals, and respect of religion; but these are scarce, the power of example is sometimes irresistible. Even among these back-settlers, their depravity is greater or less, according to what nation or province they belong. Were I to adduce proofs of this, I might be accused of partiality. If there happens to be some rich intervals, some fertile bottoms, in those remote districts, the people will there prefer tilling the land to hunting, and will attach themselves to it; but even on these fertile spots you may plainly perceive the inhabitants to acquire a great degree of rusticity and selfishness.

It is in consequence of this straggling situation, and the astonishing power it has on manners, that the backsettlers of both the Carolinas, Virginia, and many other parts, have been long a set of lawless people; it has been even dangerous to travel among them. Government can do nothing in so extensive a country, better it should wink at these irregularities, than that it should use means inconsistent with its usual mildness. Time will efface those stains: in proportion as the great body of population approaches them they will reform, and become polished and subordinate. Whatever has been said of the four New England provinces, no such degeneracy of manners has ever tarnished their annals; their back-settlers have been kept within the bounds of decency, and government, by means of wise laws, and by the influence of religion. What a detestable idea such people must have given to the natives of the Europeans! They trade with them, the worst of people are permitted to do that which none but persons of the best characters should be employed in. They get drunk with them, and often defraud the Indians. Their avarice, removed from the eyes of their superiors, knows no bounds; and aided by the little superiority of knowledge, these traders deceive them, and even sometimes shed blood. Hence those shocking violations, those sudden devastations which have so often stained our frontiers, when hundreds of innocent people have been sacrificed for the crimes of a few. It was in consequence of such behaviour, that the Indians took the hatchet against the Virginians in 1774. Thus are our first steps trod, thus are our first trees felled, in general, by the most vicious of our people; and thus the path is opened for the arrival of a second and better class, the true American freeholders; the most respectable set of people in this part of the world: respectable for their industry, their happy independence, the great share of freedom they possess, the good regulation of their families, and for extending the trade and the dominion of our mother country. . . .

Thomas Jefferson

from Notes on the State of Virginia (1785)

Many of the laws which were in force during the monarchy being relative merely to that form of government, or inculcating principles inconsistent with republicanism, the first assembly which met after the establishment of the commonwealth appointed a committee to revise the whole code, to reduce it into proper form and volume, and report it to the assembly. This work has been executed by three gentlemen, and reported; but probably will not be taken up till a restoration of peace shall leave to the legislature leisure to go through such a work.

The following are the most remarkable alterations proposed:

To change the rules of descent, so as that the lands of any person dying intestate shall be divisible equally among all his children, or other representatives, in equal degree.

To make slaves distributable among the next of kin, as other moveables.

To have all public expences, whether of the general treasury, or of a parish or county, (as for the maintenance of the poor, building bridges, court-houses, &c.) supplied by assessments on the citizens, in proportion to their property.

To hire undertakers for keeping the public roads in repair, and indemnify individuals through whose lands new roads shall be opened.

To define with precision the rules whereby aliens should become citizens, and citizens make themselves aliens.

To establish religious freedom on the broadest bottom.

To emancipate all slaves born after passing the act. The bill reported by the revisors does not itself contain this proposition; but an amendment containing it was prepared, to be offered to the legislature whenever the bill should be taken up, and further directing, that they should continue with their parents to a certain age, then be brought up, at the public expence, to tillage, arts or sciences, according to their geniusses, till the females should be eighteen, and the males twenty-one years of age, when they should be colonized to such place as the circumstances of the time should render most proper, sending them out with arms, implements of houshold and of the handicraft arts, seeds, pairs of the useful domestic animals, &c. to declare them a free and independant people, and extend to them our alliance and protection, till they shall have acquired strength; and to send vessels at the same time to other parts of the world for an equal number of white inhabitants; to induce whom to migrate hither, proper encouragements were to be proposed. It will probably be asked, Why not retain and incorporate the blacks into the state, and thus save the expence of supplying, by importation of white settlers, the vacancies they will leave? Deep rooted prejudices entertained by the whites; ten thousand recollections, by the blacks, of the injuries they have sustained; new provocations; the real distinctions which nature has made; and many other circumstances, will divide us into parties, and produce convulsions which will probably never end but in the extermination of the one or the other race. To these objections, which are political, may be added others, which are physical and moral. The first difference which strikes us is that of colour. Whether the black of the negro resides in the reticular membrane between the skin and scarf-skin, or in the scarf-skin itself; whether it proceeds from the colour of the blood, the colour of the bile, or from that of some other secretion, the difference is fixed in nature, and is as real as if its seat and cause were better known to us. And is this difference of no importance? Is it not the foundation of a greater or less share of beauty in the two races? Are not the fine mixtures of red and white, the expressions of every passion by greater or less suffusions of colour in the one, preferable to that eternal monotony, which reigns in the countenances, that immoveable veil of black which covers all the emotions of the other race? Add to these, flowing hair, a more elegant symmetry of form, their own judgment in favour of the whites, declared by their preference of them, as uniformly as is the preference of the Oran-ootan for the black women over those of his own species. The circumstance of superior beauty, is thought worthy attention in the propagation of our horses, dogs, and other domestic animals; why not in that of man? Besides those of colour, figure, and hair, there are other physical distinctions proving a difference of race. They have less hair on the face and body. They secrete less by the kidnies, and more by the glands of the skin, which gives them a very strong and disagreeable odour. This greater degree of transpiration renders them more tolerant of heat, and less so of cold, than the whites. Perhaps too a difference of structure in the pulmonary apparatus, which a late ingenious experimentalist has discovered to be the principal regulator of animal heat, may have disabled them from extricating, in the act of inspiration, so much of that fluid from the outer air, or obliged them in expiration, to part with more of it. They seem to require less sleep. A black, after hard labour through the day, will be induced by the slightest amusements to sit up till midnight, or later, though knowing he must be out with the first dawn of the morning. They are at least as brave, and more adventuresome. But this may perhaps proceed from a want of forethought, which prevents their seeing a danger till it be present. When present, they do not go through it with more coolness or steadiness than the whites. They are more ardent after their female: but love seems with them to be more an eager desire, than a tender delicate mixture of sentiment and sensation. Their griefs are transient. Those numberless afflictions, which render it doubtful whether heaven has given life to us in mercy or in wrath, are less felt, and sooner forgotten with them. In general, their existence appears to participate more of sensation than reflection. To this must be ascribed their disposition to sleep when abstracted from their diversions, and unemployed in labour. An animal whose body is at rest, and who does not reflect, must be disposed to sleep of course. Comparing them by their faculties of memory, reason, and imagination, it appears to me, that in memory they are equal to the whites; in reason much inferior, as I think one could scarcely be found capable of tracing and comprehending the investigations of Euclid; and that in imagination they are dull, tasteless, and anomalous. It would be unfair to follow them to Africa for this investigation. We will consider them here, on the same stage with the whites, and where the facts are not apocryphal on which a judgment is to be formed. It will be right to make great allowances for the difference of condition, of education, of conversation, of the sphere in which they move. Many millions of them have been brought to, and born in America. Most of them indeed have been confined to tillage, to their own homes and their own society: yet many have been so situated, that they might have availed themselves of the conversation of their masters; many have been brought up to the handicraft arts, and from that circumstance have always been associated with the whites. Some have been liberally educated, and all have lived in countries where the arts and sciences are cultivated to a considerable degree, and have had before their eyes samples of the best works from abroad. The Indians, with no advantages of this kind, will often carve figures on their pipes not destitute of design and merit. They will crayon out an animal, a plant, or a country, so as to prove the existence of a germ in their minds which only wants cultivation. They astonish you with strokes of the most sublime oratory; such as prove their reason and sentiment strong, their imagination glowing and elevated. But never yet could I find that a black had uttered a thought above the level of plain narration; never see even an elementary trait of painting or sculpture. In music they are more generally gifted than the whites with accurate ears for tune and time, and they have been found capable of imagining a small catch. Whether they will be equal to the composition of a more extensive run of melody, or of complicated harmony, is yet to be proved. Misery is often the parent of the most affecting touches in poetry. Among the blacks is misery enough, God knows, but no poetry.

The improvement of blacks in body and mind, in the first instance of their mixture with the whites, has been observed by every one, and proves that their inferiority is not the effect merely of their condition of life. . . .

Whether further observation will or will not verify the conjecture, that nature has been less bountiful to them in the endowments of the head, I believe that in those of the heart she will be found to have done them justice. That disposition to theft with which they have been branded, must be ascribed to their situation, and not to any depravity of the moral sense. The man, in whose favour no laws of property exist, probably feels himself less bound to respect those made in favour of others. When arguing for ourselves, we lay it down as a fundamental, that laws, to be just, must give a reciprocation of right: that, without this, they are mere arbitrary rules of conduct, founded in force, and not in conscience: and it is a problem which I give to the master to solve, whether the religious precepts against the violation of property were not framed for him as well as his slave? And whether the slave may not as justifiably take a little from one, who has taken all from him, as he may slay one who would slay him? That a change in the relations in which a man is placed should change his ideas of moral right and wrong, is neither new, nor peculiar to the colour of the blacks. Homer tells us it was so 2600 years ago.

'Ημισυ, γαξ τ' ἀρετῆς ἀποαίνυἱαι εὐρύθπα Zεὺs
'Aνερos, ευτ' ἄν μιν κατὰ δ ὑλιον ἥμαξ ἐλησιν.   *Od.* 17. 323.

　Jove fix'd it certain, that whatever day
　Makes man a slave, takes half his worth away.

But the slaves of which Homer speaks were whites. Notwithstanding these considerations which must weaken their respect for the laws of property, we find among them numerous instances of the most rigid integrity, and as many as among their better instructed masters, of benevolence, gratitude, and unshaken fidelity.—The opinion, that they are inferior in the faculties of reason and imagination, must be hazarded with great diffidence. To justify a general conclusion, requires many observations, even where the subject may be submitted to the Anatomical knife, to Optical glasses, to analysis by fire, or by solvents. How much more then where it is a faculty, not a substance, we are examining; where it eludes the research of all the senses; where the conditions of its existence are various and variously combined; where the effects of those which are present or absent bid defiance to calculation; let me add too, as a circumstance of great tenderness, where our conclusion would degrade a whole race of men from the rank in the scale of beings which their Creator may perhaps have given them. To our reproach it must be said, that though for a century and a half we have had under our eyes the races of black and of red men, they have never yet been viewed by us as subjects of natural history. I advance it therefore as a suspicion only, that the blacks, whether originally a distinct race, or made distinct by time and circumstances, are inferior to the whites in the endowments both of body and mind. It is not against experience to suppose, that different species of the same genus, or varieties of the same species, may possess different qualifications. Will not a lover of natural history then, one who views the gradations in all the races of animals with the eye of philosophy, excuse an effort to keep those in the department of man as distinct as nature has formed them? This unfortunate difference of colour, and perhaps of faculty, is a powerful obstacle to the emancipation of these people. Many of their advocates, while they wish to vindicate the liberty of human nature, are anxious also to preserve its dignity and beauty. Some of these, embarrassed by the question "What further is to be done with them?" join themselves in opposition with those who are actuated by sordid avarice only. Among the Romans emancipation required but one effort. The slave, when made free, might mix with, without staining the blood of his master. But with us a second is necessary, unknown to history. When freed, he is to be removed beyond the reach of mixture.

JAMES MADISON

The Federalist No. 10 (1787–1788)

November 22, 1787

To the People of the State of New York.

Among the numerous advantages promised by a well constructed union, none deserves to be more accurately developed than its tendency to break and control the violence of faction. The friend of popular governments, never finds himself so much alarmed for their character and fate, as when he contemplates their propensity to this dangerous vice. He will not fail therefore to set a due value on any plan which, without violating the principles to which he is attached, provides a proper cure for it. The instability, injustice and confusion introduced into the public councils, have in truth been the mortal diseases under which popular governments have everywhere perished, as they continue to be the favorite and fruitful topics from which the adversaries to liberty derive their most specious declamations. The valuable improvements made by the American Constitutions on the popular models, both ancient and modern, cannot certainly be too much admired; but it would be an unwarrantable partiality, to contend that they have as effectually obviated the danger on this side as was wished and expected. Complaints are every where heard from our most considerate and virtuous citizens, equally the friends of public and private faith, and of public and personal liberty; that our governments are too unstable; that the public good is disregarded in the conflicts of rival parties; and that measures are too often decided not according to the rules of justice and the rights of the minor party, but by the superior force of an interested and over-bearing majority. However anxiously we may wish that these complaints had no foundation, the evidence of known facts will not permit us to deny that they are in some degree true. It will be found indeed, on a candid review of our situation, that some of the distresses under which we labor, have been erroneously charged on the operation of our governments; but it will be found, at the same time, that other causes will not alone account for many of our heaviest misfortunes, and particularly for that prevailing and increasing distrust of public engagements, and alarm for private rights, which are echoed from one end of the continent to the other. These must be chiefly, if not wholly, effects of the unsteadiness and injustice with which a factious spirit has tainted our public administrations.

By a faction I understand a number of citizens, whether amounting to a majority or minority of the whole, who are united and actuated by some common impulse of passion, or of interest, adverse to the rights of other citizens or to the permanent and aggregate interests of the community.

There are two methods of curing the mischiefs of faction: the one, by removing its causes; the other, by controlling its effects.

There are again two methods of removing the causes of faction: the one by destroying the liberty which is essential to its existence; the other, by giving to every citizen the same opinions, the same passions, and the same interests.

It could never be more truly said than of the first remedy, that it is worse than the disease. Liberty is to faction what air is to fire, an aliment without which it instantly expires. But it could not be a less folly to abolish liberty, which is essential to political life, because it nourishes faction, than it would be to wish the annihilation of air, which is essential to animal life, because it imparts to fire its destructive agency.

The second expedient is as impracticable, as the first would be unwise. As long as the reason of man continues fallible and he is at liberty to exercise it, different opinions will be formed. As long as the connection subsists between his reason and his self-love, his opinions and his passions will have a reciprocal influence on each other; and the former will be objects to which the latter will attach themselves. The diversity in the faculties of men from which the rights of property originate, is not less an insuperable obstacle to a uniformity of interests. The protection of these faculties is the first object of government. From the protection of different and unequal faculties of acquiring property, the possession of different degrees and kinds of property immediately results; and from the influence of these on the sentiments and views of the respective proprietors, ensues a division of the society into different interests and parties.

The latent causes of faction are thus sown in the nature of man; and we see them every where brought into different degrees of activity, according to the different circumstances of civil society. A zeal for different opinions concerning religion, concerning government and many other points, as well of speculation as of practice; an attachment to different leaders ambitiously contending for preeminence and power; or to persons of other descriptions whose fortunes have been interesting to the human passions, have in turn divided mankind into parties, inflamed them with mutual animosity, and rendered them much more disposed to vex and oppress each other, than to co-operate for their common good. So strong is this propensity of mankind to fall into mutual animosities, that where no substantial occasion presents itself, the most frivolous and fanciful distinctions have been sufficient to kindle their unfriendly passions and excite their most violent conflicts. But the most common and durable source of factions has been the various and unequal distribution of property. Those who hold and those who are without property have ever formed distinct interests in society. Those who are creditors and those who are debtors fall under a like discrimination. A landed interest, a manufacturing interest, a mercantile interest, a monied interest, with many lesser interests, grow up of necessity in civilized nations and divide them into different classes, actuated by different sentiments and views. The regulation of these various and interfering interests forms the principal task of modern legislation and involves the spirit of party and faction in the necessary and ordinary operations of government.

No man is allowed to be a judge in his own cause because his interest would certainly bias his judgment and, not improbably, corrupt his integrity. With equal, nay with greater reason, a body of men are unfit to be both judges and parties at the same time; yet, what are many of the most important acts of legislation but so many judicial determinations, not indeed concerning the right of single persons but concerning the rights of large bodies of citizens; and what are the different classes of legislators but advocates and parties to the causes which they determine? Is a law proposed concerning private debts? It is a question to which the creditors are parties on one side and the debtors on the other. Justice ought to hold the balance between them. Yet the parties are and must be themselves the judges; and the most numerous party, or, in other words, the most powerful faction must be expected to prevail. Shall domestic manufactures be encouraged, and in what degree, by restrictions on foreign manufactures? are questions which would be differently decided by the landed and the manufacturing classes, and probably by neither with a sole regard to justice and the public good. The apportionment of taxes on the various descriptions of property is an act which seems to require the most exact impartiality; yet, there is perhaps no legislative act in which greater opportunity and temptation are given to a predominant party, to trample on the rules of justice. Every shilling with which they over-burden the inferior number is a shilling saved to their own pockets.

It is in vain to say that enlightened statesmen will be able to adjust these clashing interests and render them all subservient to the public good. Enlightened statesmen will not always be at the helm; Nor, in many cases, can such an adjustment be made at all, without taking into view indirect and remote considerations, which will rarely prevail over the immediate interest which one party may find in disregarding the rights of another, or the good of the whole.

The inference to which we are brought, is, that the *causes* of faction cannot be removed and that relief is only to be sought in the means of controlling its *effects.*

If a faction consists of less than a majority, relief is supplied by the republican principle, which enables the majority to defeat its sinister views by regular vote. It may clog the administration, it may convulse the society; but it will be unable to execute and mask its violence under the forms of the Constitution. When a majority is included in a faction, the form of popular government on the other hand enables it to sacrifice to its ruling passion or interest, both the public good and the rights of other citizens. To secure the public good, and private rights, against the danger of such a faction, and at the same time to preserve the spirit and the form of popular government, is then the great object to which our enquiries are directed. Let me add that it is the great desideratum, by which alone this form of government can be rescued from the opprobrium under which it has so long labored, and be recommended to the esteem and adoption of mankind.

By what means is this object attainable? Evidently by one of two only. Either the existence of the same passion or interest in a majority at the same time, must be prevented; or the majority, having such co-existent passion or interest, must be rendered, by their number and local situation, unable to concert and carry into effect schemes of oppression. If the impulse and the opportunity be suffered to coincide, we well know that neither moral nor religious motives can be relied on as an adequate control. They are not found to be such on the injustice and violence of individuals and lose their efficacy in proportion to the number combined together, that is, in proportion as their efficacy becomes needful.

From this view of the subject, it may be concluded that a pure democracy, by which I mean a society consisting of a small number of citizens who assemble and administer the government in person, can admit of no cure for the mischiefs of faction. A common passion or interest will, in almost every case, be felt by a majority of the whole; a communication and concert results from the form of government itself; and there is nothing to check the inducements to sacrifice the weaker party or an obnoxious individual. Hence it is that such democracies have ever been spectacles of turbulence and contention, have ever been found incompatible with personal security or the rights of property, and have in general been as short in their lives as they have been violent in their deaths. Theoretic politicians, who have patronized this species of government have erroneously supposed that by reducing mankind to a perfect equality in their political rights, they would at the same time be perfectly equalized and assimilated in their possessions, their opinions, and their passions.

A republic, by which I mean a government in which the scheme of representation takes place, opens a different prospect and promises the cure for which we are seeking. Let us examine the points in which it varies from pure democracy, and we shall comprehend both the nature of the cure and the efficacy which it must derive from the union.

The two great points of difference between a democracy and a republic are first, the delegation of the government, in the latter, to a small number of citizens elected by the rest; secondly, the greater number of citizens and greater sphere of country over which the latter may be extended.

The effect of the first difference is, on the one hand, to refine and enlarge the public views by passing them through the medium of a chosen body of citizens whose wisdom may best discern the true interest of their country and whose patriotism and love of justice will be least likely to sacrifice it to temporary or partial considerations. Under such a regulation, it may well happen that the public voice pronounced by the representatives of the people will be more consonant to the public good than if pronounced by the people themselves convened for the purpose. On the other hand, the effect may be inverted. Men of factious tempers, of local prejudices, or of sinister designs, may by intrigue, by corruption or by other means, first obtain the suffrages and then betray the interests of the people. The question resulting is, whether small or extensive republics are most favorable to the election of proper guardians of the public weal; and it is clearly decided in favor of the latter by two obvious considerations.

In the first place it is to be remarked that however small the republic may be, the representatives must be raised to a certain number in order to guard against the cabals of a few, and that however large it may be, they must be limited to a certain number in order to guard against the confusion of a multitude. Hence the number of representatives in the two cases, not being in proportion to that of the constituents, and being proportionally greatest in the small republic, it follows that if the proportion of fit characters be not less in the large than in the small republic, the former will present a greater option and consequently a greater probability of a fit choice.

In the next place, as each representative will be chosen by a greater number of citizens in the large than in the small republic, it will be more difficult for unworthy candidates to practise with success the vicious arts by which elections are too often carried, and the suffrages of the people being more free, will be more likely to center on men who possess the most attractive merit and the most diffusive and established characters.

It must be confessed that in this, as in most other cases, there is a mean, on both sides of which inconveniencies will be found to lie. By enlarging too much the number of electors, you render the representative too little acquainted with all their local circumstances and lesser interests; as by reducing it too much, you render him unduly attached to these, and too little fit to comprehend and pursue great and national objects. The Federal Constitution forms a happy combination in this respect; the great and aggregate interests being referred to the national, the local and particular to the state legislatures.

The other point of difference is, the greater number of citizens and extent of territory which may be brought within the compass of republican, than of democratic government; and it is this circumstance principally which renders factious combinations less to be dreaded in the former, than in the latter. The smaller the society, the fewer probably will be the distinct parties and interests composing it; the fewer the distinct parties and interests, the more frequently will a majority be found of the same party; and the smaller the number of individuals composing a majority, and the smaller the compass within which they are placed, the more easily will they concert and execute their plans of oppression. Extend the sphere, and you take in a greater variety of parties and interests; you make it less probable that a majority of the whole will have a common motive to invade the rights of other citizens; or if such a common motive exists, it will be more difficult for all who feel it to discover their own strength and to act in unison with each other. Besides other impediments, it may be remarked that where there is a consciousness of unjust or dishonorable purposes, communication is always checked by distrust, in proportion to the number whose concurrence is necessary. . . .

The influence of factious leaders may kindle a flame within their particular states, but will be unable to spread a general conflagration through the other states; a religious sect, may degenerate into a political faction in a part of the confederacy; but the variety of sects dispersed over the entire face of it, must secure the national councils against any danger from that source; a rage for paper money, for an abolition of debts, for an equal division of property, or for any other improper or wicked project, will be less apt to pervade the whole body of the union than a particular member of it; in the same proportion as such a malady is more likely to taint a particular county or district, than an entire state.

In the extent and proper structure of the union, therefore, we behold a republican remedy for the diseases most incident to republican government. And according to the degree of pleasure and pride, we feel in being republicans, ought to be our zeal in cherishing the spirit, and supporting the character of Federalists.

James Madison

The Federalist No. 51 (1787–1788)

February 6, 1788

To the People of the State of New York.

To what expedient then shall we finally resort for maintaining in practice the necessary partition of power among the several departments, as laid down in the Constitution? The only answer that can be given is that as all these exterior provisions are found to be inadequate, the defect must be supplied by so contriving the interior structure of the government as that its several constituent parts may, by their mutual relations, be the means of keeping each other in their proper places. . . .

But the great security against a gradual concentration of the several powers in the same department consists in giving to those who administer each department the necessary constitutional means, and personal motives, to resist encroachments of the others. The provision for defense must in this, as in all other cases, be made commensurate to the danger of attack. Ambition must be made to counteract ambition. The interest of the man must be connected with the constitutional rights of the place. It may be a reflection on human nature that such devices should be necessary to control the abuses of government. But what is government itself but the greatest of all reflections on human nature? If men were angels, no government would be necessary. If angels were to govern men, neither external nor internal controls on government would be necessary. In framing a government which is to be administered by men over men, the great difficulty lies in this: You must first enable the government to control the governed; and in the next place, oblige it to control itself. A dependence on the people is no doubt the primary control on the government; but experience has taught mankind the necessity of auxiliary precautions.

This policy of supplying by opposite and rival interests, the defect of better motives, might be traced through the whole system of human affairs, private as well as public. We see it particularly displayed in all the subordinate distributions of power, where the constant aim is to divide and arrange the several offices in such a manner as that each may be a check on the other, that the private interest of every individual, may be a sentinel over the public rights. These inventions of prudence cannot be less requisite in the distribution of the supreme powers of the state.

But it is not possible to give to each department an equal power of self defense. In republican government the legislative authority, necessarily, predominates. The remedy for this inconveniency is, to divide the legislature into different branches and to render them by different modes of election, and different principles of action, as little connected with each other as the nature of their common functions and their common dependence on the society will admit. . . .

There are moreover two considerations particularly applicable to the federal system of America, which place that system in a very interesting point of view.

First. In a single republic, all the power surrendered by the people is submitted to the administration of a single government; and usurpations are guarded against by a division of the government into distinct and separate departments. In the compound republic of America, the power surrendered by the people is first divided between two distinct governments, and then the portion allotted to each, subdivided among distinct and separate departments. Hence a double security arises to the rights of the people. The different governments will control each other at the same time that each will be controlled by itself.

Second. It is of great importance in a republic not only to guard the society against the oppression of its rulers but to guard one part of the society against the injustice of the other part. Different interests necessarily exist in different classes of citizens. If a majority be united by a common interest, the rights of the minority will be insecure. . . . In a society under the forms of which the stronger faction can readily unite and oppress the weaker, anarchy may as truly be said to reign, as in a state of nature where the weaker individual is not secured against the violence of the stronger. And as in the latter state even the stronger individuals are prompted by the uncertainty of their condition, to submit to a government which may protect the weak as well as themselves, so in the former state, will the more powerful factions or parties be gradually induced by a like motive, to wish for a government which will protect all parties, the weaker as well as the more powerful. It can be little doubted that if the state of Rhode Island was separated from the confederacy and left to itself, the insecurity of rights under the popular form of government within such narrow limits would be displayed by such reiterated oppressions of factious majorities that some power altogether independent of the people would soon be called for by the voice of the very factions whose misrule had proved the necessity of it. In the extended republic of the United States, and among the great variety of interests, parties and sects which it embraces, a coalition of a majority of the whole society could seldom take place on any other principles than those of justice and the general good; and there being thus less danger to a minor from the will of the major party, there must be less pretext also, to provide for the security of the former, by introducing into the government a will not dependent on the latter, or in other words, a will independent of the society itself. It is no less certain than it is important, notwithstanding the contrary opinions which have been entertained, that the larger the society, provided it lie within a practicable sphere, the more duly capable it will be of self government. And happily for the *republican cause,* the practicable sphere may be carried to a very great extent by a judicious modification and mixture of the *federal principle.*

Publius

NOAH WEBSTER

from On the Education of Youth in America (1790)

Education is a subject which has been exhausted by the ablest writers, both among the ancients and moderns. I am not vain enough to suppose I can suggest any new ideas upon so trite a theme as Education in general; but perhaps the manner of conducting the youth in America may be capable of some improvement. Our constitutions of civil government are not yet firmly established; our national character is not yet formed; and it is an object of vast magnitude that systems of Education should be adopted and pursued, which may not only diffuse a knowledge of the sciences, but may implant, in the minds of the American youth, the principles of virtue and of liberty; and inspire them with just and liberal ideas of government, and with an inviolable attachment to their own country. It now becomes every American to examin the modes of Education in Europe, to see how far they are applicable in this country, and whether it is not possible to make some valuable alterations, adapted to our local and political circumstances. Let us examin the subject in two views. First, as it respects arts and sciences. Secondly, as it is connected with morals and government. In each of these articles, let us see what errors may be found, and what improvements suggested, in our present practice.

The first error that I would mention, is, a too general attention to the dead languages, with a neglect of our own.

This practice proceeds probably from the common use of the Greek and Roman tongues, before the English was brought to perfection. There was a long period of time, when these languages were almost the only repositories of science in Europe. Men, who had a taste for learning, were under a necessity of recurring to the sources, the Greek and Roman authors. These will ever be held in the highest estimation both for stile and sentiment; but the most valuable of them have English translations, which, if they do not contain all the elegance, communicate all the ideas of the originals. The English language, perhaps, at this moment, is the repository of as much learning, as one half the languages of Europe. In copiousness it exceeds all modern tongues; and though inferior to the Greek and French in softness and harmony, yet it exceeds the French in variety; it almost equals the Greek and Roman in energy, and falls very little short of any language in the regularity of its construction. . . .

It is not my wish to discountenance totally the study of the dead languages. On the other hand I should urge a more close attention to them, among young men who are designed for the learned professions. The poets, the orators, the philosophers and the historians of Greece and Rome, furnish the most excellent models of Stile, and the richest treasures of Science. . . .

But my meaning is, that the dead languages are not necessary for men of business, merchants, mechanics, planters, &c. nor of utility sufficient to indemnify them for the expense of time and money which is requisite to acquire a tolerable acquaintance with the Greek and Roman authors. Merchants often have occasion for a knowledge of some foreign living language, as, the French, the

Italian, the Spanish, or the German; but men, whose business is wholly domestic, have little or no use for any language but their own; much less, for languages known only in books. . . .

But young gentlemen are not all designed for the same line of business, and why should they pursue the same studies? Why should a merchant trouble himself with the rules of Greek and Roman syntax, or a planter puzzle his head with conic sections? Life is too short to acquire, and the mind of man too feeble to contain, the whole circle of sciences. The greatest genius on earth, not even a Bacon, can be a perfect master of *every* branch; but any moderate genius may, by suitable application, be perfect in any *one* branch. By attempting therefore to teach young gentlemen every thing, we make the most of them mere smatterers in science. In order to qualify persons to figure in any profession, it is necessary that they should attend closely to those branches of learning which lead to it.

There are some arts and sciences which are necessary for every man. Every man should be able to speak and write his native tongue with correctness; and have some knowledge of mathematics. The rules of arithmetic are indispensably requisite. But besides the learning which is of common utility, lads should be directed to pursue those branches which are connected more immediately with the business for which they are destined.

It would be very useful for the farming part of the community, to furnish country schools with some easy system of practical husbandry. By repeatedly reading some book of this kind, the mind would be stored with ideas, which might not indeed be understood in youth, but which would be called into practice in some subsequent period of life. This would lead the mind to the subject of agriculture, and pave the way for improvements.

Young gentlemen, designed for the mercantile line, after having learned to write and speak English correctly, might attend to French, Italian, or such other living language, as they will probably want in the course of business. These languages should be learned early in youth, while the organs are yet pliable; otherwise the pronunciation will probably be imperfect. These studies might be succeeded by some attention to chronology, and a regular application to geography, mathematics, history, the general regulations of commercial nations, principles of advance in trade, of insurance, and to the general principles of government. . . .

Such a system of English Education is also much preferable to a university Education, even with the usual honors; for it might be finished so early as to leave young persons time to serve a regular apprenticeship, without which no person should enter upon business. But by the time a university Education is completed, young men commonly commence *gentlemen;* their age and their pride will not suffer them to go thro the drudgery of a compting house, and they enter upon business without the requisite accomplishments. Indeed it appears to me that what is now called a *liberal Education,* disqualifies a man for business. Habits are formed in youth and by practice; and as business is, in some measure, mechanical, every person should be exercised in his employment, in an early period of life, that his habits may be formed by the time his apprenticeship expires. An Education in a university interferes with the forming of these habits; and perhaps forms opposite habits; the mind may contract a fondness for ease, for pleasure or for books, which no efforts can overcome. An academic Education, which should furnish the youth with some ideas of men and things, and leave time for an apprenticeship, before the age of twenty one years, would in my opinion, be the most eligible for young men who are designed for activ employments. . . .

The rod is often necessary in school; especially after the children have been accustomed to disobedience and a licentious behavior at home. All government originates in families, and if neglected there, it will hardly exist in society; but the want of it must be supplied by the rod in school, the penal laws of the state, and the terrors of divine wrath from the pulpit. The government both of families and schools should be absolute. There should, in families, be no appeal from one parent to another, with the prospect of pardon for offences. The one should always vindicate, at least apparently, the conduct of the other. In schools the master should be absolute in command; for it is utterly impossible for any man to support order and discipline among children, who are indulged with an appeal to their parents. A proper subordination in families would generally supersede the necessity of severity in schools; and a strict discipline in both is the best foundation of good order in political society. . . .

The only practicable method to reform mankind, is to begin with children; to banish, if possible, from their company, every low bred, drunken, immoral character. Virtue and vice will not grow together in a great degree, but they will grow where they are planted, and when one has taken root, it is not easily supplanted by the other. The great art of correcting mankind therefore, consists in prepossessing the mind with good principles.

For this reason society requires that the Education of youth should be watched with the most scrupulous attention. Education, in a great measure, forms the moral characters of men, and morals are the basis of government. Education should therefore be the first care of a Legislature; not merely the institution of schools, but the furnishing of them with the best men for teachers. A good system of Education should be the first article in the code of political regulations; for it is much easier to introduce and establish an effectual system for preserving morals, than to correct, by penal statutes, the ill effects of a bad system. I am so fully persuaded of this, that I shall almost adore that great man, who shall change our practice and opinions, and make it respectable for the first and best men to superintend the Education of youth.

Another defect in our schools, which, since the revolution, is become inexcuseable, is the want of proper books. The collections which are now used consist of essays that respect foreign and ancient nations. The minds of youth are perpetually led to the history of Greece and Rome or to Great Britain; boys are constantly repeating the declamations of Demosthenes and Cicero, or debates upon some political question in the British Parliment. These are excellent specimens of good sense, polished stile and perfect oratory; but they are not interesting to children. They cannot be very useful, except to young gentlemen who want them as models of reasoning and eloquence, in the pulpit or at the bar.

But every child in America should be acquainted with his own country. He should read books that furnish him with ideas that will be useful to him in life and practice. As soon as he opens his lips, he should lisp the praise of liberty, and of those illustrious heroes and statesmen, who have wrought a revolution in her favor.

A selection of essays, respecting the settlement and geography of America; the history of the late revolution and of the most remarkable characters and events that distinguished it, and a compendium of the principles of the federal and provincial governments, should be the principal school book in the United States. These are interesting objects to every man; they call home the minds of youth and fix them upon the interests of their own country, and they assist in forming attachments to it, as well as in enlarging the understanding. . . .

In several States, we find laws passed, establishing provisions for colleges and academies, where people of property may educate their sons; but no provision is made for instructing the poorer rank of people, even in reading and writing. Yet in these same States, every citizen who is worth a few shillings annually, is entitled to vote for legislators. This appears to me a most glaring solecism in government. The constitutions are *republican,* and the laws of education are *monarchical.* The *former* extend civil rights to every honest industrious man; the *latter* deprive a large proportion of the citizens of a most valuable privilege.

In our American republics, where governments is in the hands of the people knowlege should be universally diffused by means of public schools. Of such consequence is it to society, that the people who make laws, should be well informed, that I conceive no Legislature can be justified in neglecting proper establishments for this purpose.

When I speak of a diffusion of knowlege, I do not mean merely a knowlege of spelling books, and the New Testament. An acquaintance with ethics, and with the general principles of law, commerce, money and government, is necessary for the yeomanry of a republican state. This acquaintance they might obtain by means of books calculated for schools, and read by the children, during the winter months, and by the circulation of public papers. . . .

It may be true that all men cannot be legislators; but the more generally knowlege is diffused among the substantial yeomanry, the more perfect will be the laws of a republican state.

Every small district should be furnished with a school, at least four months in a year; when boys are not otherwise employed. This school should be kept by the most reputable and well informed man in the district. Here children should be taught the usual branches of learning; submission to superiors and to laws; the moral or social duties; the history and transactions of their own country; the principles of liberty and government. Here the rough manners of the wilderness should be softened, and the principles of virtue and good behavior inculcated. The *virtues* of men are of more consequence to society than their *abilities;* and for this reason, the *heart* should be cultivated with more assiduity than the *head*.

Such a general system of education is neither impracticable nor difficult; and excepting the formation of a federal government that shall be efficient and permanent, it demands the first attention of American patriots. Until such a system shall be adopted and pursued, until the Statesman and Divine shall unite their efforts in *forming* the human mind, rather than in loping its excressences, after it has been neglected; until Legislators discover that the only way to make good citizens and subjects, is to nourish them from infancy; and until parents shall be convinced that the *worst* of men are not the proper teachers to make the *best;* mankind cannot know to what a degree of perfection society and government may be carried. America affords the fairest opportunities for making the experiment and opens the most encouraging prospect of success.

In a system of education, that should embrace every part of the community, the female sex claim no inconsiderable share of our attention.

The women in America (to their honor it is mentioned) are not generally above the care of educating their own children. Their own education should therefore enable them to implant in the tender mind, such sentiments of virtue, propriety and dignity, as are suited to the freedom of our governments. Children should be treated as children, but as children that are, in a future time, to be men and women. By treating them as if they were always to remain children, we very often see their childishness adhere to them, even in middle life. The silly language called *baby talk,* in which most persons are initiated in infancy, often breaks out in discourse, at the age of forty, and makes a man appear very ridiculous. In the same manner, vulgar, obscene and illiberal ideas, imbibed in a nursery or a kitchen, often give a tincture to the conduct through life. In order to prevent every evil bias, the ladies, whose province it is to direct the inclinations of children on their first appearance, and to choose their nurses, should be possessed, not only of amiable manners, but of just sentiments and enlarged understandings.

But the influence of women in forming the dispositions of youth, is not the sole reason why their education should be particularly guarded; their influence in controling the manners of a nation, is another powerful reason. Women, once abandoned, may be instrumental in corrupting society; but such is the delicacy of the sex, and such the restraints which custom imposes upon them, that they are generally the last to be corrupted. There are innumerable instances of men, who have been restrained from a vicious life, and even of very abandoned men, who have been reclaimed, by their attachment to ladies of virtue. A fondness for the company and conversation of ladies of character, may be considered as a young man's best security against the attractives of a dissipated life. A man who is attached to *good* company, seldom frequents that which is *bad*. For this reason, society requires that females should be well educated, and extend their influence as far as possible over the other sex.

But a distinction is to be made between a *good* education, and a *showy* one; for an education, merely superficial, is a proof of corruption of taste, and has a mischievous influence on manners. The education of females, like that of males, should be adapted to the principles of the government, and correspond with the stage of society. Education in Paris differs from that in Petersburg, and the education of females in London or Paris should not be a model for the Americans to copy.

In all nations a *good* education, is that which renders the ladies correct in their manners, respectable in their families, and agreeable in society. That education is always *wrong,* which raises a woman above the duties of her station.

In America, female education should have for its object what is *useful.* Young ladies should be taught to speak and write their own language with purity and elegance; an article in which they are often deficient. The French language is not necessary for ladies. In some cases it is convenient, but, in general, it may be considered as an article of luxury. As an accomplishment, it may be studied by those whose attention is not employed about more important concerns.

Some knowledge of arithmetic is necessary for every lady. Geography should never be neglected. Belles Letters learning seems to correspond with the dispositions of most females. A taste for Poetry and fine writing should be cultivated; for we expect the most delicate sentiments from the pens of that sex, which is possessed of the finest feelings.

A course of reading can hardly be prescribed for all ladies. But it should be remarked, that this sex cannot be too well acquainted with the writers upon human life and manners. The Spectator should fill the first place in every lady's library. Other volumes of periodical papers, tho inferior to the Spectator, should be read; and some of the best histories.

With respect to novels, so much admired by the young, and so generally condemned by the old, what shall I say? Perhaps it may be said with truth, that some of them are useful, many of them pernicious, and most of them trifling. A hundred volumes of modern novels may be read, without acquiring a new idea. Some of them contain entertaining stories, and where the descriptions are drawn from nature, and from characters and events in themselves innocent, the perusal of them may be harmless. . . .

In the large towns in America, music, drawing and dancing, constitute a part of female education. They, however, hold a subordinate rank; for my fair friends will pardon me, when I declare, that no man ever marries a woman for her performance on a harpsichord, or her figure in a minuet. However ambitious a woman may be to command admiration *abroad,* her real merit is known only at *home.* Admiration is useless, when it is not supported by domestic worth. But real honor and permanent esteem, are always secured by those who preside over their own families with dignity. . . .

Americans, unshackle your minds, and act like independent beings. You have been children long enough, subject to the control, and subservient to the interest of a haughty parent. You have now an interest of your own to augment and defend: You have an empire to raise and support by your exertions, and a national character to establish and extend by your wisdom and virtues. To effect these great objects, it is necessary to frame a liberal plan of policy, and built it on a broad system of education. Before this system can be formed and embraced, the Americans must *believe,* and *act* from the belief, that it is dishonorable to waste life in mimicking the follies of other nations and basking in the sunshine of foreign glory.

Judith Sargent Murray

from On the Equality of the Sexes (1790)

Is it upon mature consideration we adopt the idea, that nature is thus partial in her distributions? Is it indeed a fact, that she hath yielded to one half of the human species so unquestionable a mental superiority? I know that to both sexes elevated understandings, and the reverse, are common. But, suffer me to ask, in what the minds of females are so notoriously deficient, or unequal. May not the intellectual powers be ranged under their four heads—imagination, reason, memory and judgement. The province of imagination has long since been surrendered up to us, and we have been crowned undoubted sovereigns of the regions of fancy. Invention is perhaps the most arduous effort of the mind; this branch of imagination hath been particularly ceded to us, and we have been time out of mind invested with that creative faculty. Observe the variety of fashions (here I bar the contemptuous smile) which distinguish and adorn the female world; how continually are they changing, insomuch that they almost render the whole man's assertion problematical, and we are ready to say, *there is something new under the sun.* Now, what a playfulness, what an exuberance of fancy, what strength of inventive imagination, doth this continual variation discover? . . . Another instance of our creative powers, is our talent for slander; how ingenious are we at inventive scandal? what a formidable story can we in a moment fabricate merely from the force of a prolifick imagination? how many reputations, in the fertile brain of a female, have been utterly despoiled? how industrious are we at improving a hint? suspicion how easily do we convert into conviction, and conviction, embellished by the power of eloquence, stalks abroad to the surprise and confusion of unsuspecting innocence. Perhaps it will be asked if I furnish these facts as instances of excellency in our sex. Certainly not; but as proofs of a creative faculty, of a lively imagination. Assuredly great activity of mind is thereby discovered, and was this activity properly directed, what beneficial effects would follow. Is the needle and kitchen sufficient to employ the operations of a soul thus organized? I should conceive not. Nay, it is a truth that those very departments leave the intelligent principle vacant, and at liberty for speculation. Are we deficient in reason? We can only reason from what we blow, and if opportunity of acquiring knowledge hath been denied us, the inferiority of our sex cannot fairly be deduced from thence. Memory, I believe, will be allowed us in common, since every one's experience must testify, that a loquacious old woman is as frequently met with, as a communicative old man; their subjects are alike drawn from the fund of other times, and the transactions of their youth, or of maturer life, entertain, or perhaps fatigue you, in the evening of their lives. "But our judgment is not so strong—we do not distinguish so well." Yet it may be questioned, from what doth this superiority, in thus discriminating faculty of the soul, proceed. May we not trace its source in the difference of education, and continued advantages? Will it be said that the judgment of a male of two years old, is more sage than that of a female's of the same age? I believe the reverse is generally observed to be true. But from that period what partiality! how is the one exalted and the other depressed, by the contrary modes of education which are adopted! the one is taught to aspire, and the other is early confined and limited. As their years increase, the sister must be wholly domesticated, while the brother is led by the hand through all the flowery paths of science. . . . At length arrived at womanhood, the uncultivated fair one feels a void, which the employments allotted her are by no means capable of filling. What can she do? to books, she may not apply; or if she doth, *to those only of the novel kind,* lest she merit the appellation of a *learned lady;* and what ideas have been affixed to this term, the observation of many can testify. Fashion, scandal and sometimes what is still more reprehensible, are then called in to her relief; and who can say to what lengths the liberties she takes may proceed. Meantime she herself is most unhappy; she feels the want of a cultivated mind. Is she single, she in vain seeks to fill up time from sexual employments or amusements. Is she united to a person whose soul nature made equal to her own, education hath set him so far above her, that in those entertainments which are productive of such rational felicity, she is not qualified to accompany him. She experiences a mortifying consciousness of inferiority, which embitters every enjoyment. Doth the person to whom her adverse fate hath consigned her, possess a mind incapable of improvement, she is equally wretched, in being so closely connected with an individual whom she cannot but despise. Now, was she permitted the same instructors as her brother, (with an eye however to their particular departments) for the employment of a rational mind an ample field would be opened. In astronomy she might catch a glimpse of the immensity of the Deity, and thence she would form amazing conceptions of the august and supreme Intelligence. In geography she would admire Jehova in the midst of his benevolence; thus adapting this globe to the various wants and amusements of its inhabitants. In natural philosophy she would adore the infinite majesty of heaven, clothed in condescension; and as she traversed the reptile world, she would hail the goodness of a creating God. A mind, thus filled, would have little room for the trifles with which our sex are, with too much justice, accused of amusing themselves, and they would thus be rendered fit companions for those, who should one day wear them as their crown. Fashions, in their variety, would then give place to conjectures, which might perhaps conduce to the improvement of the literary world; and there would be no leisure for slander or detraction. . . .

Will it be urged that those acquirements would supersede our domestick duties, I answer that every requisite in female economy is easily attained; and, with truth I can add, that when once attained, they require no further *mental attention.* Nay, while we are pursuing the needle, or the superintendency of the family, I repeat, that our minds are at full liberty for reflection; that imagination may exert itself in full vigor; and that if a just foundation early laid, our ideas will then be worthy of rational beings. If we were industrious we might easily find time to arrange them upon paper, or should avocations press too hard for such an indulgence, the hours allotted for conversation would at least become more refined and rational. Should it still be vociferated, "Your domestick employments are sufficient"—I would calmly ask, is it reasonable, that a candidate for immortality, for the joys of heaven, an intelligent being, who is to spend an eternity in contemplating the works of Deity, should at present be so degraded, as to be allowed no other ideas, than those which are suggested by the mechanism of a pudding, or the sewing of the seams of a garment? Pity that all such censurers of female improvement do not go one step further, and deny their future existence; to be consistent they surely ought.

Yes, ye lordly, ye haughty sex, our souls are by nature *equal* to yours; the same breath of God animates, enlivens, and invigorates us; and that we are not fallen lower than yourselves, let those witness who have greatly towered above the various discouragements by which they have been so heavily oppressed; and though I am unacquainted with the list of celebrated characters on either side, yet from the observations I have made in the contracted circle in which I have moved, I dare confidently believe, that from the commencement of time to the present day, there hath been as many females, as males, who, by the *mere force of natural powers,* have merited the crown of applause; who *thus unassisted,* have seized the wreath of fame. I know there are who assert, that as the animal powers of the one sex are superiour, of course their mental faculties also must be stronger; thus attributing strength of mind to the transient organization of this earth born tenement. But if this reasoning is just, man must be content to yield the palm to many of the brute creation, since by not a few of his brethren of the field, he is far surpassed in bodily strength. Moreover, was this argument admitted, it would prove too much, for occular demonstration evinceth, that there are many robust masculine ladies, and effeminate gentlemen. . . . Besides, were we to grant that animal strength proved anything, taking into consideration the accustomed impartiality of nature, we should be induced to imagine, that she had invested the female mind with superiour strength as an equivalent for the bodily powers of man. But waving this however palpable advantage, for *equality* only, we wish to contend.

CONSTANTIA

Benjamin Banneker and Thomas Jefferson

Letters (1791)

Maryland, Baltimore County, August 19, 1791.

SIR,

I am fully sensible of the greatness of that freedom, which I take with you on the present occasion; a liberty which seemed to me scarcely allowable, when I reflected on that distinguished and dignified station in which you stand, and the almost general prejudice and prepossession, which is so prevalent in the world against those of my complexion.

I suppose it is a truth too well attested to you, to need a proof here, that we are a race of beings, who have long labored under the abuse and censure of the world; that we have long been looked upon with an eye of contempt; and that we have long been considered rather as brutish than human, and scarcely capable of mental endowments.

Sir, I hope I may safely admit, in consequence of that report which hath reached me, that you are a man far less inflexible in sentiments of this nature, than many others; that you are measurably friendly, and well disposed towards us; and that you are willing and ready to lend your aid and assistance to our relief, from those many distresses, and numerous calamities, to which we are reduced.

Now Sir, if this is founded in truth, I apprehend you will embrace every opportunity, to eradicate that train of absurd and false ideas and opinions, which so generally prevails with respect to us; and that your sentiments are concurrent with mine, which are, that one universal Father hath given being to us all; and that he hath not only made us all of one flesh, but that he hath also, without partiality, afforded us all the same sensations and endowed us all with the same faculties; and that however variable we may be in society or religion, however diversified in situation or color, we are all of the same family, and stand in the same relation to him.

Sir, if these are sentiments of which you are fully persuaded, I hope you cannot but acknowledge, that it is the indispensible duty of those, who maintain for themselves the rights of human nature, and who possess the obligations of Christianity, to extend their power and influence to the relief of every part of the human race, from whatever burden or oppression they may unjustly labor under; and this, I apprehend, a full conviction of the truth and obligation of these principles should lead all to.

Sir, I have long been convinced, that if your love for yourselves, and for those inestimable laws, which preserved to you the rights of human nature, was founded on sincerity, you could not but be solicitous, that every individual, of whatever rank or distinction, might with you equally enjoy the blessings thereof; neither could you rest satisfied short of the most active effusion of your exertions, in order to their promotion from any state of degradation, to which the unjustifiable cruelty and barbarism of men may have reduced them.

Sir, I freely and cheerfully acknowledge, that I am of the African race, and in that color which is natural to them of the deepest dye; and it is under a sense of the most profound gratitude to the Supreme Ruler of the Universe, that I now confess to you, that I am not under that state of tyrannical thraldom, and inhuman captivity, to which too many of my brethren are doomed, but that I have abundantly tasted of the fruition of those blessings, which proceed from that free and unequalled liberty with which you are favored; and which, I hope, you will willingly allow you have mercifully received, from the immediate hand of that Being, from whom proceedeth every good and perfect Gift.

Sir, suffer me to recal to your mind that time, in which the arms and tyranny of the British crown were exerted, with every powerful effort, in order to reduce you to a state of servitude: look back, I entreat you, on the variety of dangers to which you were exposed; reflect on that time, in which every human aid appeared unavailable, and in which even hope and fortitude wore the aspect of inability to the conflict, and you cannot but be led to a serious and grateful sense of your miraculous and providential preservation; you cannot but acknowledge, that the present freedom and tranquility which you enjoy you have mercifully received, and that it is the peculiar blessing of Heaven.

This, Sir, was a time when you clearly saw into the injustice of a state of slavery, and in which you had just apprehensions of the horrors of its condition. It was now that your abhorrence thereof was so excited, that you publicly held forth this true and invaluable doctrine, which is worthy to be recorded and remembered in all succeeding ages: "We hold these truths to be self-evident, that all men are created equal; that they are endowed by their Creator with certain unalienable rights, and that among these are, life, liberty, and the pursuit of happiness."

Here was a time, in which your tender feelings for yourselves had engaged you thus to declare, you were then impressed with proper ideas of the great violation of liberty, and the free possession of those blessings, to which you were entitled by nature; but, Sir, how pitiable is it to reflect, that although you were so fully convinced of the benevolence of the Father of Mankind, and of his equal and impartial distribution of these rights and privileges, which he hath conferred upon them, that you should at the same time counteract his mercies, in detaining by fraud and violence so numerous a part of my brethren, under groaning captivity and cruel oppression, that you should at the same time be found guilty of that most criminal act, which you professedly detested in others, with respect to yourselves.

I suppose that your knowledge of the situation of my brethren, is too extensive to need a recital here; neither shall I presume to prescribe methods by which they may be relieved, otherwise than by recommending to you and all others, to wean yourselves from those narrow prejudices which you have imbibed with respect to them, and as Job proposed to his friends, "put your soul in their souls' stead;" thus shall your hearts be enlarged with kindness and benevolence towards them; and thus shall you need neither the direction of myself or others, in what manner to proceed herein.

And now, Sir, although my sympathy and affection for my brethren hath caused my enlargement thus far, I ardently hope, that your candor and generosity will plead with you in my behalf, when I make known to you, that it was not originally my design; but having taken up my pen in order to direct to you, as a present, a copy of an Almanac, which I have calculated for the succeeding year, I was unexpectedly and unavoidably led thereto.

This calculation is the production of my arduous study, in this my advanced stage of life; for having long had unbounded desires to become acquainted with the secrets of nature, I have had to gratify my curiosity herein, through my own assiduous application to Astronomical Study, in which I need not recount to you the many difficulties and disadvantages, which I have had to encounter.

And although I had almost declined to make my calculation for the ensuing year, in consequence of that time which I had allotted therefor, being taken up at the Federal Territory, by the request of Mr. Andrew Ellicott, yet finding myself under several engagements to Printers of this state, to whom I had communicated my design, on my return to my place of residence, I industriously applied myself thereto, which I hope I have accomplished with correctness and accuracy; a copy of which I have taken the liberty to direct to you, and which I humbly request you will favorably receive; and although you may have the opportunity of perusing it after its publication, yet I choose to send it to you in manuscript previous thereto, that thereby you might not only have an earlier inspection, but that you might also view it in my own hand writing . . . . **To**

–Benjamin Banneker

Philadelphia Aug. 30. 1791.

SIR

I thank you sincerely for your letter of the 19th instant and for the Almanac it contained. No body wishes more than I do to see such proofs as you exhibit, that nature has given to our black brethren, talents equal to those of the other colors of men, and that the appearance of a want of them is owing merely to the degraded condition of their existence, both in Africa & America. I can add with truth, that no body wishes more ardently to see a good system commenced for raising the condition both of their body & mind to what it ought to be, as fast as the imbecility of their present existence, and other circumstances which cannot be neglected, will admit. I have taken the liberty of sending your Almanac to Monsieur de Condorcet, Secretary of the Academy of Sciences at Paris, and member of the Philanthropic society, because I considered it as a document to which your whole colour had a right for their justification against the doubts which have been entertained of them. I am with great esteem, Sir Your most obed^t humble serv^t.

–Thomas Jefferson

America Guided by Wisdom by Benjamin Turner. Reprinted by permission of Chicago Historical Society.

4. Freedoms and Slaveries, 1820–1860

War News from Mexico, 1848 by Richard Caton Woodville. The Manoogian Collection. Photograph © Board of Trustees, National Gallery of Art, Washington. Courtesy of National Gallery of Art, Washington.

In 1848 the Mexican-American War ended with the United States in possession of California and much of the West. The same year, artist Richard Caton Woodville imagined how Americans might have reacted to news of victory. Beneath the pediment of the "American Hotel," men of all ages listen to a young comrade read from the newspaper, as several African Americans—one a raggedly clad child—listen from the steps and a white woman peers in from the right side. *War News from Mexico* was part of a new movement in American art: "genre" paintings depicting ordinary people in scenes from everyday life. In one sense, Woodville's painting showed how changes in communication were linking Americans together as never before. Newspaper-reading, which had occurred in America since Benjamin Franklin's day, was now ubiquitous; the Mexican-American War was the first American conflict to be reported in the papers by war correspondents. The small "Post Office" sign on the left pillar heralded another change: mail now traveled inexpensively across most of the United States, a far cry from fifty years before. Consider, too, the visual space of this painting: a series of rectangles, moving out from the newspaper in the center to the frame of the building to the frame of the entire picture. The medium is the message: the news, and the paper that reports it, draw a community together. However, the building's frame also segments that community—a suggestion, perhaps, of the larger national division that the Mexican-American War helped to bring about.

Chronology

1803:	Louisiana Purchase
1808:	Congress prohibits U.S. participation in international slave trade
1817–1825:	Erie Canal constructed
1819–1820:	Missouri Crisis and Compromise
1823:	Lowell, Massachusetts, mills open
1830:	Congress passes Indian Removal Act
1831:	Nat Turner's revolt in Virginia William Lloyd Garrison begins publishing abolitionist newspaper *The Liberator*
1834:	Cyrus McCormick patents the McCormick reaper First strike at Lowell mills
1835:	Southern legislatures complete tightening of "black codes" Texas revolts against Mexico
1844:	Samuel F. B. Morse operates first telegraph
1845:	Beginning of Irish potato famine and heavy Irish immigration Texas annexed to the U.S. as a slave state
1846–1848:	Mexican-American War
1848:	Women's Rights Convention at Seneca Falls, New York
1850:	Compromise of 1850
1851:	Harriet Beecher Stowe's *Uncle Tom's Cabin* published
1854:	Republican Party formed, with "free soil" platform
1857:	Supreme Court decision in *Dred Scott v. Sanford*
1860:	Abraham Lincoln elected President (November) South Carolina secedes from Union (December); 10 other states follow
1861–1865:	Civil War

Introduction

In 1853, the New York artist Asher B. Durand (1796–1883) painted *Progress*, a testament to a changing America. *Progress* depicted a landscape—the favorite subject of American artists in the mid-nineteenth century. For these painters, the nation's landscape (or their imaginative recreations of it) became America's answer to European history-painting. The United States might not have centuries of historical events to capture in art, but it had landscapes that represented both unspoiled natural beauty and opportunities for new human endeavor. Many of these artists, who included Thomas Cole, Frederick Church, and many others besides Durand, worked in and around New York's Hudson River Valley; they later came to be called the Hudson River School. But their subjects ranged from Maine to California. In *Progress*, Durand offered a landscape with two sides. In the right foreground (the front, bottom section) bustled modernization: roads with covered wagons, a canal, a railroad. Further back in the painting appeared a town that seemed to exemplify "The Advance of Civilization"—which was the alternate title for the painting. In the left foreground, watching all this development, stood a cluster of Indians on a cliff, amid rocks and living and dead trees. Indians were familiar sights in American landscape paintings: their presence helped identify the scenes as "American." But in this case, Durand's Indians were physically separated from the march of "progress." Could they take part in the scenes on the left? Apparently not: they would have to fall (or jump) off that cliff to get there.

The developments in Asher Durand's painting were just one manifestation of how America changed between 1800 and 1865. In one sense, the United States were becoming more "united" than they had been after the Revolution, when "United States" was more a rhetorical term than an actuality. Religious denominations like the Baptists and Methodists, the two most successful at attracting new believers, crossed local and state boundaries. So did the Democratic and Whig political parties that came of age around 1840. The most dramatic force for union was the transportation revolution that Durand depicted: improved roads (gravel-based, with tree stumps cleared away), canals that connected major bodies of water (notably the Erie Canal across New York state), and finally railroads. Railroads changed the way Americans conceived of distance, and they developed quickly: from seventy-three miles of track in the entire country in 1830 to over thirty thousand in 1860. The bulk of railroad-building occurred in the northern and midwestern states, creating regional networks of commerce. Noah Webster and Alexander Hamilton's dream was beginning to be realized, but a strong federal government had little to do with this unification. The national government possessed little presence in Americans' everyday lives, except for the post office. In fact, the government's major actions—acquiring land through treaties (with Native American tribes and with France, in the Louisiana Purchase) and by force (Indian wars, the Mexican War of the 1840s)—reinforced the localism of American society, by adding more land for people to settle, far from existing centers of government. This was Thomas Jefferson's agrarian vision: to keep the United States agricultural and localistic, with government at a minimum. On the eve of the Civil War, though urban dwellers numbered a fifth of the population (from five percent in 1800), the vast majority of Americans lived in places of 2500 inhabitants or fewer.

In these years, another member of the Revolutionary generation—Benjamin Franklin—became as famous as he had ever been in his lifetime. Biographies, children's schoolbooks, and history books all hailed the Pennsylvanian sage who had invented bifocal eyeglasses, founded the first library and fire company in North America, and signed both the Declaration of Independence and the Constitution. Above all, however, the image of Benjamin Franklin in nineteenth-century

America was not the Enlightenment scientist or the Revolutionary patriot, but a *new* idea: that of the "self-made man," whose industriousness, sobriety, and ingenuity had allowed him to rise from obscurity as the son of a Boston candle-maker to fame, fortune, and greatness. For young men in the new republic (from the adoption of the Constitution in 1788 to the outbreak of the Civil War in 1861), Franklin became the model for success—success in a new kind of society, which Franklin in his own lifetime had only begun to experience.

At the heart of this new society was the concept of "individualism." Individualism, a word coined in the 1830s by the French nobleman Alexis De Tocqueville (1805–1859) to describe the United States, was the idea that every individual had the capacity and opportunity to become successful through individual efforts. Individuals were "free agents," free to make moral, economic, and political choices for themselves. In one sense, this spirit emerged from the American Revolution, even if that revolution had been limited in its social consequences. In another, it emerged from the Enlightenment idea that human beings could use reason to understand and affect their world.

In a third sense, it emerged from specific developments unleashed by the Constitution and other events of the early republic. For instance, the First Amendment to the Constitution guaranteed that "Congress shall make no law respecting an establishment of religion, or prohibiting the free exercise thereof." In 1791 this was a revolutionary concept: nearly every European nation of the time and many of the new United States had established churches, supported by the government and recognized as the state religion. The Constitution, in effect, licensed a religious free market—and almost immediately diverse denominations began to compete for members, holding massive revival meetings and publishing thousands of religious pamphlets and tracts. Similarly, within forty years of the Constitution most states passed liberal suffrage laws, removing property qualifications for voting. As a result, by 1840 most white men could cast ballots—creating a political free market in which political parties competed in elections, using many of the same tactics as the religious denominations. A "market society" had emerged—not just a capitalist market economy in which individuals bought and sold products and services, but also a society in which many aspects of social relations (like religion and politics) resembled the market pattern.

To many people the development of a market society represented progress, freedom, and opportunity. In the United States, more of the population voted and owned property than in any nation in Europe. But even Alexis De Tocqueville (1805–1859), who had first coined the term "individualism" to describe Americans, was skeptical of its side effects. According to Tocqueville, Americans were forever restless and discontented in the midst of their prosperity: with the opportunity to get ahead came anxieties that people in more rigidly structured societies had never known. Equality of opportunity came at the expense of security about one's social position (even if it was a subordinate one); with freedom to rise came the chance of failure. The constant quest for more money or the latest fashions also met with challenge from a group of writers and thinkers who called themselves the Transcendentalists. Drawing from European Romanticism, Transcendentalist authors argued that "individualism" as practiced by most Americans had become little more than a rat race, a set of expectations imposed by the emerging market. Only through intellectual liberation—the attempt to cultivate "individuality," the ideas and traits that made one unique—could individuals transcend society's artificial constraints. When Ralph Waldo Emerson (1803–1882), the leading Transcendentalist philosopher, wrote about "Self-Reliance," he was speaking not of Benjamin Franklin's model, but of a different concept of the individual. Similarly, Emerson's friend Henry David Thoreau (1817–1862) refused to pay his taxes in protest over slavery and the Mexican War, then wrote about it in his essay "On Civil Disobedience." Thoreau suggested that an individual could—must—challenge society's conventions and rules when he considered them unjust.

Other challenges to market society came from radically different quarters. Both George Fitzhugh (1806–1881), a prominent defender of slavery, and workingmen's groups in the North argued that capitalism exploited its laborers for the profit of the owners of capital, a concept similar to the one Karl Marx was simultaneously developing in Europe. Indeed, the very newness of capitalism—as an economic system, it had existed for less than a century—may have made it seem more threatening to those who had been part of other ways of life. Craft workers accustomed to gaining a skill through the time-honored process of apprenticeship, then establishing their own shops and training the next generation of apprentices, found the rising mechanization of their crafts (and the increasing use of unskilled laborers to perform tasks at low wages) unsettling. To these workers, including the group in Charlestown, Massachusetts, that called itself the Workingmen's Party, the opportunity to establish one's own shop was ebbing, not expanding. Fitzhugh's critique of capitalism, to be sure, was part of his defense of Southern slavery, and his portrayals of slavery omitted its brutality. Nonetheless, it is important to recognize that his argument dealt with Northern society as much as with his native Virginia.

Women's places in this new market society were as varied as men's: it is impossible to define "women's role" in any monolithic way. After the Revolution, numerous writers championed "republican motherhood," the idea that women had a civic role in the United States as the principal creators of new generations of citizens. As a result, these authors argued, American women needed to be educated more seriously than women in other nations or in earlier times: they needed to learn history, science, and literature, as well as the more traditional domestic duties. In the 1820s and 1830s, these ideas shifted into the "cult of domesticity," the idea that home was the happiest place on earth, where children's education took place and where women ruled. It is easy, from a twenty-first-century vantage point, to dismiss the idea of domesticity as archaic; in the 1820s, however, it seemed progressive to many women and men. In earlier agricultural families, after all, home and work were completely intertwined, and both were dominated by the father and husband. Particularly in cities and towns where men increasingly left home to go to work, women were achieving a new form of authority in the home. With this new place of authority came the idea that women were morally superior to men—precisely because they were not part of the competitive, morally corrosive world of the economic marketplace.

If domesticity could suggest that women's place was in the home, it could equally imply that women had a larger moral role to play in society. And thousands of women did, moving into teaching, charitable work, and social reform activity. Among the principal proponents of this active, educated, *and* domestic American womanhood was Catharine Beecher (1800–1878), daughter of the celebrated minister Lyman Beecher and sister of Harriet Beecher Stowe, who would in 1851 write *Uncle Tom's Cabin*, the bestselling abolitionist novel that stirred the waters of sectional conflict. But domesticity was not available to all women. Maria W. Stewart (1803–1879), a black woman born in Connecticut and widowed in her mid-twenties, did at least two things that were nearly unheard of for women, let alone black women: she gave lectures to mixed groups of black men and women, and she used her literacy to write essays about the conditions of African Americans. Some of her lectures and essays appeared in *The Liberator*, the abolitionist newspaper published by William Lloyd Garrison. In the lecture printed here, "Why Sit Ye Here and Die," Stewart encouraged white women and black men to consider the condition of black women, a plight that reflected their race, their gender, and their economic status.

As Stewart's lecture suggested, racism toward blacks was rampant in the non-slaveholding, self-consciously "progressive" North as well as in the South. Indeed, the very concept of progress depends on a concept of backwardness: to see oneself as progressive implies a comparison with someone else. In nineteenth-century America, that someone else was often defined by race or ethnicity. New immigrants from Ireland and Germany, who came to the United States in the tens of thousands between 1845 and 1860, often met with discrimination; many native-born citizens especially saw the Catholic Irish as degraded. Similar images of Native Americans flourished in these years: white Americans widely viewed Indians as unwilling or unable to engage in the ways of so-called "civilized" society. African Americans inhabited the bottom of white America's racial hierarchy. Many whites considered them mentally inferior, incapable of surviving in freedom. (Communities of free blacks in the North belied this view.) Others acknowledged the humanity of African Americans but feared that slaves would suffer if freed, because of their lack of education and the racism prevalent in white society.

When Alexis De Tocqueville visited the United States in the 1830s, he paid much attention to relations among the "three races" of North America: European Americans, African Americans, and Native Americans. His perceptions, printed here, captured the differing forms of race relations. In the 1820s, the government of Georgia sought to expel the Cherokee population that lived, as a separate nation, within its borders. Eventually, defying the Supreme Court, President Andrew Jackson ordered expulsion, and the Cherokees and four other tribes were forcibly removed to the "Indian Territory" (which would become the state of Oklahoma). The Cherokees, who had established an advanced agricultural society in Georgia, were divided over the prospect of moving. Before the removal order, the Cherokee newspaper editor Elias Boudinot (c. 1803–1839) appealed to the United States government by explaining the nature of his culture. While Boudinot emphasized how Cherokees were becoming more "American," the slave Nat Turner (1800–1831) had no such opportunity. Owned by a master in Southampton County, Virginia, Turner experienced religious revelations that ultimately induced him to lead a slave rebellion in late August 1831. By the time white authorities crushed the rebellion, some two hundred people were dead: about sixty whites and more than twice that number of blacks, slave and free. Turner himself was executed on November 11, but not before he met with the local lawyer and slaveowner Thomas R. Gray. Gray wrote down their conversations, and had them published as *The Confessions of Nat Turner* two weeks after Turner's execution. When reading this document, it is important to consider how Gray's own conceptions influenced the way he arranged and told the story.

Nat Turner's rebellion, the last major slave revolt in the American South, helped change southerners' defense of slavery. Slaveowners soon adopted a "positive defense" of their peculiar institution: slavery, many of them now argued, was a benevolent institution that protected inferior beings who would otherwise be unable to protect themselves. George Fitzhugh would become one of the chief exponents of this view, but thirty years of commentators had made the same point. At the same time, the abolitionist movement sought to galvanize northerners against slavery—and to convince slaveholders themselves to free their slaves. Abolitionists never countenanced slave rebellion *a la* Nat Turner: their foremost African-American spokesman, Frederick Douglass, appealed to northern white audience who would have been horrified by the specter of black men with weapons. Still, abolitionists constituted a tiny, often-ridiculed minority among mid-nineteenth-century Americans.

For some women abolitionists, participating in a movement to emancipate slaves led to questioning their own status. Even some abolitionists believed that women abolitionists should deliver speeches only to female audiences. In 1848, a group of women and men (including Frederick Douglass) met at Seneca Falls, New York, to discuss women's rights. Most of them had participated in abolitionism for over a decade. Elizabeth Cady Stanton (1815–1902) drafted the Seneca Falls "Declaration of Sentiments," which sixty-eight women and thirty-two men signed. Like the abolitionists, the Seneca Falls declaration met with far more derision than praise. Advocates of a different kind of "women's rights" responded. As editor of the popular magazine *Godey's Lady's Book*, Sarah Josepha Hale (1788–1879) was among the most influential women of the day. She used her "Editor's Table" column in January 1850 to remind readers that her magazines had always advocated a powerful, but distinct, role for women. Sojourner Truth (1797–1883) agreed with the objectives of the Seneca Falls convention, but wondered whether its notions of equality applied to African-

American women too. Born in slavery with the name Isabella, she took the name Sojourner Truth to reflect her mission as a free woman: a traveling preacher speaking God's revealed truth. In 1851 Truth spoke before a women's rights convention in Akron, Ohio. Her address was soon reported in an abolitionist newspaper, and narrated nearly thirty years later in her biography, *Narrative of Sojourner Truth.* Both versions appear here; because Truth never learned to read or write, we must rely upon others' accounts of her oratory.

The Mexican War of 1846–1848 proved to be a critical turning point in the struggle over slavery. The war became a media event, reported by newspapers across the nation and depicted in countless engravings of the battles and biographies of the generals. When the war ended, the United States had won much of Mexico's territory, including California. The issue of whether California would become a free or a slave state led to the Compromise of 1850—which admitted California to the Union as a free state, and enacted a strict Fugitive Slave Law that could force Northerners to participate in catching and returning escaped slaves. This law led Harriet Beecher Stowe to write *Uncle Tom's Cabin* (1851) in protest; the book became the biggest seller in American history to that point. In fact, Stowe's book was to the abolitionist movement what Thomas Paine's *Common Sense* had been to the independence movement seventy-five years before: it galvanized public opinion against slavery, and intensified the conflict between North and South. During the 1850s, a series of events further estranged the sections, persuading many Northerners that a "slave power conspiracy" sought to control the federal government. Bloody warfare erupted in Kansas Territory over whether this future state should be open to slavery. The Supreme Court's 1857 decision in *Dred Scott v. Sanford* suggested that a master could take his slaves anywhere—even into free states—and retain ownership of them. At the same time, the rise of the new Republican party—pledged to bar slavery from new territories or states—persuaded Southerners that a "black Republican" conspiracy aimed to surround the South and ultimately to destroy its economic system and way of life. When the Republicans won the White House and Congress in 1860, seven Southern states (South Carolina, Mississippi, Florida, Alabama, Georgia, Louisiana, and Texas) seceded from the Union. When new president Abraham Lincoln sent an expedition to supply Fort Sumter, off the South Carolina coast, in April 1861, South Carolina troops bombarded the fort, and civil war had begun. Virginia, North Carolina, Tennessee, and Arkansas soon joined the seceding states.

Abraham Lincoln (1809–1865), the first President from the new Republican party, exemplified Northern attitudes about race. Lincoln's home state mirrored the nation: northern Illinois, populated by transplanted New Englanders who tended to abhor slavery, bordered Michigan and Canada; southern Illinois, across the Ohio River from Kentucky and Missouri, consisted largely of emigrants from Virginia, Kentucky, or Tennessee, all slave states. Abraham Lincoln thus dealt with the divisions over slavery throughout his political life, unlike politicians in states like South Carolina or Massachusetts where such divisions barely existed. He became a member of the Republican party soon after its founding in 1854, but he was decidedly not an abolitionist. Like other middle-of-the-road Republicans, he believed that slavery should not expand into new territories but should be allowed to continue where it already existed. (This stance helps explain why he, rather than a stauncher abolitionist, was his party's presidential candidate in 1860.) As president, he entered the Civil War with one objective: to save the Union at any cost. Over time, he moved toward emancipating the slaves, for political, military, and moral reasons. The works printed here reveal Lincoln's beliefs as they evolved during the war.

The Civil War transformed American society. Over six hundred thousand soldiers lost their lives (more than two thirds to diseases contracted in camps, battlefields, and army hospitals). Nearly another half million returned home grievously wounded. The total casualties amounted to over seven percent of all the males in the United States. When the war ended, slavery was no more; slaves—the principal form of Southern capital—now owned themselves. The North had reconquered the rebellious states, and attempted to reconstruct them, by providing freed slaves with education and voting rights and thus preparing them for life in individualistic market society. Though this effort largely ended when federal troops pulled out of the Southern states, it contributed to the origins of a Southern educational system that would produce many of the African-American professionals and leaders of the coming generations. In the North, the war accelerated the growth of industry and railroads. Because the South, which had always opposed measures that strengthened the federal government's power, was temporarily out of the Union, Congress passed and President Lincoln signed a series of laws that expanded the scope of government action. The Homestead Act offered one hundred sixty acres of public land to any farmer who paid a small fee and cultivated the land for five years, the transcontinental railroad act established the first coast-to-coast railroad, and the Morrill Act laid the foundations of land-grant colleges and universities.

Perhaps as dramatic was a deceptively simple change in the way Americans talked about their country. Before the war, most Americans would have used the plural—"The United States *are* fighting a war"—emphasizing the separateness of the states, not the singleness of the union. After the war, the United States became a singular noun—"The United States *is* fighting a war"—and Americans came to refer to their country as a "nation," a single entity, not simply a divisible "union" of separate states.

Ralph Waldo Emerson
from "Self Reliance" (1841)

I read the other day some verses written by an eminent painter which were original and not conventional. The soul always hears an admonition in such lines, let the subject be what it may. The sentiment they instil is of more value than any thought they may contain. To believe your own thought, to believe that what is true for you in your private heart is true for all men,—that is genius. Speak your latent conviction, and it shall be the universal sense; for the inmost in due time becomes the outmost, and our first thought is rendered back to us by the trumpets of the Last Judgment. Familiar as the voice of the mind is to each, the highest merit we ascribe to Moses, Plato and Milton is that they set at naught books and traditions, and spoke not what men but what *they* thought. A man should learn to detect and watch that gleam of light which flashes across his mind from within, more than the lustre of the firmament of bards and sages. Yet he dismisses without notice his thought, because it is his. In every work of genius we recognize our own rejected thoughts; they come back to us with a certain alienated majesty. Great works of art have no more affecting lesson for us than this. They teach us to abide by our spontaneous impression with good-humored inflexibility then most when the whole cry of voices is on the other side. Else to-morrow a stranger will say with masterly good sense precisely what we have thought and felt all the time, and we shall be forced to take with shame our own opinion from another.

There is a time in every man's education when he arrives at the conviction that envy is ignorance; that imitation is suicide; that he must take himself for better or worse as his portion; that though the wide universe is full of good, no kernel of nourishing corn can come to him but through his toil bestowed on that plot of ground which is given to him to till. The power which resides in him is new in nature, and none but he knows what that is which he can do, nor does he know until he has tried. Not for nothing one face, one character, one fact, makes much impression on him, and another none. This sculpture in the memory is not without preestablished harmony. The eye was placed where one ray should fall, that it might testify of that particular ray. We but half express ourselves, and are ashamed of that divine idea which each of us represents. It may be safely trusted as proportionate and of good issues, so it be faithfully imparted, but God will not have his work made manifest by cowards. A man is relieved and gay when he has put his heart into his work and done his best; but what he has said or done otherwise shall give him no peace. It is a deliverance which does not deliver. In the attempt his genius deserts him; no muse befriends; no invention, no hope.

Trust thyself: every heart vibrates to that iron string. Accept the place the divine providence has found for you, the society of your contemporaries, the connection of events. Great men have always done so, and confided themselves childlike to the genius of their age, betraying their perception that the absolutely trustworthy was seated at their heart, working through their hands, predominating in all their being. And we are now men, and must accept in the highest mind the same transcendent destiny; and not minors and invalids in a protected corner, not cowards fleeing before a revolution, but guides, redeemers and benefactors, obeying the Almighty effort and advancing on Chaos and the Dark.

What pretty oracles nature yields us on this text in the face and behavior of children, babes, and even brutes! That divided and rebel mind, that distrust of a sentiment because our arithmetic has computed the strength and means opposed to our purpose, these have not. Their mind being whole, their eye is as yet unconquered, and when we look in their faces we are disconcerted. Infancy conforms to nobody; all conform to it; so that one babe commonly makes four or five out of the adults who prattle and play to it. So God has armed youth and puberty and manhood no less with its own piquancy and charm, and made it enviable and gracious and its claims not to be put by, if it will stand by itself. Do not think the youth has no force, because he cannot speak to you and me. Hark! in the next room his voice is sufficiently clear and emphatic. It seems he knows how to speak to his contemporaries. Bashful or bold then, he will know how to make us seniors very unnecessary. . . .

These are the voices which we hear in solitude, but they grow faint and inaudible as we enter into the world. Society everywhere is in conspiracy against the manhood of every one of its members. Society is a joint-stock company, in which the members agree, for the better securing of his bread to each shareholder, to surrender the liberty and culture of the eater. The virtue in most request is conformity. Self-reliance is its aversion. It loves not realities and creators, but names and customs.

Whoso would be a man, must be a nonconformist. He who would gather immortal palms must not be hindered by the name of goodness, but must explore if it be goodness. Nothing is at last sacred but the integrity of your own mind. Absolve you to yourself, and you shall have the suffrage of the world. I remember an answer which when quite young I was prompted to make to a valued adviser who was wont to importune me with the dear old doctrines of the church. On my saying, "What have I to do with the sacredness of traditions, if I live wholly from within?" my friend suggested,—"But these impulses may be from below, not from above." I replied, "They do not seem to me to be such; but if I am the Devil's child, I will live then from the Devil." No law can be sacred to me but that of my nature. Good and bad are but names very readily transferable to that or this; the only right is what is after my constitution; the only wrong what is against it. A man is to carry himself in the presence of all opposition as if every thing were titular and ephemeral but he. I am ashamed to think how easily we capitulate to badges and names, to large societies and dead institutions. Every decent and well-spoken individual affects and sways me more than is right. I ought to go upright and vital, and speak the rude truth in all ways. If malice and vanity wear the coat of philanthropy, shall that pass? If an angry bigot assumes this bountiful cause of Abolition, and comes to me with his last news from Barbadoes, why should I not say to him, "Go love thy infant; love thy wood-chopper; be good-natured and modest; have that grace; and never varnish your hard, uncharitable ambition with this incredible tenderness for black folk a thousand miles off. Thy love afar is spite at home." Rough and graceless would be such greeting, but truth is handsomer than the affectation of love. Your goodness must have some edge to it,—else it is none. The doctrine of hatred must be preached, as the counteraction of the doctrine of love, when that pules and whines. I shun father and mother and wife and brother when my genius calls me. I would write on the lintels of the door-post, *Whim.* I hope it is somewhat better than whim at last, but we cannot spend the day in explanation. Expect me not to show cause why I seek or why I exclude company. Then again, do not tell me, as a good man did to-day, of my obligation to put all poor men in good situations. Are they *my* poor? I tell thee, thou foolish philanthropist, that I grudge the dollar, the dime, the cent I give to such men as do not belong to me and to whom I do not belong. There is a class of persons to whom by all spiritual affinity I am bought and sold; for them I will go to prison if need be; but your miscellaneous popular charities; the education at college of fools; the building of meeting-houses to the vain end to which many now stand; alms to sots, and the thousand-fold Relief Societies;—though I confess with shame I sometimes succumb and give the dollar, it is a wicked dollar, which by and by I shall have the manhood to withhold.

Virtues are, in the popular estimate, rather the exception than the rule. There is the man *and* his virtues. Men do what is called a good action, as some piece of courage or charity, much as they would pay a fine in expiation of daily nonappearance on parade. Their works are done as an apology or extenuation of their living in the world,—as invalids and the insane pay a high board. Their virtues are penances. I do not wish to expiate, but to live. My life is for itself and not for a spectacle. I much prefer that it should be of a lower strain, so it be genuine and equal, than that it should be glittering and unsteady. I wish it to be sound and sweet, and not to need diet and bleeding. I ask primary evidence that you are a man, and refuse this appeal from the man to his actions. I know that for myself it makes no difference whether I do or forbear those actions which are reckoned excellent. I cannot consent to pay for a privilege where I have intrinsic right. Few and mean as my gifts may be, I actually am, and do not need for my own assurance or the assurance of my fellows any secondary testimony.

What I must do is all that concerns me, not what the people think. This rule, equally arduous in actual and in intellectual life, may serve for the whole distinction between greatness and meanness. It is the harder because you will always find those who think they know what is your duty better than you know it. It is easy in the world to live after the world's opinion; it is easy in solitude to live after our own; but the great man is he who in the midst of the crowd keeps with perfect sweetness the independence of solitude.

The objection to conforming to usages that have become dead to you is that it scatters your force. It loses your time and blurs the impression of your character. If you maintain a dead church, contribute to a dead Bible-society, vote with a great party either for the government or against it, spread your table like base housekeepers,—under all these screens I have difficulty to detect the precise man you are: and of course so much force is withdrawn from your proper life. But do your work, and I shall know you. Do your work, and you shall reinforce yourself. A man must consider what a blind-man's buff is this game of conformity. If I know your sect I anticipate your argument. I hear a preacher announce for his text and topic the expediency of one of the institutions of his church. Do I not know beforehand that not possibly can he say a new and spontaneous word? Do I not know that with all this ostentation of examining the grounds of the institution he will do no such thing? Do I not know that he is pledged to himself not to look but at one side, the permitted side, not as a man, but as a parish minister? He is a retained attorney, and these airs of the bench are the emptiest affectation. Well, most men have bound their eyes with one or another handkerchief, and attached themselves to some one of these communities of opinion. This conformity makes them not false in a few particulars, authors of a few lies, but false in all particulars. Their every truth is not quite true. Their two is not the real two, their four not the real four; so that every word they say chagrins us and we know not where to begin to set them right. Meantime nature is not slow to equip us in the prison-uniform of the party to which we adhere. We come to wear one cut of face and figure, and acquire by degrees the gentlest asinine expression. There is a mortifying experience in particular, which does not fail to wreak itself also in the general history; I mean "the foolish face of praise," the forced smile which we put on in company where we do not feel at ease, in answer to conversation which does not interest us. The muscles, not spontaneously moved but moved by a low usurping wilfulness, grow tight about the outline of the face, with the most disagreeable sensation.

For nonconformity the world whips you with its displeasure. And therefore a man must know how to estimate a sour face. The bystanders look askance on him in the public street or in the friend's parlor. If this aversion had its origin in contempt and resistance like his own he might well go home with a sad countenance; but the sour faces of the multitude, like their sweet faces, have no deep cause, but are put on and off as the wind blows and a newspaper directs. Yet is the discontent of the multitude more formidable than that of the senate and the college. It is easy enough for a firm man who knows the world to brook the rage of the cultivated classes. Their rage is decorous and prudent, for they are timid, as being very vulnerable themselves. But when to their feminine rage the indignation of the people is added, when the ignorant and the poor are aroused, when the unintelligent brute force that lies at the bottom of society is made to growl and mow, it needs the habit of magnanimity and religion to treat it godlike as a trifle of no concernment.

The other terror that scares us from self-trust is our consistency; a reverence for our past act or word because the eyes of others have no other data for computing our orbit than our past acts, and we are loth to disappoint them.

But why should you keep your head over your shoulder? Why drag about this corpse of your memory, lest you contradict somewhat you have stated in this or that public place? Suppose you should contradict yourself; what then? It seems to be a rule of wisdom never to rely on your memory alone, scarcely even in acts of pure memory, but to bring the past for judgment into the thousand-eyed present, and live ever in a new day. In your metaphysics you have denied personality to the Deity, yet when the devout motions of the soul come, yield to them heart and life, though they should clothe God with shape and color. Leave your theory, as Joseph his coat in the hand of the harlot, and flee.

A foolish consistency is the hobgoblin of little minds, adored by little statesmen and philosophers and divines. With consistency a great soul has simply nothing to do. He may as well concern himself with his shadow on the wall. Speak what you think now in hard words and to-morrow speak what to-morrow thinks in hard words again, though it contradict everything you said to-day.—"Ah, so you shall be sure to be misunderstood."—Is it so bad then to be misunderstood? Pythagoras was misunderstood, and Socrates, and Jesus, and Luther, and Copernicus, and Galileo, and Newton, and every pure and wise spirit that ever took flesh. To be great is to be misunderstood. . . .

Society is a wave. The wave moves onward, but the water of which it is composed does not. The same particle does not rise from the valley to the ridge. Its unity is only phenomenal. The persons who make up a nation to-day, next year die, and their experience dies with them.

And so, the reliance on Property, including the reliance on governments which protect it, is the want of self-reliance. Men have looked away from themselves and at things so long that they have come to esteem the religious, learned and civil institutions as guards of property, and they deprecate assaults on these, because they feel them to be assaults on property. They measure their esteem of each other by what each has, and not by what each is. But a cultivated man becomes ashamed of his property, out of new respect for his nature. Especially he hates what he has if he sees that it is accidental,—came to him by inheritance, or gift, or crime; then he feels that it is not having; it does not belong to him, has no root in him and merely lies there because no revolution or no robber takes it away. But that which a man is, does always by necessity acquire; and what the man acquires, is living property, which does not wait the beck of rulers, or mobs, or revolutions, or fire, or storm, or bankruptcies, but perpetually renews itself wherever the man breathes. "Thy lot or portion of life," said the Caliph Ali, "is seeking after thee; therefore be at rest from seeking after it." Our dependence on these foreign goods leads us to our slavish respect for numbers. The political parties meet in numerous conventions; the greater the concourse and with each new uproar of announcement, The delegation from Essex! The Democrats from New Hampshire! The Whigs of Maine! the young patriot feels himself stronger than before by a new thousand of eyes and arms. In like manner the reformers summon conventions and vote and resolve in multitude. Not so, O friends! will the God deign to enter and inhabit you, but by a method precisely the reverse. It is only as a man puts off all foreign support and stands alone that I see him to be strong and to pre-vail. He is weaker by every recruit to his banner. Is not a man better than a town? Ask nothing of men, and, in the endless mutation, thou only firm column must presently appear the upholder of all that surrounds thee. He who knows that power is inborn, that he is weak because he has looked for good out of him and elsewhere, and, so perceiving, throws himself unhesitatingly on his thought, instantly rights himself, stands in the erect position, commands his limbs, works mira-cles; just as a man who stands on his feet is stronger than a man who stands on his head.

So use all that is called Fortune. Most men gamble with her, and gain all, and lose all, as her wheel rolls. But do thou leave as unlawful these winnings, and deal with Cause and Effect, the chancellors of God. In the Will work and acquire, and thou hast chained the wheel of Chance, and shall sit hereafter out of fear from her rotations. A political victory, a rise of rents, the recovery of your sick or the return of your absent friend, or some other favorable event raises your spirits, and you think good days are preparing for you. Do not believe it. Nothing can bring you peace but yourself. Nothing can bring you peace but the triumph of principles.

HENRY DAVID THOREAU

from "On Civil Disobedience" (1849)

I heartily accept the motto,—"That government is best which governs least"; and I should like to see it acted up to more rapidly and systematically. Carried out, it finally amounts to this, which I also believe,—"That government is best which governs not at all"; and when men are prepared for it, that will be the kind of government which they will have. Government is at best but an expedient; but most governments are usually, and all governments are sometimes, inexpedient. The objections which have been brought against a standing army, and they are many and weighty, and deserve to prevail, may also at last be brought against a standing government. The standing army is only an arm of the standing government. The government itself, which is only the mode which the people have chosen to execute their will, is equally liable to be abused and perverted before the people can act through it. Witness the present Mexican war, the work of comparatively a few individuals using the standing government as their tool; for, in the outset, the people would not have consented to this measure.

This American government,—what is it but a tradition, though a recent one, endeavoring to transmit itself unimpaired to posterity, but each instant losing some of its integrity? It has not the vitality and force of a single living man; for a single man can bend it to his will. It is a sort of wooden gun to the people themselves. But it is not the less necessary for this; for the people must have some complicated machinery or other, and hear its din, to satisfy that idea of government which they have. Governments show thus how successfully men can be imposed on, even impose on themselves, for their own advantage. It is excellent, we must all allow. Yet this government never of itself furthered any enterprise, but by the alacrity with which it got out of its way. *It* does not keep the country free. *It* does not settle the West. *It* does not educate. The character inherent in the American people has done all that has been accomplished; and it would have done somewhat more, if the government had not sometimes got in its way. For government is an expedient by which men would fain succeed in letting one another alone; and, as has been said, when it is most expedient, the governed are most let alone by it. . . .

But, to speak practically and as a citizen, unlike those who call themselves no-government men, I ask for, not at once no government, but *at once* a better government. Let every man make known what kind of government would command his respect, and that will be one step toward obtaining it.

After all, the practical reason why, when the power is once in the hands of the people, a majority are permitted, and for a long period continue, to rule, is not because they are most likely to be in the right, nor because this seems fairest to the minority, but because they are physically the strongest. But a government in which the majority rule in all cases cannot be based on justice, even as far as men understand it. Can there not be a government in which majorities do not virtually decide right and wrong, but conscience?—in which majorities decide only those questions to which the rule of expediency is applicable? Must the citizen ever for a moment, or in the least degree, resign his conscience to the legislator? Why has every man a conscience, then? I think that we should be men first, and subjects afterward. It is not desirable to cultivate a respect for the law, so much as for the right. The only obligation which I have the right to assume, is to do at any time what I think right. It is truly enough said, that a corporation has no conscience; but a corporation of conscientious men is a corporation *with* a conscience. Law never made men a whit more just; and, by means of their respect for it, even the well-disposed are daily made the agents of injustice. A common and natural result of an undue respect for law is, that you may see a file of soldiers, colonel, captain, corporal, privates, powder-monkeys, and all, marching in admirable order over hill and dale to the wars, against their wills, ay, against their common sense and consciences, which makes it very steep marching indeed, and produces a palpitation of the heart. . . .

The mass of men serve the state thus, not as men mainly, but as machines, with their bodies. They are the standing army, and the militia, jailers, constables, posse comitatus, &c. In most cases there is no free exercise whatever of the judgment or of the moral sense; but they put themselves on a level with wood and earth and stones; and wooden men can perhaps be manufactured that will serve the purpose as well. Such command no more respect than men of straw or a lump of dirt. They have the same sort of worth only as horses and dogs. Yet such as these even are commonly esteemed good citizens. Others,—as most legislators, politicians, lawyers, ministers, and officeholders,—serve the state chiefly with their heads; and, as they rarely make any moral distinctions, they are as likely to serve the Devil, without *intending* it, as God. A very few, as heroes, patriots, martyrs, reformers in the great sense, and *men,* serve the state with their consciences also, and so necessarily resist it for the most part; and they are commonly treated as enemies by it. . . .

How does it become a man to behave toward this American government to-day? I answer, that he cannot without disgrace be associated with it. I cannot for an instant recognize that political organization as my government which is the *slave's* government also.

All men recognize the right of revolution; that is, the right to refuse allegiance to, and to resist, the government, when its tyranny or its inefficiency are great and unendurable. But almost all say that such is not the case now. But such was the case, they think, in the Revolution of '75. If one were to tell me that this was a bad government because it taxed certain foreign commodities brought to its ports, it is most probable that I should not make an ado about it, for I can do without them. All machines have their friction; and possibly this does enough good to counterbalance the evil. At any rate, it is a great evil to make a stir about it. But when the friction comes to have its machine, and oppression and robbery are organized, I say, let us not have such a machine any longer. In other words, when a sixth of the population of a nation which has undertaken to be the refuge of liberty are slaves, and a whole country is unjustly overrun and conquered by a foreign army, and subjected to military law, I think that it is not too soon for honest men to rebel and revolutionize. What makes this duty the more urgent is the fact, that the country so overrun is not our own, but ours is the invading army. . . .

Practically speaking, the opponents to a reform in Massachusetts are not a hundred thousand politicians at the South, but a hundred thousand merchants and farmers here, who are more interested in commerce and agriculture than they are in humanity, and are not prepared to do justice to the slave and to Mexico, *cost what it may.* I quarrel not with far-off foes, but with those who, near at home, co-operate with, and do the bidding of, those far away, and without whom the latter would be harmless. We are accustomed to say, that the mass of men are unprepared; but improvement is slow, because the few are not materially wiser or better than the many. It is not so important that many should be as good as you, as that there be some absolute goodness somewhere; for that will leaven the whole lump. There are thousands who are *in opinion* opposed to slavery and to the war, who yet in effect do nothing to put an end to them; who, esteeming themselves children of Washington and Franklin, sit down with their hands in their pockets, and say that they know not what to do, and do nothing; who even postpone the question of freedom to the question of free-trade, and quietly read the prices-current along with the latest advices from Mexico, after dinner, and, it may be, fall asleep over them both. What is the price-current of an honest man and a patriot to-day? They hesitate, and they regret, and sometimes they petition; but they do nothing in earnest and with effect. They will wait, well disposed, for others to remedy the evil, that they may no longer have it to regret. At most, they give only a cheap vote, and a feeble countenance and God-speed, to the right, as it goes by them. There are nine hundred and ninety-nine patrons of virtue to one virtuous man. But it is easier to deal with the real possessor of a thing than with the temporary guardian of it.

All voting is a sort of gaming, like checkers or backgammon, with a slight moral tinge to it, a playing with right and wrong, with moral questions; and betting naturally accompanies it. The character of the voters is not staked. I cast my vote, perchance, as I think right; but I am not vitally concerned that that right should prevail. I am willing to leave it to the majority. Its obligation, therefore, never exceeds that of expediency. Even voting *for the right* is *doing* nothing for it. It is only expressing to men feebly your desire that it should prevail. A wise man will not leave the right to the mercy of chance, nor wish it to prevail through the power of the majority. There is but little virtue in the action of masses of men. When the majority shall at length vote for the abolition of slavery, it will be because they are indifferent to slavery, or because there is but little slavery left to be abolished by their vote. *They* will then be the only slaves. Only *his* vote can hasten the abolition of slavery who asserts his own freedom by his vote. . . .

It is not a man's duty, as a matter of course, to devote himself to the eradication of any, even the most enormous wrong; he may still properly have other concerns to engage him; but it is his duty, at least, to wash his hands of it, and, if he gives it no thought longer, not to give it practically his support. If I devote myself to other pursuits and contemplations, I must first see, at least, that I do not pursue them sitting upon another man's shoulders. I must get off him first, that he may pursue his contemplations too. See what gross inconsistency is tolerated. I have heard some of my townsmen say, "I should like to have them order me out to help put down an insurrection of the slaves, or to march to Mexico;—see if I would go"; and yet these very men have each, directly by their allegiance, and so indirectly, at least, by their money, furnished a substitute. The soldier is applauded who refuses to serve in an unjust war by those who do not refuse to sustain the unjust government which makes the war; is applauded by those whose own act and authority he disregards and sets at naught; as if the State were penitent to that degree that it hired one to scourge it while it sinned, but not to that degree that it left off sinning for a moment. Thus, under the name of Order and Civil Government, we are all made at last to pay homage to and support our own meanness. After the first blush of sin comes its indifference; and from immoral it becomes, as it were, *un*moral, and not quite unnecessary to that life which we have made.

The broadest and most prevalent error requires the most disinterested virtue to sustain it. The slight reproach to which the virtue of patriotism is commonly liable, the noble are most likely to incur. Those who, while they disapprove of the character and measures of a government, yield to it their allegiance and support, are undoubtedly its most conscientious supporters, and so frequently the most serious obstacles to reform. Some are petitioning the State to dissolve the Union, to disregard the requisitions of the President. Why do they not dissolve it themselves,—the union between themselves and the State,—and refuse to pay their quota into its treasury? Do not they stand in the same relation to the State, that the State does to the Union? And have not the same reasons prevented the State from resisting the Union, which have prevented them from resisting the State?

How can a man be satisfied to entertain an opinion merely, and enjoy *it*? Is there any enjoyment in it, if his opinion is that he is aggrieved? If you are cheated out of a single dollar by your neighbor, you do not rest satisfied with knowing that you are cheated, or with saying that you are cheated, or even with petitioning him to pay you your due; but you take effectual steps at once to obtain the full amount, and see that you are never cheated again. Action from principle, the perception and the performance of right, changes things and relations; it is essentially revolutionary, and does not consist wholly with anything which was. It not only divides states and churches, it divides families; ay, it divides the *individual,* separating the diabolical in him from the divine.

Unjust laws exist: shall we be content to obey them, or shall we endeavor to amend them, and obey them until we have succeeded, or shall we transgress them at once? Men generally, under such a government as this, think that they ought to wait until they have persuaded the majority to alter them. They think that, if they should resist, the remedy would be worse than the evil. But it is the fault of the government itself that the remedy *is* worse than the evil. *It* makes it worse. Why is it not more apt to anticipate and provide for reform? Why does it not cherish its wise minority? Why does it cry and resist before it is hurt? Why does it not encourage its citizens to be on the alert to point out its faults, and *do* better than it would have them? Why does it always crucify Christ, and excommunicate Copernicus and Luther, and pronounce Washington and Franklin rebels? . . .

If the injustice is part of the necessary friction of the machine of government, let it go, let it go: perchance it will wear smooth,—certainly the machine will wear out. If the injustice has a spring, or a pulley, or a rope, or a crank, exclusively for itself, then perhaps you may consider whether the remedy will not be worse than the evil; but if it is of such a nature that it requires you to be the agent of injustice to another, then, I say, break the law. Let your life be a counter friction to stop the machine. What I have to do is to see, at any rate, that I do not lend myself to the wrong which I condemn.

As for adopting the ways which the State has provided for remedying the evil, I know not of such ways. They take too much time, and a man's life will be gone. I have other affairs to attend to. I came into this world, not chiefly to make this a good place to live in, but to live in it, be it good or bad. A man has not everything to do, but something; and because he cannot do *everything,* it is not necessary that he should do *something* wrong. It is not my business to be petitioning the Governor or the Legislature any more than it is theirs to petition me; and, if they should not hear my petition, what should I do then? But in this case the State has provided no way: its very Constitution is the evil. This may seem to be harsh and stubborn and unconciliatory; but it is to treat with the utmost kindness and consideration the only spirit that can appreciate or deserves it. So is all change for the better, like birth and death, which convulse the body.

I do not hesitate to say, that those who call themselves Abolitionists should at once effectually withdraw their support, both in person and property, from the government of Massachusetts, and not wait till they constitute a majority of one, before they suffer the right to prevail through them. I think that it is enough if they have God on their side, without waiting for that other one. Moreover, any man more right than his neighbors constitutes a majority of one already.

I meet this American government, or its representative, the State government, directly, and face to face, once a year—no more—in the person of its tax-gatherer; this is the only mode in which a man situated as I am necessarily meets it; and it then says distinctly, Recognize me; and the simplest, the most effectual, and, in the present posture of affairs, the indispensablest mode of treating with it on this head, of expressing your little satisfaction with and love for it, is to deny it then. My civil neighbor, the tax-gatherer, is the very man I have to deal with,—for it is, after all, with men and not with parchment that I quarrel,— and he has voluntarily chosen to be an agent of the government. How shall he ever know well what he is and does as an officer of the government, or as a man, until he is obliged to consider whether he shall treat me, his neighbor, for whom he has respect, as a neighbor and well-disposed man, or as a maniac and disturber of the peace, and see if he can get over this obstruction to his neighborliness without a ruder and more impetuous thought or speech corresponding with his action. I know this well, that if one thousand, if one hundred, if ten men whom I could name,—if ten *honest* men only,—ay, if *one* HONEST man, in this State of Massachusetts, *ceasing to hold slaves,* were actually to withdraw from this copartnership, and be locked up in the county jail therefor, it would be the abolition of slavery in America. For it matters not how small the beginning may seem to be: what is once well done is done forever. But we love better to talk about it: that we say is our mission. Reform keeps many scores of newspapers in its service, but not one man. If my esteemed neighbor, the State's ambassador, who will devote his days to the settlement of the question of human rights in the Council Chamber, instead of being threatened with the prisons of Carolina, were to sit down the prisoner of Massachusetts, that State which is so anxious to foist the sin of slavery upon her sister,—though at present she can discover only an act of inhospitality to be the ground of a quarrel with her,—the Legislature would not wholly waive the subject the following winter.

Under a government which imprisons any unjustly, the true place for a just man is also a prison. The proper place to-day, the only place which Massachusetts has provided for her freer and less desponding spirits, is in her prisons, to be put out and locked out of the State by her own act, as they have already put themselves out by their principles. It is there that the fugitive slave, and the Mexican prisoner on parole, and the Indian come to plead the wrongs of his race, should find them; on that separate, but more free and honorable ground, where the State places those who are not *with* her, but *against* her,—the only house in a slave State in which a free man can abide with honor. If any think that their influence would be lost there, and their voices no longer afflict the ear of the State, that they would not be as an enemy within its walls, they do not know by how much truth is stronger than error, nor how much more eloquently and effectively he can combat injustice who has experienced a little in his own person. Cast your whole vote, not a strip of paper merely, but your whole influence. A minority is powerless while it conforms to the majority; it is not even a minority then; but it is irresistible when it clogs by its whole weight. If the alternative is to keep all just men in prison, or give up war and slavery, the State will not hesitate which to choose. If a thousand men were not to pay their tax-bills this year, that would not be a violent and bloody measure, as it would be to pay them, and enable the State to commit violence and shed innocent blood. This is, in fact, the definition of a peaceable revolution, if any such is possible. If the tax-gatherer, or any other public officer, asks me, as one has done, "But what shall I do?" my answer is, "If you really wish to do anything, resign your office." When the subject has refused allegiance, and the officer has resigned his office, then the revolution is accomplished. But even suppose blood should flow. Is there not a sort of blood shed when the conscience is wounded? Through this wound a man's real manhood and immortality flow out, and he bleeds to an everlasting death. I see this blood flowing now. . . .

Some years ago, the State met me in behalf of the Church, and commanded me to pay a certain sum toward the support of a clergyman whose preaching my father attended, but never I myself. "Pay," it said, "or be locked up in the jail." I declined to pay. But, unfortunately, another man saw fit to pay it. I did not see why the schoolmaster should be taxed to support the priest, and not the priest the schoolmaster; for I was not the State's schoolmaster, but I supported myself by voluntary subscription. I did not see why the lyceum should not present its tax-bill, and have the State to back its demand, as well as the Church. However, at the request of the selectmen, I condescended to make some such statement as this in writing:— "Know all men by these presents, that I, Henry Thoreau, do not wish to be regarded as a member of any incorporated society which I have not joined." This I gave to the town clerk; and he has it. The State, having thus learned that I did not wish to be regarded as a member of that church, has never made a like demand on me since; though it said that it must adhere to its original presumption that time. If I had known how to name them, I should then have signed off in detail from all the societies which I never signed on to; but I did not know where to find a complete list.

I have paid no poll-tax for six years. I was put into a jail once on this account, for one night; and, as I stood considering the walls of solid stone, two or three feet thick, the door of wood and iron, a foot thick, and the iron grating which strained the light, I could not help being struck with the foolishness of that institution which treated me as if I were mere flesh and blood and bones, to be locked up. I wondered that it should have concluded at length that this was the best use it could put me to, and had never thought to avail itself of my services in some way. I saw that, if there was a wall of stone between me and my townsmen, there was a still more difficult one to climb or break through, before they could get to be as free as I was. I did not for a moment feel confined, and the walls seemed a great waste of stone and mortar. I felt as if I alone of all my townsmen had paid my tax. They plainly did not know how to treat me, but behaved like persons who are underbred. In every threat and in every compliment there was a blunder; for they thought that my chief desire was to stand the other side of that stone wall. I could not but smile to see how industriously they locked the door on my meditations, which followed them out again without let or hindrance, and *they* were really all that was dangerous. As they could not reach me, they had resolved to punish my body; just as boys, if they cannot come at some person against whom they have a spite, will abuse his dog. I saw that the State was half-witted, that it was timid as a lone woman with her silver spoons, and that it did not know its friends from its foes, and I lost all my remaining respect for it, and pitied it. . . .

The authority of government, even such as I am willing to submit to,—for I will cheerfully obey those who know and can do better than I, and in many things even those who neither know nor can do so well,—is still an impure one: to be strictly just, it must have the sanction and consent of the governed. It can have no pure right over my person and property but what I concede to it. The progress from an absolute to a limited monarchy, from a limited monarchy to a democracy, is a progress toward a true respect for the individual. Even the Chinese philosopher was wise enough to regard the individual as the basis of the empire. Is a democracy, such as we know it, the last improvement possible in government? Is it not possible to take a step further towards recognizing and organizing the rights of man? There will never be a really free and enlightened State, until the State comes to recognize the individual as a higher and independent power, from which all its own power and authority are derived, and treats him accordingly. I please myself with imagining a State at last which can afford to be just to all men, and to treat the individual with respect as a neighbor; which even would not think it inconsistent with its own repose, if a few were to live aloof from it, not meddling with it, nor embraced by it, who fulfilled all the duties of neighbors and fellowmen. A State which bore this kind of fruit, and suffered it to drop off as fast as it ripened, would prepare the way for a still more perfect and glorious State, which also I have imagined, but not yet anywhere seen.

Progress (The Advance of Civilization), 1853 by Asher B. Durand, Warner Collection.

Progress (The Advance of Civilization), 1853 by Asher B. Durand, Warner Collection.
Details: left foreground (above); right foreground (below).

Address of the Workingmen's Party of Charlestown, Massachusetts (1840)

"BRETHREN:—The time seems to have arrived, when we, the real workingmen of the country, should pause, and survey our condition; ascertain our actual state, what are our rights, and the means of securing their full enjoyment.

"We are in this country, as in all others, the great majority of the population. We are the real producers. By our toil and sweat, our skill and industry, is produced all the wealth of the community. We have felled the primeval forests of this western world, converted them into fruitful fields, and planted the rose in the wilderness. We have erected these cities and villages which smile where lately was the Indian's wigwam, or the lair of the wild beast. We have called into existence American manufactures, and been the instruments by which Commerce has amassed her treasures; our labor has digged the canals, and constructed the railways, which are intersecting the country in all directions, and opening its resources. We have built and manned the ships which navigate every ocean, and furnished the houses of the rich with all their comforts and luxuries. Our labor has done it all. And yet what is our condition? We toil on from morning to night, from one year's end to another, increasing our exertions with each year, and with each day, and still we are the poor and dependent. Here, as everywhere else, they, who pocket the proceeds of our labor, look upon us as the lower class, and term us the mob. We are but laborers, operatives, *vulgar* workingmen. We are poor. Our wages barely suffice to supply us the necessaries of life. We rarely have either leisure or opportunity to cultivate our minds, or to acquire that general knowledge of men and things, which no human being should grow up without. We are doomed by our position to grow up ignorant, and often in total neglect of all our nobler endowments. Our rights and interests attract no general attention. Legislators have no leisure to attend to our wants. And politicians have no further concern with us, than to wheedle us out of our votes by fair speeches and vague promises. The great concern is to take care of the rich and prosperous, the educated and powerful—of those who fill the high places of society, ride in carriages, sit on cushioned seats, and feast their dainty palates on luxuries culled from every clime. The wants of these are urgent. *Their* rights, privileges, and interests will brook no delay. But we, we, who bear all the burdens of society, pay all the revenues of Government, and the incomes of the rich, why we may go our way till a more convenient season.

"Now, Brethren, against this state of things, we enter a loud, an indignant protest. Our pockets may be empty, our faces may be sunburnt, and our hands may be hard; but we are men, with the souls of men, and the rights of men. There is a spirit within us, that assures us we were not born to be slaves; that we were not made merely to toil and sweat, to endure hunger, and cold, and nakedness, and death, that the few might grow fat on our labors and sufferings, and then turn round and kick us. We feel that we were made for something better, and that we have a right to aspire to something higher. An apostle has said, "If any man will not work, neither shall he eat." And this we believe should apply to one man as well as to another. Why, if we must bear all the burthens of society, shall we not in common justice enjoy all its blessings?

"Brethren, we have reflected on our condition, and we have come to the conclusion, that it is not the true condition of men. We are made of the same blood with those who work us as they do their horses and oxen, and who value us only for the profit they can derive from our labors. As pure blood courses in our veins as in theirs; as generous, as noble emotions swell our bosoms, and we have by nature capacities, to say the least, every way equal to theirs. Why then are they regarded as the better sort? Why then do they fatten on our labors? Why then are they rich and we poor? Why shall not our condition be as good as theirs? Why shall they call themselves our masters, and work us for their profit? . . .

"How stands the case with us? We labor more hours and with more intensity than we did formerly. We are aided by the discoveries of science and the introduction of machinery which gives to our labor a thousand fold additional power of production; and yet our condition relatively to the capitalist does by no means become better. There is scarcely a country in Europe where, in proportion to the labor they perform, the laboring classes are worse off than they are here. If we worked no more hours in a day, no more days in a week, and with no more intensity, than do the Italian peasants, we should find ourselves in a condition scarcely superior to theirs. We receive only about the same proportion of the proceeds of our labor.

"Moreover everything is tending to reduce the workingmen of this country to the condition they are sunk to in the old world. And what is that condition? In England, Scotland, and Wales, fourteen millions of the population, it is said, are obliged to subsist on an annual income of about ninety dollars a year and under. Five millions of these subsist on an annual income of less than twenty-five dollars each. In some counties in England, prior to the new poor laws, the paupers amounted to 63 per cent on the whole population, and in Liverpool every third individual was in indigence. Of Ireland, we need say nothing more than that one third of the whole population experience a deficiency of even third rate potatoes for thirty weeks out of fifty-two. In France, out of a population of about thirty-two millions, nearly thirty-one millions receive an annual income of under seventy-five dollars each; seven millions five hundred thousand, under twenty-five dollars; seven millions five hundred thousand, about eighteen dollars each. The expense of living is higher in England than in this country, and probably about one fourth less in France. But what must be the condition of the laboring classes even in France, where it is better than in England, and perhaps as good as in any country in Europe with the exception of Belgium?

"Now, what saves us from a similar condition? We are saved from a similar condition mainly by the paucity of our numbers, and the superior freedom of our industry, which creates a greater competition among capitalists, and therefore a greater demand for laborers. But this competition is less among manufacturers than it was. The principal manufacturers having adopted in regard to labor nearly uniform prices, rarely bid upon one another. The multiplication of large corporations is rapidly changing the whole character of our laboring population, by bringing them under the control of corporate bodies. These corporations check individual enterprise, lessen competition between individual capitalists, bind the capitalists together in close affinity of interest, and enable them to exert a sovereign control over the prices of labor. Let these corporations continue to increase for a few years longer, and they will be able to reduce our wages to the minimum of human subsistence. There will grow up around them a population bearing but little resemblance to that which won our political independence. It will be enfeebled in mind and body, and without either the mental or physical energy to shift its employment, or to make a firm stand for the amelioration of its condition.

"Hitherto the great mass of our laboring population has been bred in the agricultural districts, and consequently could easily shift from the city or the factory village to the farm. But this will not continue to be the case for another generation. Nor is this all. Lands are monopolized; the whole earth is foreclosed. However well disposed the laborer might be to cultivate the soil, he has not the means of becoming its owner. He has no spot on which to erect him a cabin, or on which he may raise a few potatoes to feed his wife and little ones; for the broad hands of the few cover it all over.

"Nor can we stop here. It would seem that the more we produced the better should be our condition. But this is not the fact except for short seasons. We suffer from over-production. To-day the supply is small, and the demand is brisk, we find employment and receive tolerable wages. But a hundred capitalists have rushed simultaneously into the work of producing; all hands are employed; forthwith the demand is supplied; the market is glutted; sales are diminished; and the diminished sales return upon us in the shape of a reduction of wages. To make up for this reduction of wages, we must labor more hours, or with greater intensity, and increase the amount of our production; and this increased amount of production, returns upon us again in the shape of a still farther reduction of our wages; and thus on, till they are reduced to the lowest point compatible with our existence.

"Brethren, put these things together, and tell us, if the natural tendency in this country is not to reduce us, and that at no distant day, to the miserable condition of the laboring classes in the old world? We stand on the declivity; we have already begun to descend! What is to save us?

"Brethren, this is a question of fearful import to us and our children. It is a question we must put to ourselves in sober earnest. It is a question we must put *now,* for a little more delay and it will be TOO LATE. Is it not already too late? God forbid! We will not believe it too late; but we feel that not a moment is to be lost. Now or never, must our salvation be secured. How shall it be done?

"Brethren, our salvation must, through the blessing of God, come from ourselves. It is useless to expect it from those whom our labors enrich. It is for their interest to augment our numbers and our poverty. It is their interest to purchase our labor at the lowest rate possible; it is ours to sell it at the highest rate possible. Their interest and ours, then, stand in direct opposition to each other. The greater our numbers, the more necessitous our condition, the greater is the facility with which they can obtain laborers, and the lower the price they are obliged to pay for labor. The fewer our numbers, the more independent our condition, the higher is the price we can demand and obtain for our labor. This refutes the pretensions of the aristocracy, that their interests and ours are one and the same. As men, as human beings, no doubt their interest and ours are the same; but their interests as capitalists, and ours as laborers, are directly opposite, and mutually destructive. In fact there is less identity of interest between the capitalists and us, than there is between the master and the slave. The slave is the master's property, and it is for the master's interest to take care of his property; it is for his interest to give his slave a sufficiency of food, and to be careful not to overwork him; for the sickness or death of his slave would be a loss of property. The same principle, which leads a man to take good care of his horses, sheep, and oxen, would lead him to take good care of his slaves. But the capitalist has no other interest in us, than to get as much labor out of us as possible. We are hired men, and hired men, like hired horses, have no souls. If a man owns the horse he drives, he will take care not to injure him; but if the horse be a hired one, what he will do, is told in a common saying, "Hired horses have no souls; drive on." "Hired men have no souls; drive on." If we sicken and die, the loss is ours, not the employer's. *There are enough more ready to take our places.*

"Brethren, we conjure you, therefore, not to believe a word of what is said about your interest and that of your employers being the same. Your interests and theirs are in the nature of things, hostile and irreconcilable. Then do not look to them for relief. Be not so mad as to suppose that they will voluntarily work out your salvation for you. You must expect them to be governed mainly by their own interests, and must never rely on their doing, as a body, what it is not for their interest to do. If then you have ever expected the capitalist, the accumulator, contractor, and employer, to conspire to elevate your condition, expect it no longer. As well might the poor and depressed have expected the Gospel, which is good news to the poor, from the scribes and pharisees, the chief priests and elders, who crucified Jesus for proclaiming it."

GEORGE FITZHUGH

from Cannibals All! or, Slaves Without Masters (1857)

We are, all, North and South, engaged in the White Slave Trade, and he who succeeds best, is esteemed most respectable. It is far more cruel than the Black Slave Trade, because it exacts more of its slaves, and neither protects nor governs them. We boast, that it exacts more, when we say, "that the *profits* made from employing free labor are greater than those from slave labor." The profits, made from free labor, are the amount of the products of such labor, which the employer, by means of the command which capital or skill gives him, takes away, exacts or "exploitates" from the free laborer. The profits of slave labor are that portion of the products of such labor which the power of the master enables him to appropriate. These profits are less, because the master allows the slave to retain a larger share of the results of his own labor, than do the employers of free labor. But we not only boast that the White Slave Trade is more exacting and fraudulent (in fact, though not in intention,) than Black Slavery; but we also boast, that it is more cruel, in leaving the laborer to take care of himself and family out of the pittance which skill or capital have allowed him to retain. When the day's labor is ended, he is free, but is overburdened with the cares of family and household, which make his freedom an empty and delusive mockery. But his employer is really free, and may enjoy the profits made by others' labor, without a care, or a trouble, as to their well-being. The negro slave is free, too, when the labors of the day are over, and free in mind as well as body; for the master provides food, raiment, house, fuel, and everything else necessary to the physical well-being of himself and family. The master's labors commence just when the slave's end. No wonder men should prefer white slavery to capital, to negro slavery, since it is more profitable, and is free from all the cares and labors of black slave-holding.

Now, reader, if you wish to know yourself—to "descant on your own deformity"—read on. But if you would cherish self-conceit, self-esteem, or self-appreciation, throw down our book; for we will dispel illusions which have promoted your happiness, and shew you that what you have considered and practiced as virtue, is little better than moral Cannibalism. But you will find yourself in numerous and respectable company; for all good and respectable people are "Cannibals all," who do not labor, or who are successfully trying to live without labor, on the unrequited labor of other people:— Whilst low, bad, and disreputable people, are those who labor to support themselves, and to support said respectable people besides. Throwing the negro slaves out of the account, and society is divided in Christendom into four classes: The rich, or independent respectable people, who live well and labor not at all; the professional and skillful respectable people, who do a little light work, for enormous wages; the poor hard-working people, who support every body, and starve themselves; and the poor thieves, swindlers and sturdy beggars, who live like gentlemen, without labor, on the labor of other people. The gentlemen exploitate, which being done on a large scale, and requiring a great many victims, is highly respectable—whilst the rogues and beggars take so little from others, that they fare little better than those who labor.

But, reader, we do not wish to fire into the flock. "Thou art the man!" You are a Cannibal! and if a successful one, pride yourself on the number of your victims, quite as much as any Feejee chieftain, who breakfasts, dines and sups on human flesh.—And your conscience smites you, if you have failed to succeed, quite as much as his, when he returns from an unsuccessful foray.

Probably, you are a lawyer, or a merchant, or a doctor, who have made by your business fifty thousand dollars, and retired to live on your capital. But, mark! not to spend your capital. That would be vulgar, disreputable, criminal. That would be, to live by your own labor; for your capital is your amassed labor. That would be, to do as common working men do; for they take the pittance which their employers leave them, to live on. They live by labor; for they exchange the results of their own labor for the products of other people's labor. It is, no doubt, an honest, vulgar way of living; but not at all a respectable way. The respectable way of living is, to make other people work for you, and to pay them nothing for so doing—and to have no concern about them after their work is done. Hence, white slave-holding is much more respectable than negro slavery—for the master works nearly as hard for the negro, as he for the master. But you, my virtuous, respectable reader, exact three thousand dollars per annum from white labor, (for your income is the product of white labor,) and make not one cent of return in any form. You retain your capital, and never labor, and yet live in luxury on the labor of others. Capital commands labor, as the master does the slave. Neither pays for labor; but the master permits the slave to retain a larger allowance from the proceeds of his own labor, and hence "free labor is cheaper than slave labor." You, with the command over labor which your capital gives you, are a slave owner—a master, without the obligations of a master. They who work for you, who create your income, are slaves, without the rights of slaves. Slaves without a master! Whilst you were engaged in amassing your capital, in seeking to become independent, you were in the White Slave Trade. To become independent, is to be able to make other people support you, without being obliged to labor for *them*. Now, what man in society is not seeking to attain this situation? He who attains it, is a slave owner, in the worst sense. He who is in pursuit of it, is engaged in the slave trade. You, reader, belong to the one or other class. The men without property, in free society, are theoretically in a worse condition than slaves. Practically, their condition corresponds with this theory, as history and statistics every where demonstrate. The capitalists, in free society, live in ten times the luxury and show that Southern masters do, because the slaves to capital work harder and cost less, than negro slaves.

The negro slaves of the South are the happiest, and, in some sense, the freest people in the world. The children and the aged and infirm work not at all, and yet have all the comforts and necessaries of life provided for them. They enjoy liberty, because they are oppressed neither by care nor labor. The women do little hard work, and are protected from the despotism of their husbands by their masters. The negro men and stout boys work, on the average, in good weather, not more than nine hours a day. The balance of their time is spent in perfect abandon. Besides, they have their Sabbaths and holidays. White men, with so much of license and liberty, would die of ennui; but negroes luxuriate in corporeal and mental repose. With their faces upturned to the sun, they can sleep at any hour; and quiet sleep is the greatest of human enjoyments. "Blessed be the man who invented sleep." 'Tis happiness in itself—and results from contentment with the present, and confident assurance of the future. We do not know whether free laborers ever sleep. They are fools to do so; for, whilst they sleep, the wily and watchful capitalist is devising means to ensnare and exploitate them. The free laborer must work or starve. He is more of a slave than the negro, because he works longer and harder for less allowance than the slave, and has no holiday, because the cares of life with him begin when its labors end. He has no liberty, and not a single right. We know, 'tis often said, air and water, are common property, which all have equal right to participate and enjoy; but this is utterly false. The appropriation of the lands carries with it the appropriation of all on or above the lands, *usque ad cœlum, aut ad inferos.* A man cannot breathe the air, without a place to breathe it from, and all places are appropriated. All water is private property "to the middle of the stream," except the ocean, and that is not fit to drink.

Free laborers have not a thousandth part of the rights and liberties of negro slaves. Indeed, they have not a single right or a single liberty, unless it be the right or liberty to die. But the reader may think that he and other capitalists and employers are freer than negro slaves. Your capital would soon vanish, if you dared indulge in the liberty and abandon of negroes. You hold your wealth and position by the tenure of constant watchfulness, care and circumspection. You never labor; but you are never free.

Where a few own the soil, they have unlimited power over the balance of society, until domestic slavery comes in, to compel them to permit this balance of society to draw a sufficient and comfortable living from "terra mater." Free society, asserts the right of a few to the earth—slavery, maintains that it belongs, in different degrees, to all. . . .

"Property in man" is what all are struggling to obtain. Why should they not be obliged to take care of man, their property, as they do of their horses and their hounds, their cattle and their sheep. Now, under the delusive name of liberty, you work him, "from morn to dewy eve"—from infancy to old age—then turn him out to starve. You treat your horses and hounds better. Capital is a cruel master. The free slave trade, the commonest, yet the cruellest of trades. . . .

'Tis an historical fact, that this family association, this patriarchal government, for purposes of defence against enemies from without, gradually merges into larger associations of men under a common government or ruler. This latter is the almost universal, and we may thence infer, natural and normal condition of civilized man. In this state of society there is no liberty for the masses. Liberty has been exchanged by nature for security.

What is falsely called Free Society, is a very recent invention. It proposes to make the weak, ignorant and poor, free, by turning them loose in a world owned exclusively by the few (whom nature and education have made strong, and whom property has made stronger,) to get a living. In the fanciful state of nature, where property is unappropriated, the strong have no weapons but superior physical and mental power with which to oppress the weak. Their power of oppression is increased a thousand fold, when they become the exclusive owners of the earth and all the things thereon. They are masters without the obligations of masters, and the poor are slaves without the rights of slaves.

It is generally conceded, even by abolitionists, that the serfs of Europe were liberated because the multitude of laborers, and their competition as freemen to get employment, had rendered free labor cheaper than slave labor. But, strange to say, few seem to have seen that this is in fact asserting that they were less free after emancipation than before. Their obligation to labor was increased; for they were compelled to labor more than before to obtain a livelihood, else their free labor would not have been cheaper than their labor as slaves. They lost something in liberty, and everything in rights—for emancipation liberated or released the masters from all their burdens, cares and liabilities, whilst it in creased both the labors and the cares of the liberated serf. . . .

We do not agree with the authors of the Declaration of Independence, that governments "derive their just powers from the consent of the governed." The women, the children, the negroes, and but few of the non-property holders were consulted, or consented to the Revolution, or the governments that ensued from its success. As to these, the new governments were self-elected despotisms, and the governing class self-elected despots. Those governments originated in force, and have been continued by force. All governments must originate in force, and be continued by force. The very term, government, implies that it is carried on against the consent of the governed. Fathers do not derive their authority, as heads of families, from the consent of wife and children, nor do they govern their families by their consent. They never take the vote of the family as to the labors to be performed, the moneys to be expended, or as to anything else. Masters dare not take the vote of slaves, as to their government. If they did, constant holiday, dissipation and extravagance would be the result. Captains of ships are not appointed by the consent of the crew, and never take their vote, even in "doubling Cape Horn." If they did, the crew would generally vote to get drunk, and the ship would never weather the cape. Not even in the most democratic countries are soldiers governed by their consent, nor is their vote taken on the eve of battle. They have some how lost (or never had) the "inalienable rights of life, liberty and the pursuit of happiness;" and, whether Americans or Russians, are forced into battle, without and often against their consent. The ancient republics were governed by a small class of adult male citizens, who assumed and exercised the government, without the consent of the governed. The South is governed just as those ancient republics were. In the county in which we live, there are eighteen thousand souls, and only twelve hundred voters. But we twelve hundred, the governors, never asked and never intend to ask the consent of the sixteen thousand eight hundred whom we govern. Were we to do so, we should soon have an "organized anarchy." The governments of Europe could not exist a week without the positive force of standing armies.

They are all governments of force, not of consent. Even in our North, the women, children, and free negroes, constitute four-fifths of the population; and they are all governed without their consent. But they mean to correct this gross and glaring iniquity at the North. They hold that all men, women, and negroes, and smart children, are equals, and entitled to equal rights. The widows and free negroes begin to vote in some of those States, and they will have to let all colors and sexes and ages vote soon, or give up the glorious principles of human equality and universal emancipation.

The experiment which they will make, we fear, is absurd in theory, and the symptoms of approaching anarchy and agrarianism among them, leave no doubt that its practical operation will be no better than its theory. Anti-rentism, "vote-myself-a-farm" ism, and all the other isms, are but the spattering drops that precede a social deluge.

Abolition ultimates in "Consent Government;" Consent Government in Anarchy, Free Love, Agrarianism, &c., &c., and "Self-elected despotism," winds up the play. . . .

A like danger threatens North and South, proceeding from the same source. Abolitionism is maturing what Political Economy began. With inexorable sequence "Let Alone" is made to usher in No-Government. North and South our danger is the same, and our remedies, though differing in degree, must in character be the same. "Let Alone" must be repudiated, if we would have any Government. We must, in all sections, act upon the principle that the world is "too little governed." You of the North need not institute negro slavery; far less reduce white men to the state of negro slavery. But the masses require more of protection, and the masses and philosophers equally require more of control. . . .

CATHARINE BEECHER

from A Treatise on Domestic Economy (1841)

Chapter I.

The Peculiar Responsibilities of American Women.

There are some reasons, why American women should feel an interest in the support of the democratic institutions of their Country, which it is important that they should consider. The great maxim, which is the basis of all our civil and political institutions, is, that "all men are created equal," and that they are equally entitled to "life, liberty, and the pursuit of happiness."

But it can readily be seen, that this is only another mode of expressing the fundamental principle which the Great Ruler of the Universe has established, as the law of His eternal government. "Thou shalt love they neighbor as thyself;" and "Whatsoever ye would that men should dó to you, do ye even so to them," are the Scripture forms, by which the Supreme Lawgiver requires that each individual of our race shall regard the happiness of others, as of the same value as his own; and which forbid any institution, in private or civil life, which secures advantages to one class, by sacrificing the interests of another.

The principles of democracy, then, are identical with the principles of Christianity.

But, in order that each individual may pursue and secure the highest degree of happiness within his reach, unimpeded by the selfish interests of others, a system of laws must be established, which sustain certain relations and dependencies in social and civil life. What these relations and their attending obligations shall be, are to be determined, not with reference to the wishes and interests of a few, but solely with reference to the general good of all; so that each individual shall have his own interest, as well as the public benefit, secured by them.

For this purpose, it is needful that certain relations be sustained, which involve the duties of subordination. There must be the magistrate and the subject, one of whom is the superior, and the other the inferior. There must be the relations of husband and wife, parent and child, teacher and pupil, employer and employed, each involving the relative duties of subordination. The superior, in certain particulars, is to direct, and the inferior is to yield obedience. Society could never go forward, harmoniously, nor could any craft or profession be successfully pursued, unless these superior and subordinate relations be instituted and sustained.

But who shall take the higher, and who the subordinate, stations in social and civil life? This matter, in the case of parents and children, is decided by the Creator. He has given children to the control of parents, as their superiors, and to them they remain subordinate, to a certain age, or so long as they are members of their household. And parents can delegate such a portion of their authority to teachers and employers, as the interests of their children require.

In most other cases, in a truly democratic state, each individual is allowed to choose for himself, who shall take the position of his superior. No woman is forced to obey any husband but the one she chooses for herself; nor is she obliged to take a husband, if she prefers to remain single. So every domestic, and every artisan or laborer, after passing from parental control, can choose the employer to whom he is to accord obedience, or, if he prefers to relinquish certain advantages, he can remain without taking a subordinate place to any employer.

Each subject, also, has equal power with every other, to decide who shall be his superior as a ruler. The weakest, the poorest, the most illiterate, has the same opportunity to determine this question, as the richest, the most learned, and the most exalted.

And the various privileges that wealth secures, are equally open to all classes. Every man may aim at riches, unimpeded by any law or institution which secures peculiar privileges to a favored class, at the expense of another. Every law, and even institution, is tested by examining whether it secures equal advantages to all; and, if the people become convinced that any regulation sacrifices the good of the majority to the interests of the smaller number, they have power to abolish it.

The institutions of monarchical and aristocratic nations are based on precisely opposite principles. They secure, to certain small and favored classes, advantages, which can be maintained, only by sacrificing the interests of the great mass of the people. Thus, the throne and aristocracy of England are supported by laws and customs, which burden the lower classes with taxes, so enormous, as to deprive them of all the luxuries, and of most of the comforts, of life. Poor dwellings, scanty food, unhealthy employments, excessive labor, and entire destitution of the means and time for education, are appointed for the lower classes, that a few may live in palaces, and riot in every indulgence.

The tendencies of democratic institutions, in reference to the rights and interests of the female sex, have been fully developed in the United States; and it is in this aspect, that the subject is one of peculiar interest to American women. In this Country, it is established, both by opinion and by practice, that woman has an equal interest in all social and civil concerns; and that no domestic, civil, or political, institution, is right, which sacrifices her interest to promote that of the other sex. But in order to secure her the more firmly in all these privileges, it is decided, that, in the domestic relation, she take a subordinate station, and that, in civil and political concerns, her interests be intrusted to the other sex, without her taking any part in voting, or in making and administering laws. The result of this order of things has been fairly tested, and is thus portrayed by M. De Tocqueville, a writer, who, for intelligence, fidelity, and ability, ranks second to none.

"There are people in Europe, who, confounding together the different characteristics of the sexes, would make of man and woman, beings not only equal, but alike. They would give to both the same functions, impose on both the same duties, and grant to both the same rights. They would mix them in all things—their business, their occupations, their pleasures. It may readily be conceived that, by thus attempting to make one sex equal to the other, both are degraded; and, from so preposterous a medley of the works of Nature, nothing could ever result, but weak men and disorderly women.

"It is not thus that the Americans understand the species of democratic equality, which may be established between the sexes. They admit, that, as Nature has appointed such wide differences between the physical and moral constitutions of man and woman, her manifest design was, to give a distinct employment to their various faculties; and they hold, that improvement does not consist in making beings so dissimilar do pretty nearly the same things, but in getting each of them to fulfil their respective tasks, in the best possible manner. The Americans have applied to the sexes the great principle of political economy, which governs the manufactories of our age, by carefully dividing the duties of man from those of woman, in order that the great work of society may be the better carried on. . . .

"Thus the Americans do not think that man and woman have either the duty, or the right, to perform the same offices, but they show an equal regard for both their respective parts; and, though their lot is different, they consider both of them, as beings of equal value. They do not give to the courage of woman the same form, or the same direction, as to that of man; but they never doubt her courage: and if they hold that man and his partner ought not always to exercise their intellect and understanding in the same manner, they at least believe the understanding of the one to be as sound as that of the other, and her intellect to be as clear. Thus, then, while they have allowed the social inferiority of woman to subsist, they have done all they could to raise her, morally and intellectually, to the level of man; and, in this respect, they appear to me to have excellently understood the true principle of democratic improvement.

"As for myself, I do not hesitate to avow, that, although the women of the United States are confined within the narrow circle of domestic life, and their situation is, in some respects, one of extreme dependence, I have nowhere seen women occupying a loftier position; and if I were asked, now I am drawing to the close of this work, in which I have spoken of so many important things done by the Americans, to what the singular prosperity and growing strength of that people ought mainly to be attributed, I should reply,—*to the superiority of their women.*"

This testimony of a foreigner, who has had abundant opportunities of making a comparison, is sanctioned by the assent of all candid and intelligent men, who have enjoyed similar opportunities.

It appears, then, that it is in America, alone, that women are raised to an equality with the other sex; and that, both in theory and practice, their interests are regarded as of equal value. They are made subordinate in station, only where a regard to their best interests demands it, while, as if in compensation for this, by custom and courtesy, they are always treated as superiors. Universally, in this Country, through every class of society, precedence is given to woman, in all the comforts, conveniences, and courtesies, of life.

In civil and political affairs, American women take no interest or concern, except so far as they sympathize with their family and personal friends; but in all cases, in which they do feel a concern, their opinions and feelings have a consideration, equal, or even superior, to that of the other sex.

In matters pertaining to the education of their children, in the selection and support of a clergyman, in all benevolent enterprises, and in all questions relating to morals or manners, they have a superior influence. In such concerns, it would be impossible to carry a point, contrary to their judgment and feelings; while an enterprise, sustained by them, will seldom fail of success.

If those who are bewailing themselves over the fancied wrongs and injuries of women in this Nation, could only see things as they are, they would know, that, whatever remnants of a barbarous or aristocratic age may remain in our civil institutions, in reference to the interests of women, it is only because they are ignorant of them, or do not use their influence to have them rectified; for it is very certain that there is nothing reasonable, which American women would unite in asking, that would not readily be bestowed.

The preceding remarks, then, illustrate the position, that the democratic institutions of this Country are in reality no other than the principles of Christianity carried into operation, and that they tend to place woman in her true position in society, as having equal rights with the other sex; and that, in fact, they have secured to American women a lofty and fortunate position, which, as yet, has been attained by the women of no other nation. . . .

The success of democratic institutions, as is conceded by all, depends upon the intellectual and moral character of the mass of the people. If they are intelligent and virtuous, democracy is a blessing; but if they are ignorant and wicked, it is only a curse, and as much more dreadful than any other form of civil government, as a thousand tyrants are more to be dreaded than one. It is equally conceded, that the formation of the moral and intellectual character of the young is committed mainly to the female hand. The mother forms the character of the future man; the sister bends the fibres that are hereafter to be the forest tree; the wife sways the heart, whose energies may turn for good or for evil the destinies of a nation. Let the women of a country be made virtuous and intelligent, and the men will certainly be the same. The proper education of a man decides the welfare of an individual; but educate a woman, and the interests of a whole family are secured.

If this be so, as none will deny, then to American women, more than to any others on earth, is committed the exalted privilege of extending over the world those blessed influences, which are to renovate degraded man, and "clothe all climes with beauty."

No American woman, then, has any occasion for feeling that hers is an humble or insignificant lot. The value of what an individual accomplishes, is to be estimated by the importance of the enterprise achieved, and not by the particular position of the laborer. The drops of heaven which freshen the earth, are each of equal value, whether they fall in the lowland meadow, or the princely parterre. The builders of a temple are of equal importance, whether they labor on the foundations, or toil upon the dome.

Thus, also, with those labors which are to be made effectual in the regeneration of the Earth. And it is by forming a habit of regarding the apparently insignificant efforts of each isolated laborer, in a comprehensive manner, as indispensible portions of a grand result, that the minds of all, however humble their sphere of service, can be invigorated and cheered. The woman, who is rearing a family of children; the woman, who labors in the schoolroom; the woman, who, in her retired chamber, earns, with her needle, the mite, which contributes to the intellectual and moral elevation of her Country; even the humble domestic, whose example and influence may be moulding and forming young minds, while her faithful services sustain a prosperous domestic state;—each and all may be animated by the consciousness, that they are agents in accomplishing the greatest work that ever was committed to human responsibility. It is the building of a glorious temple, whose base shall be coextensive with the bounds of the earth, whose summit shall pierce the skies, whose splendor shall beam on all lands; and those who hew the lowliest stone, as much as those who carve the highest capital, will be equally honored, when its top-stone shall be laid, with new rejoicings of the morning stars, and shoutings of the sons of God.

Maria W. Stewart

"Why Sit Ye Here and Die?" (1832)

WHY SIT YE HERE and die? If we say we will go to a foreign land, the famine and the pestilence are there, and there we shall die. If we sit here, we shall die. Come, let us plead our cause before the whites: if they save us alive, we shall live—and if they kill us, we shall but die.

Methinks I heard a spiritual interrogation—"Who shall go forward, and take off the reproach that is cast upon the people of color? Shall it be a woman?" And my heart made this reply—"If it is thy will, be it even so, Lord Jesus?"

I have heard much respecting the horrors of slavery; but may heaven forbid that the generality of my color throughout these United States should experience any more of its horrors than to be a servant of servants, or hewers of wood and drawers of water! Tell us no more of southern slavery; for with few exceptions, although I may be very erroneous in my opinion, yet I consider our condition but little better than that. Yet, after all, methinks there are no chains so galling as the chains of ignorance—no fetters so binding as those that bind the soul, and exclude it from the vast field of usefulness and scientific knowledge. O, had I received the advantages of early education, my ideas would, ere now, have expanded far and wide; but, alas! I possess nothing but moral capability—no teachings but the teaching of the Holy Spirit.

I have asked several individuals of my sex, who transact business for themselves, if providing our girls were to give them the most satisfactory references, they would not be willing to grant them an equal opportunity with others? Their reply has been—for their own part, they had no objection, but as it was not the custom, were they to take them into their employ, they would be in danger of losing the public patronage.

And such is the powerful force of prejudice. Let our girls possess what amiable qualities of soul they may, let their characters be fair and spotless as innocence itself; let their natural taste and ingenuity be what they may; it is impossible for scarce an individual of them to rise above the condition of servants. Ah! why is this cruel and unfeeling distinction? Is it merely because God has made our complexion to vary? If it be, O shame to soft, relenting humanity! "Tell it not in Gath! publish it not in the streets of Askelon!" Yet, after all, methinks were the American free people of color to turn their attention more assiduously to moral worth and intellectual improvement, this would be the result: prejudice would gradually diminish, and the whites would be compelled to say, unloose those fetters!

Though black their skins as shades of night,
Their hearts are pure, their souls are white.

Few white persons of either sex, who are calculated for any thing else, are willing to spend their lives and bury their talents in performing mean, servile labor. And such is the horrible idea that I entertain respecting a life of servitude, that if I conceived of there being no possibility of my rising above the condition of a servant, I would gladly hail death as a welcome messenger. O, horrible idea, indeed! to possess noble souls aspiring after high and honorable acquirements, yet confined by the chains of ignorance and poverty to lives of continual drudgery and toil. Neither do I know of any who have enriched themselves by spending their lives as house-domestics, washing windows, shaking carpets, brushing boots, or tending upon gentlemen's tables. I can but die for expressing my sentiments; and I am as willing to die by the sword as the pestilence; for I am a true born American; your blood flows in my veins, and your spirit fires my breast. . . .

Take us generally as a people, we are neither lazy nor idle; and considering how little we have to excite or stimulate us, I am almost astonished that there are so many industrious and ambitious ones to be found: although I acknowledge, with extreme sorrow, that there are some who never were and never will be serviceable to society. And have you not a similar class among yourselves?

Again. It was asserted that we were "a ragged set, crying for liberty." I reply to it, the whites have so long and so loudly proclaimed the theme of equal rights and privileges, that our souls have caught the flame also, ragged as we are. As far as our merit deserves, we feel a common desire to rise above the condition of servants and drudges. I have learnt, by bitter experience, that continual hard labor deadens the energies of the soul, and benumbs the faculties of the mind; the ideas become confined, the mind barren, and, like the scorching sands of Arabia, produces nothing; or, like the uncultivated soil, brings forth thorns and thistles.

Again. Continual hard labor irritates our tempers and sours our dispositions; the whole system becomes worn out with toll and fatigue; nature herself becomes almost exhausted, and we care but little whether we live or die. It is true, that the free people of color throughout these United States are neither bought nor sold, nor under the lash of the cruel driver; many obtain a comfortable support; but few, if any, have an opportunity of becoming rich and independent; and the employments we most pursue are as unprofitable to us as the spider's web or the floating bubbles that vanish into air. As servants, we are respected; but let us presume to aspire any higher, our employer regards us no longer. And were it not that the King Eternal has declared that Ethiopia shall stretch forth her hands unto God, I should indeed despair.

I do not consider it derogatory, my friends, for persons to live out to service. There are many whose inclination leads them to aspire no higher; and I would highly commend the performance of almost anything for an honest livelihood; but where constitutional strength is wanting, labor of this kind, in its mildest form, is painful. And doubtless many are the prayers that have ascended to heaven from Afric's daughters for strength to perform their work. Oh, many are the tears that have been shed for the want of that strength! Most of our color have dragged out a miserable existence of servitude from the cradle to the grave. And what literary acquirements can be made, or useful knowledge derived, from either maps, books or charts, by those who continually drudge from Monday morning until Sunday noon? O, ye fairer sisters, whose hands are never soiled, whose nerves and muscles are never strained, go learn by experience! Had we the opportunity that you have had, to improve our moral and mental faculties, what would have hindered our intellects from being as bright, and our manners from being as dignified as yours? Had it been our lot to have been nursed in the lap of affluence and ease, and to have basked beneath the smiles and sunshine of fortune, should we not have naturally supposed that we were never made to toil? And why are not our forms as delicate, and our constitutions as slender as yours? Is not the workmanship as curious and complete? Have pity upon us, have pity upon us, O ye who have hearts to feel for others' woes; for the hand of God has touched us. Owing to the disadvantages under which we labor, there are many flowers among us that are

born to bloom unseen,
And waste their fragrance on the desert air.

My beloved brethren, as Christ has died in vain for those who will not accept of offered mercy, so will it be vain for the advocates of freedom to spend their breath in our behalf, unless with united hearts and souls you make some mighty efforts to raise your sons and daughters from the horrible state of servitude and degradation in which they are placed. It is upon you that woman depends; she can do but little besides using her influence; and it is for her sake and yours that I have come forward and made myself a hissing and a reproach among the people; for I am also one of the wretched and miserable daughters of the descendants of fallen Africa. Do you ask, why are you wretched and miserable? I reply, look at many of the most worthy and interesting of us doomed to spend our lives in gentlemen's kitchens. Look at our young men, smart, active and energetic, with souls filled with ambitious fire; if they look forward, alas! what are their prospects? They can be nothing but the humblest laborer, on account of their dark complexion; hence many of them lose their ambition, and become worthless. Look at our middle-aged men, clad in their rusty plaids and coats; in winter, every cent they earn goes to buy their wood and pay their rent; their poor wives also toil beyond their strength, to help support their families. Look at our aged sires, whose heads are whitened with the frosts of seventy winters, with their old wood-saws on their backs. Alas, what keeps us so? Prejudice, ignorance and poverty. But ah! methinks our oppression is soon to come to an end; yea, before the Majesty of heaven our groans and cries have reached the ears of the Lord of Sabaoth. As the prayers and tears of Christians will avail the finally impenitent nothing; neither will the prayers and tears of the friends of humanity avail us any thing, unless we possess a spirit of virtuous emulation within our breasts. Did the pilgrims, when they first landed on these shores, quietly compose themselves, and say, "the Britons have all the money and all the power, and we must continue their servants forever?" Did they sluggishly sigh, and say, "our lot is hard, the Indians own the soil, and we cannot cultivate it?" No; they first made powerful efforts to raise themselves, and then God raised up those illustrious patriots, Washington and Lafayette, to assist and defend them. And, my brethren, have you made a powerful effort? Have you prayed the Legislature for mercy's sake to grant you all the rights and privileges of free citizens, that your daughters may rise to that degree of respectability which true merit deserves, and your sons above the servile situations which most of them fill?

ALEXIS DETOCQUEVILLE

from Democracy in America (1835)

If we reasoned from what passes in the world, we should almost say that the European is to the other races of mankind, what man is to the lower animals;—he makes them subservient to his use; and when he cannot subdue, he destroys them. Oppression has at one stroke deprived the descendants of the Africans of almost all the privileges of humanity. The negro of the United States has lost all remembrance of his country; the language which his forefathers spoke is never heard around him; he abjured their religion and forgot their customs when he ceased to belong to Africa, without acquiring any claim to European privileges. But he remains half-way between the two communities, sold by the one, repulsed by the other; finding not a spot in the universe to call by the name of country, except the faint image of a home which the shelter of his master's roof affords.

The negro has no family; woman is merely the temporary companion of his pleasures, and his children are upon an equality with himself from the moment of their birth. Am I to call it a proof of God's mercy, or a visitation of his wrath, that man in certain states appears to be insensible to his extreme wretchedness, and almost affects with a depraved taste the cause of his misfortunes? The negro, who is plunged in this abyss of evils, scarcely feels his own calamitous situation. Violence made him a slave, and the habit of servitude gives him the thoughts and desires of a slave; he admires his tyrants more than he hates them, and finds his joy and his pride in the servile imitation of those who oppress him: his understanding is degraded to the level of his soul.

The negro enters upon slavery as soon as he is born; nay, he may have been purchased in the womb, and have begun his slavery before he began his existence. Equally devoid of wants and of enjoyment, and useless to himself, he learns, with his first notions of existence, that he is the property of another who has an interest in preserving his life, and that the care of it does not devolve upon himself; even the power of thought appears to him a useless gift of Providence, and he quietly enjoys the privileges of his debasement.

If he becomes free, independence is often felt by him to be a heavier burden than slavery; for having learned, in the course of his life, to submit to everything except reason, he is too much unacquainted with her dictates to obey them. A thousand new desires beset him, and he is destitute of the knowledge and energy necessary to resist them: these are masters which it is necessary to contend with, and he has learned only to submit and obey. In short, he sinks to such a depth of wretchedness, that while servitude brutalizes, liberty destroys him.

Oppression has been no less fatal to the Indian than to the negro race, but its effects are different. Before the arrival of the white men in the New World, the inhabitants of North America lived quietly in their woods, enduring the vicissitudes, and practising the virtues and vices common to savage nations. The Europeans, having dispersed the Indian tribes and driven them into the deserts, condemned them to a wandering life full of inexpressible sufferings.

Savage nations are only controlled by opinion and by custom. When the North American Indians had lost their sentiment of attachment to their country; when their families were dispersed, their traditions obscured, and the chain of their recollections broken; when all their habits were changed, and their wants increased beyond measure, European tyranny rendered them more disorderly and less civilized than they were before. The moral and physical condition of these tribes continually grew worse, and they became more barbarous as they became more wretched. Nevertheless the Europeans have not been able to metamorphose the character of the Indians; and though they have had power to destroy them, they have never been able to make them submit to the rules of civilized society.

The lot of the negro is placed on the extreme limit of servitude, while that of the Indian lies on the uttermost verge of liberty; and slavery does not produce more fatal effects upon the first, than independence upon the second. The negro has lost all property in his own person, and he cannot dispose of his existence without committing a sort of fraud: but the savage is his own master as soon as he is able to act; parental authority is scarcely known to him; he has never bent his will to that of any of his kind, nor learned the difference between voluntary obedience and a shameful subjection; and the very name of law is unknown to him. To be free, with him, signifies to escape from all the shackles of society. As he delights in this barbarous independence, and would rather perish than sacrifice the least part of it, civilization has little power over him.

The negro makes a thousand fruitless efforts to insinuate himself among men who repulse him; he conforms to the taste of his oppressors, adopts their opinions, and hopes by imitating them to form a part of their community. Having been told from infancy that his race is naturally inferior to that of the whites, he assents to the proposition, and is ashamed of his own nature. In each of his features he discovers a trace of slavery, and, if it were in his power, he would willingly rid himself of everything that makes him what he is.

The Indian, on the contrary, has his imagination inflated with the pretended nobility of his origin, and lives and dies in the midst of these dreams of pride. Far from desiring to conform his habits to ours, he loves his savage life as the distinguishing mark of his race, and he repels every advance to civilization, less perhaps from the hatred which he entertains for it, than from a dread of resembling the Europeans. While he has nothing to oppose to our perfection in the arts but the resources of the desert, to our tactics nothing but undisciplined courage; while our well-digested plans are met by the spontaneous instincts of savage life, who can wonder if he fails in this unequal contest?

The negro, who earnestly desires to mingle his race with that of the European, cannot effect it; while the Indian, who might succeed to a certain extent, disdains to make the attempt. The servility of the one dooms him to slavery, the pride of the other to death. . . .

The ejectment of the Indians very often takes place at the present day, in a regular, and, as it were, a legal manner. When the European population begins to approach the limit of the desert inhabited by a savage tribe, the government of the United States usually despatches envoys to them, who assemble the Indians in a large plain, and having first eaten and drunk with them, accost them in the following manner: "What have you to do in the land of your fathers? Before long you must dig up their bones in order to live. In what respect is the country you inhabit better than another? Are there no woods, marshes, or prairies, except where you dwell? And can you live nowhere but under your own sun? Beyond those mountains which you see at the horizon, beyond the lake which bounds your territory on the west, there lie vast countries where beasts of chase are found in great abundance; sell your land to us, and go to live happily in those solitudes." After holding this language, they spread before the eyes of the Indians fire-arms, woollen garments, kegs of brandy, glass necklaces, bracelets of tinsel, ear-rings, and looking-glasses. If, when they have beheld all these riches, they still hesitate, it is insinuated that they have not the means of refusing their required consent, and that the government itself will not long have the power of protecting them in their rights. What are they to do? Half convinced, and half compelled, they go to inhabit new deserts, where the importunate whites will not let them remain ten years in tranquillity. In this manner do the Americans obtain at a very low price whole provinces, which the richest sovereigns of Europe could not purchase.

These are great evils, and it must be added that they appear to me to be irremediable. I believe that the Indian nations of North America are doomed to perish; and that whenever the Europeans shall be established on the shores of the Pacific ocean, that race of men will be no more. The Indians had only the two alternatives of war or civilization; in other words, they must either have destroyed the Europeans or become their equals.

At the first settlement of the colonies they might have found it possible, by uniting their forces, to deliver themselves from the small bodies of strangers who landed on their continent. They several times attempted to do it, and were on the point of succeeding; but the disproportion of their resources, at the present day, when compared with those of the whites, is too great to allow such an enterprise to be thought of. Nevertheless, there do arise from time to time among the Indians men of penetration, who foresee the final destiny which awaits the native population, and who exert themselves to unite all the tribes in common hostility to the Europeans; but their efforts are unavailing. Those tribes which are in the neighbourhood of the whites, are too much weakened to offer an effectual resistance; while the others, giving way to that childish carelessness of the morrow which characterizes savage life, wait for the near approach of danger before they prepare to meet it: some are unable, the others are unwilling to exert themselves.

It is easy to foresee that the Indians will never conform to civilization; or that it will be too late, whenever they may be inclined to make the experiment.

Civilization is the result of a long social process which takes place in the same spot, and is handed down from one generation to another, each one profiting by the experience of the last. Of all nations, those submit to civilization with the most difficulty, which habitually live by the chase. Pastoral tribes, indeed, often change their place of abode; but they follow a regular order in their migrations, and often return again to their old stations, while the dwelling of the hunter varies with that of the animals he pursues.

Several attempts have been made to diffuse knowledge among the Indians, without controlling their wandering propensities; by the Jesuits in Canada, and by the puritans in New England; but none of these endeavours were crowned by any lasting success. Civilization began in the cabin, but it soon retired to expire in the woods; the great error of these legislators of the Indians was their not understanding, that in order to succeed in civilizing a people, it is first necessary to fix it; which cannot be done without inducing it to cultivate the soil: the Indians ought in the first place to have been accustomed to agriculture. But not only are they destitute of this indispensable preliminary to civilization, they would even have great difficulty in acquiring it. Men who have once abandoned themselves to the restless and adventurous life of the hunter, feel an insurmountable disgust for the constant and regular labour which tillage requires. We see this proved in the bosom of our own society; but it is far more visible among peoples whose partiality for the chase is a part of their national character.

Independently of this general difficulty, there is another which applies peculiarly to the Indians; they consider labour not merely as an evil, but as a disgrace; so that their pride prevents them from becoming civilized, as much as their indolence.

There is no Indian so wretched as not to retain, under his hut of bark, a lofty idea of his personal worth; he considers the cares of industry and labour as degrading occupations; he compares the husbandman to the ox which traces the furrow; and even in our most ingenious handicraft, he can see nothing but the labour of slaves. Not that he is devoid of admiration for the power and intellectual greatness of the whites; but although the result of our efforts surprises him, he contemns the means by which we obtain it; and while he acknowledges our ascendency, he still believes in his superiority. War and hunting are the only pursuits which appear to him worthy to be the occupations of a man. The Indian, in the dreary solitude of his woods, cherishes the same ideas, the same opinions, as the noble of the middle ages in his castle, and he only requires to become a conqueror to complete the resemblance: thus, however strange it may seem, it is in the forests of the New World, and not among the Europeans who people its coasts, that the ancient prejudices of Europe are still in existence. . . .

If the Indian tribes which now inhabit the heart of the continent could summon up energy enough to attempt to civilize themselves, they might possibly succeed. Superior already to the barbarous nations which surround them, they would gradually gain strength and experience; and when the Europeans should appear upon their borders, they would be in a state, if not to maintain their independence, at least to assert their right to the soil, and to incorporate themselves with the conquerors. But it is the misfortune of Indians to be brought into contact with a civilized people, which is also (it may be owned) the most avaricious nation on the globe, while they are still semi-barbarian: to find despots in their instructers, and to receive knowledge from the hand of oppression. Living in the freedom of the woods, the North American Indian was destitute, but he had no feeling of inferiority toward any one; as soon, however, as he desires to penetrate into the social scale of the whites, he takes the lowest rank in society, for he enters ignorant and poor within the pale of science and wealth. After having led a life of agitation, beset with evils and dangers, but at the same time filled with proud emotions, he is obliged to submit to a wearisome, obscure, and degraded state, and to gain the bread which nourishes him by hard and ignoble labour; such are in his eyes the only results of which civilization can boast: and even this much he is not sure to obtain.

When the Indians undertake to imitate their European neighbours, and to till the earth like the settlers, they are immediately exposed to a very formidable competition. The white man is skilled in the craft of agriculture; the Indian is a rough beginner in an art with which he is unacquainted. The former reaps abundant crops without difficulty, the latter meets with a thousand obstacles in raising the fruits of the earth.

The European is placed among a population whose wants he knows and partakes. The savage is isolated in the midst of a hostile people, with whose manners, language, and laws, he is imperfectly acquainted, but without whose assistance he cannot live. He can only procure the materials of comfort by bartering his commodities against the goods of the European, for the assistance of his countrymen is wholly insufficient to supply his wants. When the Indian wishes to sell the produce of his labour, he cannot always meet with a purchaser, while the European readily finds a market; and the former can only produce at a considerable cost, that which the latter vends at a very low rate. Thus the Indian has no sooner escaped those evils to which barbarous nations are exposed, than he is subjected to the still greater miseries of civilized communities; and he finds it scarcely less difficult to live in the midst of our abundance, than in the depth of his own wilderness.

He has not yet lost the habits of his erratic life; the traditions of his fathers and his passion for the chase are still alive within him. The wild enjoyments which formerly animated him in the woods painfully excite his troubled imagination; and his former privations appear to be less keen, his former perils less appalling. He contrasts the independence which he possessed among his equals with the servile position which he occupies in civilized society. On the other hand, the solitudes which were so long his free home are still at hand; a few hours' march will bring him back to them once more. The whites offer him a sum, which seems to him to be considerable, for the ground which he has begun to clear. This money of the Europeans may possibly furnish him with the means of a happy and peaceful subsistence in remote regions; and he quits the plough, resumes his native arms, and returns to the wilderness for ever. The condition of the Creeks and Cherokees, to which I have already alluded, sufficiently corroborates the truth of this deplorable picture.

The Indians in the little which they have done, have unquestionably displayed as much natural genius as the peoples of Europe in their most important designs; but nations as well as men require time to learn, whatever may be their intelligence and their zeal. While the savages were engaged in the work of civilization, the Europeans continued to surround them on every side, and to confine them within narrower limits; the two races gradually met, and they are now in immediate juxtaposition to each other. The Indian is already superior to his barbarous parent, but he is still very far below his white neighbour. With their resources and acquired knowledge, the Europeans soon appropriated to themselves most of the advantages which the natives might have derived from the possession of the soil: they have settled in the country, they have purchased land at a very low rate or have occupied it by force, and the Indians have been ruined by a competition which they had not the means of resisting. They were isolated in their own country, and their race only constituted a colony of troublesome aliens in the midst of a numerous and domineering people.

Washington said in one of his messages to congress, "We are more enlightened and powerful than the Indian nations, we are therefore bound in honour to treat them with kindness and even with generosity." But this virtuous and high-minded policy has not been followed. The rapacity of the settlers is usually backed by the tyranny of the government. Although the Cherokees and the Creeks are established upon the territory which they inhabited before the settlement of the Europeans, and although the Americans have frequently treated with them as with foreign nations, the surrounding states have not consented to acknowledge them as independent peoples, and attempts have been made to subject these children of the woods to Anglo-American magistrates, laws, and customs. Destitution had driven these unfortunate Indians to civilization, and oppression now drives them back to their former condition; many of them abandon the soil which they had begun to clear, and return to their savage course of life. . . .

Such is the language of the Indians: their assertions are true, their forebodings inevitable. From whichever side we consider the destinies of the aborigines of North America, their calamities appear to be irremediable: if they continue barbarous, they are forced to retire: if they attempt to civilize their manners, the contact of a more civilized community subjects them to oppression and destitution. They perish if they continue to wander from waste to waste, and if they attempt to settle, they still must perish; the assistance of Europeans is necessary to instruct them, but the approach of Europeans corrupts and repels them into savage life; they refuse to change their habits as long as their solitudes are their own, and it is too late to change them when they are constrained to submit.

The Spaniards pursued the Indians with blood-hounds, like wild beasts; they sacked the New World with no more temper or compassion than a city taken by storm: but destruction must cease, and phrensy be stayed; the remnant of the Indian population, which had escaped the massacre, mixed with its conquerors and adopted in the end their religion and their manners. The conduct of the Americans of the United States toward the aborigines is characterized, on the other hand, by a singular attachment to the formalities of law. Provided that the Indians retain their barbarous condition, the Americans take no part in their affairs: they treat them as independent nations, and do not possess themselves of their hunting grounds without a treaty of purchase: and if an Indian nation happens to be so encroached upon as to be unable to subsist upon its territory, they afford it brotherly assistance in transporting it to a grave sufficiently remote from the land of its fathers.

The Spaniards were unable to exterminate the Indian race by those unparalleled atrocities which brand them with indelible shame, nor did they even succeed in wholly depriving it of its rights; but the Americans of the United States have accomplished this twofold purpose with singular felicity; tranquilly, legally, philanthropically, without shedding blood, and without violating a single great principle of morality in the eyes of the world. It is impossible to destroy men with more respect for the laws of humanity. . . .

The Indians will perish in the same isolated condition in which they have lived; but the destiny of the negroes is in some measure interwoven with that of the Europeans. These two races are attached to each other without intermingling; and they are alike unable entirely to separate or to combine. The most formidable of all the ills which threaten the future existence of the United

States, arises from the presence of a black population upon its territory; and in contemplating the causes of the present embarrassments or of the future dangers of the United States, the observer is invariably led to consider this as a primary fact.

The permanent evils to which mankind is subjected are usually produced by the vehement or the increasing efforts of men; but there is one calamity which penetrated furtively into the world, and which was at first scarcely distinguishable amid the ordinary abuses of power: it originated with an individual whose name history has not preserved; it was wafted like some accursed germe upon a portion of the soil, but it afterward nurtured itself, grew without effort, and spreads naturally with the society to which it belongs. I need scarcely add that this calamity is slavery. Christianity suppressed slavery, but the Christians of the sixteenth century re-established it—as an exception, indeed, to their social system, and restricted to one of the races of mankind; but the wound thus inflicted upon humanity, though less extensive, was at the same time rendered far more difficult of cure.

It is important to make an accurate distinction between slavery itself, and its consequences. The immediate evils which are produced by slavery were very nearly the same in antiquity as they are among the moderns; but the consequences of these evils were different. The slave, among the ancients, belonged to the same race as his master, and he was often the superior of the two in education and instruction. Freedom was the only distinction between them; and when freedom was conferred, they were easily confounded together. The ancients, then, had a very simple means of avoiding slavery and its evil consequences, which was that of affranchisement; and they succeeded as soon as they adopted this measure generally. Not but, in ancient states, the vestiges of servitude subsisted for some time after servitude itself was abolished. There is a natural prejudice which prompts men to despise whomsoever has been their inferior, long after he is become their equal; and the real inequality which is produced by fortune or by law, is always succeeded by an imaginary inequality which is implanted in the manners of the people. Nevertheless, this secondary consequence of slavery was limited to a certain term among the ancients; for the freedman bore so entire a resemblance to those born free, that it soon became impossible to distinguish him from among them.

The greatest difficulty in antiquity was that of altering the law; among the moderns it is that of altering the manners; and, as far as we are concerned, the real obstacles begin where those of the ancients left off. This arises from the circumstance that, among the moderns, the abstract and transient fact of slavery is fatally united to the physical and permanent fact of colour. The tradition of slavery dishonours the race, and the peculiarity of the race perpetuates the tradition of slavery. No African has ever voluntarily emigrated to the shores of the New World; whence it must be inferred, that all the blacks who are now to be found in that hemisphere are either slaves or freedmen. Thus the negro transmits the eternal mark of his ignominy to all his descendants; and although the law may abolish slavery, God alone can obliterate the traces of its existence. . . .

The first negroes were imported into Virginia about the year 1621. In America, therefore, as well as in the rest of the globe, slavery originated in the south. Thence it spread from one settlement to another; but the number of slaves diminished toward the northern states, and the negro population was always very limited in New England.

A century had scarcely elapsed since the foundation of the colonies, when the attention of the planters was struck by the extraordinary fact, that the provinces which were comparatively destitute of slaves, increased in population, in wealth, and in prosperity, more rapidly than those which contained the greatest number of negroes. In the former, however, the inhabitants were obliged to cultivate the soil themselves, or by hired labourers; in the latter, they were furnished with hands for which they paid no wages; yet, although labour and expense were on the one side, and ease with economy on the other, the former were in possession of the most advantageous system. This consequence seemed to be the more difficult to explain, since the settlers, who all belonged to the same European race, had the same habits, the same civilization, the same laws, and their shades of difference were extremely slight.

Time, however, continued to advance; and the Anglo-Americans, spreading beyond the coasts of the Atlantic ocean, penetrated farther and farther into the solitudes of the west; they met with a new soil and an unwonted climate; the obstacles which opposed them were of the most various character; their races intermingled, the inhabitants of the south went up toward the north, those of the north descended to the south; but in the midst of all these causes, the same result recurred at every step; and in general, the colonies in which there were no slaves became more populous and more rich than those in which slavery flourished. The more progress was made, the more it was shown that slavery, which is so cruel to the slave, is prejudicial to the master. . . .

The influence of slavery extends still farther; it affects the character of the master, and imparts a peculiar tendency to his ideas and his tastes. Upon both banks of the Ohio, the character of the inhabitants is enterprising and energetic; but this vigour is very differently exercised in the two states. The white inhabitant of Ohio, who is obliged to subsist by his own exertions, regards temporal prosperity as the principal aim of his existence; and as the country which he occupies presents inexhaustible resources to his industry, and ever-varying lures to his activity, his acquisitive ardour surpasses the ordinary limits of human cupidity: he is tormented by the desire of wealth, and he boldly enters upon every path which fortune opens to him; he becomes a sailor, pioneer, an artisan, or a labourer, with the same indifference, and he supports, with equal constancy, the fatigues and the dangers incidental to these various professions; the resources of his intelligence are astonishing, and his avidity in the pursuit of gain amounts to a species of heroism.

But the Kentuckian scorns not only labour, but all the undertakings which labour promotes; as he lives in an idle independence, his tastes are those of an idle man; money loses a portion of its value in his eyes; he covets wealth much less than pleasure and excitement; and the energy which his neighbour devotes to gain, turns with him to a passionate love of field sports and military exercises; he delights in violent bodily exertion, he is familiar with the use of arms, and is accustomed from a very early age to expose his life in single combat. Thus slavery not only prevents the whites from becoming opulent, but even from desiring to become so. . . .

If I were called upon to predict what will probably occur at some future time, I should say, that the abolition of slavery in the south, will, in the common course of things, increase the repugnance of the white population for the men of colour. I found this opinion upon the analogous observation which I already had occasion to make in the north. I there remarked, that the white inhabitants of the north avoid the negroes with increasing care, in proportion as the legal barriers of separation are removed by the legislature; and why should not the same result take place in the south? In the north, the whites are deterred from intermingling with the blacks by the fear of an imaginary danger; in the south where the danger would be real, I cannot imagine that the fear would be less general. . . .

I am obliged to confess that I do not regard the abolition of slavery as a means of warding off the struggle of the two races in the United States. The negroes may long remain slaves without complaining; but if they are once raised to the level of freemen, they will soon revolt at being deprived of all their civil rights; and as they cannot become the equals of the whites, they will speedily declare themselves as enemies. In the north everything contributed to facilitate the emancipation of the slaves; and slavery was abolished, without placing the free negroes in a position which could become formidable, since their number was too small for them ever to claim the exercise of their rights. But such is not the case in the south. The question of slavery was a question of commerce and manufacture for the slave-owners in the north; for those of the south, it is a question of life and death. God forbid that I should seek to justify the principle of negro slavery, as has been done by some American writers! But I only observe that all the countries which formerly adopted that execrable principle are not equally able to abandon it at the present time.

When I contemplate the condition of the south, I can only discover two alternatives which may be adopted by the white inhabitants of those states; viz, either to emancipate the negroes, and to intermingle with them; or, remaining isolated from them, to keep them in a state of slavery as long as possible. All intermediate measures seem to me likely to terminate, and that shortly, in the most horrible of civil wars, and perhaps in the extirpation of one or other of the two races. Such is the view which the Americans of the south take of the question, and they act consistently with it. As they are determined not to mingle with the negroes, they refuse to emancipate them. . . .

The legislation of the southern states, with regard to slaves, presents at the present day such unparalleled atrocities, as suffice to show how radically the laws of humanity have been perverted, and to betray the desperate position of the community in which that legislation has been promulgated. The Americans of this portion of the Union have not, indeed, augmented the hardships of slavery; they have, on the contrary, bettered the physical condition of the slaves. The only means by which the ancients maintained slavery were fetters and death; the Americans of the south of the Union have discovered more intellectual securities for the duration of their power. They have employed their despotism and their violence against the human mind. In antiquity, precautions were taken to prevent the slave from breaking his chains; at the present day measures are adopted to deprive him even of the desire of freedom. The ancients kept the bodies of their slaves in bondage, but they placed no restraint upon the mind and no check upon education; and they acted consistently with their established principle, since a natural termination of slavery then existed, and one day or other the slave might be set free, and become the equal of his master. But the Americans of the south, who do not admit that the negroes can ever be commingled with themselves, have forbidden them to be taught to read or to write, under severe penalties; and as they will not raise them to their own level, they sink them as nearly as possible to that of the brutes. . . .

Whatever may be the efforts of the Americans of the south to maintain slavery, they will not always succeed. Slavery, which is now confined to a single tract of the civilized earth, which is attacked by Christianity as unjust, and by political economy as prejudicial, and which is now contrasted with democratic liberties and the information of our age, cannot survive. By the choice of the master or the will of the slave, it will cease; and in either case great calamities may be expected to ensue. If liberty be refused to the negroes of the south, they will in the end seize it for themselves by force; if it be given, they will abuse it ere long.

ELIAS BOUDINOT

from "An Address to the Whites" (1826)

To those who are unacquainted with the manners, habits, and improvements of the Aborigines of this country, the term *Indian* is pregnant with ideas the most repelling and degrading. But such impressions, originating as they frequently do, from infant prejudices, although they hold too true when applied to some, do great injustices to many of this race of beings.

Some there are, perhaps even in this enlightened assembly, who at the bare sight of an Indian, or at the mention of the name, would throw back their imaginations to ancient times, to the ravages of savage warfare, to the yells pronounced over the mangled bodies of women and children, thus creating an opinion, inapplicable and highly injurious to those for whose temporal interest and eternal welfare, I come to plead.

What is an Indian? Is he not formed of the same materials with yourself? For "of one blood God created all the nations that dwell on the face of the earth." Though it be true that he is ignorant, that he is a heathen, that he is a savage; yet he is no more than all others have been under similar circumstances. Eighteen centuries ago what were the inhabitants of Great Britain?

You here behold an *Indian*, my kindred are *Indians,* and my fathers sleeping in the wilderness grave—they too were *Indians.* But I am not as my fathers were—broader means and nobler influences have fallen upon me. Yet I was not born as thousands are, in a stately dome and amid the congratulations of the great, for on a little hill, in a lonely cabin, overspread by the forest oak, I first drew my breath; and in a language unknown to learned and polished nations, I learnt to lisp my fond mother's name. In after days, I have had greater advantages than most of my race; and I now stand before you delegated by my native country to seek her interest, to labour for her respectability, and by my public efforts to assist in raising her to an equal standing with other nations of the earth.

The time has arrived when speculations and conjectures as to the practicability of civilizing the Indians must forever cease. A period is fast approaching when the stale remark—"Do what you will, an Indian will still be an Indian," must be placed no more in speech. With whatever plausibility this popular objection may have heretofore been made, every candid mind must now be sensible that it can no longer be uttered, except by those who are uninformed with respect to us, who are strongly prejudiced against us, or who are filled with vindictive feelings towards us for the present history of the Indians, particularly of that nation to which I belong, most incontrovertibly establishes the fallacy of this remark. . . .

My design is to offer a few disconnected facts relative to the present improved state, and to the ultimate prospects of that particular tribe called Cherokees to which I belong.

The Cherokee nation lies within the chartered limits of the states of Georgia, Tennessee, and Alabama. Its extent as defined by treaties is about 200 miles in length from East to West, and about 120 in breadth. This country which is supposed to contain about 10,000,000 of acres exhibits great varieties of surface, the most part being hilly and mountainous, affording soil of no value. The vallies, however, are well watered and afford excellent land, in many parts particularly on the large streams, that of the first quality. The climate is temperate and healthy, indeed I would not be guilty of exaggeration were I to say, that the advantages which this country possesses to render it salubrious, are many and superior. Those lofty and barren mountains, defying the labour and ingenuity of man, and supposed by some as placed there only to exhibit omnipotence, contribute to the healthiness and beauty of the surrounding plains, and give to us that free air and pure water which distinguish our country. Those advantages, calculated to make the inhabitants healthy, vigorous, and intelligent, cannot fail to cause this country to become interesting. And there can be no doubt that the Cherokee Nation, however obscure and trifling it may now appear, will finally become, if not under its present occupants, one of the Garden spots of America. And here, let me be indulged in the fond wish, that she may thus become under those who now possess her; and ever be fostered, regulated and protected by the generous government of the United States.

The population of the Cherokee Nation increased from the year 1810 to that of 1824, 2000 exclusive of those who emigrated in 1818 and 19 to the west of the Mississippi—of those who reside on the Arkansas the number is supposed to be about 5000.

The rise of these people in their movement towards civilization may be traced as far back as the relinquishment of their towns; when game became incompetent to their support, by reason of the surrounding white population. They then betook themselves to the woods, commenced the opening of small clearings, and the raising of stock; still however following the chase. Game has since become so scarce that little dependence for subsistence can be placed upon it. They have gradually and I could almost say universally forsaken their ancient employment. In fact, there is not a single family in the nation, that can be said to subsist on the slender support which the wilderness would afford. The love and the practice of hunting are not now carried to a higher degree, than among all frontier people whether white or red. It cannot be doubted, however, that there are many who have commenced a life of agricultural labour from mere necessity, and if they could, would gladly resume their former course of living. But these are individual feelings and ought to be passed over.

On the other hand it cannot be doubted that the nation is improving, rapidly improving in all those particulars which must finally constitute the inhabitants an industrious and intelligent people.

It is a matter of surprise to me, and must be to all those who are properly acquainted with the condition of the Aborigines of this country, that the Cherokees have advanced so far and so rapidly in civilization. But there are yet powerful obstacles, both within and without, to be surmounted in the march of improvement. The prejudices in regard to them in the general community are strong and lasting. The evil effects of their intercourse with their immediate white neighbours, who differ from them chiefly in name, are easily to be seen, and it is evident that from this intercourse proceed those demoralizing practices which in order to surmount, peculiar and unremitting efforts are necessary. In defiance, however, of these obstacles the Cherokees have improved and are still rapidly improving. To give you a further view of their condition, I will here repeat some of the articles of the two statistical tables taken at different periods.

In 1810 There were 19,500 cattle; 6,100 horses; 19,600 swine; 1,037 sheep, 467 looms; 1,600 spinning wheels; 30 waggons; 500 ploughs; 3 saw-mills; 13 grist-mills etc. At this time there are 22,000 cattle; 7,600 Horses; 46,000 swine; 2,500 sheep; 762 looms; 2488 spinning wheels; 172 waggons; 2,943 ploughs; 10 saw-mills; 31 grist-mills; 62 Blacksmith-shops; 8 cotton machines; 18 schools; 18 ferries; and a number of public roads. In one district there were, last winter, upwards of 0000 volumes of good books; and 11 different periodical papers both religious and political, which were taken and read. On the public roads there are many decent Inns, and few houses for convenience, etc., would disgrace any country. Most of the schools are under the care and tuition of christian missionaries, of different denominations, who have been of great service to the nation, by inculcating moral and religious principles into the minds of the rising generation. In many places the word of God is regularly preached and explained, both by missionaries and natives; and there are numbers who have publicly professed their belief and interest in the merits of the great Saviour of the world. It is worthy of remark, that in no ignorant country have the missionaries undergone less trouble and difficulty, in spreading a knowledge of the Bible, than in this. Here, they have been welcomed and encouraged by the proper authorities of the nation, their persons have been protected, and in very few instances have some individual vagabonds threatened violence to them. Indeed it may be said with truth, that among no heathen people has the faithful minister of God experienced greater success, greater reward for his labour, than in this. He is surrounded by attentive hearers, the words which flow from his lips are not spent in vain. The Cherokees have had no established religion of their own, and perhaps to this circumstance we may attribute, in part, the facilities with which missionaries have pursued their ends. They cannot be called idolators; for they never worshipped Images. They believed in a Supreme Being, the Creator of all, the God of the white, the red, and the black man. They also believed in the existence of an evil spirit who resided, as they thought, in the setting sun, the future place of all who in their life time had done iniquitously. Their prayers were addressed alone to the Supreme Being, and which if written would fill a large volume, and display much sincerity, beauty and sublimity. When the ancient customs of the Cherokees were in their full force, no warrior thought himself secure, unless he had addressed his guardian angel; no hunter could hope for success, unless before the rising sun he had asked the assistance of his God, and on his return at eve had offered his sacrifice to him.

There are three things of late occurance, which must certainly place the Cherokee Nation in a fair light, and act as a powerful argument in favor of Indian improvement.

First. The invention of letters.

Second. The translation of the New Testament into Cherokee.

And Third. The organization of a Government.

The Cherokee mode of writing lately invented by George Guest, who could not read any language nor speak any other than his own, consists of eighty-six characters, principally syllabic, the combinations of which form all the words of the language. Their terms may be greatly simplified, yet they answer all the purposes of writing, and already many natives use them.

The translation of the New Testament, together with Guest's mode of writing, has swept away that barrier which has long existed, and opened a spacious channel for the instruction of adult Cherokees. Persons of all ages and classes may now read the precepts of the Almighty in their own language. Before it is long, there will scarcely be an individual in the nation who can say, "I know not God neither understand I what thou sayest," for all shall know him from the greatest to the least. The aged warrior over whom has rolled three score and ten years of savage life, will grace the temple of God with his hoary head; and the little child yet on the breast of its pious mother shall learn to lisp its Maker's name.

The shrill sound of the Savage yell shall die away as the roaring of far distant thunder; and Heaven wrought music will gladden the affrighted wilderness. "The solitary places will be glad for them, and the desert shall rejoice and blossom as a rose." Already do we see the morning star, forerunner of approaching dawn, rising over the tops of those deep forests in which for ages have echoed the warrior's whoop. But has not God said it, and will he not do it? The Almighty decrees his purposes, and man cannot with all his ingenuity and device countervail them. They are more fixed in their course than the rolling sun—more durable than the everlasting mountains.

The Government, though defective in many respects, is well suited to the condition of the inhabitants. As they rise in information and refinement, changes in it must follow, until they arrive at that state of advancement, when I trust they will be admitted into all the privileges of the American family.

The Cherokee Nation is divided into eight districts, in each of which are established courts of justice, where all disputed cases are decided by a Jury, under the direction of a circuit Judge, who has jurisdiction over two districts. Sheriffs and other public officers are appointed to execute the decisions of the courts, collect debts, and arrest thieves and other criminals. Appeals may be taken to the Superior Court, held annually at the seat of Government. The Legislative authority is vested in a General Court, which consists of the National Committee and Council. The National Committee consists of thirteen members, who are generally men of sound sense and fine talents. The National Council consists of thirty-two members, beside the speaker, who act as the representatives of the people. Every bill passing these two bodies, becomes the law of the land. Clerks are appointed to do the writings, and record the proceedings of the Council. The executive power is vested in two principal chiefs, who hold their office during good behaviour, and sanction all the decisions of the legislative council. Many of the laws display some degree of civilization, and establish the respectability of the nation.

Polygamy is abolished. Female chastity and honor are protected by law. The Sabbath is respected by the Council during session. Mechanics are encouraged by law. The practice of putting aged persons to death for witchcraft is abolished and murder has now become a governmental crime. . . .

When before did a nation of Indians step forward and ask for the means of civilization? The Cherokee authorities have adopted the measures already stated, with a sincere desire to make their nation an intelligent and a virtuous people, and with a full hope that those who have already pointed out to them the road of happiness, will now assist them to pursue it. With that assistance, what are the prospects of the Cherokees? Are they not indeed glorious, compared to that deep darkness in which the nobler qualities of their souls have slept. Yes, methinks I can view my native country, rising from the ashes of her degradation, wearing her purified and beautiful garments, and taking her seat with the nations of the earth. I can behold her sons bursting the fetters of ignorance and unshackling her from the vices of heathenism. She is at this instant, risen like the first morning sun, which grows brighter and brighter, until it reaches its fulness of glory.

She will become not a great, but a faithful ally of the United States. In times of peace she will plead the common liberties of America. In times of war her intrepid sons will sacrifice their lives in your defence. And because she will be useful to you in coming time, she asks you to assist her in her present struggles. She asks not for greatness; she seeks not wealth, she pleads only for assistance to become respectable as a nation, to enlighten and ennoble her sons, and to ornament her daughters with modesty and virtue. She pleads for this assistance, too, because on her destiny hangs that of many nations. If she completes her civilization—then may we hope that all our nations will—then, indeed, may true patriots be encouraged in their efforts to make this world of the West, one continuous abode of enlightened, free, and happy people.

But if the Cherokee Nation fail in her struggle, if she die away, then all hopes are blasted, and falls the fabric of Indian civilization. Their fathers were born in darkness, and have died in darkness; without your assistance so will their sons. You, see, however, where the probability rests. Is there a soul whose narrowness will not permit the exercise of charity on such an occasion? Where is he that can withhold his mite from an object so noble? Who can prefer a little of his silver and gold, to the welfare of nations of his fellow beings? Human wealth perishes with our clay, but that wealth gained in charity still remains on earth, to enrich our names, when we are gone, and will be remembered in Heaven, when the miser and his coffers have mouldered together in their kindred earth. The works of a generous mind sweeten the cup of affliction; they enlighten the dreary way to the cold tomb; they blunt the sting of death, and smooth his passage to the unknown world. When all the kingdoms of this earth shall die away and their beauty and power shall perish, his name shall live and shine as a twinkling star; those for whose benefit be done his deeds of charity shall call him blessed, and they shall add honor to his immortal head.

There are, with regard to the Cherokee and other tribes, two alternatives; they must either become civilized and happy, or sharing the fate of many kindred nations, become extinct. If the General Government continue its protection, and the American people assist them in their humble efforts, they will, they must rise. Yes, under such protection, and with such assistance, the Indian must rise like the Phoenix, after having wallowed for ages in ignorance and barbarity. But should this Government withdraw its care, and the American people their aid, then, to use the words of a writer, "they will go the way that so many tribes have gone before them; for the hordes that still linger about the shores of Huron, and the tributary streams of the Mississippi, will share the fate of those tribes that once lorded it along the proud banks of the Hudson; of that gigantic race that are said to have existed on the borders of the Susquehanna; of those various nations that flourished about the Potomac and the Rhappahannoc, and that peopled the forests of the vast valley of Shenandoah. They will vanish like a vapour from the face of the earth, their very history will be lost in forgetfulness, and places that now know them will know them no more."

There is, in Indian history, something very melancholy, and which seems to establish a mournful precedent for the future events of the few sons of the forest, now scattered over this vast continent. We have seen every where the poor aborigines melt away before the white population. I merely speak of the fact, without at all referring to the cause. We have seen, I say, one family after another, one tribe after another, nation after nation, pass away; until only a few solitary creatures are left to tell the sad story of extinction.

Shall this precedent be followed? I ask you, shall red men live, or shall they be swept from the earth? With you and this public at large, the decision chiefly rests. Must they perish? Must they all, like the unfortunate Creeks, (victims of the unchristian policy of certain persons,) go down in sorrow to their grave?

They hang upon your mercy as to a garment. Will you push them from you, or will you save them? Let humanity answer.

NAT TURNER

from *The Confessions of Nat Turner* (1831)

Agreeable to his appointment, on the evening he was committed to prison, with permission of the jailer, I [Thomas Gray] visited NAT on Tuesday the 1st November, when, without being questioned at all, he commenced his narrative in the following words:—

Sir,—You have asked me to give a history of the motives which induced me to undertake the late insurrection, as you call it—To do so I must go back to the days of my infancy, and even before I was born. I was thirty-one years of age the 2d of October last, and born the property of Benj. Turner, of this county. In my childhood a circumstance occurred which made an indelible impression on my mind, and laid the ground work of that enthusiasm which has terminated so fatally to many, both white and black, and for which I am about to atone at the gallows. It is here necessary to relate this circumstance—trifling as it may seem, it was the commencement of that belief which has grown with time, and even now, sir, in this dungeon, helpless and forsaken as I am, I cannot divest myself of. Being at play with other children, when three or four years old, I was telling them something, which my mother overhearing, said it had happened before I was born—I stuck to my story, however, and related somethings which went, in her opinion, to confirm it—others being called on were greatly astonished, knowing that these had happened, and caused them to say in my hearing, I surely would a prophet, as the Lord had shewn me things that had happened before my birth. . . .

And about this time I had a vision—and I saw white spirits and black spirits engaged in battle, and the sun was darkened—the thunder rolled in the Heavens, and blood flowed in streams—and I heard a voice saying, "Such is your luck, such you are called to see, and let it come rough or smooth, you must surely bare it." I now withdrew myself as much as my situation would permit, from the intercourse of my fellow servants, for the avowed purpose of serving the Spirit more fully—and it appeared to me, and reminded me of the things it had already shown me, and that it would then reveal to me the knowledge of the elements, the revolution of the planets, the operation of tides, and changes of the seasons. After this revelation in the year 1825, and the knowledge of the elements being made known to me, I sought more than ever to obtain true holiness before the great day of judgment should appear, and then I began to receive the true knowledge of faith. And from the first steps of righteousness until the last, was I made perfect; and the Holy Ghost was with me, and said, "Behold me as I stand in the Heavens—and I looked and saw the forms of men in different attitudes—and there were lights in the sky to which the children of darkness gave other names than what they really were—for they were the lights of the Saviour's hands, stretched forth from east to west, even as they were extended on the cross of Calvary for the redemption of sinners. And I wondered greatly at these miracles, and prayed to be informed of a certainty of the meaning thereof—and shortly afterwards, while laboring in the field, I discovered drops of blood on the corn as though it were dew from heaven—and I communicated it to many, both white and black, in the neighborhood—and I then found on the leaves in the woods hieroglyphic characters, and numbers, with the forms of men in different attitudes, portrayed in blood, and representing the figures I had seen before in the heavens. And now the Holy Ghost had revealed itself to me, and made plain the miracles it had shown me—For as the blood of Christ had been shed on this earth, and had ascended to heaven for the salvation of sinners, and was now returning to earth again in the form of dew—and as the leaves on the trees bore the impressions of the figures I had seen in the heavens, it was plain to me that the Saviour was about to lay down the yoke he had borne for the sins of men, and the great day of judgment was at hand. . . .

Since the commencement of 1830, I had been living with Mr. Joseph Travis, who was to me a kind master, and placed the greatest confidence in me; in fact, I had no cause to complain of his treatment of me. On Saturday evening, the 20th of August, it was agreed between Henry, Hark and myself, to prepare a dinner the next day for the men we expected, and then to concert a plan, as we had not yet determined on any. Hark, on the following morning, brought a pig, and Henry brandy, and being joined by Sam, Nelson, Will and Jack, they prepared in the woods a dinner, where, about three o'clock, I joined them.

Q. Why were you so backward in joining them.

A. The same reason that had caused me not to mix with them for years before.

I saluted them on coming up, and asked Will how came he there, he answered, his life was worth no more than others, and his liberty as dear to him. I asked him if he thought to obtain it? He said he would, or lose his life. This was enough to put him in full confidence. Jack, I knew, was only a tool in the hands of Hark. It was quickly agreed we should commence at home (Mr. J. Travis') on that night, and until we had armed and equipped ourselves, and gathered sufficient force, neither age nor sex was to be spared, (which was invariably adhered to.) We remained at the feast, until about two hours in the night, when we went to the house and found Austin; they all went to the cider press and drank, except myself. On returning to the house, Hank went to the door with an axe, for the purpose of breaking it open , as we knew we were strong enough to murder the family, if they were awaked by the noise; but reflecting that it might create an alarm in the neighborhood, we determined to enter the house secretly, and murder them whilst sleeping. Hark got a ladder and set it against the chimney, on which I ascended, and hoisting a window, entered and came down stairs, unbarred the door, and removed the guns from their places. It was then observed that I must spill the first blood. On which, armed with a hatchet, and accompanied by Will, I entered my master's chamber, it being dark, I could not give a death blow, the hatchet glanced from his head, he sprang from the bed, and called his wife, it was his last word, Will laid him dead, with a blow of his axe, and Mrs. Travis shared the same fate, as she lay in bed. The murder of this family, five in number, was the work of a moment, not one of them awoke; there was a little infant sleeping in a cradle, that was forgotten, until we had left the house and gone some distance, when Henry and Will returned and killed it; we got here, four guns that would shoot, and several old muskets, with a pound or two of powder. We remained some time at the barn, where we paraded; I formed them in a line as soldiers, and after carrying them off to Mr. Salathur Francis', about six hundred yards distant, Sam and Will went to the door and knocked. Mr. Francis asked who was there, Sam replied it was him, and he had a letter for him, on which he got up and came to the door; they immediately seized him, and dragging him out a little from the door, he was dispatched by repeated blows on the head; there was no other white person in the family. We started from there for Mrs. Reese's, maintaining the most perfect silence on our march, where finding the door unlocked, we entered, and murdered Mrs. Reese in her bed, while sleeping; her son awoke, but it was only to sleep the sleep of death; he had only time to say who is that, and he was no more. From Mrs. Reese's we went to Mrs. Turner's, a mile distant, which we reached about sunrise, on Monday morning. Henry, Austin, and Sam, went to the still, where, finding Mr. Peebles, Austin shot him, and the rest of us went to the house; as we approached, the family discovered us, and shut the door. Vain hope! Will, with one stroke of his axe, opened it, and we entered and found Mrs. Turner and Mrs. Newsome in the middle of a room, almost frightened to death. Will immediately killed Mrs. Turner, with one blow of his axe. I took Mrs. Newsome by the hand, and with the sword I had when I was apprehended, I struck her several blows over the head, but not being able to kill her, as the sword was dull. Will turning around and discovering it, despatched her also. A general destruction of property and search for money and ammunition, always succeeded the murders. By this time my company amounted to fifteen, and nine men mounted, who started for Mrs. White-head's, (the other six were to go through a by way to Mr. Bryant's, and rejoin us at Mrs. White-head's,) as we approached the house we discovered Mr. Richard Whitehead standing in the cotton patch, near the lane fence; we called him over into the land, and Will, the executioner, was near at hand, with his fatal axe, to send him to an untimely grave.

I here proceeded to make some inquiries of him, after assuring him of the certain death that awaited him, and that concealment would only bring destruction on the innocent as well as guilty, of his own color, if he knew of any extensive or concerted plan. His answer was, I do not. When I questioned him as to the insurrection in North Carolina happening about the same time, he denied any knowledge of it; and when I looked him in the face as though I would search his inmost thoughts, he replied, "I see sir, you doubt my word; but can you not think the same ideas, and strange appearances about this time in the heaven's might prompt others, as well as myself, to this undertaking." I now had much conversation with and asked him many questions, having forborne to do so previously, except in the cases noted in parenthesis; but during his statement, I had, unnoticed by him, taken notes as to some particular circumstances, and having the advantage of his statement before me in writing, on the evening of the third day that I had been with him, I began a cross examination, and found his statement corroborated by every circumstance coming within my own knowledge or the confessions of others whom had been either killed or executed, and whom he had not seen nor had any knowledge since 22d of August last, he expressed himself fully satisfied as to the impracticability of his attempt. It has been said he was ignorant and cowardly, and that his object was to murder and rob for the purpose of obtaining money to make his escape. It is notorious, that he was never known to have a dollar in his life; to swear an oath, or drink a drop or spirits.

As to his ignorance, he certainly never had advantages of education, but he can read and write, (it was taught him by his parents,) and for natural intelligence and quickness of apprehension, is surpassed by few men I have even seen. As to his being a coward, his reason as given for not resisting Mr. Phipps, shows the decision of his character. When he saw Mr. Phipps present his gun, he said he knew it was impossible for him to escape as the woods were full of men; he therefore thought it was better to surrender, and trust to fortune for his escape. He is a complete fanatic, or plays his part most admirably. On other subjects he possesses an uncommon share of intelligence, with a mind capable of attaining any thing; but warped and perverted by the influence of early impressions. He is below the ordinary in stature, though strong and active, having the true negro face, every feature of which is strongly marked. I shall not attempt to describe the effect of his narrative, as told and commented on by himself, in the condemned hole of the prison. The calm, deliberate composure with which he spoke of his late deeds and intentions, the expression of his fiend-like face when excited by enthusiasm, still bearing the stains of the blood of helpless innocence about him; clothed with rags and covered with chains; yet daring to raise his manacled hands to heaven, with a spirit soaring above the attributes of man; I looked on him and my blood curdled in my veins.

The Commonwealth, vs. Nat Turner.	}	Charged with making insurrection, and plotting to take away the lives of divers free white persons, &c. on the 22d of August, 1831.

The court composed of—, having met for the trial of Nat Turner, the prisoner was brought in and arraigned, and upon his arraignment pleaded *Not guilty*; saying to his counsel to that he did not feel so.

On the part of the Commonwealth, Levi Waller was introduced, who being sworn, deposed as follows: (*agreeably to Nat's own Confession.*) Col. Trezvant {the committing magistrate} was then introduced, who being sworn, narrated Nat's Confession to him, as follows: (*his Confession as given to Mr. Gray.*) The prisoner introduced no evidence, and the case was submitted without argument to the court, who having found him guilty, Jeremiah Cobb, Esq. Chairman, pronounced the sentence of the court, in the following words: "Nat Turner! Stand up. Have you anything to say why sentence of death should not be pronounced against you?"

Ans. I have not. I have made a full confession to Mr. Gray, and I have nothing more to say.

Attend then to the sentence of the court. You have been arraigned and tried before this court, and convicted of one of the highest crimes in our criminal code. You have been convicted of plotting in cold blood, the indiscriminate destruction of men, of helpless women, and of infant children. The evidence before us leaves not a shadow of doubt, but that your hands were often imbrued in the blood of the innocent; and your own confessions tells us that they were stained with the blood of a Master; in your own language, "too indulgent." Could I stop here, your crime would be sufficiently aggravated. But the original contriver of a plan, deep and deadly, one that never can be effected, you managed so far to put it into execution, as to deprive us of many of our most valuable citizens; and this was done when they were asleep, and defenceless; under circumstances shocking to humanity. And while upon this part of the subject, I cannot but call your attention to the poor misguided wretches who have gone before you. They are not few in number—they were your bosom associates; and the blood of all cries aloud, and calls upon you, as the author of their misfortune. Yes! You forced them unprepared, from Time to Eternity. Borne down by this load of guilt, your only justification is, that you were led away by fanaticism. If this be true, from my soul I pity you; and while you have my sympathies, I am, nevertheless called upon to pass the sentence of the court. The time between this and your execution, will necessarily be very short; and your only hope must be in another world. The judgement of the court is, that you be taken hence to the jail from whence you came, thence to the place of execution, and on Friday next, between the hours of 10 A.M. and 2 P.M. be hung by the neck until you are dead! dead! dead[!] and may the Lord have mercy upon your soul.

WOMEN'S RIGHTS CONVENTION, SENECA FALLS, NEW YORK
Declaration of Sentiments (1848)

1. Declaration of Sentiments

When, in the course of human events, it becomes necessary for one portion of the family of man to assume among the people of the earth a position different from that which they have hitherto occupied, but one to which the laws of nature and of nature's God entitle them, a decent respect to the opinions of mankind requires that they should declare the causes that impel them to such a course.

We hold these truths to be self-evident: that all men and women are created equal; that they are endowed by their Creator with certain inalienable rights; that among these are life, liberty, and the pursuit of happiness; that to secure these rights governments are instituted, deriving their just powers from the consent of the governed. Whenever any form of government becomes destructive of these ends, it is the right of those who suffer from it to refuse allegiance to it, and to insist upon the institution of a new government, laying its foundation on such principles, and organizing its powers in such form, as to them shall seem most likely to effect their safety and happiness. Prudence, indeed, will dictate that governments long established should not be changed for light and transient causes; and accordingly all experience hath shown that mankind are more disposed to suffer while evils are sufferable, than to right themselves by abolishing the forms to which they are accustomed. But when a long train of causes and usurpations, pursuing invariably the same object, evinces a design to reduce them under absolute despotism, it is their duty to throw off such government, and to provide new guards for the future security. Such has been the patient sufferance of the women under this government, and such is now the necessity which constrains them to demand the equal station to which they are entitled.

The history of mankind is a history of repeated injuries and usurpations on the part of man toward woman, having in direct object the establishment of an absolute tyranny over her. To prove this, let facts be submitted to a candid world.

He has never permitted her to exercise her inalienable right to the elective franchise.

He has compelled her to submit to laws, in the formation of which she had no voice.

He has withheld from her rights which are given to the most ignorant and degraded men—both natives and foreigners.

Having deprived her of this first right of a citizen, the elective franchise, thereby leaving her without representation in the halls of legislation, he has oppressed her on all sides.

He has made her, if married, in the eye of the law, civilly dead.

He has taken from her all right in property, even to the wages she earns.

He has made her, morally, an irresponsible being, as she can commit many crimes with impunity, provided they be done in the presence of her husband. In the covenant of marriage, she is compelled to promise obedience to her husband, he becoming, to all intents and purposes, her master—the law giving him power to deprive her of her liberty, and to administer chastisement.

He has so framed the laws of divorce, as to what shall be the proper causes, and in case of separation, to whom the guardianship of the children shall be given, as to be wholly regardless of the happiness of women—the law, in all uses, going upon a false supposition of the supremacy of man, and giving all power into his hands.

After depriving her of all rights as a married woman, if single, and the owner of property, he has taxed her to support a government which recognizes her only when her property can be made profitable to it.

He has monopolized nearly all the profitable employment, and from those she is permitted to follow, she receives but a scanty remuneration. He closes against her all the avenues to wealth and distinction which he considers most honorable to himself. As a teacher of theology, medicine, or law, she is not known.

He has denied her the facilities for obtaining a thorough education, all colleges being closed against her.

He allows her in Church, as well as State, but in a subordinate position, claiming Apostolic authority for her exclusion from the ministry, and, with some exceptions, from any public participation in the affairs of the Church.

He has created a false public sentiment by giving to the world a different code of morals for men and women, by which moral delinquencies which exclude women from society, are not only tolerated, but deemed of little account in man.

He has usurped the prerogative of Jehovah himself, claiming it as his right to assign for her a sphere of action, when that belongs to her conscience and to her God.

He has endeavored, in every way that he could, to destroy her confidence in her own powers, to lessen her self-respect and to make her willing to lead a dependent and abject life.

Now, in view of this entire disfranchisement of one-half the people of this country, their social and religious degradation—in view of the unjust laws above mentioned, and because women do feel themselves aggrieved, oppressed, and fraudulently deprived of their most sacred rights, we insist that they have immediate admission to all the rights and privileges which belong to them as citizens of the United States.

In entering upon the great work before us, we anticipate no small amount of misconception, misrepresentation, and ridicule; but we shall use every instrumentality within our power to effect our object. We shall employ agents, circulate tracts, petition the State and National legislatures, and endeavor to enlist the pulpit and the press on our behalf. We hope this Convention will be followed by a series of Conventions embracing every part of the country.

2. Resolutions

WHEREAS, The great precept of nature is conceded to be, that "man shall purse his own true and substantial happiness." Blackstone in his Commentaries remarks, that this law of Nature being coeval with mankind, and dictated by God himself, is of course superior in obligation to any other. It is binding over all the globe, in all countries and at all times; no human laws are of any validity if contrary to this, and such of them as are valid, derive all their force, and all their validity, and all their authority, mediately and immediately, from this original; therefore,

Resolved, That all laws which prevent woman from occupying such a station in society as her conscience shall dictate, or which place her in a position inferior to that of man, are contrary to the great precept of nature, and therefore of no force or authority.

Resolved, That woman is man's equal—was intended to be so by the Creator, and the highest good of the race demands that she should be recognized as such.

Resolved, That the women of this country ought to be enlightened in regard to the laws under which they live, that they may no longer publish their degradation by declaring themselves satisfied with their present position, nor their ignorance, by asserting that they have all the rights they want.

Resolved, That inasmuch as man, while claiming for himself intellectual superiority, does accord to woman moral superiority, it is pre-eminently his duty to encourage her to speak and teach, as she has an opportunity, in all religious assemblies.

Resolved, That the same amount of virtue, delicacy, and refinement of behavior that is required of woman in the social state, should also be required of man, and the same transgressions should be visited with equal severity on both man and woman.

Resolved, That the objection of indelicacy and impropriety, which is so often brought against woman when she addresses a public audience, comes with a very ill-grace from those who encourage, by their attendance, her appearance on the stage, in the concert, or in feats of the circus.

Resolved, That woman has too long rested satisfied in the circumscribed limits which corrupt customs and a perverted application of the Scriptures have marked out for her, and that it is time she should move in the enlarged sphere which her great Creator has assigned her.

Resolved, That is the duty of the women of this country to secure to themselves their sacred right to the elective franchise.

Resolved, That the equality of human rights results necessarily from the fact of the identity of the race in capabilities and responsibilities.

Resolved, That the speedy success of our cause depends upon the zealous and untiring efforts of both men and women, for the overthrow of the monopoly of the pulpit, and for the securing to women an equal participation with men in the various trades, professions, and commerce.

Resolved, therefore, That, being invested by the creator with the same capabilities, and the same consciousness of responsibility for their exercise, it is demonstrably the right and duty of woman, equally with man, to promote every righteous cause by every righteous means; and especially in regard to the great subjects of morals and religion, it is self-evidently her right to participate with her brother in teaching them, both in private and in public, by writing and by speaking, by any instrumentalities proper to be used, and in any assemblies proper to be held; and this being a self-evident truth growing out of the divinely implanted principles of human nature, any custom or authority adverse to it, whether modern or wearing the hoary sanction of antiquity, is to be regarded as a self-evident falsehood, and at war with mankind.

Sarah Josepha Hale

"Editor's Table," from *Godey's Lady's Book*,
(1850)

THE beginning of a new volume and a new year naturally excites the inquiry—What have we to do? To answer this question rightly, we must well understand, not only what we have done, but also what we have intended to accomplish. What has been our aim? The Lady's Book has had, from the first, but one grand design—to subserve the best interests of Woman.

What a wonderful change in public opinion concerning the powers of the female mind has been effected since our journal was first published! Then—that is, twenty years ago—very little interest was taken in female education. The subject of "woman's rights" had been foolishly and clamorously urged by a few, who, with a "zeal without knowledge" or discretion, would have broken down the barriers of true modesty, and destroyed the retiring graces of woman's nature, in which her most beneficial influence is concealed, like the flower in its calyx.

Gently to unfold this flower, as the sun's rays in the spring warm and expand the rose till its beauty is seen and its sweet incense induces the admirer to preserve it for its virtues as well as its loveliness, has been the work of the Lady's Book.

And now, who questions the beneficial influence of woman's cultivated intellect? or doubts the great effect it is to exercise on the improvement and happiness of the world?

We are intending, in this Table, to serve up a few of the recent opinions of English and American writers on these interesting subjects—Woman, and her intellectual and moral influence, selected from works not, probably, yet seen by the greater portion of our readers. And first from a true poet:—

> Woman is not undeveloped man,
> But diverse: could we make her as the man,
> Sweet love were slain, whose dearest bond is this,
> Not like to like, but like in difference:
> Yet in the long years like must they grow;
> The man be more of woman, she of man;
> He gain in sweetness and in moral height,
> Nor lose the wrestling thews that throw the world;
> She mental breadth, nor fail in childward care:
> More as the double-natured poet each;
> Till, at the last, she set herself to man
> Like perfect music unto noble words;
> And so these twain, upon the skirts of Time,
> Sit side by side, full-summed in all their powers,
> Dispensing harvest, sowing the To-be,

Self-reverent each, and reverencing each,
Distinct in individualities,
But like each other, even as those who love.
Then comes the statelier Eden back to men;
Then reigns the world's great bridals chaste and calm;
Then springs the crowning race of humankind.
May these things be!—Tennyson's *Princess*.

The difference between the mental qualities of the sexes is owing, we apprehend, far more to education than to nature. At all events, there is no such natural difference as warrants the distinction we make in the mental discipline we provide for them. There are certain professional studies with which no one thinks of vexing the mind of any one, man or woman, but those who intend to practice the professions; but why, in a good English library, there should be one-half of it, and that the better half, which a young woman is not expected to read—this we never could understand, and never reflect on with common patience. Why may not a Locke, or a Paley, or a Dugald Stewart, train the mind of the future Mother of a family? Or why may not an intelligent young woman be a companion for her brother or her husband in his more serious moods of thought, as well as in his gayer and more trifling? Would the world lose anything of social happiness or moral refinement by this intellectual equality of the two sexes? You vex the memory of a young girl with dictionaries and vocabularies without end; you tax her memory in every conceivable manner; and, at an after age, you give the literature of sentiment freely to her pillage; but that which should step between the two—the culture of the reason—this is entirely forbidden. . . . —*Blackwood's Magazine*.

But matters are mending, and will continue to mend. There are so many women of richly cultivated minds who have distinguished themselves in letters or in society, and made it highly feminine to be intelligent as well as good, and to have elevated as well as amiable feelings, that, by and by, the whole sex must adopt a new standard of education. It must, we presume, be by leaders of their own, starting out of their own body, that the rest of the soft and timid flock must be led.—*Ibid*.

The mothers of this generation must form the men and women of the next. No degree of masculine cultivation can make up for a lack of mental and physical development in woman. It is the mother who gives the elements of greatness. Every day's observation teaches us this lesson; and no society, no nation can advance where the culture, and all that goes to form the character of woman, are neglected; and no nation can fail of greatness where women are held in genuine respect.

We have said little of the "Rights of Woman." Her first right is to education, in its widest, sense—to such education as will give her the full development of all her personal, mental, and moral qualities. Having that, there will be no longer any question about her rights; and rights are liable to be perverted to wrongs when we are incapable of rightly exercising them. Give woman health, beauty, high intelligence, and that purity of soul and benevolence of heart which belong to her nature, and she would have no difficulty in making her proper place in society; for she would have the forming of the thought, and taste, and moral sentiment of the world. It seems hard to regenerate the world; but the work would be easy, if we could but see the means which God has appointed. We have only to give full play and free development to the love principle, which finds its form and expression in the pure nature of woman, in order to reform the world.

There is no danger that we shall ever esteem too highly, honor too much, or treat with a too tender consideration, the mothers of our race. No chivalry was ever extravagant; it was only misguided. The impulse was holy, but misdirected. That impulse gave us civilization; the same chivalric feeling, with more enlightenment, will give us that state of society that glows in beauty in our radiant dreams of the future. Physically and morally, God has made woman worthy to be the mother of mankind. Her nature is as exalted as her function. Love, and truth, and purity are the instincts of her being. Religion is the grand impulse of her soul. Even in her present imperfect state, after ages of neglect and suffering, she commands our admiration, and receives our love and worship. All that is truly good and beautiful in society, we owe to woman. The regeneration of the race, and the opening of a higher and happier existence to mankind, are sufficient motives to influence us in using all our exertions to improve the condition of woman; while her elevation and happiness will be the most gratifying feature of a new order of society.

Woman must be the motive power of all human progress. Man may be, to whatever extent we please to contend, the head and hands of any true movement; but woman must be its warm heart. Hers is the empire of the affections; and her attractions are sufficient to elevate the world, if she be only elevated to the vantage-ground that belongs to her. If woman, for the past century, had not been shut out from her rightful share of the advantages of education and opportunities for culture, the world would have made more rapid advances. The great mistake of men has been, to leave her behind, and to endeavor to get along without her. Such a one-sided advance is impossible. Woman must advance step by step with man; in some things, she must even lead and guide him, or there can be no advancement. For man to endeavor to move on alone, leaving his "better half' to lag behind him, can only produce discord, mischief, and misery. Humanity becomes a divided body, without a living soul.

If any difference be allowed in the means of education and the facilities for improvement, it should be in favor of the female sex; for, in the period of our youth, it is the highest ambition of every man to make himself agreeable, acceptable to, and worthy of the other sex. The intelligence and refinement of woman, therefore, would secure the education and elevation of man, in the present generation, by the law of sexual attraction, while it would still more secure the improvement of both sexes of the coming generations, by the laws of hereditary descent.

As philosophers, recognizing the laws of the material and moral universe; as philanthropists, seeking the elevation and happiness of our species; as Christians, having faith in the goodness and wisdom of God, and in the temporal and eternal salvation of his children—we should work earnestly to undo the wrongs of ages, and give to woman that place in society for which God designed her; and that opportunity for the development of her gifts and graces which would secure her own happiness, fulfill the promise of the future, and make her the glory of the race, in that condition of social order and moral harmony to which all the attractions of humanity tend, and in which the highest earthly destiny of the human race shall be accomplished.—Thomas L. Nicholas.

Our selections are from masculine writers; and from hundreds of others, of the highest genius and most eminent fame, similar sentiments might be quoted. We are encouraged and guided by this popular opinion. THE LADY'S BOOK (including the Boston Lady's Magazine) was the first avowed advocate of the holy cause of woman's intellectual progress; it has been the pioneer in the wonderful change of public sentiment respecting female education, and the employment of female talent in the work of educating the young.

We intend to go on, sustained and accelerated by this universal encouragement, till our grand aim is accomplished, till female education shall receive the same careful attention and liberal support from public legislation as are bestowed on that of the other sex.

Such is the mission of the Lady's Book for 1850. Does not every Lady in America wish success to her own Book? We are sure its readers do; and, in return, this number is charged with the greetings of its editors to all their friends. May each and all enjoy a happy New Year!

Ar'n't I a Woman? Speech to the Women's Rights Convention in Akron, Ohio, 1851 (1851 and 1878)

From *The Anti-Slavery Bugle,* June 21, 1851

One of the most unique and interesting speeches of the Convention was made by Sojourner Truth, an emancipated slave. It is impossible to transfer it to paper, or convey any adequate idea of the effect it produced upon the audience. Those only can appreciate it who saw her powerful form, her whole-souled, earnest gesture, and listened to her strong and truthful tones. She came forward to the platform and addressing the President said with great simplicity: "May I say a few words?" Receiving an affirmative answer, she proceeded:

I want to say a few words about this matter. I am a woman's rights. I have as much muscle as any man, and can do as much work as any man. I have plowed and reaped and husked and chopped and mowed, and can any man do more than that? I have heard much about the sexes being equal. I can carry as much as any man, and can eat as much too, if I can get it. I am as strong as any man that is now. As for intellect, all I can say is, if woman have a pint, and man a quart—why can't she have her little pint full? You need not be afraid to give us our rights for fear we will take too much,—for we can't take more than our pint'll hold. The poor men seem to be all in confusion, and don't know what to do. Why children, if you have woman's rights, give it to her and you will feel better. You will have your own rights, and they won't be so much trouble. I can't read, but I can hear. I have heard the bible and have learned that Eve caused man to sin. Well, if woman upset the world, do give her a chance to set it right side up again. The Lady has spoken about Jesus, how he never spurned woman from him, and she was right. When Lazarus died, Mary and Martha came to him with faith and love and besought him to raise their brother. And Jesus wept and Lazarus came forth. And how came Jesus into the world? Through God who created him and a woman who bore him. Man, where is your part? But the women are coming up blessed be God and a few of the men are coming up with them. But man is in a tight place, the poor slave is on him, woman is coming on him, he is surely between a hawk and a buzzard.

From *The Narrative of Sojourner Truth,* 1878

In the year 1851 she left her home in Northampton, Mass., for a lecturing tour in Western New York. accompanied by the Hon. George Thompson of England, and other distinguished abolitionists. To advocate the cause of the enslaved at this period was both unpopular and unsafe. Their meetings were frequently disturbed or broken up by the pro-slavery mob, and their lives imperiled. At such times, Sojourner fearlessly maintained her ground, and by her dignified manner and opportune remarks would disperse the rabble and restore order.

She spent several months in Western New York, making Rochester her head-quarters. Leaving this State, she traveled westward, and the next glimpse we get of her is in a Woman's Rights Convention at Akron, Ohio. Mrs. Frances D. Gage, who presided at that meeting, relates the following:—

"The cause was unpopular then. The leaders of the movement trembled on seeing a tall, gaunt black woman, in a gray dress and white turban, surmounted by an uncouth sun-bonnet, march deliberately into the church, walk with the air of a queen up the aisle, and take her seat upon the pulpit steps. A buzz of disapprobation was heard all over the house, and such words as these fell upon listening ears:

"'An abolition affair!' 'Woman's rights and niggers!' 'We told you so!' 'Go it, old darkey!'

"I chanced upon that occasion to wear my first laurels in public life as president of the meeting. At my request, order was restored and the business of the hour went on. The morning session was held; the evening exercises came and went. Old Sojourner, quiet and reticent as the 'Libyan Statue,' sat crouched against the wall on the corner of the pulpit stairs, her sun-bonnet shading her eyes, her elbows on her knees, and her chin resting upon her broad, hard palm. At intermission she was busy, selling "*The Life of Sojourner Truth*," a narrative of her own strange and adventurous life. Again and again timorous and trembling ones came to me and said with earnestness, 'Don't let her speak, Mrs. Gage, it will ruin us. Every newspaper in the land will have our cause mixed with abolition and niggers, and we shall be utterly denounced.' My only answer was, 'We shall see when the time comes.'

"The second day the work waxed warm. Methodist, Baptist, Episcopal, Presbyterian, and Universalist ministers came in to hear and discuss the resolutions presented. One claimed superior rights and privileges for man on the ground of superior intellect; another, because of the manhood of Christ. 'If God had desired the equality of woman, he would have given some token of his will through the birth, life, and death of the Saviour.' Another gave us a theological view of the sin of our first mother. There were few women in those days that dared to 'speak in meeting,' and the august teachers of the people were seeming to get the better of us, while the boys in the galleries and the sneerers among the pews were hugely enjoying the discomfiture, as they supposed, of the 'strong minded.' Some of the tender-skinned friends were on the point of losing dignity, and the atmosphere of the convention betokened a storm.

"Slowly from her seat in the corner rose Sojourner Truth, who, till now, had scarcely lifted her head. 'Don't let her speak!' gasped half a dozen in my ear. She moved slowly and solemnly to the front, laid her old bonnet at her feet, and turned her great, speaking eyes to me. There was a hissing sound of disapprobation above and below. I rose and announced 'Sojourner Truth,' and begged the audience to keep silence for a few moments. The tumult subsided at once, and every eye was fixed on this almost Amazon form, which stood nearly six feet high, head erect, and eye piercing the upper air, like one in a dream. At her first word, there was a profound hush. She spoke in deep tones, which, though not loud, reached every ear in the house, and away through the throng at the doors and windows:—

"'Well, chilern, whar dar is so much racket dar must be something out o' kilter. I tink dat 'twixt de niggers of de Souf and de women at de Norf all a talkin' 'bout rights, de white men will be in a fix pretty soon. But what's all dis here talkin' 'bout? Dat man ober dar say dat women needs to be helped into carriages, and lifted ober ditches, and to have de best place every whar. Nobody eber help me into carriages, or ober mud puddles, or gives me any best place [and raising herself to her full height and her voice to a pitch like rolling thunder, she asked], and ar'n't I a woman? Look at me! Look at my arm! [And she bared her right arm to the shoulder, showing her tremendous muscular power.] I have plowed, and planted, and gathered into barns, and no man could head me—and ar'n't I a woman? I could work as much and eat as much as a man (when I could get it), and bear de lash as well—and ar'nt I a woman? I have borne thirteen chilern and seen 'em mos' all sold off into slavery, and when I cried out with a mother's grief, none but Jesus heard—and ar'n't I a woman? Den dey talks 'bout dis ting in de head—what dis dey call it?' 'Intellect,' whispered some one near. 'Dat's it honey. What's dat got to do with women's rights or niggers' rights? If my cup won't hold but a pint and yourn holds a quart, wouldn't ye be mean not to let me have my little half-measure full?' And she pointed her significant finger and sent a keen glance at the minister who had made the argument. The cheering was long and loud.

"'Den dat little man in black dar, he say women can't have as much rights as man, cause Christ want a woman. Whar did your Christ come from?' Rolling thunder could not have stilled that crowd as did those deep, wonderful tones, as she stood there with outstretched arms and eye of fire. Raising her voice still louder, she repeated, 'Whar did your Christ come from? From God and a woman. Man had nothing to do with him.' Oh! what a rebuke she gave the little man.

" 'Turning again to another objector, she took up the defense of mother Eve. I cannot follow her through it all. It was pointed, and witty, and solemn, eliciting at almost every sentence deafening applause; and she ended by asserting that 'if de fust woman God ever made was strong enough to turn the world upside down, all 'lone, dese togedder [and she glanced her eye over us], ought to be able to turn it back and get it right side up again, and now dey is asking to do it, de men better let em.' Long-continued cheering. 'Bleeged to ye for hearin' on me, and now ole Sojourner ha'n't got nothing more to say.'

"Amid roars of applause, she turned to her corner, leaving more than one of us with streaming eyes and hearts beating with gratitude. She had taken us up in her strong arms and carried us safely over the slough of difficulty, turning the whole tide in our favor. I have never in my life seen anything like the magical influence that subdued the mobbish spirit of the day and turned the jibes and sneers of an excited crowd into notes of respect and admiration. Hundreds rushed up to shake hands, and congratulate the glorious old mother and bid her God speed on her mission of 'testifying again concerning the wickedness of this 'ere people.'"

ABRAHAM LINCOLN

Letter to Horace Greeley (August 22, 1862)

Hon. Horace Greeley: Executive Mansion,
Dear Sir   Washington, August 22, 1862.
I have just read yours of the 19th, addressed to myself through the New-York Tribune. If there be in it any statements, or assumptions of fact, which I may know to be erroneous, I do not, now and here, controvert them. If there be in it any inferences which I may believe to be falsely drawn, I do not now and here, argue against them. If there be perceptable in it an impatient and dictatorial tone, I waive it in deference to an old friend, whose heart I have always supposed to be right.

As to the policy I "seem to be pursuing" as you say, I have not meant to leave any one in doubt.

I would save the Union. I would save it the shortest way under the Constitution. The sooner the national authority can be restored; the nearer the Union will be "the Union as it was." If there be those who would not save the Union, unless they could at the same time *save* slavery, I do not agree with them. If there be those who would not save the Union unless they could at the same time *destroy* slavery, I do not agree with them. My paramount object in this struggle *is* to save the Union, and is *not* either to save or to destroy slavery. If I could save the Union without freeing *any* slave I would do it, and if I could save it by freeing *all* the slaves I would do it; and if I could save it by freeing some and leaving others alone I would also do that. What I do about slavery, and the colored race, I do because I believe it helps to save the Union; and what I forbear, I forbear because I do *not* believe it would help to save the Union. I shall do *less* whenever I shall believe what I am doing hurts the cause, and I shall do *more* whenever I shall believe doing more will help the cause. I shall try to correct errors when shown to be errors; and I shall adopt new views so fast as they shall appear to be true views.

I have here stated my purpose according to my view of *official* duty; and I intend no modification of my oft-expressed *personal* wish that all men every where could be free. Yours,
                                                                       A. Lincoln

Abraham Lincoln

Emancipation Proclamation (January 1, 1863)

. . . Whereas on the 22d day of September, A.D. 1862, a proclamation was issued by the President of the United States, containing, among other things, the following, to wit:

"That on the 1st day of January, A.D. 1863, all persons held as slaves within any State or designated part of a State the people whereof shall them be in rebellion against the United States shall be then, thenceforward, and forever free; and the executive government of the United States, including the military and naval authority thereof, will recognize and maintain the freedom of such persons and will do no act or acts to repress such persons, or any of them, in any efforts they may make for their actual freedom.

"That the executive will on the 1st day of January aforesaid, by proclamation, designate the State and parts of States, if any, in which the people thereof, respectively, shall then be in rebellion against the United States; and the fact that any State or the people thereof shall on that day be in good faith represented in the Congress of the United States by members chosen thereto at elections wherein a majority of the qualified voters of such States shall have participated shall, in the absence of strong countervailing testimony, be deemed conclusive evidence that such State and the people thereof are not then in rebellion against the United States."

Now, therefore, I, Abraham Lincoln, President of the United States, by virtue of the power in me vested as Commander-in-Chief of the Army and Navy of the United States in time of actual armed rebellion against the authority and government of the United States, and as a fit and necessary war measure for suppressing said rebellion, do, on this 1st day of January, AD. 1863, and in accordance with my purpose so to do, publicly proclaimed for the full period of hundred days from the first day above mentioned, order and designate as the States and parts of States wherein the people thereof, respectively, are this day in rebellion against the United States the following, to wit:

Arkansas, Texas, Louisiana (except the parishes of St. Bernard, Plaquemines, Jefferson, St. John, St. Charles . . . and Orleans, including the city of New Orleans), Mississippi, Alabama, Florida, Georgia, South Carolina, North Carolina, and Virginia (except the forty-eight counties designated as West Virginia, and also the counties of Berkeley, Accomac, Northampton, Elizabeth City, York, Princess Anne, and Norfolk, including the cities of Norfolk and Portsmouth), and which excepted parts are for the present left precisely as if this proclamation were not issued.

And by virtue of the power and for the purpose aforesaid, I do order and declare that all persons held as slaves within said designated States and parts of States are, and henceforward shall be, free; and that the Executive Government of the United States, including the military and naval authorities thereof, will recognize and maintain the freedom of said persons.

And I hereby enjoin upon the people so declared to be free to abstain from all violence, unless in necessary self-defense; and I recommend to them that, in all cases when allowed, they labor faithfully for reasonable wages.

And I further declare and make known that such persons of suitable conditions will be received into the armed service of the United States to garrison forts, positions, stations, and other places, and to man vessels of all sorts in said service.

And upon this act, sincerely believed to be an act of justice, warranted by the Constitution upon military necessity, I invoke the considerate judgment of mankind and the gracious favor of Almighty God. . . .

Abraham Lincoln

Gettysburg Address (November 19, 1863)

Four score and seven years ago our fathers brought forth on this continent, a new nation, conceived in Liberty, and dedicated to the proposition that all men are created equal.

Now we are engaged in a great civil war, testing whether that nation, or any nation so conceived and so dedicated, can long endure. We are met on a great battle-field of that war. We have come to dedicate a portion of that field, as a final resting place for those who here gave their lives that that nation might live. It is altogether fitting and proper that we should do this.

But, in a larger sense, we can not dedicate—we can not consecrate—we can not hallow—this ground. The brave men, living and dead, who struggled here, have consecrated it, far above our poor power to add or detract. The world will little note, nor long remember what we say here, but it can never forget what they did here. It is for us the living, rather, to be dedicated here to the unfinished work which they who fought here have thus far so nobly advanced. It is rather for us to be here dedicated to the great task remaining before us—that from these honored dead we take increased devotion to that cause for which they gave the last full measure of devotion—that we here highly resolve that these dead shall not have died in vain—that this nation, under God, shall have a new birth of freedom—and that government of the people, by the people, for the people, shall not perish from the earth.

Abraham Lincoln
November 19, 1863

ABRAHAM LINCOLN

Second Inaugural Address (March 4, 1865)

Fellow Countrymen:

At this second appearing to take the oath of the presidential office, there is less occasion for an extended address than there was at the first. Then a statement, somewhat in detail, of a course to be pursued, seemed fitting and proper. Now, at the expiration of four years, during which public declarations have been constantly called forth on every point and phase of the great contest which still absorbs the attention, and engrosses the enerergies [*sic*] of the nation, little that is new could be presented. The progress of our arms, upon which all else chiefly depends, is as well known to the public as to myself; and it is, I trust, reasonably satisfactory and encouraging to all. With high hope for the future, no prediction in regard to it is ventured.

On the occasion corresponding to this four years ago, all thoughts were anxiously directed to an impending civil-war. All dreaded it—all sought to avert it. While the inaugural address was being delivered from this place, devoted altogether to *saving* the Union without war, insurgent agents were in the city seeking to *destroy* it without war—seeking to dissol[v]e the Union, and divide effects, by negotiation. Both parties deprecated war; but one of them would *make* war rather than let the nation survive; and others would *accept* war rather than let it perish. And the war came.

One eighth of the whole population were colored slaves, not distributed generally over the Union, but localized in the Southern part of it. These slaves constituted a peculiar and powerful interest. All knew that this interest was, somehow, the cause of the war. To strengthen, perpetuate, and extend this interest was the object for which the insurgents would rend the Union, even by war; while the government claimed no right to do more than to restrict the territorial enlargement of it. Neither party expected for the war, the magnitude, or the duration, which it has already attained. Neither anticipated that the *cause* of the conflict might cease with, or even before, the conflict itself should cease. Each looked for an easier triumph, and a result less fundamental and astounding. Both read the same Bible, and pray to the same God; and each invokes His aid against the other. It may seem strange that any men should dare ask a just God's assistance in wringing their bread from the sweat of other men's faces; but let us judge not that we will be not judged. The prayers of both could not be answered; that of neither has been answered fully. The Almighty has His own purposes. "Woe unto the world because of offences! for it must needs be that offences come; but woe to that man by whom the offence cometh!" If we shall suppose that American Slavery is one of those offences which, in the providence of God, must needs come, but which, having continued through His appointed time, He now wills to remove, and that He gives to both North and South, this terrible war, as the woe due to those by whom the offence came, shall we discern therein any departure from those divine attributes which the believers in a Living God always ascribe to Him? Fondly do we hope—fervently do we pray—that this mighty scourge of war may speedily pass away. Yet, if God wills that it continue, until all the wealth piled by the bond-man's two hundred and fifty years of unrequited toil shall be sunk, and until every drop of blood drawn with the lash, shall be paid by another drawn with the sword, as was said three thousand years ago, so still it must be said "the judgments of the Lord, are true and righteous altogether."

With malice toward none; with charity for all; with firmness in the right, as God gives us to see the right, let us strive on to finish the work we are in; to bind up the nation's wounds; to care for him who shall have borne the battle, and for his widow, and his orphan—to do all which may achieve and cherish a just, and a lasting peace, among ourselves, and with all nations.

March 4, 1865

5. Defining "American" amid Social Change, 1865–1920

American Progress, 1874 by John Gast. Copyright © 2000 by Christie's Images, New York. Courtesy of Christie's Images.

The artist John Gast painted *American Progress* in the very years when gold was discovered in the Black Hills of the Dakota Territory. This discovery set off new warfare between the Sioux and the U.S. Army, which had turned its energies to Indian wars once the Civil War ended. Made into a lithograph, Gast's painting soon found its way into the pages of an American geography book. Like Asher B. Durand's 1853 *Progress*, this painting suggested American development. Here, however, everything seems in motion. The hunters in the foreground, the covered wagon and stagecoach and trains in the middleground, even the farmers tilling the land and tending the cattle: all seem to move west. The Indians on the left, along with the buffalo behind them, appear to flee this "progress." And above the scene floats Lady Liberty, an American star in her flaxen hair, a book in her hand, as she strings telegraph wire from pole to pole across the continent. Images such as this one portrayed American progress not just as the triumph of American transportation, communication, and economy, but also as a masculine drive west. The only woman here is an allegorical figure, the representation of the United States as a goddess. Not all is harmonious here: note how the sky moves from sunshine in the east to smoky clouds in the west. Was this the gunsmoke of the Indian wars? Perhaps, but Gast's *American Progress* is what takes place after the West is won— or, from the Indians' perspective, lost: now light can come to the "wilderness," a familiar refrain in late-nine-

Chronology

1862:   Homestead Act makes free land available to settlers

1865–1870:   13th, 14th, and 15th Amendments to Constitution ratified

1874–1875:   Sioux battles in Black Hills of Dakotas

1876:   Alexander Graham Bell patents the telephone

1881:   Helen Hunt Jackson, *A Century of Dishonor*
Booker T. Washington founds Tuskegee Institute, Alabama

1882:   Chinese Exclusion Act passed

1887:   Dawes Severalty Act

1888:   Edward Bellamy, *Looking Backward*

1889:   Jane Addams founds Hull-House in Chicago

1890:   U.S. census announces end of the frontier line

1890s–1915:   Progressive Era in local and state governments: municipal services, anti-corruption drives

1896:   *Plessy v. Ferguson* decision upholds racial segregation

1898:   Spanish-American War

1901:   Theodore Roosevelt becomes President

1901–1915:   Progressive Era in national government: conservation, Pure Food & Drug Act, anti-trust actions

1903:   U.S. obtains Panama Canal rights (canal opens 1914)

1909:   National Association for the Advancement of Colored People (NAACP) founded

1914–1918:   World War I in Europe (U.S. involvement 1917–1918)

1919:   18th Amendment (Prohibition) ratified

1920:   19th Amendment (woman suffrage) ratified

Introduction

The implications contained in the 1890 report of the Bureau of the Census were sobering. The enumeration of the population had indicated that there no longer existed a frontier region remaining to be explored and settled. Demographers found that they could not draw a line through a map of the United States to identify any major region with fewer than two white persons per square mile. One of the great stories of human migration was coming to an end: the story in Nathaniel Currier and James Ives's popular 1868 lithograph *Across the Continent: "Westward the Course of Empire Takes Its Way"* had occurred from the old frontiers of the Great Lakes to the newest ones in the Rocky Mountain states. As the twentieth century approached, this development forced Americans to think about the future from a new perspective, that of a society dominated by industrial production and large cities. Horace Greeley's oft-quoted admonition to the urban poor of New York City—"Go West, young man, Go West"—no longer rang true. Americans now had to look elsewhere for a haven from the dangers and constraints of a society increasingly affected by technological change and governed by bureaucratic institutions. How could such a society reconcile its profoundly altered conditions with its earlier concepts of individual opportunity? And could new forms of technology and social organization—sometimes promising, sometimes threatening—be harnessed for the good of mankind?

Consolidation, the creation of an entirely new scale of operation, was the overarching theme of the fifty-five years after the Civil War. In some ways, what happened between 1865 and 1920 continued and escalated what had started before the war: the growth of factories, the beginnings of an immigrant working class, the advance of the railroads. But it was quantitatively different. By 1900, some railroad companies had work forces in the tens of thousands; industrial work possessed an increasing anonymity, a decreasing sense of craft. And twenty-five million immigrants—more than the nation's entire population in 1850—came to the United States between 1865 and 1915, most of them from countries in southern and eastern Europe whose inhabitants had never before left for America. The change was qualitatively different as well: stockholders without any personal connection to factory work owned the corporations that controlled industries like steel, coal, and railroads. Owners neither managed nor labored in the factories and mines that their capital had financed; in this development was born the modern corporate structure. Agriculture witnessed parallel changes: the new realities of the marketplace came to subvert Jefferson's vision of a peaceful, harmonious, and rewarding agrarian society dominated by an independent yeomanry. Controlled by remote national and international commodities markets, improved technologies that could drive small farmers out of business, and the national railroad network (the new middleman between farmers and the consumers of their products), farming in America was becoming another form of commerce, not a special way of life. Finally, urban America ballooned: in 1920, the U.S. census showed for the first time that a majority of Americans lived in cities.

For over fifty years, beginning in 1862, a Methodist minister named Russell H. Conwell (1843–1925) delivered a sermon called "Acres of Diamonds," to audiences across the United States. Conwell, the foremost proponent of the "Gospel of Wealth," argued that the United States afforded unlimited opportunities for those who followed the path of hard work and ingenuity—and that those who failed to find those opportunities were shirking their God-given duty. It is worth considering whether this sermon was as applicable when Conwell gave it in 1915 as it had been when he first wrote it. A similar philosophy emerged in "Social Darwinism," which applied Charles Darwin's biological theories to the social world. William Graham Sumner, the Yale professor who was

America's most prominent Social Darwinist, explained this doctrine in his best-selling *What Social Classes Owe to Each Other* (1883): "Certain ills belong to the hardships of human life. They are natural. They are a part of the struggle with Nature for existence. . . . We have never supposed that *laissez-faire* would give us perfect happiness." Both the Gospel of Wealth and Social Darwinism provided justifications for the late-nineteenth-century industrialists and tycoons who were consolidating the economy under their control.

At the same time, the domination of American society by a tiny number of successful entrepreneurs and businessmen—and those men's lavish uses of their enormous wealth—met with satire and criticism from other writers. Mark Twain and Charles Dudley Warner called the era "The Gilded Age," referring to the new millionaires' tendency to show off their wealth in extravagant consumption. Edward Bellamy (1850–1898) portrayed this society more harshly in his utopian novel *Looking Backward 2000–1887*, whose main character traveled in time to the year 2000, when the greed and inequality of the 1880s had been replaced by a technologically advanced, egalitarian America. In Bellamy's first chapter, printed here, this character describes American society, circa 1887.

Four centuries after Columbus's arrival in the New World, a young historian at the University of Wisconsin actually *was* looking backward—and forward. Frederick Jackson Turner (1861–1932) responded in 1893 to the census bureau's announcement by pondering the ways in which the frontier experience had shaped American values and institutions. Turner, who delivered his address "The Significance of the Frontier in American History" to the American Historical Association, was part of the new breed of college-trained professional men and women that included the social workers, engineers, and economists of his day. Like them and like Edward Bellamy, he subscribed to the idea that environment—the conditions in which a person lived—played at least as substantial a role in shaping experience as did individual characteristics. How would a new American environment, without the "frontier" of the past, shape citizens of the future?

Numerous reform movements, collectively known as "Progressivism," asked this question. "Progressive" reformers believed not only that environments helped shape the people who lived in them, but also that human beings could reshape those environments—and thus transform lives. They disagreed with Social Darwinists, who argued that the basic contours of society (such as "survival of the fittest") were fixed. Instead, Progressives believed that problems were often social rather than individual, solvable rather than intractable. Social science was among their most powerful tools: by studying a problem (often using quantitative methods), they believed, they could propose effective solutions. This Progressive movement both energized and transformed America. Political reformers battled the corruption of machine politicians, and social workers lobbied for tenement inspection laws, protection for laboring children and women, and a ten-hour day in mines and factories. Engineers designed new street and water systems, making sewer disposal and public parks a high form of public improvement. City managers sought to bring business expertise to the business of running America's cities. In all these realms, the "expert"—trained in newly professionalized social sciences like social work, engineering, nursing, and economics—became glorified. Early in the new century, President Theodore Roosevelt attempted to break up powerful monopolies with the anti-trust provisions of the Sherman Act, and when his trust-busting proved ineffective he turned to a "New Nationalism" to justify firmer federal control of America's corporations.

One of the first major social movements of the post-Civil-War years was "Indian reform." After the war, the United States moved most of its remaining army to the West, where railroad companies were crossing the Plains and Rockies and where scattered mineral strikes (such as gold in the South Dakota territory in the 1870s) attracted American citizens and companies seeking quick fortunes. In the process, Americans encountered the Native American tribes still living in those regions. The government's official policy in these years was "agency status": Indians were encouraged to become dependent on the federal Indian Bureau for their livelihood: giving up their lands, living on reservations maintained by the government, receiving food and other provisions from government agents. Resistance to these policies, as well as to encroaching white people, led to warfare between the Civil War and 1890. At the same time, white reformers argued that the United States had treated American Indians shamefully ever since the Revolution. *A Century of Dishonor*, a study by the poet and novelist Helen Hunt Jackson (1830–1885), galvanized the Indian reform movement. Jackson traced how the United States had broken all its treaties with Indian nations and then failed to provide adequately for Indians on reservations. This movement won the support of some Native American writers and speakers, including Sarah Winnemucca, a Northern Paiute woman from Nevada, who delivered speeches from San Francisco to Boston. Indian reformers believed in overhauling the reservation system by giving land to Indian heads of households or adult males. This proposal became law in the 1887 Dawes Severalty Act, encouraging Indians to practice agriculture and embrace private property. Reformers also wanted Indian children to be taught English, Christianity, and mechanical or agricultural skills. In short, their solution was "Americanization." Some Indians welcomed this plan. Others objected that the reformers, however well intentioned, sought to eradicate Indian cultures.

A similar debate ensued about—and among—the new immigrants. The largest number of immigrants lived in cities. No place housed more than New York City, where people of dozens of nationalities lived within a few square miles of each other, most of them in ethnic neighborhoods (which might be as small as a few square blocks). One of the most effective reports about everyday conditions in the new urban-industrial order came from the pen and camera of journalist Jacob Riis (1849–1914), a Danish immigrant who movingly informed his readers "how the other half lived" in the slums and tenements of New York City's Lower East Side. Along with fellow Progressives, Riis believed that improvements in living conditions could help immigrants survive and succeed. Equally important, Riis believed that immigrants should become "Americans" by attending public schools and adopting "American" ways. (He titled his own 1901 autobiography *The Making of an American*.) The author Abraham Cahan (1860–1951) was a Jewish immigrant from Vilna, Lithuania, who arrived in the United States on June 6, 1882. Like thousands of other immigrants, Cahan worked in factories and became involved in labor unions. Cahan became best known for his novels *Yekl, A Tale of the New York Ghetto* and *The Rise of David Levinsky*, which told of Eastern European immigrants. He also contributed regular newspaper articles to the *New York Commercial Advertiser*, two of which appear here. Like Riis's photos, these articles were created for a white, middle-class audience. But unlike Riis's pictures, Cahan's stories presented immigrants (including himself) as people with their own voices, helping to shape a new America as the nation became a world power.

What happened to immigrants' native cultures as these new Americans experienced the United States? The philosopher Horace Kallen (1882–1974) offered one theory. Kallen, the son of Latvian Jewish immigrants, spent much of his life considering what "American" meant to new immigrants, and the ways they could maintain their ethnic heritages in the United States. For Kallen, the issue was generational: the children and grandchildren of immigrants each moved through stages of "American-ness." We can see generational elements as well in the vernacular (or "folk") rhymes of Chinese immigrants. Chinese immigrants had a different experience than Europeans did. They had first come to the west coast in the 1850s, attracted by news of the gold rush; hence their term for America, "Jinshan" or "Gold Mountain." Mostly from the Cantonese region in southeastern China, these migrants engaged in a variety of economic pursuits: service industries in San Francisco, mines in eastern California and Nevada, railroad-building, farming. By 1870, however, prejudice against the Chinese rose as more white Americans migrated west to seek their own fortunes—an easier trip, thanks to the transcontinental railroad completed in 1869. In 1882 the

United States government passed the Chinese Exclusion Act restricting Chinese immigration. As the act was enforced, Chinese people in America were not allowed to become naturalized citizens or to own land. Other discriminatory laws—denying legal immigrants the right to re-enter the United States if they went home to visit families, arresting others for not carrying proper identification—encouraged many Chinese immigrants to leave. (It is worth noting that a large percentage of all immigrants, perhaps as many as one third, returned to their native countries: their aim was never to become "Americans.") In 1880, 132,000 Chinese lived in America; their population dropped under 90,000 by 1900 and to just 61,639 in 1920. Still, a Chinese community survived in northern California—complete with a literary culture that included Chinese-language schools, newspapers, and books, such as the *Jinshan ge ji* almanacs where the vernacular rhymes here first appeared in print. These verses have been translated from the Chinese language in which they were originally published; in their original Chinese, they had a 46-syllable pattern somewhat similar to certain types of Chinese folk songs. Individual writers are not known, because the almanacs did not identify them (following a traditional Chinese practice).

So the Northeast grew more urban and polyglot, and the West swelled with new residents while debating whether Native Americans and Chinese immigrants could become "American." What of the South? The region defeated in the Civil War experienced change of its own. Above all, a third of the southern population, enslaved before 1865, was now free. African Americans "owned themselves" now, and they sought to remake themselves as "Americans": citizens, independent producers, full-fledged families with legal marriages. The South itself remained predominantly agricultural, although the tobacco and textile industries expanded from the 1880s on. The end of Reconstruction ushered in a new period of white racism, characterized by violence and the attempt to strip African Americans of the rights supposedly guaranteed by the Fourteenth (citizenship) and Fifteenth (voting) Amendments to the Constitution. Most whites, including intellectuals and political reformers, North and South, ignored the problems of African Americans throughout these years. Blacks were subjected to a devastating system of segregation and discrimination—Jim Crow laws, a "separate but equal" doctrine established by the Supreme Court, systematic disenfranchisement, and the brutal lynching of several thousand blacks between 1890 and 1910. For all their reformist zeal, most Progressives failed to address these conditions. Reactions to these conditions by black leaders diverged. The major themes of that response are reflected in the conflicting views of Booker T. Washington (1856–1915) and W. E. B. DuBois (1868–1963), the preeminent African American leaders of the era. Washington, an educator who founded Tuskegee Institute in Alabama for African Americans, delivered his most famous address before an all-white audience at the Atlanta Exposition of 1895. DuBois, the first African American to receive a doctorate from Harvard University and one of the founders of the National Association for the Advancement of Colored People, became Washington's harshest critic.

Women were prominent among Progressive reformers; in the process of combating social ills, many women became increasingly attuned to their own unequal place in American society. Charlotte Perkins Stetson Gilman (1860–1935), the nation's foremost feminist speaker and writer, echoed the languages of Darwinian theory and social science. Her 1900 book *Women and Economics*, subtitled "A Study of the Economic Relation Between Men and Women as a Factor in Social Evolution," described women's place in society and how it was changing. One element of the change lay in education: after the Civil War, an increasing number of American women attended college—and found careers in the emerging social-science professions. To be sure, these were mostly middle- and upper-class women, but many of them turned their attention to the lives of their less-privileged sisters: the women (and their children) who worked for meager wages in sweatshops and factories, the immigrant women seeking to raise children in a new land. Through social-scientific investigations, they helped expose labor conditions and pushed for child-labor laws; they founded "settlement houses" to assist and educate working-class and immigrant women and families. One of these college-educated, middle-class women was Margaret Murray Washington (1865–1825), Booker T. Washington's wife. A graduate of Fisk University (an African-American college established after the Civil War), she became "lady principal" at her future husband's Tuskegee Institute in 1890. She helped found the Tuskegee Woman's Club (1895) and the National Federation of Afro-American Women (1896), and served as president of the National Association of Colored Women from 1912 to 1918. In a 1904 article in *Outlook* magazine, Washington wrote mainly about educated women like herself—but she also referred to the situation of more ordinary African-American women. Some of these women reformers led the renewed movement for woman suffrage, granted in the Nineteenth Amendment to the Constitution (1920). But women's participation in Progressivism was far broader than suffrage.

The final voice in this chapter belongs to another college-educated woman. Jane Addams (1860–1935) founded Hull-House, a settlement house in Chicago, in 1889 and remained its resident director until she died forty-six years later. Nobody had created the profession of "social work" yet, but Addams became effectively America's first great social worker—and the first woman to win the Nobel Peace Prize, in 1931. As she wrote in true Progressive spirit, "The Settlement then, is an experimental effort to aid in the solution of the social and industrial problems which are engendered by the modern conditions of life in a great city." Every day 2,000 people came to Hull-House: children for art or dance or exercise classes, men and women out of work or seeking practical education, immigrants and native-born Americans, parents and children. Scholars from universities used Hull-House as a laboratory for the social sciences; leaders of Chicago society visited. In short, Addams and Hull-House sought to bridge the gap between society's "halves," the groups that were becoming so separate as America became ever more urban, ever more industrial, ever more polyglot.

RUSSELL CONWELL

from "Acres of Diamonds" (1862)

. . . I often wish I could see the younger people, and would that the Academy had been filled tonight with our high-school scholars, and our grammar-school scholars, that I could have them to talk to. While I would have preferred such an audience as that, because they are most susceptible, as they have not grown up into their prejudices as we have, they have not gotten into any custom that they cannot break, they have not met with any failures as we have; and while I could perhaps do such an audience as that more good than I can do grown-up people, yet I will do the best I can with the material I have. I say to you that you have 'acres of diamonds' in Philadelphia right where you now live. 'Oh,' but you say, 'you cannot know much about your city if you think there are any "acres of diamonds" here'. . . .

[T]he opportunity to get rich, to attain unto great wealth, is here in Philadelphia now, within the reach of almost every man and woman who hears me speak tonight, and I mean just what I say. I have not come to this platform even under these circumstances to recite something to you. I have come to tell you what in God's sight I believe to be the truth, and if the years of life have been of any value to me in the attainment of common sense, I know I am right; that the men and women sitting here, who found it difficult perhaps to buy a ticket to this lecture or gathering to-night, have within their reach 'acres of diamonds,' opportunities to get largely wealthy. There never was a place on earth more adapted than the city of Philadelphia to-day, and never in the history of the world did a poor man without capital have such an opportunity to get rich quickly and honestly as he has now in our city. I say it is the truth, and I want you to accept it as such; for if you think I have come to simply recite something, then I would better not be here. I have no time to waste in any such talk, but to say the things I believe, and unless some of you get richer for what I am saying tonight my time is wasted.

I say that you ought to get rich, and it is your duty to get rich. How many of my pious brethren say to me, 'Do you, a Christian minister, spend your time going up and down the country advising young people to get rich, to get money?' 'Yes, of course I do.' They say, 'Isn't that awful! Why don't you preach the gospel instead of preaching about man's making money?' 'Because to make money honestly is to preach the gospel.' That is the reason. The men who get rich may be the most honest men you find in the community.

'Oh,' but says some young man here to-night, 'I have been told all my life that if a person has money he is very dishonest and dishonorable and mean and contemptible.' My friend, that is the reason why you have none, because you have that idea of people. The foundation of your faith is altogether false. Let me say here clearly, and say it briefly, though subject to discussion which I have not time for here, ninety-eight out of one hundred of the rich men of America are honest. That is why they are rich. That is why they are trusted with money. That is why they carry on great enterprises and find plenty of people to work with them. . . .

For a man to have money, even in large sums, is not an inconsistent thing. We preach against covetousness, and you know we do, in the pulpit, and oftentimes preach against it so long and use the terms about 'filthy lucre' so extremely that Christians get the idea that when we stand in the pulpit we believe it is wicked for any man to have money . . . until the collection-basket goes around, and then we almost swear at the people because they don't give more money. Oh, the inconsistency of such doctrines as that!

Money is power, and you ought to be reasonably ambitious to have it. You ought because you can do more good with it than you could without it. Money printed your Bible, money builds your churches, money sends your missionaries, and money pays your preachers, and you would not have many of them, either, if you did not pay them. I am always willing that my church should raise my salary, because the church that pays the largest salary always raises it the easiest. You never knew an exception to it in your life. The man who gets the largest salary can do the most good with the power that is furnished to him. Of course he can if his spirit be right to use it for what it is given to him.

I say, then, you ought to have money. If you can honestly attain unto riches in Philadelphia, it is your Christian and godly duty to do so. It is an awful mistake of these pious people to think you must be awfully poor in order to be pious.

Some men say, 'Don't you sympathize with the poor people?' Of course I do, or else I would not have been lecturing these years. I won't give in but what I sympathize with the poor, but the number of poor who are to be sympathized with is very small. To sympathize with a man whom God has punished for his sins, thus to help him when God would still continue a just punishment, is to do wrong, no doubt about it, and we do that more than we help those who are deserving. While we should sympathize with God's poor—that is, those who cannot help themselves—let us remember there is not a poor person in the United States who was not made poor by his own shortcomings, or by the shortcomings of someone else. It is all wrong to be poor, anyhow. . . .

I think I will leave that behind me now and answer the question of nearly all of you who are asking, 'Is there opportunity to get rich in Philadelphia?' Well, now, how simple a thing it is to see where it is, and the instant you see where it is it is yours. Some old gentleman gets up back there and says, 'Mr. Conwell, have you lived in Philadelphia for thirty-one years and don't know that the time has gone by when you can make anything in this city?' 'No, I don't think it is.' 'Yes, it is; I have tried it.' 'What business are you in?' 'I kept a store here for twenty years, and never made over a thousand dollars in the whole twenty years.'

'Well, then, you can measure the good you have been to this city by what this city has paid you, because a man can judge very well what he is worth by what he receives; that is, in what he is to the world at this time. If you have not made over a thousand dollars in twenty years in Philadelphia, it would have been better for Philadelphia if they had kicked you out of the city nineteen years and nine months ago. A man has no right to keep a store in Philadelphia twenty years and not make at least five hundred thousand dollars, even though it be a corner grocery up-town.' You say, 'You cannot make five thousand dollars in a store now.' Oh, my friends, if you will just take only four blocks around you, and find out what the people want and what you ought to supply and set them down with your pencil, and figure up the profits you would make if you did supply them, you would very soon see it. There is wealth right within the sound of your voice. . . .

But let me hasten to one other greater thought. 'Show me the great men and women who live in Philadelphia.' A gentleman over there will get up and say: 'We don't have any great men in Philadelphia. They don't live here. They live away off in Rome or St. Petersburg or London or Manayunk, or anywhere else but here in our town.' I have come now to the apex of my thought. I have come now to the heart of the whole matter and to the center of my struggle: Why isn't Philadelphia a greater city in its greater wealth? Why does New York excel Philadelphia? People say, 'Because of her harbor.' Why do many other cities of the United States get ahead of Philadelphia now? There is only one answer, and that is because our own people talk down their own city.

If there ever was a community on earth that has to be forced ahead, it is the city of Philadelphia. If we are to have a boulevard, talk it down; if we are going to have better schools, talk them down; if you wish to have wise legislation, talk it down; talk all the proposed improvements down. That is the only great wrong that I can lay at the feet of the magnificent Philadelphia that has been so universally kind to me. I say it is time we turn around in our city and begin to talk up the things that are in our city, and begin to set them before the world as the people of Chicago, New York, St. Louis, and San Francisco do. Oh, if we only could get that spirit out among our people, that we can do things in Philadelphia and do them well! . . .

FREDERICK JACKSON TURNER

from "The Significance of the Frontier in American History" (1893)

In a recent bulletin of the Superintendent of the Census for 1890 appear these significant words: "Up to and including 1880 the country had a frontier of settlement, but at present the unsettled area has been so broken into by isolated bodies of settlement that there can hardly be said to be a frontier line. In the discussion of its extent, its westward movement, etc., it can not, therefore, any longer have a place in the census reports." This brief official statement marks the closing of a great historic movement. Up to our own day American history has been in a large degree the history of the colonization of the Great West. The existence of an area of free land, its continuous recession, and the advance of American settlement westward, explain American development.

Behind institutions, behind constitutional forms and modifications, lie the vital forces that call these organs into life and shape them to meet changing conditions. The peculiarity of American institutions is, the fact that they have been compelled to adapt themselves to the changes of an expanding people—to the changes involved in crossing a continent, in winning a wilderness, and in developing at each area of this progress out of the primitive economic and political conditions of the frontier into the complexity of city life. Said Calhoun in 1817, "We are great, and rapidly—I was about to say fearfully—growing!" So saying, he touched the distinguishing feature of American life. All peoples show development; the germ theory of politics has been sufficiently emphasized. In the case of most nations, however, the development has occurred in a limited area; and if the nation has expanded, it has met other growing peoples whom it has conquered. But in the case of the United States we have a different phenomenon. Limiting our attention to the Atlantic coast, we have the familiar phenomenon of the evolution of institutions in a limited area, such as the rise of representative government; the differentiation of simple colonial governments into complex organs; the progress from primitive industrial society, without division of labor, up to manufacturing civilization. But we have in addition to this a recurrence of the process of evolution in each western area reached in the process of expansion. Thus American development has exhibited not merely advance along a single line, but a return to primitive conditions on a continually advancing frontier line, and a new development for that area. American social development has been continually beginning over again on the frontier. This perennial rebirth, this fluidity of American life, this expansion westward with its new opportunities, its continuous touch with the simplicity of primitive society, furnish the forces dominating the American character. . . .

First we note that the frontier promoted the formation of a composite nationality for the American people. The coast was preponderantly English, but the later tides of continental immigration flowed across to the free lands. This was the case from the early colonial days. The Scotch-Irish and the Palatine Germans, or "Pennsylvania Dutch," furnished the dominant element in the stock of the colonial frontier. With these peoples were also the freed indented servants, or redemptioners, who at the expiration of their time of service passed to the frontier. . . . In the crucible of the frontier the immigrants were Americanized, liberated, and fused into a mixed race, English in neither nationality nor characteristics. The process has gone on from the early days to our own. . . .

The legislation which most developed the powers of the national government, and played the largest part in its activity, was conditioned on the frontier. Writers have discussed the subjects of tariff, land, and internal improvement, as subsidiary to the slavery question. But when American history comes to be rightly viewed it will be seen that slavery question is an incident. . . . The growth of nationalism and the evolution of American political institutions were dependent on the advance of the frontier. . . .

The pioneer needed the goods of the coast, and so the grand series of internal improvement and railroad legislation began, with potent nationalizing effects. Over internal improvements occurred great debates, in which grave constitutional questions were discussed. Sectional groupings appear in the votes, profoundly significant for the historian. Loose construction increased as the nation marched westward. But the West was not content with bringing the farm to the factory. Under the lead of Clay—"Harry of the West"—protective tariffs were passed, with the cry of bringing the factory to the farm. The disposition of the public lands was a third important subject of national legislation influenced by the frontier.

The public domain has been a force of profound importance in the nationalization and development of the government. The effects of the struggle of the landed and the landless States, and of the Ordinance of 1787, need no discussion. Administratively the frontier called out some of the highest and most vitalizing activities of the general government. The purchase of Louisiana was perhaps the constitutional turning point in the history of the Republic, inasmuch as it afforded both a new era for national legislation and the occasion of the downfall of the policy of strict construction. But the purchase of Louisiana was called out by frontier needs and demands. As frontier States accrued to the Union the national power grew. . . .

But it was not merely in legislative action that the frontier worked against the sectionalism of the coast. The economic and social characteristics of the frontier worked against sectionalism. The men of the frontier had closer resemblances to the Middle region than to either of the other sections. Pennsylvania had been the seed-plot of frontier emigration, and, although she passed on her settlers along the Great Valley into the west of Virginia and the Carolinas, yet the industrial society of these Southern frontiersmen was always more like that of the Middle region than like that of the tidewater portion of the South, which later came to spread its industrial type throughout the South.

The Middle region, entered by New York harbor, was an open door to all Europe. The tidewater part of the South represented typical Englishmen, modified by a warm climate and servile labor, and living in baronial fashion on great plantations; New England stood for a special English movement—Puritanism. The Middle region was less English than the other sections. It had a wide mixture of nationalities, a varied society, the mixed town and county system of local government, a varied economic life, many religious sects. In short, it was a region mediating between New England and the South, and the East and the West. It represented that composite nationality which the contemporary United States exhibits, that juxtaposition of non-English groups, occupying a valley or a little settlement, and presenting reflections of the map of Europe in their variety. It was democratic and nonsectional, if not national; "easy, tolerant, and contented"; rooted strongly in material prosperity. It was typical of the modern United States. . . .

But the most important effect of the frontier has been in the promotion of democracy here and in Europe. As has been indicated, the frontier is productive of individualism. Complex society is precipitated by the wilderness into a kind of primitive organization based on the family. The tendency is anti-social. It produces antipathy to control, and particularly to any direct control. The tax-gatherer is viewed as a representative of oppression. Prof. Osgood, in an able article, has pointed out that the frontier conditions prevalent in the colonies are important factors in the explanation of the American Revolution, where individual liberty was sometimes confused with absence of all effective government. The same conditions aid in explaining the difficulty of instituting a strong government in the period of the confederacy. The frontier individualism has from the beginning promoted democracy.

The frontier States that came into the Union in the first quarter of a century of its existence came in with democratic suffrage provisions, and had reactive effects of the highest importance upon the older States whose peoples were being attracted there. An extension of the franchise became essential. It was *western* New York that forced an extension of suffrage in the constitutional convention of that State in 1821; and it was *western* Virginia that compelled the tide-water region to put a more liberal suffrage provision in the constitution framed in 1830, and to give to the frontier region a more nearly proportionate representation with the tide-water aristocracy. The rise of democracy as an effective force in the nation came in with western preponderance under Jackson and William Henry Harrison, and it meant the triumph of the frontier—with all of its good and with all of its evil elements. . . .

So long as free land exists, the opportunity for a competency exists, and economic power secures political power. But the democracy born of free land, strong in selfishness and individualism, intolerant of administrative experience and education, and pressing individual liberty beyond its proper bounds, has its dangers as well as its benefits. Individualism in America has allowed a laxity in regard to governmental affairs which has rendered possible the spoils system and all the manifest evils that follow from the lack of a highly developed civic spirit. In this connection may be noted also the influence of frontier conditions in permitting lax business honor, inflated paper currency and wild-cat banking. The colonial and revolutionary frontier was the region whence emanated many of the worst forms of an evil currency. . . .

From the conditions of frontier life came intellectual traits of profound importance. The works of travelers along each frontier from colonial days onward describe certain common traits, and these traits have, while softening down, still persisted as survivals in the place of their origin, even when a higher social organization succeeded. The result is that to the frontier the American intellect owes its striking characteristics. That coarseness and strength combined with acuteness and inquisitiveness; that practical, inventive turn of mind, quick to find expedients; that masterful grasp of material things, lacking in the artistic but powerful to effect great ends; that restless, nervous energy; that dominant individualism, working for good and for evil, and withal that buoyancy and exuberance which comes with freedom—these are traits of the frontier, or traits called out elsewhere because of the existence of the frontier. Since the days when the fleet of Columbus sailed into the waters of the New World, America has been another name for opportunity, and the people of the United States have taken their tone from the incessant expansion which has not only been open but has even been forced upon them. He would be a rash prophet who should assert that the expansive character of American life has now entirely ceased. Movement has been its dominant fact, and, unless this training has no effect upon a people, the American energy will continually demand a wider field for its exercise. But never again will such gifts of free land offer themselves. For a moment, at the frontier, the bonds of custom are broken and unrestraint is triumphant. There is not *tabula rasa*. The stubborn American environment is there with its imperious summons to accept its conditions; the inherited ways of doing things are also there; and yet, in spite of environment, and in spite of custom, each frontier did indeed furnish a new field of opportunity, a gate of escape from the bondage of the past; and freshness, and confidence, and scorn of older society, impatience of its restraints and its ideas, and indifference to its lessons, have accompanied the frontier. What the Mediterranean Sea was to the Greeks, breaking the bond of custom, offering new experiences, calling out new institutions and activities, that, and more, the ever retreating frontier has been to the United States directly, and to the nations of Europe more remotely. And now, four centuries from the discovery of America, at the end of a hundred years of life under the Constitution, the frontier has gone, and with its going has closed the first period of American history.

Across the Continent: Westward the Course of Empire Takes Its Way, 1868 by Francis F. Palmer.
Courtesy of Thomas Gilcrease Institute of American History and Art.

HELEN HUNT JACKSON

from A Century of Dishonor (1881)

There are within the limits of the United States between two hundred and fifty and three hundred thousand Indians, exclusive of those in Alaska. The names of the different tribes and bands, as entered in the statistical tables of the Indian Office Reports, number nearly three hundred. One of the most careful estimates which have been made of their numbers and localities gives them as follows: "In Minnesota and States east of the Mississippi, about 32,500; in Nebraska, Kansas, and the Indian Territory, 70,650; in the Territories of Dakota, Montana, Wyoming, and Idaho, 65,000; in Nevada and the Territories of Colorado, New Mexico, Utah, and Arizona, 84,000; and on the Pacific slope, 48,000."

Of these, 130,000 are self-supporting on their own reservations, "receiving nothing from the Government except interest on their own moneys, or annuities granted them in consideration of the cession of their lands to the United States."*

This fact alone would seem sufficient to dispose forever of the accusation, so persistently brought against the Indian, that he will not work.

Of the remainder, 84,000 are partially supported by the Government—the interest money due them and their annuities, as provided by treaty, being inadequate to their subsistence on the reservations where they are confined. In many cases, however, these Indians furnish a large part of their support—the White River Utes, for instance, who are reported by the Indian Bureau as getting sixty-six percent of their living by "root-digging, hunting, and fishing;" the Squaxin band, in Washington Territory, as earning seventy-five percent, and the Chippewas of Lake Superior as earning fifty percent in the same way. These facts also would seem to dispose of the accusation that the Indian will not work.

There are about 55,000 who never visit an agency, over whom the Government does not pretend to have either control or care. These 55,000 "subsist by hunting, fishing, on roots, nuts, berries, etc., and by begging and stealing"; and this also seems to dispose of the accusation that the Indian will not "work for a living." There remains a small portion, about 31,000, that are entirely subsisted by the Government.

There is not among these three hundred bands of Indians one which has not suffered cruelly at the hands of either of the Government or of white settlers. The poorer, the more insignificant, the more helpless the band, the more certain the cruelty and outrage to which they have been subjected. This is especially true of the bands on the Pacific slope. These Indians found themselves of a sudden surrounded by and caught up in the great influx of gold-seeking settlers, as helpless creatures on a shore are caught up in a tidal wave. There was not time for the Government to make treaties; not even time for communities to make laws. The tale of the wrongs, the oppressions, the murders of the Pacific-slope Indians in the last thirty years would be a volume by itself, and is too monstrous to be believed.

---

*Annual Report of Indian Commission for 1872.

It makes little difference, however, where one opens the record of the history of the Indians; every page and every year has its dark stain. The story of one tribe is the story of all, varied only by differences of time and place; but neither time nor place makes any difference in the main facts. Colorado is as greedy and unjust in 1880 as was Georgia in 1830, and Ohio in 1795; and the United States Government breaks promises now as deftly as then, and with an added ingenuity from long practice.

One of its strongest supports in so doing is the wide-spread sentiment among the people of dislike to the Indian, of impatience with his presence as a "barrier to civilization," and distrust of it as a possible danger. The old tales of the frontier life, with its horrors of Indian warfare, have gradually, by two or three generations' telling, produced in the average mind something like an hereditary instinct of unquestioning and unreasoning aversion which it is almost impossible to dislodge or soften.

There are hundreds of pages of unimpeachable testimony on the side of the Indian; but it goes for nothing, is set down as sentimentalism or partisanship, tossed aside and forgotten.

President after president has appointed commission after commission to inquire into and report upon Indian affairs, and to make suggestions as to the best methods of managing them. The reports are filled with eloquent statements of wrongs done to the Indians, of perfidies on the part of the Government; they counsel, as earnestly as words can, a trial of the simple and unperplexing expedients of telling truth, keeping promises, making fair bargains, dealing justly in all ways and all things. These reports are bound up with the Government's Annual Reports, and that is the end of them. It would probably be no exaggeration to say that not one American citizen out of ten thousand ever sees them or knows that they exist, and yet any one of them, circulated throughout the country, read by the right-thinking, right-feeling men and women of this land, would be of itself a "campaign document" that would initiate a revolution which would not subside until the Indians' wrongs were, so far as is now left possible, righted.

In 1869 President Grant appointed a commission of nine men, representing the influence and philanthropy of six leading States, to visit the different Indian reservations, and to "examine all matters appertaining to Indian affairs."

In the report of this commission are such paragraphs as the following: "To assert that 'the Indian will not work' is as true as it would be to say that the white man will not work.

"Why should the Indian be expected to plant corn, fence lands, build houses, or do anything but get food from day to day, when experience has taught him that the product of his labor will be seized by the white man to-morrow? The most industrious white man would become a drone under similar circumstances. Nevertheless, many of the Indians" (the commissioners might more forcibly have said 130,000 of the Indians) "are already at work, and furnish ample refutation of the assertion that 'the Indian will not work.' There is no escape from the inexorable logic of facts.

"The history of the Government connections with the Indians is a shameful record of broken treaties and unfulfilled promises. The history of the border white man's connection with the Indians is a sickening record of murder, outrage, robbery, and wrongs committed by the former, as the rule, and occasional savage outbreaks and unspeakable barbarous deeds of retaliation by the latter, as the exception.

"Taught by the Government that they had rights entitled to respect, when those rights have been assailed by the rapacity of the white man, the arm which should have been raised to protect them has ever been ready to sustain the aggressor.

"The testimony of some of the highest military officers of the United States is on record to the effect that, in our Indian wars, almost without exception, the first aggressions have been made by the white man; and the assertion is supported by every civilian of reputation who has studied the subject. In addition to the class of robbers and outlaws who find impunity in their nefarious pursuits on the frontiers, there is a large class of professedly reputable men who use every means in their power to bring on Indian wars for the sake of the profit to be realized from the presence of troops and the expenditure of Government funds in their midst. They proclaim death to the Indians at all times in words and publications, making no distinction between the innocent and the guilty. They irate the lowest class of men to the perpetration of the darkest deeds against their victims, and as judges and jurymen shield them from the justice due to their crimes. Every crime committed by a white man against an Indian is concealed or palliated. Every offence committed by an Indian against a white man is borne on the wings of the post or the telegraph to the remotest corner of the land, clothed with all the horrors which the reality or imagination can throw around it. Against such influences as these the people of the United States need to be warned."

To assume that it would be easy, or by any one sudden stroke of legislative policy possible, to undo the mischief and hurt of the long past, set the Indian policy of the country right for the future, and make the Indians at once safe and happy, is the blunder of a hasty and uninformed judgment. The notion which seems to be growing more prevalent, that simply to make all Indians at once citizens of the United States would be a sovereign and instantaneous panacea for all their ills and all the Government's perplexities, is a very inconsiderate one. To administer complete citizenship of a sudden, all round, to all Indians, barbarous and civilized alike, would be as grotesque a blunder as to dose them all round with any one medicine, irrespective of the symptoms and needs of their diseases. It would kill more than it would cure. Nevertheless, it is true, as was well stated by one of the superintendents of Indian Affairs in 1857, that, "so long as they are not citizens of the United States, their rights of property must remain insecure against invasion. The doors of the federal tribunals being barred against them while wards and dependents, they can only exercise the rights of free government, or give to those who make, execute, and construe the few laws they are allowed to enact, dignity sufficient to make them respectable. While they continue individually to gather the crumbs that fall from the table of the United States, idleness, improvidence, and indebtedness will be the rule, and industry, thrift, and freedom from debt the exception. The utter absence of individual title to particular lands deprives every one among them of the chief incentive to labor and exertion—the very mainspring on which the prosperity of a people depends."

All judicious plans and measures for their safety and salvation must embody provisions for their becoming citizens as fast as they are fit, and must protect them till then in every right and particular in which our laws protect other "persons" who are not citizens.

There is a disposition in a certain class of minds to be impatient with any protestation against wrong which is unaccompanied or unprepared with a quick and exact scheme of remedy. This is illogical. When pioneers in a new country find a tract of poisonous and swampy wilderness to be reclaimed, they do not withhold their hands from fire and axe till they see clearly which way roads should run, where good water will spring, and what crops will best grow on the redeemed land. They first clear the swamp. So with this poisonous and baffling part of the domain of our national affairs—let us first "clear the swamp."

However great perplexity and difficulty there may be in the details of any and every plan possible for doing at this late day anything like justice to the Indian, however hard it may be for good statesmen and good men to agree upon the things that ought to be done, there certainly is, or ought to be, no perplexity whatever, no difficulty whatever, in agreeing upon certain things that ought not to be done, and which must cease to be done before the first steps can be taken toward righting the wrongs, curing the ills, and wiping out the disgrace to us of the present condition of our Indians.

Cheating, robbing, breaking promises—these three are clearly things which must cease to be done. One more thing, also, and that is the refusal of the protection of the law to the Indian's rights of property, "of life, liberty, and the pursuit of happiness."

When these four things have ceased to be done, time, statesmanship, philanthropy, and Christianity can slowly and surely do the rest. Till these four things have ceased to be done, statesmanship and philanthropy alike must work in vain, and even Christianity can reap but small harvest.

EDWARD BELLAMY

Looking Backward 2000–1887, Chapter I (1888)

I first saw the light in the city of Boston in the year 1857. "What!" you say, "eighteen fifty-seven? That is an odd slip. He means nineteen fifty-seven, of course." I beg pardon, but there is no mistake. It was about four in the afternoon of December the 26th, one day after Christmas, in the year 1857, not 1957, that I first breathed the east wind of Boston, which, I assure the reader, was at that remote period marked by the same penetrating quality characterizing it in the present year of grace, 2000.

These statements seem so absurd on their face, especially when I add that I am a young man apparently of about thirty years of age, that no person can be blamed for refusing to read another word of what promises to be a mere imposition upon his credulity. Nevertheless I earnestly assure the reader that no imposition is intended, and will undertake, if he shall follow me a few pages, to entirely convince him of this. If I may, then, provisionally assume, with the pledge of justifying the assumption, that I know better than the reader when I was born, I will go on with my narrative. As every schoolboy knows, in the latter part of the nineteenth century the civilization of to-day, or anything like it, did not exist, although the elements which were to develop it were already in ferment. Nothing had, however, occurred to modify the immemorial division of society into the four classes, or nations, as they may be more fitly called, since the differences between them were far greater than those between any nations nowadays, of the rich and the poor, the educated and the ignorant. I myself was rich and also educated, and possessed, therefore, all the elements of happiness enjoyed by the most fortunate in that age. Living in luxury, and occupied only with the pursuit of the pleasures and refinements of life, I derived the means of my support from the labor of others, rendering no sort of service in return. My parents and grand-parents had lived in the same way, and I expected that my descendants, if I had any, would enjoy a like easy existence.

But how could I live without service to the world? you ask. Why should the world have supported in utter idleness one who was able to render service? The answer is that my great-grandfather had accumulated a sum of money on which his descendants had ever since lived. The sum, you will naturally infer, must have been very large not to have been exhausted in supporting three generations in idleness. This, however, was not the fact. The sum had been originally by no means large. It was, in fact, much larger now that three generations had been supported upon it in idleness, than it was at first. This mystery of use without consumption, of warmth without combustion, seems like magic, but was merely an ingenious application of the art now happily lost but carried to great perfection by your ancestors, of shifting the burden of one's support on the shoulders of others. The man who had accomplished this, and it was the end all sought, was said to live on the income of his investments. To explain at this point how the ancient methods of industry made this possible would delay us too much. I shall only stop now to say that interest on investments was a species of tax in perpetuity upon the product of those engaged in industry which a person possessing or inheriting money was able to levy. It must not be supposed that an arrangement which seems so unnatural and preposterous according to modern notions was never criticised by your ancestors. It had been the effort of lawgivers and prophets from the earliest ages to abolish interest, or at least to limit it to the smallest possible rate. All these efforts had, however, failed, as they necessarily must so long as the ancient social organizations prevailed. At the time of which I write, the latter part of the nineteenth century, governments had generally given up trying to regulate the subject at all.

By way of attempting to give the reader some general impression of the way people lived together in those days, and especially of the relations of the rich and poor to one another, perhaps I cannot do better than to compare society as it then was to a prodigious coach which the masses of humanity were harnessed to and dragged toilsomely along a very hilly and sandy road. The driver was hunger, and permitted no lagging, though the pace was necessarily very slow. Despite the difficulty of drawing the coach at all along so hard a road, the top was covered with passengers who never got down, even at the steepest ascents. These seats on top were very breezy and comfortable. Well up out of the dust, their occupants could enjoy the scenery at their leisure, or critically discuss the merits of the straining team. Naturally such places were in great demand and the competition for them was keen, every one seeking as the first end in life to secure a seat on the coach for himself and to leave it to his child after him. By the rule of the coach a man could leave his seat to whom he wished, but on the other hand there were many accidents by which it might at any time be wholly lost. For all that they were so easy, the seats were very insecure, and at every sudden jolt of the coach persons were slipping out of them and falling to the ground, where they were instantly compelled to take hold of the rope and help to drag the coach on which they had before ridden so pleasantly. It was naturally regarded as a terrible misfortune to lose one's seat, and the apprehension that this might happen to them or their friends was a constant cloud upon the happiness of those who rode.

But did they think only of themselves? you ask. Was not their very luxury rendered intolerable to them by comparison with the lot of their brothers and sisters in the harness, and the knowledge that their own weight added to their toil? Had they no compassion for fellow beings from whom fortune only distinguished them? Oh, yes; commiseration was frequently expressed by those who rode for those who had to pull the coach, especially when the vehicle came to a bad place in the road, as it was constantly doing, or to a particularly steep hill. At such times, the desperate straining of the team, their agonized leaping and plunging under the pitiless lashing of hunger, the many who fainted at the rope and were trampled in the mire, made a very distressing spectacle, which often called forth highly creditable displays of feeling on the top of the coach. At such times the passengers would call down encouragingly to the toilers of the rope, exhorting them to patience, and holding out hopes of possible compensation in another world for the hardness of their lot, while others contributed to buy salves and liniments for the crippled and injured. It was agreed that it was a great pity that the coach should be so hard to pull, and there was a sense of general relief when the specially bad piece of road was gotten over. This relief was not, indeed, wholly on account of the team, for there was always some danger at these bad places of a general overturn in which all would lose their seats.

It must in truth be admitted that the main effect of the spectacle of the misery of the toilers at the rope was to enhance the passengers' sense of the value of their seats upon the coach, and to cause them to hold on to them more desperately than before. If the passengers could only have felt assured that neither they nor their friends would ever fall from the top, it is probable that, beyond contributing to the funds for liniments and bandages, they would have troubled themselves extremely little about those who dragged the coach.

I am well aware that this will appear to the men and women of the twentieth century an incredible inhumanity, but there are two facts, both very curious, which partly explain it. In the first place, it was firmly and sincerely believed that there was no other way in which Society could get along, except the many pulled at the rope and the few rode, and not only this, but that no very radical improvement even was possible, either in the harness, the coach, the roadway, or the distribution of the toil. It had always been as it was, and it always would be so. It was a pity, but it could not be helped, and philosophy forbade wasting compassion on what was beyond remedy.

The other fact is yet more curious, consisting in a singular hallucination which those on the top of the coach generally shared, that they were not exactly like their brothers and sisters who pulled at the rope, but of finer clay, in some way belonging to a higher order of beings who might justly expect to be drawn. This seems unaccountable, but, as I once rode on this very coach and shared that very hallucination, I ought to be believed. The strangest thing about the hallucination was that those who had but just climbed up from the ground, before they had outgrown the marks of the rope upon their hands, began to fall under its influence. As for those whose parents and grand-parents before them had been so fortunate as to keep their seats on the top, the conviction they cherished of the essential difference between their sort of humanity and the common article was absolute. The effect of such a delusion in moderating fellow feeling for the sufferings of the mass of men into a distant and philosophical compassion is obvious. To it I refer as the only extenuation I can offer for the indifference which, at the period I write of, marked my own attitude toward the misery of my brothers.

In 1887 I came to my thirtieth year. Although still unmarried, I was engaged to wed Edith Bartlett. She, like myself, rode on the top of the coach. That is to say, not to encumber ourselves further with an illustration which has, I hope, served its purpose of giving the reader some general impression of how we lived then, her family was wealthy. In that age, when money alone commanded all that was agreeable and refined in life, it was enough for a woman to be rich to have suitors; but Edith Bartlett was beautiful and graceful also.

My lady readers, I am aware, will protest at this. "Handsome she might have been," I hear them saying, "but graceful never, in the costumes which were the fashion at that period, when the head covering was a dizzy structure a foot tall, and the almost incredible extension of the skirt behind by means of artificial contrivances more thoroughly dehumanized the form than any former device of dressmakers. Fancy any one graceful in such a costume!" The point is certainly well taken, and I can only reply that while the ladies of the twentieth century are lovely demonstrations of the effect of appropriate drapery in accenting feminine graces, my recollection of their great-grandmothers enables me to maintain that no deformity of costume can wholly disguise them.

Our marriage only waited on the completion of the house which I was building for our occupancy in one of the most desirable parts of the city, that is to say, a part chiefly inhabited by the rich. For it must be understood that the comparative desirability of different parts of Boston for residence depended then, not on natural features, but on the character of the neighboring population. Each class or nation lived by itself, in quarters of its own. A rich man living among the poor, an educated man among the uneducated, was like one living in isolation among a jealous and alien race. When the house had been begun, its completion by the winter of 1886 had been expected. The spring of the following year found it, however, yet incomplete, and my marriage still a thing of the future. The cause of a delay calculated to be particularly exasperating to an ardent lover was a series of strikes, that is to say, concerted refusals to work on the part of the brick-layers, masons, carpenters, painters, plumbers, and other trades concerned in house building. What the specific causes of these strikes were I do not remember. Strikes had become so common at that period that people had ceased to inquire into their particular grounds. In one department of industry or another, they had been nearly incessant ever since the great business crisis of 1873. In fact it had come to be the exceptional thing to see any class of laborers pursue their avocation steadily for more than a few months at a time.

The reader who observes the dates alluded to will of course recognize in these disturbances of industry the first and incoherent phase of the great movement which ended in the establishment of the modern industrial system with all its social consequences. This is all so plain in the retrospect that a child can understand it, but not being prophets, we of that day had no clear idea what was happening to us. What we did see was that industrially the country was in a very queer way. The relation between the workingman and the employer, between labor and capital, appeared in some unaccountable manner to have become dislocated. The working classes had quite suddenly and very generally become infected with a profound discontent with their condition, and an idea that it could be greatly bettered if they only knew how to go about it. On every side, with one accord, they preferred demands for higher pay, shorter hours, better dwellings, better educational advantages, and a share in the refinements and luxuries of life, demands which it was impossible to see the way to granting unless the world were to become a great deal richer than it then was. Though they knew something of what they wanted, they knew nothing of how to accomplish it, and the eager enthusiasm with which they thronged about any one who seemed likely to give them any light on the subject lent sudden reputation to many would-be leaders, some of whom had little enough light to give. However chimerical the aspirations of the laboring classes might be deemed, the devotion with which they supported one another in the strikes, which were their chief weapon, and the sacrifices which they underwent to carry them out left no doubt of their dead earnestness.

As to the final outcome of the labor troubles, which was the phrase by which the movement I have described was most commonly referred to, the opinions of the people of my class differed according to individual temperament. The sanguine argued very forcibly that it was in the very nature of things impossible that the new hopes of the workingmen could be satisfied, simply because the world had not the wherewithal to satisfy them. It was only because the masses worked very hard and lived on short commons that the race did not starve outright, and no considerable improvement in their condition was possible while the world, as a whole, remained so poor. It was not the capitalists whom the laboring men were contending with, these maintained, but the iron-bound environment of humanity, and it was merely a question of the thickness of their skulls when they would discover the fact and make up their minds to endure what they could not cure.

The less sanguine admitted all this. Of course the workingmen's aspirations were impossible of fulfillment for natural reasons, but there were grounds to fear that they would not discover this fact until they had made a sad mess of society. They had the votes and the power to do so if they pleased, and their leaders meant they should. Some of these desponding observers went so far as to predict an impending social cataclysm. Humanity, they argued, having climbed to the top round of the ladder of civilization, was about to take a header into chaos, after which it would doubtless pick itself up, turn round, and begin to climb again. Repeated experiences of this sort in historic and prehistoric times possibly accounted for the puzzling bumps on the human cranium. Human history, like all great movements, was cyclical, and returned to the point of beginning. The idea of indefinite progress in a right line was a chimera of the imagination, with no analogue in nature. The parabola of a comet was perhaps a yet better illustration of the career of humanity. Tending upward and sunward from the aphelion of barbarism, the race attained the perihelion of civilization only to plunge downward once more to its nether goal in the regions of chaos.

This, of course, was an extreme opinion, but I remember serious men among my acquaintances who, in discussing the signs of the times, adopted a very similar tone. It was no doubt the common opinion of thoughtful men that society was approaching a critical period which might result in great changes. The labor troubles, their causes, course, and cure, took lead of all other topics in the public prints, and in serious conversation.

The nervous tension of the public mind could not have been more strikingly illustrated than it was by the alarm resulting from the talk of a small band of men who called themselves anarchists, and proposed to terrify the American people into adopting their ideas by threats of violence, as if a mighty nation which had but just put down a rebellion of half its own numbers, in order to maintain its political system, were likely to adopt a new social system out of fear.

As one of the wealthy, with a large stake in the existing order of things, I naturally shared the apprehensions of my class. The particular grievance I had against the working classes at the time of which I write, on account of the effect of their strikes in postponing my wedded bliss, no doubt lent a special animosity to my feeling toward them.

JACOB RIIS

from How the Other Half Lives (1890)

Long ago it was said that "one half of the world does not know how the other half lives." That was true then. It did not know because it did not care. The half that was on top cared little for the struggles, and less for the fate of those who were underneath, so long as it was able to hold them there and keep its own seat. There came a time when the discomfort and crowding below were so great, and the consequent upheavals so violent, that it was no longer an easy thing to do, and then the upper half fell to inquiring what was the matter. Information on the subject has been accumulating rapidly since, and the whole world has had its hands full answering for its old ignorance.

In New York, the youngest of the world's great cities, that time came later than elsewhere, because the crowding had not been so great. There were those who believed that it would never come; but their hopes were vain. Greed and reckless selfishness wrought like results here as in the cities of older lands. "When the great riot occurred in 1863," so reads the testimony of the Secretary of the Prison Association of New York before a legislative committee appointed to investigate causes of the increase of crime in the State twenty-five years ago, "every hiding-place and nursery of crime discovered itself by immediate and active participation in the operations of the mob. Those very places and domiciles, and all that are like them, are to-day nurseries of crime, and of the vices and disorderly courses which lead to crime. By far the largest part—eighty per cent. at least—of crimes against property and against the person are perpetrated by individuals who have either lost connection with home life, or never had any, or whose *homes had ceased to be sufficiently separate, decent, and desirable to afford what are regarded as ordinary wholesome influences of home and family.* . . . The younger criminals seem to come almost exclusively from the worst tenement house districts, that is, when traced back to the very places where they had their homes in the city here." Of one thing New York made sure at that early stage of the inquiry: the boundary line of the Other Half lies through the tenements.

It is ten years and over, now, since that line divided New York's population evenly. To-day three-fourths of its people live in the tenements, and the nineteenth century drift of the population to the cities is sending ever-increasing multitudes to crowd them. The fifteen thousand tenant houses that were the despair of the sanitarian in the past generation have swelled into thirty-seven thousand, and more than twelve hundred thousand persons call them home. The one way out he saw—rapid transit to the suburbs—has brought no relief. We know now that there is no way out; that the "system" that was the evil offspring of public neglect and private greed has come to stay, a storm-centre forever of our civilization. Nothing is left but to make the best of a bad bargain.

What the tenements are and how they grew to what they are, we shall see hereafter. The story is dark enough, drawn from the plain public records, to send a chill to any heart. If it shall appear that the sufferings and the sins of the "other half," and the evil they breed, are but as a just punishment upon the community that gave it no other choice, it will be because that is the truth. The boundary line lies there because, while the forces for good on one side vastly outweigh the bad—it were not well otherwise—in the tenements all the influences make for evil; because they are the hot-beds of the epidemics that carry death to rich and poor alike; the nurseries of pauperism and crime that fill our jails and police courts; that throw off a scum of forty thousand human wrecks to the island asylums and workhouses year by year; that turned out in the last eight years a round half million beggars to prey upon our charities; that maintain a standing army of ten thousand tramps with all that that implies; because, above all, they touch the family life with deadly moral contagion. This is their worst crime, inseparable from the system. That we have to own it the child of our own wrong does not excuse it, even though it gives it claim upon our utmost patience and tenderest charity.

What are you going to do about it? is the question of to-day. It was asked once of our city in taunting defiance by a band of political cutthroats, the legitimate outgrowth of life on the tenement-house level. Law and order found the answer then and prevailed. With our enormously swelling population held in this galling bondage, will that answer always be given ? It will depend on how fully the situation that prompted the challenge is grasped. Forty per cent. of the distress among the poor, said a recent official report, is due to drunkenness. But the first legislative committee ever appointed to probe this sore went deeper down and uncovered its roots. The "conclusion forced itself upon it that certain conditions and associations of human life and habitation are the prolific parents of corresponding habits and morals," and it recommended "the prevention of drunkenness by providing for every man a clean and comfortable home." Years after, a sanitary inquiry brought to light the fact that "more than one-half of the tenements with two-thirds of their population were held by owners who made the keeping of them a business, *generally a speculation*. The owner was seeking a certain percentage on his outlay, and that percentage very rarely fell below fifteen per cent., and frequently exceeded thirty. . . . The complaint was universal among the tenants that they were entirely uncared for, and that the only answer to their requests to have the place put in order by repairs and necessary improvements was that they must pay their rent or leave. The agent's instructions were simple but emphatic: 'Collect the rent in advance, or, failing, eject the occupants.' " Upon such a stock grew this upas-tree. Small wonder the fruit is bitter. The remedy that shall be an effective answer to the coming appeal for justice must proceed from the public conscience. Neither legislation nor charity can cover the ground. The greed of capital that wrought the evil must itself undo it, as far as it can now be undone. Homes must be built for the working masses by those who employ their labor; but tenements must cease to be "good property" in the old, heartless sense. "Philanthropy and five per cent." is the penance exacted.

If this is true from a purely economic point of view, what then of the outlook from the Christian standpoint? Not long ago a great meeting was held in this city, of all denominations of religious faith, to discuss the question how to lay hold of these teeming masses in the tenements with Christian influences, to which they are now too often strangers. Might not the conference have found in the warning of one Brooklyn builder, who has invested his capital on this plan and made it pay more than a money interest, a hint worth heeding: "How shall the love of God be understood by those who have been nurtured in sight only of the greed of man?"

Mulberry Bend by Jacob Riis, The Jacob Riis Collection. Reprinted by permission of Museum of the City of New York.

Bottle Alley by Jacob Riis, The Jacob Riis Collection. Reprinted by permission of Museum of the City of New York.

Room in a Tenement Flat by Jacob Riis, The Jacob Riis Collection. Reprinted by permission of Museum of the City of New York.

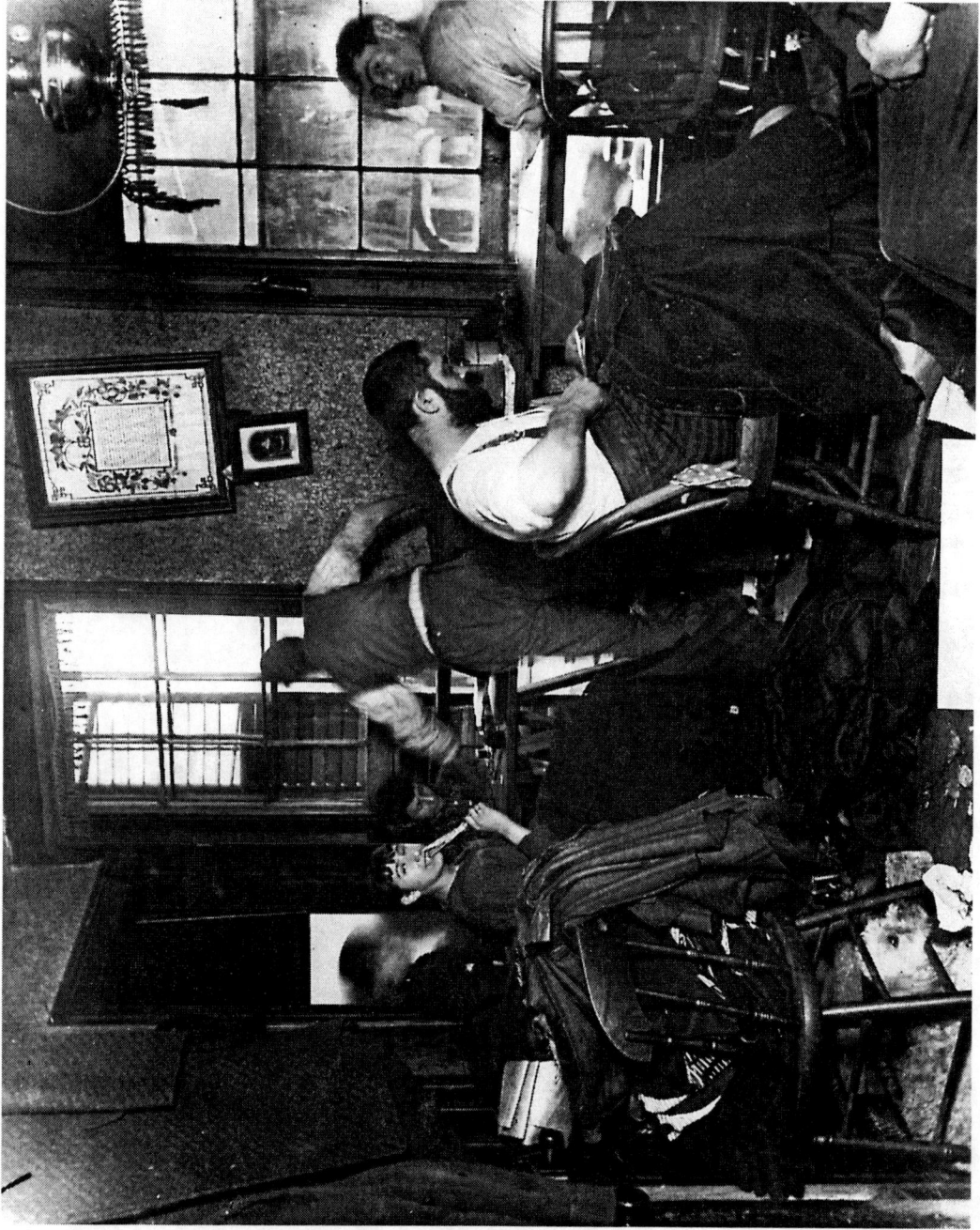

Knee-pants at Forty-Five Cents a Dozen at Ludlow Street Sweater Shop by Jacob Riis, The Jacob Riis Collection. Reprinted by permission of Museum of the City of New York.

Abraham Cahan

"The God of Israel Is Getting Even with Them"
(May 14,1898)

The ghetto never does things by halves, and its war feeling manifests itself with an oriental exuberance which keeps the neighborhood in a constant effervescence of excitement. The crowds in front of the bulletin boards of the four Yiddish dailies in this world within a world are not quite so large, perhaps, as the throngs on Park Row, but this numerical inferiority is more than made up in violence of gesticulation and vehemence of verbal expression. The Jews are glad to see Spain defeated. They have a double reason for it. Apart from considering themselves Americans and loving their adopted country as the only one in the world where the unhappy children of Israel find a home, they have an old account to settle with the Spaniards.

"Serve them right! Serve them right!" said a patriarchal old tailor, speaking of Manila. "They tortured the Jews and banished them from their land, and now the God of Israel is getting even with them. It is an old story, more than four hundred years old, but the High One never forgets, you know. You see, the Lord could have smashed them long ago, and even now He could have made some other power the messenger of Spain's ruin. Why, then, did it fall to the lot of the United States to settle her? You don't know? Well, I'll tell you. Who should avenge the blood of Israel? Russia, which is just as bad to the Jews as Spain was? Germany, Austria or any other country which is eaten up with anti-Semitism as a bad apple is with worms? England isn't a bad country, but what good does she do our people? The United States is the only land that has been a real mother to us. So God thought He might as well give the Americans the job. The friends of Israel getting square on His enemies, see?"

The younger and more educated part of the East Side population are against Spain because they are Americans and because they sympathize with the cause of free Cuba, but to the older folks, especially such as are initiated into the intricacies of Talmudic lore, a victory like Dewey's is as much of a triumph to the Jewish race as it is to the American people.

Perhaps the most interesting things in this connection are the prayers offered in behalf of American arms in the synagogues of Russia. The Saturday service usually includes a prayer for the health of the ruler of the country in which the worshippers dwell, and according to letters received from Russia and Poland, some of the Jewish congregations in these countries have now added to the benediction which they chant for the health of the Czar a hymn blessing President McKinley and the American nation and praying for their triumph over Spain. . . .

Thousands of Jews have enlisted in the various volunteer recruiting stations. Many of these can now be seen drilling at Peekskill or Camp Black, and many more are impatiently waiting to be called. A characteristic episode was related by one of the well-known lawyers of the East Side. A poor tailor of forty-five, who had seen fire in the Russo-Turkish War, became so excited over the conflict between the United States and Spain that he made up his mind to go to the front.

"Are you crazy?" asked his wife, pointing to their four children.

"I can't help it, my dear," was the old soldier's reply. "God and good people will take care of you and the young ones. My blood is up. If I had to face death for Russia, which has done nothing but evil to our people, how much more readily ought I to fight for this country, which has been so good to us? Ah! you are only a woman. What do you know about these things? I am going to enlist." And he did.

One old housewife, who has been some ten years in this country, without seeing anything of it beyond her tenement house and the Hester Street markets, was slow to understand what the whole trouble was about.

"War?" she asked in amazement. "America going to shed blood, too? Why, they have no Czar here, so who has quarreled with the King of Spain?"

After the situation was explained to her at length she asked again: "Cuba? And where is Cuba? Did you not say yourself that Cuba was also America, and don't I know that America belongs to the President, so where does the Spanish King come in after all?"

Another old matron, whose Americanized son had enlisted, thought it was only a joke. "No, mother, it is not a joke," the boy declared in English, to which she answered in Yiddish, as usual: "It is not a joke? What then is it? Is that what we came away from Russia for—to become soldiers here? We might as well stay at home."

The boy explained that Russia never was the home of the Jews, while in America they were as good as the Gentiles, and that being an American he must fight for his country.

ABRAHAM CAHAN

"Imagined America" (August 6, 1898)

I do not know through what association of ideas the image came into my head, but I remember distinctly that the word America would call to my mind a luxuriant many-colored meadow, with swarms of tall people hurrying hither and thither along narrow footpaths. They were all young and beardless and all men. Why the scene contained not a single woman I can explain no more than I can account for the color of the spring overcoats the men wore, which were exclusively gray.

When a child, I was fond of Cooper's and Mayne Reid's stories, which I read in a Russian translation, and it may be that something in some of these stories it was which painted the meadow and the gray-coated people in my mind. Later I read of Washington and Lincoln and liked them both. When Garfield was assassinated I read the news in a St. Petersburg paper. I can almost see the page and the upper part of the column in which the despatch was printed and the feeling of indignation with which I was discussing it with my classmates. We were all more or less "tainted" with nihilism, and while we applauded those who blew up the palace of our own Czar, the man who would lay his hand on the chosen representative of a free people was in our eyes nothing short of a demon.

By the time I had made up my mind to emigrate, the portraits of Washington, Lincoln and Garfield, as I had seen them in illustrated books and weeklies, had been added to the image of America in my head. By a strain of memory I can recall these portraits looming somewhere over my rich-colored meadow and my gray overcoats.

I knew some people who could speak English, but I do not think I ever heard them speak it. At all events, I never had any personal impression as to how that language sounded. But then, Turgenev says somewhere in his writings that English is the language of birds, so, accepting that, I would imagine Englishman twittering, warbling and chirping in their efforts to produce French words. This had nothing to do with my beardless Americans, however, whom I somehow could not get to speak the "language of birds." To be sure, I was aware that my gray-coated young fellows were of the same stock and spoke the same tongue as the inhabitants of Great Britain, but the composite picture of the English nation in my brain was so distinct from my image of an American that I could not get them to speak the same language either, and if the truth must be told, my gray-coated Yankee must have been a dumb creature, for I do not seem ever to have thought of him as speaking or singing or doing anything except push his way through that bright-hued meadow of his.

I set foot on American soil on a scorching day in June, and the first American I saw was an old customs officer, with a white beard and in the blue uniform of his office. The beardless men in gray vanished as if at the stroke of a magic wand, but then, gleaming green, fresh and beautiful, not many yards off, was the shore of Staten Island, and, while I was uttering exclamations of enchantment in chorus with my fellow passengers, I asked myself whether my dream of a meadow had not come true.

Still, pretty as America was, it somehow did not seem to be genuine, and much as I admired the shore I had a lurking impression that it was not the same sort of grass, trees, flowers, sod as in Europe, that it was more or less artificial, flimsy, ephemeral, as if a good European rainstorm could wipe it all off as a wet sponge would a colored picture made with colored chalk on a blackboard.

I remember joking of the seeming unreality of things in my new home. "The ice here is not cold," I would say, "the sugar is not sweet and the water is not wet." And a homesick German thereupon added in the words of a favorite poet of his that America was a country where "the birds had no sing, the flowers no fragrance, and the men no hearts." Why I should have doubted the actuality of things in the New World I do not know. Now that I try to account for that vague, hidden suspicion which the very sky and clouds of New York aroused in me, it occurs to me that it may have been due to my deep-rooted notion of America as something so far removed from my world that it must look entirely different from it. If Staten Island had the appearance which its reflection had in the water, if the trees and the cliffs were all upside down, I should have been surprised but satisfied.

However it may be, although I expressed my doubts as to the reality of nature in the strange land in jest, and although the logic of my mind and all I knew of things natural and artificial told me that the trees were trees and the grass grass, still these doubts remained intact, and from their remote corner in my soul they made me scrutinize the verdure to see if it was the genuine article. One of the first things I beheld on the pier as we were landed was a big Maltese cat. I can just see her squatting by the side of the gangplank and eyeing me as I came down. Nor shall I ever forget the queer sense of joy which the sight of her gave me. "Why, they have cats here!" I exclaimed to myself. "And just like ours, too!" I felt like flinging myself upon the little creature, hugging her, shaking her paw and introducing myself to her as a fellow-countryman. At the next instant, however, I was surveying that same cat to make sure that she was really a cat like our cats at home, a living creature and not a mechanical imitation of one; the more so since I knew of the prevalence of machinery in the United States, and of the inventive genius of its people. I had read of the artificial hatching of chickens, and by a stretch of imagination I could see artificial dogs and artificial cats. Of course, I knew that this cat was a genuine one, and I inwardly made fun of my suspicions as well as of my joy, but the suspicions held their own, and altogether I was two men in one.

"Oh, come, it's a cat; can't you see?" said one.

"Of course it is. Who says it isn't?" the other retorted with cowardly insincerity.

When I found myself on the street and my eye fell on an old rickety building, I experienced a feeling akin to surprise. I could only conceive of America as a brand-new country, and everything in it, everything made by man, at least, was to be spick and span, while here was an old house, weather-beaten and somewhat misshapen with age. How did it get time to grow old?

The first American who left an impression on me was a tall, gray-haired missionary whom I saw preaching from a bench on Union or Madison Square—I do not remember which. One of his hands was bandaged, and as he stood against the blue sky with the disabled member resting against his breast and his flowing beard looming dazzlingly white in a flood of sunshine, this picture at once moved me to pity and thrilled me with reverence. The old man's speech at first impressed me like the monotonous thrumming noise which is produced by playing upon the loose end of a thin, flexible strip of steel whose other end is made fast to some stationary object. A dignified, reverent sort of monotony it was at first, and I liked it as well as the metallic ring in the man's voice. As I stood listening to it I had a sense of being in the presence of self-denying piety, and again I was wondering whether it was not a sort of *fata morgana*. My idea of America had so little to do with what I now saw before me that I was timidly asking myself whether the man was a genuine man, his beard a genuine beard, the bandages on his hand real bandages. But presently he began to speak faster, and the illusion fled. His English now sounded in my ears like the snapping noise made by running a stick across the rods of a metal gate or fence. The sound at once became annoying to me, and the man was suddenly transformed into a heartless, vulgar, supercilious creature. His voice set my teeth on edge, and I remember the malicious feeling with which I set to analyzing it. "How does he get that confounded metallic sound of his?" I asked myself, and after listening a few minutes I made the discovery that he pronounced the "R" utterly unlike any people I had known. "Do they all speak like that?" I said to myself with disgust, trying to imitate him for sheer hatred, and getting all the more disgusted with him because I failed.

The preacher's manner, his scant gesticulations, the way he aimed his fist at the air and then brought it down on nothing, his projecting lower lip when he shut his mouth, his gray eyes, everything about him seemed to me intensely repulsive and anything but human. He struck me as a species of frog, and try as I would, I could not get myself to imagine that the sounds he uttered were words and that the crowd around him understood their meaning.

Subsequently, when I had mastered English enough to understand the old preacher and to make myself understood, more or less, to him, I made his acquaintance, and my original impressions gave way to others. I found him to be a very pleasant and interesting man. I liked him, and my second image of him is one of my dearest portraits in my mental album of American races.

Horace M. Kallen

from "Democracy Versus the Melting Pot" (1915)

All immigrants and their offspring are by the way of undergoing "Americanization" if they remain in one place in the country long enough—say six or seven years. The general notion of "Americanization" appears to signify the adoption of the American variety of English speech, American clothes and manners, the American attitude in politics. "Americanization" signifies, in short, the disappearance of the external differences upon which so much race-prejudice often feeds. It appears to imply the fusion of the various bloods, and a transmutation by "the miracle of assimilation" of Jews, Slavs, Poles, Frenchmen, Germans, Hindus, Scandinavians and so on into beings similar in background, tradition, outlook and spirit to the descendants of the British colonists, the "Anglo-Saxon" stock. Broadly speaking, these elements of Americanism are somewhat external, the effect of environment; largely internal, the effect of heredity, social and personal. Thus American economic individualism, American traditional *laissez-faire* policy is largely the effect of environment; where nature offers more than enough potential wealth to go round, there is no immediate need for regulating distribution. . . .

. . . At his core, no human being, even in a "state of nature," is a mere mathematical unit of action like the "economic man." Behind him in time and tremendously in him in quality, are his ancestors; around him in space are his relatives and kin, carrying in common with him the inherited organic set from a remoter common ancestry. In all these he lives and moves and has his being. They constitute his, literally, *natio,* the inwardness of his nativity, and in Europe every inch of his non-human environment wears the effects of their action upon it and breathes their spirit. The America he comes to, beside Europe, is Nature virgin and inviolate: it does not guide him with ancestral blazings: externally he is cut off from the past. Not so internally: whatever else he changes, he cannot change his grandfather. Moreover, he comes rarely alone; he comes companioned with his fellow nationals; and he comes to no strangers, but to kin and friends who have gone before. If he is able to excel, he soon achieves a local habitation. There he encounters the native American to whom he is merely a Dutchman, a Mick, a frog, a wop, a dago, a hunky, or a sheeny and no more; and he encounters these others who are unlike him, dealing with him as a lower and outlandish creature. Then, be he even the rudest and most primeval peasant, heretofore totally unconscious of his nationality, of his categorical difference from many men and similarity to some, he must inevitably become conscious of it. Thus, in the industrial and congested towns of the United States, where there are real and large contacts between immigrant nationalities, the first effect appears to be an intensification of spiritual dissimilarities, always to the disadvantage of the dissimilarities.

The second generation, consequently, devotes itself feverishly to the attainment of similarity. The social tradition of its parents is lost by attrition or thrown off for advantage. The merest externals of the new one are acquired—via the street and the public school. But as the public school imparts it, or as the social settlement imparts it, it is not really a *life;* it is an abstraction, an arrangement of words. America is a word: as a historic fact, or as a democratic ideal of life, it is not realized at all. At best and at worst—now that the captains of industry are showing disturbance over the mess they have made, and "vocational training" is becoming a part of the public educational program—the prospective American learns a trade, acquiring at his most impressionable age the habit of being a cog in the industrial machine. . . .

The array of forces for and against that likemindedness which is the stuff and essence of nationality seems to align itself as follows. For it there work social imitations of the upper by the lower classes, the facility of communications, the national pastimes of baseball and motion-picture, the mobility of population, the cheapness of printing and the public schools. Against it there work the primary ethnic and cultural differences with which the population starts, its stratification over an enormous extent of country, and most powerfully, its industrial and economic stratification. The United States are an English-speaking country but in no intimate and utter way, as is New Zealand or Australia or even Canada. English seems to Americans what Latin used to be to the Roman provinces and to the middle ages—the language of the upper and dominant class, the vehicle and symbol of culture: for much of the population it is a sort of Esperanto or Ido, a *lingua franca* necessary less in the free than the business contacts of the daily life. The American mass is composed of elementals, peasants . . . —with, in a word, the proletarian foundation material of all forms of civilization. Their self-consciousness as groups is comparatively weak, although their organization and control of their individual members are often very strong. This is a factor which favors their "assimilation," for the more cultivated a group is the more it is aware of its individuality, and the less willing it is to surrender that individuality—one need think only of the Puritans themselves, leaving Holland for fear of absorption into the Dutch population; of the Creoles and the Pennsylvania Germans of this country, or of the Jews, anywhere. Peasants, on the other hand, having nothing much consciously to surrender in taking over a new culture, feel no necessary break and find the transition easy. They accomplish it, other things being equal, in a generation. It is the shock of confrontation with other ethnic groups and the natural feeling of aliency reinforced by social discrimination and economic exploitation that generate in them an intenser group-consciousness, which then militates against "Americanization" by rendering more important than ever the two factors to which the spiritual expression of the proletarian has been largely confined. These factors are language and religion. Religion is, of course, no more a "universal" than language. The history of Christianity makes evident enough how religion is modified, even inverted, by race, place and time. It becomes a principle of separation, often the sole repository of the national spirit, almost always the conservator of the national language and of the tradition that is passed on with the language to succeeding generations. Among immigrants, hence, religion and language tend to be coordinate: a single expression of the spontaneous and instinctive cultural life of the masses, and the primary inward factors making against assimilation. . . .

. . . At the present time there seems to be no dominant American mind other than the industrial and theological. The spirit of the land is inarticulate, not a voice but a chorus of many voices each singing a rather different tune. How to get order into this cacophony is the question for all persons who are concerned about those things which alone justify wealth and power; for all who are concerned about justice, the arts, literature, philosophy, science. What must, what can, what *shall* this cacaphony become—a unison or a harmony?

For decidedly, the older America, whose voice and whose spirit were New England, has, by virtue of business, of communications, of the immigrant, gone beyond recall. Americans of British stock still are prevailingly the artists and thinkers of the land, but they work, each for himself, without common vision or ideals. They have no *ethos* any more. The older tradition has passed from a life into a memory, and the newer one, so far as it has an Anglo-Saxon base, is holding its own beside more and more formidable competitors, the expression in appropriate form of the national inheritances of the various populations concentrated in various states of the Union, populations of whom their national self-consciousness is perhaps the chief spiritual asset, as their labor-power is their chief economic asset. Think of the Creoles in the south and the French-Canadians in the north, clinging to French for countless generations and maintaining, however weakly, spiritual and social contacts with the mother-country; of the Germans with their *Deutschtum*, their *Männer-chore, Turnvereine,* and *Schüzenfeste;* of the generally separate Jews; of the intensely nationalistic Irish; of the Pennsylvania Germans; of the indomitably narrow Poles and even more indomitably flexible Bohemians; of the 30,000 Belgians in Wisconsin with their "Belgian" language, a mixture of Walloon and Flemish welded by reaction to a strange social environment. Except in such cases as the town of Lead, South Dakota, the great ethnic groups of proletarians, thrown upon themselves in a new setting, generate from among themselves the other social classes which Mr. Ross and his kind so sadly miss among them: their shopkeepers, their physicians, their attorneys, their journalists and their national and political leaders, who form the links between them and the greater American society. They develop their own literature or become conscious of that of the mother country. As they grow more prosperous and "Americanized," as they become freed from the stigma of "foreigner," they develop group self-respect: the wop changes into a proud Italian, the hunky into an intensely nationalist Slav. They learn, or they recall, the spiritual heritage of their nationality. Their cultural abjectness gives way to cultural pride and the public schools, the libraries and the clubs become beset with demands for texts in the national language and literature. . . .

Immigrants appear to pass through four phases in the course of being automatically Americanized. In the first phase they exhibit economic eagerness, the greedy hunger of the unfed. Since external differences are a handicap in the economic struggle, they "assimilate," seeking thus to facilitate the attainment of economic independence. Once the proletarian level of such independence is reached, the process of assimilation slows down and tends to come to a stop. The immigrant group is still a national group, modified, sometimes improved, by environmental influences, but otherwise a solitary spiritual unit, which is seeking to find its way out on its own social level. This search brings to light permanent group distinctions and the immigrant, like the Anglo-Saxon American, is thrown back upon himself and his ancestry. Then a process of dissimilation begins. The arts, life and ideals of the nationality become central and paramount; ethnic and national differences change in status from disadvantages to distinctions. All the while the immigrant has been uttering his life in the English language and behaving like an American in matters economic and political, and continues to do so. The institutions of the Republic have become the liberating cause and the background for the rise of the cultural consciousness and social autonomy of the immigrant Irishman, German, Scandinavian, Jew, Pole or Bohemian. On the whole, the automatic processes of Americanization have not repressed nationality. These processes have liberated nationality, and more or less gratified it.

Hence, what troubles Mr. Ross and so many other American citizens of British stock is not really inequality; what troubles them is *difference.* Only things that are *alike* in fact and not abstractly, and only men that are alike in origin and in feeling and not abstractly, can possess the equality which maintains that inward unanimity of sentiment and outlook which make a homogeneous national culture. The writers of the American Declaration of Independence and of the Constitution of the United States were not confronted by the practical fact of ethnic dissimilarity among the whites of the country. Their descendants are confronted by it. Its existence, acceptance and development are some of the inevitable consequences of the democratic principle on which the American theory of government is based, and the result at the present writing is to many worthies very unpleasant. Democratism and the federal principle have worked together with economic greed and ethnic snobbishness to people the land with all the nationalities of Europe, and to convert the early American nationality into the present American *nation.* For in effect the United States are in the process of becoming a federal state not merely as a union of geographical and administrative unities, but also as a cooperation of cultural diversities, as a federation or commonwealth of national cultures. . . .

America is, in fact, at the parting of the ways. Two genuine social alternatives are before Americans, either of which they may realize if they will. In social construction the will is father to the fact, for the fact is hardly ever anything more, under the grace of accident and luck, than the concord or conflict of wills. What do Americans *will* to make of the United States—a unison, singing the old British theme "America," the America of the New England School? or a harmony, in which that theme shall be dominant, perhaps, among others, but one among many, not the only one?

The mind reverts helplessly to the historic attempts at unison in Europe—the heroic failure of the pan-Hellenists, of the Romans, the disintegration and the diversification of the Christian church, for a time the most successful unison in history; the present-day failures of Germany and of Russia. In the United States, however, the whole social situation is favorable as it has never been at any time elsewhere—everything is favorable but the basic law of America itself, and the spirit of the American institutions. To achieve unison—it can be achieved—would be to violate these. For the end determines the means and the means transmute the end, and this end would involve no other means than those used by Germany in Poland, in Schleswig-Holstein, and Alsace-Lorraine; by Russia in the Jewish Pale, in Poland, in Finland; by Austria among the Slavs; by Turkey among the Arabs, Armenians and Greeks. Fundamentally it would require the complete nationalization of education, the abolition of every form of parochial and private school, the abolition of instruction in other tongues than English, and the concentration of the teaching of history and literature upon the English tradition. The other institutions of society would require treatment analogous to that administered by Germany to her European acquisitions. And all of this, even if meeting with no resistance, would not completely guarantee the survival as a unison of the older Americanism. For the program would be applied to diverse ethnic types under changing conditions, and the reconstruction that, with the best will, they might spontaneously make of the tradition would more likely than not be a far cry from the original. It is, already.

The notion that the program might be realized by radical and even forced miscegenation, by the creation of the melting-pot by law, and thus by the development of the new "American race" is . . . as mystically optimistic as it is ignorant. . . . There is nothing more to be said to the pious stupidity that identifies recency with goodness. The unison to be achieved cannot be a unison of ethnic types. It must be, if it is to be at all, a unison of social and historic interests, established by the complete cutting-off of the ancestral memories of the American populations, the enforced, exclusive use of the English language and English and American history in the schools and in the daily life.

The attainment of the other alternative, a harmony, also requires concerted public action. But the action would do no violence to the ideals of American fundamental law and the spirit of American institutions nor to the qualities of men. It would seek simply to eliminate the waste and the stupidity of the social organization, by way of freeing and strengthening the strong forces actually in operation. Taking for its point of departure the existing ethnic and cultural groups it would seek to provide conditions under which each might attain the cultural perfection that is *proper to its kind.* The provision of such conditions has been said to be the primary intent of American fundamental law and the function of American institutions. And all of the various nationalities which compose the American nation must be taught first of all this fact, which used perhaps to be, to patriotic minds, the outstanding ideal content of "Americanism"—that democracy means self-realization through self-control, self-discipline, and that one is impossible without the other. . . .

. . . What is inalienable in the life of mankind is its intrinsic positive quality—its psychophysical inheritance. Men may change their clothes, their politics, their wives, their religions, their philosophies, to a greater or lesser extent; they cannot change their grandfathers. Jews or Poles or Anglo-Saxons, in order to cease being Jews or Poles or Anglo-Saxons, would have to cease to be, while they could cease to be citizens or church members or carpenters or lawyers without ceasing to be. The selfhood which is inalienable in them, and for the realization of which they require "inalienable" liberty is ancestrally determined, and the happiness which they pursue has its form implied in ancestral endowment. This is what, actually, democracy in operation assumes. . . . Its form would be that of the federal republic; its substance a democracy of nationalities, cooperating voluntarily and autonomously through common institutions in the enterprise of self-realization through the perfection of men according to their kind. The common language of the commonwealth, the language of its great tradition, would be English, but each nationality would have for its emotional and involuntary life its own peculiar dialect or speech, its own individual and inevitable esthetic and intellectual forms. The political and economic life of the commonwealth is a single unit and serves as the foundation and background for the realization of the distinctive individuality of each *natio* that composes it and of the pooling of these in a harmony above them all. Thus "American civilization" may come to mean the perfection of the cooperative harmonies of "European civilization"—the waste, the squalor and the distress of Europe being eliminated—a multiplicity in a unity, an orchestration of mankind. As in an orchestra every type of instrument has its specific *timbre* and *tonality,* founded in its substance and form; as every type has its appropriate theme and melody in the whole symphony, so in society, each ethnic group may be the natural instrument, its temper and culture may be its theme and melody and the harmony and dissonances and discords of them all may make the symphony of civilization. With this difference: a musical symphony is written before it is played; in the symphony of civilization the playing is the writing, so that there is nothing so fixed and inevitable about its progressions as in music, so that within the limits set by nature and luck they may vary at will, and the range and variety of the harmonies may become wider and richer and more beautiful—or the reverse.

But the question is, do the dominant classes in America want such a society? The alternative is actually before them. Can they choose wisely? Or will vanity blind them and fear constrain, turning the promise of freedom into the fact of tyranny, and once more vindicating the ancient habit of men and aborting the hope of the world?

JINSHAN GE JI ALMANACS

Vernacular Poems by Chinese Immigrants

(1911 and 1915)

4　At home I was in poverty,
　　　constantly worried about firewood and rice.
　I borrowed money
　　　to come to Gold Mountain.
　Immigration officers cross-examined me;
　　　no way could I get through.
　Deported to this island,
　　　like a convicted criminal.
　Here—
　Mournful sighs fill the gloomy room.
　A nation weak; her people often humiliated
　Like animals, tortured and destroyed at others'
　　　whim.

家貧柴米思。○貸本來金山⑴。
閒員審問脫身難。○撥往埃崙⑶。
到此間。○闇室長嗟嘆。
國弱被人多辱慢。○儼然畜類任推殘。

（一）金山：美國
（二）撥：參看歌#3
（三）埃崙：音譯「島」；
指天使島

JSGJ I.14a

12　So, liberty is your national principle;
　Why do you practice autocracy?
　You don't uphold justice, you Americans,
　You detain me in prison, guard me closely.
　Your officials are wolves and tigers,
　All ruthless, all wanting to bite me.
　An innocent man implicated, such an injustice!
　When can I get out of this prison and free
　　　my mind?

自由爲國例。○何事學專制。
不持公理美人兮。○困我監牢嚴密睇⑴。
狼虎差。○橫行更欲噬。
罪及無辜眞惡抵⑵。○幾時出獄開心懷。

（一）睇：參看歌#10
（二）惡抵：難以抵受，參看歌#10

JSGJ I.13b

34　Since coming to the frontier land,
　I have taken all kinds of abuse from the
　　　barbarians.
　I have come across the horizon to the Flowery
　　　Flag Nation;
　The surroundings still fill me with thoughts
　　　of home.
　Don't despair:
　All we need is profit and money.
　Should our purses be stuffed with gold,
　We'll pick out a date and have our homebound
　　　whip ready.

自到邊疆地。○受盡番奴欺。
天涯走過至花旗⑴。○觸景依然懷故里。
莫傷氣。○祇爭財與利。
黃金擲入荷包裡。○整定歸鞭有日期。

（一）花旗：參看歌#3

JSGJ I.12a

193

46   Since you've sojourned to America, Husband,
     My heart aches for you all the time.
     Unable to share my feelings, my brows are
          besieged with sorrow;
     I grieve that we're at opposite ends of the
          earth.
     Mourning at midnight,
     I cannot fall asleep in the gauze-tented bed.
     Thinking, wondering, O, who is the trusted
          friend?
     Who will deliver my message to the Flowery Flag
          Nation?

76   My friends, remember by all means:
     Don't let yourselves be stranded in a foreign country.
     Brows besieged by sorrow from frequent worries
          of home;
     Thousands of miles of clouds and mountains further
          impede a gloomy stay.
     Separation brings out misery.
     Have your belongings always packed and ready.
     A journey to America is only a search for wealth.
     Return to the old country quickly, to avoid
          going astray.

87   Drifting all this way to seek some gain,
     I've forsaken my family for a long time.
     No need to linger in the Flowery Flag Nation,
     Pack up my belongings and go home!
     This is truly my wish:
     Leave this barbaric land on the earliest possible
          day.
     It can't be compared to the warmth of home;
     My heart cares only for the day of my return.

100 At the moment, I hardly have enough grub to
          eat.
     But I won't take it as fate, my final destiny.
     I don't believe I will live like this till my hair
          turns white;
     It's only the low ebb in my life.
     When luck strikes,
     With the whole world behind me,
     I will be rich in a few years' turn.
     And then, I will buy property and build a
          Western mansion.

自君遊歐美。妾每心記記。
幽懷難遮鎖愁眉。惱恨天涯隔兩地。
午夜悲。羅幃難入寐。
籌度執爲賢知己。代奴傳語到花旗。

JSGJ I.50a

（一）裡：作「李」

勿困他邦地。同人要緊記。
家居復望鎖愁眉。暗滯雲山千萬里。
睽生悲。速整隨行裡。(一)
只爲求財經旅美。早回故國免流離。

JSGJ I.11b

（一）花旗：麥香歌#3

漂身來覓利。家人久拋棄。
何須依戀在花旗。(一)收拾行裝旋故里。
儂所冀。早離番邦地。
桑梓殷情無可比。一心懷念轉歸期。

JSGJ I.12b

（二）（一）
唔 睇
信 透
： ：
不 看
相 透
信

目下難餬口。造化睇未透。(一)
唔信這樣到白頭。祇因眼前命不偶。
運氣湊。世界還在後。
轉過幾年富且厚。怎時置業起洋樓。

JSGJ II.44a

118 Since I left South China,
I have changed my clothes to the Western style.
I seek praise for being neat and fashionable
Though I have yet to speak with an American
  tongue.
Smart in appearance—
Who dares to call me an ignorant fool?
A loose gown with wide sleeves brings only
  scurrilous remarks
And it gets you nowhere, even if you are modern
  in education.

自從離兩廣。服色轉西裝。
爭誇齊整兼在行。誰散話褒慈。（四）
週身光（三）。
閒袖長袍招誹謗。縱深新學亦收庄（五）
。

（一）花語：花旗話，即英語
（二）未噲：還不會
（三）光：光鮮
（四）褒慈：土氣傻瓜
（五）收庄：不能作主持

JSGJ I.11a

126 American ways are very extreme.
This worn writing brush cannot reveal them
  all.
Just let me show you one ridiculous example
  in brief,
And I must warn you, gentlemen, before you
  die of shock from hearing this news:
There was a lawless shrew—
She bullied and humiliated her inept husband;
She divorced him, seized and sold the family property;
Then, she openly found and married another man!

歐美風俗屬。禿筆寫唔細（一）
。
舉彼荒唐事略提。恐令男界開驚斃。
不法妻。欺凌愚拙婿。
分拆還佔家產賣。公然另擇別郎締。

（一）細：作「唔」，唔哂：不完

JSGJ II.30a

134 In all earnestness, I speak to all my sisters:
Why be so easily discouraged?
From now on, superior talents will arise among
  us women;
Men and women will have equal rights, and that
  will not change!
Won't that be wonderful?
A life without oppression!
We can choose our own mate, be he a wise man
  or a fool.
Even our parents can't interfere with us anymore!

敬告眾姊妹。何必心先灰。
從今巾幗起高才。男婦平權無更改。
得意哉。身處專制外。
夫婿智愚隨我採。縱然爹媽阻唔來（一）
。

（一）阻唔來：阻止不了

JSGJ II.2a

135 Following the practice of the Western countries,
I am free to make my marriage choice.
I cheer that the obsolete rituals are abolished.
No longer can matchmakers manipulate our lives.
It's a brand new world.
I am married in a civilized way.
I have found a good husband on my own, as I have
  wished.
Our hearts and views are at one, our brows beam
  with joy.

取法泰西例。隨我結夫妻。
革除古禮實歡懷。免使媒婆來舟柴。
新世界。文明諧伉儷（一）
。
在己如意速佳婿。同心同德樂眉齊
。

（一）儷：作「儀」

JSGJ II.2b

BOOKER T. WASHINGTON
Atlanta Exposition Speech (1895)

One-third of the population of the South is of the Negro race. No enterprise seeking the material, civil, or moral welfare of this section can disregard this element of our population and reach the highest success. I but convey to you, Mr. President and Directors, the sentiment of the masses of my race when I say that in no way have the value and manhood of the American Negro been more fittingly and generously recognized than by the managers of the magnificent Exposition at every stage of its progress. It is a recognition that will do more to cement the friendship of the two races than any occurrence since the dawn of our freedom.

Not only this, but the opportunity here afforded will awaken among us a new era of industrial progress. Ignorant and inexperienced, it is not strange that in the first years of our new life we began at the top instead of at the bottom; that a seat in Congress or the state legislature was more sought than real estate or industrial skill; that the political convention or stump speaking had more attractions than starting a dairy farm or truck garden.

A ship lost at sea for many days suddenly sighted a friendly vessel. From the mast of the unfortunate vessel was seen a signal, "Water, water; we die of thirst!" The answer from the friendly vessel at once came back, "Cast down your bucket where you are." A second time the signal, 'Water, water; send us water!" ran up from the distressed vessel, and was answered, "Cast down your bucket where you are." And a third and fourth signal for water was answered, "Cast down your bucket where you are." The captain of the distressed vessel, at last heeding the injunction, cast down his bucket, and it came up full of fresh sparkling water from the mouth of the Amazon River. To those of my race who depend on bettering their condition in a foreign land or who underestimate the importance of cultivating friendly relations with the Southern white man, who is their next-door neighbour, I would say: "Cast down your bucket where you are"—cast it down in making friends in every manly way of the people of all races by whom we are surrounded.

Cast it down in agriculture, mechanics, in commerce, in domestic service, and in the professions. And in this connection it is well to bear in mind that whatever other sins the South may be called to bear, when it comes to business, pure and simple, it is in the South that the Negro is given a man's chance in the commercial world, and in nothing is this Exposition more eloquent than in emphasizing this chance. Our greatest danger is that in the great leap from slavery to freedom we may overlook the fact that the masses of us are to live by the productions of our hands, and fail to keep in mind that we shall prosper in proportion as we learn to dignify and glorify common labour and put brains and skill into the common occupations of life; shall prosper in proportion as we learn to draw the line between the superficial and the substantial, the ornamental gewgaws of life and the useful. No race can prosper till it learns that there is as much dignity in tilling a field as in writing a poem. It is at the bottom of life we must begin, and not at the top. Nor should we permit our grievances to overshadow our opportunities.

To those of the white race who look to the incoming of those of foreign birth and strange tongue and habits for the prosperity of the South, were I permitted I would repeat what I say to my own race, "Cast down your bucket where you are." Cast it down among the eight millions of Negroes whose habits you know, whose fidelity and love you have tested in days when to have proved treacherous meant the ruin of your firesides. Cast down your bucket among these people who have, without strikes and labour wars, tilled your fields, cleared your forests, builded your railroads and cities, and brought forth treasures from the bowels of the earth, and helped make possible this magnificent representation of the progress of the South. Casting down your bucket among my people, helping and encouraging them as you are doing on these grounds, and to education of head, hand, and heart, you will find that they will buy your surplus land, make blossom the waste places in your fields, and run your factories. While doing this, you can be sure in the future, as in the past, that you and your families will be surrounded by the most patient, faithful, law-abiding, and unresentful people that the world has seen. As we have proved our loyalty to you in the past, in nursing your children, watching by the sick-bed of your mothers and fathers, and often following them with tear-dimmed eyes to their graves, so in the future, in our humble way, we shall stand by you with a devotion that no foreigner can approach, ready to lay down our lives, if need be, in defence of yours, interlacing our industrial, commercial, civil, and religious life with yours in a way that shall make the interests of both races one. In all things that are purely social we can be as separate as the fingers, yet one as the hand in all things essential to mutual progress.

There is no defence or security for any of us except in the highest intelligence and development of all. If anywhere there are efforts tending to curtail the fullest growth of the Negro, let these efforts be turned into stimulating, encouraging, and making him the most useful and intelligent citizen. Effort or means so invested will pay a thousand per cent interest. These efforts will be twice blessed—"blessing him that gives and him that takes."

There is no escape through law of man or God from the inevitable:—

> *The laws of changeless justice bind*
> *Oppressor with oppressed;*
> *And close as sin and suffering joined*
> *We march to fate abreast.*

Nearly sixteen millions of hands will aid you in pulling the load upward, or they will pull against you the load downward. We shall constitute one-third and more of the ignorance and crime of the South, or one-third its intelligence and progress; we shall contribute one-third to the business and industrial prosperity of the South, or we shall prove a veritable body of death, stagnating, depressing, retarding every effort to advance the body politic.

Gentlemen of the Exposition, as we present to you our humble effort at an exhibition of our progress, you must not expect overmuch. Starting thirty years ago with ownership here and there in a few quilts and pumpkins and chickens (gathered from miscellaneous sources), remember the path that has led from these to the inventions and production of agricultural implements, buggies, steam-engines, newspapers, books, statuary, carving, paintings, the management of drug-stores and banks, has not been trodden without contact with thorns and thistles. While we take pride in what we exhibit as a result of our independent efforts, we do not for a moment forget that our part in this exhibition would fall far short of your expectations but for the constant help that has come to our educational life, not only from the Southern states, but especially from Northern philanthropists, who have made their gifts a constant stream of blessing and encouragement.

The wisest among my race understand that the agitation of questions of social equality is the extremest folly, and that progress in the enjoyment of all the privileges that will come to us must be the result of severe and constant struggle rather than of artificial forcing. No race that has anything to contribute to the markets of the world is long in any degree ostracized. It is important and right that all privileges of the law be ours, but it is vastly more important that we be prepared for the exercises of these privileges. The opportunity to earn a dollar in a factory just now is worth infinitely more than the opportunity to spend a dollar in an opera-house.

In conclusion, may I repeat that nothing in thirty years has given us more hope and encouragement, and drawn us so near to you of the white race, as this opportunity offered by the Exposition; and here bending, as it were, over the altar that represents the results of the struggles of your race and mine, both starting practically empty-handed three decades ago, I pledge that in your effort to work out the great and intricate problem which God has laid at the doors of the South, you shall have at all times the patient, sympathetic help of my race; only let this be constantly in mind, that, while from representations in these buildings of the product of field, of forest, of mine, of factory, letters, and art, much good will come, yet far above and beyond material benefits will be that higher good, that, let us pray God, will come, in a blotting out of sectional differences and racial animosities and suspicions, in a determination to administer absolute justice, in a willing obedience among all classes to the mandates of law. This, this, coupled with our material prosperity, will bring into our beloved South a new heaven and a new earth.

W. E. B. DuBois

from "Of Mr. Booker T. Washington and Others," from *The Souls of Black Folk* (1903)

Easily the most striking thing in the history of the American Negro since 1876 is the ascendancy of Mr. Booker T. Washington. It began at the time when war memories and ideals were rapidly passing; a day of astonishing commercial development was dawning; a sense of doubt and hesitation overtook the freedmen's sons,—then it was that his leading began. Mr. Washington came, with a single definite programme, at the psychological moment when the nation was a little ashamed of having bestowed so much sentiment on Negroes, and was concentrating its energies on Dollars. His programme of industrial education, conciliation of the South, and submission and silence as to civil and political rights, was not wholly original; the Free Negroes from 1830 up to war-time had striven to build industrial schools, and the American Missionary Association had from the first taught various trades; and Price and others had sought a way of honorable alliance with the best of the Southerners. But Mr. Washington first indissolubly linked these things; he put enthusiasm, unlimited energy, and perfect faith into this programme, and changed it from a by-path into a veritable Way of Life. And the tale of the methods by which he did this is a fascinating study of human life.

It startled the nation to hear a Negro advocating such a programme after many decades of bitter complaint; it startled and won the applause of the South, it interested and won the admiration of the North; and after a confused murmur of protest, it silenced if it did not convert the Negroes themselves.

To gain the sympathy and coöperation of the various elements comprising the white South was Mr. Washington's first task; and this, at the time Tuskegee was founded, seemed, for a black man, well-nigh impossible. And yet ten years later it was done in the word spoken at Atlanta: "In all things purely social we can be as separate as the five fingers, and yet one as the hand in all things essential to mutual progress." This "Atlanta Compromise" is by all odds the most notable thing in Mr. Washington's career. The South interpreted it in different ways: the radicals received it as a complete surrender of the demand for civil and political equality; the conservatives, as a generously conceived working basis for mutual understanding. So both approved it, and to-day its author is certainly the most distinguished Southerner since Jefferson Davis, and the one with the largest personal following.

Next to this achievement comes Mr. Washington's work in gaining place and consideration in the North. Others less shrewd and tactful had formerly essayed to sit on these two stools and had fallen between them; but as Mr. Washington knew the heart of the South from birth and training, so by singular insight he intuitively grasped the spirit of the age which was dominating the North. And so thoroughly did he learn the speech and thought of triumphant commercialism, and the ideals of material prosperity, that the picture of a lone black boy poring over a French grammar amid the weeds and dirt of a neglected home soon seemed to him the acme of absurdities. One wonders what Socrates and St. Francis of Assisi would say to this.

And yet this very singleness of vision and thorough oneness with his age is a mark of the successful man. It is as though Nature must needs make men narrow in order to give them force. So Mr. Washington's cult has gained unquestioning followers, his work has wonderfully prospered, his friends are legion, and his enemies are confounded. To-day he stands as the one recognized spokesman of his ten million fellows, and one of the most notable figures in a nation of seventy millions. One hesitates, therefore, to criticise a life which, beginning with so little, has done so much. And yet the time is come when one may speak in all sincerity and utter courtesy of the mistakes and shortcomings of Mr. Washington's career, as well as of his triumphs, without being thought captious or envious, and without forgetting that it is easier to do ill than well in the world. . . .

Booker T. Washington arose as essentially the leader not of one race but of two,—a compromiser between the South, the North, and the Negro. Naturally the Negroes resented, at first bitterly, signs of compromise which surrendered their civil and political rights, even though this was to be exchanged for larger chances of economic development. The rich and dominating North, however, was not only weary of the race problem, but was investing largely in Southern enterprises, and welcomed any method of peaceful coöperation. Thus, by national opinion, the Negroes began to recognize Mr. Washington's leadership; and the voice of criticism was hushed.

Mr. Washington represents in Negro thought the old attitude of adjustment and submission; but adjustment at such a peculiar time as to make his programme unique. This is an age of unusual economic development, and Mr. Washington's programme naturally takes an economic cast, becoming a gospel of Work and Money to such an extent as apparently almost completely to overshadow the higher aims of life. Moreover, this is an age when the more advanced races are coming in closer contact with the less developed races, and the race-feeling is therefore intensified; and Mr. Washington's programme practically accepts the alleged inferiority of the Negro races. Again, in our own land, the reaction from the sentiment of war time has given impetus to race-prejudice against Negroes, and Mr. Washington withdraws many of the high demands of Negroes as men and American citizens. In other periods of intensified prejudice all the Negro's tendency to self-assertion has been called forth; at this period a policy of submission is advocated. In the history of nearly all other races and peoples the doctrine preached at such crises has been that manly self-respect is worth more than lands and houses, and that a people who voluntarily surrender such respect, or cease striving for it, are not worth civilizing.

In answer to this, it has been claimed that the Negro can survive only through submission. Mr. Washington distinctly asks that black people give up, at least for the present, three things,—

First, political power,

Second, insistence on civil rights,

Third, higher education of Negro youth,—

and concentrate all their energies on industrial education, the accumulation of wealth, and the conciliation of the South. This policy has been courageously and insistently advocated for over fifteen years, and has been triumphant for perhaps ten years. As a result of this tender of the palm-branch, what has been the return? In these years there have occurred:

1. The disfranchisement of the Negro.

2. The legal creation of a distinct status of civil inferiority for the Negro.

3. The steady withdrawal of aid from institutions for the higher training of the Negro.

These movements are not, to be sure, direct results of Mr. Washington's teachings; but his propaganda has, without a shadow of doubt, helped their speedier accomplishment. The question then comes: Is it possible, and probable, that nine millions of men can make effective progress in economic lines if they are deprived of political rights, made a servile caste, and allowed only the most meagre chance for developing their exceptional men? If history and reason give any distinct answer to these questions, it is an emphatic *No.* And Mr. Washington thus faces the triple paradox of his career:

1. He is striving nobly to make Negro artisans businessmen and property-owners; but it is utterly impossible, under modern competitive methods, for workingmen and property-owners to defend their rights and exist without the right of suffrage.

2. He insists on thrift and self-respect, but at the same time counsels a silent submission to civic inferiority such as is bound to sap the manhood of any race in the long run.

3. He advocates common-school and industrial training, and depreciates institutions of higher learning; but neither the Negro common-schools, nor Tuskegee itself, could remain open a day were it not for teachers trained in Negro colleges, or trained by their graduates.

This triple paradox in Mr. Washington's position is the object of criticism by two classes of colored Americans. One class is spiritually descended from Toussaint the Savior, through Gabriel, Vesey, and Turner, and they represent the attitude of revolt and revenge; they hate the white South blindly and distrust the white race generally, and so far as they agree on definite action, think that the Negro's only hope lies in emigration beyond the borders of the United States. And yet, by the irony of fate, nothing has more effectually made this programme seem hopeless than the recent course of the United States toward weaker and darker peoples in the West Indies, Hawaii, and the Philippines,—for where in the world may we go and be safe from lying and brute force?

The other class of Negroes who cannot agree with Mr. Washington has hitherto said little aloud. They deprecate the sight of scattered counsels, of internal disagreement; and especially they dislike making their just criticism of a useful and earnest man an excuse for a general discharge of venom from small-minded opponents. Nevertheless, the questions involved are so fundamental and serious that it is difficult to see how men like the Grimkes, Kelly Miller, J. W. E. Bowen, and other representatives of this group, can much longer be silent. Such men feel in conscience bound to ask of this nation three things:

1. The right to vote.
2. Civic equality.
3. The education of youth according to ability.

They acknowledge Mr. Washington's invaluable service in counselling patience and courtesy in such demands; they do not ask that ignorant black men vote when ignorant whites are debarred, or that any reasonable restrictions in the suffrage should not be applied; they know that the low social level of the mass of the race is responsible for much discrimination against it, but they also know, and the nation knows, that relentless color-prejudice is more often a cause than a result of the Negro's degradation; they seek the abatement of this relic of barbarism, and not its systematic encouragement and pampering by all agencies of social power from the Associated Press to the Church of Christ. They advocate, with Mr. Washington, a broad system of Negro common schools supplemented by thorough industrial training; but they are surprised that a man of Mr. Washington's insight cannot see that no such educational system ever has rested or can rest on any other basis than that of the well-equipped college and university, and they insist that there is a demand for a few such institutions throughout the South to train the best of the Negro youth as teachers, professional men, and leaders.

This group of men honor Mr. Washington for his attitude of conciliation toward the white South; they accept the "Atlanta Compromise" in its broadest interpretation; they recognize, with him, many signs of promise, many men of high purpose and fair judgment, in this section; they know that no easy task has been laid upon a region already tottering under heavy burdens. But, nevertheless, they insist that the way to truth and right lies in straightforward honesty, not in indiscriminate flattery; in praising those of the South who do well and criticising uncompromisingly those who do ill; in taking advantage of the opportunities at hand and urging their fellows to do the same, but at the same time in remembering that only a firm adherence to their higher ideals and aspirations will ever keep those ideals within the realm of possibility. They do not expect that the free right to vote, to enjoy civic rights, and to be educated, will come in a moment; they do not expect to see the bias and prejudices of years disappear at the blast of a trumpet; but they are absolutely certain that the way for a people to gain their reasonable rights is not by voluntarily throwing them away and insisting that they do not want them; that the way for a people to gain respect is not by continually belittling and ridiculing themselves; that, on the contrary, Negroes must insist continually, in season and out of season, that voting is necessary to modern manhood, that color discrimination is barbarism, and that black boys need education as well as white boys.

In failing thus to state plainly and unequivocally the legitimate demands of their people, even at the cost of opposing an honored leader, the thinking classes of American Negroes would shirk a heavy responsibility,—a responsibility to themselves, a responsibility to the struggling masses, a responsibility to the darker races of men whose future depends so largely on this American experiment, but especially a responsibility to this nation,—this common Fatherland. It is wrong to encourage a man or a people in evil-doing; it is wrong to aid and abet a national crime simply because it is unpopular not to do so. The growing spirit of kindliness and reconciliation between the North and South after the frightful difference of a generation ago ought to be a source of deep congratulation to all, and especially to those whose mistreatment caused the war; but if that reconciliation is to be marked by the industrial slavery and civic death of those same black men, with permanent legislation into a position of inferiority, then those black men, if they are really men, are called upon by every consideration of patriotism and loyalty to oppose such a course by all civilized methods, even though such opposition involves disagreement with Mr. Booker T. Washington. We have no right to sit silently by while the inevitable seeds are sown for a harvest of disaster to our children, black and white. . . .

It would be unjust to Mr. Washington not to acknowledge that in several instances he has opposed movements in the South which were unjust to the Negro; he sent memorials to the Louisiana and Alabama constitutional conventions, he has spoken against lynching, and in other ways has openly or silently set his influence against sinister schemes and unfortunate happenings. Notwithstanding this, it is equally true to assert that on the whole the distinct impression left by Mr. Washington's propaganda is, first, that the South is justified in its present attitude toward the Negro because of the Negro's degradation; secondly, that the prime cause of the Negro's failure to rise more quickly is his wrong education in the past; and, thirdly, that his future rise depends primarily on his own efforts. Each of these propositions is a dangerous half-truth. The supplementary truths must never be lost sight of: first, slavery and race-prejudice are potent if not sufficient causes of the Negro's position; second, industrial and common-school training were necessarily slow in planting because they had to await the black teachers trained by higher institutions,—it being extremely doubtful if any essentially different development was possible, and certainly a Tuskegee was unthinkable before 1880; and, third, while it is a great truth to say that the Negro must strive and strive mightily to help himself, it is equally true that unless his striving be not simply seconded, but rather aroused and encouraged, by the initiative of the richer and wiser environing group, he cannot hope for great success.

In his failure to realize and impress this last point, Mr. Washington is especially to be criticised. His doctrine has tended to make the whites, North and South, shift the burden of the Negro problem to the Negro's shoulders and stand aside as critical and rather pessimistic spectators; when in fact the burden belongs to the nation, and the hands of none of us are clean if we bend not our energies to righting these great wrongs.

The South ought to be led, by candid and honest criticism, to assert her better self and do her full duty to the race she has cruelly wronged and is still wronging. The North—her co-partner in guilt—cannot salve her conscience by plastering it with gold. We cannot settle this problem by diplomacy and suaveness, by "policy" alone. If worse come to worst, can the moral fibre of this country survive the slow throttling and murder of nine millions of men?

The black men of America have a duty to perform, a duty stern and delicate,—a forward movement to oppose a part of the work of their greatest leader. So far as Mr. Washington preaches Thrift, Patience, and Industrial Training for the masses, we must hold up his hands and strive with him, rejoicing in his honors and glorying in the strength of this Joshua called of God and of man to lead the headless host. But so far as Mr. Washington apologizes for injustice, North or South, does not rightly value the privilege and duty of voting, belittles the emasculating effects of caste distinctions, and opposes the higher training and ambition of our brighter minds,—so far as he, the South, or the Nation, does this,—we must unceasingly and firmly oppose them. By every civilized and peaceful method we must strive for the rights which the world accords to men, clinging unwaveringly to those great words which the sons of the Fathers would fain forget: "We hold these truths to be self-evident: That all men are created equal; that they are endowed by their Creator with certain unalienable rights; that among these are life, liberty, and the pursuit of happiness."

Charlotte Perkins Stetson (Gilman)

from Women and Economics: A Study of the Economic Relation Between Men and Women as a Factor in Social Evolution (1900)

The path of history is strewn with fossils and faint relics of extinct races—races which died of what the sociologist would call internal diseases rather than natural causes. This, too, has been clear to the observer in all ages. It has been easily seen that there was something in our own behavior which did us more harm than any external difficulty; but what we have not seen is the natural cause of our unnatural conduct, and how most easily to alter it.

Rudely classifying the principal fields of human difficulty, we find one large proportion lies in the sex-relation, and another in the economic relation, between the individual constituents of society. To speak broadly, the troubles of life as we find them are mainly traceable to the heart or the purse. The other horror of our lives—disease—comes back often to these causes,—to something wrong either in economic relation or in sex-relation. To be ill-fed or ill-bred, or both, is largely what makes us the sickly race we are. In this wrong breeding, this maladjustment of the sex-relation in humanity, what are the principal features? We see in social evolution two main lines of action in this department of life. One is a gradual orderly development of monogamous marriage, as the form of sex-union best calculated to advance the interests of the individual and of society. It should be clearly understood that this is a natural development, inevitable in the course of social progress; not an artificial condition, enforced by laws of our making. Monogamy is found among birds and mammals: it is just as natural a condition as polygamy or promiscuity or any other form of sex-union; and its permanence and integrity are introduced and increased by the needs of the young and the advantage to the race, just as any other form of reproduction was introduced. Our moral concepts rest primarily on facts. The moral quality of monogamous marriage depends on its true advantage to the individual and to society. If it were not the best form of marriage for our racial good, it would not be right. All the way up, from the promiscuous horde of savages, with their miscellaneous matings, to the lifelong devotion of romantic love, social life has been evolving a type of sex-union best suited to develope and improve the individual and the race. This is an orderly process, and a pleasant one, involving only such comparative pain and difficulty as always attend the assumption of new processes and the extinction of the old; but accompanied by far more joy than pain. . . .

Natural selection develops race. Sexual selection develops sex. Sex-development is one throughout its varied forms, tending only to reproduce what is. But race-development rises ever in higher and higher manifestation of energy. As sexes, we share our distinction with the animal kingdom almost to the beginning of life, and with the vegetable world as well. As races, we differ in ascending degree; and the human race stands highest in the scale of life so far.

When, then, it can be shown that sex-distinction in the human race is so excessive as not only to affect injuriously its own purposes, but to check and pervert the progress of the race, it becomes a matter for most serious consideration. Nothing could be more inevitable, however, under our sexuo-economic relation. By the economic dependence of the human female upon the male, the balance of forces is altered. Natural selection no longer checks the action of sexual selection, but co-operates with it. Where both sexes obtain their food through the same exertions, from the same sources, under the same conditions, both sexes are acted upon alike, and developed alike by their environment. Where the two sexes obtain their food under different conditions, and where that difference consists in one of them being fed by the other, then the feeding sex becomes the environment of the fed. Man, in supporting woman, has become her economic environment. Under natural selection, every creature is modified to its environment, developing perforce the qualities needed to obtain its livelihood under that environment. Man, as the feeder of woman, becomes the strongest modifying force in her economic condition. Under sexual selection the human creature is of course modified to its mate, as with all creatures. When the mate becomes also the master, when economic necessity is added to sex-attraction, we have the two great evolutionary forces acting together to the same end; namely, to develop sex-distinction in the human female. For, in her position of economic dependence in the sex-relation, sex-distinction is with her not only a means of attracting a mate, as with all creatures, but a means of getting her livelihood, as is the case with no other creature under heaven. Because of the economic dependence of the human female on her mate, she is modified to sex to an excessive degree. This excessive modification she transmits to her children; and so is steadily implanted in the human constitution the morbid tendency to excess in this relation, which has acted so universally upon us in all ages, in spite of our best efforts to restrain it. It is not the normal sex-tendency, common to all creatures, but an abnormal sex-tendency, produced and maintained by the abnormal economic relation which makes one sex get its living from the other by the exercise of sex-functions. This is the immediate effect upon individuals of the peculiar sexuo-economic relation which obtains among us. . . .

From the time our children are born, we use every means known to accentuate sex-distinction in both boy and girl; and the reason that the boy is not so hopelessly marked by it as the girl is that he has the whole field of human expression open to him besides. In our steady insistence on proclaiming sex-distinction we have grown to consider most human attributes as masculine attributes, for the simple reason that they were allowed to men and forbidden to women. . . .

All the varied activities of economic production and distribution, all our arts and industries, crafts and trades, all our growth in science, discovery, government, religion,—these are along the line of self-preservation: these are, or should be, common to both sexes. To teach, to rule, to make, to decorate, to distribute,—these are not sex-functions: they are race-functions. Yet so inordinate is the sex-distinction of the human race that the whole field of human progress has been considered a masculine prerogative. What could more absolutely prove the excessive sex-distinction of the human race? That this difference should surge over all its natural boundaries and blazon itself across every act of life, so that every step of the human creature is marked "male" or "female,"—surely, this is enough to show our over-sexed condition.

This excessive distinction shows itself again in a marked precocity of development. Our little children, our very babies, show signs of it when the young of other creatures are serenely asexual in general appearance and habit. We eagerly note this precocity. We are proud of it. We carefully encourage it by precept and example, taking pains to develop the sex-instinct in little children, and think no harm. One of the first things we force upon the child's dawning consciousness is the fact that he is a boy or that she is a girl, and that, therefore, each must regard everything from a different point of view. They must be dressed differently, not on account of their personal needs, which are exactly similar at this period, but so that neither they, nor any one beholding them, may for a moment forget the distinction of sex. . . .

That the girl-child should be so dressed as to require a difference in care and behavior, resting wholly on the fact that she is a girl,—a fact not otherwise present to her thought at that age,—is a precocious insistence upon sex-distinction, most unwholesome in its results. Boys and girls are expected, also, to behave differently to each other, and to people in general,—a behavior to be briefly described in two words. To the boy we say, "Do"; to the girl, "Don't." The little boy must "take care" of the little girl, even if she is larger than he is. "Why?" he asks. Because he is a boy. Because of sex. Surely, if she is the stronger, she ought to take care of him, especially as the protective instinct is purely feminine in a normal race. It is not long before the boy learns his lesson. He is a boy, going to be a man; and that means all. "I thank the Lord that I was not born a woman," runs the Hebrew prayer. She is a girl, "only a girl," "nothing but a girl," and going to be a woman,—only a woman. Boys are encouraged from the beginning to show the feelings supposed to be proper to their sex. When our infant son bangs about, roars, and smashes things, we say proudly that he is "a regular boy!" When our infant daughter coquettes with visitors, or wails in maternal agony because her brother has broken her doll, whose sawdust remains she nurses with piteous care, we say proudly that "she is a perfect little mother already!" What business has a little girl with the instincts of maternity? No more than the little boy should have with the instincts of paternity. They are sex-instincts, and should not appear till the period of adolescence. The most normal girl is the "tom-boy,"—whose numbers increase among us in these wiser days,—a healthy young creature, who is human through and through, not feminine till it is time to be. The most normal boy has calmness and gentleness as well as vigor and courage. He is a human creature as well as a male creature, and not aggressively masculine till it is time to be. Childhood is not the period for these marked manifestations of sex. That we exhibit them, that we admire and encourage them, shows our over-sexed condition.

When man began to feed and defend woman, she ceased proportionately to feed and defend herself. When he stood between her and her physical environment, she ceased proportionately to feel the influence of that environment and respond to it. When he became her immediate and all-important environment, she began proportionately to respond to this new influence, and to be modified accordingly. In a free state, speed was of as great advantage to the female as to the male, both in enabling her to catch prey and in preventing her from being caught by enemies; but, in her new condition, speed was a disadvantage. She was not allowed to do the catching, and it profited her to be caught by her new master. The human female was cut off from the direct action of natural selection, that mighty force which heretofore had acted on male and female alike with inexorable and beneficial effect, developing strength, developing skill, developing endurance, developing courage,—in a word, developing species. . . .

To the young man confronting life the world is wide. Such powers as he has he may use, must use. If he chooses wrong at first, he may choose again, and yet again. Not effective or successful in one channel, he may do better in another. The growing, varied needs of all mankind call on him for the varied service in which he finds his growth. What he wants to be, he may strive to be. What he wants to get, he may strive to get. Wealth, power, social distinction, fame,—what he wants he can try for.

To the young woman confronting life there is the same world beyond, there are the same human energies and human desires and ambition within. But all that she may wish to have, all that she may wish to do, must come through a single channel and a single choice. Wealth, anger, social distinction, fame,—not only these, but home and happiness, reputation, ease and pleasure, her bread and butter,—all, must come to her through a small gold ring. This is a heavy pressure. It has accumulated behind her through heredity, and continued about her through environment. It has been subtly trained into her through education, till she herself has come to think it a right condition, and pours its influence upon her daughter with creasing impetus. Is it any wonder that women are over-sexed? But for the constant inheritance from the more human male, we should have been queen bees, indeed, long before this. But the daughter of the soldier and the sailor, of the artist, the inventor, the great merchant, has inherited in body and brain her share of his development in each generation, and so stayed somewhat human for all her femininity. . . .

The inevitable trend of human life is toward higher civilization; but, while that civilization is confined to one sex, it inevitably exaggerates sex-distinction, until the increasing evil of this condition is stronger than all the good of the civilization attained, and the nation falls. Civilization, be it understood, does not consist in the acquisition of luxuries. Social development is an organic development. A civilized State is one in which the citizens live in organic industrial relation. The more full, free, subtle, and easy that relation; the more perfect the differentiation of labor and exchange of product, with their correlative institutions,—the more perfect is that civilization. To eat, drink, sleep, and keep warm,—these are common to all animals, whether the animal couches in a bed of leaves or one of eiderdown, sleeps in the sun to avoid the wind or builds a furnace-heated house, lies in wait for game or orders a dinner at a hotel. These are but individual animal processes. Whether one lays an egg or a million eggs, whether one bears a cub, a kitten, or a baby, whether one broods its chickens, guards its litter, or tends a nursery full of children, these are but individual animal processes. But to serve each other more and more widely; to live only by such service; to develope special functions, so that we depend for our living on society's return for services that can be of no direct use to ourselves,—this is civilization, our human glory and race-distinction.

All this human progress has been accomplished by men. Women have been left behind, outside, below, having no social relation whatever, merely the sex-relation, whereby they lived. Let us bear in mind that all the tender ties of family are ties of blood, of sex-relationship. A friend, a comrade, a partner,—this is a human relative. Father, mother, son, daughter, sister, brother, husband, wife,—these are sex-relatives. Blood is thicker than water, we say. True. But ties of blood are not those that ring the world with the succeeding waves of progressive religion, art, science, commerce, education, all that makes us human. Man is the human creature. Woman has been checked, starved, aborted in human growth; and the swelling forces of race-development have been driven back in each generation to work in her through sex-functions alone.

This is the way in which the sexuo-economic relation has operated in our species, checking race-development in half of us, and stimulating sex-development in both.

. . . Fortunately, the laws of social evolution do not wait for our recognition or acceptance, they go straight on. And this greater and more important change than the world has ever seen, this slow emergence of the long subverted human female to full racial equality has been going on about us full long enough to be observed. It is seen more prominently in this country than in any other, for many reasons.

The Anglo-Saxon blood, that English mixture of which Tennyson sings,—"Saxon and Norman and Dane though we be,"—is the most powerful expression of the latest current of fresh racial life from the north,—from those sturdy races where the women were more like men, and the men no less manly because of it. The strong, fresh spirit of religious revolt in the new church that protested against and broke loose from the old, woke and stirred the soul of woman as well as the soul of man, and in the equality of martyrdom the sexes learned to stand side by side. Then, in the daring and exposure, the strenuous labor and bitter hardship of the pioneer life of the early settlers, woman's very presence was at a premium; and her labor had a high economic value. Sex-dependence was almost unfelt. She who moulded the bullets, and loaded the guns while the men fired them, was co-defender of the home and young. She who carded and dyed and wove and spun was co-provider for the family. Men and women prayed together, worked together, and fought together in comparative equality. More than all, the development of democracy has brought to us the fullest individualization that the world has ever seen. Although politically expressed by men alone, the character it has produced is inherited by their daughters. The Federal Democracy in its organic union, reacting upon individuals, has so strengthened, freed, emboldened, the human soul in America that we have thrown off slavery, and with the same impulse have set in motion the long struggle toward securing woman's fuller equality before the law.

This struggle has been carried on unflaggingly for fifty years, and fast nears its victorious end. It is not only in the four States where full suffrage is exercised by both sexes, nor in the twenty-four where partial suffrage is given to women, that we are to count progress; but in the changes legal and social, mental and physical, which mark the advance of the mother of the world toward her full place. Have we not all observed the change even in size of the modern woman, with its accompanying strength and agility? . . . Women are growing honester, braver, stronger, more healthful and skilful and able and free, more human in all ways.

The change in education is in large part a cause of this, and progressively a consequence. Day by day the bars go down. More and more the field lies open for the mind of woman to glean all it can, and it has responded most eagerly. Not only our pupils, but our teachers, are mainly women. And the clearness and strength of the brain of the woman prove continually the injustice of the clamorous contempt long poured upon what was scornfully called "the female mind." There is no female mind. The brain is not an organ of sex. As well speak of a female liver. . . .

In the fiction of to-day women are continually taking larger place in the action of the story. They are given personal characteristics beyond those of physical beauty. And they are no longer content simply to *be*: they *do*. They are showing qualities of bravery, endurance, strength, foresight, and power for the swift execution of well-conceived plans. They have ideas and purposes of their own; and even when, as in so many cases described by the more reactionary novelists, the efforts of the heroine are shown to be entirely futile, and she comes back with a rush to the self-effacement of marriage with economic dependence, still the efforts were there. Disapprove as he may, use his art to oppose and contemn as he may, the true novelist is forced to chronicle the distinctive features of his time; and no feature is more distinctive of this time than the increasing individualization of women. With lighter touch, but with equally unerring truth, the wit and humor of the day show the same development. The majority of our current jokes on women turn on their "newness," their advance.

Women have been led under pressure of necessity into a most reluctant entrance upon fields of economic activity. The sluggish and greedy disposition bred of long ages of dependence has by no means welcomed the change. Most women still work only as they "have to," until they can marry and "be supported." Men, too, liking the power that goes with money, and the poor quality of gratitude and affection bought with it, resent and oppose the change; but all this disturbs very little the course of social progress.

A truer spirit is the increasing desire of young girls to be independent, to have a career of their own, at least for a while, and the growing objection of countless wives to the pitiful asking for money, to the beggary of their position. More and more do fathers give their daughters, and husbands their wives, a definite allowance,—a separate bank account,—something which they can play is all their own. The spirit of personal independence in the women of to-day is sure proof that a change has come.

For a while the introduction of machinery which took away from the home so many industries deprived women of any importance as an economic factor; but presently she arose, and followed her lost wheel and loom to their new place, the mill. To-day there is hardly an industry in the land in which some women are not found. Everywhere throughout America are women workers outside the unpaid labor of the home, the last census giving three million of them. This is so patent a fact, and makes itself felt in so many ways by so many persons, that it is frequently and widely discussed. Without here going into its immediate advantages or disadvantages from an industrial point of view, it is merely instanced as an undeniable proof of the radical change in the economic position of women that is advancing upon us. She is assuming new relations from year to year before our eyes; but we, seeing all social facts from a personal point of view, have failed to appreciate the nature of the change.

Consider, too, the altered family relation which attends this movement. Entirely aside from the strained relation in marriage, the other branches of family life feel the strange new forces, and respond to them. "When I was a girl," sighs the gray-haired mother, "we sisters all sat and sewed while mother read to us. Now every one of my daughter has a different club!" She sighs, be it observed. We invariably object to changed conditions in those departments of life where we have established ethical values. For all the daughters to sew while the mother read aloud to them was esteemed right; and, therefore, the radiating diffusion of daughters among clubs is esteemed wrong,—a danger to home life. In the period of the common sewing and reading the women so assembled were closely allied in industrial and intellectual development as well as in family relationship. They all could do the same work, and liked to do it. They all could read the same book, and liked to read it. (And reading, half a century ago, was still considered half a virtue and the other half a fine art.) Hence the ease with which this group of women entered upon their common work and common pleasure.

The growing individualization of democratic life brings inevitable change to our daughters as well as to our sons. Girls do not all like to sew, many do not know how. Now to sit sewing together, instead of being a harmonizing process, would generate different degrees of restlessness, of distaste, and of nervous irritation. And, as to the reading aloud, it is not so easy now to choose a book that a well-educated family of modern girls and their mother would all enjoy together. As the race become more specialized, more differentiated, the simple lines of relation in family life draw with less force, and the more complex lines of relation in social life draw with more force; and this is a perfectly natural and desirable process for women as well as for men. . . .

The rapid extension of function in the modern woman has nothing to do with any exchange of masculine and feminine traits: it is simply an advance in human development of traits common to both sexes, and is wholly good in its results. No one who looks at the life about us can fail to see the alteration going on. It is a pity that we so fail to estimate its value. On the other hand, the growth and kindling intensity of the social consciousness among us all is as conspicuous a feature of modern life as the change in women's position, and closely allied therewith. . . .

Social sympathy and thought are growing more intense and active every day. In our cumbrous efforts at international arbitration, in the half-hearted alliances and agreements between great peoples, in the linking of humanity together across ocean and mountain and desert plain by steam and electricity, in the establishment of such world-functions as the international postal service,—in these, externally, our social unity has begun to act. In the more familiar field of personal life, who has not seen how unceasingly many of us are occupied in the interests of the community, even to the injury of our own? The rising manifestations of social interest among women were covered with ridicule at first, through such characters as Mrs. Jellyby or Mrs. Pardiggle, although a few women who were so great and so identified with religion and philanthropy as to command respect, women like the saintly Elizabeth Fry, Florence Nightingale, and Clara Barton, escaped. But both belong to the same age, are part of the same phenomena. To-day there is hardly a woman of intelligence in all America, to say nothing of other countries, who is not definitely and actively concerned in some social interest, who does not recognize some duty besides those incident to her own blood relationship. . . .

One of the most valuable features of this vast line of progress is the new heroism it is pouring into life. The crumbling and flattening of ambitions and ideals under pressure of our modern business life is a patent fact. We are growing to surrender taste and conscience and honor itself to the demands of business success, prostituting the noblest talents to the most ignoble uses with that last excuse of cowardice,—"A man must live." Into this phase of life comes a new spirit,—the spirit of such women as Elizabeth Cady Stanton and Susan B. Anthony; of Dr. Elizabeth Blackwell and her splendid sisterhood; of all the women who have battled and suffered for half a century, forcing their way, with sacrifices never to be told, into the field of freedom so long denied them,—not for themselves alone, but for one another. We have loudly cried out at the injury to the home and family which are supposed to follow such a course. We have unsparingly ridiculed the unattractive and unfeminine among these vanguard workers. But few have thought what manner of spirit it must take to leave the dear old easy paths so long trodden by so many feet, and go to hew out new ones alone. The nature of the effort involved and the nature of the opposition incurred conduced to lessen the soft charms and graces of the ultra-feminine state; but the women who follow and climb swiftly up the steps which these great leaders so laboriously built may do the new work in the new places, and still keep much of what these strenuous heroes had to lose. . . .

The gates are nearly all open, at least in some places; and the racial activities of women are free to develop as rapidly as the nature of the case will allow. The main struggle now is with the distorted nature of the creature herself. Grand as are the women who embody at whatever cost the highest spirit of the age, there still remains to us the heavy legacy of the years behind,—the innumerable weak and little women, with the aspirations of an affectionate guinea pig. The soul of woman must speak through the long accumulation of her intensified sex-nature, through the uncertain impulses of a starved and thwarted class. She must recognize that she is handicapped. She must understand her difficulty, and meet it bravely and firmly.

But this is a matter for personal volition, for subjective consciousness. The thing to see and to rejoice in is that, with and without their conscious volition, with or without the approval and assistance of men, in spite of that crowing imbecility of history,—the banded opposition of some women to the advance of the others,—the female of our race is making sure and rapid progress in human development.

Margaret Murray Washington

from "The Gain in the Life of Negro Women" (1904)

In the many-tongued discussion of negro problems there is no fallacy so common or so insidious as that by which a proposition found true of a particular group of negroes is, in virtue of that fact, proclaimed true of all or of the great mass. To maintain that since from the negroes in a certain town no superior class has emerged, the negroes of America have no superior class—to maintain that is to feel with the Africans that, because the white slave-catchers were merciless, all white men are merciless. The specific problem which is the subject of this paper—Gain in the Life of Negro Women—is often similarly befuddled. There are 8,840,789 negroes in this country, of whom 4,447,568 are women. These women live in States from Massachusetts to Mississippi; some live on plantations, some in towns, some in cities; some are ignorant, some intelligent; some are rich, some poor; some good, some bad. To make propositions that will hold true of these many and essentially different groups of negro women is a task which I do not essay—a task to which Edmund Burke referred when he said that no man can indict a whole race of people.

Moreover, you can no more find the "average" negro woman than you can multiply eggs by treaties. Just as eggs are different from treaties, so good negro women are different from bad negro women, and no average can be struck. The best we can do is to estimate the size of the various groups of negro women, but even this is not enough; the influence, efficiency, significance of one superior woman's life may be indefinitely more than that of ten dull drudges. And so the statistical method could not do justice to this essentially human problem; statistics negate individuality.

I propose to speak of the superior class of negro women, and roughly to indicate something of the import of their organized endeavor.

Every census teems with information that testifies to the material and spiritual gain of the negro population and notably of negro women. To cite a few illustrations from school enrollment, I may say that in the census year [1900] 1,096,774 negroes attended school, of whom 510,007 were males and 586,767 were females; 27,858 females as against 28,268 males attended school from two to three months; 160,231 females as against 136,028 males attended school from four to five months; and 227,546 females as against 187,173 males attended school six months and more. These figures indicate the well-known fact that girls attend school more continuously than boys; the boys must go to work while the girls are in school.

In the one hundred public high schools for negroes, 3,659 girls as against 2,974 boys were enrolled in elementary grades, and in secondary grades 3,933 girls and 1,634 boys. In these schools 154 girls were enrolled in the business course; 792 in the classical course; 1,098 girls in the scientific course. In the normal course of the high schools there were 221 girls and 65 boys. In the industrial training courses there were 709 girls and 550 boys. 501 girls and 177 boys graduated in 1900—1 from the high-school course.

In the secondary and higher schools of the colored race there were 13,306 females and 9,587 males in elementary grades; 7,383 females and 6,164 males in the secondary grades; 740 females and 2,339 males in the collegiate course. In secondary and higher schools there were 17,138 colored students receiving the industrial training, of whom 11,012 were females.

These young negro women have not come through the schools on "flowery beds of ease." While their mothers and fathers of the generation of yesterday have not been able to give them that home training essential to the best development, they have by the sweat of their brows aided their boys and girls to get the education for which they themselves had yearned in vain. The average young negro woman has either helped her parents on the cotton patch or her mother with her laundry work, during vacation, and in that way has helped to defray her expenses through school. The large majority have worked their way through school in spite of the heavy odds against them. Better home training might have aided them the better to meet the problems confronting them in their lives and service.

At any rate, the schools are each year appreciably increasing the number of educated women of negro blood. The educational provision is of course dangerously inadequate; thus, I know of a great Southern State where there has not for years been a nearly sufficient number of candidates for positions as teachers who could meet the minimum requirements. However, the proportion of educated negro women to-day is very much greater than in 1860. The crucial question is always whether, in the environment in which the negro school or college girl eventually finds herself, she will be able to maintain in her life the ideals of school and college. A superior class of negro women, realizing this situation, have organized a system of clubs to meet the difficulty in some measure. The educated negro girl, these women say, must not go back to the blanket! The woman's club organizes the social life of educated negro women on rational principles, and urges those women to intelligent social service. From this point of view, and from many others, the club movement is interesting.

The club movement among negro women, with social betterment as the aim, began fifteen years ago. So educative was the force that a National Association was organized in 1895. To-day West Virginia, Ohio, Iowa, Pennsylvania, Illinois, Missouri, Mississippi, and Alabama have State federations. The Northeastern Federation of forty-five clubs confines its work to the Northeast. The Southern Federation of two hundred and twenty-five clubs is devoted to work in the Southern States, but its clubs are affiliated with the National organization.

The work of the individual club is varied. The largest of these have departments directed by women interested in certain phases of uplift—free kindergartens, day nurseries, temperance, prison work, social purity, Mothers' Unions, and the like. The intellectual development has an outlet by discussions of live topics. Here is a typical evening's programme of one of these clubs:

Music, Vocal.

Russia, Past and Present.

Quartet.

The Representative People of Russia.

Life of the Russian Peasant Women as Compared with that of Negro Women.

Instrumental Music.

Our women are wide awake to the necessity of social culture, and no more pleasing feature is there than to receive their friends in their best attire in tastefully furnished reception-rooms. This is a diversion on the club programme perhaps once a year. But the earnest, faithful work of these women in their chosen fields of labor is the aim of their existence. By their efforts free kindergartens, day nurseries, sewing and cooking schools, are supported. Hundreds of untaught mothers living with their children in their cabin homes or in the crowded tenements of the cities are taught how to live. In some of the large towns weekly meetings are held with an average attendance of one hundred and fifty women. . . .

For the past five years the Southern Federation of Colored Women's Clubs has met in the cities of Montgomery, Alabama; Atlanta, Georgia; Vicksburg, Mississippi; New Orleans, Louisiana; and recently in Jacksonville, Florida. After each yearly meeting the impetus gained in the work has been wonderful. Club life has a strong hold in all the cities and States of the South. Each year the new accessions come better prepared to lend a hand in the service. Mothers, business women, school-teachers, are equally active in their efforts to reach out after those who should be awakened to the necessity of proper home making and training for their children.

In the story of the evolution of a club woman in one of our periodicals the trend of the club idea of the white woman seems to take her away from home duties. But our negro women are American daughters of aliens whose home life has not generations of culture behind it, and our work must be practical.

Yet a large percentage of our negro women preside in homes of their own in all these cities where the Southern Federation of Negro Women's Clubs has been privileged to meet. The majority of these club women have helped their husbands to purchase homes by their thrift and economy. Many of these residences are situated on prominent streets. They are well-designed, painted cottages of six and eight rooms, with bath and hot and cold water contrivances, well ventilated, and constructed with an eye to sanitary arrangements. These homes are tastefully furnished.

The hostesses who have entertained the delegations of the Federation as the years have passed, not only know how to keep house, but how to cook and serve well-prepared meals properly in well-appointed dining-rooms. The same women have attended the daily sessions of the conventions, and are those who give the addresses of welcome, direct the federated clubs of the city, and conduct those Mothers' Conferences that are proving vital helps. These women are the leaders in the side trips, trolley rides, and local receptions given as recreations to the visiting workers. They are women following their chosen pursuits—dressmaking, millinery, manicuring. They are clerks, stenographers, trained nurses, teachers, workers in every field of labor that helps them to make a living and buy homes. In many of our largest cities a goodly percentage of the bank depositors are negro women. This means a nest-egg for the purchase and ownership of homes. The negro women are unmodern in that they assume a share in working to pay for homes for their families. In many instances young married couples unite their savings in buying homes—in this order of helpmate may lie some of the reason for gain in the sacredness of the marriage tie. . . .

Our young woman is already taking her place in various spheres of life, regardless of precedent. Her training fits her for home life and the larger social service of the school-room. She does with her might what her hands find to do. A college girl directs a steam laundry or makes soap in a large laundering establishment. She has spent four years at Greek and Latin, but has charge of a broom factory where girls are manufacturing brooms of all sorts and sizes. She has gained all the training possible in the schools of her native heath, and by arduous sacrifice has worked her way through the best New England schools of domestic science that she might be thoroughly prepared to teach. She has a laboratory for her theory classes in cooking. She teaches practical cooking daily to large classes of white-capped, white-aproned girls, with individual towels and holders, and at the end of each week in one school alone four hundred and fifty negro girls have learned to cook by doing. No more helpful encouragement has come for this work than the testimonials from white women of the South interested in the improvement of some of these girls.

Young negro women are teaching hundreds of their sisters the same principles of dressmaking and millinery that they were taught in the training-schools of Pratt and Teachers' College. And these young women are not misfits. They are not despondent in their calling. They are putting in brain with the would-be drudgery, and are making marked success of industries where women with fewer advantages might have failed to show their pupils the true dignity of labor.

The present indications of advance in the life of negro women are most hopeful for the future of the race. With the home training that is becoming possible, with the training that our schools afford, with the inheritance of true worth that made the parents do their utmost to bequeath to their children honest, upright lives, the young negro women will possess that wealth of character that will be the means eventually of dispelling the greatest barriers that may confront the race. . . .

It remains with the greater mass of our women to make the weal or woe come quickly or linger. But the signs of the times are bright. The educative forces are at work. The greater mass is being leavened, and we thank God that there will be no retrograde. There has been none and there will be none!

JANE ADDAMS

from Twenty Years at Hull-House (1910)

Throughout our school years we were always keenly conscious of the growing development of Rockford Seminary into a college. The opportunity for our Alma Mater to take her place in the new movement of full college education for women filled us with enthusiasm, and it became a driving ambition with the undergraduates to share in this new and glorious undertaking. We gravely decided that it was important that some of the students should be ready to receive the bachelor's degree the very first moment that the charter of the school should secure the right to confer it. Two of us, therefore, took a course in mathematics, advanced beyond anything previously given in the school, from one of those early young women working for a Ph.D., who was temporarily teaching in Rockford that she might study more mathematics in Leipzig. . . .

In line with this policy of placing a woman's college on an equality with the other colleges of the state, we applied for an opportunity to compete in the intercollegiate oratorical contest of Illinois, and we succeeded in having Rockford admitted as the first woman's college. When I was finally selected as the orator, I was somewhat dismayed to find that, representing not only one school but college women in general, I could not resent the brutal frankness with which my oratorical possibilities were discussed by the enthusiastic group who would allow no personal feeling to stand in the way of progress, especially the progress of Woman's Cause. I was told among other things that I had an intolerable habit of dropping my voice at the end of a sentence in the most feminine, apologetic and even deprecatory manner which would probably lose Woman the first place.

Woman certainly did lose the first place and stood fifth, exactly in the dreary middle, but the ignominious position may not have been solely due to bad mannerisms, for a prior place was easily accorded to William Jennings Bryan, who not only thrilled his auditors with an almost prophetic anticipation of the cross of gold, but with a moral earnestness which we had mistakenly assumed would be the unique possession of the feminine orator. . . .

I do not wish to take callow writing too seriously, but I reproduce from an oratorical contest the following bit of premature pragmatism, doubtless due much more to temperament than to perception, because I am still ready to subscribe to it, although the grandiloquent style is, I hope, a thing of the past: "Those who believe that Justice is but a poetical longing within us, the enthusiast who thinks it will come in the form of a millennium, those who see it established by the strong arm of a hero, are not those who have comprehended the vast truths of life. The actual Justice must come by trained intelligence, by broadened sympathies toward the individual man or woman who crosses our path; one item added to another is the only method by which to build up a conception lofty enough to be of use in the world." . . .

Toward the end of our four years' course we debated much as to what we were to be, and long before the end of my schooldays it was quite settled in my mind that I should study medicine and "live with the poor." This conclusion of course was the result of many things, perhaps epitomized in my graduating essay on "Cassandra" and her tragic fate "always to be in the right, and always to be disbelieved and rejected."

This state of affairs, it may readily be guessed, the essay held to be an example of the feminine trait of mind called intuition, "an accurate perception of Truth and Justice, which rests contented in itself and will make no effort to confirm itself or to organize through existing knowledge." The essay then proceeds—I am forced to admit, with overmuch conviction—with the statement that woman can only "grow accurate and intelligible by the thorough study of at least one branch of physical science, for only with eyes thus accustomed to the search for truth can she detect all self-deceit and fancy in herself and learn to express herself without dogmatism." So much for the first part of the thesis. Having thus "gained accuracy, would woman bring this force to bear throughout morals and justice, then she must find in active labor the promptings and inspirations that come from growing insight." I was quite certain that by following these directions carefully, in the end the contemporary woman would find "her faculties clear and acute from the study of science, and her hand upon the magnetic chain of humanity."

This veneration for science portrayed in my final essay was doubtless the result of the statements the textbooks were then making of what was called the theory of evolution, the acceptance of which even thirty years after the publication of Darwin's *Origin of Species* had about it a touch of intellectual adventure. We knew, for instance, that our science teacher had accepted this theory, but we had a strong suspicion that the teacher of Butler's *Analogy* had not. We chafed at the meagerness of the college library in this direction, and I used to bring back in my handbag books belonging to an advanced brother-in-law who had studied medicine in Germany and who therefore was quite emancipated. The first gift I made when I came into possession of my small estate the year after I left school was a thousand dollars to the library of Rockford College, with the stipulation that it be spent for scientific books. In the long vacations I pressed plants, stuffed birds, and pounded rocks in some vague belief that I was approximating the new method, and yet when my stepbrother who was becoming a real scientist, tried to carry me along with him into the merest outskirts of the methods of research, it at once became evident that I had no aptitude and was unable to follow intelligently Darwin's careful observations on the earthworm. I made a heroic effort, although candor compels me to state that I never would have finished if I had not been pulled and pushed by my really ardent companion, who in addition to a multitude of earthworms and a fine microscope, possessed untiring tact with one of flagging zeal.

As our boarding-school days neared the end, in the consciousness of approaching separation we vowed eternal allegiance to our "early ideals," and promised each other we would "never abandon them without conscious justification," and we often warned each other of "the perils of self-tradition."

Whatever may have been the perils of self-tradition, I certainly did not escape them, for it required eight years—from the time I left Rockford in the summer of 1881 until Hull-House was opened in the autumn of 1899—to formulate my convictions even in the least satisfactory manner, much less to reduce them to a plan for action. During most of that time I was absolutely at sea so far as any moral purpose was concerned, clinging only to the desire to live in a really living world and refusing to be content with a shadowy intellectual or aesthetic reflection of it. . . .

* * *

Four fifths of the children brought into the Juvenile Court in Chicago are the children of foreigners. The Germans are the greatest offenders, Polish next. Do their children suffer from the excess of virtue in those parents so eager to own a house and lot? One often sees a grasping parent in the court, utterly broken down when the Americanized youth who has been brought to grief clings as piteously to his peasant father as if he were still a frightened little boy in the steerage.

Many of these children have come to grief through their premature fling into city life, having thrown off parental control as they have impatiently discarded foreign ways. Boys of ten and twelve will refuse to sleep at home, preferring the freedom of an old brewery vault or an empty warehouse to the obedience required by their parents, and for days these boys will live on the milk and bread which they steal from the back porches after the early morning delivery. Such children complain that there is "no fun" at home. One little chap who was given a vacant lot to cultivate by the City Garden Association insisted upon raising only popcorn and tried to present the entire crop to Hull-House "to be used for the parties," with the stipulation that he would have "to be invited every single time."

Then there are little groups of dissipated young men who pride themselves upon their ability to live without working and who despise all the honest and sober ways of their immigrant parents. They are at once a menace and a center of demoralization. Certainly the bewildered parents, unable to speak English and ignorant of the city, whose children have disappeared for days or weeks, have often come to Hull-House, evincing that agony which fairly separates the marrow from the bone, as if they had discovered a new type of suffering, devoid of the healing in familiar sorrows. It is as if they did not know how to search for the children without the assistance of the children themselves. Perhaps the most pathetic aspect of such cases is their revelation of the premature dependence of the older and wiser upon the young and foolish, which is in itself often responsible for the situation because it has given the children an undue sense of their own importance and a false security that they can take care of themselves.

On the other hand, an Italian girl who has had lessons in cooking at the public school will help her mother to connect the entire family with American food and household habits. That the mother has never baked bread in Italy—only mixed it in her own house and then taken it out to the village oven—makes all the more valuable her daughter's understanding of the complicated cooking stove. The same thing is true of the girl who learns to sew in the public school, and more than anything else, perhaps, of the girl who receives the first simple instruction in the care of little children—that skillful care which every tenement house baby requires if he is to be pulled through his second summer. As a result of this teaching I recall a young girl who carefully explained to her Italian mother that the reason the babies in Italy were so healthy and the babies in Chicago were so sickly, was not, as her mother had firmly insisted, because her babies in Italy had goat's milk and her babies in America had cow's milk, but because the milk in Italy was clean and the milk in Chicago was dirty. She said that when you milked your own goat before the door, you knew that the milk was clean, but when you bought milk from the grocery store after it had been carried for many miles in the country, you couldn't tell whether it was fit for the baby to drink until the men from the City Hall who had watched it all the way said that it was all right.

Thus through civic instruction in the public schools, the Italian woman slowly became urbanized in the sense in which the word was used by her own Latin ancestors, and thus the habits of her entire family were modified. The public schools in the immigrant colonies deserve all the praise as Americanizing agencies which can be bestowed upon them, and there is little doubt that the fast-changing curriculum in the direction of the vacation-school experiments will react more directly upon such households.

It is difficult to write of the relation of the older and most foreign-looking immigrants to the children of other people—the Italians whose fruitcarts are upset simply because they are "dagoes" or the Russian peddlers who are stoned and sometimes badly injured because it has become a code of honor in a gang of boys to thus express their derision. The members of a Protective Association of Jewish Peddlers organized at Hull-House related daily experiences in which old age had been treated with such irreverence, cherished dignity with such disrespect, that a listener caught the passion of Lear in the old texts, as a platitude enunciated by a man who discovers in it his own experience thrills us as no unfamiliar phrases can possibly do. The Greeks are filled with amazed rage when their very name is flung at them as an opprobrious epithet. Doubtless these difficulties would be much minimized in America, if we faced our own race problem with courage and intelligence, and these very Mediterranean immigrants might give us valuable help. Certainly they are less conscious than the Anglo-Saxon of color distinctions, perhaps because of their traditional familiarity with Carthage and Egypt. They listened with respect and enthusiasm to a scholarly address delivered by Professor Du Bois at Hull-House on a Lincoln's birthday, with apparently no consciousness of that race difference which color seems to accentuate so absurdly, and upon my return from various conferences held in the interest of "the advancement of colored people," I have had many illuminating conversations with my cosmopolitan neighbors.

The celebration of national events has always been a source of new understanding and companionship with the members of the contiguous foreign colonies not only between them and their American neighbors but between them and their own children. One of our earliest Italian events was a rousing commemoration of Garibaldi's birthday, and his imposing bust, presented to Hull-House that evening, was long the chief ornament of our front hall. It called forth great enthusiasm from the *connazionali* whom Ruskin calls, not the "common people" of Italy, but the "companion people" because of their power for swift sympathy.

A huge Hellenic meeting held at Hull-House, in which the achievements of the classic period were set forth both in Greek and English by scholars of well-known repute, brought us into a new sense of fellowship with all our Greek neighbors. As the mayor of Chicago was seated upon the right hand of the dignified senior priest of the Greek Church and they were greeted alternately in the national hymns of America and Greece, one felt a curious sense of the possibility of transplanting to new and crude Chicago some of the traditions of Athens itself, so deeply cherished in the hearts of this group of citizens.

The Greeks indeed gravely consider their traditions as their most precious possession and more than once in meetings of protest held by the Greek colony against the aggressions of the Bulgarians in Macedonia, I have heard it urged that the Bulgarians are trying to establish a protectorate, not only for their immediate advantage, but that they may claim a glorious history for the "barbarous country." It is said that on the basis of this protectorate, they are already teaching in their schools that Alexander the Great was a Bulgarian and that it will be but a short time before they claim Aristotle himself, an indignity the Greeks will never suffer!

To me personally the celebration of the hundredth anniversary of Mazzini's birth was a matter of great interest. Throughout the world that day Italians who believed in a United Italy came together. They recalled the hopes of this man who, with all his devotion to his country was still more devoted to humanity and who dedicated to the workingmen of Italy an appeal so philosophical, so filled with a yearning for righteousness, that it transcended all national boundaries and became a bugle call for "The Duties of Man." A copy of this document was given to every school child in the public schools of Italy on this one hundredth anniversary, and as the Chicago branch of the Society of Young Italy marched into our largest hall and presented to Hull-House an heroic bust of Mazzini, I found myself devoutly hoping that the Italian youth, who have committed their future to America, might indeed become "the Apostle of the fraternity of nations" and that our American citizenship might be built without disturbing these foundations which were laid of old time.

6. The Emergence of Modern America, 1920–1945

The Louisville Flood, 1937 by Margaret Bourke-White. Gift of Sean Callahan. Photograph Copyright © 2000 by Whitney Museum of American Art. Courtesy of Whitney Museum of American Art.

By the time Margaret Bourke-White snapped this picture of African Americans waiting for flood relief during the Great Depression, photography was a century old. Ever since Jacob Riis in the 1880s, photographers had used their art for social purposes: showing the wealthier classes "how the other half lives," capturing the conditions of child laborers in factories. In the 1930s, a new generation of photographers—Dorothea Lange, Gordon Parks, Walker Evans, Bourke-White—made photo-journalism a career. They published their pictures for new magazines such as *Time* and *Life*, and they worked with New Deal federal agencies to investigate American poverty during the Great Depression. These photographs were never neutral, never simply objective statements of life "as it was": photographers used the realistic effect of the camera, and their own power to create images, to tell specific stories. In every possible way, *The Louisville Flood* exposes the black-and-white contrasts in American life. The billboard seems like an advertisement from the prosperous 1920s, or a harbinger of the post-World War II suburban (and mostly white) middle class. But in the midst of depression and natural catastrophe, those cheerful, well-dressed parents, children, and dog mock the real people standing beneath them, who are after all men and women and children too. If "There's no way like the American Way," which way does Bourke-White's photograph point? The billboard's car seems to move forward, while the relief line shuffles off to the right, with no clear beginning or end. Or perhaps, like the American economy of the 1930s, the line stands still, some people staring at Bourke-White's camera—and thus at the viewer—while others look ahead toward an uncertain future.

Chronology

1920: U.S. census reports that urban population is greater than rural population for the first time

1923: Equal Rights Amendment is first introduced in Congress

1924: National Origins Act tightens immigration quotas first established in 1921

1925: Scopes trial (Dayton, Tennessee) pits religious fundamentalism against modernity

1927: *The Jazz Singer*, first feature-length movie with sound

1929: Stock market crash begins Great Depression (1929–1939)

1932: Franklin D. Roosevelt elected President

1933: New Deal begins
roughly 13 million workers unemployed
21st Amendment repeals Prohibition
Adolf Hitler seizes power in Germany

1934: Indian Reorganization Act repeals Dawes Severalty Act and reasserts status of Indian tribes as semi-sovereign nations

1935: Dust storms turn the southern Great Plains into the Dust Bowl

1938: Fair Labor Standards Act establishes first federal minimum wage

1939: World War II breaks out in Europe
John Steinbeck, *The Grapes of Wrath*

1941: Japanese attack Pearl Harbor, Hawaii; U.S. enters World War II

1941: Executive order forbids racial discrimination in defense industries and government

1942: Executive order mandates internment of Japanese Americans

1945: Germany surrenders (May)
U.S. drops atomic bombs on Hiroshima and Nagasaki; Japan surrenders (August)

Introduction

During the quarter century from the Peace Conference in 1919 to the end of the Second World War in 1945, American society went through three distinct and dramatic phases: economic growth and substantial social change during the 1920s; widespread unemployment and severe economic malaise in the 1930s; and finally five years in which American society re-energized itself to win the Second World War . . . three distinct eras, but each intricately connected to the others. What a tumultuous twenty-five years!

Following the end of the Great War on November 11, 1918, the American people entered into a decade of unprecedented economic growth. A booming industrial economy cranked out a seemingly endless number of new products that elevated the national standard of living and in turn changed the way the American people lived. A booming stock market produced a sense of economic euphoria that swept up most doubters in a spectacular rise in stock prices. Although the rising economic tide did not lift all boats (as a group, farmers and industrial workers did not share in the economic bonanza), a substantial number of Americans saw a marked improvement in their standard of living. For example, the percentage of houses with electricity increased from 16% in 1919 to 69% in 1929, and by decade's end more than 50% of houses contained indoor plumbing. Technological advances touched many lives. Such amenities as electric refrigerators and stoves, vacuum cleaners, and irons replaced the ice box, wood burning kitchen stove, hand-held rug dust beaters, and the cumbersome five-pound, cast-iron, implement used to press clothes. In the evenings families gathered around radio receivers to listen to news reports, situation comedies, detective escapades, and musical programs. They even whistled along with the new—if dubious— phenomenon of singing commercials.

Americans also enjoyed enhanced mobility. They enthusiastically embraced the mass-produced automobiles pouring off Detroit assembly lines; by decade's end twenty-nine million registered automobiles prowled the streets and roads of America, nearly one vehicle for every four residents. Additionally, four million trucks changed the way commerce delivered goods, setting in motion the long but sure decline of the once-omnipotent transcontinental trunk railroad lines. Life in such "typical" American communities as Muncie, Indiana, as described and interpreted by the cultural anthropologists Robert and Helen Lynd (1882–1970, 1896–1982) was transformed by the new technologies that came to Main Street.

The soaring economy left social and economic reformers without much of a constituency. The American people turned their back on the fervent appeals of progressives to continue the reforms that had flourished during the first fifteen years of the new century but had run aground during the war. Where they had earlier rallied to Theodore Roosevelt's inspired progressive bombast and Woodrow Wilson's eloquent appeals for New Freedom economic reforms, the American people now elevated business executives to the highest of approval ratings. Even the eccentric if sometimes reactionary and ruthless automobile magnate, Henry Ford, was buoyed by a boomlet urging him to run for president in 1924. If he could build a reliable automobile that cost less than $500, so the reasoning went, why couldn't he operate the federal government just as efficiently?

The siren calls for reform gave way to a groundswell of support for "Normalcy," a curious phrase coined by Warren G. Harding during the presidential campaign of 1920 that pointed the way toward a restoration of the businessman as the dominant force in the nation's political and social structure. The nation needed, President Harding solemnly affirmed in his inaugural address, "restoration rather than reform." Labor union leaders struggled to maintain their small memberships in the face of hostile courts, political leaders, and public opinion; anything akin to left-leaning radicalism engendered widespread public condemnation. Advocates for protecting women workers and excluding children from the labor force no longer enjoyed widespread popular support. Women's rights took a new tack in 1923 with the introduction of a proposed Constitutional amendment entitled the Equal Rights Amendment. The debate between veteran social reformer Florence Kelley (1859–1932) and Elsie Hill (1884–1970) over the merits of the amendment provides interesting perspectives on an issue that remains alive in the 21st century. Spokesmen for beleaguered African Americans, laboring under oppressive segregation laws and practices throughout the forty-eight states, could not generate public support even for such a fundamental law as making lynching a federal crime. An isolationist and sometimes xenophobic Congress passed restrictions upon immigration in 1921 and 1924 based upon quota systems that precluded nearly all immigration save token numbers of western Europeans. Throughout the South and Midwest a revived Ku Klux Klan grew even larger than it had been during Reconstruction, attracting an estimated six million members by 1925. The American people furiously debated such contentious issues as laws forbidding the teaching of the theories of evolution in the public schools, and the 18th Amendment to the Constitution that made it a federal crime to transport and sell alcoholic beverages across state lines.

Sinclair Lewis (1885–1951) sought to expose such attitudes, especially in his deliciously satirical novel detailing the private anxieties of a realtor named George F. Babbitt. To Lewis's chagrin, many readers found this shallow resident of the Midwestern town of Zenith to be a person not to be sneered at, but rather to be admired, even emulated! In the excerpt here Babbitt speaks to a local real estate sales and booster club about the qualities he believes desirable for a community leader. In 1925 the pioneering Madison Avenue advertising executive, Bruce Barton (1886–1967), created a sensation with his unusual biography of Jesus Christ, entitled *The Man Nobody Knows*. In this biography Barton suggests that Jesus was "the founder of modern business," a leader who "picked up twelve men from the bottom ranks of business and forged them into an organization that conquered the world." This heretofore unrecognized Jesus not only created an aggressive twelve-man sales force, but with his use of parables created the concept of contemporary advertising, including sales slogans; his talents even extended to that of after-dinner speaker. Given the best-selling popularity of Barton's book (it was the first "book of the month" selection of the new mail-order club), is it any wonder most Americans agreed with President Calvin Coolidge's crisp comment, "America's business is business"?

Many leading intellectuals were so depressed with a society that idolized the anti-Semitic automobile manufacturer Henry Ford, cheered the execution in 1927 of two radical Italian immigrants, Nicola Sacco and Bartolomeo Vanzetti, and overwhelmingly rejected membership in the League of Nations, that they fled to Europe to symbolize their alienation with a "Philistine" America. One of the leading progressive intellectuals of the time, Walter Weyl, co-founder of the progressive opinion journal, *The New Republic*, lamented that progressives had been so beaten down by the forces of Babbittry and Normalcy that they had been reduced to a small minority of "tired radicals."

The intellectuals' disillusionment was symbolized by the devastating satire that journalist H. L. Mencken visited upon many vulnerable and inviting targets. In his syndicated newspaper column and the magazine, *The American Mercury*, this Baltimore-based journalist denounced popular fundamentalist ministers, such as Aimee Semple McPherson and Billy Sunday, as frauds, nominated the neighborhood bootlegger as his candidate for hero of the decade, advocated the legalization of prostitution, denounced anti-immigrant legislation with the suggestion that the Statue of Liberty should be taken out to sea beyond the three-mile limit and sunk, railed against the "fundamentalist Pope" William Jennings Bryan for supporting a Tennessee law making it illegal to teach the Darwinian theories of evolution in the public schools, and caustically dismissed the conservative middle classes as "homo boobiens" and the "booboisie." Mencken's assault upon Babbittry proved popular with college students and the urbane "smart set," but his critique rolled off the general American public like so much water off a duck.

What Mencken missed, of course, was the fact that beneath the veneer of Babbittry, serious things were being accomplished in a rapidly changing America. Breakthroughs in medical science made surgical procedures much more reliable, and psychiatry came of age with the widespread acceptance of the new theories of psychoanalysis advanced by Sigmund Freud. The Post Office introduced air-mail delivery, and the American people thrilled to the first trans-Atlantic flight in 1927 by youthful pilot Charles Lindbergh—"The Lone Eagle." The laboratories of American universities and corporations produced a wide array of new products and materials, including synthetic fibers, plastics, lacquers, and cellophane. Americans now wore wrist watches and lit their smokes with safety matches and mechanical lighters. Even the prototype of the television set was operable by the end of the decade, although the slow pace of technology transfer precluded its widespread use until after the Second World War. The African American scientist George Washington Carver demonstrated the potential of applied research when he discovered new uses for the pedestrian peanut and sweet potato, producing such diverse items as shaving lotion, axle grease, shoe polish, and glue.

Nowhere did the pace of change and "progress" occur more rapidly than in the cities. Significantly, the Census of 1920 had reported that for the first time a majority of Americans now lived in urban areas. In the cities the improved technologies of structural steel construction and the electric elevator produced new skylines punctuated by soaring skyscrapers. The towering 102-story Empire State Building in New York City captured the nation's attention, but the Bank of Manhattan (71 stories) and the Chrysler Building (77 stories) had already elevated New Yorkers' horizons. In the Midwest the innovative real estate developer, J. C. Nichols, constructed the nation's first automobile-oriented shopping center, located on the southern edge of Kansas City. Nichols used this pleasant and attractive commercial area as the anchor for an upscale suburban housing development that attracted eager buyers. His concept of suburban development was soon emulated across the nation—although often with less concern for the aesthetic qualities than he built into the attractive Spanish motif of the Country Club Plaza. All across urban America, the automobile stimulated the migration of the white middle and upper classes to the suburbs—a phenomenon that would grow exponentially after 1945 and not reach its apex until the 1990s.

Although important members of America's intellectual and artistic elite fled to the Left Bank of Paris in a symbolic rejection of the dominant lowbrow culture they perceived, in reality American letters flourished during the 1920s. It was a time of enormous creative energy, as witnessed by the writings of Sinclair Lewis, Ellen Glasgow, Thomas Wolfe, John Dos Passos, F. Scott Fitzgerald, Eugene O'Neill, Willa Cather, Sherwood Anderson, William Faulkner, and T. S. Eliot. Of special significance was the explosion of literary and musical creativity in the recently settled African American community located on the northern side of Manhattan Island. What was termed the "Harlem Renaissance" signaled the arrival of such distinguished African American writers as Countee Cullen (1903–1946), Langston Hughes (1902–1967), Claude McKay, James Weldon Johnson, and Jean Toomer, as well as the expressly American music genre of jazz brought to general public awareness by such talents as Duke Ellington and Louis Armstrong. These talented artists and writers not only drew heavily upon their African and American slave roots but implicitly sent out the message that their race was worthy of respect and admiration. Perhaps the poet Langston Hughes best summarized the significance of the Harlem Renaissance when he wrote one single, simple, but powerful sentence: "I am a Negro—and beautiful."

For much of the decade the upward movement of economic charts also seemed to be a thing of beauty. In his Inaugural Address in 1929 the new president, Herbert Hoover, expressed the optimism of a nation when he said, "We in America today are nearer the final triumph over poverty than ever before in the history of the land. The poorhouse is vanishing from among us."

Less than eight months later, however, the economy began a traumatic downward spiral that eventually engulfed the nation in economic disaster. The 1920s had witnessed unprecedented economic growth and expansion that introduced Americans to the wonders of a consumer-oriented, middle-class life style. But the "Roaring Twenties" ended with a resounding thud, as the stock market lost 50% of its valuation within three months after the devastation wrought on "Black Tuesday," October 29, 1929. This spectacular crash was only the beginning, however, as the market continued an agonizing plummet that did not bottom out until 1933. The losses were mind-boggling by any measurement. The Dow Jones Industrial Average had lost 75% of its value, and some major blue chip stocks suffered even more. General Motors stock fell from 92 to 8, U. S. Steel from 262 to 22, and Montgomery Ward from 138 to 4.

By 1933 fully 26% of the work force was unemployed, with no prospects for the future. Poorhouses were now flourishing, as were rag-tag communities of shacks, tents, and cardboard boxes, housing hundreds of thousands of the nation's disinherited in what the baffled and bewildered, frightened and angry residents derisively called Hoovervilles. Mortgage foreclosures across the nation's farmlands became commonplace, and the heart of the American economy, located in its complex system of federal and state banks, proved to be especially vulnerable. By 1933 more than 6,000 banks across the land had shuttered their doors forever, with untold billions of dollars in customer deposits having vanished. Long bread lines of the unemployed now formed in cities outside of makeshift soup kitchens; a telling icon for the new era, unemployed men wearing their three-piece business suits stood on street corners and sold apples.

Unemployment spread like a cancer throughout the industrial belt of the Midwest and Northeast, while farm prices plummeted to such lows that the cost of shipping commodities to market exceeded the price they would bring on the open agricultural markets. In the conservative Republican heartland of Iowa, farm leader Milo Reno led a "Farm Strike" that saw farmers pour fresh milk into ditches rather than ship it to market in a futile effort to raise wholesale milk prices. Angry farmers across the Midwest formed into vigilante forces to prevent sheriffs from foreclosing on heavily mortgaged farms. Just four years after Herbert Hoover so confidently assumed the presidency, his successor, Franklin D. Roosevelt (1882–1945), had to reassure a frightened nation that, "The only thing we have to fear is fear itself—nameless, unreasoning, unjustified terror which paralyzes needed efforts to convert retreat into advance."

Despite widespread hardship and suffering, most Americans remained unmoved by impassioned radicals urging them to support a bewildering array of reforms and panaceas that covered the ideological spectrum. Instead, they adhered to a middle-ground approach pursed by President Franklin D. Roosevelt and his New Deal administration. Although those on the right condemned the New Deal as "socialistic" or worse, the essential truth is that the New Deal was inherently conservative in its approach to its central mission of providing relief to the suffering and generating economic recovery. Although the new president was not afraid to experiment with new ideas, he largely did so within carefully drawn limits. In the final analysis, his helter-skelter program was, more than anything else, designed to restore and protect the established economic system of corporate capitalism.

Because the New Deal did not push the outer limits of possible recovery effort, American society limped along throughout the 1930s under the weight of double-digit unemployment, stilled factories, drought-riddled farmlands, and frazzled banking and financial systems. Novelist John Steinbeck's *The Grapes of Wrath* told the saga of an Oklahoma farm family's dispossession from their land and subsequent migration to an uncertain future in the agribusiness heart of California's sprawling San Joaquin Valley. In this classic novel Steinbeck (1902–1968) presented another image of capitalism's impact on classic American individualism. His powerful 1936 essay, "Dubious Battle in California," appeared in a major opinion journal three years before the publication of his novel. Steinbeck's journalistic description of the problems confronting the "Okies" anticipated his emotional and tragic novel about the Joad family as it moved westward along a dusty Route 66 in a dilapidated vehicle seeking refuge in a seductively beckoning, but ultimately hostile, California.

Despite the New Deal's highly publicized efforts to revive the severely wounded economy, the much-sought-after recovery did not occur. As late as 1939 unemployment remained at the unacceptable level of 15%. Ten years after the Great Crash, the specter of depression—widespread malnutrition, an army of hobos traversing the land, foreclosures of millions of homes and farms, and hopelessly shattered lives—remained much in evidence. The New Deal had helped, but its limitations were evident everywhere. A consensus of historians and economists have since concluded that it was the essential conservatism of the president that helped prevent the funding of public works programs at sufficient levels to produce economic recovery. As Roosevelt told the Congress in 1935, "Continued dependence upon relief induces a spiritual and moral disintegration fundamentally destructive to the national fibre. To dole out relief in this way is to administer a narcotic, a subtle destroyer of the human spirit. The federal government must and shall quit this business of relief." His predecessor, the repudiated Herbert Hoover, could not have stated it more eloquently.

Although its efforts to provide relief were inadequate, and although it failed to re-establish a vigorous economy, the New Deal nonetheless produced important reforms that changed the structure of American society. The New Deal greatly expanded the role of the federal government in the daily lives of the American people. The government now assumed the responsibility for providing a foundation of security for the American businessman, farmer, and worker. The initial legislative output in the spring of 1933 was prodigious, producing far-reaching new programs that included efforts to increase commodity prices through encouraging reduced production (Agricultural Adjustment Administration), the far-ranging public power and conservation effort in the southeastern United States (Tennessee Valley Authority), a program to employ the nation's jobless youth in enhancing conservation efforts (Civilian Conservation Corps), and several programs to employ the nation's idle work force (Public Works Administration, Civilian Works Administration, and Works Progress Administration), and an ill-designed and quickly scuttled effort to encourage cooperation and reduce competition among manufacturers (National Recovery Administration).

In subsequent years the Administration reversed more than a half century of federal policy by encouraging the development of independent labor unions (Wagner Labor Act), established programs to provide for dependent children, the physically handicapped, and the elderly (Social Security Act), created the nation's first minimum wage law (at 25 cents an hour!), and established the standard work week at 40 hours. Federal deposit insurance for savings and loans and banks improved institutional stability for the nation's financial markets, as did the creation of the stock and bond market watchdog Securities and Exchange Commission. Prospective home owners benefitted from Federal Housing Administration sponsored mortgage insurance and low down-payment requirements, the Home Owners Loan Corporation assisted 4 million hard-pressed families to refinance their mortgages, and the Public Housing Authority initiated a program to provide decent housing for low income families. All told, the New Deal responded to public demand that the government assume the responsibility for managing the economy to provide a modicum of security for business, labor, and consumer.

Minorities received only modest attention from the Roosevelt Administration. Although Roosevelt appointed several African Americans to mid-level administrative roles (the so-called "Black

Cabinet"), his reform program did not truly assist the nation's largest racial minority, preferring instead to offer a few highly publicized but largely cosmetic initiatives. One of the more noteworthy efforts on behalf of minorities occurred under the leadership of John Collier (1884–1968), who as Director of the Bureau of Indian Affairs established a new initiative to help Native Americans preserve their heritage and become more self-reliant. His essential ideas are excerpted here from his 1938 annual report. Contrast his agenda, however well intentioned, with the one presented in 1933 by a member of the Teton Sioux, Luther Standing Bear (1868–1939).

By 1939 the New Deal reform impulse had largely spent itself, and President Roosevelt now devoted most of his attention to the rapidly unraveling world situation. In the Far East, the Imperial Government of Japan had already enjoyed major military success along the coast of China and in Manchuria, and when Roosevelt attempted to pressure the Japanese government to reverse those developments, relations between the rival powers in the Pacific rapidly deteriorated. Hamstrung by strong isolationist sentiment in Congress, the president was unable to respond to German rearmament—a direct violation of the Treaty of Versailles—under the fascist government of Adolf Hitler. After joint British, French, and American efforts to appease Hitler's thirst for additional territory and power failed, on September 1, 1939, German forces moved into Poland. England and France immediately declared war. For the next two years American politics was consumed by the great debate over whether the United States should assist the Allies, an action that Roosevelt and his internationalist supporters urged upon Congress. Public opinion slowly swung away from the isolationists, especially after Hitler's spectacular *blitzkrieg* attack that brought France to its knees in June of 1940.

Events eventually worked to FDR's advantage. As Hitler mounted his massive bombing campaign of London and British military bases, public opinion expressed deep concern over the ability of the British to withstand an anticipated Nazi invasion. Roosevelt received grudging approval from Congress to initiate the nation's first peacetime draft in October of 1940, during the midst of his campaign for an unprecedented third term. That same autumn FDR also stretched his Constitutional authority to the limit by transferring command of fifty outdated destroyers to Britain to help prepare for the anticipated German invasion of English soil (the program proved more symbolic than reality, as only six ships were ever delivered). In return the United States obtained 99-year leases on some small military bases in the Caribbean, ostensibly to help protect the Panama Canal. Roosevelt understood, however, that public opinion still precluded his taking the nation into the war.

The decision of the Japanese high command to attack the United States naval base at Pearl Harbor ended the debate over America's role in the war. On December 7, 1941, early on a Sunday morning, wave after wave of Japanese aircraft bombed and strafed the American fleet in the shallow harbor of the Hawaiian island of Oahu, sinking or heavily damaging eighteen major ships, killing 2,403 Americans. At nearby Hickam Field, a major Army Air Force base, 300 fighter aircraft were destroyed or seriously damaged. Denouncing the attack as "a day that will live in infamy," on December 8th President Roosevelt asked Congress to declare war on Japan. Three days later Hitler declared war on the United States and the battle was joined.

The American people built an enormous military arsenal, converting most of the nation's agricultural and industrial capacity to the war effort. They displayed very little of the emotionalism and enthusiasm that had accompanied American entrance into World War I. The full-scale production effort quickly ended the unemployment that had plagued the nation for more than a decade; this quick economic turnabout strengthened the arguments of activist-inclined economists that the American economy could be successfully monitored and controlled. The defense production figures were staggering. Consider the construction of aircraft: by mid-1945 American industry had delivered 18,000 B-24s; 12,600 B-17s; 3,800 enormous B-29 Superfortress bombers, and more than

200,000 fighter aircraft and transport airplanes . . . in all 299,293 military aircraft between 1940 and 1945. The Navy put 1,556 new major vessels on line while an additional 5,777 merchant ships were manufactured to supply American soldiers and sailors around the world. The amazing list goes on and on: 634,569 jeeps, 6 and a half million rifles, 88,000 tanks, 2,310,000 trucks, and 40 billion bullets. And three atomic bombs.

The war production effort quickly wiped out the lingering effects of the Great Depression. Workers not only enjoyed better paying jobs, but many earned overtime. One group of Americans, however, never had the opportunity to participate in the war effort. Due to intense anti-Japanese sentiment fueled by a half-century legacy of racial discrimination in California, 110,000 American citizens of Japanese heritage were incarcerated in the months immediately following Pearl Harbor for fear that they might be potential spies or saboteurs. In 1943 the Supreme Court upheld this outrageous violation of their civil liberties. Before the war, teenager Hisaye Yamamoto (1921–) wrote a poem about her loyalty to the United States; during the internment, one of its victims, Ted Nakashima, described his sentiments in an article for *The New Republic*.

The fifteen million men and women who served in the Armed Forces put the equipment to good use. Following the grand strategy of concentrating upon the defeat of Germany first, the Navy by mid-1943 had won the most important battle of the war—in the North Atlantic—clearing the shipping lanes to Great Britain of Nazi submarines, whose early successes had threatened to turn the tide of war away from the Allies. On June 6, 1944, the Allies launched the greatest single military operation in the history of mankind under the command of General Dwight D. Eisenhower—the invasion of Normandy. Its ultimate success was a testimony to the productive capacity of the United States: 6,483 naval vessels churned across the English Channel in the dark of night. As the first rays of dawn appeared, stunned Nazi defenders saw row upon row of ships filled with men and equipment that stretched beyond the hazy horizon. The subsequent carnage on the beaches that fateful day, as so vividly described by journalist Ernie Pyle (1900–1945), was incredible. By day's end troops had clawed out a beachhead, having scaled the towering cliffs above the beach littered with dead men and incredible amounts of debris despite withering machine gun fire. More than 6,000 Americans died at Omaha Beach that first day, many of them dying not from enemy fire but by drowning in the furiously churning tides. Within a few weeks a major breakthrough occurred and the Allied forces resolutely pushed eastward toward Germany. After another ten months of fighting—and devastating fire bombing that virtually obliterated major German cities—on May 5, 1945, Germany surrendered.

Halfway around the world, the war still raged on. The island-hopping strategy in the South Pacific was enjoying success, but in battle after battle Japanese defenders fought with great tenacity. The original strategy of the Japanese high command was, after disabling the American Pacific fleet at Pearl Harbor, to establish a defensive perimeter around its resource-rich new possessions by using its modern fleet as a shield, ultimately wearing down the American resolve and forcing a negotiated settlement that would give Japan control of its recent conquests in Southeast Asia. The Japanese were tenacious and extracted high costs as the Americans steadily advanced westward, island after bloody island, under the leadership of General Douglas MacArthur and Admiral Chester Nimitz. In 1945 the Japanese defenders fought ferociously, refusing to surrender in the face of death, defending the two small but strategic islands of Iwo Jima and Okinawa.

The unflagging determination of the Japanese island defenders, the terrifying reports of thousands of death-wish *kamikaze* attacks that sank 36 American ships and damaged 368 others and killed 4,900 sailors and wounded a like number, and widely reported statements by Japanese military leaders that surrender would never occur, led American military planners to seek alternatives to the planned amphibious invasion of the Japanese mainland scheduled for November of 1945.

Estimates within the War Department placed potential American casualties as high as the unacceptable level of 1,500,000. A few top American officials hoped that the secret Manhattan Engineering Project, the code name for the atomic bomb research and development project, would provide a solution to their dilemma. A prototype bomb, giving off the power of 20,000 tons of TNT, was first tested successfully on July 16, 1945, in the remote Sonoran desert near the small town of Alamogordo, New Mexico.

The prospect of unacceptable levels of American casualties during an invasion, the many atrocities committed by the Japanese upon American prisoners of war, and an all-too-evident, racially inspired dislike of the perpetrators of Pearl Harbor that pervaded much of American public opinion, all contributed to the decision by President Harry S. Truman (1884–1972) to use the newly developed atomic bomb upon two Japanese cities. Although the wisdom of the decision to bomb civilian targets has been debated ever since, the new president and his top advisors never had any doubt that the new weapon of mass destruction should be used. This was, after all, a war in which the official American objective was the "unconditional surrender" of the enemy. President Truman would later write, "Make no mistake about it. I regarded the bomb as a military weapon and never had any doubt that it should be used." On August 6, 1945, Truman's order was carried out and a bomb was dropped over the city of Hiroshima, killing 40,000 people instantly, while another 140,000 died of burns and radiation within a few days. Three days later a second bomb fell on Nagasaki, killing an estimated 200,000. Five days later, following rancorous debate between political moderates and hard-line military leaders, the Japanese agreed to the Allied terms of surrender.

The war thus ended on the ominous note of nuclear weaponry. An estimated 20 million persons had died in the conflict, including 320,000 American men and women. The American people's hope, as President Roosevelt so ambitiously outlined in his 1944 State of the Union Message, that they could enjoy the fruits of victory free from fears of future wars and protected by new levels of government-provided economic security, would not be realized. Instead, they faced an uncertain economic future at home, while the rapidly deteriorating relationship with wartime ally Soviet Union seemed especially ominous. However much they might have desired to return once more to a time of Normalcy, the American people understood that such refuge was no longer possible. As they pondered an uncertain future, the specter of a man-made mushroom cloud lurked over their shoulders. The tumultuous roller-coaster ride of the previous quarter century had not yet ended.

SINCLAIR LEWIS

"Our Ideal Citizen," from *Babbitt* (1922)

Our Ideal Citizen—I picture him first and foremost as being busier than a bird-dog, not wasting a lot of good time in day-dreaming or going to sassiety teas or kicking about things that are none of his business, but putting the zip into some store or profession or art. At night he lights up a good cigar, and climbs into the little old 'bus, and maybe cusses the carburetor, and shoots out home. He mows the lawn, or sneaks in some practice putting, and then he's ready for dinner. After dinner he tells the kiddies a story, or takes the family to the movies, or plays a few fists of bridge, or reads the evening paper, and a chapter or two of some good lively Western novel if he has a taste for litera-ture, and maybe the folks next-door drop in and they sit and visit about their friends and the topics of the day. Then he goes happily to bed, his conscience clear, having contributed his mite to the prosperity of the city and to his own bank-account.

In politics and religion this Sane Citizen is the canniest man on earth; and in the arts he invari-ably has a natural taste which makes him pick out the best, every time. In no country in the world will you find so many reproductions of the Old Masters and of well-known paintings on parlor walls as in these United States. No country has anything like our number of phonographs, with not only dance records and comic but also the best operas, such as Verdi, rendered by the world's highest-paid singers.

In other countries, art and literature are left to a lot of shabby bums living in attics and feeding on booze and spaghetti, but in America the successful writer or picture-painter is indistinguishable from any other decent business man; and I, for one, am only too glad that the man who has the rare skill to season his message with interesting reading matter and who shows both purpose and pep in handling his literary wares has a chance to drag down his fifty thousand bucks a year, to mingle with the biggest executives on terms of perfect equality, and to show as big a house and as swell a car as any Captain of Industry! But, mind you, it's the appreciation of the Regular Guy who I have been depicting which has made this possible, and you got to hand as much credit to him as to the authors themselves.

Finally, but most important, our Standardized Citizen, even if he is a bachelor, is a lover of the Little Ones, a supporter of the hearthstone which is the basic foundation of our civilization, first, last, and all the time, and the thing that most distinguishes us from the decayed nations of Europe.

I have never yet toured Europe—and as a matter of fact, I don't know that I care to such an awful lot, as long as there's our own mighty cities and mountains to be seen—but, the way I figure it out, there must be a good many of our own sort of folks abroad. Indeed, one of the most enthusi-astic Rotarians I ever met boosted the tenets of one-hundred-per-cent pep in a burr that smacked o' bonny Scutlond and all ye bonny braes o' Bobby Burns. But same time, one thing that distin-guishes us from our good brothers, the hustlers over there, is that they're willing to take a lot off the snobs and journalists and politicians, while the modern American business man knows how to talk right up for himself, knows how to make it good and plenty clear that he intends to run the works. He doesn't have to call in some highbrow hired-man when it's necessary for him to answer the crooked critics of the sane and efficient life. He's not dumb, like the old-fashioned merchant. He's got a vocabulary and a punch.

With all modesty, I want to stand up here as a representative business man and gently whisper, "Here's our kind of folks! Here's the specifications of the Standardized American Citizen! Here's the new generation of Americans: fellows with hair on their chests and smiles in their eyes and adding-machines in their offices. We're not doing any boasting, but we like ourselves first-rate, and if you don't like us, look out—better get under cover before the cyclone hits town!"

So! In my clumsy way I have tried to sketch the Real He-man, the fellow with Zip and Bang. And it's because Zenith has so large a proportion of such men that it's the most stable, the greatest of our cities. New York also has its thousands of Real Folks, but New York is cursed with unnumbered foreigners. So are Chicago and San Francisco. Oh, we have a golden roster of cities—Detroit and Cleveland with their renowned factories, Cincinnati with its great machine-tool and soap products, Pittsburg and Birmingham with their steel, Kansas City and Minneapolis and Omaha that open their bountiful gates on the bosom of the ocean-like wheatlands, and countless other magnificent sister-cities, for, by the last census, there were no less than sixty-eight glorious American burgs with a population of over one hundred thousand! And all these cities stand together for power and purity, and against foreign ideas and communism—Atlanta with Hartford, Rochester with Denver, Milwaukee with Indianapolis, Los Angeles with Scranton, Portland, Maine, with Portland, Oregon. A good live wire from Baltimore or Seattle or Duluth is the twin-brother of every like fellow booster from Buffalo or Akron, Fort Worth or Oskaloosa!

But it's here in Zenith, the home for manly men and womanly women and bright kids, that you find the largest proportion of these Regular Guys, and that's what sets it in a class by itself; that's why Zenith will be remembered in history as having set the pace for a civilization that shall endure when the old time-killing ways are gone forever and the day of earnest efficient endeavor shall have dawned all round the world!

Some time I hope folks will quit handing all the credit to a lot of moth-eaten, mildewed, out-of-date, old, European dumps, and give proper credit to the famous Zenith spirit, that clean fighting determination to win Success that has made the little old Zip City celebrated in every land and clime, wherever condensed milk and pasteboard cartons are known! Believe me, the world has fallen too long for these worn-out countries that aren't producing anything but bootblacks and scenery and booze, that haven't got one bathroom per hundred people, and that don't know a loose-leaf ledger from a slip-cover; and it's just about time for some Zenithite to get his back up and holler for a show-down!

I tell you, Zenith and her sister-cities are producing a new type of civilization. There are many resemblances between Zenith and these other burgs, and I'm darn glad of it! The extraordinary, growing, and sane standardization of stores, offices, streets, hotels, clothes, and newspapers throughout the United States shows how strong and enduring a type is ours. . . .

Yes, sir, these other burgs are our true partners in the great game of vital living. But let's not have any mistake about this. I claim that Zenith is the best partner and the fastest-growing partner of the whole caboodle. I trust I may be pardoned if I give a few statistics to back up my claims. If they are old stuff to any of you, yet the tidings of prosperity, like the good news of the Bible, never become tedious to the ears of a real hustler, no matter how oft the sweet story is told! Every intelligent person knows that Zenith manufactures more condensed milk and evaporated cream, more paper boxes, and more lighting-fixtures, than any other city in the United States, if not in the world. But it is not so universally known that we also stand second in the manufacture of package-butter, sixth in the giant realm of motors and automobiles, and somewhere about third in cheese, leather findings, tar roofing, breakfast food, and overalls!

Our greatness, however, lies not alone in punchful prosperity but equally in that public spirit, that forward-looking idealism and brotherhood, which has marked Zenith ever since its foundation by the Fathers. We have a right, indeed we have a duty toward our fair city, to announce broadcast the facts about our high schools, characterized by their complete plants and the finest school-ventilating systems in the country, bar none; our magnificent new hotels and banks and the paintings and carved marble in their lobbies; and the Second National Tower, the second highest business building in any inland city in the entire country. When I add that we have an unparalleled number of miles of paved streets, bathrooms, vacuum cleaners, and all the other signs of civilization; that our library and art museum are well supported and housed in convenient and roomy buildings; that our park-system is more than up to par, with its handsome driveways adorned with grass, shrubs, and statuary, then I give a hint of the all-round unlimited greatness of Zenith!

I believe, however, in keeping the best to the last. When I remind you that we have one motor car for every five and seven-eighths persons in the city, then I give a rock-ribbed practical indication of the kind of progress and braininess which is synonymous with the name Zenith!

But the way of the righteous is not all roses. Before I close I must call your attention to a problem we have to face, this coming year. The worst menace to sound government is not the avowed socialists but a lot of cowards who work under cover—the long-haired gentry who call themselves "liberals" and "radicals" and "non-partisan" and "intelligentsia" and God only knows how many other trick names! Irresponsible teachers and professors constitute the worst of this whole gang, and I am ashamed to say that several of them are on the faculty of our great State University! The U. is my own Alma Mater, and I am proud to be known as an alumni, but there are certain instructors there who seem to think we ought to turn the conduct of the nation over to hoboes and roustabouts.

Those profs are the snakes to be scotched—they and all their milk-and-water ilk! The American business man is generous to a fault, but one thing he does demand of all teachers and lecturers and journalists: if we're going to pay them our good money, they've got to help us by selling efficiency and whooping it up for rational prosperity! And when it comes to these blab-mouth, fault-finding, pessimistic, cynical University teachers, let me tell you that during this golden coming year it's just as much our duty to bring influence to have those cusses fired as it is to sell all the real estate and gather in all the good shekels we can.

Not till that is done will our sons and daughters see that the ideal of American manhood and culture isn't a lot of cranks sitting around chewing the rag about their Rights and their Wrongs, but a God-fearing, hustling, successful, two-fisted Regular Guy, who belongs to some church with pep and piety to it, who belongs to the Boosters or the Rotarians or the Kiwanis, to the Elks or Moose or Red Men or Knights of Columbus or any one of a score of organizations of good, jolly, kidding, laughing, sweating, upstanding, lend-a-handing Royal Good Fellows, who plays hard and works hard, and whose answer to his critics is a square-toed boot that'll teach the grouches and smart alecks to respect the He-man and get out and root for Uncle Samuel, U.S.A.!

Robert S. Lynd and Helen M. Lynd

"Inventions Re-Making Leisure," from *Middletown: A Study in Modern American Culture* (1929)

"Why on earth do you need to study what's changing in this country?" said a lifelong resident and shrewd observer of the Middle West. "I can tell you what's happening in just four letters: A-U-T-O!" . . .

The first real automobile appeared in Middletown in 1900. About 1906 it was estimated that "there are probably 200 in the city and county." At the close of 1923 there were 6,221 passenger cars in the city, one for every 6.1 persons, or roughly two for every three families. Of these 6,221 cars, 41 per cent. were Fords; 54 per cent. of the total were cars of models of 1920 or later, and 17 per cent. models earlier than 1917. These cars average a bit over 5,000 miles a year. For some of the workers and some of the business class, use of the automobile is a seasonal matter, but the increase in surfaced roads and in closed cars is rapidly making the car a year-round tool for leisure-time as well as getting-a-living activities. As, at the turn of the century, business class people began to feel apologetic if they did not have a telephone, so ownership of an automobile has now reached the point of being an accepted essential of normal living.

Into the equilibrium of habits which constitutes for each individual some integration in living has come this new habit, upsetting old adjustments, and blasting its way through such accustomed and unquestioned dicta as "Rain or shine, I never miss a Sunday morning at church"; "A high school boy does not need much spending money"; "I don't need exercise, walking to the office keeps me fit"; "I wouldn't think of moving out of town and being so far from my friends"; "Parents ought always to know where their children are." The newcomer is most quickly and amicably incorporated into those regions of behavior in which men are engaged in doing impersonal, matter-of-fact things; much more contested is its advent where emotionally charged sanctions and taboos are concerned. No one questions the use of the auto for transporting groceries, getting to one's place of work or to the golf course, or in place of the porch for "cooling off after supper" on a hot summer evening; however much the activities concerned with getting a living may be altered by the fact that a factory can draw from workmen within a radius of forty-five miles, or however much old labor union men resent the intrusion of this new alternate way of spending an evening, these things are hardly major issues. But when auto riding tends to replace the traditional call in the family parlor as a way of approach between the unmarried, "the home is endangered," and all-day Sunday motor trips are a "threat against the church"; it is in the activities concerned with the home and religion that the automobile occasions the greatest emotional conflicts.

Group-sanctioned values are disturbed by the inroads of the automobile upon the family budget. A case in point is the not uncommon practice of mortgaging a home to buy an automobile.

Data on automobile ownership were secured from 123 working class families. Of these, sixty have cars. Forty-one of the sixty own their homes. Twenty-six of these forty-one families have mortgages on their homes. Forty of the sixty-three families who do not own a car own their homes. Twenty-nine of these have mortgages on their homes. Obviously other factors are involved in many of Middletown's mortgages. That the automobile does represent a real choice in the minds of some at least is suggested by the acid retort of one citizen to the question about car ownership: "No, sir, we've *not* got a car. *That's* why we've got a home." According to an officer of a Middletown automobile financing company, 75 to 90 per cent. of the cars purchased locally are bought on time payment, and a working man earning $35.00 a week frequently plans to use one week's pay each month as payment for his car. . . .

Many families feel that an automobile is justified as an agency holding the family group together. "I never feel as close to my family as when we are all together in the car," said one business class mother, and one or two spoke of giving up Country Club membership or other recreations to get a car for this reason. "We don't spend anything on recreation except for the car. We save every place we can and put the money into the car. It keeps the family together," was an opinion voiced more than once. Sixty-one per cent. of 337 boys and 60 per cent. of 423 girls in the three upper years of the high school say that they motor more often with their parents than without them. . . .

The threat which the automobile presents to some anxious parents is suggested by the fact that of thirty girls brought before the juvenile court in the twelve months preceding September 1, 1924, charged with "sex crimes," for whom the place where the offense occurred was given in the records, nineteen were listed as having committed the offense in an automobile. Here again the automobile appears to some as an "enemy" of the home and society. . . .

Like the automobile, the motion picture is more to Middletown than simply a new way of doing an old thing; it has added new dimensions to the city's leisure. To be sure, the spectacle-watching habit was strong upon Middletown in the nineties. Whenever they had a chance people turned out to a "show," but chances were relatively fewer. Fourteen times during January, 1890, for instance, the Opera House was opened for performances ranging from *Uncle Tom's Cabin* to *The Black Crook*, before the paper announced that "there will not be any more attractions at the Opera House for nearly two weeks." In July there were no "attractions"; a half dozen were scattered through August and September; there were twelve in October.

Today nine motion picture theaters operate from 1 to 11 P.M. seven days a week summer and winter; four of the nine give three different programs a week, the other five having two a week; thus twenty-two different programs with a total of over 300 performances are available to Middletown every week in the year. In addition, during January, 1923, there were three plays in Middletown and four motion pictures in other places than the regular theaters, in July three plays and one additional movie, in October two plays and one movie.

About two and three-fourths times the city's entire population attended the nine motion picture theaters during the month of July, 1923, the "valley" month of the year, and four and one-half times the total population in the "peak" month of December. Of 395 boys and 457 girls in the three upper years of the high school who stated how many times they had attended the movies in "the last seven days," a characteristic week in mid-November, 30 per cent. of the boys and 39 per cent. of the girls had not attended, 31 and 29 per cent. respectively had been only once, 22 and 21 per cent. respectively two times, 10 and 7 per cent. three times, and 7 and 4 per cent. four or more times. According to the housewives interviewed regarding the custom in their own families, in three of the forty business class families interviewed and in thirty-eight of the 122 working class families no member "goes at all" to the movies. One family in ten in each group goes as an entire family once a week or oftener; the two parents go together without their children once a week or oftener in four business class families (one in ten), and in two working class families (one in sixty) ; in fifteen business class families and in thirty-eight working class families the children were said by their mothers to go without their parents one or more times weekly.

In short, the frequency of movie attendance of high school boys and girls is about equal, business class families tend to go more often than do working class families, and children of both groups attend more often without their parents than do all the individuals or other combinations of family members put together. The decentralizing tendency of the movies upon the family, suggested by this last, is further indicated by the fact that only 21 per cent. of 337 boys and 33 per cent. of 423 girls in the three upper years of the high school go to the movies more often with their parents than without them. On the other hand, the comment is frequently heard in Middletown that movies have cut into lodge attendance, and it is probable that time formerly spent in lodges, saloons, and unions is now being spent in part at the movies, at least occasionally with other members of the family. Like the automobile and radio, the movies, by breaking up leisure time into an individual, family, or small group affair, represent a counter movement to the trend toward organization so marked in clubs and other leisure-time pursuits. . . .

Next largest are the crowds which come to see the sensational society films. The kind of vicarious living brought to Middletown by these films may be inferred from such titles as; "Alimony— brilliant men, beautiful jazz babies, champagne baths, midnight revels, petting parties in the purple dawn, all ending in one terrific smashing climax that makes you gasp"; "Married Flirts— Husbands: Do you flirt? Does your wife always know where you are? Are you faithful to your vows? Wives: What's your hubby doing? Do you know? Do you worry? Watch out for Married Flirts." So fast do these flow across the silver screen that, e.g., at one time The Daring Years, Sinners in Silk, Women Who Give, and The Price She Paid were all running synchronously, and at another "Name the Man—a story of betrayed womanhood, Rouged Lips, and The Queen of Sin. While Western "action" films and a million-dollar spectacle like The Covered Wagon or The Hunchback of Notre Dame draw heavy houses, and while managers lament that there are too few of the popular comedy films, it is the film with burning "heart interest," that packs Middletown's motion picture houses week after week. Young Middletown enters eagerly into the vivid experience of Flaming Youth: "neckers, petters, white kisses, red kisses, pleasure-mad daughters, sensation-craving mothers, by an author who didn't dare sign his name; the truth bold, naked, sensational"—so ran the press advertisement—under the spell of the powerful conditioning medium of pictures presented with music and all possible heightening of the emotional content, and the added factor of sharing this experience with a "date" in a darkened room. Meanwhile, Down into the Sea in Ships, a costly spectacle of whaling adventure, failed at the leading theater "because," the exhibitor explained, "the whale is really the hero in the film and there wasn't enough 'heart interest' for the women.". . .

Though less widely diffused as yet than automobile owning or movie attendance, the radio nevertheless is rapidly crowding its way in among the necessities in the family standard of living. Not the least remarkable feature of this new invention is its accessibility. Here skill and ingenuity can in part offset money as an open sesame to swift sharing of the enjoyments of the wealthy. With but little equipment one can call the life of the rest of the world from the air, and this equipment can be purchased piecemeal at the ten-cent store. Far from being simply one more means of passive enjoyment, the radio has given rise to much ingenious manipulative activity. In a count of representative sections of Middletown, it was found that, of 303 homes in twenty-eight blocks in the "best section" of town, inhabited almost entirely by the business class, 12 per cent. had radios; of 518 workers' homes in sixty-four blocks, 6 per cent. had radios. . . .

In the flux of competing habits that are oscillating the members of the family now towards and now away from the home, radio occupies an intermediate position. Twenty-five per cent. of 337 high school boys and 22 per cent. of 423 high school girls said that they listen more often to the radio with their parents than without them, and, as pointed out above, 20 per cent. of 274 boys in the three upper years of the high school answered "radio" to the question, "In what thing that you are doing at home this fall are you most interested?"—more than gave any other answer. More than one mother said that her family used to scatter in the evening—"but now we all sit around and listen to the radio."

Likewise the place of the radio in relation to Middletown's other leisure habits is not wholly clear. As it becomes more perfected, cheaper, and a more accepted part of life, it may cease to call forth so much active, constructive ingenuity and become one more form of passive enjoyment. Doubtless it will continue to play a mighty role in lifting Middletown out of the humdrum of every day; it is beginning to take over that function of the great political rallies or the trips by the train-load to the state capital to hear a noted speaker or to see a monument dedicated that a generation ago helped to set the average man in a wide place. But it seems not unlikely that, while furnishing a new means of diversified enjoyment, it will at the same time operate, with national advertising, syndicated newspapers, and other means of large-scale diffusion, as yet another means of standardizing many of Middletown's habits. Indeed, at no point is one brought up more sharply against the impossibility of studying Middletown as a self-contained, self-starting community than when one watches these space-binding leisure-time inventions imported from without—automobile, motion picture, and radio—reshaping the city.

FLORENCE KELLEY AND ELSIE HILL

"Shall Women Be Equal Before the Law?"
from *The Nation* (1922)

Yes!

The removal of all forms of the subjection of women is the purpose to which the National Woman's Party is dedicated. Its present campaign to remove the discriminations against women in the laws of the United States is but the beginning of its determined effort to secure the freedom of women, an integral part of the struggle for human liberty for which women are first of all responsible. Its interest lies in the final release of woman from the class of a dependent, subservient being to which early civilization committed her.

The laws of various States at present hold her in that class. They deny her a control of her children equal to the father's; they deny her, if married, the right to her own earnings; they punish her for offenses for which men go unpunished; they exclude her from public office and from public institutions to the support of which her taxes contribute. These laws are not the creation of this age, but the fact that they are still tolerated on our statute books and that in some States their removal is vigorously resisted shows the hold of old traditions upon us. Since the passage of the Suffrage Amendment the incongruity of these laws, dating back many centuries, has become more than ever marked. . . .

The National Woman's Party believes that it is a vital social need to do away with these discriminations against women and is devoting its energies to that end. The removal of the discriminations and not the method by which they are removed is the thing upon which the Woman's Party insists. It has under consideration an amendment to the Federal Constitution which, if adopted, would remove them at one stroke, but it is at present endeavoring to secure their removal in the individual States by a blanket bill, which is the most direct State method. . . .

Elsie Hill

No!

Sex is a biological fact. The political rights of citizens are not property dependent upon sex, but social and domestic relations and industrial activities are. All modern-minded people desire that women should have full political equality and like opportunity in business and the professions. No enlightened person desires that they should be excluded from jury duty or denied the equal guardianship of children, or that unjust inheritance laws or discriminations against wives should be perpetuated.

The inescapable facts are, however, that men do not bear children, are freed from the burdens of maternity, and are not susceptible, in the same measure as women, to poisons now increasingly characteristic of certain industries, and to the universal poison of fatigue. These are differences so far reaching, so fundamental, that it is grotesque to ignore them. Women cannot be made men by act of the legislature or by amendment of the Federal Constitution. This is no matter of today or to-morrow. The inherent differences are permanent. Women will always need many laws different from those needed by men.

The effort to enact the blanket bill in defiance of all biological differences recklessly imperils the special laws for women as such, for wives, for mothers, and for wage-earners. . . .

Why should wage-earning women be thus forbidden to get laws for their own health and welfare and that of their unborn children? Why should they be made subject to the preferences of wage-earning men? Is not this of great and growing importance when the number of women wage-earners, already counted by millions, increases by leaps and bounds from one census to the next? And when the industries involving exposure to poisons are increasing faster than ever? And when the overwork of mothers is one recognized cause of the high infant death-rate? And when the rise in the mortality of mothers in childbirth continues?

If there were no other way of promoting more perfect equality for women, an argument could perhaps be sustained for taking these risks. But why take them when every desirable measure attainable through the blanket bill can be enacted in the ordinary way? . . .

Florence Kelley

BRUCE BARTON

"Jesus as Advertising Man," from *The Man Nobody Knows* (1925)

Every advertising man ought to study the parables of Jesus in the same fashion, schooling himself in their language and learning these four big elements of their power.

1. First of all they are marvelously condensed, as all good advertising must be. . . .

How often you must read and read before you discover just what it is that the advertiser wants you to do. Jesus had no introductions. A single sentence grips your attention; three or four more tell the story; one or two more and the application is driven home. When he wanted a new disciple he said simply "Follow me." When he sought to explain the deepest philosophic mystery—the personality and character of God—he said, "A king made a banquet and invited many guests. God is that king and you are the guests; the Kingdom of Heaven is happiness—a banquet to be enjoyed." . . .

Jesus hated prosy dullness. He praised the Centurion who was anxious not to waste his time; the only prayer which he publicly commended was uttered by a poor publican who rarely cried out, "God, be merciful to me a sinner." A seven word prayer, Jesus called it a good one. A sixty-eight word prayer, he said, contained all that men needed to say or God to hear. What would be his verdict on most of our prayers and our speeches and our advertisements?

2. His language was marvelously simple—a second great essential. There is hardly a sentence in his teaching which a child can not understand. His illustrations were all drawn from the commonest experiences of life; "a sower went forth to sow"; "a certain man had two sons"; "a man built his house on the sands"; "the kingdom of heaven is like a grain of mustard seed." The absence of adjectives is striking. . . .

Jesus used few qualifying words and no long ones. We referred a minute ago to those three literary masterpieces, *The Lord's Prayer, The Twenty-Third Psalm, The Gettysburg* Address. Recall their phraseology:

Our Father which art in Heaven, hallowed be thy name

* * *

The Lord is my shepherd; I shall not want

* * *

Four score and seven years ago

Not a single three-syllable word; hardly any two-syllable words. All the greatest things in human life are one-syllable things—love, joy, hope, home, child, wife, trust, faith, God—and the great advertisements generally speaking, are those in which the most small words are found.

3. Sincerity glistened like sunshine through every sentence he uttered; sincerity is the third essential. . . .

Jesus was notably tolerant of almost all kinds of sinners. . . .

But for one sin he had no mercy. He denounced the *insincerity* of the Pharisees in phrases which sting like the lash of a whip. They thought they had a first mortgage on the Kingdom of Heaven, and he told them scornfully that only those who become like little children have any chance of entering in. . . .

Much brass has been sounded and many cymbals tinkled in the name of advertising; but the advertisements which persuade people to act are written by men who have an abiding respect for the intelligence of their readers, and a deep sincerity regarding the merits of the goods they have to sell. . . .

4. Finally he knew the necessity for repetition and practiced it. . . .

It has been said that "reputation is repetition." No important truth can be impressed the minds of any large number of people by being said only once. The thoughts which Jesus had to give the world were revolutionary, but they were few in number. "God is your father," he said, "caring more for the welfare of every one of you than any human father can possibly care for his children. His Kingdom is happiness! his rule is love." This is what be had to teach, but he knew the necessity of driving it home from every possible angle. So in one of his stories God is the shepherd searching the wilds for one wandering sheep; in another, the Father welcoming home a prodigal boy; in another a King who forgives his debtors large amounts and expects them to be forgiving in turn—*many* stories, *many* advertisements, but the same big Idea. . . .

So we have the main points of his business philosophy:
1. Whoever will be great must render great service.
2. Whoever will find himself at the top must be willing to lose himself at the bottom.
3. The big rewards come to those who travel the second, undemanded mile. . . .

Countee Cullen

"A Song of Praise" (1925)

(For one who praised his lady's being fair.)

You have not heard my love's dark throat,
  Slow-fluting like a reed,
Release the perfect golden note
  She caged there for my need.

Her walk is like the replica
  Of some barbaric dance
Wherein the soul of Africa
  Is winged with arrogance.

And yet so light she steps across
  The ways her sure feet pass,
She does not dent the smoothest moss
  Or bend the thinnest grass.

My love is dark as yours is fair,
  Yet lovelier I hold her
Than listless maids with pallid hair,
  And blood that's thin and colder.

You-proud-and-to-be-pitied one,
  Gaze on her and despair;
Then seal your lips until the sun
  Discovers one as fair.

COUNTEE CULLEN

"Incident" (1925)

(For Eric Walrond)

Once riding in old Baltimore,
  Heart-filled, head-filled with glee,
I saw a Baltimorean
  Keep looking straight at me.

Now I was eight and very small,
  And he was no whit bigger,
And so I smiled, but he poked out
  His tongue, and called me, "Nigger."

I saw the whole of Baltimore
  From May until December;
Of all the things the happened there
  That's all that I remember.

COUNTEE CULLEN
"Heritage" (1925)

(For Harold Jackman)

What is Africa to me:
Copper sun or scarlet sea,
Jungle star or jungle track,
Strong bronzed me, or regal black
Women from whose loins I sprang
When the birds of Eden sang?
One three centuries removed
From the scenes his father loved,
Spicy grove, cinnamon tree,
What is Africa to me?

So I lie, who all day long
Want no sound except the song
Sung by wild barbaric birds
Goading massive jungle herds,
Juggernauts of flesh that pass
Trampling tall defiant grass
Where young forest lovers lie
Plighting troth beneath the sky.
So I lie, who always hear,
Though I cram against my ear
Both my thumbs, and keep them there,
Great drums throbbing through the air.
So I die, whose fount of pride,
Dear distress, and joy allied
Is my somber flesh and skin,
With the dark blood dammed within
Like great pulsing tides of wine
That, I fear, must burst the fine
Channels of the chafing net
Where they surge and roam and fret.
Africa? A book one thumbs
Listlessly, till slumber comes.

Unremembered are her bats
Circling through the night, her cats
Crouching in the river reeds,
Stalking gentle flesh that feeds
By the river brink; no more
Does the bugle-throated roar
Cry that monarch claws have leapt
From the scabbards where they slept.
Silver snakes that once a year
Doff the lovely coats you wear,
Seek no covert in your fear
Lest a mortal eye should see;
What's your nakedness to me?
Here no leprous flowers rear
Fierce corollas in the air;
Here no bodies sleek and wet
Dripping mingled rain and sweat,
Tread the savage measures of
Jungle boys and girls in love.
What is last year's snow to me
Last year's anything? The tree
Budding yearly must forget
How its past arose or set—
Bough and blossom, flower, fruit
Even what shy bird with mute
Wonder at her travail there,
Meekly labored in its hair.
One three centuries removed
From the scenes his fathers loved,
Spicy grove, cinnamon tree,
What is Africa to me?

So I lie, who finds no peace
Night or day, no slight release
From the unremittant beat
Made by cruel padded feet
Walking through my body's street.
Up and down they go, and back,
Treading out a jungle track.
So I lie, who never quite
Safely sleep from rain at night—
I can never rest at all
When the rain begins to fall;
Like a soul gone mad with pain
I must match its weird refrain;
Ever must I twist and squirm
Writhing like a baited worm,
While its primal measures drip
Through my body, crying, "Strip!

Doff this new exuberance.
Come and dance the Lover's Dance!"
In an old remembered way
Rain works on me night and day.
Quaint, outlandish heathen gods
Black men fashion out of rods,
Clay, and brittle bits of stone,
In a likeness like their own
My conversion came high-priced;
I belong to Jesus Christ,
Preacher of humility;
Heathen gods are naught to me.

Father, Son, and Holy Ghost,
So I make an idle boast;
Jesus of the twice-turned cheek,
Lamb of God, although I speak
With my mouth thus, in my heart
Do I play a double part.
Ever at Thy glowing altar
Must my heart grow sick and falter,
Wishing He I served were black,
Thinking then it would not lack
Precedent of pain to guide it,
Let who would or might deride it;
Surely then this flesh would know
Yours had borne a kindred woe.
Lord, I fashion dark gods, too,
Daring even to give You
Dark despairing features where,
Crowned with dark rebellious hair,
Patience wavers just so much as
Mortal grief compels, while touches
Quick and hot, of anger, rise
To smitten cheek and weary eyes.
Lord, forgive me if my need
Sometimes shapes all human creed.
All day long and all night through,
One thing only must I do:
Quench my pride and cool my blood,
Lest I perish in the flood.
Lest a hidden ember set
Timber that I thought was wet
Burning like the dryest flax,
Melting like the merest wax,
Lest the grave restore its dead.
Not yet has my heart or head
In the least way realized
They and I are civilized.

Langston Hughes

"The Negro Speaks of Rivers" (1920)

I've known rivers:
I've known rivers ancient as the world and older than the
    flow of human blood in human veins.

My soul has grown deep like the rivers.

I bathed in the Euphrates when dawns were young.
I built my hut near the Congo and it lulled me to sleep.
I looked upon the Nile and raised the pyramids above it.
I heard the singing of the Mississippi when Abe Lincoln
    went down to New Orleans, and I've seen its muddy
    bosom turn all golden in the sunset.

I've known rivers:
Ancient, dusky rivers.

My soul has grown deep like the rivers.

LANGSTON HUGHES

"The Weary Blues" (1923)

Droning a drowsy syncopated tune,
Rocking back and forth to a mellow croon,
    I heard a Negro play.
Down on Lenox Avenue the other night
By the pale dull pallor of an old gas light
    He did a lazy sway. . . .
    He did a lazy sway. . . .
To the tune o' those Weary Blues.
With his ebony hands on each ivory key
He made that poor piano moan with melody.
    O Blues!
Swaying to and fro on his rickety stool
He played that sad raggy tune like a musical fool.
    Sweet Blues!
Coming from a black man's soul.
    O Blues!
In a deep song voice with a melancholy tone
I heard that Negro sing, that old piano moan—
    "Ain't got nobody in all this world,
    Ain't got nobody but ma self.
    I's gwine to quit ma frownin'
    And put ma troubles on the shelf."
Thump, thump, thump, went his foot on the floor.
He played a few chords then he sang some more—
    "I got the Weary Blues
    And I can't be satisfied.
    Got the Weary Blues
    And can't be satisfied—
    I ain't happy no mo'
    And I wish that I had died."
And far into the night he crooned that tune.
The stars went out and so did the moon.
The singer stopped playing and went to bed
While the Weary Blues echoed through his head.
He slept like a rock or a man that's dead.

JOHN STEINBECK

"Dubious Battle in California,"
from *The Nation* (1936)

In sixty years a complete revolution has taken place in California agriculture. Once its principal products were hay and cattle. Today fruits and vegetables are its most profitable crops. With the change in the nature of farming there has come a parallel change in the nature and amount of the labor necessary to carry it on. Truck gardens, while they give a heavy yield per acre, require much more labor and equipment than the raising of hay and livestock. At the same time these crops are seasonal, which means that they are largely handled by migratory workers. Along with the intensification of farming made necessary by truck gardening has come another important development. The number of large-scale farms, involving the investment of thousands of dollars, has increased; so has the number of very small farms of from five to ten acres. But the middle farm, of from 100 to 300 acres is in process of elimination.

There are in California, therefore, two distinct classes of farmers widely separated in standard of living, desires, needs, and sympathies: the very small farmer who more often than not takes the side of the workers in disputes and the speculative farmer, like A. J. Chandler, publisher of the Los Angeles *Times*, or like Herbert Hoover and William Randolph Hearst, absentee owners who possess huge sections of land. Allied with these large individual growers have been the big incorporated farms, owned by their stockholders and farmed by instructed managers, and a large number of bank farms, acquired by foreclosure and operated by Superintendents whose labor policy is dictated by the bank. For example, the Bank of America is very nearly the largest farm owner and operator in the state of California.

These two classes have little or no common ground; while the small farmer is likely to belong to the grange, the speculative farmer belongs to some such organization as the Associated Farmers of California, which is closely tied to the state Chamber of Commerce. This group has as its major activity resistance to any attempt of farm labor to organize. Its avowed purpose has been the distribution of news reports and leaflets tending to show that every attempt to organize agricultural workers was the work of red agitators and that every organization was Communist inspired.

The completion of the transcontinental railroads left in the country many thousands of Chinese and some Hindus who had been imported for the work. At about the same time the increase of fruit crops, with their heavy seasonal need for pickers, created a demand for this mass of cheap labor. These people, however, did not long remain on the land. They migrated to the cities, rented small plots of land there, and, worst of all, organized in the so-called "Tongs," which were able to direct their efforts as a group. Soon the whites were inflamed to race hatred, riots broke out against the Chinese, and repressive activities were undertaken all over the state, until these people, who had been a tractable and cheap source of labor, were driven from the fields.

To take the place of the Chinese, the Japanese were encouraged to come into California; and they, even more than the Chinese, showed an ability not only to obtain land for their subsistence but to organize. The "Yellow Peril" agitation was the result. Then, soon after the turn of the century Mexicans were imported in great numbers. For a while they were industrious workers, until the process of importing twice as many as were needed in order to depress wages made their earnings drop below any conceivable living standard. In such conditions they did what the others had done; they began to organize. The large growers immediately opened fire on them. The newspapers were full of the radicalism of the Mexican unions. Riots became common in the Imperial Valley and in the grape country in and adjacent to Kern County. Another wave of importations was arranged, from the Philippine Islands, and the cycle was repeated—wage depression due to abundant labor, organization, and the inevitable race hatred and riots.

This brings us almost to the present. The drought in the Middle West has very recently made available an enormous amount of cheap labor. Workers have been coming to California in nondescript cars from Oklahoma, Nebraska, Texas, and other states, parts of which have been rendered uninhabitable by drought. Poverty-stricken after the destruction of their farms, their last reserves used up in making the trip, they have arrived so beaten and destitute that they have been willing at first to work under any conditions and for any wages offered. This migration started on a considerable scale about two years ago and is increasing all the time.

For a time it looked as though the present cycle would be identical with the earlier ones, but there are several factors in this influx which differentiate it from the others. In the first place, the migrants are undeniably American and not deportable. In the second place, they were not lured to California by a promise of good wages, but are refugees as surely as though they had fled from destruction by an invader. In the third place, they are not drawn from a peon class, but have either owned small farms or been farm hands in the early American sense, in which the "hand" is a member of the employing family. They have one fixed idea, and that is to acquire land and settle on it. Probably the most important difference is that they are not easily intimidated. They are courageous, intelligent, and resourceful. Having gone through the horrors of the drought and with immense effort having escaped from it, they cannot be herded, attacked, starved, or frightened as all the others were.

Let us see what the emigrants from the dust bowl find when they arrive in California. The ranks of permanent and settled labor are filled. In most cases all resources have been spent in making the trip from the dust bowl. Unlike the Chinese and the Filipinos, the men rarely come alone. They bring wives and children, now and then a few chickens and their pitiful household goods, though in most cases these have been sold to buy gasoline for the trip. It is quite usual for a man, his wife, and from three to eight children to arrive in California with no possessions but the rattletrap car they travel in and the ragged clothes on their bodies. They often lack bedding and cooking utensils.

During the spring, summer, and part of the fall the man may find some kind of agricultural work. The top pay for a successful year will not be over $400, and if he has any trouble or is not agile, strong, and quick it may well be only $150. It will be seen that rent is out of the question. Clothes cannot be bought. Every available cent must go for food and a reserve to move the car from harvest to harvest. The migrant will stop in one of two federal camps, in a state camp, in houses put up by the large or small farmers, or in the notorious squatters' camps. In the state and federal camps he will find sanitary arrangements and a place to pitch his tent. The camps maintained by the large farmers are of two classes—houses which are rented to the workers at what are called nominal prices, $4 to $8 a month, and camp grounds which are little if any better than the squatters' camps. Since rent is such a problem, let us see how the houses are fitted. Ordinarily there is one room, no running water; one toilet and one bathroom are provided for two or three hundred persons. Indeed, one large farmer was accused in a Growers' Association meeting of being "kind of communistic" because he advocated separate toilets for men and women. Some of the large ranches maintain what are called model workers' houses. One such ranch, run by a very prominent man, has neat single-room houses built of whitewashed adobe. They are said to have cost $500 apiece. They are rented for $5 a month. This ranch pays twenty cents an hour as opposed to the thirty cents paid at other ranches and indorsed by the grange in the community. Since this rugged individual is saving 33 1/3 percent of his labor cost and still charging $5 a month rent for his houses, it will be readily seen that he is getting a very fair return on his money besides being generally praised as a philanthropist. The reputation of this ranch, however, is that the migrants stay only long enough to get money to buy gasoline with, and then move on.

The small farmers are not able to maintain camps of any comfort or with any sanitary facilities except one or two holes dug for toilets. The final resource is the squatters' camp, usually located on the bank of some watercourse. The people pack into them. They use the watercourse for drinking, bathing, washing their clothes, and to receive their refuse, with the result that epidemics start easily and are difficult to check. Stanislaus County, for example, has a nice culture of hookworm in the mud by its squatters' camp. The people in these camps, because of long-continued privation, are in no shape to fight illness. It is often said that no one starves in the United States, yet in Santa Clara County last year five babies were certified by the local coroner to have died of "malnutrition," the modern word for starvation, and the less shocking word, although in its connotation it is perhaps more horrible since it indicates that the suffering has been long drawn out.

In these squatters' camps the immigrant will find squalor beyond anything he has yet had to experience and intimidation almost unchecked. At one camp it is the custom of deputy sheriffs, who are also employees of a great ranch nearby, to drive by the camp for hours at a time, staring into the tents as though trying to memorize faces. The communities in which these camps exist want migratory workers to come for the month required to pick the harvest, and to move on when it is over. If they do not move on, they are urged to with guns.

These are some of the conditions California offers the refugees from the dust bowl. But the refugees are even less content with the starvation wages and the rural slums than were the Chinese, the Filipinos, and the Mexicans. Having their families with them, they are not so mobile as the earlier immigrants were. If starvation sets in, the whole family starves, instead of just one man. Therefore they have been quick to see that they must organize for their own safety.

Attempts to organize have been met with a savagery from the large growers beyond anything yet attempted. In Kern County a short time ago a group met to organize under the A. F. of L. They made out their form and petition for a charter and put it in the mail for Washington. That night a representative of Associated Farmers wired Washington for information concerning a charter granted to these workers. The Washington office naturally replied that it had no knowledge of such a charter. In the Bakersfield papers the next day appeared a story that the A. F. of L. denied the affiliation; consequently the proposed union must be of Communist origin.

But the use of the term communism as a bugbear has nearly lost its sting. An official of a speculative-farmer group, when asked what he meant by a Communist replied: "Why, he's the guy that wants twenty-five cents an hour when we're paying twenty." This realistic and cynical definition has finally been understood by the workers, so that the term is no longer the frightening thing it was. And when a county judge said, "California agriculture demands that we create and maintain a peonage," the future of unorganized agricultural labor was made clear to every man in the field.

The usual repressive measures have been used against these migrants: shooting by deputy sheriffs in "self-defense," jailing without charge, refusal of trial by jury, torture and beating by night riders. But even in the short time that these American migrants have been out here there has been a change. It is understood that they are being attacked not because they want higher wages, not because they are Communists, but simply because they want to organize. And to the men, since this defines the thing not to be allowed, it also defines the thing that is completely necessary to the safety of the workers.

This season has seen the beginning of a new form of intimidation not used before. It is the whispering campaign which proved so successful among business rivals. As in business, it is particularly deadly here because its source cannot be traced and because it is easily spread. One of the items of this campaign is the rumor that in the event of labor troubles the deputy sheriffs inducted to break up picket lines will be armed not with tear gas but with poison gas. The second is aimed at the women and marks a new low in tactics. It is to the effect that in the event of labor troubles the water supply used by strikers will be infected with typhoid germs. The fact that these bits of information are current over a good part of the state indicates that they have been widely planted.

The effect has been far from that desired. There is now in California anger instead of fear. The stupidity of the large grower has changed terror into defensive fury. The granges, working close to the soil and to the men, and knowing the temper of the men of this new race, have tried to put through wages that will allow a living, however small. But the large growers, who have been shown to be the only group making a considerable profit from agriculture, are devoting their money to tear gas and rifle ammunition. The men will organize and the large growers will meet organization with force. It is easy to prophesy this. In Kern County the grange has voted $1 a hundred pounds for cotton pickers for the first picking. The Associated Farmers have not yielded from seventy-five cents. There is tension in the valley, and fear for the future.

It is fervently to be hoped that the great group of migrant workers so necessary to the harvesting of California's crops may be given the right to live decently, that they may not be so badgered, tormented, and hurt that in the end they become avengers of the hundreds of thousands who have been tortured and starved before them.

JOHN STEINBECK

The Grapes of Wrath, Chapter 5 (1939)

The owners of the land came onto the land, or more often a spokesman for the owners came. They came in closed cars, and they felt the dry earth with their fingers, and sometimes they drove big earth augers into the ground for soil tests. The tenants, from their sun-beaten dooryards, watched uneasily when the closed cars drove along the fields. And at last the owner men drove into the dooryards and sat in their cars to talk out of the windows. The tenant men stood beside the cars for a while, and then squatted on their hams and found sticks with which to mark the dust.

In the open doors the women stood looking out, and behind them the children—corn-headed children, with wide eyes, one bare foot on top of the other bare foot, and the toes working. The women and the children watched their men talking to the owner men. They were silent.

Some of the owner men were kind because they hated what they had to do, and some of them were angry because they hated to be cruel, and some of them were cold because they had long ago found that one could not be an owner unless one were cold. And all of them were caught in something larger than themselves. Some of them hated the mathematics that drove them, and some were afraid, and some worshiped the mathematics because it provided a refuge from thought and from feeling. If a bank or a finance company owned the land, the owner man said, the Bank—or the Company—needs—wants—insists—must have—as though the Bank or the Company were a monster, with thought and feeling, which had ensnared them. These last would take no responsibility for the banks or the companies because they were men and slaves, while the banks were machines and masters all at the same time. Some of the owner men were a little proud to be slaves to such cold and powerful masters. The owner men sat in the cars and explained. You know the land is poor. You've scrabbled at it long enough, God knows.

The squatting tenant men nodded and wondered and drew figures in the dust, and yes, they knew, God knows. If the dust only wouldn't fly. If the top would only stay on the soil, it might not be so bad.

The owner men went on leading to their point: You know the land's getting poorer. You know what cotton does to the land; robs it, sucks all the blood out of it.

The squatters nodded—they knew, God knew. If they could only rotate the crops they might pump blood back into the land.

Well, it's too late. And the owner men explained the workings and the thinkings of the monster that was stronger than they were. A man can hold land if he can just eat and pay taxes; he can do that.

Yes, he can do that until his crops fail one day and he has to borrow money from the bank.

But—you see, a bank or a company can't do that, because those creatures don't breathe air, don't eat side-meat. They breathe profits; they eat the interest on money. If they don't get it, they die the way you die without air, without side-meat. It is a sad thing, but it is so, It is just so.

The squatting men raised their eyes to understand. Can't we just hang on? Maybe the next year will be a good year. God knows how much cotton next year. And with all the wars—God knows what price cotton will bring. Don't they make explosives out of cotton? And uniforms? Get enough wars and cotton'll hit the ceiling. Next year, maybe. They looked up questioningly.

We can't depend on it. The bank—the monster has to have profits all the time. It can't wait. It'll die. No, taxes go on. When the monster stops growing, it dies. It can't stay one size.

Soft fingers began to tap the sill of the car window, and the hard fingers tightened on the restless drawing sticks. In the doorways of the sun-beaten tenant houses, women sighed and then shifted feet so that the one that had been down was now on top, and the toes working. Dogs came sniffing near the owner cars and wetted on all four tires one after another. And chickens lay in the sunny dust and fluffed their feathers to get the cleansing dust down to the skin. In the little sties the pigs grunted inquiringly over the muddy remnants of the slops.

The squatting men looked down again. What do you want us to do? We can't take less share of the crop—we're half starved now. The kids are hungry all the time. We got no clothes, torn an' ragged. If all the neighbors weren't the same, we'd be ashamed to go to meeting.

And at last the owner men came to the point. The tenant system won't work any more. One man on a tractor can take the place of twelve or fourteen families. Pay him a wage and take all the crop. We have to do it. We don't like to do it. But the monster's sick. Something's happened to the monster.

But you'll kill the land with cotton.

We know. We've got to take cotton quick before the land dies. Then we'll sell the land. Lots of families in the East would like to own a piece of land.

The tenant men looked up alarmed. But what'll happen to us? How'll we eat?

You'll have to get off the land. The plows'll go through the dooryard.

And now the squatting men stood up angrily. Grampa took up the land, and he had to kill the Indians and drive them away. And Pa was born here, and he killed weeds and snakes. Then a bad year came and he had to borrow a little money. An' we was born here. There in the door—our children born here. And Pa had to borrow money. The bank owned the land then, but we stayed and we got a little bit of what we raised.

We know that—all that. It's not us, it's the bank. A bank isn't like a man. Or an owner with fifty thousand acres, he isn't like a man either. That's the monster.

Sure, cried the tenant men, but it's our land. We measured it and broke it up. We were born on it, and we got killed on it, died on it. Even if it's no good, it's still ours. That's what makes it ours—being born on it, working it, dying on it. That makes ownership, not a paper with numbers on it.

We're sorry. It's not us. It's the monster. The bank isn't like a man.

Yes, but the bank is only made of men.

No, you're wrong there—quite wrong there. The bank is something else than men. It happens that every man in a bank hates what the bank does, and yet the bank does it. The bank is something more than men, I tell you. It's the monster. Men made it, but they can't control it.

The tenants cried, Grampa killed Indians, Pa killed snakes for the land. Maybe we can kill banks—they're worse than Indians and snakes. Maybe we got to fight to keep our land, like Pa and Grampa did.

And now the owner men grew angry. You'll have to go.

But it's ours, the tenant men cried. We—

No. The bank, the monster owns it. You'll have to go.

We'll get our guns, like Grampa when the Indians came. What then?

Well—first the sheriff, and then the troops. You'll be stealing if you try to stay, you'll be murderers if you kill to stay. The monster isn't men, but it can make men do what it wants.

But if we go, where'll we go? How'll we go? We got no money.

We're sorry, said the owner men. The bank, the fifty-thousand-acre owner can't be responsible. You're on land that isn't yours. Once over the line maybe you can pick cotton in the fall. Maybe you can go on relief. Why don't you go on west to California? There's work there, and it never gets cold. Why, you can reach out anywhere and pick an orange. Why, there's always some kind of crop to work in. Why don't you go there? And the owner men started their cars and rolled away.

The tenant men squatted down to their hams again to mark the dust with a stick, to figure, to wonder. Their sunburned faces were dark, and their sun-whipped eyes were light. The women moved cautiously out of the doorways toward their men, and the children crept behind the women, cautiously, ready to run. The bigger boys squatted beside their fathers, because that made them men. After a time the women asked, What did he want?

And the men looked up for a second, and the smolder of pain was in their eyes. We got to get off. A tractor and a superintendent. Like factories.

Where'll we go? the women asked.

We don't know. We don't know.

And the women went quickly, quietly back into the houses and herded the children ahead of them. They knew that a man so hurt and so perplexed may turn in anger, even on people he loves. They left the men alone to figure and to wonder in the dust.

After a time perhaps the tenant man looked about—at the pump put in ten years ago, with a goose-neck handle and iron flowers on the spout, at the chopping block where a thousand chickens had been killed, at the hand plow lying in the shed, and the patent crib hanging in the rafters over it.

The children crowded about the women in the houses. What we going to do, Ma? Where we going to go?

The women said, We don't know, yet. Go out and play. But don't go near your father. He might whale you if you go near him. And the women went on with the work, but all the time they watched the men squatting in the dust—perplexed and figuring.

The tractors came over the roads and into the fields, great crawlers moving like insects, having the incredible strength of insects. They crawled over the ground, laying the track and rolling on it and picking it up. Diesel tractors, puttering while they stood idle; they thundered when they moved, and then settled down to a droning roar. Snub-nosed monsters, raising the dust and sticking their snouts into it, straight down the country, across the country, through fences, through dooryards, in and out of gullies in straight lines. They did not run on the ground, but on their own roadbeds. They ignored hills and gulches, water courses, fences, houses.

The man sitting in the iron seat did not look like a man; gloved, goggled, rubber dust mask over nose and mouth, he was part of the monster, a robot in the seat. The thunder of the cylinders sounded through the country, became one with the air and the earth, so that earth and air muttered in sympathetic vibration. The driver could not control it—straight across country it went, cutting through a dozen farms and straight back. A twitch at the controls could swerve the cat', but the driver's hands could not twitch because the monster that built the tractor, the monster that sent the tractor out, had somehow got into the driver's hands, into his brain and muscle, had goggled him and muzzled him—goggled his mind, muzzled his speech, goggled his perception, muzzled his protest. He could not see the land as it was, he could not smell the land as it smelled; his feet did not stamp the clods or feel the warmth and power of the earth. He sat in an iron seat and stepped on iron pedals. He could not cheer or beat or curse or encourage the extension of his power, and because of this he could not cheer or whip or curse or encourage himself. He did not know or own or trust or beseech the land. If a seed dropped did not germinate, it was nothing. If the young thrusting plant withered in drought or drowned in a flood of rain, it was no more to the driver than to the tractor.

He loved the land no more than the bank loved the land. He could admire the tractor—its machined surfaces, its surge of power, the roar of its detonating cylinders; but it was not his tractor. Behind the tractor rolled the shining disks, cutting the earth with blades—not plowing but surgery, pushing the cut earth to the right where the second row of disks cut it and pushed it to the left; slicing blades shining, polished by the cut earth. And pulled behind the disks, the harrows combing with iron teeth so that the little clods broke up and the earth lay smooth. Behind the harrows, the long seeders—twelve curved iron penes erected in the foundry, orgasms set by gears, raping methodically, raping without passion. The driver sat in his iron seat and he was proud of the straight lines he did not will, proud of the tractor he did not own or love, proud of the power he could not control. And when that crop grew, and was harvested, no man had crumbled a hot clod in his fingers and let the earth sift past his fingertips. No man had touched the seed, or lusted for the growth. Men ate what they had not raised, had no connection with the bread. The land bore under iron, and under iron gradually died; for it was not loved or hated, it had no prayers or curses.

At noon the tractor driver stopped sometimes near a tenant house and opened his lunch: sandwiches wrapped in waxed paper, white bread, pickle, cheese, Spam, a piece of pie branded like an engine part. He ate without relish. And tenants not yet moved away came out to see him, looked curiously while the goggles were taken off, and the rubber dust mask, leaving white circles around the eyes and a large white circle around nose and mouth. The exhaust of the tractor puttered on, for fuel is so cheap it is more efficient to leave the engine running than to heat the Diesel nose for a new start. Curious children crowded close, ragged children who ate their fried dough as they watched. They watched hungrily the unwrapping of the sandwiches, and their hunger-sharpened noses smelled the pickle, cheese, and Spam. They didn't speak to the driver. They watched his hand as it carried food to his mouth. They did not watch him chewing; their eyes followed the hand that held the sandwich. After a while the tenant who could not leave the place came out and squatted in the shade beside the tractor.

"Why! you're Joe Davis's boy!"

"Sure," the driver said.

"Well, what you doing this kind of work for—against your own people?"

"Three dollars a day. I got damn sick of creeping for my dinner—and not getting it. I got a wife and kids. We got to eat. Three dollars a day, and it comes every day."

"That's right," the tenant said. "But for your three dollars a day fifteen or twenty families can't eat at all. Nearly a hundred people have to go out and wander on the roads for your three dollars a day. Is that right?"

And the driver said, "Can't think of that. Got to think of my own kids. Three dollars a day, and it comes every day. Times are changing, mister, don't you know? Can't make a living on the land unless you've got two, five, ten thousand acres and a tractor. Crop land isn't for little guys like us any more. You don't kick up a howl because you can't make Fords, or because you're not the telephone company. Well, crops are like that now. Nothing to do about it. You try to get three dollars a day someplace. That's the only way."

The tenant pondered. "Funny thing how it is. If a man owns a little property, that property is him, it's part of him, and it's like him. If he owns property only so he can walk on it and handle it and be sad when it isn't doing well, and feel fine when the rain falls on it, that property is him, and some way he's bigger because he owns it. Even if he isn't successful he's big with his property. That is so."

And the tenant pondered more. "But let a man get property he doesn't see, or can't take time to get his fingers in, or can't be there to walk on it—why, then the property is the man. He can't do what he wants, he can't think what he wants. The property is the man, stronger than he is. And he is small, not big. Only his possessions are big—and he's the servant of his property. That is so, too."

The driver munched the branded pie and threw the crust away. "Times are changed, don't you know? Thinking about stuff like that don't feed the kids. Get your three dollars a day, feed your kids. You got no call to worry about anybody's kids but your own. You get a reputation for talking like that, and you'll never get three dollars a day. Big shots won't give you three dollars a day if you worry about anything but your three dollars a day."

"Nearly a hundred people on the road for your three dollars. Where will we go?"

"And that reminds me," the driver said. "you better get out soon. I'm going through the dooryard after dinner."

"You filled in the well this morning."

"I know. Had to keep the line straight. But I'm going through the dooryard after dinner. Got to keep the lines straight. And—well, you know Joe Davis, my old man, so I'll tell you this. I got orders wherever there's a family not moved out—if I have an accident—you know, get too close and cave the house in a little—well, I might get a couple of dollars. And my youngest kid never had no shoes yet."

"I built it with my hands. Straightened old nails to put the sheathing on. Rafters are wired to the stringers with baling wire. It's mine. I built it. You bump it down—I'll be in the window with a rifle. You even come too close and I'll pot you like a rabbit."

"It's not me. There's nothing I can do. I'll lose my job if I don't do it. And look—suppose you kill me? They'll just hang you, but long before you're hung there'll be another guy on the tractor, and he'll bump the house down. You're not killing the right guy."

"That's so," the tenant said. "Who gave you orders? I'll go after him. He's the one to kill."

"You're wrong. He got his orders from the bank. The bank told him, 'Clear those people out or it's your job.'"

"Well, there's a president of the bank. There's a board of directors. I'll fill up the magazine of the rifle and go into the bank."

The driver said, "Fellow was telling me the bank gets orders from the East. The orders were, 'Make the land show profit or we'll close you up.'"

"But where does it stop? Who can we shoot? I don't aim to starve to death before I kill the man that's starving me."

"I don't know. Maybe there's nobody to shoot. Maybe the thing isn't men at all. Maybe, like you said, the property's doing it. Anyway I told you my orders."

"I got to figure," the tenant said. "We all got to figure. There's some way to stop this. It's not like lightning or earthquakes. We've got a bad thing made by men, and by God that's something we can change." The tenant sat in his doorway, and the driver thundered his engine and started off, tracks falling and curving, harrows combing, and the phalli of the seeder slipping into the ground. Across the dooryard the tractor cut, and the hard, foot-beaten ground was seeded field, and the tractor cut through again; the uncut space was ten feet wide. And back he came. The iron guard bit into the house-corner, crumbled the wall, and wrenched the little house from its foundation so that it fell sideways, crushed like a bug. And the driver was goggled and a rubber mask covered his nose and mouth. The tractor cut a straight line on, and the air and the ground vibrated with its thunder. The tenant man stared after it, his rifle in his hand. His wife was beside him, and the quiet children behind. And all of them stared after the tractor.

JOHN COLLIER

from Report of the Commissioner on Indian Affairs (1938)

In all our colorful American life there is no group around which there so steadfastly persists an aura compounded of glamour, suspicion and romance, as the Indian. For generations, the Indian has been, and is today, the center of an amazing series of wonderings, fears, legends, hopes.

Yet those who have worked with Indians know that they are neither the cruel, warlike, irreligious savages imagined by some, nor are they the "fortunate children of nature's bounty" described by tourists who see them for an hour at some glowing ceremonial. We find the Indians, in all the basic forces and forms of life, human beings like ourselves. The majority of them are very poor people living under severely simple conditions. We know them to be deeply religious. We know them to be possessed of all the powers, intelligence, and genius within the range of human endowment. Just as we yearn to live out our own lives in our own ways, so, too, do the Indians, in their ways.

For nearly 300 years white Americans, in our zeal to carve out a nation made to order, have dealt with the Indians on the erroneous, yet tragic, assumption that the Indians were a dying race—to be liquidated. We took away their best lands; broke treaties, promises; tossed them the most nearly worthless scraps of a continent that had once been wholly theirs. But we did not liquidate their spirit. The vital spark which kept them alive was hardy. So hardy, indeed, that we now face an astounding, heartening fact.

The Indians Are No Longer a Dying Race

Actually, the Indians, on the evidence of Federal census rolls of the past 8 years, are increasing at almost twice the rate of the population as a whole.

With this fact before us, our whole attitude toward the Indians has necessarily undergone a profound change. Dead is the centuries-old notion that the sooner we eliminated this doomed race, preferably humanely, the better. No longer can we, with even the most generous intentions, pour millions of dollars and vast reservoirs of energy, sympathy, and effort into any unproductive attempts at some single, artificial permanent solution of the Indian problem. No longer can we naively talk of or think of the "Indian problem." Our task is to help Indians meet the myriad of complex, interrelated, mutually dependant situations which develop among them, according to the very best light we can get on those happenings—much as we deal with our own perplexities and opportunities.

We, therefore, define our Indian policy somewhat as follows: So productively to use the moneys appropriated by the Congress for Indians, as to enable them, on good, adequate lands of their own, to earn decent livelihoods and lead self-respecting, organized lives in harmony with their own aims and ideals, as an integral part of American life. Under such a policy, the ideal end result will be the ultimate disappearance of any need for Government aid or supervision. . . .

So intimately is all of Indian life tied up with the land and its utilization that to think of Indians is to think of land. The two are inseparable. Upon the land and its intelligent use depends the main future of the American Indian.

The Indian feels toward his land not a mere ownership sense but a devotion and veneration befitting what is not only a home but a refuge. At least 9 out of 10 Indians remain on or near the land. When times are good, a certain number drift away to town or city to work for wages. When times become bad, home to the reservation the Indian comes, and to the comparative security which he knows is waiting for him. The Indian still has much to learn in adjusting himself to the strains of competition amid an acquisitive society; but he long ago learned how to contend with the stresses of nature. Not only does the Indian's major source of livelihood derive from the land, but his social and political organizations are rooted in the soil.

A major aim, then, of the Indian Service is to help the Indians to keep and consolidate what lands they now have and to provide more and better lands upon which they may effectively carry on their lives. Just as important is the task of helping the Indian make such use of his land as will conserve the land, insure Indian self-support, and safeguard or build up the Indian's social life. Many subsequent chapters of this report deal with this latter task. . . .

Reorganization and Self-Government Activities

It is necessary to restate from time to time the historical processes underlying the administration of Indian affairs. It is necessary because repeatedly the question is raised as to why Indian lands should be tax-exempt, or why the United States should administer health, education, and other social services for the Indian population. In brief, why should the Indian be under guardianship?

Why Indians' Special Status?

European colonizers and their descendants brought to America ideas of land ownership, morality, government, and religion which were meaningless to the native American. In time these ideas became dominant to the exclusion of Indian habits of thought. Since we were a humane Nation and were not bent on destroying the Indians, we assumed the responsibility of showing them how our ideas operated. We wanted them to learn our ways so that they could exist side by side with us. In other words, we instituted a system of Indian education which is with us today.

We took away from the Indian all but a tiny fraction of his wealth in land, water, and other resources, and even his food supply, insofar as that consisted of game and wild products; and by doing so we charged ourselves with the responsibility of keeping the Indian from starvation.

Furthermore, since the Indian's understanding of property differed from ours, it was obvious that he would not long retain the little property left him if he was not protected. That made it necessary to erect trust-barriers around him which would prevent predatory men from making off with the means by which the Indian was to be taught a new way of existing.

By placing trust-barriers around Indian property, we exempted his land from State and local taxation. In taking this action we were subjecting the Indian to possible discrimination on the part of the States which would have resulted in leaving him without health care, education, roads, or any of the services which a State renders its people. States and local communities cannot furnish services without revenue. Once again, then, it became necessary for the Federal Government to assume an obligation toward the Indian tribes whose property it was seeking to protect.

These are the factors which Congress and the courts have borne in mind when they have dealt with Indian questions. The historical process has been long and involved. A mass of rules and regulations has accumulated and is today operative in the Indian Service. It is not an inert mass, as so often is assumed. There are within it directional drives, the aim of which has always been to solve or to cure the fundamental dislocation of a people overwhelmed by a superior force.

We are now at work developing a policy which we believe to be broad enough and sound enough to achieve, if continued, the purpose for which the Indian Service has always worked—the Indian's adjustment to his new world and a termination of his "problem." That policy is based on two ideas—organization, and a fuller use of land. Out of organization will come greater participation in the management of property and domestic affairs; and out of land use, which contemplates the purchase of land for those now landless and credit to carry on operations, will come better living conditions. Fundamental to the program is a recognition of the right of Indian culture to survive and enrich the daily life of the individual and the group. Not humanitarianism alone, but a belief that human beings are at their best when they are left at peace in those matters of conscience which come closest to them, prompts this attitude. . . .

LUTHER STANDING BEAR
from Land of the Spotted Eagle (1933)

The feathered and blanketed figure of the American Indian has come to symbolize the American continent. He is the man who through centuries has been moulded and sculpted by the same hand that shaped its mountains, forests, and plains, and marked the course of its rivers.

The American Indian is of the soil, whether it be the region of forests, plains, pueblos, or mesas. He fits into the landscape, for the hand that fashioned the continent also fashioned the man for his surroundings. He once grew as naturally as the wild sunflowers; he belongs just as the buffalo belonged.

With a physique that fitted, the man developed fitting skills—crafts which today are called American. And the body had a soul, also formed and moulded by the same master hand of harmony. Out of the Indian approach to existence there came a great freedom—an intense and absorbing love for nature; a respect for life; enriching faith in a Supreme Power; and principles of truth, honesty, generosity, equity, and brotherhood as a guide to mundane relations. . . .

The white man does not understand the Indian for the reason that he does not understand America. He is too far removed from its formative processes. The roots of the tree of his life have not yet grasped the rock and soil. The white man is still troubled with primitive fears; he still has in his consciousness the perils of this frontier continent, some of its fastnesses not yet having yielded to his questing footsteps and inquiring eyes. He shudders still with the memory of the loss of his forefathers upon its scorching deserts and forbidding mountaintops. The man from Europe is still a foreigner and an alien. And he still hates the man who questioned his path across the continent.

But in the Indian the spirit of the land is still vested; it will be until other men are able to divine and meet its rhythm. Men must be born and reborn to belong. Their bodies must be formed of the dust of their forefathers' bones.

The attempted transformation of the Indian by the white man and the chaos that has resulted are but the fruits of the white man's disobedience of a fundamental and spiritual law. The pressure that has been brought to bear upon the native people, since the cessation of armed conflict, in the attempt to force conformity of custom and habit has caused a reaction more destructive than war, and the injury has not only affected the Indian, but has extended to the white population as well. Tyranny, stupidity, and lack of vision have brought about the situation now alluded to as the "Indian Problem."

There is, I insist, no Indian problem as created by the Indian himself. Every problem that exists today in regard to the native population is due to the white man's cast of mind, which is unable, at least reluctant, to seek understanding and achieve adjustment in a new and a significant environment into which it has so recently come.

The white man excused his presence here by saying that he had been guided by the will of his God; and in so saying absolved himself of all responsibility for his appearance in a land occupied by other men.

Then, too, his law was a written law; his divine decalogue reposed in a book. And what better proof that his advent into this country and his subsequent acts were the result of divine will! He brought the Word! There ensued a blind worship of written history, of books, of the written word, that has denuded the spoken word of its power and sacredness. The written word became established as a criterion of the superior man—a symbol of emotional fineness. The man who could write his name on a piece of paper, whether or not he possessed the spiritual fineness to honor those words in speech, was by some miraculous formula a more highly developed and sensitized person than the one who had never had a pen in hand, but whose spoken word was inviolable and whose sense of honor and truth was paramount. With false reasoning was the quality of human character measured by man's ability to make with an implement a mark upon paper. But granting this mode of reasoning be correct and just, then where are to be placed the thousands of illiterate whites who are unable to read and write? Are they, too, 'savages'? Is not humanness a matter of heart and mind, and is it not evident in the form of relationship with men? Is not kindness more powerful than arrogance; and truth more powerful than the sword?

True, the white man brought great change. But the varied fruits of his civilization, though highly colored and inviting, are sickening and deadening. And if it be the part of civilization to maim, rob, and thwart, then what is progress? . . .

After subjugation, after dispossession, there was cast the last abuse upon the people who so entirely resented their wrongs and punishments, and that was the stamping and the labeling of them as savages. To make this label stick has been the task of the white race and the greatest salve that it has been able to apply to its sore and troubled conscience now hardened through the habitual practice of injustice.

But all the years of calling the Indian a savage has never made him one; all the denial of his virtues has never taken them from him; and the very resistance he has made to save the things inalienably his has been his saving strength—that which will stand him in need when justice does make its belated appearance and he undertakes rehabilitation.

All sorts of feeble excuses are heard for the continued subjection of the Indian. One of the most common is that he is not yet ready to accept the society of the white man—that he is not yet ready to mingle as a social entity.

This, I maintain, is beside the question. The matter is not one of making over the external Indian into the likeness of the white race—a process detrimental to both races. Who can say that the white man's way is better for the Indian? Where resides the human judgment with the competence to weigh and value Indian ideals and spiritual concepts; or substitute for them other values?

Then, has the white man's social order been so harmonious and ideal as to merit the respect of the Indian, and for that matter the thinking class of the white race? Is it wise to urge upon the Indian a foreign social form? Let none but the Indian answer!

Rather, let the white brother face about and cast his mental eye upon a new angle of vision. Let him look upon the Indian world as a human world; then let him see to it that human rights be accorded to the Indians. And this for the purpose of retaining for his own order of society a measure of humanity. . . .

The spiritual health and existence of the Indian was maintained by song, magic, ritual, dance, symbolism, oratory (or council), design, handicraft, and folk-story.

Manifestly, to check or thwart this expression is to bring about spiritual decline. And it is in this condition of decline that the Indian people are today. There is but a feeble effort among the Sioux to keep alive their traditional songs and dances, while among other tribes there is but a half-hearted attempt to offset the influence of the Government school and at the same time recover from the crushing and stifling régime of the Indian Bureau.

One has but to speak of Indian verse to receive uncomprehending and unbelieving glances. Yet the Indian loved verse and into this mode of expression went his deepest feelings. Only a few ardent and advanced students seem interested; nevertheless, they have given in book form enough Indian translations to set forth the character and quality of Indian verse.

Oratory receives a little better understanding on the part of the white public, owing to the fact that oratorical compilations include those of Indian orators.

Hard as it seemingly is for the white man's ear to sense the differences, Indian songs are as varied as the many emotions which inspire them, for no two of them are alike. For instance, the Song of Victory is spirited and the notes high and remindful of an unrestrained hunter or warrior riding exultantly over the prairies. On the other hand, the song of the *Cano unye* is solemn and full of urge, for it is meant to inspire the young men to deeds of valor. Then there are the songs of death and the spiritual songs which are connected with the ceremony of initiation. These are full of the spirit of praise and worship, and so strong are some of these invocations that the very air seems as if surcharged with the presence of the Big Holy.

The Indian loved to worship. From birth to death he revered his surroundings. He considered himself born in the luxurious lap of Mother Earth and no place was to him humble. There was nothing between him and the Big Holy. The contact was immediate and personal, and the blessings of Wakan Tanka flowed over the Indian like rain showered from the sky. Wakan Tanka was not aloof, apart, and ever seeking to quell evil forces. He did not punish the animals and the birds, and likewise He did not punish man. He was not a punishing God. For there was never a question as to the supremacy of an evil power over and above the power of Good. There was but one ruling power, and that was *Good.*

Of course, none but an adoring one could dance for days with his face to the sacred sun, and that time is all but done. We cannot have back the days of the buffalo and beaver; we cannot win back our clean blood-stream and superb health, and we can never again expect that beautiful *rapport* we once had with Nature. The springs and lakes have dried and the mountains are bare of forests. The plow has changed the face of the world. Wi-wila is dead! No more may we heal our sick and comfort our dying with a strength founded on faith, for even the animals now fear us, and fear supplants faith.

And the Indian wants to dance! It is his way of expressing devotion, of communing with unseen power, and in keeping his tribal identity. When the Lakota heart was filled with high emotion, he danced. When he felt the benediction of the warming rays of the sun, he danced. When his blood ran hot with success of the hunt or chase, he danced. When his heart was filled with pity for the orphan, the lonely father, or bereaved mother, he danced. All the joys and exaltations of life, all his gratefulness and thankfulness, all his acknowledgments of the mysterious power that guided life, and all his aspirations for a better life, culminated in one great dance—the Sun Dance.

When the Indian has forgotten the music of his forefathers, when the sound of the tomtom is no more, when noisy jazz has drowned the melody of the flute, he will be a dead Indian. When the memory of his heroes are no longer told in story, and he forsakes the beautiful white buckskin for factory shoddy, he will be dead. When from him has been taken all that is his, all that he has visioned in nature, all that has come to him from infinite sources, he then, truly, will be a dead Indian. His spirit will be gone, and though he walk crowded streets, he will, in truth, be—*dead!*

But all this must not perish; it must live, to the end that America shall be educated no longer to regard native production of whatever tribe—folk-story, basketry, pottery, dance, song, poetry—as curios, and native artists as curiosities. For who but the man indigenous to the soil could produce its song, story, and folk-tale; who but the man who loved the dust beneath his feet could shape it and put it into undying, ceramic form; who but he who loved the reeds that grew beside still waters, and the damp roots of shrub and tree, could save it from seasonal death, and with almost superhuman patience weave it into enduring objects of beauty—into timeless art!

Regarding the "civilization" that has been thrust upon me since the days of reservation, it has not added one whit to my sense of justice; to my reverence for the rights of life; to my love for truth, honesty, and generosity; nor to my faith in Wakan Tanka—God of the Lakotas. For after all the great religions have been preached and expounded, or have been revealed by brilliant scholars, or have been written in books and embellished in fine language with finer covers, man—all man—is still confronted with the Great Mystery.

So if today I had a young mind to direct, to start on the journey of life, and I was faced with the duty of choosing between the natural way of my forefathers and that of the white man's present way of civilization, I would, for its welfare, unhesitatingly set that child's feet in the path of my forefathers. I would raise him to be an Indian!

ERNIE PYLE

from Brave Men (1944)

Owing to a last-minute alteration in the arrangements, I didn't arrive on the beachhead until the morning after D-day, after our first wave of assault troops had hit the shore.

By the time we got there the beaches had been taken and the fighting had moved a couple of miles inland. All that remained on the beach was some sniping and artillery fire, and the occasional startling blast of a mine geysering brown sand into the air. That plus a gigantic and pitiful litter of wreckage along miles of shore line.

Submerged tanks and overturned boats and burned trucks and shell-shattered jeeps and sad little personal belongings were strewn all over those bitter sands. That plus the bodies of soldiers lying in rows covered with blankets, the toes of their shoes sticking up in a line as though on drill. And other bodies, uncollected, still sprawling grotesquely in the sand or half hidden by the high grass beyond the beach. That plus an intense, grim determination of work-weary men to get that chaotic beach organized and get all the vital supplies and the reinforcements moving more rapidly over it from the stacked-up ships standing in droves out to sea.

After it was over it seemed to me a pure miracle that we ever took the beach at all. For some of our units it was easy, but in the special sector where I landed our troops faced such odds that our getting ashore was like my whipping Joe Louis down to a pulp. The men who did it on that beach were men of the First and Twenty-ninth Divisions.

I want to tell you what the opening of the second front in that one sector entailed, so that you can know and appreciate and forever be humbly grateful to those both dead and alive who did it for you.

Ashore, facing us, were more enemy troops than we had in our assault waves. The advantages were all theirs, the disadvantages all ours. The Germans were dug into positions they had been working on for months, although they were not entirely complete. A 100-foot bluff a couple of hundred yards back from the beach had great concrete gun emplacements built right into the hilltop. These opened to the sides instead of to the front, thus making it hard for naval fire from the sea to reach them. They could shoot parallel with the shore and cover every foot of it for miles with artillery fire.

Then they had hidden machine-gun nests on the forward slopes, with crossfire taking in every inch of the beach. These nests were connected by networks of trenches, so that the German gunners could move about without exposing themselves.

Throughout the length of the beach, running zigzag a couple of hundred yards back from the shore line, was an immense V-shaped ditch fifteen feet deep. Nothing could cross it, not even men on foot, until fills had been made. And in other places at the far end of the beach, where the ground was flatter, they had great concrete walls. These were blasted by our naval gun-fire or by explosives set by hand after we got ashore.

Our only exits from the beach were several swales or valleys, each about a hundred yards wide. The Germans made the most of those funnellike traps, sowing them with buried mines. They also contained barbed-wire entanglements with mines attached, hidden ditches, and machine guns firing from the slopes.

All this was on the shore. But our men had to go through a maze nearly as deadly before they even got ashore. Underwater obstacles were terrific. Under the water the Germans had whole fields of evil devices to catch our boats. Several days after the landing we had cleared only channels through them and still could not approach the whole length of the beach with our ships. Even then some ship or boat would hit one of those mines and be knocked out of commission.

The Germans had masses of great six-pronged spiders—made of railroad iron and standing shoulder-high—just beneath the surface of the water, for our landing craft to run into. They had huge logs buried in the sand, pointing upward and outward, their tops just below the water. Attached to the logs were mines.

In addition to these obstacles they had floating mines offshore, land mines buried in the sand of the beach, and more mines in checkerboard rows in the tall grass beyond the sand. And the enemy had four men on shore for every three men we had approaching the shore.

And yet we got on. . . .

Our men simply could not get past the beach. They were pinned down right on the water's edge by an inhuman wall of fire from the bluff. Our first waves were on that beach for hours, instead of a few minutes, before they could begin working inland.

The foxholes were still there—dug at the very edge of the water, in the sand and the small jumbled rocks that formed parts of the beach.

Medical corpsmen attended the wounded as best they could. Men were killed as they stepped out of landing craft. An officer whom I knew got a bullet through the head just as the door of his landing craft was let down. Some men were drowned.

The first crack in the beach defenses was finally accomplished by terrific and wonderful naval gunfire, which knocked out the big emplacements. Epic stories have been told of destroyers that ran right up into shallow water and had it out point-blank with the big guns in those concrete emplacements ashore.

When the heavy fire stopped, our men were organized by their officers and pushed on inland, circling machine-gun nests land taking them from the rear.

As one officer said, the only way to take a beach is to face it and keep going. It is costly at first, but it's the only way. If the men are pinned down on the beach, dug in and out of action, they might as well not be there at all. They hold up the waves behind them, and nothing is being gained.

Our men were pinned down for a while, but finally they stood up and went through, and so we took that beach and accomplished our landing. . . .

I took a walk along the historic coast of Normandy in the country of France. It was a lovely day for strolling along the seashore. Men were sleeping on the sand, some of them sleeping forever. Men were floating in the water, but they didn't know they were in the water, for they were dead.

The water was full of squishy little jellyfish about the size of a man's hand. Millions of them. In the center of each of them was a green design exactly like a four-leafed clover. The good-luck emblem. Sure. Hell, yes.

I walked for a mile and a half along the water's edge of our many-miled invasion beach. I walked slowly, for the detail on that beach was infinite.

The wreckage was vast and startling. The awful waste and destruction of war, even aside from the loss of human life, has always been one of its outstanding features to those who are in it. Anything and everything is expendable. And we did expend on our beachhead in Normandy during those first few hours.

For a mile out from the beach there were scores of tanks and trucks and boats that were not visible, for they were at the bottom of the water—swamped by overloading, or hit by shells, or sunk by mines. Most of their crews were lost.

There were trucks tipped half over and swamped, partly sunken barges, and the angled-up corners of jeeps, and small landing craft half submerged. And at low tide you could still see those vicious six-pronged iron snares that helped snag and wreck them.

On the beach itself, high and dry, were all kinds of wrecked vehicles. There were tanks that had only just made the beach before being knocked out. There were jeeps that had burned to a dull gray. There were big derricks on caterpillar treads that didn't quite make it. There were half-tracks carrying office equipment that had been made into a shambles by a single shell hit, their interiors still holding the useless equipage of smashed typewriters, telephones, office files.

There were LCTs turned completely upside down, and lying on their backs, and how they got that way I don't know. There were boats stacked on top of each other, their sides caved in, their suspension doors knocked off.

In this shore-line museum of carnage there were abandoned rolls of barbed wire and smashed bulldozers and big stacks of thrown-away life belts and piles of shells still waiting to be moved. In the water floated empty life rafts and soldiers' packs and ration boxes, and mysterious oranges. On the beach lay snarled rolls of telephone wire and big rolls of steel matting and stacks of broken, rusting rifles.

On the beach lay, expended, sufficient men and mechanism for a small war. They were gone forever now. And yet we could afford it.

We could afford it because we were on, we had our toe hold, and behind us there were such enormous replacements for this wreckage on the beach that you could hardly conceive of the sum total. Men and equipment were flowing from England in such a gigantic stream that it made the waste on the beachhead seem like nothing at all, really nothing at all.

But there was another and more human litter. It extended in a thin little line, just like a high-water mark, for miles along the beach. This was the strewn personal gear, gear that would never be needed again by those who fought and died to give us our entrance into Europe.

There in a jumbled row for mile on mile were soldiers' packs. There were socks and shoe polish, sewing kits, diaries, Bibles, hand grenades. There were the latest letters from home, with the address on each one neatly razored out—one of the security precautions enforced before the boys embarked.

There were toothbrushes and razors, and snapshots of families back home staring up at you from the sand. There were pocketbooks, metal mirrors, extra trousers, and bloody, abandoned shoes. There were broken-handled shovels, and portable radios smashed almost beyond recognition, and mine detectors twisted and ruined.

There were torn pistol belts and canvas water buckets, first-aid kits, and jumbled heaps of life belts. I picked up a pocket Bible with a soldier's name in it, and put it in my jacket. I carried it half a mile or so and then put it back down on the, beach. I don't know why I picked it up, or why I put it down again.

Soldiers carry strange things ashore with them. In every invasion there is at least one soldier hitting the beach at H-hour with a banjo slung over his shoulder. The most ironic piece of equipment marking our beach—this beach first of despair, then of victory—was a tennis racket that some soldier had brought along. It lay lonesomely on the sand, clamped in its press, not a string broken.

Two of the most dominant items in the beach refuse were cigarettes and writing paper. Each soldier was issued a carton of cigarettes just before he started. That day those cartons by the thousand, water-soaked and spilled out, marked the line of our first savage blow. . . .

The strong, swirling tides of the Normandy coast line shifted the contours of the sandy beach as they moved in and out. They carried soldiers' bodies out to sea, and later they returned them. They covered the corpses of heroes with sand, and then in their whims they uncovered them.

As I plowed out over the wet sand, I walked around what seemed to be a couple of pieces of driftwood sticking out of the sand. But they weren't driftwood. They were a soldier's two feet. He was completely covered except for his feet; the toes of his GI shoes pointed toward the land he had come so far to see, and which he saw so briefly. . . .

Hisaye Yamamoto

"Et Ego in America Vixi" (1941)

My skin is sun-gold
My cheekbones are proud
My eyes slant darkly
And my hair is touched
With the dusky bloom of purple plums.
The soul of me is enrapt
To see the wisteria in blue-violet cluster
The heart of me breathless
At the fragile beauty of an ageless vase.
But my heart flows over
My throat chokes in reverent wonder
At the unfurled glory of a flag—
    Red as the sun
    White as the almond blossom
    Blue as the clear summer sky.

TED NAKASHIMA

"Concentration Camp, U.S. Style," from *The New Republic* (1943)

Unfortunately in this land of liberty, I was born of Japanese parents; born in Seattle of a mother and father who have been in this country since 1901. Fine parents, who brought up their children in the best American way of life. My mother served with the Volunteer Red Cross Service in the last war—my father, an editor, has spoken and written Americanism for forty years.

Our family is almost typical of the other unfortunates here at the camp. The oldest son, a licensed architect, was educated at the University of Washington, has a master's degree from the Massachusetts Institute of Technology, and is a scholarship graduate of the American School of Fine Arts in Fontainebleau, France. He is now in camp in Oregon with his wife and three-months-old child. He had just completed designing a much-needed defense housing project at Vancouver, Washington.

The second son is an M.D. He served his internship in a New York hospital, is married, and has two fine sons. The folks banked on him, because he was the smartest of us three boys. The army took him a month after he opened his office. He is now a lieutenant in the Medical Corps, somewhere in the South.

I am the third son, the dumbest of the lot, but still smart enough to hold down a job as an architectural draftsman. I have just finished building a new home and had lived in it three weeks. My desk was just cleared of work done for the Army Engineers, another stack of 391 defense houses was waiting (a rush job), when the order came to pack up and leave for this resettlement center called "Camp Harmony."

Mary, the only girl in the family, and her year-old son, "Butch," are with our parents—interned in the stables of the Livestock Exposition Buildings in Portland.

Now that you can picture our thoroughly American background, let me describe our new home.

The resettlement center is actually a penitentiary—armed guards in towers with spotlights and deadly tommy guns, fifteen feet of barbed-wire fences, everyone confined to quarters at nine, lights out at ten o'clock. The guards are ordered to shoot anyone who approaches within twenty feet of the fences. No one is allowed to take the two-block-long hike to the latrines after nine, under any circumstances.

The apartments, as the army calls them, are two-block-long stables, with windows on one side. Floors are . . . two-by-fours laid directly on the mud, which is everywhere. The stalls are about eighteen by twenty-one feet; some contain families of six or seven persons. Partitions are seven feet high, leaving a four-foot opening above. The rooms aren't too bad, almost fit to live in for a short while.

The food and sanitation problems are the worst. We have had absolutely no fresh meat, vegetables or butter since we came here. Mealtime queues extend for blocks; standing in a rainswept line, feet in the mud, waiting for the scant portions of canned wieners and boiled potatoes, hash for breakfast or canned wieners and beans for dinner. Milk only for the kids. Coffee or tea dosed with saltpeter and stale bread are the adults' staples. Dirty, unwiped dishes, greasy silver, a starchy diet, no butter, no milk, bawling kids, mud, wet mud that stinks when it dries, no vegetables—a sad thing for the people who raised them in such abundance. Memories of a crisp head of lettuce with our special olive oil, vinegar, garlic and cheese dressing.

Today one of the surface sewage-disposal pipes broke and the sewage flowed down the streets. Kids play in the water. Shower baths without hot water. Stinking mud and slops everywhere.

Can this be the same America we left a few weeks ago?

As I write, I can remember our little bathroom—light coral walls. My wife painting them, and the spilled paint in her hair. The open towel shelving and the pretty shower curtains which we put up the day before we left. How sanitary and clean we left it for the airlines pilot and his young wife who are now enjoying the fruits of our labor.

It all seems so futile, struggling, trying to live our old lives under this useless, regimented life. The senselessness of all the inactive manpower. Electricians, plumbers, draftsmen, mechanics, carpenters, painters, farmers—every trade-men who are able and willing to do all they can to lick the Axis. Thousands of men and women in these camps, energetic, quick, alert, eager for hard, constructive work, waiting for the army to do something for us, an army that won't give us butter.

I can't take it! I have 391 defense houses to be drawn. I left a fine American home which we built with our own hands. I left . . . good friends, friends who would swear by us. I don't have enough of that Japanese heritage *ga-man*—a code of silent suffering and ability to stand pain.

Oddly enough I still have a bit of faith in army promises of good treatment and Mrs. Roosevelt's pledge of a future worthy of good American citizens. I'm banking another $67 of income tax on the future. Sometimes I want to spend the money I have set aside for income tax on a bit of butter or ice cream or something good that I might have smuggled through the gates, but I can't do it when I think that every dollar I can put into "the fight to lick the Japs," the sooner I will be home again. I must forget my stomach.

What really hurts most is the constant reference to us evacués as "Japs." "Japs" are the guys we are fighting. We're on this side and we want to help.

Why won't America let us?

Franklin D. Roosevelt

State of the Union Message (January 11, 1944)

To the Congress of the United States:

This Nation in the past two years has become an active partner in the world's greatest war against human slavery.

We have joined with like-minded people in order to defend ourselves in a world that has been gravely threatened with gangster rule.

But I do not think that any of us Americans can be content with mere survival. Sacrifices that we and our allies are making impose upon us all a sacred obligation to see to it that out of this war we and our children will gain something better than mere survival.

We are united in determination that this war shall not be followed by another interim which leads to new disaster—that we shall not repeat the tragic errors of ostrich isolationism—that we shall not repeat the excesses of the wild twenties when this Nation went for a joyride on a roller coaster which ended in a tragic crash. . . .

It is our duty now to begin to lay the plans and determine the strategy for the winning of a lasting peace and the establishment of an American standard of living higher than ever before known. We cannot be content, no matter how high that general standard of living may be, if some fraction of our people—whether it be one-third or one-fifth or one-tenth—is ill-fed, ill-clothed, ill-housed, and insecure.

This Republic had its beginning, and grew to its present strength, under the protection of certain inalienable political rights—among them the right of free speech, free press, free worship, trial by jury, freedom from unreasonable searches and seizures. They were our rights to life and liberty.

As our Nation has grown in size and stature, however—as our industrial economy expanded—these political rights proved inadequate to assure us equality in the pursuit of happiness.

We have come to a clear realization of the fact that true individual freedom cannot exist without economic security and independence. "Necessitous men are not free men." People who are hungry and out of a job are the stuff of which dictatorships are made.

In our day these economic truths have been accepted as self-evident. We have accepted, so to speak, a second Bill of Rights under which a new basis of security and prosperity can be established for all—regardless of station, race, or creed.

Among these are:

The right to a useful and remunerative job in the industries or shops or farms or mines of the Nation;

The right to earn enough to provide adequate food and clothing and recreation;

The right of every farmer to raise and sell his products at a return which will give him and his family a decent living;

The right of every businessman, large and small, to trade in an atmosphere of freedom from unfair competition and domination by monopolies at home or abroad;

The right of every family to a decent home;

The right to adequate medical care and the opportunity to achieve and enjoy good health;

The right to adequate protection from the economic fears of old age, sickness, accident, and unemployment;

The right to a good education.

All of these rights spell security. And after this war is won, we must be prepared to move forward, in the implementation of these rights, to new goals of human happiness and well-being.

America's own rightful place in the world depends in large part upon how fully these and similar rights have been carried into practice for our citizens. For unless there is security here at home there cannot be lasting peace in the world.

One of the great American industrialists of our day—a man who has rendered yeoman service to his country in this crisis—recently emphasized the grave dangers of rightist reaction in this Nation. All clear-thinking businessmen share his concern. Indeed, if such reaction should develop—if history were to repeat itself and we were to return to the so-called normalcy of the 1920's—then it is certain that, even though we shall have conquered our enemies on the battlefields abroad, we shall have yielded to the spirit of fascism here at home.

I ask the Congress to explore the means for implementing this economic bill of rights—for it is definitely the responsibility of the Congress so to do. Many of these problems are already before committees of the Congress in the form of proposed legislation. I shall from time to time communicate with the Congress with respect to these and further proposals. In the event that no adequate program of progress is evolved, I am certain that the Nation will be conscious of the fact.

Our fighting men abroad—and their families at home—expect such a program and have the right to insist upon it. It is to their demands that this Government should pay heed rather than to the whining demands of selfish pressure groups who seek to feather their nests while young Americans are dying.

The foreign policy that we have been following—the policy that guided us at Moscow, Cairo, and Teheran—is based on the common-sense principle which was best expressed by Benjamin Franklin on July 4, 1776: "We must all hang together, or assuredly we shall all hang separately."

I have often said that there are no two fronts for America in this war. There is only one front. There is one line of unity which extends from the hearts of the people at home to the men of our attacking forces in our farthest outposts. When we speak of our total effort, we speak of the factory and the field and the mine as well as of the battleground—we speak of the soldier and the civilian, the citizen and his Government.

Each and every one of us has a solemn obligation under God to serve this Nation in its most critical hour—to keep this Nation great—to make this Nation greater in a better world.

Harry S. Truman

On the Decision to Drop the Atomic Bombs (1955)

The historic message of the first explosion of an atomic bomb was flashed to me in a message from Secretary of War Stimson on the morning of July 16. The most secret and the most daring enterprise of the war had succeeded. We were now in possession of a weapon that would not only revolutionize war but could alter the course of history and civilization. This news reached me at Potsdam the day after I had arrived for the conference of the Big Three.

Preparations were being rushed for the test atomic explosion at Alamogordo, New Mexico, at the time I had to leave for Europe, and on the voyage over I had been anxiously awaiting word on the results. I had been told of many predictions by the scientists, but no one was certain of the outcome of this full-scale atomic explosion. As I read the message from Stimson, I realized that the test not only met the most optimistic expectation of the scientists but that the United States had in its possession an explosive force of unparalleled power.

Stimson flew to Potsdam the next day to see me and brought with him the full details of the test. I received him at once and called in Secretary of State Byrnes, Admiral Leahy, General Marshall, General Arnold, and Admiral King to join us at my office at the Little White House. We reviewed our military strategy in the light of this revolutionary development. We were not ready to make use of this weapon against the Japanese, although we did not know as yet what effect the new weapon might have, physically or psychologically, when used against the enemy. For that reason the military advised that we go ahead with the existing military plans for the invasion of the Japanese home islands.

At Potsdam, as elsewhere, the secret of the atomic bomb was kept closely guarded. We did not extend the very small circle of Americans who knew about it. Churchill naturally knew about the atomic bomb project from its very beginning, because it had involved the pooling of British and American technical skill.

On July 24 I casually mentioned to Stalin that we had a new weapon of unusual destructive force. The Russian Premier showed no special interest. All he said was that he was glad to hear it and hoped we would make "good use of it against the Japanese."

A month before the test explosion of the atomic bomb the service Secretaries and the Joint Chiefs of Staff had laid their detailed plans for the defeat of Japan before me for approval. There had apparently been some differences of opinion as to the best route to be followed, but these had evidently been reconciled, for when General Marshall had presented his plan for a two-phase invasion of Japan, Admiral King and General Arnold had supported the proposal heartily.

The Army plan envisaged an amphibious landing in the fall of 1945 on the island of Kyushu, the southernmost of the Japanese home islands. This would be accomplished by our Sixth Army, under the command of General Walter Krueger. The first landing would then be followed approximately four months later by a second great invasion, which would be carried out by our Eighth and Tenth Armies, followed by the First Army transferred from Europe, all of which would go ashore in the Kanto plains area near Tokyo. In all, it had been estimated that it would require until the late fall of 1946 to bring Japan to her knees.

This was a formidable conception, and all of us realized fully that the fighting would be fierce and the losses heavy. But it was hoped that some of Japan's forces would continue to be preoccupied in China and others would be prevented from reinforcing the home islands if Russia were to enter the war.

There was, of course, always the possibility that the Japanese might choose to surrender sooner. Our air and fleet units had begun to inflict heavy damage on industrial and urban sites in Japan proper. Except in China, the armies of the Mikado had been pushed back everywhere in relentless successions of defeats.

Acting Secretary of State Grew had spoken to me in late May about issuing a proclamation that would urge the Japanese to surrender but would assure them that we would permit the Emperor to remain as head of the state. Grew backed this with arguments taken from his ten years' experience as our Ambassador in Japan, and I told him that I had already given thought to this matter myself and that it seemed to me a sound idea. Grew had a draft of a proclamation with him, and I instructed him to send it by the customary channels to the Joint Chiefs and the State-War-Navy Coordinating Committee in order that we might get the opinions of all concerned before I made my decision.

On June 18 Grew reported that the proposal had met with the approval of his Cabinet colleagues and of the Joint Chiefs. The military leaders also discussed the subject with me when they reported the same day. Grew, however, favored issuing the proclamation at once, to coincide with the closing of the campaign on Okinawa, while the service chiefs were of the opinion that we should wait until we were ready to follow a Japanese refusal with the actual assault of our invasion forces.

It was my decision then that the proclamation to Japan should be issued from the forthcoming conference at Potsdam. This, I believed, would clearly demonstrate to Japan and to the world that the Allies were united in their purpose. By that time, also, we might know more about two matters of significance for our future effort: the participation of the Soviet Union and the atomic bomb. We knew that the bomb would receive its first test in mid-July. If the test of the bomb was successful, I wanted to afford Japan a clear chance to end the fighting before we made use of this newly gained power. If the test should fail, then it would be even more important to us to bring about a surrender before we had to make a physical conquest of Japan. General Marshall told me that it might cost half a million American lives to force the enemy's surrender on his home grounds.

But the test was now successful. The entire development of the atomic bomb had been dictated by military considerations. The idea of the atomic bomb had been suggested to President Roosevelt by the famous and brilliant Dr. Albert Einstein, and its development turned out to be a vast undertaking. It was the achievement of the combined efforts of science, industry, labor, and the military, and it had no parallel in history. The men in charge and their staffs worked under extremely high pressure, and the whole enormous task required the services of more than one hundred thousand men and immense quantities of material. It required over two and a half years and necessitated the expenditure of two and a half billions of dollars.

Only a handful of the thousands of men who worked in these plants knew what they were producing. So strict was the secrecy imposed that even some of the highest-ranking officials in Washington had not the slightest idea of what was going on. I did not. Before 1939 it had been generally agreed among scientists that it was theoretically possible to release energy from the atom. In 1940 we had begun to pool with Great Britain all scientific knowledge useful to war, although Britain was at war at that time and we were not. Following this—in 1942—we learned that the Germans were at work on a method to harness atomic energy for use as a weapon of war. This, we understood, was to be added to the V-1 and V-2 rockets with which they hoped to conquer the world. They failed, of course, and for this we can thank Providence. But now a race was on to make the atomic bomb—a race that became "the battle of the laboratories."

It was under the general policy of pooling knowledge between our nation and Great Britain that research on the atomic bomb started in such feverish secrecy. American and British scientists joined in the race against the Germans. We in America had available a great number of distinguished scientists in many related fields of knowledge, and we also had another great advantage. We could provide the tremendous industrial and economic resources required for the project—a vastly expensive project—without injury to our war production program. Furthermore, our plants were far removed from the reach of enemy bombing. Britain, whose scientists had initiated the project and were contributing much of the original atomic data, was constantly exposed to enemy bombing and, when she started the atomic research, also faced the possibility of invasion.

For these reasons Roosevelt and Churchill agreed to pool the research and concentrate all of the work on the development of the project within the United States. Working together with the British, we thus made it possible to achieve a great scientific triumph in the field of atomic energy. Nevertheless, basic and historic as this event was, it had to be considered at the time as relatively incidental to the far-flung war we were fighting in the Pacific at terrible cost in American lives.

We could hope for a miracle, but the daily tragedy of a bitter war crowded in on us. We labored to construct a weapon of such overpowering force that the enemy could be forced to yield swiftly once we could resort to it. This was the primary aim of our secret and vast effort. But we also had to carry out the enormous effort of our basic and traditional military plans.

The task of creating the atomic bomb had been entrusted to a special unit of the Army Corps of Engineers, the so-called Manhattan District, headed by Major General Leslie R. Groves. The primary effort, however, had come from British and American scientists working in laboratories and offices scattered throughout the nation.

Dr. J. Robert Oppenheimer, the distinguished physicist from the University of California, had set up the key establishment in the whole process at Los Alamos, New Mexico. More than any other one man, Oppenheimer is to be credited with the achievement of the completed bomb.

My own knowledge of these developments had come about only after I became President, when Secretary Stimson had given me the full story. He had told me at that time that the project was nearing completion and that a bomb could be expected within another four months. It was at his suggestion, too, that I had then set up a committee of top men and had asked them to study with great care the implications the new weapon might have for us . . . .

This committee was assisted by a group of scientists, of whom those most prominently connected with the development of the atomic bomb were Dr. Oppenheimer, Dr. Arthur H. Compton, Dr. E. O. Lawrence, and the Italian-born Dr. Enrico Fermi. The conclusions reached by these men, both in the advisory committee of scientists and in the larger committee, were brought to me by Secretary Stimson on June 1.

It was their recommendation that the bomb be used against the enemy as soon as it could be done. They recommended further that it should be used without specific warning and against a target that would clearly show its devastating strength. I had realized, of course, that, an atomic bomb explosion would inflict damage and casualties beyond imagination. On the other hand, the scientific advisers of the committee reported, "We can propose no technical demonstration likely to bring an end to the war; we see no acceptable alternative to direct military use." It was their conclusion that no technical demonstration they might propose, such as over a deserted island, would be likely to bring the war to an end. It had to be used against an enemy target.

The final decision of where and when to use the atomic bomb was up to me. Let there be no mistake about it. I regarded the bomb as a military weapon and never had any doubt that it should be used. The top military advisers to the President recommended its use, and when I talked to Churchill he unhesitatingly told me that he favored the use of the atomic bomb if it might aid to end the war.

In deciding to use this bomb I wanted to make sure that it would be used as a weapon of war in the manner prescribed by the laws of war. That meant that I wanted it dropped on a military target. I had told Stimson that the bomb should be dropped as nearly as possibly upon a war production center of prime military importance.

Stimson's staff had prepared a list of cities in Japan that might serve as targets. Kyoto, though favored by General Arnold as a center of military activity, was eliminated when Secretary Stimson pointed out that it was a cultural and religious shrine of the Japanese.

Four cities were finally recommended as targets: Hiroshima, Kokura, Niigata, and Nagasaki. They were listed in that order as targets for the first attack. The order of selection was in accordance with the military importance of these cities, but allowance would be given for weather conditions at the time of the bombing. Before the selected targets were approved as proper for military purposes, I personally went over them in detail with Stimson, Marshall, and Arnold, and we discussed the matter of timing and the final choice of the first target.

General Spaatz, who commanded the Strategic Air Forces, which would deliver the bomb on the target, was given some latitude as, to when and on which of the four targets the bomb would be dropped. That was because of weather and other operational considerations.

With this order the wheels were set in motion for the first use of an atomic weapon against a military target. I had made the decision. I also instructed Stimson that the order would stand unless I notified him that the Japanese reply to our ultimatum was acceptable.

On August 9 the second atom bomb was dropped, this time on Nagasaki. We gave the Japanese three days in which to make up their minds to surrender, and the bombing would have been held off another two days had weather permitted. During those three days we indicated that we meant business. On August 7 the 20th Air Force sent out a bomber force of some one hundred and thirty B-29's, and on the eighth it reported four hundred and twenty B-29's in day and night attacks. The choice of targets for the second atom bomb was first Kokura, with Nagasaki second. The third city on the list, Niigata, had been ruled out as too distant. By the time Kokura was reached the weather had closed in, and after three runs over the spot without a glimpse of the target, with gas running short, a try was made for the second choice, Nagasaki. There, too, the weather had closed in, but an opening in the clouds gave the bombardier his chance, and Nagasaki was successfully bombed.

This second demonstration of the power of the atomic bomb apparently threw Tokyo into a panic, for the next morning brought the first indication that the Japanese Empire was ready to surrender.

7. America Since 1945

100 Cans, 1962 by Andy Warhol. Albright-Knox Gallery of Art. Courtesy of Art Resource, New York.

In 1999, the Campbell's Soup Company announced that it was changing its familiar can label. Customers lamented the passing of a design they had known for two generations. In a sense, the Campbell's label had been a tiny beacon of stability in an era of massive change: movements for equal rights for African Americans, women, Native Americans, Chicanos, gays and lesbians; social protest against the Vietnam War and the destruction of the natural environment. But that red-and-white label with its gold seal was something else, too: a canny advertising maneuver. Brand-name advertising had its roots in the late nineteenth century, but the post-World War II boom elevated consumer goods to new heights. A ubiquitous design, a catchy slogan ("Coke is it"), or a celebrity endorsement (Michael Jordan) could mean the difference between success or failure on the supermarket or department-store shelves. What would become of art—long identified with individuality, originality, and personal vision—in an age when products and images were reproduced mechanically for a mass public, and when many artists made their living in the advertising business? Andy Warhol's "Pop Art" offered one answer: make art about standardization itself. Warhol's most famous painting depicted a solitary can of Campbell's Tomato Soup. His images of Marilyn Monroe—the same face, in different colors and backgrounds—made a similar point about celebrity. In a movie-star culture, a famous face was a brand name too. In *100 Cans*, Warhol used beef noodle soup but the point was the same: the endless reproduction of the same products, packaged in the same labels, symbolized an era when even the houses in suburban subdivisions were pre-fabricated.

Chronology

1945:	World War II ends
1946:	Churchill's "Iron Curtain" speech, announcing the Cold War
1947:	House Un-American Activities Committee hearings in Hollywood Jackie Robinson becomes first African American in major-league baseball
1948:	President Truman issues order desegregating the armed forces
1950–1953:	Korean War
1950–1954:	McCarthy Senate hearings
1954:	French surrender at Dien Bien Phu; North and South Vietnam created U.S. explodes first hydrogen bomb *Brown v. Board of Education of Topeka* overturns *Plessy v. Ferguson*
1955:	Jonas Salk pioneers polio vaccine
1955–1956:	Montgomery bus boycott
1956:	Interstate Highway System authorized
1960:	John F. Kennedy elected President Sit-in movement begins at a lunch counter in Greensboro, N.C.
1962:	Betty Friedan, *The Feminine Mystique*
1963:	Martin Luther King, "I Have a Dream" speech President Kennedy assassinated
1964:	President Johnson signs Civil Rights Act Tonkin Gulf Resolution authorizes escalation of U.S. military presence in Vietnam
1965:	Malcolm X assassinated Voting Rights Act signed into law
1965–1968:	Race-based riots in major cities, from Los Angeles (Watts) to Newark
1966:	Black Panther Party formed Opposition to Vietnam War escalates

1968: Martin Luther King, Jr., assassinated
Richard Nixon elected President

1969: Woodstock music festival: high tide of counterculture
Stonewall Riot in Greenwich Village (New York) sparks gay liberation movement

1973: Paris Peace Agreement ends U.S. involvement in Vietnam War
Roe v. Wade legalizes abortion
Arab oil embargo sparks U.S. oil crisis

1974: President Ricahrd Nixon resigns in the wake of the Watergate scandals

1975: Communist government assumes control of South Viet Nam

1979: Oil shortagesagain plague American society
Inflation reaches double-digit levels
Three Mile Island nuclear reactor suffers major melt-down

1981: Ronald Reagan assumes presidency and institutes major tax cuts to stimulate a
stagnant economy

1981: AIDS first identified by medical researchers

1986: Iran-Contra Scandal is uncovered

1987: United States and Soviet union agree to major reduction in nuclear weapons

1989: Soviet Union dissolves
Berlin Wall dismantled
Tiananmen Square massacre in Beijing

1991: Persian Gulf War

1990s: Dow Jones Industrial Average more than triples
Internet, World Wide Web, and cell telephones
transform communications world wide

1995: Federal Building in Oklahoma City bombed by Anti-Government domestic terrorists

1996: Clinton administration passes welfare reform package

1999: President Clinton commits American troops to Kosovo

Introduction

The Second World War stands as the great watershed of 20th century American history, a time of fundamental and pervasive change, equal in impact to the Civil War of the nineteenth century. The intensive national defense mobilization of industry and agriculture not only produced the resources and equipment necessary for victory over formidable foes, but in the process unleashed a powerful set of political, social, and economic forces that substantially altered the structure of the nation.

The remarkable economic expansion created by the war effort rippled through American society for decades to come. Although many economists and government planners feared a return to a depressed economy at war's end, the obverse occurred. Fifteen years' pent-up demand for major consumer items kicked the postwar economy into high gear. For years Americans had deferred the purchase of homes, automobiles, appliances, and other large ticket items. The demand for consumer products, coupled with the maintenance of a high-profile defense posture as a result of the onset of the Cold War, produced an extended period of economic expansion unlike any previous era in the nation's history. (In fact, from 1943 forward, companies had been anticipating this demand, even encouraging its development, as the advertisement for Norge refrigerators in this chapter illustrates.)

The result was an economic revolution that greatly expanded the middle class, cut the number of Americans living in poverty by half, and produced an unprecedented high standard of living. By 1960 Americans were talking proudly about their "affluent society" and contemplating the meaning of the new "white-collar" class of service workers and managers. This new class of middle managers wielded increased influence within a society becoming ever more complex. Policy makers noted approvingly the onset of "automation," which reduced the need for human labor doing repetitive tasks and substituted sophisticated machines, many of them controlled by the first generation of "main frame" computers.

Some influential social critics, however, saw negative factors within the postwar "consumer culture." Social psychologists like Harvard University's David Riesman pondered the decline of traditional American opportunism and individualism, or as he put it, the relative decline of "inner-directed" self-starters and the growing preponderance of "outer-directed," upward-bound, mid-level corporate managers who instinctively sought the approval of their peers by engaging in what seemed to be a mind-numbing "conformity." *Fortune Magazine's* senior associate editor, William Whyte, stirred a national controversy in 1956 with his caustic description of the "Organization Man." This middle-manager type seemed always mindful of how others perceived his ability to work cooperatively within "group settings," a practice that Whyte believed stifled business ingenuity and was producing a new generation of cautious decision makers, fearful of being perceived as independent thinkers. In light of the incredible levels of imagination and creativity that have characterized the American economic expansion of the 1990s, these mid-century fears seem hopelessly misplaced, but perhaps such warnings awakened the American people to the danger.

The new consumer-culture lifestyle was most visible in the vast tracts of new suburban developments that extended outward from central cities in ever-expanding concentric rings. The lure of the suburbs is captured in a 1950 essay by Ralph G. Martin. His essay is greatly influenced by the enthusiasm for the new housing developments evidenced by veterans who returned home after the war, eager to "settle down" and get on with their married lives in a brand new home financed through the G.I. Bill. Contractor William Levitt showed the way to a new suburban environment with his enormous development on Long Island, fifteen miles from New York City. His crews routinely erected a new Cape Cod facsimile tract house in less than two weeks, ready for the happy new mortgage holder to move in. By 1950 Levitt had turned a large patch of potato fields into a package suburban community containing 17,400 new houses and 82,000 residents.

That the houses in Levittown looked almost identical gave eager buyers scant pause, but it heightened social commentators' fears about a new form of drab sameness. As a *New York Times* writer noted, "Levittown houses were social creations more than architectural ones—they turned the detached, single family house from a distant dream into a real possibility for thousands of middle-class American families." Levittown became the prototype for middle-class housing developments across the country. Builders generally evidenced little concern for aesthetics. "There's a green one and a pink one, and a blue one and a yellow one, and they're all made out of ticky-tacky, and they all look just the same," went the oft-repeated lament from folk singer Malvina Reynolds' popular song. Novelist John Keats denounced the new suburbs as a nightmare "conceived in error, nurtured by greed. . . . They destroy established cities and trade patterns, pose dangerous problems for the areas they invade, and actually drive made myriads of housewives shut up in them." Such criticisms, however, were ignored, and by 1965 more Americans lived in suburbs than in the core central cities.

Limited access, multi-lane freeway systems connected the increasingly sprawling cities, strongly encouraging the abandonment of mass transit systems in favor of the ubiquitous automobile. Congress knuckled under to the Highway Lobby of automobile manufacturers, oil companies, automobile clubs, and highway construction interests when it passed without a dissenting vote the Interstate Highway Act of 1956. This important bill authorized construction of 42,500 miles of multi-lane, limited access expressways that would connect all cities in the United States of over 100,000 residents. Ford Motor Company, like many automobile and oil companies, promoted the Interstate system, as indicated by its advertisement reproduced in this chapter. The interstate highway system, which became the most expensive government project in American history, ensured that the United States would become ever more auto- and petroleum-dependent, a situation that many would lament during the gasoline shortages of the 1970s, when prices soared and cars lined up for blocks waiting to get gasoline on their government-rationed days. America's postwar consumer culture increasingly revolved around the automobile, spawning a new "drive-in" culture that included fast food emporiums, long-distance commuting, and the sparkling new Meccas of the consumer-oriented society—the regional shopping malls located at major suburban intersections of the Interstate.

Supported by the implicit approval seen each day on commercial television programs like "Leave It to Beaver" and "Father Knows Best," a remarkable new suburban lifestyle spread across America. The sharp criticisms of this lifestyle and its attendant values, including those offered by the poet Allen Ginsburg (1926–1997), largely fell on deaf ears. Suburban parents, enjoying the material comforts of their split-level or ranch style homes, were not swayed by such criticisms—although writers of the "Beat" movement, like Ginsburg, would soon find a following among alienated intellectuals. Suburbanites were more likely to appreciate Gertrude Crampton's (1927–) children's book *Tootle*, which taught the next generations of organization men and women the virtues of conforming to established values and not questioning authority.

The ascendant economy might have sharply reduced poverty in America, but it never came close to eradicating it. In the early 1960s, social critic Michael Harrington (1928-1989) urged Americans to look beyond the affluent suburbs to "the other America," where poverty was largely hidden from view on Indian reservations, in the hills and backwoods of Appalachia, in small farm towns that had fallen upon economic hard times, and especially in deteriorating inner cities. Harrington's powerful narrative made many affluent readers uncomfortable and greatly influenced the thinking of liberal political leaders during the 1960s, many of whom (like President Lyndon Johnson) believed that poverty could be eliminated by a federal War on Poverty.

Other voices also challenged dominant social values during the 1960s. *The Feminine Mystique* (1963) by suburban housewife Betty Friedan (1921–), a pivotal work in the newly revitalized women's movement, reflected the long-suppressed feelings of millions of middle class women. During World War II, many industrial employers had hired women to work on the assembly lines and in other non-traditional settings in order to meet high production quotas. When the war ended, however, it was expected that they abandon employment and return to their traditional roles of homemaker and mother, thus opening up jobs for returning veterans. Although that happened to a great extent, millions of women did not easily forget the satisfactions derived from holding a job outside the home, feeling the rise in self-confidence and satisfaction as they cashed paychecks that they had earned. The greatly expanded realm of women's work during the war substantially influenced attitudes that helped produce the feminist movement in the 1960s; Friedan's best-selling book appealed as well to a new generation of young middle-class women who were not to be content merely with the challenges of being housewife and mother.

A second challenge to America's smug complacency emerged among college students, especially those enrolled in many of the nation's elite universities. Students for a Democratic Society, formed in 1962 with its idealistic manifesto, the Port Huron Statement, sought to rally America's college-age students behind social reform. This organization initially mobilized support for the civil-rights crusade, though after 1965 much of its energies were spent opposing the war in Vietnam. A third challenge came from artists associated with the "Pop Art" movement of the 1960s, notably Andy Warhol. Ed Ruscha's *Standard Station* made a similar statement with another symbol of modern culture; was Ruscha's empty gas station a celebration of car culture, or something else entirely?

One of major results of the social protests of the 1960s was a revitalized environmental movement. Rooted in the conservation movement of the earlier progressive era, it took on a much broader and comprehensive outlook during the 1960s. Rachel Carson's impassioned book *Silent Spring* (1962) alerted Americans to the serious damage that pesticides and other chemicals inflicted on bird life, wild animals, and the nation's food and water supply. Much to the shock of the American people, even their proud national bird, the bald eagle, had become threatened with extinction due to such deadly pesticides as DDT. The movement crested with a nationwide Earth Day in 1970. By 1973 the administration of Republican President Richard Nixon had guided to passage several important laws to protect the nation's environment from pollution of air, water, and soil. The centerpiece of this effort was the establishment of the Environmental Protection Agency in 1970, an umbrella agency to enforce such new laws as the Clean Air Act (1970), the Water Pollution Control Act (1972), the Pesticides Control Act (1972), and the Endangered Species Act (1973). One of the leaders in the new movement was scientist-activist Barry Commoner (1917–), whose 1971 book, *The Closing Circle: Nature, Man and Technology*, excerpted here, presented an environmental call to arms.

Just as World War II laid the groundwork for the rise of the consumer culture, so too did it stimulate the civil-rights movement. During the war, the United States government successfully mobilized its resources to overcome the racist doctrines of Nazism, but it did so with a segregated work force and military, a paradox that stands as one of the great ironies of American history. During the war civil-rights leaders (who had been challenging segregationist laws in the federal courts for decades, but with only marginal success), galvanized their forces, gained confidence from increased white liberal support, armed themselves with new strategies, and vowed to build a new era of racial equality. In 1941 the African American labor leader, A. Philip Randolph, exposed the evils of job discrimination by proposing a March on Washington. President Roosevelt shortly thereafter issued an executive order to investigate allegations of discrimination in defense industries, and in return Randolph called off the protest, but civil- rights leaders now recognized the potential of direct action. Other events of the war and immediate postwar years gave further impetus to the movement. Two major books about the insidious and pervasive racism in America, Carey McWilliams' *Brothers Under the Skin* (1943) and Gunnar Myrdal's epic *The American Dilemma* (1944), shattered liberal white complacency about American racism. Major wartime race riots in Harlem and Detroit, and the "zoot suit riots" against Hispanics in Los Angeles, further increased concern about traditional racial customs and laws. Thus events during the war set in motion the drama that would become the civil rights movement.

In the spring of 1947, when Branch Rickey, president of professional baseball's Brooklyn Dodgers, fielded the first African American player in the National League since the 1880s, an entire nation watched intently. The bravery of Jackie Robinson (1919–1972) in the face of sustained racial harassment inspired millions of blacks and whites alike, and helped prepare the American people for the impending dismantling of institutionalized segregation; although Organized Baseball was (and remains) a very conservative entity, the desegregation of the "national pastime" in 1947 was one of the first and most significant postwar steps to end institutionalized segregation in the United States. So was President Harry Truman's desegregation of the American armed forces a year later.

During the 1950s the civil rights movement gained momentum with a stunning unanimous decision by the Supreme Court on May 17, 1954. In *Brown v. Board of Education of Topeka, Kansas*, the Court declared unconstitutional one of the bulwarks of America's system of racial segregation by ordering the integration of the nation's public school systems. The following year the nation's attention was focused upon a dramatic confrontation between a privately owned bus system in Montgomery, Alabama, and that city's African American residents protesting segregated seating on the city's only bus system. Leading the boycott was a young Baptist minister, Martin Luther King, Jr. (1929–1968). After 18 embittered months, during which time King was arrested, harassed, and threatened with assassination, the white bus company capitulated. National television news coverage of the protest soon produced a veritable explosion of other demonstrations and protests across the South—and violent counterattacks by white segregationists. Television coverage of these sensational events greatly expanded public awareness and support for the movement, particularly in the North where millions were exposed to the viciousness of Southern segregation for the first time.

As the selections here reveal, the drive for civil rights was anything but monolithic. At center stage was King, who advocated a strategy of non-violence and peaceful resistance to laws and customs that denied African Americans equal opportunity. King's approach was aimed primarily at discriminatory Southern state and local laws, and his message was deeply rooted in the Southern Baptist culture in which he had been raised as the son of a minister. Although the movement he led had many targets, special emphasis was placed upon gaining the right-to-vote for millions of blacks who were unable to exercise the fundamental right of citizenship, and upon ending the discrimination long practiced by hotels, restaurants, stores, transportation systems, and other public accommodations. King's charisma and leadership style led to his frequent arrests by Southern police departments intent upon maintaining the racial *status quo*. It was during one of those incarcerations in Birmingham in 1963, that King wrote a letter to a group of white ministers who had urged him to be patient in his quest for racial justice. In this classic letter, King eloquently made his case for pressing forward in the fight against racism and segregation.

In sharp contrast, the leadership of Malcolm X (1925–1965), the charismatic Black Muslim, reflected the views of Northern, urban blacks who felt little in common with Dr. King's teachings. Stokeley Carmichael (1941–1998), who began his activist career as a college-age disciple of King, moved in new directions by the mid-1960s, after witnessing a seemingly endless number of bombings, beatings, and murders of civil rights activists—and after recognizing that America's racial problem lay not just in the legally segregated South, but in the North were there were far fewer discriminatory laws but widespread *de facto* segregation practices controlling access to housing, employment, education, and public accommodations. By 1965 Carmichael and the Student Non-Violent Coordinating Committee had openly broken with King, brusquely challenging the goal of racial integration, placing greater emphasis upon economic rather than political and civil rights, and arguing that violence in self-defense was justified and reasonable.

Much of this new thinking was subsumed under the powerful slogan of "Black Power," resulting in the frequent alienation of heretofore supportive white allies in the civil-rights movement. Riots and looting by black protestors—most of them in their teens and twenties—first erupted in August of 1965 in the south central Los Angeles black neighborhood of Watts. During the next three "long hot summers" series of major racially-inspired riots ripped through many American cities, including Newark Detroit, Cincinnati, Cleveland, and Washington, D. C. All told more than 200 violent episodes worthy of the federal government's definition of "civil disturbance" had occurred in cities across the United States by the end of 1968. In 1968 a special presidential commission appointed by President Lyndon Johnson to study the riots and make policy recommendations to the Congress and himself, concluded that the United States had become "two societies, one black, one white, separate and unequal." The Commission singled out "white racism" as the root problem of race relations in America: "What white Americans have never fully understood—but what the Negro can never forget—is that white society is deeply implicated in the ghetto. White institutions created it, white institutions maintain it, and white society condones it." More than three decades later, the debate continues with little expectation of easy or early resolution.

The civil-rights movement peaked in 1964-5 under the determined leadership of President Lyndon Johnson. He assumed the presidency on November 22, 1963, after the assassination of President John F. Kennedy, and pledged himself to honor Kennedy's memory by convincing Congress to pass legislation that Kennedy had endorsed. The Civil Rights Act of 1964 prohibited segregation in public accommodations (hotels, restaurants, theaters, and other commercial places) as well as barring discrimination in employment and authorizing the Department of Justice to file suits to achieve school integration. In 1965 another major victory was achieved with legislation providing federal protection for voting rights for minorities. Within a few years the structure of Southern politics had been fundamentally altered. Although these measures were important, they did not satisfy the rapidly escalating expectations of African Americans, especially in addressing underlying economic conditions.

Johnson's commitment to civil rights was merely one part of his larger vision of building a "Great Society." A protege of Franklin Roosevelt as a young congressman during the 1930s, Johnson wanted not only to extend, but greatly expand his mentor's liberal dream. His programs included a "War on Poverty" that he launched with great fanfare in 1965, massive increases in federal funding for public schools and higher education, programs to stimulate the development of the arts and humanities, and the rebuilding of decaying inner cities with such innovative programs as "model cities" where the residents affected would have a major say in how assistance funds were to be spent. In retrospect, the outpouring of Great Society legislation during the mid-sixties constituted the culmination of the progressive-liberal agenda of the twentieth century. There would be scant further liberal reforms of this type in the last three decades of the 20th century as neo-conservative policies gained credence and popular public support.

The presidency of Ronald Reagan during the 1980s constituted a major psychological shift away from big government reform programs, and in the mid-1990s President Bill Clinton led a reform movement within the Democratic Party that downplayed federal programs and emphasized cuts in federal taxes and the shift of decision-making from Washington, D. C., to state houses. Firing a dramatic first shot of his re-election campaign in his January 1996 State of the Union Message, Clinton declared that "the era of big government is over." Much to the dismay of his party's once dominant liberal wing, Clinton worked with conservatives and moderates of both parties to gain passage of the Work Opportunity Reconciliation Act of 1996, that he intended would "end welfare as we know it." And indeed it did, tightening up on child-support grants to single parents, limiting any person to five years of government assistance during a lifetime, and authorizing state welfare agencies to cut off support to any recipient of public assistance who did not obtain a job after two years of uninterrupted public support.

Although rising income levels and growing public dissatisfaction with the much-publicized failures and waste of liberal reform programs would have prevented the achievement of Johnson's grandiose plans for a Great Society, his own administration's handling of the twenty-year-old anti-communist foreign policy led to a dramatic loss of support for liberal causes even before he left office in 1969. When Johnson took office, the government of South Vietnam had for years been under siege by Viet Cong guerrilla forces and the communist government of North Vietnam. Johnson, it is important to remember, had matured as a Washington political leader during the formative years of the Cold War. He had supported without question the foreign policies established by President Harry S. Truman to "contain" communism, particularly the Soviet Union, and like most political leaders of his generation he was a dedicated "Cold Warrior." He subscribed to the liberal credo that envisioned America as protecting "freedom" (*i. e.* democratic, capitalistic governments) around the globe.

During the early 1950s Johnson had watched with frustration and anger as Republican Joseph McCarthy severely damaged the Democrats with his reckless (and unproven) charges of communist influence and infiltration of the highest levels of the government. True to his anti-communist roots and determined not to permit a recurrence of McCarthyism, Johnson informed top advisors within twenty-four hours of becoming president that he would not allow South Vietnam to be taken by communist forces. In that moment, he determined his administration's fate.

Following his landslide victory over conservative Republican Barry Goldwater in the 1964 presidential election, in which he branded his opponent as a dangerous warmonger, Johnson ordered a large military intervention into the civil war in South Vietnam. In February 1965 operation "Rolling Thunder" was instituted, a massive bombing operation that saw more explosive power dropped upon non-urban North Vietnam military targets than was dropped upon Germany during the Second World War. He simultaneously committed 50,000 American ground troops to fight in Vietnam, and four months later secretly committed an additional 50,000. Johnson had committed the United States to a full-scale military commitment, risking in the process the prestige of his presidency on a futile effort to somehow salvage a corrupt, unpopular, and tottering government of South Vietnam.

Contrary to the assurances of military and intelligence leaders that a speedy victory would be easily won , Johnson soon learned that there was no easy way out. The United States, in the name of containing communism, had gotten deeply involved in a civil war whose murky roots stretched back to the mid-1940s. Each American escalation was met with an even more determined response by the enemy. Saturation bombings, widespread use of destructive defoliants like "Agent Orange," annual expenditures that rose to $20 billion, the eventual deployment of more than 700,000 troops by 1968, and even the destruction of entire villages suspected of harboring Viet Cong guerrillas, all proved futile. American troops found themselves ill prepared for guerrilla warfare, and military morale rapidly deteriorated as months and then years went by without any real progress. Public support also waned. Public-opinion polls decidedly favored American intervention at the time of the initial escalation in 1965; in August of 1964 only two members of congress had voted against the pivotal Gulf of Tonkin resolution authorizing the president to take whatever actions deemed necessary to repel the North Vietnamese forces. But as the war continued with no end in sight, as the enemy gave no sign of bending even before carpet bombing of their homeland, and as American casualties mounted, public support began to ebb. By 1968 the nation was convulsed in angry debate. Large antiwar demonstrations occurred on college campuses, and in New York City public demonstrations by antiwar "doves" were met with angry, and occasionally physical, responses from "hawks" who supported Johnson's policy.

The turning point in the war was the unexpected "Tet" offensive by the joint forces of the Viet Cong and North Vietnamese army in January of 1968 that at one point saw the enemy penetrate the American embassy grounds in Saigon. At first the Tet offensive caught the Americans and Army of South Vietnam by complete surprise and inflicted major damage to American military bases. Although the Tet offensive eventually resulted in a decisive American military victory, it proved disastrous for Johnson at home because it showed, contrary to many official assurances, that there was no "light at the end of the tunnel." As the television images showed a resurgent enemy force, public opinion turned sharply against the war. Johnson was forced to forego a campaign for re-election, and the Democratic Party became so bitterly divided over Johnson's Vietnam policy that Republican Richard M. Nixon won the presidential election. After trying various military and diplomatic initiatives, all unsuccessful, Nixon eventually decided to turn the war over to the South Vietnamese and began a systematic withdrawal of American troops. By 1973 most Americans had left, and two years later Ho Chi Minh's North Vietnamese forces unified the country under communist rule.

The war did major damage to the fabric of American society, dividing families and friends, setting off a period of economic inflation and unemployment that baffled economists, and shattering Lyndon Johnson's dream of building a Great Society. Among those who suffered were the veterans who came home to an ungrateful, even hostile reception. The vast majority of the 1,600,000 Americans who served in Vietnam came from the nation's poorest and least influential families. Even the decision to memorialize the more than 58,000 Americans who died on that distant battlefield produced a major controversy. The legacy of the war continues to cast a long shadow over American society, as the moving epilogue of Marilyn Young's (1937–) *The Vietnam Wars, 1945–1990* makes clear.

The Vietnam War, of course, was a logical extension of America's Cold War policy of containment. In 1947 President Harry Truman had told Congress that the United States had to support "free peoples who are resisting attempted subjugation by armed minorities or outside pressures," and in his eloquent inaugural address in 1961 John F. Kennedy had emphasized the willingness of the American people to "pay any price, bear any burden, meet any hardship, support any friend, oppose any foe to assure the survival and the success of liberty." After nearly half a century, the Cold War ended abruptly in the late 1980s with the collapse of Communist governments in Eastern Europe, and finally in 1991 with the dissolution of the Soviet Union itself. Overnight, the world was a much different place. As new instabilities arose around the globe during the 1990s, the world became perhaps an even more dangerous place than during the long confrontation between the Soviet Union and the United States. The aftermath of the Cold War has witnessed the emergence of global markets, major advances in communications and satellite surveillance, and the firing of ethnic, religious, and nationalistic passions, producing an array of new problems and potentials unimaginable even at the time of the collapse of the Soviet Union.

What the future holds for the 21st century—given the accelerating rate of scientific, economic, and political change—is anyone's guess. However, there is little question that the debates and struggles that lie ahead will be well grounded in the constantly evolving traditions that have become integral to the unique society that is America.

RALPH G. MARTIN

"Life in the New Suburbia," from
The New York Times Magazine (1950)

You can still remember walking up to your new house, in this new Long Island development, that day it was legally yours. You didn't see the unlandscaped mud on your lawn, you saw thick green grass and flowers, all kinds of flowers. And when you opened the door—what a feeling it can be to put a key in the door and open it!—you didn't see the emptiness, you saw a cozy furniture arrangement around the fireplace. Looking out of the huge living room window, you didn't see the tractors busy leveling the land, you saw a future park, all dressed up in thick trees and birds, so many, many birds. And as you walked around the room, just touching things, it was so easy to imagine noises in the silence—your wife busy in the kitchen making another fancy dessert, the crying of a brand-new baby. . . .

The idyll of a first home in the suburbs—it is that—but this is not the familiar suburb which comprises a little of everything from a General Grant mansard to a three-room "ranch house." This is one of those new developments with a pattern all its own. Our development sprang up—and there are dozens like it on Long Island—mostly to accommodate veterans who wanted a place away from the in-laws, far from exorbitant rents in dank Manhattan basements. The notable characteristic of these developments is that they emerge out of nothingness and in a few months a community is formed. The result is a new way of living—and a new kind of person, what might be called the Development Type.

Of course, it's not *the* country. It's not Bucks County, Pa., or Old Lyme, Conn., with the tinkling brook running past the doorstep. More likely to be seen here is a neighbor, quite friendly, sunning his newborn in front of his own house, one or two hundred feet away. And near by, more houses, hundreds of them, and more kids. Nor is it like one of Long Island's old semi-country townships, some of which have been thriving outside New York City since before the Revolution. Those neighboring communities have both old folks and new folks, old houses and new houses, grandmas, tall trees, overstuffed attics and Established Ways.

It does, however, have some of the charm of any country village. When you walk around at night, this place is a cork blanket. No buses, no streetcars, no jangling taxis, no baby-sitter parties blaring out of the windows.

"I'm lucky. I work out here. I don't go to the city unless I have to," said Lester Grolnick, an "old-timer" who has lived here since the community was born, several years ago. "I've developed the hick attitude, I guess. All of a sudden now, I get overwhelmed by the hustle and bustle. I'm so used to the quiet that when I go to visit my folks in Brooklyn, I can't sleep because of the street noise. Honest. And I was born in Brooklyn, lived there all my life. Can you beat it?"

Our particular development sits on a flat stretch of land, about thirty miles from New York and halfway from either the north or south shores of Long Island. When we talk of the Island, we usually mean only Nassau and Suffolk Counties, both outside the city limits, stretching out about 100 miles long, twenty miles wide. Since 1940, Nassau alone has had almost a 50 percent population increase. In the past two years, there have been a dozen brand new communities created out of farmland, with whole new sections added to twenty-five other communities—actually, 60,000 new homes since 1947.

My community isn't just a bedroom of New York City, even though it's only fifty minutes away. Every day it becomes more of a separate place. It has a new bank, a post-office, a telephone building. Two more schools are getting ready to open, several more churches, always more clubs. The local paper has announced a concert series. A veterans organization picked its own local beauty queen. Stassen and Lehman both thought it important enough to make a special speech here the same night before election. They're even bringing a grand opera company here.

Who wants Coney Island, when it's always ten degrees cooler here, when all you have to do is walk a few blocks to your nearest swimming pool? (There will be one huge pool for every 1,000 homes.) Who has to go to Broadway for first-run movies, if you can find them in near-by towns? If you're a joiner, you have more than two dozen clubs to choose from here, including the recipe-traders at the Home Bureau, the singers at the Major and Minors, the hard-fighting Home Owners Association, and even a Dartmouth Club.

Or maybe you like to dance? It doesn't cost a nickel at the Village Green restaurant every Saturday night. Somebody once explained the big turnouts by saying, "I guess we're all at the same dance age."

They're alike in so many other ways. Besides being in the same age group (25–35), almost every one of the 9,000 homes has at least one child (and only 100 of the 8,000 children are old enough for high school). Nobody keeps up with the Joneses because they almost all have the same income (about $4,000 average). Nobody talks about the war much, because they've all been in it. And most of the men have the same Long Island Rail Road commuting problem—which many have solved by car pools. All this helps cement neighbors into friends.

The Howard Handlers have lived here only since September, but when Howard talks about his neighbors—welding boss John Phillips, city fireman Tom Carney and air-conditioning expert Dick Hollis—you'd think he was talking about his closest kin.

"Phillips' wife had a birthday last night and what a time we all had," Howard said. "Hollis brought over his kid and put him in the same bed with the Phillips' two kids and then he took out his guitar and played and played and we just sang all night long.

"I tell ya, the four of us really have it worked out. When the girls go to a garden club meeting, we boys get together and baby-sit and play pinochle. Or one night we'll all go bowling down at the Village Green. And now we're all taking some of these adult education courses down at the school one night a week. Dick and I are taking a course in 'How to Finish Your Attic' and John's learning photography."

He told how they shared everything they learned: the best stuff to clean tile floors, the cheapest insurance for their thermopane windows, that there was a small ventilator opening that should be screened to keep out field mice. When Howard brought back fresh flowers from his mother, all four homes got some. Each woman already had spliced a piece of her potted plant to give to the others. They even compared electric bills to see if any one bill was out of line.

"See that door windbreaker," said Howard proudly. "It got loose, so Hollis made angle irons for all four of us. And when I wanted to buy a garbage can, he wouldn't let me. He made me that one out of a fifty-pound grease drum. Now isn't that a beautiful garbage can?"

People who lived for years in apartment houses without ever really knowing their neighbors come here and start living Dale Carnegie. For newcomers it sometimes becomes overwhelming. You come home from work to find your neighbor (whom you hadn't yet met) had put your milk in her refrigerator so the sun wouldn't spoil it. If you don't have a car, neighbors with cars are always asking your wife, "I'm going shopping. Do you want to come along?"

Before you can ask somebody for the neighbor's lawnmower, he usually volunteers it. One woman left her faucet running and came back to a flooded kitchen, but six neighbors were already mopping it up. If your car gets stuck here, don't worry, the next car that comes along will stop to help. When polio victim Norman Modell came out of the hospital, and needed some strong arms to support him while he tried to walk again, he had all the volunteers he needed.

Perhaps all this explains why Mrs. Edwin Niles said, "For the first time since I left Fordyce, Ark., I really feel at home."

There's a small-town friendliness at the Village Greens (there are three so far, more coming up fast). Modernly styled, the Green is the shopping center for each area—and something more. People are always stopping to talk to each other there. Nobody rushes.

This is a paradise for children. "There are so many babies here that you would think everybody would be blase about them," said Mrs. Alice Miller. "Still, when a new one is coming, all the neighbors make a fuss over you. I had to go to the hospital soon after I moved in, and neighbors I hadn't even met yet just came in and took over. They pack your bags, drive you to the hospital if your husband's working, take care of your other baby if you have one. And they wouldn't let me buy anything for it either. The carriage isn't mine and neither is the crib, and my other neighbor said we could have those baby scales as long as we need them. Somebody here always has a baby a year older."

The slightly older ones never had it so good. If they leave their toys on the walk sometimes, or if they overrun into somebody's back yard—there's a deep, patient understanding by the neighbors, because they probably also have a child. Children have space to run in, grass to roll in, wading pools, playgrounds. Mothers don't worry too much about cars, because there's almost no transient traffic. People who drive to finance a summer playground for the children.

While the PTA concentrates on an individual school, the AAUW canvasses the broader picture. They get acquainted with top school board officials, learn about local tax structure and county government, invite an expert to tell them how to start a town library.

This "our town" spirit takes on a sharper focus when people talk about their homes. The houses take on the personalities of their owners. Different kinds of garages, a concrete patio, a huge wagon wheel, a rustic fence, an unusual signpost, special flower arrangements, and every home has a different paint job. Working around the house isn't a chore, it's mixed up with a deep feeling of pride.

"Now he knows how to hammer a nail," said Betty Gurwitz, pointing to her husband. "And he knows all about the nitrogen content of the soil. You should have seen our tomatoes. We didn't buy a single tomato, and we eat a lot of them."

Her husband rubbed his chin reflectively. "We had corn, too," he added, "but it wasn't successful this year. Didn't have enough space. Next year I'll try several varieties so I can have cross-pollination. Which reminds me, I need more mulch." He laughed at himself. "Mulch—that's a hot one. I never even heard the word before I came here."

But not everybody's happy here. Slightly more than half the homes are rented and there's a small population turnover. Some people leave because they think it's too rural; they want more excitement, more Broadway. Some families grow so large that they need a bigger place than these 4½-room homes (although some homes have attics converted into two more, a room over the garage, a utility room in back of it).

One woman moved because "a house isn't a house if it doesn't have a basement," even though she admitted the radiant heating was wonderful. Another woman was moving back to New York "because I like to live where I can walk with my baby carriage and see stores instead of houses."

For others it's a financial question. Monthly payment for home owners is $58, which covers equity, interest, taxes, everything but heat and electricity. But there's always the monthly commutation ticket ($17) plus bus and subway fares, unless you've connected with a car pool. Another frequently brought up criticism is that this town isn't typical of the real world. You can tell your child about old people, but you can't show him any. The same is almost true of teen-agers.

Some people move back to the city because they find these small communities too friendly. They're introverts who like invisible moats around their homes, or else they don't know how to cope with overexuberant neighbors who insist on coming in without knocking. Usually, though, people here who want moats, have them—without moving.

But people have other reasons for moving. You have to live in a house for a while before you find the kinks in it. Maybe your wife will develop a phobia about always walking on hard tile? Or maybe you get sensitive about having an overlarge living room window when your view is nothing but the overlarge living room window of your neighbor? Or maybe it's the size of the rooms, or the layout, or perhaps your wife never did like the fireplaces?

Norge Company Advertisement. Reprinted from *Ladies Home Companion,* Copyright © 1943. Reprinted by permission of Norge Company.

After a while you may find all kinds of things you'd like to change, especially if your repair bills are high. The dream house is always a continuous dream. Houses aren't like cars—you can't trade them in every year. For most people here, this is it. For others, this first home is only the first step, a sort of education in what a house is. If their income grows as big as their expected family, then they plan to build what they really want.

The case for this sort of new semi-rural community isn't clearcut. It depends on who you are. But if you want a place where you can walk safely down the street with a pet live duck; if you want a place where you can start a small symphony orchestra simply by writing a letter to the editor, as automobile salesman Lawrence Eliscu did; if you like to get up in the morning and go right out into the fresh air—not smoke or dirt, but real fresh air; if you prefer folk dances to the juke box, buttercups to Broadway; if all your life you've unconsciously been running away from the pushing, blaring hurry of the city—then this is for you.

How many cloverleafs will grow tomorrow?

THE RED MEN went single-file among the great old trees in shallow trench-like trails; the trails broadened when the white men came because they liked to walk two abreast, talking.

Those were the simple beginnings of the American Road, in colonial times. The roads spread slowly but surely, for roads unite those people who live apart—and yet for three centuries the roads were wretched things by our standards today.

The first "Good Roads Movement" came with the bicycle; indignant wheelmen organized themselves in the 1890's to try to get a few stretches of smooth going. But little was done until Henry Ford began trundling his way around sleepy Detroit in his odd-looking little horseless carriage.

Then, under the impact of the automobile, began the real American Road. The unimportant little Bureau of Public Roads suddenly became enormously important. States set up highway commissions; men debated over what kind of oil to spread on the gravel of new roads. In 1904 the whole United States spent less than $80,000,000 on road improvement. In 1950 the U. S. spent more than fifty times as much on its streets and highways—but still only half enough.

In the last 50 years, the American Road has grown into a network of 3,322,000 miles long, a network on which the Ford Motor Company alone has put over 35,000,000 cars, a substantial part of the traffic which is the very life-stream of the nation.

Much remains to be done. The job of building America is endless. Too many streets in which wagons could scrape comfortably past each other are now inadequate for the huge trucks moving vital food and materials. Many a road or street has its sharp right angles instead of gentle curves —when it was built, the curves would have cut across some farmer's field. The angles are still there, even though the farmer's field has long since been grown over with skyscrapers or blocks of city homes.

We need more of those superb new turnpikes, expressways and super-highways with their overpasses and underpasses, and glittering huge silver-steel bridges that soar across the rivers of the land.

They must keep growing day by day and mile by mile toward a future of highway safety and of free-moving traffic. The day is coming when motorists will travel from coast to coast in a whole new dimension of safety and comfort, for every community is determined to make the American Road better in every way that modern highway engineering can devise.

Thus triumphing over time, space and geography, this generation has somehow stubbornly produced its way out of a thousand different crises; it goes hopefully pushing on down the American Road toward the dream of a brighter and better future for all mankind. The Ford Motor Company affirms its faith in this generation, and its belief in the American Road as a path toward progress and peace.

Ford Motor Company

FORD · LINCOLN · MERCURY CARS · FORD TRUCKS AND TRACTORS

◄ CITY CANYONS are as wide as two wagons; modern traffic needs space for speed.

THE CLOVERLEAF, the engineer's masterpiece, is a symbol of modern civilization; it shows that a community is determined to save lives—as well as time and trouble. ►

Ford Motor Company Advertisement. Reprinted from *Life*, Copyright © June 2, 1952.
Reprinted by permission of Ford Motor Company.

Ford Motor Company advertisement, 1952.

"Tootle" (1945)

Far, far to the west of everywhere is the village of Lower Trainswitch. All the baby locomotives go there to learn to be big locomotives. The young locomotives steam up and down the tracks, trying to call out the long, sad *ToooOoooot* of the big locomotives. But the best they can do is a gay little *Tootle*.

Lower Trainswitch has a fine school for engines. There are lessons in Whistle Blowing, Stopping for a Red Flag Waving, Puffing Loudly When Starting, Coming Around Curves Safely, Screeching When Stopping, and Clicking and Clacking Over the Rails.

Of all the things that are taught in the Lower Trainswitch School for Locomotives, the most important is, of course, Staying on the Rails No Matter What.

The head of the school is an old engineer named Bill. Bill always tells the new locomotives that he will not be angry if they sometimes spill the soup pulling the diner, or if they turn the milk to butter now and then. But they will never, never be good trains unless they get 100 A+ in Staying on the Rails No Matter What. All the baby engines work very hard to get 100 A+ in Staying on the Rails. After a few weeks not one of the engines in the Lower Trainswitch School for Trains would even think of getting off the rails, no matter—well, no matter what.

One day a new locomotive named Tootle came to school.

"Here is the finest baby I've seen since old 600," thought Bill. He patted the gleaming young locomotive and said, "How would you like to grow up to be the Flyer between New York and Chicago?"

"If a Flyer goes very fast, I should like to be one," Tootle answered. "I love to go fast. Watch me."

He raced all around the roundhouse.

"Good! Good!" said Bill. "You must study Whistle Blowing, Puffing Loudly When Starting, Stopping for a Red Flag Waving, and Pulling the Diner without Spilling the Soup.

"But most of all you must study Staying on the Rails No Matter What. Remember, you can't be a Flyer unless you get 100 A+ in Staying on the Rails."

Tootle promised that he would remember and that he would work very hard.

He did, too.

He even worked hard at Stopping for a Red Flag Waving. Tootle did not like those lessons at all. There is nothing a locomotive hates more than stopping.

But Bill said that no locomotive ever, ever kept going when he saw a red flag waving.

One day, while Tootle was practicing for his lesson in Staying on the Rails No Matter What, a dreadful thing happened.

He looked across the meadow he was running through and saw a fine, strong black horse.

"Race you to the river," shouted the black horse, and kicked up his heels.

Away went the horse. His black tail streamed out behind him, and his mane tossed in the wind. Oh, how he could run!

"Here I go," said Tootle to himself.

"If I am going to be a Flyer, I can't let a horse beat me," he puffed. "Everyone at school will laugh at me."

His wheels turned so fast that they were silver streaks. The cars lurched and bumped together. And just as Tootle was sure he could win, the tracks made a great curve.

"Oh, Whistle!" cried Tootle. "That horse will beat me now. He'll run straight while I take the Great Curve."

Then the Dreadful Thing happened. After all that Bill had said about Staying on the Rails No Matter What, Tootle jumped off the tracks and raced alongside the black horse!

The race ended in a tie. Both Tootle and the black horse were happy. They stood on the bank of the river and talked.

"It's nice here in the meadow." Tootle said.

When Tootle got back to school, he said nothing about leaving the rails. But he thought about it that night in the roundhouse.

"Tomorrow I will work hard," decided Tootle. "I will not even think of leaving the rails, no matter what."

And he did work hard. He practiced tootling so much that the Mayor Himself ran up the hill, his green coattails flapping, and said that everyone in the village had a headache and would he please stop TOOTLING.

So Tootle was sent to practice Staying on the Rails No Matter What.

As he came to the Great Curve, Tootle looked across the meadow. It was full of buttercups.

"It's like a big yellow carpet. How I should like to play in them and hold one under my searchlight to see if I like butter!" thought Tootle. "But no, I am going to be a Flyer and I must practice Staying on the Rails No Matter What!"

Tootle clicked and clacked around the Great Curve. His wheels began to say over and over again, "Do you like butter? Do you?"

"I don't know," said Tootle crossly. "But I'm going to find out."

He stopped much faster than any good Flyer ever does, unless he is stopping for a Red Flag Waving. He hopped off the tracks and bumped along the meadow to the yellow buttercups.

"What fun!" said Tootle.

And he danced around and around and held one of the buttercups under his searchlight.

"I do like butter!" cried Tootle. "I do!"

At last the sun began to go down, and it was time to hurry to the roundhouse.

That evening while the Chief Oiler was playing checkers with old Bill, he said, "It's queer. It's very queer, but I found grass between Tootle's front wheels today."

"Hmm," said Bill. "There must be grass growing on the tracks."

"Not on our tracks," said the Day Watchman, who spent his days watching the tracks and his nights watching Bill and the Chief Oiler play checkers.

Bill's face was stern. "Tootle knows he must get 100 A+ in Staying on the Rails No Matter What, if he is going to be a Flyer."

Next day Tootle played all day in the meadow. He watched a green frog and he made a daisy chain. He found a rain barrel, and he said softly, "Toot!" "TOOT!" shouted the barrel. "Why, I sound like a flyer already!" cried Tootle.

That night the First Assistant Oiler said he had found a daisy in Tootle's bell. The day after that, the Second Assistant Oiler said that he had found hollyhock flowers floating in Tootle's eight bowls of soup.

And then the Mayor Himself said that he had seen Tootle chasing butterflies in the Meadow. The Mayor Himself said that Tootle had looked very silly, too.

Early one morning Bill had a long, long talk with the Mayor Himself.

When the Mayor Himself left the Lower Trainswitch School for Locomotives, he laughed all the way to the village.

"Bill's plan will surely put Tootle back on the track," he chuckled.

Bill ran from one store to the next, buying ten yards of this and twenty yards of that and all you have of the other. The Chief Oiler and the First, Second, and Third Assistant Oilers were hammering and sawing instead of oiling and polishing. And Tootle? Well, Tootle was in the meadow watching the butterflies flying and wishing he could dip and soar as they did.

Not a store in Lower Trainswitch was open the next day and not a person was at home. By the time the sun came up, every villager was hiding in the meadow along the tracks. And each of them had a red flag. It had taken all the red goods in Lower Trainswitch, and hard work by the Oilers, but there was a red flag for everyone.

Soon Tootle came tootling happily down the tracks. When he came to the meadow, he hopped off the tracks and rolled along the grass. Just as he was thinking what a beautiful day it was, a red flag poked up from the grass and waved hard. Tootle stopped, for every locomotive knows he must Stop for a Red Flag Waving.

"I'll go another way," said Tootle.

He turned to the left, and up came another waving red flag, this time from the middle of the buttercups.

When he went to the right, there was another red flag waving.

There were red flags waving from the buttercups, in the daisies, under the trees, near the bluebirds' nest, and even one behind the rain barrel. And, of course, Tootle had to stop for each one, for a locomotive must always Stop for a Red Flag Waving.

"Red flags," muttered Tootle. "This meadow is full of red flags. How can I have any fun?"

"Whenever I start, I have to stop. Why did I think this meadow was such a fine place? Why don't I ever see a green flag?"

Just as the tears were ready to slide out of his boiler, Tootle happened to look back over his coal car. On the tracks stood Bill, and in his hand was a big green flag. "Oh!" said Tootle.

He puffed up to Bill and stopped.

"This is the place for me," said Tootle. "There is nothing but red flags for locomotives that get off their tracks."

"Hurray!" shouted the people of Lower Trainswitch, and jumped up from their hiding places. "Hurray for Tootle the Flyer!"

Now Tootle is a famous Two-Miles-a-Minute Flyer. The young locomotives listen to his advice.

"Work hard," he tells them. "Always remember to Stop for a Red Flag Waving. But most of all, Stay on the Rails No Matter What."

JACKIE ROBINSON

"The Struggles of Spring Training," from *Jackie Robinson: My Story* (1948)

We had a tough time getting to Daytona Beach. At one point we had to give up our seats because the Army still had priority on planes. So we took a train to Jacksonville, and when we got there we found we'd have to go the rest of the way by bus. We didn't like the bus, and we particularly didn't like the back seat when there were empty seats near the center. Florida law designates where Negroes are to ride in public conveyances. The law says: "Back seat." We rode there.

When we arrived in Daytona Beach we were met at the bus station by Wendell Smith, sports editor of *The Pittsburgh Courier*, and Billy Rowe, a photographer for the same paper. They had been there about four days and had arranged housing accommodations and other necessities. With them was Johnny Wright, a good friend of mine and a pitcher for the Homestead Grays of the Negro National League. Mr. Rickey had signed Johnny to a Montreal contract not long after he had signed me. Johnny had come up with a good record in the Negro National League and had been a star pitcher for a Navy team in 1945.

They took us to the home of a prominent Negro family. The rest of the team usually stayed at a big hotel on the ocean front, but this particular time they were quartered at Sanford, Florida, where the Dodger organization was looking over at least two hundred players.

As a result of our transportation difficulties, I was two days late. I learned from Smith and Rowe that Mr. Rickey was a bit upset about my late arrival; so we decided to get up early next morning and drive to Sanford, which is some twenty miles south of Daytona Beach.

We arrived in Sanford the next morning about ten o'clock, but instead of going to the ball park, we decided to go to the home of Mr. Brock, a well-to-do Negro citizen of the town and call Mr. Rickey. We had to feel our way in this entire matter. We didn't want to cause a commotion or upset anything by walking into the park and surprising everyone. It was no secret that Johnny and I were going to be there, but we felt it best to remain as inconspicuous as possible.

Smith called Mr. Rickey at his hotel and he told us we should get over to the park as soon as possible. We took our shoes and gloves and hurried over. Clyde Sukeforth met us. We shook hands. "Go right into the dressing room and get your uniforms," he said. "Babe Hamburger, our clubhouse man, is in there. He'll see that you get fixed up."

I glanced at the players on the field. They had come from every section of the country—two hundred men out there, all hoping some day to become members of the Brooklyn Dodgers. Some were tossing balls to each other; others were hitting fungoes to the outfielders; still others were running around the field conditioning their legs. Suddenly I felt uncomfortably conspicuous standing there. Every single man on the field seemed to be staring at Johnny Wright and me. . . .

We ducked into the clubhouse. It was empty save for one man, a big, fat fellow. I felt a bit tense and I'm sure Johnny did, too. We were ill at ease and didn't know exactly what to do next. The man saw us then and came right over and introduced himself. "Hiya, fellows," he said with a big, broad smile on his face. "I'm Babe Hamburger . . . Robinson and Wright, eh? Well, that's swell. Which one is Robinson?"

I put out my hand and he gave it a hearty shake. "This is Johnny Wright," I said. Johnny shook Babe's big, soft mitt.

"Well, fellows," he said, "I'm not exactly what you'd call a part of this great experiment, but I'm gonna give you some advice anyway. Just go out there and do your best. Don't get tense. Just be yourselves."

Be ourselves? Here in the heart of the race-conscious South? . . . Johnny and I both realized that this was hostile territory—that anything could happen any time to a Negro who thought he could play ball with white men on an equal basis. It was going to be difficult to relax and behave naturally. But we assured Babe we'd try. . . .

We finally got dressed and headed for the field. Waiting for us was a group of reporters from New York, Pittsburgh, Baltimore, Montreal, and Brooklyn. They surrounded us and started firing questions:

"What are you going to do if the pitchers start throwing at you?" one of them asked.

"The same thing everyone else does," I answered, smiling. "Duck!"

The next morning we were up bright and early. We went out to the park in a taxi and this time dressed with the rest of the players. Practice that day was a bit long, but not at all strenuous.

When we got back to Brock's, Johnny and I found Wendell Smith and Billy Rowe, our newspaper friends from Pittsburgh, waiting for us. Usually, they joked and kidded with us a lot; but that night they were both exceptionally quiet and sober. We all ate together. The conversation dragged until I began to feel uncomfortable. . . .

Rowe got up from the table suddenly and said to Smith, "I'm going to fill up with gas." He had a red Pontiac that he used to cover his assignments.

"We should be able to get out of here in fifteen or twenty minutes," Smith said. "Daytona isn't far, either."

"You guys leaving us?" I asked curiously.

"No," Smith said. "We're all going to Daytona." . . .

"What about practice in the morning?" I asked. "After all, we came here to make the Montreal Club."

I was angry. What was this all about, anyway? No one had told us to move on to Daytona. . . . After all, things had been going beautifully. The first two days of practice had passed without a single incident. Surely we weren't being rejected after only a two-day trial! We were just beginning to loosen up a bit. The tenseness was going away, I was beginning to feel free and good inside.

As I sat there getting sorer by the minute, I heard Smith talking on the telephone: "Yes, Mr. Rickey," he said, "I'm with them now. We're pulling out for Daytona in about twenty minutes. Just as soon as they get their bags packed." I heard Rowe's car pull up in the driveway. . . .

We piled into the car and started for Daytona. Rowe was driving and Smith was sitting beside him. Johnny was in the back with me. None of us said a word. We stopped at the main intersection of the town for a traffic light. A group of men were standing on the street corner in their shirt sleeves. It looked like a typical small-town bull session.

I suddenly decided that Sanford wasn't a bad town at all. The people had been friendly to us. Apparently they liked ball players. The men on the corner turned to look at us. Easy-going guys, curious over where we were going—certainly not hostile, I thought. I smiled at them. I actually felt like waving.

Rowe broke the silence for the first time as the light changed and we picked up speed. "How can people like that call themselves Americans!" he said bitterly. . . .

"Now just a minute," I said "They haven't done anything to us. They're nice people as far as I'm concerned." . . .

"Yeah," Smith said, swinging around and looking us in the face. His eyes were blazing with anger. "Sure, they liked you. They were in love with you. . . . That's why we're leaving."

"What do you mean?" I asked.

"I don't get it," chimed in Johnny.

"You will," Rowe said. "You will."

"Look," Smith said, "we didn't want to tell you guys because we didn't want to upset you. We want you to make this ball club. But . . . we're leaving this town because we've been told to get out. They won't stand for Negro ball players on the same field with whites!" . . .

The expulsion from Sanford was a humiliating experience. I found myself wishing I had never gotten mixed up in the whole business. When the club moved into Daytona, our permanent training base, what hope was there that I would not be kicked out of town just as I had been in Sanford? I was sure that as soon as I walked out on the field, an objection would be raised. I didn't want to go through that all over again. What could I do? Quit? . . . I wanted to; but I just didn't have the nerve to walk out on all the people who were counting on me—my family and close friends, Mr. Rickey, the fourteen million Negroes from coast to coast, the legion of understanding white people. Dejected as I was, I just had to stick it out.

The rest of the team was quartered in a big hotel overlooking the Atlantic Ocean. I stayed in the home of a private family in the Negro section of the town. When we finished practice, I'd go home and play cards with Smith, Rowe, and my wife. Once in a while we'd go to a movie. There was only one Negro movie in town and the picture ran for three days. Consequently we'd see two pictures a week. Often there was absolutely nothing to do. Our life was so restricted and monotonous that sometimes we would go to see the same movie twice.

Now and then some of the local Negroes would invite us to dinner or for a game of cards. There was also a USO Club near-by and some evenings I'd go there to play table tennis or pinochle. But no matter how I tried I couldn't find a sufficient diversion to preoccupy me. I found myself stewing over the problems which I knew were bound to confront me sooner or later. . . .

We were scheduled to play an exhibition game with the Jersey City Giants in Jacksonville. We made the trip by bus, and when we arrived at the park there was a big crowd waiting outside. We climbed out and went over to the players' gate leading onto the field. It was locked. We couldn't get in; nor, apparently, could the waiting fans.

"What's wrong here?" [Montreal manager] Hopper asked a man standing near-by.

"The game's been called off," the man said. "The Bureau of Recreation won't let the game be played because you've got colored guys on your club."

Mel Jones got hold of Charley Stoneham, the Jersey City business manager, and found that the man's report was correct. George Robinson, executive secretary of the Bureau of Recreation, had informed the Jersey City club that he would not allow the game to be played. There was nothing for us to do but drive back to Daytona. . . .

ALLEN GINSBERG

from "Howl" (1956)

I

I saw the best minds of my generation destroyed by madness, starving hysterical naked,

dragging themselves through the negro streets at dawn looking for an angry fix,

angelheaded hipsters burning for the ancient heavenly connection to the starry dynamo in the
machinery of night,

who poverty and tatters and hollow-eyed and high sat up smoking in the supernatural darkness
of cold-water flats floating across the tops of cities contemplating jazz,

who bared their brains to Heaven under the El and saw
Mohammedan angels staggering on tenement roofs illuminated,

who passed through universities with radiant cool eyes hallucinating
Arkansas and Blake-light tragedy among the scholars of war,

who were expelled from the academies for crazy & publishing obscene odes on the windows of
the skull,

who cowered in unshaven rooms in underwear, burning their money in wastebaskets and
listening to the Terror through the wall,

who got busted in their pubic beards returning through Laredo with a belt of marijuana for New York,

who ate fire in paint hotels or drank turpentine in Paradise Alley, death, or purgatoried their
torsos night after night

with dreams, with drugs, with waking nightmares, alcohol and cock and endless balls,

incomparable blind streets of shuddering cloud and lightning in the mind leaping toward poles
of Canada & Paterson, illuminating all the motionless world of Time between,

Peyote solidities of halls, backyard green tree cemetery dawns, wine drunkenness over the
rooftops, storefront boroughs of teahead joyride neon blinking traffic light, sun and moon
and tree vibrations in the roaring winter dusks of Brooklyn, ashcan rantings and kind king
light of mind

who chained themselves to subways for the endless ride from Battery to holy Bronx on
benzedrine until the noise of wheels and children brought them down shuddering mouth-
wracked and battered bleak of brain all drained of brilliance in the drear light of Zoo,

who sank all night in submarine light of Bickford's floated out and sat through the stale beer
afternoon in desolate Fugazzi's, listening to the crack of doom on the hydrogen jukebox,

who talked continuously seventy hours from park to pad to bar to Bellevue to museum to the
Brooklyn Bridge,

a lost battalion of platonic conversationalists jumping down the stoops off fire escapes off
windowsills off Empire State out of the moon,

yacketayakking screaming vomiting whispering facts and memories and anecdotes and eyeball
kicks and shocks of hospitals and jails and wars,

whole intellects disgorged in total recall for seven days and nights with brilliant eyes, meat for
the Synagogue cast on the pavement,
who vanished into nowhere Zen New Jersey leaving a trail of ambiguous picture postcards of
Atlantic City Hall,
suffering Eastern sweats and Tangerian bone-grindings and migraines of China underjunk-
withdrawal in Newark's bleak furnished room,
who wandered around and around at midnight in the railroad yard wondering where to go, and
went, leaving no broken hearts,
who lit cigarettes in boxcars boxcars boxcars racketing through snow toward lonesome farms in
grandfather night,
who studied Plotinus Poe St. John of the Cross telepathy and bop kabbalah because the cosmos
instinctively vibrated at their feet in Kansas,
who loned it through the streets of Idaho seeking visionary indian angels who were visionary
indian angels,
who thought they were only mad when Baltimore gleamed in supernatural ecstasy,
who jumped in limousines with the Chinaman of Oklahoma on the impulse of winter midnight
streetlight smalltown rain,
who lounged hungry and lonesome through Houston seeking jazz or sex or soup, and followed
the brilliant Spaniard to converse about America and Eternity, a hopeless task, and so took
ship to Africa,
who disappeared into the volcanoes of Mexico leaving behind nothing but the shadow of
dungarees and the lava and ash of poetry scattered in fireplace Chicago,
who reappeared on the West Coast investigating the FBI in beards and shorts with big pacifist
eyes sexy in their dark skin passing out incomprehensible leaflets,
who burned cigarette holes in their arms protesting the narcotic tobacco haze of Capitalism,
who distributed Supercommunist pamphlets in Union Square weeping and undressing while the
sirens of Los Alamos wailed them down, and wailed down Wall, and the Staten Island ferry
also wailed,
who broke down crying in white gymnasiums naked and trembling before the machinery of
other skeletons
who bit detectives in the neck and shrieked with delight in policecars for committing no crime
but their own wild cooking pederasty and intoxication,
who howled on their knees in the subway and were dragged off the roof waving genitals and
manuscripts,
who let themselves be fucked in the ass by saintly motorcyclists, and screamed with joy,
who blew and were blown by those human seraphim, the sailors, caresses of Atlantic and
Caribbean love,
who balled in the morning in the evenings in rosegardens and the grass of public parks and
cemeteries scattering their semen freely to whomever come who may,
who hiccuped endlessly trying to giggle but wound up with a sob behind a partition in a Turkish
Bath when the blond & naked angel came to pierce them with a sword,
who lost their loveboys to the three old shrews of fate the one eyed shrew of the heterosexual
dollar the one eyed shrew that winks out of the womb and the one eyed shrew that does
nothing but sit on her ass and snip the intellectual golden threads of the craftsman's loom,
who copulated ecstatic and insatiate with a bottle of beer a sweetheart a package of cigarettes a
candle and fell off the bed, and continued along the floor and down the hall and ended
fainting on the wall with a vision of ultimate cunt and come eluding the last gyzym of
consciousness,

who sweetened the snatches of a million girls trembling in the sunset, and were red eyed in the
    morning but prepared to sweeten the snatch of the sunrise, flashing buttocks under barns
    and naked in the lake,

who went out whoring through Colorado in myriad stolen night-cars, N.C., secret hero of these
    poems, cocksman and Adonis of Denver—joy to the memory of his innumerable lays of girls
    in empty lots & diner backyards, moviehouses' rickety rows, on mountaintops in caves or
    with gaunt waitresses in familiar roadside lonely petticoat upliftings & especially secret gas-
    station solipsisms of johns, & hometown alleys too,

who faded out in vast sordid movies, were shifted in dreams, woke on a sudden Manhattan, and
    picked themselves up out of basements hungover with heartless Tokay and horrors of Third
    Avenue iron dreams & stumbled to unemployment offices,

who walked all night with their shoes full of blood on the snowbank docks waiting for a door in
    the East River to open to a room full of streamheat and opium,

who created great suicidal dramas on the apartment cliff-banks of the Hudson under the wartime
    blue floodlight of the moon & their heads shall be crowned with laurel in oblivion,

who ate the lamb stew of the imagination or digested the crab at the muddy bottom of the rivers
    of Bowery,

who wept at the romance of the streets with their pushcarts full of onions and bad music,

who sat in boxes breathing in the darkness under the bridge, and rose up to build harpsichords in
    their lofts,

who coughed on the sixth floor of Harlem crowned with flame under the tubercular sky
    surrounded by orange crates of theology,

who scribbled all night rocking and rolling over lofty incantations which in the yellow morning
    were stanzas of gibberish,

who cooked rotten animals lung heart feet tail borsht & tortillas dreaming of the pure vegetable
    kingdom,

who plunged themselves under meat trucks looking for an egg,

who threw their watches off the roof to cast their ballot for Eternity outside of Time, & alarm
    clocks fell on their heads every day for the next decade,

who cut their wrists three times successively unsuccessfully, gave up and were forced to open
    antique stores where they thought they were growing old and cried,

who were burned alive in their innocent flannel suits on Madison Avenue amid blasts of leaden
    verse & the tanked-up clatter of the iron regiments of fashion & the nitroglycerine shrieks of
    the fairies of advertising & the mustard gas of sinister intelligent editors, or were run down
    by the drunken taxicabs of Absolute Reality,

who jumped off the Brooklyn Bridge this actually happened and walked away unknown and
    forgotten into the ghostly daze of Chinatown soup alleyways & firetrucks, not even one free
    beer,

who sang out of their windows in despair, fell out of the subway window, jumped in the filthy
    Passaic, leaped on negroes, cried all over the street, danced on broken wineglasses barefoot
    smashed phonograph records of nostalgic European 1930s German jazz finished the whiskey
    and threw up groaning into the bloody toilet, moans in their ears and the blast of colossal
    steamwhistles,

who barreled down the highways of the past journeying to each other's hotrod-Golgotha jail-
    solitude watch or Birmingham jazz incarnation,

who drove crosscountry seventytwo hours to find out if I had a vision or you had a vision or he
    had a vision to find out Eternity,

who journeyed to Denver, who died in Denver, who came back to Denver & waited in vain, who watched over Denver & brooded & loned in Denver and finally went away to find out the Time, & now Denver is lonesome for her heroes,

who fell on their knees in hopeless cathedrals praying for each other's salvation and light and breasts, until the soul illuminated its hair for a second,

who crashed through their minds in jail waiting for impossible criminals with golden heads and the charm of reality in their hearts who sang sweet blues to Alcatraz,

who retired to Mexico to cultivate a habit, or Rocky Mount to tender Buddha or Tangiers to boys or Southern Pacific to the black locomotive or Harvard to Narcissus to Woodlawn to the daisychain or grave,

who demanded sanity trials accusing the radio of hypnotism & were left with their insanity & their hands & a hung jury,

who threw potato salad at CCNY lecturers on Dadaism and subsequently presented themselves on the granite steps of the madhouse with shaven heads and harlequin speech of suicide, demanding instantaneous lobotomy.

and who were given instead the concrete void of insulin Metrazol electricity hydrotherapy psychotherapy occupational therapy pingpong & amnesia,

who in humorless protest overturned only one symbolic pingpong table, resting briefly in catatonia,

returning years later truly bald except for a wig of blood, and tears and fingers, to the visible madman doom of the wards of the madtowns of the East,

Pilgrim State's Rockland's and Greystone's foetid halls, bickering with the echoes of the soul, rocking and rolling in the midnight solitude-bench dolmen-realms of love, dream of life a nightmare, bodies turned to stone as heavy as the moon,

with mother finally ******, and the last fantastic book flung out of the tenement window, and the last door closed at 4 a.m. and the last telephone slammed at the wall in reply and the last furnished room emptied down to the last piece of mental furniture, a yellow paper rose twisted on a wire hanger in the closet, and even that imaginary, nothing but a hopeful little bit of hallucination—

ah, Carl, while you are not safe I am not safe, and now you're really in the total animal soup of time—

and who therefore ran through the icy street obsessed with a sudden flash of the alchemy of the use of the ellipse the catalog the meter & the vibrating plane,

who dreamt and made incarnate gaps in Time & Space through images juxtaposed, and trapped the archangel of the soul between 2 visual images and joined the elemental verbs and set the noun and dash of consciousness together jumping with sensation of Pater Omnipotens Aeterna Deus

to recreate the syntax and measure of poor human prose and stand before you speechless and intelligent and shaking with shame, rejected yet confessing out the soul to conform to the rhythm of thought in his naked and endless head,

the madman bum and angel beat in Time, unknown, yet putting down here what might be left to say in time come after death,

and rose reincarnate in the ghostly clothes of jazz in the goldhorn shadow of the band and blew the suffering of America's naked mind for love into an eli eli lamma lamma sabacthani saxophone cry that shivered the cities down to the last radio

with the absolute heart of the poem of life butchered out of their own bodies good to eat a thousand years.

MICHAEL HARRINGTON

"The Invisible Land"
from *The Other America* (1962)

There is a familiar America. It is celebrated in speeches and advertised on television and in the magazines. It has the highest mass standard of living the world has ever known.

In the 1950's this America worried about itself, yet even its anxieties were products of abundance. The title of a brilliant book was widely misinterpreted, and the familiar America began to call itself "the affluent society." There was introspection about Madison Avenue and tail fins; there was discussion of the emotional suffering taking place in the suburbs. In all this, there was an implicit assumption that the basic grinding economic problems had been solved in the United States. In this theory the nation's problems were no longer a matter of basic human needs, of food, shelter, and clothing. Now they were seen as qualitative, a question of learning to live decently amid luxury.

While this discussion was carried on, there existed another America. In it dwelt somewhere between 40,000,000 and 50,000,000 citizens of this land. They were poor. They still are.

To be sure, the other America is not impoverished in the same sense as those poor nations where millions cling to hunger as a defense against starvation. This country has escaped such extremes. That does not change the fact that tens of millions of Americans are, at this very moment, maimed in body and spirit, existing at levels beneath those necessary for human decency. If these people are not starving, they are hungry, and sometimes fat with hunger, for that is what cheap foods do. They are without adequate housing and education and medical care. . . .

The millions who are poor in the United States tend to become increasingly invisible. Here is a great mass of people, yet it takes an effort of the intellect and will even to see them. . . .

The other America, the America of poverty, is hidden today in a way that it never was before. Its millions are socially invisible to the rest of us. No wonder that so many misinterpreted Galbraith's title and assumed that "the affluent society" meant that everyone had a decent standard of life. The misinterpretation was true as far as the actual day-to-day lives of two-thirds of the nation were concerned. Thus, one must begin a description of the other America by understanding why we do not see it.

There are perennial reasons that make the other America an invisible land.

Poverty is often off the beaten track. It always has been. The ordinary tourist never left the main highway, and today he rides interstate turnpikes. He does not go into the valleys of Pennsylvania where the towns look like movie sets of Wales in the thirties. He does not see the company houses in rows, the rutted roads (the poor always have bad roads whether they live in the city, in towns, or on farms), and everything is black and dirty. And even if he were to pass through such a place by accident, the tourist would not meet the unemployed men in the bar or the women coming home from a runaway sweatshop.

Then too, beauty and myths are perennial masks of poverty. The traveler comes to the Appalachians in the lovely season. He sees the hills, the streams, the foliage—but not the poor. Or perhaps he looks at a run-down mountain house and, remembering Rousseau rather than seeing with his eyes, decides that "those people" are truly fortunate to be living the way they are and that they are lucky to be exempt from the strains and tensions of the middle class. The only problem is that "those people," the quaint inhabitants of those hills, are undereducated, underprivileged, lack medical care, and are in the process of being forced from the land into a life in the cities, where they are misfits.

These are normal and obvious causes of the invisibility of the poor. They operated a generation ago; they will be functioning a generation hence. It is more important to understand that the very development of American society is creating a new kind of blindness about poverty. The poor are increasingly slipping out of the very experience and consciousness of the nation.

If the middle class never did like ugliness and poverty, it was at least aware of them. "Across the tracks" was not a very long way to go. There were forays into the slums at Christmas time; there were charitable organizations that brought contact with the poor. Occasionally, almost everyone passed through the Negro ghetto or the blocks of tenements, if only to get downtown to work or to entertainment.

Now the American city has been transformed. The poor still inhabit the miserable housing in the central area, but they are increasingly isolated from contact with, or sight of, anybody else. Middle-class women coming in from Suburbia on a rare trip may catch the merest glimpse of the other America on the way to an evening at the theater, but their children are segregated in suburban schools. The business or professional man may drive along the fringes of slums in a car or bus, but it is not an important experience to him. The failures, the unskilled, the disabled, the aged, and the minorities are right there, across the tracks, where they have always been. But hardly anyone else is.

In short, the very development of the American city has removed poverty from the living, emotional experience of millions upon millions of middle-class Americans. Living out in the suburbs, it is easy to assume that ours is, indeed, an affluent society.

This new segregation of poverty is compounded by a well-meaning ignorance. A good many concerned and sympathetic Americans are aware that there is much discussion of urban renewal. Suddenly, driving through the city, they notice that a familiar slum has been torn down and that there are towering, modern buildings where once there had been tenements or hovels. There is a warm feeling of satisfaction, of pride in the way things are working out: the poor, it is obvious, are being taken care of. . . .

. . . the poor are politically invisible. It is one of the cruelest ironies of social life in advanced countries that the dispossessed at the bottom of society are unable to speak for themselves. The people of the other America do not, by far and large, belong to unions, to fraternal organizations, or to political parties. They are without lobbies of their own; they put forward no legislative program. As a group, they are atomized. They have no face; they have no voice. . . .

Out of the thirties came the welfare state. Its creation had been stimulated by mass impoverishment and misery, yet it helped the poor least of all. Laws like unemployment compensation, the Wagner Act, the various farm programs, all these were designed for the middle third in the cities, for the organized workers, and for the upper third in the country, for the big market farmers. If a man works in an extremely low-paying job, he may not even be covered by social security or other welfare programs. If he receives unemployment compensation, the payment is scaled down according to his low earnings.

One of the major laws that was designed to cover everyone, rich and poor, was social security. But even here the other Americans suffered discrimination. Over the years social security payments have not even provided a subsistence level of life. The middle third have been able to supplement the Federal pension through private plans negotiated by unions, through joining medical insurance schemes like Blue Cross, and so on. The poor have not been able to do so. They lead a bitter life, and then have to pay for that fact in old age.

Indeed, the paradox that the welfare state benefits those least who need help most is but a single instance of a persistent irony in the other America. Even when the money finally trickles down, even when a school is built in a poor neighborhood, for instance, the poor are still deprived. Their entire environment, their life, their values, do not prepare them to take advantage of the new opportunity. The parents are anxious for the children to go to work; the pupils are pent up, waiting for the moment when their education has complied with the law. . . .

What shall we tell the American poor, once we have seen them? Shall we say to them that they are better off than the Indian poor, the Italian poor, the Russian poor? That is one answer, but it is heartless. I should put it another way. I want to tell every well-fed and optimistic American that it is intolerable that so many millions should be maimed in body and in spirit when it is not necessary that they should be. My standard of comparison is not how much worse things used to be. It is how much better they could be if only we were stirred.

BETTY FRIEDAN

from The Feminine Mystique (1962)

The problem lay buried, unspoken, for many years in the minds of American women. It was a strange stirring, a sense of dissatisfaction, a yearning that women suffered in the middle of the twentieth century in the United States. Each suburban wife struggled with it alone. As she made the beds, shopped for groceries, matched slipcover material, ate peanut butter sandwiches with her children, chauffeured Cub Scouts and Brownies, lay beside her husband at night—she was afraid to ask even of herself the silent question—"Is this all?"

For over fifteen years there was no word of this yearning in the millions of words written about women, for women, in all the columns, books and articles by experts telling women their role was to seek fulfillment as wives and mothers. Over and over women heard in voices of tradition and of Freudian sophistication that they could desire no greater destiny than to glory in their own femininity. Experts told them how to catch a man and keep him, how to breastfeed children and handle their toilet training, how to cope with sibling rivalry and adolescent rebellion; how to buy a dishwasher, bake bread, cook gourmet snails, and build a swimming pool with their own hands; how to dress, look, and act more feminine and make marriage more exciting; how to keep their husbands from dying young and their sons from growing into delinquents. They were taught to pity the neurotic, unfeminine, unhappy women who wanted to be poets or physicists or presidents. They learned that truly feminine women do not want careers, higher education, political rights—the independence and the opportunities that the old-fashioned feminists fought for. Some women, in their forties and fifties, still remembered painfully giving up those dreams, but most of the younger women no longer even thought about them. A thousand expert voices applauded their femininity, their adjustment, their new maturity. All they had to do was devote their lives from earliest girlhood to finding a husband and bearing children.

By the end of the nineteen-fifties, the average marriage age of women in America dropped to 20, and was still dropping, into the teens. Fourteen million girls were engaged by 17. The proportion of women attending college in comparison with men dropped from 47 per cent in 1920 to 35 per cent in 1958. A century earlier, women had fought for higher education; now girls went to college to get a husband. By the mid-fifties, 60 per cent dropped out of college to marry, or because they were afraid too much education would be a marriage bar. Colleges built dormitories for "married students," but the students were almost always the husbands. A new degree was instituted for the wives —"Ph.T." (Putting Husband Through).

Then American girls began getting married in high school. And the women's magazines, deploring the unhappy statistics about these young marriages, urged that courses on marriage, and marriage counselors, be installed in the high schools. Girls started going steady at twelve and thirteen, in junior high. Manufacturers put out brassieres with false bosoms of foam rubber for little girls of ten. And an advertisement for a child's dress, sizes 3–6x, in the *New York Times* in the fall of 1960, said: "She Too Can Join the Man-Trap Set."

By the end of the fifties, the United States birthrate was overtaking India's. The birth-control movement, renamed Planned Parenthood, was asked to find a method whereby women who had been advised that a third or fourth baby would be born dead or defective might have it anyhow. Statisticians were especially astounded at the fantastic increase in the number of babies among college women. Where once they had two children, now they had four, five, six. Women who had once wanted careers were now making careers out of having babies. So rejoiced *Life* magazine in a 1956 paean to the movement of American women back to the home.

In a New York hospital, a woman had a nervous breakdown when she found she could not breastfeed her baby. In other hospitals, women dying of cancer refused a drug which research had proved might save their lives: its side effects were said to be unfeminine. "If I have only one life, let me live it as a blonde," a larger-than-life-sized picture of a pretty, vacuous woman proclaimed from newspaper, magazine, and drugstore ads. And across America, three out of every ten women dyed their hair blonde. They ate a chalk called Metrecal, instead of food, to shrink to the size of the thin young models. Department-store buyers reported that American women, since 1939, had become three and four sizes smaller. "Women are out to fit the clothes, instead of vice-versa," one buyer said.

Interior decorators were designing kitchens with mosaic murals and original paintings, for kitchens were once again the center of women's lives. Home sewing became a million-dollar industry. Many women no longer left their homes, except to shop, chauffeur their children, or attend a social engagement with their husbands. Girls were growing up in America without ever having jobs outside the home. In the late fifties, a sociological phenomenon was suddenly remarked: a third of American women now worked, but most were no longer young and very few were pursuing careers. They were married women who held part-time jobs, selling or secretarial, to put their husbands through school, their sons through college, or to help pay the mortgage. Or they were widows supporting families. Fewer and fewer women were entering professional work. The shortages in the nursing, social work, and teaching professions caused crises in almost every American city. Concerned over the Soviet Union's lead in the space race, scientists noted that America's greatest source of unused brainpower was women. But girls would not study physics: it was "unfeminine." A girl refused a science fellowship at Johns Hopkins to take a job in a real-estate office. All she wanted, she said, was what every other American girl wanted—to get married, have four children and live in a nice house in a nice suburb.

The suburban housewife—she was the dream image of the young American women and the envy, it was said, of women all over the world. The American housewife—freed by science and labor-saving appliances from the drudgery, the dangers of childbirth and the illnesses of her grandmother. She was healthy, beautiful, educated, concerned only about her husband, her children, her home. She had found true feminine fulfillment. As a housewife and mother, she was respected as a full and equal partner to man in his world. She was free to choose automobiles, clothes, appliances, supermarkets; she had everything that women ever dreamed of.

In the fifteen years after World War II, this mystique of feminine fulfillment became the cherished and self-perpetuating core of contemporary American culture. Millions of women lived their lives in the image of those pretty pictures of the American suburban housewife, kissing their husbands goodbye in front of the picture window, depositing their stationwagonsful of children at school, and smiling as they ran the new electric waxer over the spotless kitchen floor. They baked their own bread, sewed their own and their children's clothes, kept their new washing machines and dryers running all day. They changed the sheets on the beds twice a week instead of once, took the rug-hooking class in adult education, and pitied their poor frustrated mothers, who had dreamed of having a career. Their only dream was to be perfect wives and mothers; their highest ambition to have five children and a beautiful house, their only fight to get and keep their husbands. They had no thought for the unfeminine problems of the world outside the home; they wanted the men to make the major decisions. They gloried in their role as women, and wrote proudly on the census blank: "Occupation: housewife."

For over fifteen years, the words written for women, and the words women used when they talked to each other, while their husbands sat on the other side of the room and talked shop or politics or septic tanks, were about problems with their children, or how to keep their husbands happy, or improve their children's school, or cook chicken or make slipcovers. Nobody argued whether women were inferior or superior to men; they were simply different. Words like "emancipation" and "career" sounded strange and embarrassing; no one had used them for years. When a Frenchwoman named Simone de Beauvoir wrote a book called *The Second Sex,* an American critic commented that she obviously "didn't know what life was all about," and besides, she was talking about French women. The "woman problem" in America no longer existed.

If a woman had a problem in the 1950's and 1960's, she knew that something must be wrong with her marriage, or with herself. Other women were satisfied with their lives, she thought. What kind of a woman was she if she did not feel this mysterious fulfillment waxing the kitchen floor? She was so ashamed to admit her dissatisfaction that she never knew how many other women shared it. If she tried to tell her husband, he didn't understand what she was talking about. She did not really understand it herself. For over fifteen years women in America found it harder to talk about this problem than about sex. Even the psychoanalysts had no name for it. When a woman went to a psychiatrist for help, as many women did, she would say, "I'm so ashamed," or "I must be hopelessly neurotic." "I don't know what's wrong with women today," a suburban psychiatrist said uneasily. "I only know something is wrong because most of my patients happen to be women. And their problem isn't sexual." Most women with this problem did not go to see a psychoanalyst, however. "There's nothing wrong really," they kept telling themselves. "There isn't any problem."

But on an April morning in 1959, I heard a mother of four, having coffee with four other mothers in a suburban development fifteen miles from New York, say in a tone of quiet desperation, "the problem." And the others knew, without words, that she was not talking about a problem with her husband, or her children, or her home. Suddenly they realized they all shared the same problem, the problem that has no name. They began, hesitantly, to talk about it. Later, after they had picked up their children at nursery school and taken them home to nap, two of the women cried, in sheer relief, just to know they were not alone.

Gradually I came to realize that the problem that has no name was shared by countless women in America. As a magazine writer I often interviewed women about problems with their children, or their marriages, or their houses, or their communities. But after a while I began to recognize the telltale signs of this other problem. I saw the same signs in suburban ranch houses and split-levels on Long Island and in New Jersey and Westchester County; in colonial houses in a small Massachusetts town; on patios in Memphis; in suburban and city apartments; in living rooms in the Midwest. Sometimes I sensed the problem, not as a reporter, but as a suburban housewife, for during this time I was also bringing up my own three children in Rockland County, New York. I heard echoes of the problem in college dormitories and semi-private maternity wards, at PTA meetings and luncheons of the League of Women Voters, at suburban cocktail parties, in station wagons waiting for trains, and in snatches of conversation overheard at Schrafft's. The groping words I heard from other women, on quiet afternoons when children were at school or on quiet evenings when husbands worked late, I think I understood first as a woman long before I understood their larger social and psychological implications.

Just what was this problem that has no name? What were the words women used when they tried to express it? Sometimes a woman would say "I feel empty somehow . . . incomplete." Or she would say, "I feel as if I don't exist." Sometimes she blotted out the feeling with a tranquilizer.

Sometimes she thought the problem was with her husband, or her children, or that what she really needed was to redecorate her house, or move to a better neighborhood, or have an affair, or another baby. Sometimes, she went to a doctor with symptoms she could hardly describe: "A tired feeling . . . I get so angry with the children it scares me . . . I feel like crying without any reason." (A Cleveland doctor called it "the housewife's syndrome.") A number of women told me about great bleeding blisters that break out on their hands and arms. "I call it the housewife's blight," said a family doctor in Pennsylvania. "I see it so often lately in these young women with four, five and six children who bury themselves in their dishpans. But it isn't caused by detergent and it isn't cured by cortisone."

Sometimes a woman would tell me that the feeling gets so strong she runs out of the house and walks through the streets. Or she stays inside her house and cries. Or her children tell her a joke, and she doesn't laugh because she doesn't hear it. I talked to women who had spent years on the analyst's couch, working out their "adjustment to the feminine role," their blocks to "fulfillment as a wife and mother." But the desperate tone in these women's voices, and the look in their eyes, was the same as the tone and the look of other women, who were sure they had no problem, even though they did have a strange feeling of desperation. . . .

In 1960, the problem that has no name burst like a boil through the image of the happy American housewife. In the television commercials the pretty housewives still beamed over their foaming dishpans and *Time*'s cover story on "The Suburban Wife, an American Phenomenon" protested: "Having too good a time . . . to believe that they should be unhappy." But the actual unhappiness of the American housewife was suddenly being reported—from the *New York Times* and *Newsweek* to *Good Housekeeping* and CBS Television ("The Trapped Housewife"), although almost everybody who talked about it found some superficial reason to dismiss it. It was attributed to incompetent appliance repairmen (*New York Times*), or the distances children must be chauffeured in the suburbs (*Time*), or too much PTA (*Redbook*). Some said it was the old problem—education: more and more women had education, which naturally made them unhappy in their role as housewives. "The road from Freud to Frigidaire, from Sophocles to Spock, has turned out to be a bumpy one," reported the *New York Times* (June 28, 1960). "Many young women—certainly not all—whose education plunged them into a world of ideas feel stifled in their homes. They find their routine lives out of joint with their training. Like shut-ins, they feel left out. In the last year, the problem of the educated housewife has provided the meat of dozens of speeches made by troubled presidents of women's colleges who maintain, in the face of complaints, that sixteen years of academic training is realistic preparation for wifehood and motherhood." . . .

The year American women's discontent boiled over, it was also reported (*Look*) that the more than 21,000,000 American women who are single, widowed, or divorced do not cease even after fifty their frenzied, desperate search for a man. And the search begins early—for seventy per cent of all American women now marry before they are twenty-four. A pretty twenty-five-year-old secretary took thirty-five different jobs in six months in the futile hope of finding a husband. Women were moving from one political club to another, taking evening courses in accounting or sailing, learning to play golf or ski, joining a number of churches in succession, going to bars alone, in their ceaseless search for a man.

Of the growing thousands of women currently getting private psychiatric help in the United States, the married ones were reported dissatisfied with their marriages, the unmarried ones suffering from anxiety and, finally, depression. Strangely, a number of psychiatrists stated that, in their experience, unmarried women patients were happier than married ones. So the door of all those pretty suburban houses opened a crack to permit a glimpse of uncounted thousands of American housewives who suffered alone from a problem that suddenly everyone was talking about, and beginning to take for granted, as one of those unreal problems in American life that can never be solved—like the hydrogen bomb. By 1962 the plight of the trapped American housewife had become a national parlor game. Whole issues of magazines, newspaper columns, books learned and frivolous, educational conferences and television panels were devoted to the problem.

Even so, most men, and some women, still did not know that this problem was real. But those who had faced it honestly knew that all the superficial remedies, the sympathetic advice, the scolding words and the cheering words were somehow drowning the problem in unreality. A bitter laugh was beginning to be heard from American women. They were admired, envied, pitied, theorized over until they were sick of it, offered drastic solutions or silly choices that no one could take seriously. They got all kinds of advice from the growing armies of marriage and child-guidance counselors, psychotherapists, and armchair psychologists, on how to adjust to their role as housewives. No other road to fulfillment was offered to American women in the middle of the twentieth century. Most adjusted to their role and suffered or ignored the problem that has no name. It can be less painful, for a woman, not to hear the strange, dissatisfied voice stirring within her.

It is no longer possible to ignore that voice, to dismiss the desperation of so many American women. This is not what being a woman means, no matter what the experts say. For human suffering there is a reason; perhaps the reason has not been found because the right questions have not been asked, or pressed far enough. I do not accept the answer that there is no problem because American women have luxuries that women in other times and lands never dreamed of; part of the strange newness of the problem is that it cannot be understood in terms of the age-old material problems of man: poverty, sickness, hunger, cold. The women who suffer this problem have a hunger that food cannot fill. It persists in women whose husbands are struggling internes and law clerks, or prosperous doctors and lawyers; in wives of workers and executives who make $5,000 a year or $50,000. It is not caused by lack of material advantages; it may not even be felt by women preoccupied with desperate problems of hunger, poverty or illness. And women who think it will be solved by more money, a bigger house, a second car, moving to a better suburb, often discover it gets worse.

It is no longer possible today to blame the problem on loss of femininity: to say that education and independence and equality with men have made American women unfeminine. I have heard so many women try to deny this dissatisfied voice within themselves because it does not fit the pretty picture of femininity the experts have given them. I think, in fact, that this is the first clue to the mystery: the problem cannot be understood in the generally accepted terms by which scientists have studied women, doctors have treated them, counselors have advised them, and writers have written about them. Women who suffer this problem, in whom this voice is stirring, have lived their whole lives in the pursuit of feminine fulfillment. They are not career women (although career women may have other problems); they are women whose greatest ambition has been marriage and children. For the oldest of these women, these daughters of the American middle class, no other dream was possible. The ones in their forties and fifties who once had other dreams gave them up and threw themselves joyously into life as housewives. For the youngest, the new wives and mothers, this was the only dream. They are the ones who quit high school and college to marry, or marked time in some job in which they had no real interest until they married. These women are very "feminine" in the usual sense, and yet they still suffer the problem. . . .

Can the problem that has no name be somehow related to the domestic routine of the housewife? When a woman tries to put the problem into words, she often merely describes the daily life she leads. What is there in this recital of comfortable domestic detail that could possibly cause such a feeling of desperation? Is she trapped simply by the enormous demands of her role as modern housewife: wife, mistress, mother, nurse, consumer, cook, chauffeur; expert on interior decoration, child care, appliance repair, furniture refinishing, nutrition, and education? Her day is fragmented as she rushes from dishwasher to washing machine to telephone to dryer to station wagon to supermarket, and delivers Johnny to the Little League field, takes Janey to dancing class, gets the lawnmower fixed and meets the 6:45. She can never spend more than 15 minutes on any one thing; she has no time to read books, only magazines; even if she had time, she has lost the power to concentrate. At the end of the day, she is so terribly tired that sometimes her husband has to take over and put the children to bed.

This terrible tiredness took so many women to doctors in the 1950's that one decided to investigate it. He found, surprisingly, that his patients suffering from "housewife's fatigue" slept more than an adult needed to sleep—as much as ten hours a day—and that the actual energy they expended on housework did not tax their capacity. The real problem must be something else, he decided—perhaps boredom. Some doctors told their women patients they must get out of the house for a day, treat themselves to a movie in town. Others prescribed tranquilizers. Many suburban housewives were taking tranquilizers like cough drops. "You wake up in the morning, and you feel as if there's no point in going on another day like this. So you take a tranquilizer because it makes you not care so much that it's pointless."

It is easy to see the concrete details that trap the suburban housewife, the continual demands on her time. But the chains that bind her in her trap are chains in her own mind and spirit. They are chains made up of mistaken ideas and misinterpreted facts, of incomplete truths and unreal choices. They are not easily seen and not easily shaken off.

How can any woman see the whole truth within the bounds of her own life? How can she believe that voice inside herself, when it denies the conventional, accepted truths by which she has been living? And yet the women I have talked to, who are finally listening to that inner voice, seem in some incredible way to be groping through to a truth that has defied the experts.

I think the experts in a great many fields have been holding pieces of that truth under their microscopes for a long time without realizing it. I found pieces of it in certain new research and theoretical developments in psychological, social and biological science whose implications for women seem never to have been examined. I found many clues by talking to suburban doctors, gynecologists, obstetricians, child-guidance clinicians, pediatricians, high-school guidance counselors, college professors, marriage counselors, psychiatrists and ministers—questioning them not on their theories, but on their actual experience in treating American women. I became aware of a growing body of evidence, much of which has not been reported publicly because it does not fit current modes of thought about women—evidence which throws into question the standards of feminine normality, feminine adjustment, feminine fulfillment, and feminine maturity by which most women are still trying to live.

I began to see in a strange new light the American return to early marriage and the large families that are causing the population explosion; the recent movement to natural childbirth and breastfeeding; suburban conformity, and the new neuroses, character pathologies and sexual problems being reported by the doctors. I began to see new dimensions to old problems that have long been taken for granted among women: menstrual difficulties, sexual frigidity, promiscuity, pregnancy fears, childbirth depression, the high incidence of emotional breakdown and suicide among women in their twenties and thirties, the menopause crises, the so-called passivity and immaturity of American men, the discrepancy between women's tested intellectual abilities in childhood and their adult achievement, the changing incidence of adult sexual orgasm in American women, and persistent problems in psychotherapy and in women's education.

If I am right, the problem that has no name stirring in the minds of so many American women today is not a matter of loss of femininity or too much education, or the demands of domesticity. It is far more important than anyone recognizes. It is the key to these other new and old problems which have been torturing women and their husbands and children, and puzzling their doctors and educators for years. It may well be the key to our future as a nation and a culture. We can no longer ignore that voice within women that says: "I want something more than my husband and my children and my home."

Students for a Democratic Society
from Port Huron Statement (1962)

We are people of this generation, bred in at least modest comfort, housed now in universities, looking uncomfortably to the world we inherit.

When we were kids the United States was the wealthiest and strongest country in the world; the only one with the atom bomb, the least scarred by modern war, an initiator of the United Nations that we thought would distribute Western influence throughout the world. Freedom and equality for each individual, government of, by, and for the people . . . these American values we found good, principles by which we could live as men. Many of us began maturing in complacency.

As we grew, however, our comfort was penetrated by events too troubling to dismiss. First, the permeating and victimizing fact of human degradation, symbolized by the Southern struggle against racial bigotry, compelled most of us from silence to activism. Second, the enclosing fact of the Cold War, symbolized by the presence of the Bomb, brought awareness that we ourselves, and our friends, and millions of abstract "others" we knew more directly because of our common peril, might die at any time. We might deliberately ignore, or avoid, or fail to feel all other human problems, but not these two, for these were too immediate and crushing in their impact, too challenging in the demand that we as individuals take the responsibility for encounter and resolution.

While these and other problems either directly oppressed us or rankled our consciences and became our own subjective concerns, we began to see complicated and disturbing paradoxes in our surrounding America. The declaration "all men are created equal . . ." rang hollow before the facts of Negro life in the South and the big cities of the North. The proclaimed peaceful intentions of the United States contradicted its economic and military investments in the Cold War status quo.

We witnessed, and continue to witness, other paradoxes. With nuclear energy whole cities can easily be powered, yet the dominant nation-states seem more likely to unleash destruction greater than that incurred in all wars of human history. Although our own technology is destroying old and creating new forms of social organization, men still tolerate meaningless work and idleness. While two-thirds of mankind suffers undernourishment, our own upper classes revel amidst superfluous abundance. Although world population is expected to double in forty years, the nations still tolerate anarchy as a major principle of international conduct and uncontrolled exploitation governs the sapping of the earth's physical resources. Although mankind desperately needs revolutionary leadership, America rests in national stalemate, its goals ambiguous and tradition-bound instead of informed and clear, its democratic system apathetic and manipulated rather than "of, by, and for the people."

Not only did tarnish appear on our image of American virtue, not only did disillusion occur when the hypocrisy of American ideals was discovered, but we began to sense that what we had originally seen as the American Golden Age was actually the decline of an era. The worldwide outbreak of revolution against colonialism and imperialism, the entrenchment of totalitarian states, the menace of war, overpopulation, international disorder, supertechnology—these trends were testing the tenacity of our own commitment to democracy and freedom and our abilities to visualize their application to a world in upheaval. . . .

We would replace power rooted in possession, privilege, or circumstance by power and uniqueness rooted in love, reflectiveness, reason, and creativity. As a *social system* we seek the establishment of a democracy of individual participation, governed by two central aims: that the individual share in those social decisions determining the quality and direction of his life; that society be organized to encourage independence in men and provide the media for their common participation.

In a participatory democracy, the political life would be based in several root principles:

that decision-making of basic social consequence be carried on by public groupings;

that politics be seen positively, as the art of collectively creating an acceptable pattern of social relations;

that politics has the function of bringing people out of isolation and into community, thus being a necessary, though not sufficient, means of finding meaning in personal life;

that the political order should serve to clarify problems in a way instrumental to their solution; it should provide outlets for the expression of personal grievance and aspiration; opposing views should be organized so as to illuminate choices and facilitate the attainment of goals; channels should be commonly available to relate men to knowledge and to power so that private problems . . . from bad recreation facilities to personal alienation . . . are formulated as general issues.

The economic sphere would have as its basis the principles:

that work should involve incentives worthier than money or survival. It should be educative, not stultifying; creative, not mechanical; self-directed, not manipulated, encouraging independence, a respect for others, a sense of dignity and a willingness to accept social responsibility, since it is this experience that has crucial influence on habits, perceptions and individual ethics;

that the economic experience is so personally decisive that the individual must share in its full determination;

that the economy itself is of such social importance that its major resources and means of production should be open to democratic participation and subject to democratic social regulation.

Like the political and economic ones, major social institutions—cultural, educational, rehabilitative, and others—should be generally organized with the well-being and dignity of man as the essential measure of success.

In social change or interchange, we find violence to be abhorrent because it requires generally the transformation of the target, be it a human being or a community of people, into a depersonalized object of hate. It is imperative that the means of violence be abolished and the institutions—local, national, international—that encourage nonviolence as a condition of conflict be developed. . . .

"Students don't even give a damn about the apathy," one has said. Apathy toward apathy begets a privately constructed universe, a place of systematic study schedules, two nights each week for beer, a girl or two, and early marriage; a framework infused with personality, warmth, and under control, no matter how unsatisfying otherwise.

Under these conditions university life loses all relevance to some. Four hundred thousand of our classmates leave college every year.

But apathy is not simply an attitude; it is a product of social institutions, and of the structure and organization of higher education itself. The extra curricular life is ordered according to *in loco parentis* theory, which ratifies the administration as the moral guardian of the young.

The accompanying "let's pretend" theory of student extracurricular affairs validates student government as a training center for those who want to spend their lives in political pretense, and discourages initiative from the more articulate, honest, and sensitive students. The bounds and style of controversy are delimited before controversy begins. The university "prepares" the student for "citizenship" through perpetual rehearsals and, usually, through emasculation of what creative spirit there is in the individual.

The academic life contains reinforcing counterparts to the way in which extracurricular life is organized. The academic world is founded on a teacher-student relation analogous to the parent-child relation which characterizes *in loco parentis*. Further, academia includes a radical separation of the student from the material of study. That which is studied, the social reality, is "objectified" to sterility, dividing the student from life—just as he is restrained in active involvements by the deans controlling student government. The specialization of function and knowledge, admittedly necessary to our complex technological and social structure, has produced an exaggerated compartmentalization of study and understanding. This has contributed to an overly parochial view, by faculty, of the role of its research and scholarship, to a discontinuous and truncated understanding, by students, of the surrounding social order; and to a loss of personal attachment, by nearly all, to the worth of study as a humanistic enterprise. . . .

The American political system is not the democratic model of which its glorifiers speak. In actuality it frustrates democracy by confusing the individual citizen, paralyzing policy discussion, and consolidating the irresponsible power of military and business interests.

A crucial feature of the political apparatus in America is that greater differences are harbored within each major party than the differences existing between them. Instead of two parties presenting distinctive and significant differences of approach, what dominates the system is a natural interlocking of Democrats from Southern states with the more conservative elements of the Republican Party. This arrangement of forces is blessed by the seniority system of Congress which guarantees Congressional committee domination by conservatives—ten of seventeen committees in the Senate and thirteen of twenty-one in the House of Representatives are chaired currently by Dixiecrats.

The party overlap, however, is not the only structural antagonist of democracy in politics. First, the localized nature of the party system does not encourage discussion of national and international issues: thus problems are not raised by and for people, and political representatives usually are unfettered from any responsibilities to the general public except those regarding parochial matters. Second, whole constituencies are divested of the full political power they might have: many Negroes in the South are prevented from voting, migrant workers are disenfranchised by various residence requirements, some urban and suburban dwellers are victimized by gerrymandering, and poor people are too often without the power to obtain political representation. Third, the focus of political attention is significantly distorted by the enormous lobby force, composed predominantly of business interests, spending hundreds of millions each year in an attempt to conform facts about productivity, agriculture, defense, and social services, to the wants of private economic groupings.

What emerges from the party contradiction and insulation of privately held power is the organized political stalemate: calcification dominates flexibility as the principle of parliamentary organization, frustration is the expectancy of legislators intending liberal reform, and Congress becomes less and less central to national decision-making, especially in the area of foreign policy. In this context, confusion and blurring is built into the formulation of issues, long-range priorities are not discussed in the rational manner needed for policy-making, the politics of personality and "image" become a more important mechanism than the construction of issues in a way that affords each voter a challenging and real option. The American voter is buffeted from all directions by pseudo-problems, by the structurally initiated sense that nothing political is subject to human mastery. Worried by his mundane problems which never get solved, but constrained by the common belief that politics is an agonizingly slow accommodation of views, he quits all pretense of bothering.

A most alarming fact is that few, if any, politicians are calling for changes in these conditions. . . .

In such a setting of status quo politics, where most if not all government activity is rationalized in Cold War anti-Communist terms, it is somewhat natural that discontented, super-patriotic groups would emerge through political channels and explain their ultra-conservatism as the best means of Victory over Communism. They have become a politically influential force within the Republican Party, at a national level through Senator Goldwater, and at a local level through their important social and economic roles. Their political views are defined generally as the opposite of the supposed views of Communists: complete individual freedom in the economic sphere, nonparticipation by the government in the machinery of production. But actually "anti-Communism" becomes an umbrella by which to protest liberalism, internationalism, welfareism, the active civil rights and labor movements. It is to the disgrace of the United States that such a movement should become a prominent kind of public participation in the modern world—but, ironically, it is somewhat to the interests of the United States that such a movement should be a public constituency pointed toward realignment of the political parties, demanding a conservative Republican Party in the South and an exclusion of the "leftist" elements of the national G.O.P.

Martin Luther King

"Letter from Birmingham Jail" (1963)

My Dear Fellow Clergymen:

While confined here in the Birmingham city jail, I came across your recent statement calling my present activities "unwise and untimely." Seldom do I pause to answer criticism of my work and ideas. If I sought to answer all the criticisms that cross my desk, my secretaries would have little time for anything other than such correspondence in the course of the day, and I would have no time for constructive work. But since I feel that you are men of genuine good will and your criticisms are sincerely set forth, I want to try to answer your statement in what I hope will be patient and reasonable terms.

I think I should indicate why I am here in Birmingham, since you have been influenced by the view which argues, against "outsiders coming in." I have the honor of serving as president of the Southern Christian Leadership Conference, an organization operating in every southern state, with headquarters in Atlanta, Georgia. We have some eighty-five affiliated organizations across the South, and one of them is the Alabama Christian Movement for Human Rights. Frequently we share staff, educational, and financial resources with our affiliates. Several months ago the affiliate here in Birmingham asked us to be on call to engage in a nonviolent direct-action program if such were deemed necessary. We readily consented, and when the hour came we lived up to our promise. So I, along with several members of my staff, am here because I was invited here. I am here because I have organizational ties here.

But more basically, I am in Birmingham because injustice is here. Just as the prophets of the eighth century B.C. left their villages and carried their "thus saith the Lord" far beyond the boundaries of their home towns, and just as the Apostle Paul left his village of Tarsus and carried the gospel of Jesus Christ to the far corners of the Greco-Roman world, so am I compelled to carry the gospel of freedom beyond my own home town. Like Paul, I must constantly respond to the Macedonian call for aid.

Moreover, I am cognizant of the interrelatedness of all communities and states. I cannot sit idly by in Atlanta and not be concerned about what happens in Birmingham. Injustice anywhere is a threat to justice everywhere. We are caught in an inescapable network of mutuality, tied in a single garment of destiny. Whatever affects one directly, affects all indirectly. Never again can we afford to live with the narrow, provincial "outside agitator" idea. Anyone who lives inside the United States can never be considered an outsider anywhere within its bounds.

You deplore the demonstrations taking place in Birmingham. But your statement, I am sorry to say, fails to express a similar concern for the conditions that brought about the demonstrations. I am sure that none of you would want to rest content with the superficial kind of social analysis that deals merely with effects and does not grapple with underlying causes. It is unfortunate that demonstrations are taking place in Birmingham, but it is even more unfortunate that the city's white power structure left the Negro community with no alternative. . . .

You may well ask, "Why direct action? Why sit-ins, marches, and so forth? Isn't negotiation a better path?" You are quite right in calling for negotiation. Indeed, this is the very purpose of direct action. Nonviolent direct action seeks to create such a crisis and foster such a tension that a community which has constantly refused to negotiate is forced to confront the issue. It seeks so to dramatize the issue that it can no longer be ignored. My citing the creation of tension as part of the work of the nonviolent-resister may sound rather shocking. But I must confess that I am not afraid of the word "tension." I have earnestly opposed violent tension, but there is a type of constructive, nonviolent tension which is necessary for growth. Just as Socrates felt that it was necessary to create a tension in the mind so that individuals would rise from the bondage of myths and half-truths to the unfettered realm of creative analysis and objective appraisal, so must we see the need for nonviolent gadflies to create the kind of tension in society that will help men rise from the dark depths of prejudice and racism to the majestic heights of understanding and brotherhood.

The purpose of our direct-action program is to create a situation so crisis-packed that it will inevitably open the door to negotiation. I therefore concur with you in your call for negotiation. Too long has our beloved Southland been bogged down in a tragic effort to live in monologue rather than dialogue. . . .

We know through painful experience that freedom is never voluntarily given by the oppressor; it must be demanded by the oppressed. Frankly, I have yet to engage in a direct-action campaign that was "well timed" in the view of those who have not suffered unduly from the disease of segregation. For years now I have heard the word "Wait!" It rings in the ears of every Negro with piercing familiarity. This "Wait" has almost always meant "Never." We must come to see, with one of our distinguished jurists, that "justice too long delayed is justice denied."

We have waited for more than 340 years for our constitutional and God-given rights. The nations of Asia and Africa are moving with jetlike speed toward gaining political independence, but we still creep at horse-and-buggy pace toward gaining a cup of coffee at a lunch counter. Perhaps it is easy for those who have never felt the stinging darts of segregation to say, "Wait." But when you have seen vicious mobs lynch your mothers and fathers at will and drown your sisters and brothers at whim; when you have seen hate-filled policemen curse, kick, and even kill your black brothers and sisters; when you see the vast majority of your twenty million Negro brothers smothering in an airtight cage of poverty in the midst of an affluent society; when you suddenly find your tongue twisted and your speech stammering as you seek to explain to your six-year-old daughter why she can't go to the public amusement park that has just been advertised on television, and see tears welling up in her eyes when she is told that Funtown is closed to colored children, and see ominous clouds of inferiority beginning to form in her little mental sky, and see her beginning to distort her personality by developing an unconscious bitterness toward white people; when you have to concoct an answer for a five-year-old son who is asking, "Daddy, why do white people treat colored people so mean?"; when you take a cross-country drive and find it necessary to sleep night after night in the uncomfortable corners of your automobile because no motel will accept you; when you are humiliated day in and day out by nagging signs reading "white" and "colored"; when your first name becomes "nigger," your middle name becomes "boy" (however old you are) and your last name becomes "John," and your wife and mother are never given the respected title "Mrs."; when you are harried by day and haunted by night by the fact that you are a Negro, living constantly at tiptoe stance, never quite knowing what to expect next, and are plagued with inner fears and outer resentments; when you are forever fighting a degenerating sense of "nobodiness"—then you will understand why we find it difficult to wait. There comes a time when the cup of endurance runs over, and men are no longer willing to be plunged into the abyss of despair. I hope, sirs, you can understand our legitimate and unavoidable impatience.

You express a great deal of anxiety over our willingness to break laws. This is certainly a legitimate concern. Since we so diligently urge people to obey the Supreme Court's decision of 1954 outlawing segregation in the public schools, at first glance it may seem rather paradoxical for us consciously to break laws. One may well ask: "How can you advocate breaking some laws and obeying others?" The answer lies in the fact that there are two types of laws: just and unjust. I would be the first to advocate obeying just laws. One has not only a legal but a moral responsibility to obey just laws. Conversely, one has a moral responsibility to disobey unjust laws. I would agree with St. Augustine that "an unjust law is no law at all."

Now, what is the difference between the two? How does one determine whether a law is just or unjust? A just law is a man-made code that squares with the moral law or the law of God. An unjust law is a code that is out of harmony with the moral law. To put it in the terms of St. Thomas Aquinas: An unjust law is a human law that is not rooted in eternal law and natural law. Any law that uplifts human personality is just. Any law that degrades human personality is unjust. All segregation statutes are unjust because segregation distorts the soul and damages the personality. It gives the segregator a false sense of superiority and the segregated a false sense of inferiority. Segregation, to use the terminology of the Jewish philosopher Martin Buber, substitutes an "I-it" relationship for an "I-thou" relationship and ends up relegating persons to the status of things. Hence segregation is not only politically, economically, and sociologically unsound, it is morally wrong and sinful. Paul Tillich has said that sin is separation. Is not segregation an existential expression of man's tragic separation, his awful estrangement, his terrible sinfulness? Thus it is that I can urge men to obey the 1954 decision of the Supreme Court, for it is morally right; and I can urge them to disobey segregation ordinances, for they are morally wrong.

Let us consider a more concrete example of just and unjust laws. An unjust law is a code that a numerical or power majority group compels a minority group to obey but does not make binding on itself. This is *difference* made legal. By the same token, a just law is a code that a majority compels a minority to follow and that it is willing to follow itself. This is *sameness* made legal. . . .

I must confess that over the past few years I have been gravely disappointed with the white moderate. I have almost reached the regrettable conclusion that the Negro's great stumbling block in his stride toward freedom is not the White Citizen's Counciler or the Ku Klux Klanner, but the white moderate, who is more devoted to "order" than to justice; who prefers a negative peace which is the absence of tension to a positive peace which is the presence of justice; who constantly says, "I agree with you in the goal you seek, but I cannot agree with your methods of direct action"; who paternalistically believes he can set the timetable for another man's freedom; who lives by a mythical concept of time and who constantly advises the Negro to wait for a "more convenient season." Shallow understanding from people of good will is more frustrating than absolute misunderstanding from people of ill will. Lukewarm acceptance is much more bewildering than outright rejection.

I had hoped that the white moderate would understand that law and order exist for the purpose of establishing justice and that when they fail in this purpose they become the dangerously structured dams that block the flow of social progress. I had hoped that the white moderate would understand that the present tension in the South is a necessary phase of the transition from an obnoxious negative peace, in which the Negro passively accepted his unjust plight, to a substantive and positive peace, in which all men will respect the dignity and worth of human personality. Actually, we who engage in nonviolent direct action are not the creators of tension. We merely bring to the surface the hidden tension that is already alive. We bring it out in the open, where it can be seen and dealt with. Like a boil that can never be cured so long as it is covered up but must be opened with all its ugliness to the natural medicines of air and light, injustice must be exposed, with all the tension its exposure creates, to the light of human conscience and the air of national opinion, before it can be cured.

In your statement you assert that our actions, even though peaceful, must be condemned because they precipitate violence. But is this a logical assertion? Isn't this like condemning a robbed man because his possession of money precipitated the evil act of robbery? Isn't this like condemning Socrates because his unswerving commitment to truth and his philosophical inquiries precipitated the act by the misguided populace in which they made him drink hemlock? Isn't this like condemning Jesus because his unique God-consciousness and never-ceasing devotion to God's will precipitated the evil act of crucifixion? We must come to see that, as the federal courts have consistently affirmed, it is wrong to urge an individual to cease his efforts to gain his basic constitutional rights because the quest may precipitate violence. Society must protect the robbed and punish the robber. . . .

I wish you had commended the Negro sit-inners and demonstrators of Birmingham for their sublime courage, their willingness to suffer, and their amazing discipline in the midst of great provocation. One day the South will recognize its real heroes. They will be the James Merediths, with the noble sense of purpose that enables them to face jeering and hostile mobs, and with the agonizing loneliness that characterizes the life of the pioneer. They will be old, oppressed, battered Negro women, symbolized in a seventy-two-year-old woman in Montgomery, Alabama, who rose up with a sense of dignity and with her people decided not to ride segregated buses, and who responded with ungrammatical profundity to one who inquired about her weariness: "My feets is tired, but my soul is at rest." They will be the young high school and college students, the young ministers of the gospel and a host of their elders, courageously and nonviolently sitting in at lunch counters and willingly going to jail for conscience sake. One day the South will know that when these disinherited children of God sat down at lunch counters, they were in reality standing up for what is best in the American dream and for the most sacred values in our Judeo-Christian heritage, thereby bringing our nation back to those great wells of democracy which were dug deep by the founding fathers in their formulation of the Constitution and the Declaration of Independence. . . .

Malcolm X

from "Message to the Grass Roots" (1965)

We want to have just an off-the-cuff chat between you and me, us. We want to talk right down to earth in a language that everybody here can easily understand. We all agree tonight, all of the speakers have agreed, that America has a very serious problem. Not only does America have a very serious problem, but our people have a very serious problem. America's problem is us. We're her problem. The only reason she has a problem is she doesn't want us here. And every time you look at yourself, be you black, brown, red or yellow, a so-called Negro, you represent a person who poses such a serious problem for America because you're not wanted. Once you face this as a fact, then you can start plotting a course that will make you appear intelligent, instead of unintelligent.

What you and I need to do is learn to forget our differences. When we come together, we don't come together as Baptists or Methodists. You don't catch hell because you're a Baptist, and you don't catch hell because you're a Methodist. You don't catch hell because you're a Methodist or Baptist, you don't catch hell because you're a Democrat or a Republican, you don't catch hell because you're a Mason or an Elk, and you sure don't catch hell because you're an American; because if you were an American, you wouldn't catch hell. You catch hell because you're a black man. You catch hell, all of us catch hell, for the same reason.

So we're all black people, so-called Negroes, second-class citizens, ex-slaves. You're nothing but an ex-slave. You don't like to be told that. But what else are you? You are ex-slaves. You didn't come here on the "Mayflower." You came here on a slave ship. In chains, like a horse, or a cow, or a chicken. And you were brought here by the people who came here on the "Mayflower," you were brought here by the so-called Pilgrims, or Founding Fathers. They were the ones who brought you here.

We have a common enemy. We have this in common: We have a common oppressor, a common exploiter, and a common discriminator. But once we all realize that we have a common enemy, then we unite—on the basis of what we have in common. And what we have foremost in common is that enemy—the white man. He's an enemy to all of us. I know some of you all think that some of them aren't enemies. Time will tell. . . .

Instead of airing our differences in public, we have to realize we're all the same family. And when you have a family squabble, you don't get out on the sidewalk. If you do, everybody calls you uncouth, unrefined, uncivilized, savage. If you don't make it at home, you settle it at home; you get in the closet, argue it out behind closed doors, and then when you come out on the street, you pose a common front, a united front. And this is what we need to do in the community, and in the city, and in the state. We need to stop airing our differences in front of the white man, put the white man out of our meetings, and then sit down and talk shop with each other. That's what we've got to do.

I would like to make a few comments concerning the difference between the black revolution and the Negro revolution. Are they both the same? And if they're not, what is the difference? What is the difference between a black revolution and a Negro revolution? First, what is a revolution? Sometimes I'm inclined to believe that many of our people are using this word "revolution" loosely, without taking careful consideration of what this word actually means, and what its historic characteristics are. When you study the historic nature of revolutions, the motive of a revolution, the objective of a revolution, the result of a revolution, and the methods used in a revolution, you may change words. You may devise another program, you may change your goal and you may change your mind.

Look at the American Revolution in 1776. That revolution was for what? For land. Why did they want land? Independence. How was it carried out? Bloodshed. Number one, it was based on land, the basis of independence. And the only way they could get it was bloodshed. The French Revolution—what was it based on? The landless against the landlord. What was it for? Land. How did they get it? Bloodshed. Was no love lost, was no compromise, was no negotiation. I'm telling you—you don't know what a revolution is. Because when you find out what it is, you'll get back in the alley, you'll get out of the way.

The Russian Revolution—what was it based on? Land; the landless against the landlord. How did they bring it about? Bloodshed. You haven't got a revolution that doesn't involve bloodshed. And you're afraid to bleed. I said, you're afraid to bleed.

As long as the white man sent you to Korea, you bled. He sent you to Germany, you bled. He sent you to the South Pacific to fight the Japanese, you bled. You bleed for white people, but when it comes to seeing your own churches being bombed and little black girls murdered, you haven't got any blood. You bleed when the white man says bleed; you bite when the white man says bite; and you bark when the white man says bark. I hate to say this about us, but it's true. How are you going to be nonviolent in Mississippi, as violent as you were in Korea? How can you justify being nonviolent in Mississippi and Alabama, when your churches are being bombed, and your little girls are being murdered, and at the same time you are going to get violent with Hitler, and Tojo, and somebody else you don't even know?

If violence is wrong in America, violence is wrong abroad. If it is wrong to be violent defending black women and black children and black babies and black men, then it is wrong for America to draft us and make us violent abroad in defense of her. And if it is right for America to draft us, and teach us how to be violent in defense of her, then it is right for you and me to do whatever is necessary to defend our own people right here in this country. . . .

So I cite these various revolutions, brothers and sisters, to show you that you don't have a peaceful revolution. You don't have a turn-the-other-cheek revolution. There's no such thing as a nonviolent revolution. The only kind of revolution that is nonviolent is the Negro revolution. The only revolution in which the goal is loving your enemy is the Negro revolution. It's the only revolution in which the goal is a desegregated lunch counter, a desegregated theater, a desegregated park, and a desegregated public toilet; you can sit down next to white folks—on the toilet. That's no revolution. Revolution is based on land. Land is the basis of all independence. Land is the basis of freedom, justice, and equality.

The white man knows what a revolution is. He knows that the black revolution is world-wide in scope and in nature. The black revolution is sweeping Asia, is sweeping Africa, is rearing its head in Latin America. The Cuban Revolution—that's a revolution. They overturned the system. Revolution is in Asia, revolution is in Africa, and the white man is screaming because he sees revolution in Latin America. How do you think he'll react to you when you learn what a real revolution is? You don't know what a revolution is. If you did, you wouldn't use that word.

Revolution is bloody, revolution is hostile, revolution knows no compromise, revolution overturns and destroys everything that gets in its way. And you, sitting around here like a knot on the wall, saying, "I'm going to love these folks no matter how much they hate me." No, you need a revolution. Whoever heard of a revolution where they lock arms, as Rev. Cleage was pointing out beautifully, singing "We Shall Overcome"? You don't do that in a revolution. You don't do any singing, you're too busy swinging. It's based on land. A revolutionary wants land so he can set up his own nation, an independent nation. These Negroes aren't asking for any nation—they're trying to crawl back on the plantation.

When you want a nation, that's called nationalism. When the white man became involved in a revolution in this country against England, what was it for? He wanted this land so he could set up another white nation. That's white nationalism. The American Revolution was white nationalism. The French Revolution was white nationalism. The Russian Revolution too—yes, it was—white nationalism. You don't think so? Why do you think Khrushchev and Mao can't get their heads together? White nationalism. All the revolutions that are going on in Asia and Africa today are based on what?—black nationalism. A revolutionary is a black nationalist. He wants a nation. I was reading some beautiful words by Rev. Cleage, pointing out why he couldn't get together with someone else in the city because all of them were afraid of being identified with black nationalism. If you're afraid of black nationalism, you're afraid of revolution. And if you love revolution, you love black nationalism. . . .

There is nothing in our book, the Koran, that teaches us to suffer peacefully. Our religion teaches us to be intelligent. Be peaceful, be courteous, obey the law, respect everyone; but if someone puts his hand on you, send him to the cemetery. That's a good religion. In fact, that's that old-time religion. That's the one that Ma and Pa used to talk about: an eye for an eye, and a tooth for a tooth, and a head for a head, and a life for a life. That's a good religion. And nobody resents that kind of religion being taught but a wolf, who intends to make you his meal.

This is the way it is with the white man in America. He's a wolf—and you're sheep. Any time a shepherd, a pastor, teaches you and me not to run from the white man and, at the same time, teaches us not to fight the white man, he's a traitor to you and me. Don't lay down a life all by itself. No, preserve your life, it's the best thing you've got. And if you've got to give it up, let it be even-steven. . . .

I would like to mention just one other thing quickly, and that is the method that the white man uses, how the white man uses the "big guns," or Negro leaders, against the Negro revolution. They are not a part of the Negro revolution. They are used against the Negro revolution.

When Martin Luther King failed to desegregate Albany, Georgia, the civil-rights struggle in America reached its low point. King became bankrupt almost, as a leader. The Southern Christian Leadership Conference was in financial trouble; and it was in trouble, period, with the people when they failed to desegregate Albany, Georgia. Other Negro civil-rights leaders of so-called national stature became fallen idols. As they became fallen idols, began to lose their prestige and influence, local Negro leaders began to stir up the masses. In Cambridge, Maryland, Gloria Richardson; in Danville, Virginia, and other parts of the country, local leaders began to stir up our people at the grass-roots level. This was never done by these Negroes of national stature. They control you, but they have never incited you or excited you. They control you, they contain you, they have kept you on the plantation.

As soon as King failed in Birmingham, Negroes took to the streets. King went out to California to a big rally and raised I don't know how many thousands of dollars. He came to Detroit and had a march and raised some more thousands of dollars. And recall, right after that Roy Wilkins attacked King. He accused King and CORE [Congress Of Racial Equality] of starting trouble everywhere and then making the NAACP [National Association for the Advancement of Colored People] get them out of jail and spend a lot of money; they accused King and CORE of raising all the money and not paying it back. This happened; I've got it in documented evidence in the newspaper. Roy started attacking King, and King started attacking Roy, and Farmer started attacking both of them. And as these Negroes of national stature began to attack each other, they began to lose their control of the Negro masses.

The Negroes were out there in the streets. They were talking about how they were going to march on Washington. Right at that time Birmingham had exploded, and the Negroes in Birmingham—remember, they also exploded. They began to stab the crackers in the back and bust them up 'side their head—yes, they did. That's when Kennedy sent in the troops, down in Birmingham. After that, Kennedy got on the television and said "this is a moral issue." That's when he said he was going to put out a civil-rights bill. And when he mentioned civil-rights bill and the Southern crackers started talking about how they were going to boycott or filibuster it, then the Negroes started talking—about what? That they were going to march on Washington, march on the Senate, march on the White House, march on the Congress, and tie it up, bring it to a halt, not let the government proceed. They even said they were going out to the airport and lay down on the runway and not let any airplanes land. I'm telling you what they said. That was revolution. That was revolution. That was the black revolution.

It was the grass roots out there in the street. It scared the white man to death, scared the white power structure in Washington, D.C., to death; I was there. When they found out that this black steamroller was going to come down on the capital, they called in Wilkins, they called in Randolph, they called in these national Negro leaders that you respect and told them, "Call it off." Kennedy said, "Look, you all are letting this thing go too far." And Old Tom said, "Boss, I can't stop it, because I didn't start it." I'm telling you what they said. They said, "I'm not even in it, much less at the head of it." They said, "These Negroes are doing things on their own. They're running ahead of us." And that old shrewd fox, he said, "If you all aren't in it, I'll put you in it. I'll put you at the head of it. I'll endorse it. I'll welcome it. I'll help it. I'll join it." . . .

It's just like when you've got some coffee that's too black, which means it's too strong. What do you do? You integrate it with cream, you make it weak. But if you pour too much cream in it, you won't even know you ever had coffee. It used to be hot, it becomes cool. It used to be strong, it becomes weak. It used to wake you up, now it puts you to sleep. This is what they did with the march on Washington. They joined it. They didn't integrate it, they infiltrated it. They joined it, became a part of it, took it over. And as they took it over, it lost its militancy. It ceased to be angry, it ceased to be hot, it ceased to be uncompromising. Why, it even ceased to be a march. It became a picnic, a circus. Nothing but a circus, with clowns and all. You had one right here in Detroit—I saw it on television—with clowns leading it, white clowns and black clowns. I know you don't like what I'm saying, but I'm going to tell you anyway. Because I can prove what I'm saying. If you think I'm telling you wrong, you bring me Martin Luther King and A. Philip Randolph and James Farmer and those other three, and see if they'll deny it over a microphone.

No, it was a sellout. It was a takeover. When James Baldwin came in from Paris, they wouldn't let him talk, because they couldn't make him go by the script. Burt Lancaster read the speech that Baldwin was supposed to make; they wouldn't let Baldwin get up there, because they know Baldwin is liable to say anything. They controlled it so tight, they told those Negroes what time to hit town, how to come, where to stop, what signs to carry, what song to sing, what speech they could make, and what speech they couldn't make; and then told them to get out of town by sundown. And every one of those Toms was out of town by sundown. Now I know you don't like my saying this. But I can back it up. It was a circus, a performance that beat anything Hollywood could ever do, the performance of the year. Reuther and those other three devils should get an Academy Award for the best actors because they acted like they really loved Negroes and fooled a whole lot of Negroes. And the six Negro leaders should get an award too, for the best supporting cast.

STOKELEY CARMICHAEL

from "What We Want" (1966)

. . . One of the tragedies of the struggle against racism is that up to now there has been no national organization which could speak to the growing militancy of young black people in the urban ghetto. There has been only a civil rights movement, whose tone of voice was adapted to an audience of liberal whites. It served as a sort of buffer zone between them and angry young blacks. None of its so-called leaders could go into a rioting community and be listened to. In a sense, I blame ourselves—together with the mass media—for what has happened in Watts, Harlem, Chicago, Cleveland, Omaha. Each time the people in those cities saw Martin Luther King get slapped, they became angry; and when they saw four little black girls bombed to death, they were angrier; and when nothing happened, they were steaming. We had nothing to offer that they could see, except to go out and be beaten again. We helped to build their frustration.

For too many years, black Americans marched and had their heads broken and got shot. They were saying to the country, "Look, you guys are supposed to be nice guys and we are only going to do what we are supposed to do—why do you beat us up, why don't you give us what we ask, why don't you straighten yourselves out?" After years of this, we are at almost the same point—because we demonstrated from a position of weakness. We cannot be expected any longer to march and have our heads broken in order to say to whites: come on, you're nice guys. For you are not nice guys. We have found you out.

An organization which claims to speak for the needs of a community—as does the Student Nonviolent Coordinating Committee—must speak in the tone of that community, not as somebody else's buffer zone. This is the significance of black power as a slogan. For once, black people are going to use the words they want to use—not just the words whites want to hear. And they will do this no matter how often the press tries to stop the use of the slogan by equating it with racism or separatism.

An organization which claims to be working for the needs of a community—as SNCC does—must work to provide that community with a position of strength from which to make its voice heard. This is the significance of black power beyond the slogan.

Black power can be clearly defined for those who do not attach the fears of white America to their questions about it. We should begin with the basic fact that black Americans have two problems: they are poor and they are black. All other problems arise from this two-sided reality: lack of education, the so-called apathy of black men. Any program to end racism must address itself to that double reality.

Almost from its beginning, SNCC sought to address itself to both conditions with a program aimed at winning political power for impoverished Southern blacks. We had to begin with politics because black Americans are a propertyless people in a country where property is valued above all. We had to work for power, because this country does not function by morality, love, and nonviolence, but by power. Thus we determined to win political power, with the idea of moving on from there into activity that would have economic effects. With power, the masses *make or participate in making* the decisions which govern their destinies, and thus create basic change in their day-to-day lives.

But if political power seemed to be the key to self-determination, it was also obvious that the key had been thrown down a deep well many years earlier. Disenfranchisement, maintained by racist terror, made it impossible to talk about organizing for political power in 1960. The right to vote had to be won, and SNCC workers devoted their energies to this from 1961 to 1965. They set up voter registration drives in the Deep South. They created pressure for the vote by holding mock elections in Mississippi in 1963 and by helping to establish the Mississippi Freedom Democratic Party (MFDP) in 1964. That struggle was eased, though not won, with the passage of the 1965 Voting Rights Act. SNCC workers could then address themselves to the question: "Who can we vote for, to have our needs met—how do we make our vote meaningful?" . . .

SNCC today is working in both North and South on programs of voter registration and independent political organizing. In some places, such as Alabama, Los Angeles, New York, Philadelphia, and New Jersey, independent organizing under the black panther symbol is in progress. The creation of a national "black panther party" must come about; it will take time to build, and it is much too early to predict its success. We have no infallible master plan and we make no claim to exclusive knowledge of how to end racism; different groups will work in their own different ways. SNCC cannot spell out the full logistics of self-determination but it can address itself to the problem by helping black communities define their needs, realize their strength, and go into action along a variety of lines which they must choose for themselves. Without knowing all the answers, it can address itself to the basic problem of poverty; to the fact that in Lowndes County, 86 white families own 90 percent of the land. What are black people in that county going to do for jobs, where are they going to get money? There must be reallocation of land, of money.

Ultimately, the economic foundations of this country must be shaken if black people are to control their lives. The colonies of the United States—and this includes the black ghettoes within its borders, north and south—must be liberated. For a century, this nation has been like an octopus of exploitation, its tentacles stretching from Mississippi to Harlem to South America, the Middle East, southern Africa, and Vietnam; the form of exploitation varies from area to area but the essential result has been the same—a powerful few have been maintained and enriched at the expense of the poor and voiceless colored masses. This pattern must be broken. As its grip loosens here and there around the world, the hopes of black Americans become more realistic. For racism to die, a totally different America must be born.

This is what the white society does not wish to face; this is why that society prefers to talk about integration. But integration speaks not at all to the problem of poverty, only to the problem of blackness. Integration today means the man who "makes it," leaving his black brothers behind in the ghetto as fast as his new sports car will take him. It has no relevance to the Harlem wino or to the cottonpicker making three dollars a day. As a lady I know in Alabama once said, "the food that Ralph Bunche eats doesn't fill my stomach."

Integration, moreover, speaks to the problem of blackness in a despicable way. As a goal, it has been based on complete acceptance of the fact that *in order to have* a decent house or education, blacks must move into a white neighborhood or send their children to a white school. This reinforces, among both black and white, the idea that "white" is automatically better and "black" is by definition inferior. This is why integration is a subterfuge for the maintenance of white supremacy. It allows the nation to focus on a handful of Southern children who get into white schools, at great price, and to ignore the 94 percent who are left behind in unimproved all-black schools. Such situations will not change until black people have power—to control their own school boards, in this case. Then Negroes become equal in a way that means something, and integration ceases to be a one-way street. Then integration doesn't mean draining skills and energies from the ghetto into white neighborhoods; then it can mean white people moving from Beverly Hills into Watts, white people joining the Lowndes County Freedom Organization. This integration becomes relevant. . . .

To most whites, black power seems to mean that the Mau Mau are coming to the suburbs at night. The Mau Mau are coming, and whites must stop them. Articles appear about plots to "get Whitey," creating an atmosphere in which "law and order must be maintained." Once again, responsibility is shifted from the oppressor to the oppressed. Other whites chide, "Don't forget—you're only 10 percent of the population; if you get too smart, we'll wipe you out." If they are liberals, they complain, "what about me?—don't you want my help any more?" These are people supposedly concerned about black Americans, but today they think first of themselves, of their feelings of rejection. Or they admonish, "you can't get anywhere without coalitions," without considering the problems of coalition with whom?; on what terms? (coalescing from weakness can mean absorption, betrayal); when? Or they accuse us of "polarizing the races" by our calls for black unity, when the true responsibility for polarization lies with whites who will not accept their responsibility as the majority power for making the democratic process work.

White America will not face the problem of color, the reality of it. The well-intended say: "We're all human, everybody is really decent, we must forget color." But color cannot be "forgotten" until its weight is recognized and dealt with. White America will not acknowledge that the ways in which this country sees itself are contradicted by being black—and always have been. Whereas most of the people who settled this country came here for freedom or for economic opportunity, blacks were brought here to be slaves. When the Lowndes County Freedom Organization chose the black panther as its symbol, it was christened by the press "the Black Panther Party"—but the Alabama Democratic Party, whose symbol is a rooster, has never been called the White Cock Party. No one ever talked about "white power" because power in this country *is* white. All this adds up to more than merely identifying a group phenomenon by some catchy name or adjective. The furor over that black panther reveals the problems that white America has with color and sex; the furor over "black power" reveals how deep racism runs and the great fear which is attached to it.

Whites will not see that I, for example, as a person oppressed because of my blackness, have common cause with other blacks who are oppressed because of blackness. This is not to say that there are no white people who see things as I do, but that it is black people I must speak to first. It must be the oppressed to whom SNCC addresses itself primarily, not to friends from the oppressing group.

From birth, black people are told a set of lies about themselves. We are told that we are lazy—yet I drive through the Delta area of Mississippi and watch black people picking cotton in the hot sun for fourteen hours. We are told, "If you work hard, you'll succeed" . . . but if that were true, black people would own this country. We are oppressed because we are black—not because we are ignorant, not because we are lazy, not because we're stupid (and got good rhythm), but because we're black. . . .

The need for psychological equality is the reason why SNCC today believes that blacks must organize in the black community. Only black people can convey the revolutionary idea that black people are able to do things themselves. Only they can help create in the community an aroused and continuing black consciousness that will provide the basis for political strength. In the past, white allies have furthered white supremacy without the whites involved realizing it—or wanting it, I think. Black people must do things for themselves; they must get poverty money they will control and spend themselves, they must conduct tutorial programs themselves so that black children can identify with black people. This is one reason Africa has such importance: The reality of black men ruling their own nations gives blacks elsewhere a sense of possibility, of power, which they do not now have. . . .

Black people do not want to "take over" this country. They don't want to "get whitey;" they just want to get him off their backs, as the saying goes. It was for example the exploitation by Jewish landlords and merchants which first created black resentment toward Jews—not Judaism. The white man is irrelevant to blacks, except as an oppressive force. Blacks want to be in his place, yet, but not in order to terrorize and lynch and starve him. They want to be in his place because that is where a decent life can be had. . . .

As for white America, perhaps it can stop crying out against "black supremacy," "black nationalism," "racism in reverse," and begin facing reality. The reality is that this nation, from top to bottom, is racist; that racism is not primarily a problem of "human relations" but of an exploitation maintained—either actively or through silence—by the society as a whole. Camus and Sartre have asked, can a man condemn himself? Can whites, particularly liberal whites, condemn themselves? Can they stop blaming us, and blame their own system? Are they capable of the shame which might become a revolutionary emotion?

We have found that they usually cannot condemn themselves, and so we have done it. But the rebuilding of this society, if at all possible, is basically the responsibility of whites—not blacks. We won't fight to save the present society, in Vietnam or anywhere else. We are just going to work, in the way *we* see fit, and on goals *we* define, not for civil rights but for all our human rights. . . .

Chicano Manifesto

I am a Chicano. What that means to me may be entirely different from what meaning the word has for you. To be Chicano is to find out something about one's self which has lain dormant, subverted, and nearly destroyed.

I am a Chicano because of a unique fusion of bloods and history and culture. I am a Chicano because I sense a rising awareness among others like myself of a fresh rebirth of self and self-in-others.

I am a Chicano because from this revived and newly created personality I draw vitality and motivation more forceful and tangible than I ever did or could have from the gringo world.

I am a Chicano in spite of scorn or derision, in spite of opposition even from my own people, many of whom do not understand and may never fathom what Chicano means.

I am a Chicano, hopeful that my acceptance and assertion of Chicanismo will mean a better life for all my people, that it will move others into making the same act of will to accept and develop a new-found identity and power. . . .

There is a mystique among us Chicanos, something that we have searched for and now have found. It draws us together, welds from insecure, disparate groups and viewpoints a common focal thought, experience, and power. For so many years we have disclaimed or claimed this or that label, sought leadership even from the Anglo, founded any number of organizations, worried over internal issues, fought for prestige and position within our little groups; and all the while the Anglo kept us in subjugation.

To be Chicano is nothing new; it is as old as our people. But it is a new way of knowing your brown brother and of understanding our brown race. To be Chicano means that a person has looked deeper into his being and sought unique ties to his brothers in la raza.

I nearly fell victim to the Anglo. My childhood was spent in the West Side barrio of San Antonio. I lived in my grandmother's house on Ruiz Street just below Zarzamora Creek. I did well in the elementary grades and learned English quickly.

Spanish was off-limits in school anyway, and teachers and relatives taught me early that my mother tongue would be of no help in making good grades and becoming a success. Yet Spanish was the language I used in playing and arguing with friends. Spanish was the language I spoke with my abuelita, my grandmother, as I ate atole on those cold mornings when I used to wake at dawn to her clattering dishes in the tiny kitchen; or when I would cringe in mock horror at old folk tales she would tell me late at night.

But the lesson took effect anyway. Then at the age of ten I went with my mother to California, to the San Francisco Bay Area where she found work during the war years, I had my first real opportunity to strip myself completely of my heritage. In California the schools I attended were all Anglo except for this little mexicanito. At least, I never knew anyone who admitted he was Mexican and I certainly never thought to ask. When my name was accented incorrectly, Réndon instead of Rendón, that was all right; finally I must have gotten tired of correcting people or just didn't bother. . . .

When my mother, who speaks both Spanish and English fluently, spoke to me in Spanish, I would respond in English. By the time I graduated from high school and prepared to enter college, the break was nearly complete. Seldom during college did I admit to being a Mexican American. Only when Latin American students pressed me about my surname did I admit my Spanish descent, or when it proved an asset in meeting coeds from Latin American countries.

My ancestry had become a shadow, fainter and fainter about me. I felt no particular allegiance to it, drew no inspiration from it, and elected generally to let it fade away. I clicked with the Anglo mind set in college, mastered it, you might say. I even became editor of the campus biweekly newspaper as a junior, and editor of the literary magazine as a senior—not bad, now that I look back, for a tortillas-and-beans Chicano upbringing to beat the Anglo at his own game.

The point of my "success," of course, was that I had been assimilated; I had bought the white man's world. After getting my diploma I was set to launch out into a career in newspaper reporting and writing. There was no thought in my mind of serving my people, telling their story, or making anything right for anybody but myself. Instead I had dreams of Pulitzer Prizes, syndicated columns, foreign correspondent assignments, front page stories—that was for me. Then something happened.

A Catholic weekly newspaper in Sacramento offered the a position as a reporter and feature writer. I had a job on a Bay Area daily as a copyboy at the time, with the opportunity to become a reporter. But I'd just been married, and there were a number of other reasons to consider: there'd be a variety of assignments, Sacramento was the state capital, it was a good town in which to raise a family, and the other job lacked promise for upward mobility. I decided to take the offer. . . .

It was my own people who rescued me. There is a large Chicano population in Sacramento, today one of the most activist in northern California, but at the time factionalized and still dependent on the social and church organizations for identity. But together we found each other.

My job soon brought me into contact with many Chicanos as well as with the recently immigrated Mexicans, located in the barrios that Sacramento had allocated to the "Mexicans." I found my people striving to survive in an alien environment among foreign people. . . . I rediscovered my own people, or perhaps they redeemed me. . . . For the first time in many years I became reimmersed in a tough, macho ambiente (an entirely Mexican male environment). Only Spanish was spoken. The effect was shattering. It was as if my tongue, after being struck dumb as a child, had been loosened. . . . I was cast in a spiritual setting which was a perfect background for reviving my Chicano soul. Reborn but imperfectly, I still had a lot to learn about myself and my people. But my understanding deepened and renewed itself as the years went by. I visited bracero camps with teams of Chicanos: sometimes with priests taking the Sacraments; sometimes only Chicanos, offering advice or assistance with badly needed food and clothing, distributed through a bingo-game technique; and on occasion, music for group singing provided by a phonograph or a guitar. Then there were barrio organization work; migrant worker programs; a rural self-help community development project; and confrontation with antipoverty agencies, with the churches, with government officials, and with cautious Chicanos, too. . . .

I owe my life to my Chicano people. They rescued me from the Anglo kiss of death, the monolingual, monocultural, and colorless gringo society. I no longer face a dilemma of identity or direction. That identity and direction have been charted for me by the Chicano—but to think I came that close to being sucked into the vacuum of the dominant society.

Chicano is a beautiful word. Chicano describes a beautiful people. Chicano has a power of its own. Chicano is a unique confluence of histories, cultures, languages, and traditions.

Chicano is the one unique word of the Mexican American people. Its derivation is strictly internal; it owes nothing to the Anglo penchant for categorizing ethnic groups. In a way, Chicano is indefinable, more a word to be understood and felt and lived than placed in a dictionary or analyzed by Anglo anthropologists, sociologists, and apologists.

Chicano has the ring of pachuco, slang, of shortening a word, which is typical of our Mexican American experience. It also echoes the harsher sounds of our native ancestors of the Mexican Valley, but is softened by the rounded-vowel endings of our Spanish forebears. It is the perfect word to characterize the mezcla that is la raza. It portrays the fact that we have come to psychological terms with circumstances which might otherwise cause emotional and social breakdowns among our people if we only straddle cultures and do not absorb them.

Chicano is a very special word. Chicano is a unique people. Chicano is a prophecy of a new day and a new world,

Standard Station, 1966 by Ed Ruscha. Collection of the Modern Art Museum of
Fort Worth, anonymous gift in memory of Sam B. Cantey, III.
Courtesy of Modern Art Museum of Fort Worth.

BARRY COMMONER
Four Laws of Ecology

In broad outline, these are the environmental cycles which govern the behavior of the three great global systems: the air, the water, and the soil. Within each of them live many thousands of different species of living things. Each species is suited to its particular environmental niche, and each, through its life processes, affects the physical and chemical properties of its immediate environment.

Each living species is also linked to many others. These links are bewildering in their variety and marvelous in their intricate detail. An animal, such as a deer, may depend on plants for food; the plants depend on the action of soil bacteria for their nutrients; the bacteria in turn live on the organic wastes dropped by the animals on the soil. At the same time, the deer is food for the mountain lion. Insects may live on the juices of plants or gather pollen from their flowers, Other insects suck blood from animals. Bacteria may live on the internal tissues of animals and plants. Fungi degrade the bodies of dead plants and animals. All this, many times multiplied and organized species by species in intricate, precise relationships, makes up the vast network of life on the earth.

The science that studies these relationships and the processes linking each living thing to the physical and chemical environment is *ecology*. It is the science of planetary housekeeping. For the environment is, so to speak, the house created on the earth *by* living things *for* living things. It is a young science and much of what it teaches has been learned from only small segments of the whole network of life on the earth. Ecology has not yet explicitly developed the kind of cohesive, simplifying generalizations exemplified by, say, the laws of physics. Nevertheless there are a number of generalizations that are already evident in what we now know about the ecospbere and that can be organized into a kind of informal set of "laws of ecology." These are described in what follows.

The First Law of Ecology:
Everything Is Connected to Everything Else

Some of the evidence that leads to this generalization has already been discussed. It reflects the existence of the elaborate network of interconnections in the ecosphere: among different living organisms, and between populations, species, and individual organisms and their physicochemical surroundings.

The single fact that an ecosystem consists of multiple interconnected parts, which act on one another, has some surprising consequences. Our ability to picture the behavior of such systems has been helped considerably by the development, even more recent than ecology, of the science of cybernetics. We owe the basic concept, and the word itself, to the inventive mind of the late Norbert Wiener.

332

The word "cybernetics" derives from the Greek word for helmsman; it is concerned with cycles of events that steer, or govern, the behavior of a system. The helmsman is part of a system that also includes the compass, the rudder, and the ship. If the ship veers off the chosen compass course, the change shows up in the movement of the compass needle. Observed and interpreted by the helmsman this event determines a subsequent one: the helmsman turns the rudder, which swings the ship back to its original course. When this happens, the compass needle returns to its original, on-course position and the cycle is complete. If the helmsman turns the rudder too far in response to a small deflection of the compass needle, the excess swing of the ship shows up in the compass—which signals the helmsman to correct his overreaction by an opposite movement. Thus the operation of this cycle stabilizes the course of the ship.

In quite a similar way, stabilizing cybernetic relations are built into an ecological cycle. Consider, for example, the fresh-water ecological cycle: fish—organic waste—bacteria of decay—inorganic products—algae—fish. Suppose that due to unusually warm summer weather there is a rapid growth of algae. This depletes the supply of inorganic nutrients so that two sectors of the cycle, algae and nutrients, are out of balance, but in opposite directions. The operation of the ecological cycle, like that of the ship, soon brings the situation back into balance. For the excess in algae increases the ease with which fish can feed on them; this reduces the algal population, increases fish waste production, and eventually leads to an increased level of nutrients when the waste decays. Thus, the levels of algae and nutrients tend to return to their original balanced position.

In such cybernetic systems the course is not maintained by rigid control, but flexibly. Thus the ship does not move unwaveringly on its path, but actually follows it in a wavelike motion that swings equally to both sides of the true course. The frequency of these swings depends on the relative speeds of the various steps in the cycle, such as the rate at which the ship responds to the rudder.

Ecological systems exhibit similar cycles, although these are often obscured by the effects of daily or seasonal variations in weather and environmental agents. The most famous examples of such ecological oscillations are the periodic fluctuations of the size of fur-bearing animal populations. For example, from trapping records in Canada it is known that the populations of rabbits and lynx follow ten-year fluctuations. When there are many rabbits the lynx prosper; the rising population of lynx increasingly ravages the rabbit population, reducing it; as the latter become scarce, there is insufficient food to support the now numerous lynx; as the lynx begin to die off, the rabbits are less fiercely hunted and increase in number. And so on. These oscillations are built into the operation of the simple cycle, in which the lynx population is positively related to the number of rabbits and the rabbit population is negatively related to the number of lynx.

In such an oscillating system there is always the danger that the whole system will collapse when an oscillation swings so wide of the balance point that the system can no longer compensate for it. Suppose, for example, in one particular swing of the rabbit-lynx cycle, the lynx manage to eat *all* the rabbits (or, for that matter, all but one). Now the rabbit population can no longer reproduce. As usual, the lynx begin to starve as the rabbits are consumed; but this time the drop in the lynx population is not followed by an increase in rabbits. The lynx then die off. The entire rabbit-lynx system collapses. . . .

The amount of stress which an ecosystem can absorb before it is driven to collapse is also a result of its various interconnections and their relative speeds of response. The more complex the ecosystem, the more successfully it can resist a stress. For example, in the rabbit-lynx system, if the lynx had an alternative source of food they might survive the sudden depletion of rabbits. In this way, branching—which establishes alternative pathways—increases the resistance of an ecosystem to stress. Most ecosystems are so complex that the cycles are not simple circular paths, but are crisscrossed with branches to form a network or a fabric of interconnections. Like a net, in which each knot is connected to others by several strands, such a fabric can resist collapse better than a simple, unbranched circle of threads—which if cut anywhere breaks down as a whole. Environmental pollution is often a sign that ecological links have been cut and that the ecosystem has been artificially simplified and made more vulnerable to stress and to final collapse.

The feedback characteristics of ecosystems result in amplification and intensification processes of considerable magnitude. For example, the fact that in food chains small organisms are eaten by bigger ones and the latter by still bigger ones inevitably results in the concentration of certain environmental constituents in the bodies of the largest organisms at the top of the food chain. Smaller organisms always exhibit much higher metabolic rates than larger ones, so that the amount of their food which is oxidized relative to the amount incorporated into the body of the organism is thereby greater. Consequently, an animal at the top of the food chain depends on the consumption of an enormously greater mass of the bodies of organisms lower down in the food chain. Therefore, any *non*metabolized material present in the lower organisms of this chain will become concentrated in the body of the top one. Thus, if the concentration of DDT (which is not readily metabolized) in the soil is 1 unit, earthworms living in the soil will achieve a concentration of from 10 to 40 units, and in woodcocks feeding on the earthworms the DDT level will rise to about 200 units.

All this results from a simple fact about ecosystems—everything is connected to everything else: the system is stabilized by its dynamic self-compensating properties; these same properties, if overstressed, can lead to a dramatic collapse; the complexity of the ecological network and its intrinsic rate of turnover determine how much it can be stressed, and for how long, without collapsing; the ecological network is an amplifier, so that a small perturbation in one place may have large, distant, long-delayed effects.

The Second Law of Ecology: Everything Must Go Somewhere

This is, of course, simply a somewhat informal restatement of a basic law of physics—that matter is indestructible. Applied to ecology, the law emphasizes that in nature there is no such thing as "waste." In every natural system, what is excreted by one organism as waste is taken up by another as food. Animals release carbon dioxide as a respiratory waste; this is an essential nutrient for green plants. Plants excrete oxygen, which is used by animals. Animal organic wastes nourish the bacteria of decay. Their wastes, inorganic materials such as nitrate, phosphate, and carbon dioxide, become algal nutrients.

A persistent effort to answer the question "Where does it go?" can yield a surprising amount of valuable information about an ecosystem. Consider, for example, the fate of a household item which contains mercury—a substance with serious environmental effects that have just recently surfaced. A dry-cell battery containing mercury is purchased, used to the point of exhaustion, and then "thrown out." But where does it really go? First it is placed in a container of rubbish; this is collected and taken to an incinerator. Here the mercury is heated; this produces mercury *vapor* which is emitted by the incinerator stack, and mercury vapor is toxic. Mercury vapor is carried by the wind, eventually brought to earth in rain or snow. Entering a mountain lake, let us say, the mercury condenses and sinks to the bottom. Here it is acted on by bacteria which convert it to methyl mercury. This is soluble and taken up by fish; since it is not metabolized, the mercury accumulates in the organs and flesh of the fish. The fish is caught and eaten by a man and the mercury becomes deposited in his organs, where it might be harmful. And so on.

This is an effective way to trace out an ecological path. It is also an excellent way to counteract the prevalent notion that something which is regarded as useless simply "goes away" when it is discarded. Nothing "goes away"; it is simply transferred from place to place, converted from one molecular form to another, acting on the life processes of any organism in which it becomes, for a time, lodged. One of the chief reasons for the present environmental crisis is that great amounts of materials have been extracted from the earth, converted into new forms, and discharged into the environment without taking into account that "everything has to go somewhere." The result, too often, is the accumulation of harmful amounts of material in places where, in nature, they do not belong.

The Third Law of Ecology: Nature Knows Best

In my experience this principle is likely to encounter considerable resistance, for it appears to contradict a deeply held idea about the unique competence of human beings. One of the most pervasive features of modern technology is the notion that it is intended to "improve on nature"—to provide food, clothing, shelter, and means of communication and expression which are superior to those available to man in nature. Stated baldly, the third law of ecology holds that any major man-made change in a natural system is likely to be *detrimental* to that system. This is a rather extreme claim; nevertheless I believe it has a good deal of merit if understood in a properly defined context.

I have found it useful to explain this principle by means of an analogy. Suppose you were to open the back of your watch, close your eyes, and poke a pencil into the exposed works. The almost certain result would be damage to the watch. Nevertheless, this result is not *absolutely* certain. There is some finite possibility that the watch was out of adjustment and that the random thrust of the pencil happened to make the precise change needed to improve it. However, this outcome is exceedingly improbable. The question at issue is: why? The answer is self-evident: there is a very considerable amount of what technologists now call "research and development" (or, more familiarly, "R & D") behind the watch. This means that over the years numerous watchmakers, each taught by a predecessor, have tried out a huge variety of detailed arrangements of watch works, have discarded those that are not compatible with the over-all operation of the system and retained the better features. In effect, the watch mechanism, as it now exists, represents a very restricted selection, from among an enormous variety of possible arrangements of component parts, of a singular organization of the watch works. Any random change made in the watch is likely to fall into the very large class of inconsistent, or harmful, arrangements which have been tried out in past watch-making experience and discarded. One might say, as a law of watches, that "the watchmaker knows best."

There is a close, and very meaningful, analogy in biological systems. It is possible to induce a certain range of random, inherited changes in a living thing by treating it with an agent, such as x-irradiation, that increases the frequency of mutations. Generally, exposure to x-rays increases the frequency of all mutations which have been observed, albeit very infrequently, in nature and can therefore be regarded as *possible* changes. What is significant, for our purpose, is the universal observation that when mutation frequency is enhanced by x-rays or other means, nearly all the mutations are harmful to the organisms and the great majority so damaging as to kill the organism before it is fully formed.

In other words, like the watch, a living organism that is forced to sustain a random change in its organization is almost certain to be damaged rather than improved. And in both cases, the explanation is the same—a great deal of "R & D." In effect there are some two to three billion years of "R & D" behind every living thing. In that time, a staggering number of new individual living things have been produced, affording in each case the opportunity to try out the suitability of some random genetic change. If the change damages the viability of the organism, it is likely to kill it before the change can be passed on to future generations. In this way, living things accumulate a complex organization of compatible parts, those possible arrangements that are not compatible with the whole are screened out over the long course of evolution. Thus, the structure of a present living thing or the organization of a current natural ecosystem is likely to be "best" in the sense that it has been so heavily screened for disadvantageous components that any new one is very likely to be worse than the present ones.

This principle is particularly relevant to the field of organic chemistry. Living things are composed of many thousands of different organic compounds, and it is sometimes imagined that at least some of these might be improved upon if they were replaced by some man-made variant of the natural substance. The third law of ecology suggests that the artificial introduction of an organic compound that does not occur in nature, but is man-made and is nevertheless active in a living system, is very likely to be harmful.

This is due to the fact that the varieties of chemical substances actually found in living things are vastly more restricted than the *possible* varieties. A striking illustration is that if one molecule each of all the possible types of proteins were made, they would together weigh more than the observable universe. Obviously there are a fantastically large number of protein types that are *not* made by living cells. And on the basis of the foregoing, one would reason that many of these possible protein types were once formed in some particular living things, found to be harmful, and rejected through the death of the experiment. In the same way, living cells synthesize fatty acids (a type of organic molecule that contains carbon chains of various lengths) with even-numbered carbon chain lengths (i.e., 4, 6, 8, etc., carbons), but no fatty acids with odd-numbered carbon chain lengths. This suggests that the latter have once been tried out and found wanting. Similarly, organic compounds that contain attached nitrogen and oxygen atoms are singularly rare in living things. This should warn us that the artificial introduction of substances of this type would be dangerous. This is indeed the case, for such substances are usually toxic and frequently carcinogenic. And, I would suppose from the fact that DDT is nowhere found in nature, that somewhere, at some time in the past, some unfortunate cell synthesized this molecule—and died.

One of the striking facts about the chemistry of living systems is that for every organic substance produced by a living organism, there exists, somewhere in nature, an enzyme capable of breaking that substance down. In effect, no organic substance is synthesized unless there is provision for its degradation; recycling is thus enforced. Thus, when a new man-made organic substance is synthesized with a molecular structure that departs significantly from the types which occur in nature, it is probable that no degradative enzyme exists, and the material tends to accumulate.

Given these considerations, it would be prudent, I believe, to regard every man-made organic chemical *not* found in nature which has a strong action on any one organism as potentially dangerous to other forms of life. Operationally, this view means that all man-made organic compounds that are at all active biologically ought to be treated as we do drugs, or rather as we *should* treat them—prudently, cautiously. Such caution or prudence is, of course, impossible when billions of pounds of the substance are produced and broadly disseminated into the ecosystem where it can reach and affect numerous organisms not under our observation, Yet this is precisely what we have done with detergents, insecticides, and herbicides. The often catastrophic results lend considerable force to the view that "Nature knows best."

The Fourth Law of Ecology: There Is No Such Thing as a Free Lunch

In my experience, this idea has proven so illuminating for environmental problems that I have borrowed it from its original source, economics. The "law" derives from a story that economists like to tell about an oil-rich potentate who decided that his new wealth needed the guidance of economic science. Accordingly he ordered his advisers, on pain of death, to produce a set of volumes containing all the wisdom of economics. When the tomes arrived, the potentate was impatient and again issued an order—to reduce all the knowledge of economics to a single volume. The story goes on in this vein, as such stories will, until the advisers are required, if they are to survive, to reduce the totality of economic science to a single sentence. This is the origin of the "free lunch" law.

In ecology, as in economics, the law is intended to warn that every gain is won at some cost. In a way, this ecological law embodies the previous three laws. Because the global ecosystem is a connected whole, in which nothing can be gained or lost and which is not subject to over-all improvement, anything extracted from it by human effort must be replaced, Payment of this price cannot be avoided; it can only be delayed. The present environmental crisis is a warning that we have delayed nearly too long.

The preceding pages provide a view of the web of life on the earth. An effort has been made to develop this view from available facts, through logical relations, into a set of comprehensive generalizations. In other words, the effort has been scientific.

Nevertheless, it is difficult to ignore the embarrassing fact that the final generalizations which emerge from all this—the four laws of ecology—are ideas that have been widely held by many people without any scientific analysis or professional authorization. The complex web in which all life is enmeshed, and man's place in it, are clearly—and beautifully—described in the poems of Walt Whitman. A great deal about the interplay of the physical features of the environment and the creatures that inhabit it can be learned from *Moby Dick*, Mark Twain is not only a marvelous source of wisdom about the nature of the environment of the United States from the Mississippi westward, but also a rather incisive critic of the irrelevance of science which loses connection to the realities of life. As the critic Leo Marx reminds us, "Anyone familiar with the work of the classic American writers (I am thinking of men like Cooper, Emerson, Thoreau, Melville, Whitman, and Mark Twain) is likely to have developed an interest in what we recently have learned to call ecology."

Unfortunately, this literary heritage has not been enough to save us from ecological disaster. After all, every American technician, industrialist, agriculturalist, or public official who has condoned or participated in the assault on the environment has read at least some of Cooper, Emerson, Thoreau, Melville, Whitman, and Mark Twain. Many of them are campers, bird-watchers, or avid fishermen, and therefore to some degree personally aware of the natural processes that the science of ecology hopes to elucidate. Nevertheless, most of them were taken unawares by the environmental crisis, failing to understand, apparently, that Thoreau's woods, Mark Twain's rivers, and Melville's oceans are *today* under attack.

The rising miasma of pollution has helped us to achieve this understanding. For, in Leo Marx's words, "The current environmental crisis has in a sense put a literal, factual, often quantifiable base under this poetic idea [i.e., the need for human harmony with nature]." This is perhaps the major value of the effort to show that the simple generalizations which have already emerged from perceptive human contact with the natural world have a valid base in the facts and principles of a science, ecology. Thus linked to science, these ideas become tools for restoring the damage inflicted on nature by the environmental crisis.

In the woods around Walden Pond or on the beaches of the Mississippi, most of the information needed to understand the natural world can be gained by personal experience. In the world of nuclear bombs, smog, and foul water, environmental understanding needs help from the scientist.

Ben B. Seligman

"Man, Work, and the Automated Feast,"
from *Commentary* (1962)

Automation is said to have ancient beginnings. To be sure, the technology from which it goes back several centuries, at least. Automatic devices in the middle 18th century included a mechanical loom for the manufacture of figured silks; James Watt's steam engine utilized a fly-ball governor which controlled the speed at which his contrivance operated; and it has been suggested that automation's basic concept—the linkage of machines—is evident in the detachable harpoon head of the Eskimo. Yet to assert that automation is simply the latest link in a great chain of industrial history obscures what is patently a new phenomenon. In the old days, industrial change developed through fission: division of labor was the key to progress and work was made available to a huge pool of unskilled persons who in the main had been forced to migrate from farm to city. Today, it is precisely these unskilled, together with semi-skilled and even some of management's people, who are displaced and poured back into the pool. Furthermore, automation represents a marked acceleration of change with so cumulative a force that this alone spells a profound difference from what went on before.

Automation is already moving with a rapidity that threatens to tear apart existing social and organizational structures; according to some observers, it will even alter the habits of thought that men have up to now prided themselves on. Such a prospect is perhaps not surprising when we consider the cataclysmic results of the 18th century's Industrial Revolution: the changes then were so swift as to constitute a whole new phenomenon. And Marx and Weber and Sombart had shown convincingly how human and social transformation accompanied technological transformation.

Now, new industrial functions, new economic forms, new work habits, and new social headaches are being created in ways that signify a kind of dialectic leap. Even John Diebold, who claims to have invented the word "automation" and whose ebullient advocacy of computer technology has done much to spread the gospel, confesses: "I believe that [automation] marks a break with past trends, a qualitative departure from the more conventional advance of technology that began with jagged pieces of flint and progressed up to the steam engine."

Why is this so? Up to recent times, technology simply sought to substitute natural force for animal or human force. In the early days, primacy of place was given to windmills and waterfalls. Then came metallurgical discoveries; and the screw and the lathe made possible the machine, essentially a contrivance which man could watch in action. But man remained at the center of the whole business, essential to both operation and control, still more or less the maker and master of materials. With automation, man not only loses irrevocably his function as *homo faber*; he no longer even possesses the character of *animal laborans*. At best, he is a sometime supervisor of a flow process. Actual control is removed from him and given to an electronic contraption whose feedbacks and servomechanisms make it possible to produce goods and manipulate information in a continuous system, without human participation.

To realize what automation implies, we must examine the kinds of machines employed and see what they do to people and organizations. Essentially, today's scientific upheaval comprises four aspects: the conversion of industrial materials into a flow; the setting of uniform standards so that output can be treated as a flow; the utilization of electronic computers with build-in feedbacks to enable the exercise of automatic control; and the application of new energy sources to the whole process. Thus, raw materials, which represent the "input" of an industry, must be handled without human hands, as in a modern meat-packing plant. Production, at one time a series of discrete steps, is completely integrated by means of transfer machines. In some cases, computers tied to cams or templates can make the producing machine follow a predetermined pattern with greater accuracy and sharper tolerances than were dreamed possible in the heyday of the skilled machinist. Computers, into which all sort of complex information can be fed by "programmers," automatically correct errors. A wide range of goods is now produced in this startling manner—chemicals, automobiles, steel, glassware, electric bulbs, television sets, beverages, and drugs, to name a few. Factories are able to function 24 hours a day, 365 days a year, while manpower needs are reduced dramatically. And with the development of nuclear energy for industrial power, manufacturers no longer need to be near their source of raw materials; they can set up their plants closer to markets, or—if they are seeking to escape the union organizer—in the most isolated of places. Yet one industry necessarily must relate itself more intimately with the next; a scantless web envelops all the entrepreneurs and their works. . . .

The automobile industry illustrates how an integrated set of machines can function. There the engine production line, for example, consists of a series of drilling, boring, and milling operations connected by transfer machines which move the engine blocks from one point to the next. Tolerances are checked automatically; if something is awry, the whole line is stopped by an electronic device. Or one can see an automatic assembly machine put the components of a television set on a printed board and then solder them into place. These are repetitive operations and their economic justification stems from the replacement market. There is not much of a style factor here and such model changes as do occur can be handled with relative ease. Yet even where variation in the product is essential, as in machine tools, the operation still can be made automatic. . . .

The key here is feedback, the simplest case of which is the home thermostat turning a furnace on and off in order to maintain a constant room temperature. In essence, signals are sent from one part of the automated line to another, correcting errors, shifting power loads, or modifying the speed of the line. No human need adjust gauges or read thermometers or press buttons. Feedback or servomechanisms do a better control job than humans, especially when many elements are involved. Whereas the human eye can follow the motion of a gauge at about two cycles a second, a servomechanism does about 100 a second. Now, marry feedback to a computer and automation is complete. The computers, really giant adding machines and calculators, receive information from the gauges and thermometers, analyze the data, and then transmit new instructions to other gauges and instruments.

Computers, whose basic concept goes back to Blaise Pascal, were developed in their electronic form during World War II to help guns hit their targets more efficiently. There are two basic types—the analog and digital computer. The former is a kind of electronic slide rule able to apply higher mathematics to problems of rates of change in various flows. However fast it might have been, for the engineer, mathematician, and operations researcher it was not fast enough. So the digital computer was devised, a machine that employs the binary number system and consequently can only add and subtract. This is no impediment, for like an electronic abacus, the digital computer sends its impulses forward at an unbelievable speed, giving it a marked advantage over the analog machine.

Moreover, digital computers have "memory" drums in which data can be stored for future use. The electrical pulses in a digital computer last less than one-millionth of a second. Information can be extracted from the memory drum in about ten-millionths of a second. . . .

By now "Detroit" automation is quite well known. Automatic machines, linked by transfer equipment, move engine blocks through a complete manufacturing process, performing 530 precision cutting and drilling operations in 14 1/2 minutes as compared to 9 hours in a conventional plant. The Chrysler Corporation's recent breakthrough on computer "balancing" of assembly lines, essentially a "combinatorial" problem, now defines each job so rigidly that little liberties like a worker's taking a few minutes out for a smoke become serious impediments to the smooth flow of cars. An automated power plant in Louisiana saved $175,000 in fuel, $100,000 in maintenance, $1.5 million in eliminating delays and mishaps, and $500,000 in labor. A Jones & Laughlin sheet-plate mill turns out strip at the speed of 70 miles an hour with no labor other than the supervision of engineers. Punch-card systems in a reversing roughing mill modify ingot shapes, and the computer even "remembers" what to do when the forms have to be changed. Foundry work, traditionally a hand operation, is now being tied to the computer. In petroleum and chemicals, the story is almost ancient: as far back as 1949 catalytic cracking plants were turning out 41,000 barrels a day with instruments and only a few workers to watch gauges. In a Texaco refinery the computer controls 26 flow rates, 72 temperatures, 3 pressure levels, and 3 gas combinations. General Electric uses segmented "automation," that is, batch production, for motors of varying models up to 30 horsepower. Ribbon machines make 800 electric bulb blanks a minute, running without end, and requiring only one worker who stands by to make an occasional adjustment. . . .

In retailing, automation starts with inventory and accounting records. Sales data are transmitted to control centers where billing, inventory, and credit information is stored. Bad credit risks are automatically checked and information returned to the sales clerk before the package can be wrapped. Sylvania and IBM have been working on automatic check-out counters for supermarkets—the number of cash registers would be reduced, as well as the number of workers. Ferris wheels, conveyor belts, chutes, and slides, all controlled by electronic computers, deliver garments from receiving platforms to stockrooms and even return the merchandise to the ground floor if necessary. Eventually we will pay our traffic penalties to a computer: in Illinois, records of driver violations are stored in a computer and the fines calculated by machine.

This, then, is the automated feast. Tasks are accomplished with unimaginable speed. Decisions are made by coded instructions and errors quickly detected. Facts are stored and extracted from memory drums. The machines learn and "perceive": they analyze stock market conditions; establish rocket flight patterns before the shot is fired into space; write television scripts that compare favorably with what is now available; compose music; translate; and play games. They combine high technical competence with just enough of an I. Q. to keep them tractable. They do precisely the kind of work to which junior executives and semi-skilled employees are usually assigned. . . .

Between 1953 and 1960, a million and a half jobs disappeared. In one plant, studied by Floyd Mann of Michigan State University, automation reduced the work force by half. In the electrical industry, output increased 21 per cent between 1953 and 1961, while employment declined 10 percent. There was a loss of 80,000 production jobs in steel during the decade of the 50's. In the shift from aircraft to missiles, 200,000 jobs went down the technological drain. For the 5-year period 1955–1960, production workers in automobile factories were down 21 percent. All this displacement occurred in an affluent society that itself went through four postwar recessions each of which left behind an increasingly hard-core residue of unemployment—3 percent in 1951–53; 4 percent in 1955–57; and 5 percent in 1959–60.

Full employment for the next 10 years means creating 12 million new jobs—25,000 a week, or almost double the number of new openings in the 1947–57 decade. Extending the period to 1961, we find that output rose 65 percent while the number of production and maintenance jobs declined. True, white collar workers increased 7 percent, but now automation is making them just as insecure. If we assume that demand in the 60's will expand at the same rate as it did in 1947–57, then output by 1970 may very well be 50 percent greater. However, if the present rate of productivity is maintained, then the number of required man-hours will have increased by 12 percent, providing only 75 million jobs at the end of the decade. Thus, about 8 million persons, 10 percent of the labor force, will have no work. And this is a moderate forecast, for should the secular growth rate fall below 3 percent per annum, as is conceivable, output will have gone up about 40 percent. Add to this the effects of automation, and the job increase by 1970 may be only 2 million, leaving a residue of perhaps 10 million persons without jobs. . . .

What is the solution? Frankly, there is none, at least none of a definitive character. The numerous suggestions for dealing with the pressing problems that stem from automation are all piecemeal, pecking at a spot here and a point there. No amount of federal fiscal tinkering will meet the immediate needs of those who are attached to a dying industry. Economic growth, while essential, will not of itself put to work again the idle coal miner, exmachinist, and troubled bookkeeper whose jobs have vanished like the first atom bomb tower. Administration economists believe that automated unemployment can be solved by turning on ordinary Keynesian tap valves: it's all a matter of failing effective demand, they assert. There seems little awareness in important circles that the American economy is undergoing deep-rooted and subtle structural changes and that it will take massive economic and social therapy to assuage the hurt. . . .

. . . One comes back to an immediate step, which though not by any means a "solution," nevertheless offers a practicable way for mitigating some of the effects of automation—the shorter work week. Mere mention of this is apt to send a shudder down the backs of administration economists and devotees of the conventional wisdom. Expressing their horror at the thought that man should have even more leisure than he now enjoys, the latter urge that a shorter work week means less production and higher costs. And in the present context of growthmanship, this is unthinkable. Arthur Goldberg, whose grasp of legal subtleties contrasts sharply with his simplistic formulations of economic issues, warned the International Ladies' Garment Workers' Union recently that fewer hours per week would ". . . impair adversely our present stable price structure [and] make our goods less competitive both at home and abroad. . . ." The enormous productive capacity of America's industry was conveniently forgotten, a capacity so enhanced by automation that it can more than compensate for the alleged loss of output. And this is to say nothing about the quality and content of contemporary "production"—that would require another essay. The point to observe now is the curious inner tension of an industrial system whose fundamental Puritan outlook demands an incessant, unremitting outpouring of goods (for what?) while at the same time it imposes dreary idleness and dismal futures on those to whom the cornucopia is directed. We may well ask, what is the feedback in this insane circle?

But to return to the shorter work week—a cursory review of its history would demonstrate how completely reasonable it is. Prior to 1860, the rule was dawn to dusk with as much as 72 hours as the weekly standard. Demands for a shorter span were met with the contention that 12 hours a day, 6 days a week had been divinely ordained in order to strengthen worker morality. Three decades later the work week had been shortened by 12 hours. In 1910, the average ranged from 51 to 55 hours, and at that time a work force of 34 million produced a Gross National Product of about $37 billion. The work week continued to shrink: in 1920, it was 48 hours; in 1929, 44 hours; and since 1946, 40 hours. By 1955, the labor force had almost doubled while GNP increased 10-fold as compared to 1910. And all the time the work week kept declining, about 13 hours in a 45-year span, or roughly 15 minutes a year.

Was anyone hurt? Did productivity lag? Has technology been impeded? The depression years aside, whatever unemployment did occur would have been unquestionably greater without the steady drop in hours. A continuation of this secular decline would cut back the normal work week by one hour every four years. According to one estimate, this might create about a million jobs a year which, together with the normal increase in job openings, could really begin to cut into the displacement caused by automation. When Harry van Arsdale of the New York electricians' union obtained a 5-hour day, he was savagely flayed for selfishness and lack of patriotism. Even the labor movement felt embarrassed. Arsdale insisted that he was only seeking to "spread the work." Now it seems, according to Theodore Kheel, the industry's arbitrator, that well over 1,000 new jobs will be made available as a result of the union's action. . . .

It is of course a common cliché that scientific advances have outrun our capacity to deal with them. Technology, the practical and material basis of life, has acquired a tidal force of its own which threatens to inundate human thought. Moreover, modern technology, as evidenced by automation, manifests no orderly growth. Its leads and lags, its uneven development, create new power centers that result in unaccustomed strains. To be sure, this has happened before, but always at immense human cost. It is this that the high priests of automation fail to grasp, while those of us who are merely by-standers can only hope that society will eventually catch up with the engineers and scientists and archons of industry who see only a handsome profit in what the machine can do.

Marilyn Young

from *The Vietnam Wars, 1945–1990* (1991)

History is a source of strength for us.
—PHAM HUY THONG TO AN AMERICAN STUDENT,
HANOI, JANUARY 1973

. . . we have always been people who dropped the past and then could not remember where it had been put.
—GLORIA EMERSON, *Winners and Losers* (1976)

Many of us have some of the war still inside us. This creates difficulties in lives.
—LE LUU, VIETNAMESE VETERAN AND NOVELIST

Over 26 million American men came of draft age during the Vietnam War; 2.15 million of them went to Vietnam, 1.6 million were in combat. Those who fought the war and died in it were disproportionately poor, badly educated, and black. (A high school dropout who enlisted had a 70 percent chance of being sent to Vietnam, a college graduate only 42 percent; until 1971, student deferments protected the majority of students from the draft altogether.) It was also a teen-aged army—over 60 percent of those who died in Vietnam were between the ages of seventeen and twenty-one, and the average age of those who served was nineteen, five to seven years younger than in other American wars.

Between 1966 and 1972, a special Great Society program—Project 100,000—scooped up over 300,000 young men previously considered ineligible for the military because of their low test scores. Project 100,000, Secretary of Defense Robert McNamara declared, was the "world's largest education of skilled men." With lower admissions scores, the "subterranean poor" would have an opportunity to serve their country in Vietnam; simultaneously, the program had the advantage of avoiding the politically unpleasant alternative of requiring students or reservists to do the same. The benefits, especially to young black men, were said to be especially striking. As Daniel Patrick Moynihan pointed out, the military was "an utterly masculine world. Given the strains of disordered and matrifocal family life in which so many Negro youth come of age, the armed forces are a dramatic and desperately needed change, a world away from women, a world run by strong men and unquestioned authority, where discipline, if harsh, is nonetheless orderly and predictable, and where rewards, if limited, are granted on the basis of performance." In its first two years of operation, 41 percent of those brought into the military through Project 100,000 were black, 80 percent had dropped out of high school, 40 percent could read at less than sixth-grade level, and 37 percent were put directly into combat. Court-martialed at double the usual rate, over eighty thousand of these veterans left the military without the skills and opportunities McNamara assured them would be theirs, and many of them with service records that would make civilian life far more difficult than if they had never served at all.

Each young man who went to war had an individual tour of duty, 365 days, and then home, on his own, with no effort on anyone's part to prepare for the shock of return, to help make the transition from war to peace, from the privileging of violence to its prohibition, from the sharp edge death brings to the life of a soldier to the ordinary daily life of a civilian, which denies death altogether. They had spoken always of coming back "to the world," counting each day "in country" which brought them closer to the end of their tour. But the homecoming was harder than any of them had expected. Later, many veterans would tell stories of having been spat upon by anti-war protesters, or having heard of veterans who were spat on. It doesn't matter how often this happened or whether it happened at all. Veterans *felt* spat upon, stigmatized, contaminated. In television dramas, veterans were not heroes welcomed back into the bosom of loving families, admiring neighborhoods, and the arms of girls who loved uniforms; they were psychotic killers, crazies with automatic weapons. It was as if the country assumed that anyone coming back from Vietnam would, even should, feel a murderous rage against the society that had sent him there. The actual veteran—tired, confused, jet-propelled from combat to domestic airport—disappeared. Or rather, he became a kind of living hologram, an image projected by conflicting interpretations of the war: a victim or an executioner, a soldier who had lost a war, a killer who should never have fought it at all.

Of course there were also just the daily bread-and-butter problems of finding work in an economy far less open than it had been when the war was young. Today, from one quarter to one third of the homeless (between one quarter and three quarters of a million men) are Vietnam-era veterans. Without training or skills, without any public sense that the country owed them anything at all, many Vietnam veterans found themselves not only unrewarded but even disadvantaged by their service records. The war had begun to unravel even as it was being fought, so that by 1971 dissent and disobedience within the armed forces were endemic. The result was a tremendous increase in the number of less than honorable discharges—"bad paper"—which have followed the 500,000 to 750,000 men who received them ever since, making it difficult for them to get and keep jobs, and depriving them of educational and even medical benefits.

The lack of skills, the bad service records, the war wounds, have been only part of the difficulty many veterans face. At first, the widespread appearance of psychological problems was named "postwar trauma" and assimilated to the literature on the problems of veterans of other wars. It soon became clear, however, that Vietnam veterans were not like veterans of other wars. As early as 1970, Vietnam Veterans Against the War organized "rap sessions," sometimes attended by sympathetic psychiatrists, to help returning soldiers deal with their experiences. Even the Veterans Administration, obviously reluctant to single out Vietnam veterans as having any particular difficulties (especially in the light of the meager benefits accorded them), reported a "greater distrust of institutions" and a "bitterness, disgust and suspicion of those in positions of authority and responsibility."

More disturbing was the persistence—or sudden onset ten or even fifteen years after the war—of symptoms of acute distress, accompanied by flashbacks, severe sleep problems, depression, and rage. "Postwar trauma" was renamed "post-traumatic stress disorder" and assimilated not to battle fatigue or shell shock but to what people experience as survivors of floods or earthquakes. A V.A. doctor estimates that as many as 700,000 veterans suffer from some form of "post-traumatic stress disorder" (or PTSD). A massive study of Vietnam-era veterans revealed that those who had been "exposed to significant amounts of combat and/or witnessed or were participants in abusive violence [against prisoners, civilians, etc.] demonstrate long term problems" with disabling memories of the war.

Veterans of other American wars, Robert Jay Lifton argued in his book *Home from the War,* had come to terms with the absurdity and evil of war by believing that *their* war "had purpose and significance beyond the immediate horrors [they] witnessed." But "the central fact of the Vietnam War," Lifton wrote in 1973 while it was still going on, "is that no one really believes in it." Although it is possible to challenge Lifton and demonstrate that soldiers in World War II also had difficulty discerning significance beyond the immediate horror of their situation, it is nevertheless true that when they got home, the purpose and significance of what they had done was universally affirmed and most were able to accept it. This was not the situation of Vietnam veterans, for even those who came home to families or communities who approved of the war were aware of those who protested against it. Moreover, the announced goals of the war—to repel an outside invader, to give the people of South Vietnam the chance to choose their own government—were daily contradicted by the soldier's sense that in fact he was himself the invader, and that "the government he had come to defend [was] hated by the people and that he [was] hated most of all."

"What kind of war is it?" Larry Rottman, poet and veteran, asked in a poem written during the war,

> when you can be pinned down
> all day in a muddy rice paddy
> while your buddies are being shot
> and a close-support Phantom jet
> who has been napalming the enemy
> wraps itself around a tree and explodes
> and you cheer inside.

"To have been in a war does not mean you understand the memories of it," Gloria Emerson has written. In published and unpublished novels, memoirs, poems, Vietnam veterans have tried to understand their memories.

For women veterans the problem was compounded by the initial inability of anyone, including themselves, to acknowledge that they too were combat veterans. No one seems to have kept close count of their numbers. The Department of Defense says 7,500 women were on active military service in Vietnam during the war; the Veterans Administration lists 11,000 women as having served there. Together with civilians working for the Red Cross or other voluntary services, the general estimate is that a total of between 33,000 and 55,000 women worked in Vietnam during the war. Like the young men who fought the war, the young women who nursed their wounds, or tried to "take their minds off the war," were confused, often defensive, almost always pained by their memories. "Our job was to look them [wounded soldiers] in the eye and convince them that everything was all right." It took practice, but "you finally built up a facade and could literally look at somebody dying and smile like Miss America or whatever we personified to them." The war gave many women responsibilities and a sense of power usually denied them in civilian life. But this new status too was confusing and even distressing in that there was no way to extricate it from the death and dehumanization that were its occasion. One nurse resisted having to treat wounded Vietnamese until one day she was forced to take care of an infant and broke down: "How, I wondered, could I ever come to believe I hated a baby?"

Lynda Van Devanter tried to join a VVAW demonstration when she returned from Vietnam, but was told, "This demonstration is only for vets." "I am a vet," she explained. "I was in Pleiku and Qui Nhon. . . ." "I . . . don't think you're supposed to march," came the answer. "But you told me it was for vets." "It is. . . . But you're not a vet."

In 1982, the Veterans Administration acknowledged that women were truly Vietnam vets: for the first time groups were established for women suffering from post-traumatic stress disorder. "She is afraid to trust again," Marilyn McMahon says in her poem "Wounds of War":

> Her days are haunted
>   by the texture of blood
>   the odor of burns
>   the face of senseless death;
> friends known and loved
>   vanished
>   abandoned.
> She sits alone in the darkened room
>   scotch her only hope.

"The war is never over," one homeless man explained to a reporter in 1987. "You drink one too many beers and it pops up. . . . Sometimes, I hope to settle down somewhere where I won't be reminded of what I've seen. But I really don't see a future for myself." Being unable to imagine a future often precludes having one. More veterans have committed suicide since the war than died in it—at least sixty thousand. Nor is the connection between their war experience and their death at all obscure. Steven L. Anderson's parents, for example, found this note next to the body of their dead son: "When I was in Vietnam, we came across a North Vietnamese soldier with a man, a woman and a three- or four-year-old girl. We had to shoot them all. I can't get the little girl's face out of my mind. I hope that God will forgive me."

In May 1971, Medal of Honor winner Dwight W. Johnson was shot dead by the owner of a store he was attempting to rob. In Vietnam, Johnson killed "five to 20 enemy soldiers, nobody knows for sure," when the tank crew he was trying to rescue blew up in front of his eyes. "When he ran out of ammunition," his obituary continues, "he killed one with the stock of his machine gun." Unskilled and jobless in Detroit, Skip Johnson's fortunes turned when he was awarded the Medal of Honor for his heroism that day. Civic notables showered him with gifts and the Army persuaded him to return to the service as a recruiter in Detroit's predominantly black high schools. But his wife noticed some changes in him, as she had in other veterans she knew: "They get quiet. It's like they don't have too much to say about what it was like over there. Maybe it's because they've killed people and they don't really know why they've killed them."

Eventually Skip Johnson went AWOL from his recruiter's job and ended up in Valley Forge VA Hospital, where the head psychiatrist reached a preliminary diagnosis: "Depression caused by post-Vietnam adjustment problem." Later, the doctor observed Johnson's guilt over having survived the tank ambush and over "winning a high honor for the one time in his life when he lost complete control of himself. He asked: 'What would happen if I lost control of myself in Detroit and behaved like I did in Vietnam?' The prospect of such an event apparently was deeply disturbing to him." The psychiatrist refrained from answering Johnson's question; but a store manager in the western end of Detroit was more forthcoming: "'I first hit him with two bullets,' the manager . . . said later. 'But he just stood there, with the gun in his hand, and said, "I'm going to kill you. . . ."' 'I kept pulling the trigger until my gun was empty.'"

Johnson's mother, thinking about her son's life and death after he was buried at Arlington National Cemetery with full military honors, wondered whether he had simply "tired of this life and needed someone else to pull the trigger."

And many of those who have not tired of their lives, nor suffered from "post-traumatic stress disorder," who have homes, jobs, families, ambitions, nevertheless find the war somehow remains central to their lives. George Swiers tried to explain this at a conference called "Vietnam Reconsidered: Lessons from a War," which was held in Los Angeles in 1983. In 1970 he had flown direct from the battlefield to San Francisco airport, a survivor of an "honest-to-god magical mystery tour."

> And so, with a bravado inspired by two hours' worth of drugs and alcohol, and his uniform disheveled beyond embarrassment, he set out to speak to his Fellow Americans. To share with them his hideous secrets, to tell them what went on daily in their names.

No one listened; no one would engage his eyes. When Swiers completely lost control, a security officer gently led him away, advising him to "have a drink, you'll feel better."

> This week, exactly thirteen years have passed since I was last in California. I return to a place [the conference] where Vietnam is all that is spoken of. And there is some measure of comfort in that. But if I have learned anything in these thirteen years, it is this: I'm not supposed to feel better.

"My friend Patrick Finnegan," Swiers went on,

> a fellow activist and former grunt, often marvels at the government's willingness to permit any Vietnam veteran reaccess to America. For we brought with us the awful, suffocating truth of the war: that lies, though they be cleverly camouflaged, neatly packed and endorsed by presidents are still lies. And that no lie checked out in a military press release could bury deep enough the death, dishonor, and defecation that was Vietnam.

For thousands of soldiers exposed to Agent Orange, Vietnam is a daily scourge, suffered in migraines, ulcerated skin rashes, liver problems, cancer. Worse, they find themselves passing on the horrors of Vietnam to another generation. "When I came home," one veteran tried to explain to a student interviewing him for a class project,

> I hated that I had anything to do with the war. But I knew that it was over. I got my life together and went on with it. I had a few nightmares, but it was a lot less than some of my friends had. I got married, had Billy and Johnny and I was doing well. . . . Then Billy grew up and that GOD DAMN pesticide shit they dropped on us came back to haunt me and my kid. He has five Mother Fuckin scars on his body from cancer. . . . My own government that I was fighting a war for is making my son suffer for their mistakes, and I have to live with the guilt, not them!! . . . I don't want to talk about this anymore.

"This is the first war that reached into our maternity wards," Tom Valelly, a veteran and Massachusetts state representative told Myra MacPherson. "The Vietnam experience does not belong to the past. The warfare we saw in Vietnam is the warfare of the future. Vietnam was a *laboratory*. Our own men were the guinea pigs." But then, as visitors to the main Saigon maternity hospital report, so were the hundreds of thousands of Vietnamese exposed to a decade of spraying. . . .

William Ehrhart returned to Vietnam in 1985, as many veterans have begun to do recently, perhaps to find an answer to a poem he wrote during the war.

> Do they think of me now
> in those strange Asian villages
> where nothing ever seemed
> quite human
> but myself
> and my few grim friends

> moving through them
> hunched in lines?
>
> When they tell stories to their children
> of the evil
> that awaits misbehavior,
> is it me they conjure?

A Vietnamese poet, after listening to Ehrhart's poem, offered one of his own:

> When there are no more bombs,
> Shall you let me go up on earth again?
> Why do you keep asking, little one . . .
> I want to see the uncles and aunts I loved,
> Are they still fighting, Mama?
> I want to see the Yankee,
> Mama, does it look like a human being?

Meeting the man against whose troops he had fought seventeen years earlier, Ehrhart, rather disarmingly, asked the Vietnamese general what he had thought of the Americans, as fighters, as warriors. "You were—brave," the general answered. Pressed for a more specific answer, the general lists American errors: fixed positions, dependency on air support; ignorance of the land. "Would it have mattered if we had done things differently?" Ehrhart asked. "'No,' he replies after a pause. 'Probably not. History was not on your side. We were fighting for our homeland. What were you fighting for?'" Remembering himself at seventeen, the "inflexible certainty of my decision, and the terrible collective ignorance of the small town that buried half a dozen of my high school classmates," Ehrhart answers, "'Nothing that really mattered.'"

After the Korean War, the poet Thomas McGrath memorialized the American war dead—"brave: ignorant: amazed: Dead in the rice paddies, dead on the nameless hills." In November 1982, the brave, ignorant, amazed dead of Vietnam were remembered at the dedication of a Vietnam Veterans Memorial. Money for the memorial had been raised by the veterans themselves; the winning design, by Maya Ying Lin, provided for two black granite walls bearing the names of the Americans who died in Vietnam. There was a protest by those who deemed the design insufficiently patriotic, and so a life-size statue of three GIs, two white, one black, was added to the original conception. Maya Ying Lin protested that it was like "drawing a moustache" on her design, but in the event, the statues have a different impact, as unpredictable as that of the wall itself.

Unlike the commemoration of the flag raising at Iwo Jima, these soldiers are flagless and exhausted. They seem to be waiting for something, but the only thing visible in the direction in which they look are the giant slabs with the names of their dead comrades. At first Bruce Weigl wondered why he had come to the dedication ceremony in Washington on Veterans Day, 1982. "I think we came," he wrote later,

> without really knowing it, to make the memorial our wailing wall. We came to find the names of those we lost in the war, as if by tracing the letters cut into the granite we could find what was left of ourselves. It turns out that, beyond all the petty debates over the monument, no veteran could turn his back on the terrible grace of Maya Lin's wall and the names of the 57,939 who died or disappeared in Vietnam from July 1959 to May 1975: America's longest most vicious sin.

What militarists deplore as the Vietnam syndrome can better be understood as a relatively unique event in American history: an inability to forget, a resistance to the everyday workings of historical amnesia, despite the serious and coordinated efforts of the government and much of the press to "heal the wounds" of the war by encouraging such forgetting, or what comes to the same thing, firm instructions on *how* to remember. At the dedication of the Vietnam Memorial, President Reagan announced that the time had come to move on, "in unity and with resolve, with the resolve to always stand for freedom, as those who fought did, and to always try to protect and preserve the peace." Harry Haines, a Vietnam veteran, terms Reagan's call the "administrative version of Vietnam memory." According to Reagan, in Vietnam Americans stood for freedom "as Americans have always stood—*and still do.*" The Vietnam War, Haines observes, is thus "normalized, the deaths are made rational, and the veterans are whole once again, stronger for their expiated burden."

To Harry Haines, the design of the memorial is ambiguous, able to contain Weigl's meaning but also that of a veteran who shouted at a group that attempted to hold a vigil for peace at the memorial: "No, not here. . . . These people died fighting against communism and for freedom. Those people [the vigil group] have no right. It's the same thing that went on with Vietnam, saying we don't belong in El Salvador." How the memorial is interpreted is part of an *ongoing* political struggle. Its meaning, Haines insists, lies "not so much in how the dead are remembered by those of us who survived Vietnam at home or abroad, but in how that remembrance is used by power to explain—to justify—sacrifices in future Vietnams."

What distinguishes many Vietnam veterans from those who fought in other U.S. wars, Peter Marin has written, is their exceptional "moral seriousness," emerging from a "direct confrontation not only with the capacity of others for violence and brutality but also with their own culpability, their sense of their own capacity for error and excess." When a friend asked Marin, as those faced with the morally serious so often do, "Well, what is it [the veterans] really want?" Marin found himself answering spontaneously, "'Justice.' That is what they want, but it is not justice for themselves—though they would like that too. They simply want justice to *exist* for there to be justice in the world. . . ." Which is why, perhaps, Tim O'Brien insists that a "true war story is never moral. It does not instruct, nor encourage virtue, nor suggest models of proper human behavior. . . . If a story seems moral do not believe it. If at the end of a war story you feel uplifted, or if you feel that some small bit of rectitude has been salvaged from the larger waste, then you have been made the victim of a very old and terrible lie. There is no rectitude whatsoever. There is no virtue."

Michael Herr, a reporter who breathed the war in as deeply as any combat soldier, wrote that it "took the war to teach it, that you were as responsible for everything you saw as you were for everything you did. The problem was that you didn't always know what you were seeing until later, maybe years later, that a lot of it never made it in at all, it just stayed stored there in your eyes." Vietnam has remained stored in the eyes of America; very slowly it is becoming possible to know what we have seen. To figure out what it might mean, to accept responsibility for it, will take much longer.

Epilogue:
Meanings of "American Traditions"
at the Turn of the Twenty-first Century

The final readings in this book, all written within the last dozen years, offer different visions of what it means to be "American" today. The first, Ronald Reagan's "Farewell Address to the American People," reveals his political beliefs as well as his interpretation of American history. Reagan's life spans the twentieth century: born in 1911, he has lived through both world wars, and came to politics in the 1960s from a career as a movie actor. As president in the 1980s, Reagan led a conservative charge against the governmental expansion that had peaked under Lyndon Johnson. No less controversial than Johnson's Great Society, Reagan's "New Federalism" sought to cut taxes, increase American military strength, and balance the budget. Despite the three-trillion-dollar deficit these policies helped produce and various scandals within his administration, Reagan remained enormously popular with the American people. As he left office in 1989, he summarized his accomplishments in his folksy style—and traced his vision of the American past back to John Winthrop's sermon aboard the *Arbella* three and a half centuries before. The second selection, Kurt Andersen's 1994 article "Las Vegas, U.S.A." from *Time* magazine, describes the development of "postmodern" America: a nation whose economy increasingly relies on its service sector, rather than on the industrial production that defined "modern" America in the middle of the century; a nation whose entertainment industry is perhaps its most powerful export to a world that idolizes Michael Jordan and wears Nikes; a nation where images stand in for realities, much as going to a "theme park" can replace seeing the real thing; and a nation whose values seem to have changed since the 1950s, and certainly since John Winthrop's day. In short, a nation that looks more and more like Las Vegas.

The last selection suggests another definition of "America." Ishmael Reed ponders our "multinational society," in which it is difficult to label people or practices as exclusively part of one ethnic identity or another. His article raises anew the question of whether the United States is a "melting pot" or something else entirely. Like Reagan, Reed looks back to the Puritans, but with a different interpretation. In doing so, he provides a reminder of larger questions about "traditions": if, for instance, the Puritans helped to found "American traditions," which traditions were they? And which traditions provide the foundations of our society in a new century?

351

Ronald Reagan

from "Farewell Address to the American People" (1989)

My fellow Americans:

This is the 34th time I'll speak to you from the Oval Office and the last. We've been together 8 years now, and soon it'll be time for me to go. But before I do, I wanted to share some thoughts, some of which I've been saving for a long time.

It's been the honor of my life to be your President. So many of you have written the past few weeks to say thanks, but I could say as much to you. Nancy and I are grateful for the opportunity you gave us to serve.

One of the things about the Presidency is that you're always somewhat apart. You spend a lot of time going by too fast in a car someone else is driving, and seeing the people through tinted glass—the parents holding up a child, and the wave you saw too late and couldn't return. And so many times I wanted to stop and reach out from behind the glass, and connect. Well, maybe I can do a little of that tonight.

People ask how I feel about leaving. And the fact is, "parting is such sweet sorrow." The sweet part is California and the ranch and freedom. The sorrow—the goodbyes, of course, and leaving this beautiful place.

You know, down the hall and up the stairs from this office is the part of the White House where the President and his family live. There are a few favorite windows I have up there that I like to stand and look out of early in the morning. The view is over the grounds here to the Washington Monument, and then the Mall and the Jefferson Memorial. But on mornings when the humidity is low, you can see past the Jefferson to the river, the Potomac, and the Virginia shore. Someone said that's the view Lincoln had when he saw the smoke rising from the Battle of Bull Run. I see more prosaic things: the grass on the banks, the morning traffic as people make their way to work, now and then a sailboat on the river.

I've been thinking a bit at that window. I've been reflecting on what the past 8 years have meant and mean. And the image that comes to mind like a refrain is a nautical one—a small story about a big ship, and a refugee, and a sailor. It was back in the early eighties, at the height of the boat people. And the sailor was hard at work on the carrier *Midway*, which was patrolling the South China Sea. The sailor, like most American servicemen, was young, smart, and fiercely observant. The crew spied on the horizon a leaky little boat. And crammed inside were refugees from Indochina hoping to get to America. The *Midway* sent a small launch to bring them to the ship and safety. As the refugees made their way through the choppy seas, one spied the sailor on deck, and stood up, and called out to him. He yelled, "Hello, American sailor. Hello, freedom man."

A small moment with a big meaning, a moment the sailor, who wrote it in a letter, couldn't get out of his mind. And, when I saw it, neither could I. Because that's what it was to be an American in the 1980s. We stood, again, for freedom. I know we always have, but in the past few years the world again—and in a way, we ourselves—rediscovered it. . . .

When you've got to the point when you can celebrate the anniversaries of your 39th birthday you can sit back sometimes, review your life, and see it flowing before you. For me there was a fork in the river and it was right in the middle of my life. I never meant to go into politics. It wasn't my intention when I was young. But I was raised to believe you had to pay your way for the blessings bestowed on you. I was happy with my career in the entertainment world, but I ultimately went into politics because I wanted to protect something precious.

Ours was the first revolution in the history of mankind that truly reversed the course of government, and with three little words: "We the People." "We the People" tell the government what to do; it doesn't tell us. "We the People" are the driver, the government is the car. And we decide where it should go, and by what route, and how fast. Almost all the world's constitutions are documents in which governments tell the people what their privileges are. Our Constitution is a document in which "We the People" tell the government what it is allowed to do. "We the People" are free. This belief has been the underlying basis for everything I've tried to do these past 8 years.

But back in the 1960's, when I began, it seemed to me that we'd begun reversing the order of things—that through more and more rules and regulations and confiscatory taxes, the government was taking more of our money, more of our options, and more of our freedom. I went into politics in part to put up my hand and say, "Stop." I was a citizen politician, and it seemed the right thing for a citizen to do.

I think we have stopped a lot of what needed stopping. And I hope we have once again reminded people that man is not free unless government is limited. There's a clear cause and effect here that is as neat and predictable as a law of physics: As government expands, liberty contracts.

Nothing is less free than pure communism—and yet we have, the past few years, forged a satisfying new closeness with the Soviet Union. I've been asked if this isn't a gamble, and my answer is no because we're basing our actions not on words but deeds. The détente of the 1970's was based not on actions but promises. They'd promise to treat their own people and the people of the world better. But the *gulag* was still the *gulag,* and the state was still expansionist, and they still waged proxy wars in Africa, Asia, and Latin America.

Well, this time, so far, it's different. President Gorbachev has brought about some internal democratic reforms and begun the withdrawal from Afghanistan. He has also freed prisoners whose names I've given him every time we've met.

But life has a way of reminding you of big things through small incidents. Once, during the heady days of the Moscow summit, Nancy and I decided to break off from the entourage one afternoon to visit the shops on Arbat Street—that's a little street just off Moscow's main shopping area. Even though our visit was a surprise, every Russian there immediately recognized us and called out our names and reached for our hands. We were just about swept away by the warmth. You could almost feel the possibilities in all that joy. But within seconds, a KGB detail pushed their way toward us and began pushing and shoving the people in the crowd. It was an interesting moment. It reminded me that while the man on the street in the Soviet Union yearns for peace, the government is Communist. And those who run it are Communists, and that means we and they view such issues as freedom and human rights very differently.

We must keep up our guard, but we must also continue to work together to lessen and eliminate tension and mistrust. My view is that President Gorbachev is different from previous Soviet leaders. I think he knows some of the things wrong with his society and is trying to fix them. We wish him well. And we'll continue to work to make sure that the Soviet Union that eventually emerges from this process is a less threatening one. What it all boils down to is this: I want the new closeness to continue. And it will, as long as we make it clear that we will continue to act in a certain way as long as they continue to act in a helpful manner. If and when they don't, at first pull your punches. If they persist, pull the plug. It's still trust but verify. It's still play, but cut the cards. It's still watch closely. And don't be afraid to see what you see.

I've been asked if I have any regrets. Well, I do. The deficit is one. I've been talking a great deal about that lately, but tonight isn't for arguments, and I'm going to hold my tongue. But an obsevation: I've had my share of victories in the Congress, but what few people noticed is that I never won anything you didn't win for me. They never saw my troops, they never saw Reagan's regiments, the American people. You won every battle with every call you made and letter you wrote demanding action. Well, action is still needed. If we're to finish the job, Reagan's regiments will have to become the Bush brigades. Soon he'll be the chief, and he'll need you every bit as much as I did.

Finally, there is a great tradition of warnings in Presidential farewells, and I've got one that's been on my mind for some time. But oddly enough it starts with one of the things I'm proudest of in the past 8 years: the resurgence of national pride that I called the new patriotism. This national feeling is good, but it won't count for much, and it won't last unless it's grounded in thoughtfulness and knowledge.

An informed patriotism is what we want. And are we doing a good enough job teaching our children what America is and what she represents in the long history of the world? Those of us who are over 35 or so years of age grew up in a different America. We were taught, very directly, what it means to be an American. And we absorbed, almost in the air, a love of country and an appreciation of its institutions. If you didn't get these things from your family you got them from the neighborhood, from the father down the street who fought in Korea or the family who lost someone at Anzio. Or you could get a sense of patriotism from school. And if all else failed you could get a sense of patriotism from the popular culture. The movies celebrated democratic values and implicitly reinforced the idea that America was special. TV was like that, too, through the mid-sixties.

But now, we're about to enter the nineties, and some things have changed. Younger parents aren't sure that an unambivalent appreciation of America is the right thing to teach modern children. And as for those who create the popular culture, well-grounded patriotism is no longer the style. Our spirit is back, but we haven't reinstitutionalized it. We've got to do a better job of getting across that America is freedom—freedom of speech, freedom of religion, freedom of enterprise. And freedom is special and rare. It's fragile; it needs production [protection].

So, we've got to teach history based not on what's in fashion but what's important—why the Pilgrims came here, who Jimmy Doolittle was, and what those 30 seconds over Tokyo meant. You know, 4 years ago on the 40th anniversary of D-day, I read a letter from a young woman writing to her late father, who'd fought on Omaha Beach. Her name was Lisa Zanatta Henn, and she said, "we will always remember, we will never forget what the boys of Normandy did." Well, let's help her keep her word. If we forget what we did, we won't know who we are. I'm warning of an eradication of the American memory that could result, ultimately, in an erosion of the American spirit. Let's start with some basics: more attention to American history and a greater emphasis on civic ritual.

And let me offer lesson number one about America: All great change in America begins at the dinner table. So, tomorrow night in the kitchen I hope the talking begins. And children, if your parents haven't been teaching you what it means to be an American, let 'em know and nail 'em on it. That would be a very American thing to do.

And that's about all I have to say tonight except for one thing. The past few days when I've been at that window upstairs, I've thought a bit of the "shining city upon a hill." The phrase comes from John Winthrop, who wrote it to describe the America he imagined. What he imagined was important because he was an early Pilgrim, an early freedom man. He journeyed here on what today we'd call a little wooden boat and like the other Pilgrims, he was looking for a home that would be free.

I've spoken of the shining city all my political life, but I don't know if I ever quite communicated what I saw when I said it. But in my mind it was a tall, proud city built on rocks stronger than oceans, windswept, God-blessed, and teeming with people of all kinds living in harmony and peace; a city with free ports that hummed with commerce and creativity. And if there had to be city walls, the walls had doors and the doors were open to anyone with the will and the heart to get here. That's how I saw it, and see it still.

And how stands the city on this winter night? More prosperous, more secure, and happier than it was 8 years ago. But more than that: After 200 years, two centuries, she still stands strong and true on the granite ridge, and her glow has held steady no matter what storm. And she's still a beacon, still a magnet for all who must have freedom, for all the pilgrims from all the lost places who are hurtling through the darkness, toward home.

We've done our part. And as I walk off into the city streets, a final word to the men and women of the Reagan revolution, the men and women across America who for 8 years did the work that brought America back. My friends: We did it. We weren't just marking time. We made a difference. We made the city stronger, we made the city freer, and we left her in good hands. All in all, not bad, not bad at all.

And so, goodbye, God bless you, and God bless the United States of America.

KURT ANDERSEN

"Las Vegas, U.S.A.," from *Time Magazine* (1994)

How can a large-spirited American not like Las Vegas, or at least smile at the notion of it? On the other hand, how can any civilized person not loathe Las Vegas, or at least recoil at its relentlessness?

How can you not love and hate a city so crazily go-go that three different, colossally theme-park-like casino-hotels (the $375 million Luxor, Steve Wynn's $475 million Treasure Island and now the $1 billion MGM Grand, the largest hotel on earth and the venue last weekend for Barbra Streisand's multimillion-dollar return to live, paid performing) have opened on the Strip in just the past three months? How can you not love and hate a city so freakishly democratic that at a hotel called the Mirage, futuristic-looking infomercial star Susan Powter and a premodern Mennonite family can pass in a corridor, neither taking note of the other? How can you not love and hate a city where the $100,000 paintings for sale at an art gallery appended to Caesars Palace (Patron: "He's a genius." Gallery employee: "Yes, he's so creative." Patron: "It gives me goose bumps") are the work of Anthony Quinn?

In no other peacetime locale are the metaphors and ironies so impossibly juicy, so ripe for the plucking. And there are always new crops of redolent, suggestive Vegas facts, of which any several—for instance: the Mirage has a $500-a-pull slot-machine salon; the lung-cancer death rate here is the second highest in the country; the suicide rate and cellular-phone usage are the highest—constitute a vivid, up-to-date sketch of the place.

But it used to be that while Las Vegas was unfailingly piquant and over the top, it was sui generis, its own highly peculiar self. Vegas in none of its various phases (ersatz Old West outpost in the 1930s and '40s, gangsters-meet-Hollywood high-life oasis in the '50s and '60s, uncool polyester dump in the '70s and early '80s) was really an accurate prism through which to regard the nation as a whole.

Now, however, as the city ricochets through its biggest boom since the Frank-and-Dino Rat Pack days of the '50s and '60s the tourist inflow has nearly doubled over the past decade, and the area remains among America's fastest growing—the hypereclectic 24-hour-a-day fantasy-themed party machine no longer seems so very exotic or extreme. High-tech spectacle, convenience, classlessness, loose money, a Nikes-and-T-shirt dress code: that's why immigrants flock to the U.S.; that's why some 20 million Americans (and 2 million foreigners) went to Vegas in 1992. "Las Vegas exists because it is a perfect reflection of America," says Steve Wynn, the city's most important and interesting resident. "You say 'Las Vegas' in Osaka or Johannesburg, anywhere in the world, and people smile, they understand. It represents all the things people in every city in America like. Here they can get it in one gulp." There is a Jorge Luis Borges story called the Aleph that describes the magical point where all places are seen from every angle. Las Vegas has become that place in America, less because of its own transformation in the past decade than because of the transformation of the nation. Las Vegas has become Americanized, and, even more, America has become Las Vegasized.

With its ecologically pious displays of white tigers and dolphins—and no topless show girls—the almost tasteful Mirage has profoundly enlarged and updated the notion of Vegas amusement since it opened in 1989. The general Las Vegas marketing spin today is that the city is fun for the whole family. It seems to be an effective p.r. line, but it's an idea that the owners of the new Luxor and MGM Grand may have taken too much to heart.

Inside the Luxor is a fake river and barges, plus several huge "participatory adventure" areas, an ersatz archaeological ride, as well as a two-story Sega virtual-reality video-game arcade. The joint has acres of casino space—but the slots and blackjack tables are, astoundingly, quite separate from and mostly concealed by the Disneyesque fun and games. The bells and whistles are more prominent and accessible than the casino itself, and are not merely a cute, quick way to divert people as they proceed into the fleecing pen. The MGM Grand has gone further: it spent hundreds of millions of dollars extra to build an adjacent but entirely separate amusement park, cramming seven rides (three involving fake rivers) and eight "themed areas" onto 33 acres, less than a 10th the size of Disney World.

The smart operators, such as Wynn, understand the proper Vegas meaning of family fun: people who won't take vacations without their children now have places to stick the kids while Mom and Dad pursue the essentially unwholesome act of squandering the family savings on cards and dice. "It's one thing for the place to be user-friendly to the whole family because the family travels together," Wynn says. "It's quite a different thing to sit down and dedicate creative design energy to build for children. I'm not, ain't gonna, not interested. I'm after Mom and Dad." Wynn's dolphins are just a '90s form of free Scotch and sodas, a cheap, subtler means of inducing people to leave their room and lose money.

But even if Vegas is not squeaky clean, even if its raison d'etre remains something other than provoking a childlike sense of wonder, the place is no longer considered racy or naughty by most people. It seems incredible today that a book in the '60s about the city was called Las Vegas, City of Sin? The change in perception is mainly because Americans' collective tolerance for vulgarity has gone way, way up. Just a decade ago, "hell" and "damn" were the most offensive words permitted on broadcast TV; today the colloquialisms "butt" and "sucks" are in daily currency on all major networks. Characters on Fox sitcoms and MTV cartoon shows snicker about their erections, and the stars of NYPD Blue can call each other "asshole." Look at Montel Williams and Geraldo. Listen to Howard Stern.

In Vegas, Wynn actually gets a little defensive about his nudity-free shows ("Hey, I'm not afraid of boobies"), the streets are hookerless, and the best-known Vegas strip club, the Palomino, lies discreetly beyond the city limits. Meanwhile, at 116 Hooters restaurants in 30 states, the whole point is the battalion of bosomy young waitresses in tight-fitting tank tops who exist as fantasy objects for a clientele of high-testosterone frat boys and young bubbas. No wonder middle Americans find the idea of bringing kids along to Vegas perfectly appropriate. How ironic that two decades after Hunter Thompson's book *Fear and Loathing in Las Vegas,* countercultural ripple effects have so raised the American prudishness threshold that Las Vegas is considered no more unseemly than any other big city.

Sixteen years, ago, Nevada was the only place in America where one could legally go to a casino, and there were just fourteen state lotteries. As recently as 1990, there were just three states with casinos, not counting those on Indian reservations; now there are nine. Lotteries have spread to 37 states. Indiana and five Mississippi River states have talked themselves into allowing gambling on riverboats—hey, it's not immoral, it's, you know, historical—and such floating casinos may soon be moored off Boston and in Philadelphia as well. Sensible, upright Minnesota, of all places, now has more casinos than Atlantic City. With only one state, Hawaii retaining a ban on gambling, and with cable-TV oligarch John Malone interested in offering gambling on the information superhighway, Vegas doesn't seem sinful, just more entertaining and shameless.

And fortunate, especially in this age of taxophobia and budget freezes. The state of Nevada now derives half its public funds from gaming-related revenues—from voluntary consumption taxes, nearly all paid by out-of-staters. Nevadans pay no state income or inheritance tax. To craven political leaders elsewhere, this looks pretty irresistible: no pain, all gain, vigorish as fiscal policy. A new report from the Center for the Study of the States concluded, however, that "gambling cannot generally produce enough tax revenue to significantly reduce reliance on other taxes or to solve a serious state fiscal problem."

One of the defining features of Las Vegas has been its 24-hour commercial culture, which arose as a corollary to 24-hour casinos: Along with the University of Nevada's basketball team, it is the great source of civic pride. It is the salient urban feature first mentioned by Harvard-educated physician Mindy Shapiro about her adopted city: "You can buy a Cuisinart or drop off your dry cleaning at 4 in the morning!" The comic magician Penn Jillette, who was performing at Bally's last week, marvels, "There are no good restaurants, but at least they're open at 3 in the morning."

But Las Vegas' retail ceaselessness is no longer singular. These days around-the-clock restaurants and supermarkets are unremarkable in hyperconvenient America, and the information superhighway, even in its current embryonic state, permits people everywhere to consume saucy entertainment—whether pay-per-view pornography or modem with strangers—at any time of the day or night.

Las Vegas was created as the world's first experiential duty-free zone, a place dedicated to the anti-Puritan pursuit of instant gratification—no waiting, no muss, no fuss. In the '30s, Nevada was famous for its uniquely quick and easy marriage (and divorce) laws. And although a certain kind of demented Barbie and Ken still make it a point to stage their weddings in Las Vegas (158,470 people married there in 1992, a majority of them out-of-staters), it is now an atavistic impulse, since the marriage and divorce laws in the rest of the U.S have long since caught up with Nevada's pioneering looseness.

When instant gratification becomes a supreme virtue, pop culture follows. Siegfried and Roy, the ur-Vegas magicians (imagine, if you dare, a hybrid of Liberace, Arnold Schwarzenegger, David Copperfield and Marlin Perkins) who perform 480 shows a year in their own theater at the Mirage, don't seem satisfied unless every trick is a show-stopper and every moment has the feel of a finale. In front of the new Treasure Island is a Caribbean-cum-Mediterranean faux village fronting a 65-ft.-deep "lagoon" in which a full-scale British man-of-war and pirate vessel every 90 minutes stage a battle with serious fires, major explosions, 22 actors, stirring music, sinking ship. It is very impressive, completely satisfying—and gives spectators pretty much everything in 15 minutes, for free, that they go to certain two-hour $65-a-seat Broadway musicals for.

In the '50s and '60s Vegas impresarios took a dying strain of vaudeville and turned it into a highly particular Vegas style. Gamblers from Duluth and Atlanta came to see only-in-Vegas entertainments: Sinatra, Streisand, stand-up comedians, the trash rococo of Liberace, both flaunting and denying his gayness; hot-ticket singers-dancers like Ann-Margret; and shows with whiffy themes that existed as mere pretexts for bring out brigages of suggestively costumed young women jiggling through clouds of pastel-colored smoke as over-amped pop tunes blared. It was cheesy glamour, to be sure, but it was rare and one of a kind.

Precisely when did Vegas values start leaching deep into the American entertainment mainstream? Was it when Sammy Davis Jr. got his own prime-time variety show on NBC in 1966, or a year later, when both Jerry Lewis and Joey Bishop had network shows running? Or in the summer of 1969, when Elvis Presley staged his famous 14-show-a-week comeback gig in Vegas?

Whenever the change began, American show business is today so pervasively Vegasy that we hardly notice anymore. The arty, sexy French-Canadian circus Cirque du Soleil had its breakthrough run in Manhattan before decamping this year to Las Vegas, and neither venue seemed unnatural. Big rock-'n-roll concerts nowadays are often as much about wowie-kozowie production values—giant video walls, neon, fireworks, suggestively costumed young men and women, clouds of pastel-colored smoke—as music. Michael Jackson's highly stylized shtick—the cosmetics, the wardrobe, the not-quite-dirty bumps and grinds, the Liberace-like gender-preference coyness—is so Vegas that the city embraced him at every turn: a Jackson impersonator is a star of the Riviera's long-running show Splash; Jackson plays a spaceship commander in one of Sega's new virtual-reality video games at the Luxor; and Siegfried and Roy got the real Jackson to compose and sing their show-closing theme song, "Mind Is the Magic." And Madonna? Her just finished Girlie Show world tour, with its Vegas-style dancers and meretricious Vegas-style lighting, is precisely as pseudosexy in 1993 as shows at the Flamingo were in 1963—decadence lite.

Back when the Rat Pack ruled, Jackie Mason played Vegas and Edward Albee was on Broadway. Today essentially idea-free spectacle—*The Phantom of the Opera*, Cats—dominates New York City's so-called legitimate theater, and stand-up comedy is ubiquitous. In the '90s, Friars Club comedians like Mason have hit Broadway shows, and Andrew Lloyd Webber's Broadway musical *Starlight Express* has been permanently installed in the showroom of the Las Vegas Hilton. The crossbreeding seems complete.

Penn and Teller are ultra-show-biz savvy New York intellectuals whose act is an ironic deconstruction of magic shows in addition to being a very impressive magic show. They first played Vegas a year ago. Penn Jillette's fondness for Vegas, like every hip baby boomer's, is sweet-and-sour, simultaneously bemused and fond. Of a traditional Vegas variety show at Bally's called Jubilee, he rants, "In the first five minutes they destroy temples and sink a giant model of the Titanic—there are 80 topless dancing women while the Titanic sinks, blast furnaces spewing fire. You look around you, and every single person in the crowd perceives it ironically. Every single person in the show perceives it ironically. It seems like everybody in Vegas nowadays is too hip to be in Vegas."

Serious connoisseurs of the surrealistically kitschy visit Graceland Wedding Chapel, where Norm Jones, the Elvis impersonator in residence, is both pleased and bewildered by the sudden popularity of the wedding ceremonies he performs for $250. Heavy-metal star Jon Bon Jovi got married there in 1989; Phil Joanou, director of the U2's concert film Rattle and Hum, was not only married at the Graceland Chapel but played a tape of his wedding onstage every night of the band's last American tour. In December 1992 three members of Def Leppard showed up at the door, one to get married and two to renew their vows.

Last year 8 million of the city's 22 million visitors were under 40, and nearly half of those were under 30. When Soul Asylum, as part of the MTV-sponsored 1993 Alternative Nation tour, landed at its last U.S. stop in Las Vegas, the band deviated from its song list to belt out Vegasy tunes like "Mandy" and "Rhinestone Cowboy." Luke Perry and Jason Priestley of "Beverly Hills, 90210," huge Tom Jones fans, recently flew to Vegas to see their hero sing, and members of the Red Hot Chili Peppers went to Las Vegas to see and meet Julio Iglesias. "Suddenly the same things I was doing five years ago that were considered pure corn are now perceived to be in," says Wayne Newton. "It's a wonderful satisfaction to finally be hip."

Long before this generation of young hipsters started reveling in the Vegas gestalt, certain intellectuals were taking seriously the city's no-holds-barred urban style. It was 25 years ago that a little-known architect and professor, Robert Venturi, returned to Yale with his two dozen student acolytes after a remarkable 10-day expedition to Las Vegas, where they stayed at the Stardust. His influential 1972 book, *Learning From Las Vegas*, immediately made Venturi famous as a heretical high-culture proponent for the ad hoc, populist design of the Strip—the giant neon' signs, the kitschy architectural allusions to ancient Rome and the Old West, any zany kind of skin-deep picturesqueness. And a decade later, the fringe tendency became a full-fledged movement: Post-Modernism.

Today almost every big-city downtown has new scrapers that endeavor to look like old sky-scrapers. Almost every suburb has a shopping center decorated with phony arches, phony pediments, phony columns. Two decades after Venturi proposed, with the intellectual's standard perverse quasi-affection, that Vegas could be a beacon for the nation's architecture, his manifesto had transformed America. Forget the Bauhaus and your house—it is the Vegas aesthetic, architecture as grandiose cartoon, that has become the American Establishment style. And so the splendidly pyramidal new Luxor and cubist new MGM Grand (both the work of local architect Veldon Simpson) do not seem so weird, since equally odd buildings now exist all over the place.

As it was being created in the '50's, Vegas' Strip was a mutant kind of American main drag, an absurdly overscaled Main Street for cars instead of people. Everywhere else in the country the shopping mall was replacing the traditional downtown. But now the Strip in Las Vegas has come full circle, its vacant stretches filling in with so many new hotels and casinos that what had been the ultimate expression of car culture has masses of tourists walking from Bally's to Caesars to Treasure Island, and from the Luxor to the Excalibur to the MGM Grand. The Strip is virtually an old-fashioned Main Street.

Meanwhile malls, the fin-de-sicle scourge of genuine Main Streets, have become preposterous Vegassy extravaganzas themselves—themed, entertainment driven, all-inclusive, overwhelming. The West Edmonton Mall in Alberta, with its 119 acres of stores and restaurants and the world's largest indoor amusement park, pulled in 22 million people in 1992, as many as visited Las Vegas; and the 16-month-old Mall of America outside Minneapolis, with 96 acres of money-spending opportunity and America's largest indoor amusement park, claimed 40 million visitors in its first year.

Yet even as the rest of America has become more and more like Las Vegas, life for Vegas residents as well as visitors is more thoroughly sugar-frosted with fantasy than any where else. "Our customers want a passive experience." says Wynn, "but romantic." Such as his ersatz South Seas restaurant, Kokomos ("Kokomos—this is better than Hawaii. There's no place in the South Pacific where the light is so perfect, so beautiful"). At the Mediterranean-themed resort Wynn envisions for the new Dunes site down the Strip, he has talked of creating a kind of raffish virtual Nazism: at a casino-restaurant modeled on Rick's casino-restaurant in Casablanca, scenes from the movie would seamlessly blend with live actors playing Bogart and the movie's other characters among the paying customers.

The new Las Vegas has even fabricated a bit of ersatz old Las Vegas: along with its Oriental- and Bahamian-themed suites, the MGM offers rooms themed according to a decorator's Vegas ideal. The Sands, one of the last intact artifacts of the Rat Pack golden era, is being remodeled to within an inch of its life. "We're going to theme, definitely," the hotel's p.r. spokeswoman said as work was beginning late last year. "But we don't know what the themes are yet."

Even civilians must theme. At the Lakes, an upscale housing complex, the developer has built a whole tract of Gothic minicastles, one next to the other. Mountain Spa, a high-end resort and corporate retreat now being plotted on 640 acres in the city's northwest, will have a "Mediterranean feel—more of a St. Tropez feel than a Mexican-American feel," says developer Jack Sommer. "I have no trouble deviating from the established regional architecture. This is Las Vegas."

The standard Las Vegas development is, like so many others throughout the country, fenced and gated—and each freestanding middle-class house is in most cases walled off from its neighbors. Such fortress domesticity, says University of Nevada at Las Vegas political scientist Bill

Thompson, "makes it hard to see your neighbors. You don't even see your neighbors to say hi. A lot of people came here to start over, to change, and they don't want people attachments. Or rather they want to make their own people attachments, not to be thrown in with people just because their house is next door."

The problem with immersing so completely into one's own virtual reality is solipsism, a kind of holistic selfishness; other people don't matter unless they are players in one's own themed fantasy. It costs $150 a month just to keep a third of an acre green, and so the per capita water usage in Las Vegas is a gluttonous 343 gal. per day, compared with 200 in Los Angeles. The 702 area code has a higher proportion of unlisted numbers than any other. And although the per capita income is the 12th highest in the U.S., the electorate last year voted against building and improving parks. Officials say they need to build 12 new schools a year through the end of the century to accommodate the projected population influx, but they fear voters will decline to pay for them. Such civic disengagement is now a national phenomenon, but Las Vegas is at the cutting edge—and always has been. Back during the city's first spurt of urban hypertrophy in the '50s, when other new cities were grandly and confidently expanding their schools and social-welfare systems, Las Vegas was pointedly stingy.

Today's casino-driven prosperity is a somewhat self-contained bubble. The state's welfare case load has risen 54% just since 1991. "We currently have 10,500 new jobs coming online," says welfare administrator Mila Florence, referring to the staffing of the Luxor, Treasure Island and MGM Grand. "The number of persons coming into the state seeking those jobs far exceeds the number of jobs available, so our agency becomes the safety net."

Nor is it just social programs the locals are disinclined to fund. Last year voters defeated a series of bond issues that would have paid for 300 new police officers, seven new police substations, 500 new jail beds and improved security in the schools. Is the crime problem bad? Yes and no. Yes in the sense that the rates for murder and other violent crimes are somewhat higher than for the nation generally. But then they always have been—as is typical of resort areas, where tourists skew the figures. What's interesting is how even in its level of violence the rest of America has come to resemble Las Vegas. The city's homicide rate was 128% higher than the nation's as recently as 1982; today the Las Vegas homicide figure is only 56% higher than the national rate. In 1982 the local rate of violent crime—rapes, robberies, assaults, as well as homicides—was 90% higher than the national figure; today it is only 17% higher.

The theming; Liberace and Michael Jackson and Siegfried and Roy; the water gluttony; the refusal to build schools and police stations. It is fair to say that Las Vegas is in denial, which probably explains the local predilection for smarmy euphemism. From Wayne Newton on down, every man in Vegas calls every woman a lady. One of the local abortion clinics is called A Lady's Needs. Signs all over McCarran Airport declare it a nonsmoking building, yet just as noticeable as the banks of slot machines is the reek of old cigarettes. It strikes almost no one as ironic that the patron of the M.B. Dalitz Religious School is the late Moe Dalitz, the celebrated gangster.

It is understandable that the citizens are a bit embarrassed by their criminal founding fathers (Steve Wynn calls the Dunes "the original home of tinhorns and scumbags"), but the nixed feelings go beyond the mob. Last year Davy-O Thompson got zoning-board approvals to establish his haircutting salon, A Little Off the Top, where the female stylists were dressed in frilly teddies or paste-on breast caps and panties. But the board of cosmetology denied him a license an hour before he was set to open, citing concerns over "safety" and "hygiene" (He was eventually allowed to operate.) A similar protest contributed to the demise recently of a car wash featuring women in thong bikinis.

"We Las Vegans have been living under the stigma of Sin City for so long that we are desperate to prove that this is a very conservative, God-fearing, average American community that, just happens to have gambling," explains Under Sheriff Eric Cooper, who along with his boss, Sheriff John Moran, has been waging a 10-year antivice campaign. "The best thing that ever happened was when the Baptists had their convention here four years ago." The category of "Escort Services" is no longer listed in the local Yellow Pages.

It isn't just sex. Las Vegans are even ambivalent about gambling. Political discourse often revolves around keeping casinos away from decent people's homes. The promotional video produced by the Nevada Development Authority makes no mention at all of casinos. Even when a casino is a part of a new development, it is described as something else. Jack Sommer's Mountain Spa, the posh pseudo-Mediterranean resort about to start construction, will have a small "European-style" casino. But, says Sommer, "it's not really a casino. I call it a gaming amenity."

Semantic nuance, it turns out, is important. "They don't see themselves as gamblers," says Steve Wynn of the new tourists he is attracting. "They think of themselves as folks who are on vacation, and while they are there—hey, let's put some money in the slot machine." Wynn hired screenwriter Jim Hart (Hook, Bram Stoker's Dracula) to write a one-hour family-adventure TV movie (NBC, Jan. 23) set at Treasure Island, and while Hart says the movie reaffirms family values and he flew his children out during production, he understands the place has an intrinsically dark edge. "You can come out for 24 hours and lose the tuition," he says. "There are a lot of desperate characters here."

For while the city is no longer the "Genet vision of hell" that John Gregory Dunne described in his book *Vegas: A Memoir of a Dark Season* 20 years ago, it is still, for the moment, a stranger place than Omaha or Sacramento or Worcester or even Atlantic City, if only because there are so many cheerfully offered temptations to lose the tuition and so many normal-looking people flirting feverishly with that risk. The mobs on the casino floors are in a kind of murmuring trance, each middle-aged housewife or young lawyer at the slots or the poker tables mentally grappling with a nonstop flow of insane hunches and wishful superstitions, continuously driven to unworthy leaps of faith that result in unwarranted bursts of self-esteem (Blackjack!) or self-loathing (Craps!).

Wynn understands the shadowy core of Las Vegas. "There will never come a day when [potential visitors] say, 'Should it be Orlando or should it be Las Vegas?' Those are two different moods. We think of our vacation in more romantic, personal terms. We're looking for sensual, extended gratification." In other words, Disney World is about tightly scripted smile-button fun for the kids; Las Vegas, despite the new theme-park accessories, remains the epicenter of the American id, still desperate to overpay schmaltzy superstars like Barbra Streisand, still focused on the darker stirrings of chance and liquor and sex.

If it is now acceptable for the whole family to come along to Las Vegas, that's because the values of America have changed, not those of Las Vegas. Deviancy really has been defined down. The new hang-loose all-American embrace of Las Vegas is either a sign that Americans have liberated themselves from troublesome old repressions and moralist hyprocrisies, or else one more symptom of the decline of Western civilization. Or maybe both.

ISHMAEL REED

"America: The Multinational Society" (1988)

> At the annual Lower East Side Jewish Festival yesterday, a Chinese woman ate a pizza slice in front of Ty Thuan Duc's Vietnamese grocery store. Beside her a Spanish-speaking family patronized a cart with two signs: "Italian Ices" and "Kosher by Rabbi Alper." And after the pastrami ran out, everybody ate knishes.
>
> (*New York Times*, 23 June 1983)

On the day before Memorial Day, 1983, a poet called me to describe a city he had just visited. He said that one section included mosques, built by the Islamic people who dwelled there. Attending his reading, he said, were large numbers of Hispanic people, forty thousand of whom lived in the same city. He was not talking about a fabled city located in some mysterious region of the world. The city he'd visited was Detroit.

A few months before, as I was leaving Houston, Texas, I heard it announced on the radio that Texas's largest minority was Mexican-American, and though a foundation recently issued a report critical of bilingual education, the taped voice used to guide the passengers on the air trams connecting terminals in Dallas Airport is in both Spanish and English. If the trend continues, a day will come when it will be difficult to travel through some sections of the country without hearing commands in both English and Spanish; after all, for some western states, Spanish was the first written language and the Spanish style lives on in the western way of life.

Shortly after my Texas trip, I sat in an auditorium located on the campus of the University of Wisconsin at Milwaukee as a Yale professor—whose original work on the influence of African cultures upon those of the Americas has led to his ostracism from some monocultural intellectual circles—walked up and down the aisle, like an old-time southern evangelist, dancing and drumming the top of the lectern, illustrating his points before some serious Afro-American intellectuals and artists who cheered and applauded his performance and his mastery of information. The professor was "white." After his lecture, he joined a group of Milwaukeeans in a conversation. All of the participants spoke Yoruban, though only the professor had ever traveled to Africa.

One of the artists told me that his paintings, which included African and Afro-American mythological symbols and imagery, were hanging in the local McDonald's restaurant. The next day I went to McDonald's and snapped pictures of smiling youngsters eating hamburgers below paintings that could grace the walls of any of the country's leading museums. The manager of the local McDonald's said, "I don't know what you boys are doing, but I like it," as he commissioned the local painters to exhibit in his restaurant.

Such blurring of cultural styles occurs in everyday life in the United States to a greater extent than anyone can imagine and is probably more prevalent than the sensational conflict between people of different backgrounds that is played up and often encouraged by the media. The result is what the Yale professor, Robert Thompson, referred to as a cultural bouillabaisse, yet members of the nation's present educational and cultural Elect still cling to the notion that the United States belongs to some vaguely defined entity they refer to as "Western civilization," by which they mean, presumably, a civilization created by the people of Europe, as if Europe can be viewed in mono-lithic terms. Is Beethoven's Ninth Symphony, which includes Turkish marches, a part of Western civilization, or the late nineteenth- and twentieth-century French paintings, whose creators were influenced by Japanese art? And what of the cubists, through whom the influence of African art changed modern painting, or the surrealists, who were so impressed with the art of the Pacific Northwest Indians that, in their map of North America, Alaska dwarfs the lower forty-eight in size?

Are the Russians, who are often criticized for their adoption of "Western" ways by Tsarist dis-sidents in exile, members of Western civilization? And what of the millions of Europeans who have black African and Asian ancestry, black Africans having occupied several countries for hundreds of years? Are these "Europeans" members of Western civilization, or the Hungarians, who origi-nated across the Urals in a place called Greater Hungary, or the Irish, who came from the Iberian Peninsula?

Even the notion that North America is part of Western civilization because our "system of government" is derived from Europe is being challenged by Native American historians who say that the founding fathers, Benjamin Franklin especially, were actually influenced by the system of government that had been adopted by the Iroquois hundreds of years prior to the arrival of large numbers of Europeans.

Western civilization, then, becomes another confusing category like Third World, or Judeo-Christian culture, as man attempts to impose his small-screen view of political and cultural reality upon a complex world. Our most publicized novelist recently said that Western civilization was the greatest achievement of mankind, an attitude that flourishes on the street level as scribbles in public restrooms: "White Power," "Niggers and Spics Suck," or "Hitler was a prophet," the latter being the most telling, for wasn't Adolph Hitler the archetypal monoculturalist who, in his pig-headed arrogance, believed that one way and one blood was so pure that it had to be protected from alien strains at all costs? Where did such an attitude, which has caused so much misery and depression in our national life, which has tainted even our noblest achievements, begin? An atti-tude that caused the incarceration of Japanese-American citizens during World War II, the persecu-tion of Chicanos and Chinese-Americans, the near-extermination of the Indians, and the murder and lynchings of thousands of Afro-Americans.

Virtuous, hardworking, pious, even though they occasionally would wander off after some fancy clothes, or rendezvous in the woods with the town prostitute, the Puritans are idealized in our schoolbooks as "a hardy band" of no-nonsense patriarchs whose discipline razed the forest and brought order to the New World (a term that annoys Native American historians). Industri-ous, responsible, it was their "Yankee ingenuity" and practicality that created the work ethic. They were simple folk who produced a number of good poets, and they set the tone for the American writing style, of lean and spare lines, long before Hemingway. They worshiped in churches whose colors blended in with the New England snow, churches with simple structures and ornate lecterns.

The Puritans were a daring lot, but they had a mean streak. They hated the theater and banned Christmas. They punished people in a cruel and inhuman manner. They killed children who dis-obeyed their parents. When they came in contact with those whom they considered heathens or aliens, they behaved in such a bizarre and irrational manner that this chapter in the American his-tory comes down to us as a late-movie horror film. They exterminated the Indians, who taught them how to survive in a world unknown to them, and their encounter with the calypso culture of Barbados resulted in what the tourist guide in Salem's Witches' House refers to as the Witchcraft Hysteria.

The Puritan legacy of hard work and meticulous accounting led to the establishment of a great industrial society; it is no wonder that the American industrial revolution began in Lowell, Massachusetts, but there was the other side, the strange and paranoid attitudes toward those different from the Elect.

The cultural attitudes of that early Elect continue to be voiced in everyday life in the United States: the president of a distinguished university, writing a letter to the *Times*, belittling the study of African civilizations; the television network that promoted its show on the Vatican art with the boast that this art represented "the finest achievements of the human spirit." A modern up-tempo state of complex rhythms that depends upon contacts with an international community can no longer behave as if it dwelled in a "Zion Wilderness" surrounded by beasts and pagans.

When I heard a schoolteacher warn the other night about the invasion of the American educational system by foreign curriculums, I wanted to yell at the television set, "Lady, they're already here." It has already begun because the world is here. The world has been arriving at these shores for at least ten thousand years from Europe, Africa, and Asia. In the late nineteenth and early twentieth centuries, large numbers of Europeans arrived, adding their cultures to those of the European, African, and Asian settlers who were already here, and recently millions have been entering the country from South America and the Caribbean, making Yale Professor Bob Thompson's bouillabaisse richer and thicker.

One of our most visionary politicians said that he envisioned a time when the United States could become the brain of the world, by which he meant the repository of all of the latest advanced information systems. I thought of that remark when an enterprising poet friend of mine called to say that he had just sold a poem to a computer magazine and that the editors were delighted to get it because they didn't carry fiction or poetry. Is that the kind of world we desire? A humdrum homogeneous world of all brains and no heart, no fiction, no poetry; a world of robots with human attendants bereft of imagination, of culture? Or does North America deserve a more exciting destiny? To become a place where the cultures of the world crisscross. This is possible because the United States is unique in the world: The world is here.